The Terry Lectures

Freud and Philosophy

FREUD AND PHILOSOPHY

An Essay on Interpretation

PAUL RICOEUR

Translated by
DENIS SAVAGE

MOTILAL BANARSIDASS PUBLISHERS
PRIVATE LIMITED • DELHI

First Indian Edition : Delhi, 2008
Earlier published by Yale University Press, New Haven and London

ISBN: 978-81-208-3305-0

MOTILAL BANARSIDASS
41 U.A. Bungalow Road, Jawahar Nagar, Delhi 110 007
8 Mahalaxmi Chamber, 22 Bhulabhai Desai Road, Mumbai 400 026
203 Royapettah High Road, Mylapore, Chennai 600 004
236, 9th Main III Block, Jayanagar, Bangalore 560 011
Sanas Plaza, 1302 Baji Rao Road, Pune 411 002
8 Camac Street, Kolkata 700 017
Ashok Rajpath, Patna 800 004
Chowk, Varanasi 221 001

Printed in India

BY JAINENDRA PRAKASH JAIN AT SHRI JAINENDRA PRESS,
A-45 NARAINA, PHASE-I, NEW DELHI 110 028
AND PUBLISHED BY NARENDRA PRAKASH JAIN FOR
MOTILAL BANARSIDASS PUBLISHERS PRIVATE LIMITED,
BUNGALOW ROAD, DELHI 110 007

The Dwight Harrington Terry Foundation Lectures on Religion in the Light of Science and Philosophy

The deed of gift declares that "the object of this foundation is not the promotion of scientific investigation and discovery, but rather the assimilation and interpretation of that which has been or shall be hereafter discovered, and its application to human welfare, especially by the building of the truths of science and philosophy into the structure of a broadened and purified religion. The founder believes that such a religion will greatly stimulate intelligent effort for the improvement of human conditions and the advancement of the race in strength and excellence of character. To this end it is desired that a series of lectures be given by men eminent in their respective departments, on ethics, the history of civilization and religion, biblical research, all sciences and branches of knowledge which have an important bearing on the subject, all the great laws of nature, especially of evolution . . . also such interpretations of literature and sociology as are in accord with the spirit of this foundation, to the end that the Christian spirit may be nurtured in the fullest light of the world's knowledge and that mankind may be helped to attain its highest possible welfare and happiness upon this earth." The present work constitutes the thirty-eighth volume published on this foundation.

CONTENTS

PREFACE

This book originates in the Terry Lectures given at Yale University in the autumn of 1961. I wish to express my deep thanks to the Lecture Committee, the Philosophy Department, the Director of the Yale University Press, and the President of Yale University for the invitation to undertake this work.

In the autumn of 1962, eight lectures given in the Cardinal Mercier Chair at the University of Louvain became the next stage of the work. I wish to thank the President of the Institut supérieur de philosophie and the colleagues who welcomed me in this chair for their criticism as well as for the indulgence they showed toward an enterprise in progress.

I now owe it to the reader to give some indication of what he may and what he may not expect from this book.

In the first place, this book deals with Freud and not with psychoanalysis. This means there are two things lacking: analytic experience itself and a consideration of the post-Freudian schools. As for the first point, it is taking a gamble, no doubt, to write about Freud without being an analyst or having been analyzed and to treat his work as a monument of our culture, as a text in which our culture is expressed and understood. The reader will have to judge whether the wager has been won or lost. As for the post-Freudian literature, I have deliberately set it aside, either because it stems from corrections brought to Freud's ideas from analytic experience that I do not have, or because it introduces new theoretical conceptions the discussion of which would have led me away from a rigorous debate with the true founder of psychoanalysis. Therefore I have treated Freud's work as a work unto itself, and have avoided discussing the conceptions of dissidents turned adversaries: Adler and Jung, or of students turned dissidents: Erich Fromm, Karen Horney, Harry Stack Sullivan, or of disciples turned creators: Melanie Klein, Jacques Lacan.

Secondly, this book is one not of psychology but of philosophy. My interest centers on the new understanding of man that Freud introduces. I place myself in the company of Roland Dalbiez,[1] my first professor of philosophy, to whom I here wish to render homage, and of Herbert Marcuse,[2] Philip Rieff,[3] and J. C. Flugel.[4]

My work differs from that of Roland Dalbiez on an essential point: I do not believe that Freud may be confined to the exploration of the less human elements in man. My enterprise stems from the opposite conviction: Psychoanalysis conflicts with every other global interpretation of the phenomenon of man because it is an interpretation of culture. On this point I am in agreement with the last three authors cited. I differ from them, however, by the nature of my philosophical preoccupation: my problem concerns the texture or structure of Freudian discourse. First, it is an epistemological problem: What is interpretation in psychoanalysis, and how is the interpretation of the signs of man interrelated with the economic explanation that claims to get at the root of desire? Second, it is a problem of reflective philosophy: What new self-understanding comes out of this interpretation, and what self is it which thus comes to self-understanding? Third, it is a dialectical problem: Does Freud's interpretation of culture exclude all others? If not, what is the rule of thought by which it can be coordinated with other interpretations without falling into eclecticism? These three questions mark the circuitous route by which I take up the problem left unresolved at the end of my *Symbolism of Evil,* namely the relationship between a hermeneutics of symbols and a philosophy of concrete reflection.

The execution of this program required that Book II, the "Reading of Freud," conducted as rigorously as possible, be kept separate

1. Roland Dalbiez, *La Méthode psychanalytique et la doctrine freudienne* (2 vols. Paris, Desclée de Brouwer, 1936). "Freud's work is the most profound analysis history has ever known of the less human elements in man" (*2*, 513).

2. Herbert Marcuse, *Eros and Civilization: A Philosophical Inquiry into Freud* (Boston, Beacon Press, 1955).

3. Philip Rieff, *Freud, the Mind of the Moralist* (New York, Viking Press, 1959).

4. J. C. Flugel, *Man, Morals and Society* (New York, International Universities Press, 1945); Peregrine Books, 1962.

from Book III, the "Philosophical Interpretation" which I propose. Thus the reader may treat the "Analytic" of Book II as a separate and self-sufficient work. In it I have tried to remain close to the Freudian text itself; to this end I have retranslated almost all the passages I cite.[5] The philosophical interpretation is placed before and after my "Reading of Freud," being divided into the questions that make up the "Problematic" of Book I and the attempts at solution that form the "Dialectic" of Book III.[6]

5. In spite of the cumbersomeness of the procedure, I have decided to cite (a) the German text in the *Gesammelte Werke* (18 vols. London, from 1940; abbreviation: *GW*) because it is the original text; (b) the *Standard Edition* (24 vols. London, from 1953; abbreviation: *SE*) because it is the only critical edition; (c) the available French translations, so that French readers can locate the citations in their context and discuss the respective translations. [Translator's note: By the author's directive, all quotations from Freud's texts will be taken from the *Standard Edition;* references to the French editions will be omitted, as being of little use to the English reader.]

6. The four problems mentioned above constitute the four levels of this "Dialectic."

TRANSLATOR'S NOTE

This translation began when my wife, Rosa, and I first translated the three lectures which Paul Ricoeur presented as the Terry Lectures. We both feel very grateful to M. Ricoeur for his friendship and for opening up to us the richness of his meditations on Freud, symbolism, and interpretation.

I have tried to make the translation conform as closely as possible to the French text. Several minor corrections were made of the original text, all of them after consultation with the author.

I wish to thank Mary Parr for reading several chapters for style, and especially Paul Lee of the University of California, Santa Cruz, for his painstaking reading of the entire manuscript and for his many helpful suggestions. I also wish to thank the Department of Philosophy of Marquette University for their secretarial help in typing the manuscript.

Denis Savage

Milwaukee, Wisconsin
November 1969

BOOK I

Problematic: The Placing of Freud

Chapter 1: Language, Symbol, and Interpretation

PSYCHOANALYSIS AND LANGUAGE

This book is a discussion or debate with Freud. Why this interest in psychoanalysis, an interest justified neither by the competence of an analyst nor by the experience of having been analyzed? The purpose of a book is never entirely justified. In any event, no one is required to display his motives or to entangle himself in a confession. To attempt it would be self-delusion. Yet, more than anyone, the philosopher cannot refuse to give his reasons. I will do so by placing my investigation within a wider field of questioning and by relating my particular interest to a common way of posing certain problems.

It seems to me there is an area today where all philosophical investigations cut across one another—the area of language. Language is the common meeting ground of Wittgenstein's investigations, the English linguistic philosophy, the phenomenology that stems from Husserl, Heidegger's investigations, the works of the Bultmannian school and of the other schools of New Testament exegesis, the works of comparative history of religion and of anthropology concerning myth, ritual, and belief—and finally, psychoanalysis.

Today we are in search of a comprehensive philosophy of language to account for the multiple functions of the human act of signifying and for their interrelationships. How can language be put to such diverse uses as mathematics and myth, physics and art? It is no accident that we ask ourselves this question today. We have at our disposal a symbolic logic, an exegetical science, an anthropology, and a psychoanalysis and, perhaps for the first time, we are able to encompass in a single question the problem of the unification of human discourse. The very progress of the aforementioned disparate disciplines has both revealed and intensified the dismemberment of that discourse. Today the unity of human language poses a problem.

Such is the broad horizon within which our investigation is set. The present study in no way pretends to offer the comprehensive philosophy of language we are waiting for. I doubt moreover that such a philosophy could be elaborated by any one man. A modern Leibniz with the ambition and capacity to achieve it would have to be an accomplished mathematician, a universal exegete, a critic versed in several of the arts, and a good psychoanalyst. While awaiting that philosopher of integral language, perhaps it is possible for us to explore some of the key connections between the disciplines concerned with language. The present essay is an attempt to contribute to that investigation.

I contend that the psychoanalyst is a leading participant in any general discussion about language. To start with, psychoanalysis belongs to our time by virtue of Freud's written work; through this medium psychoanalysis addresses itself to those who are not analysts and who have not been analyzed. I am well aware that without actual practice a reading of Freud is truncated and runs the risk of embracing only a fetish. But if the textual approach to psychoanalysis has limits which practice alone can remove, still it has the advantage of focusing attention upon an entire aspect of Freud's work that may be hidden by practice or overlooked by a science whose sole concern is to account for what goes on in the analytic relationship. A meditation on Freud's work has the advantage of revealing that work's broadest aim: not only the renovation of psychiatry, but a reinterpretation of all psychical productions pertaining to culture, from dreams, through art and morality, to religion. This is how psychoanalysis belongs to modern culture. By interpreting culture it modifies it; by giving it an instrument of reflection it stamps it with a lasting mark.

The fluctuation in Freud's writings between medical investigation and a theory of culture bears witness to the scope of the Freudian project. True, the major texts on culture are to be found in the last part of Freud's work.[1] However, psychoanalysis should not be regarded as a form of individual psychology, tardily transposed into a sociology of culture. A summary glance at the Freudian bibliography shows that the first texts on art, morality, and religion follow shortly upon *The Interpretation of Dreams* [2] and are then developed alongside the great doctrinal texts that constitute the "Papers on Metapsychology" (1913–17), *Beyond the Pleasure Principle* (1920), and *The Ego and the Id* (1923).[3] In fact, to grasp how the theory of culture is related to the theory of dreams and the neuroses, it is necessary to go back to *The Interpretation of Dreams* of 1900, for it is here that the connection with mythology and literature was first established. Ever since 1900 the *Traumdeutung* had proposed that dreams are the dreamer's private mythology and myths the waking dreams of peoples, that Sophocles' *Oedipus* and Shakespeare's *Hamlet* are to be interpreted in the same way as dreams. We shall see that this proposal presents a problem.

Whatever the outcome of this difficulty, the entrance of psychoanalysis into the general contemporary discussion about language is not due solely to its interpretation of culture. By making dreams not only the first object of his investigation but a model (in what sense we will discuss below) of all the disguised, substitutive, and fictive expressions of human wishing or desire, Freud invites us to look to dreams themselves for the various relations between desire and language. First, it is not the dream as dreamed that can be interpreted, but rather the text of the dream account; analysis attempts to substitute for this text another text that could be called

1. *The Future of an Illusion* was published in 1927, *Civilization and Its Discontents* in 1930, *Moses and Monotheism* in 1937–39.

2. *Jokes and Their Relation to the Unconscious* was published in 1905, "Obsessive Actions and Religious Practices" in 1907, *Delusions and Dreams in Jensen's "Gradiva"* in 1907, the short essay "Creative Writers and Day-dreaming" in 1908, *Leonardo da Vinci and a Memory of His Childhood* in 1910, and the very important *Totem and Taboo* in 1913.

3. "The Moses of Michelangelo" appeared in 1914, "Thoughts for the Times on War and Death" in 1915, "A Childhood Recollection from *Dichtung und Wahrheit*" in 1917, "The 'Uncanny'" in 1919, *Group Psychology and the Analysis of the Ego* in 1921.

the primitive speech of desire. Thus analysis moves from one meaning to another meaning; it is not desires as such that are placed at the center of the analysis, but rather their language. Later we will discuss how this semantics of desire relates to the dynamics expressed in the notions of discharge, repression, cathexis, etc. But it is important to stress from the start that this dynamics—or energetics, or even hydraulics—is articulated only in a semantics: the "vicissitudes of instincts," to use one of Freud's expressions, can be attained only in the vicissitudes of meaning. Therein lies the deep reason for all the analogies between dreams and wit, dreams and myth, dreams and works of art, dreams and religious "illusion," etc. All these "psychical productions" belong to the area of meaning and come under a unified question: How do desires achieve speech? How do desires make speech fail, and why do they themselves fail to speak? This new approach to the whole of human speech, to the meaning of human desire, is what entitles psychoanalysis to its place in the general debate on language.

SYMBOL AND INTERPRETATION

Is it possible to locate more exactly just where psychoanalysis enters this general debate? Having found the origin of the problem in the theme of Freud's first great book, let us also look there for a first indication of the program of psychoanalysis. We are not yet ready to enter into the book itself, but at least the title *Traumdeutung* may serve as a guide. In this composite word we are confronted with the question of dreams and the question of interpretation. Let us take the two paths of the title and follow each in turn. The interpretation is concerned with dreams: the word "dream" is not a word that closes, but a word that opens. It does not close in upon a marginal phenomenon of our psychological life, upon the fantasies of our nights, the oneiric. It opens out onto all psychical productions, those of insanity and those of culture, insofar as they are the analogues of dreams, whatever may be the degree and principle of that relationship. Along with dreams is posited what I called above the semantics of desire, a semantics that centers around a somewhat nuclear theme: as a man of desires I go forth in disguise—*larvatus prodeo.* By the same token language itself is from the outset and for the most part distorted: it means something other than what it says, it has a double meaning, it is equivocal. The dream and its analogues are thus set within a region of language that presents itself as the locus of complex significations where another meaning is both given and hidden in an immediate meaning. Let us call this region of double meaning "symbol," and reserve discussion of the equivalence for later.

The problem of double meaning is not peculiar to psychoanalysis. It is also known to the phenomenology of religion in its constant encounter with those great cosmic symbols of earth, heaven, water, life, trees, and stones, and with those strange narratives about the origin and end of things which are the myths. However, insofar as this discipline is phenomenology and not psychoanalysis, the myths, rituals, and beliefs it studies are not fables but a particular way in which man places himself in relation to fundamental reality, whatever it may be. The problem dealt with by the phenomenology of religion is not primarily the dissimulation of desire in double meaning; this discipline does not begin by regarding symbols as a distortion of language. For the phenomenology of religion, symbols are the manifestation in the sensible—in imagination, gestures, and feelings—of a further reality, the expression of a depth which both shows and hides itself. What psychoanalysis encounters primarily as the distortion of elementary meanings connected with wishes or desires, the phenomenology of religion encounters primarily as the manifestation of a depth or, to use the word immediately, leaving for later a discussion of its content and validity, the revelation of the sacred.

Within the general discussion of language a limited but important debate immediately arises—limited, certainly, because it does not raise the question of the status of univocal languages, but important, since it covers the totality of double-meaning expressions. At the same time the form of the debate is set and the key question proposed: Is the showing-hiding of double meaning always a dissimulation of what desire means, or can it sometimes be a manifestation, a revelation, of the sacred? And is this alternative itself real or illusory, provisional or definitive? This question runs throughout this book.

Before elaborating in the next chapter the terms of the debate and before sketching the method of its resolution, let us continue to explore the outlines of the problem.

Let us return to the title of the *Traumdeutung* and follow the other path of this great title. The term *Deutung* does not mean science in a general way; it means interpretation in a precise way. The word is chosen by design, and its juxtaposition with the theme of dreams is itself quite meaningful. If dreams designate—*pars pro toto*—the entire region of double-meaning expressions, the problem of interpretation in turn designates all understanding specifically concerned with the meaning of equivocal expressions. To interpret is to understand a double meaning.

In this way the place of psychoanalysis within the total sphere of language is specified: it is the area of symbols or double meanings and the area in which the various manners of interpretation confront one another. From now on we shall call this special area, broader than psychoanalysis but narrower than the theory of language as a whole which is its horizon, the "hermeneutic field." By hermeneutics we shall always understand the theory of the rules that preside over an exegesis—that is, over the interpretation of a particular text, or of a group of signs that may be viewed as a text. (We shall explain later what we mean by the notion of text and by the extension of the concept of exegesis to all signs bearing an analogy to a text.)

If then double-meaning expressions constitute the privileged theme of the hermeneutic field, it is at once clear that the problem of symbolism enters a philosophy of language by the intermediary of the act of interpretation.

But this initial decision to interrelate the problem of symbolism and the problem of interpretation raises a series of critical questions which I wish to pose at the beginning of this book. These questions will not be resolved in this chapter but will remain open to the end. It is precisely this mutual relationship that makes the hermeneutic problem a unique one; at the same time it is decisive for the definitions of symbol and interpretation. And these are anything but self-evident. The extreme confusion of vocabulary in these matters calls for a decision, for taking a position and sticking to it; and this decision entails a whole philosophy which must be brought into the open. I have decided to define, i.e. limit, the notions of symbol and interpretation through one another. Thus a symbol is a double-meaning linguistic expression that requires an interpretation, and interpretation is a work of understanding that aims at deciphering symbols. The critical discussion will be concerned with the legitimacy of seeking the semantic criterion of symbolism in the intentional structure of double meaning, and with the legitimacy of taking this structure as the privileged object of interpretation. This is what is at stake in my decision to mutually delimit the fields of symbolism and interpretation.

In the semantic discussion to follow I shall bracket the conflict that, at least on a first reading, opposes psychoanalytic interpretation, as well as any interpretation conceived as the unmasking, demystification, or reduction of illusions, to interpretation conceived as the recollection or restoration of meaning. I am interested here merely in recognizing the contours of the hermeneutic field, although a discussion that falls short of the above conflict undoubtedly remains formal and abstract. It is important at first not to dramatize the debate but rather to contain it within the strict limits of a semantic analysis that ignores the opposition between distortion and revelation.

TOWARD A CRITIQUE OF SYMBOL

Let us take up the question on the side of symbolism. Certain widespread uses of the word are totally incompatible with one another and call for a reasoned decision. The definition I propose lies between two other definitions, one too broad, the other too narrow, which we shall proceed to discuss. Moreover, it is completely distinct from the conception of symbol in symbolic logic; we shall be able to account for this third difference only after we have elaborated the problem of hermeneutics and have located this problem within a wider philosophical perspective.[4]

Too broad a definition is one that makes the "symbolic function" the general function of mediation by which the mind or consciousness constructs all its universes of perception and discourse; this definition, as is known, is the one given by Ernst Cassirer in his *Philosophy of Symbolic Forms*. We should not forget that the explicit aim of Cassirer, inspired by Kant's philosophy, was to break the too narrow framework of the transcendental method confined within the critique of the principles of Newtonian philosophy and to explore all the activities of synthesis and their corresponding realms of objectivization. But is it legitimate to use the term "symbolic" for those various "forms" of synthesis in which objects are ruled by functions, for those "forces" each of which produces and posits a world?

Let us do justice to Cassirer: he was the first to have posed the problem of the reconstruction of language. The notion of symbolic form, prior to constituting an answer, delimits a question, namely, the question of the composition of the "mediating functions" within a single function, which Cassirer calls *das Symbolische*. "The symbolic" designates the common denominator of all the ways of objectivizing, of giving meaning to reality.

But why call this function symbolic? Cassirer chose the term first of all in order to express the universality of the Copernican revolution, which substituted the question of objectivization by the mind's synthetic function for the question of reality as it is in itself. The symbolic is the universal mediation of the mind between ourselves and the real; the symbolic, above all, indicates the nonimmediacy of our apprehension of reality. The use of the term in mathematics, linguistics, and the history of religion seems to confirm that "symbolic" has this species of universality.

Furthermore, the word "symbol" seems well suited to designate the cultural instruments of our apprehension of reality: language, religion, art, science. The task of a philosophy of symbolic forms is to arbitrate the claims of absoluteness of each of these symbolic

4. See below, Ch. 3.

functions and the many antinomies of the concept of culture that result from those claims.

Finally, the word "symbol" expresses the mutation undergone by a theory of categories—space, time, cause, number, etc.—when it escapes the limits of a mere epistemology and moves from a critique of reason to a critique of culture.

I do not deny the advantages of this choice, still less the legitimacy of Cassirer's problem, although the Kantian transcendentalism which continues to govern the notions of objectivization, synthesis, and reality is prejudicial, in my opinion, to the work of description and classification of the symbolic forms. We mentioned the unique problem that Cassirer denotes by the term "symbolic" from the beginning: the problem of the unity of language and the interrelationship of its multiple functions within a single empire of discourse. But this problem seems to me better characterized by the notion of sign or signifying function.[5] How man gives meaning by filling a sensory content with meaning—that is the problem Cassirer deals with.

Is this a dispute over words? I do not think so. What is at stake in this terminological discussion is the specificity of the hermeneutic problem. By unifying all the functions of mediation under the title of "the symbolic," Cassirer makes this concept equally as broad as the concepts of reality and culture. Thus a fundamental distinction is wiped out, which constitutes, as I see it, a true dividing line: the distinction between univocal and plurivocal expressions. It is this distinction that creates the hermeneutic problem. Moreover, Anglo-Saxon linguistic philosophy will see to it that we are mindful of this division of the semantic field. If we use the term symbolic for the signifying function in its entirety, we no longer have a word to designate the group of signs whose intentional texture calls for a read-

5. As Cassirer himself says, the concept of symbol is meant to "encompass the totality of those phenomena in which the sensuous is in any way filled with meaning [*Sinnerfüllung im Sinnlichen*], in which a sensuous content, while preserving the mode of its existence and facticity [*in der Art seines Da-Seins und So-Seins*], represents a particularization and embodiment, a manifestation and incarnation of meaning." *The Philosophy of Symbolic Forms*, tr. R. Manheim (3 vols. New Haven, Yale University Press, 1957), *3*, 93. Cited in C. Hamburg, *Symbol and Reality* (The Hague, Nijhoff, 1956), p. 59.

ing of another meaning in the first, literal, and immediate meaning. As I see it the problem of the unity of language cannot validly be posed until a fixed status has been assigned to a group of expressions that share the peculiarity of designating an indirect meaning in and through a direct meaning and thus call for something like a deciphering, i.e. an interpretation, in the precise sense of the word. To mean something other than what is said—this is the symbolic function.

Let us proceed a bit further in the semantic analysis of sign and symbol. In every sign a sensory vehicle is the bearer of a signifying function that makes it stand for something else. But I will not say that I interpret the sensory sign when I understand what it says. Interpretation has to do with a more complicated intentional structure: a first meaning is set up which intends something, but this object in turn refers to something else which is intended only through the first object.

What may lead to confusion here is the fact that in a sign there is a duality, or rather two pairs of factors, which in each case go together to form the unity of the signification. First there is the structural duality of the sensory sign and the signification it carries (the signifier and the signified, in the terminology of Ferdinand de Saussure); second there is the intentional duality of the sign (both sensory and meaningful, signifier and signified) and the thing or object designated. This double duality, structural and intentional, is most clearly seen in linguistic signs of conventional institution. On the one hand, words, phonetically different according to various languages, carry identical significations or meanings; on the other hand, these significations make the sensory signs stand for something that the signs designate. We say that words, by their sensible quality, *express* significations and that, thanks to their signification, they *designate* something. The term "to signify" covers the twofold duality of expression and designation.

But this is not the duality that specifies a symbol. The duality of symbolism is of a higher degree. It is neither the duality of sensory sign and signification nor that of signification and thing, the latter duality moreover being inseparable from the former. In a symbol the duality is added to and superimposed upon the duality of sensory sign and signification as a relation of meaning to meaning; it presupposes signs that already have a primary, literal, manifest meaning. Hence I deliberately restrict the notion of symbol to double- or multiple-meaning expressions whose semantic texture is correlative to the work of interpretation that explicates their second or multiple meanings.

Though this delimitation may appear at first to break the unity seen by Cassirer between all the signifying functions, it helps to disengage an underlying unity, thus affording a starting point for a new approach to Cassirer's problem.

Let us try to give a panoramic view of the zones of emergence of symbolism thus conceived.

For my part, I encountered the problem of symbolism in the semantic study I made of the avowal of evil. I noticed that there exists no direct discourse of avowal. Evil—whether the evil one suffers or the evil one commits—is always confessed by means of indirect expressions that are taken from the sphere of everyday experience and which have the remarkable character of analogously designating another experience. I will provisionally call it the experience of the sacred. Thus in the archaic form of avowal, the image of a spot—the spot that one removes, washes, wipes away—analogously designates stain as the sinner's situation in the dimension of the sacred. That this is a symbolic expression is amply confirmed both by the expressions and by the corresponding actions of purification. None of these modes of conduct reduces itself to a mere physical cleansing; each refers to the others without exhausting its meaning in a material gesture; burning, spitting, burying, washing, expelling, each act is an equivalent of or substitute for the others, while at the same time designating something else, namely, the restoration of integrity, of purity. Thus, all the various stages of the feeling and experience of evil can be marked off by semantic stages; I have shown how one moves to the experience of sin and guilt through a series of symbolic progressions, marked off by the images of deviation, the crooked path, wandering, and rebellion; next, by the images of weight, burden, and fault; and last, by the image of slavery, which encompasses them all.

This cycle of examples concerns only one of the zones of the emergence of symbolism, the one closest to ethical reflection, constituting what might be called the symbolism of the servile will. Upon this symbolism is easily grafted a whole process of reflection that leads to St. Augustine and Luther, as well as to Pelagius or Spinoza. Elsewhere I will show the fruitfulness such reflection may have for philosophy. The concern in the present work is not the richness of a particular symbolism but the texture or structure of symbolism revealed in it. In other words, the issue here is not the problem of evil, but the epistemology of symbolism.

To carry this epistemology through successfully we must broaden our starting point and enumerate some other areas where symbols make their appearance. This inductive approach is the only possible way to begin our investigation, for we are searching for the common structure of the various manifestations of symbolic thought. The symbols we have consulted have already attained a high level of literary elaboration; they are already on the path of reflection; they already contain the seeds of a moral or tragic vision, a wisdom or a theology. Going back to less elaborated forms of symbol I discern three different modalities of symbolism, the unity of which is not immediately apparent.

I have already alluded to the conception of symbolism in the phenomenology of religion, as developed, for example, in Van der Leeuw, Maurice Leenhardt, and Mircea Eliade. Bound to rituals and myths, these symbols constitute the language of the sacred, the *verbum* of the "hierophanies." Whether it be the symbolism of the heavens, as a figure of the most high and the immense, the powerful and the immutable, the sovereign and the wise; or the symbolism of vegetation, which comes to birth, dies, and is reborn; or of water, which threatens, cleanses, or vivifies, these innumerable theophanies or hierophanies are an inexhaustible source of symbolization. But we should be careful to note that these symbols do not stand apart from language as values of immediate expression, as directly perceptible physiognomies; only in the universe of discourse do these realities take on the symbolic dimension. Even when the elements of the universe are what carry the symbol (Heaven, Earth, Water, Life, etc.), it is a word—the word of consecration, of invocation, the mythic commentary—that *declares* the cosmic expressiveness, thanks to the double meaning of the words earth, heaven, water, life, etc. The world's expressiveness achieves language through symbol as double meaning.

The situation is no different in the second zone of the emergence of symbolism, that of the oneiric, if one designates by this word the dreams of our days and our nights. It is well known that dreams are the royal road to psychoanalysis. All question of schools aside, dreams attest that we constantly mean something other than what we say; in dreams the manifest meaning endlessly refers to hidden meaning; that is what makes every dreamer a poet. From this point of view, dreams express the private archeology of the dreamer, which at times coincides with that of entire peoples; that is why Freud often limits the notion of symbol to those oneiric themes which repeat mythology.[6] But even when they do not coincide, the mythical and the oneiric have in common this structure of double meaning. The dream as a nocturnal spectacle is unknown to us; it is accessible only through the account of the waking hours. The analyst interprets this account, substituting for it another text which is, in his eyes, the thought-content of desire, i.e. what desire would say could it speak without restraint. It must be assumed, and this problem will occupy us at length, that dreams in themselves border on language, since they can be told, analyzed, interpreted.

The third zone of emergence is that of poetic imagination. I might have started here were it not for the fact that without the detour through the cosmic and oneiric, poetic imagination is the least understood of the three. Too often it has been said that imagination is the power of forming images. This is not true if by image one means the representation of an absent or unreal thing, a process of rendering present—of presentifying—the thing over there, elsewhere, or nowhere. In no way does poetic imagination reduce itself to the power of forming a mental picture of the unreal; the imagery of sensory origin merely serves as a vehicle and as material for the verbal power whose true dimension is given to us by the oneiric and the cosmic. As Bachelard says, the poetic image "places us at the origin of articulate being"; the poetic image "becomes a

6. See below, "Analytic," Part II, Ch. 3, for the discussion of the Freudian concept of symbolic dreams.

new being in our language, it expresses us by making us what it expresses."[7] This word-image, which runs through the representation-image, is symbolism.

Three times, then, the problem of symbolism has turned out to be coextensive with the problem of language itself. There is no symbolism prior to man who speaks, even though the power of symbols is rooted more deeply, in the expressiveness of the cosmos, in what desire wants to say, in the varied image-contents that men have. But in each case it is in language that the cosmos, desire, and the imaginary achieve speech. To be sure, the Psalm says: "The heavens tell the glory of God." But the heavens do not speak; or rather they speak through the prophets, they speak through hymns, they speak through liturgy. There must always be a word to take up the world and turn it into hierophany. Likewise the dreamer, in his private dream, is closed to all; he begins to instruct us only when he recounts his dream. This narrative is what presents the problem, just like the hymn of the psalmist. Thus it is the poet who shows us the birth of the word, in its hidden form in the enigmas of the cosmos and of the psyche. The power of the poet is to show forth symbols at the moment when "poetry places language in a state of emergence," to quote Bachelard again,[8] whereas ritual and myth fix symbols in their hieratic stability, and dreams close them in upon the labyrinth of desires where the dreamer loses the thread of his forbidden and mutilated discourse.

In order to give consistency and unity to these scattered manifestations of symbol, I define it by a semantic structure that these manifestations have in common, the structure of multiple meaning. Symbols occur when language produces signs of composite degree in which the meaning, not satisfied with designating some one thing, designates another meaning attainable only in and through the first intentionality.

It is here that we are tempted by another definition which this time risks being too narrow. The definition is suggested to us by some of our examples. It consists in characterizing the bond of

7. Gaston Bachelard, *La Poétique de l'espace* (Paris, Presses Universitaires de France, 1957), p. 7.
8. Ibid., p. 10.

meaning to meaning in a symbol as analogy. To revert to the examples of the symbolism of evil, is there not an analogy between spot and stain, deviation and sin, burden and fault, which would be, in a way, the analogy of the physical and the existential? Is there not also an analogy between the immensity of the heavens and the infinity of being, whatever that signifies? Is not analogy at the root of the "correspondences" of which the poet sings? Does not this definition have the authority of Platonism, Neoplatonism, and the philosophies of the analogy of being?

There is no doubt that the analogy constituting the meaning and force of many symbols is in no way reducible to a type of argument such as reasoning by analogy, in the strict sense of reasoning by proportionality. *A* is to *B* as *C* is to *D*. The analogy that may exist between the second meaning and the first meaning is not a relation I can place before me and inspect from the outside. It is not an argument; far from lending itself to formalization, it is a relation adhering to its terms. I am carried by the first meaning, directed by it, toward the second meaning; the symbolic meaning is constituted in and through the literal meaning which achieves the analogy by giving the analogue. In contrast to a likeness that we could look at from the outside, a symbol is the very movement of the primary meaning intentionally assimilating us to the symbolized, without our being able to intellectually dominate the likeness.

This correction of the notion of analogy does not suffice, however, to cover the whole field of hermeneutics. I would consider rather that analogy is but one of the relations involved between manifest and latent meaning. Psychoanalysis, as we shall see, has uncovered a variety of processes of elaboration that are operative between the apparent and the latent meaning. The dream work is singularly more complex than the classical way of analogy; so too Nietzsche and Marx have denounced a multitude of ruses and falsifications of meaning. Our entire hermeneutic problem, as we shall state in the next chapter, proceeds from this twofold possibility of an "innocent" analogical relationship or a "cunning" distortion. In discussing the psychoanalytic notion of interpretaton we will be occupied with this polarity in symbols. To have once caught sight of it is enough to prompt a search for a definition of symbol that would be narrower than Cassirer's symbolic function and at the same time wider than the analogy of the Platonic tradition and literary symbolism.

In order to arbitrate the discordance between a definition that is too "long" and a definition that is too "short," I propose to delimit the field of application of the concept of symbol by reference to the act of interpretation. A symbol exists, I shall say, where linguistic expression lends itself by its double or multiple meanings to a work of interpretation. What gives rise to this work is an intentional structure which consists not in the relation of meaning to thing but in an architecture of meaning, in a relation of meaning to meaning, of second meaning to first meaning, regardless of whether that relation be one of analogy or not, or whether the first meaning disguises or reveals the second meaning. This texture is what makes interpretation possible, although the texture itself is made evident only through the actual movement of interpretation.

This double approach to symbol through a definition that is too long and a definition that is too short leads us to the question that will be the object of the next study: What is interpretation? We have already glimpsed the disharmony intrinsic to the question. In any event, the reference of symbols to a hermeneutic understanding has a philosophic significance I would like to bring out at the end of this first investigation.

It is through interpretation, we said above, that the problem of symbols enters into the wider problem of language. However, the link with interpretation is not external to symbols, it is not superadded to them as a chance thought. No doubt a symbol is, in the Greek sense of the word, an "enigma," but as Heraclitus says, "the Master whose oracle is at Delphi does not speak, does not dissimulate; he signifies" (*οὔτε λέγει οὔτε κρύπτει ἀλλὰ σημαίνει*).[9] Enigma does not block understanding but provokes it; there is something to unfold, to "dis-implicate" in symbols. That which arouses understanding is precisely the double meaning, the intending of the second meaning in and through the first. In the figurative expressions of the servile will that constitute the symbolism of avowal I was

9. Diels-Kranz, *Die Fragmente der Vorsokratiker,* Vol. 1, *Heraclitus,* B 93.

able to show that it is the very excess of meaning in comparison to the literal expression that puts the interpretation in motion; thus, in the most archaic symbolism, the penitent spontaneously intends the meaning of stain in that of spot. In order to characterize this manner of living in and through analogy without the latter being recognized as a distinct semantic structure, one can speak of symbolic naïveté; but this naïveté is from the start moving toward interpretation by virtue of that transgression of meaning by meaning at the heart of the symbolic structure. In general terms, every *mythos* involves a latent *logos* which demands to be exhibited. That is why there are no symbols without the beginning of interpretation; where one man dreams, prophesies, or poetizes, another rises up to interpret. Interpretation organically belongs to symbolic thought and its double meaning.

This appeal to an interpretation that proceeds from symbols assures us that a reflection upon symbols falls within a philosophy of language and even within a philosophy of reason, as we shall try to show when we confront the meaning of symbol in hermeneutics with its meaning in symbolic logic. In hermeneutics symbols have their own semantics, they stimulate an intellectual activity of deciphering, of finding a hidden meaning. Far from falling outside the bounds of language, they raise feeling to meaningful articulation. Thus "avowal" has seemed to me a word that tears feeling from its mute opacity; all the stages of feeling can thus be marked off by semantic stages. Symbols are not a nonlanguage; the split between univocal and plurivocal language extends across the empire of language. That which reveals the richness or overdetermination of meaning and demonstrates that symbols belong to integral discourse is the work, perhaps interminable, of interpretation.

The time has come to say what interpretation is and how psychoanalytic interpretation enters into the conflict between interpretations. It is only at the end of this first sketch of hermeneutic understanding that we will be able to come back to the unsettled problem of the double nature, univocal and equivocal, of discourse, and also to confront the notion of symbol in hermeneutics with the notion of symbol in symbolic logic.

Chapter 2: The Conflict of Interpretations

At the end of the preceding study we asked, What is interpretation? This question governs the following one: How does psychoanalysis become involved in the conflict of interpretations? The question of interpretation, however, is no less perplexing than that of symbol. We thought we could arbitrate the differences concerning the definition of symbol by appealing to an intentional structure, the structure of double meaning, which in turn is brought to light only in the work of interpretation. But the concept of interpretation itself poses a problem.

THE CONCEPT OF INTERPRETATION

Let us first settle a difficulty which is still merely verbal and which has been implicitly resolved by our intermediate definition of symbol.

If we consult the tradition we meet with two usages; the one proposes to us a concept of interpretation that is too short, the other a concept that is too long. These two variations in the extension of the concept of interpretation reflect fairly closely the ones we considered in the definition of symbol. If we recall here the two historical roots of these discordant traditions, the *Peri Hermêneias* of Aristotle and biblical exegesis, it is because they give a rather good indication of what corrections are to be made if one is to arrive at our intermediate concept of hermeneutics.

Start with Aristotle. As is well known, the second treatise of the *Organon* is called the *Peri Hermêneias, On Interpretation*. From it stems what I call the overly "long" concept of interpretation, a concept somewhat reminiscent of symbol in the sense of the symbolic function of Cassirer and many of the moderns.[1] It is legitimate to look for the origin of our own problem in the Aristotelian notion of interpretation, even though the connection with the Aristotelian "interpretation" seems purely verbal: the word itself figures only in the title; what is more, it designates not a science dealing with significations but signification itself, that of nouns, verbs, propositions, and discourse in general. Interpretation is any voiced sound endowed with significance—every *phônê sêmantikê,* every *vox significativa.*[2] In this sense nouns, and verbs also,[3] are of themselves already interpretations, since in them we utter something. But the simple utterance or *phasis* is only a part taken from the total meaning of the *logos;* the complete meaning of *hermêneia* appears only in the complex enunciation, the sentence, which Aristotle calls *logos* and which covers commands, wishes, and questions as well as declarative discourse or *apophansis. Hermêneia,* in the *complete* sense, is the signification of the sentence. But in the *strong* sense of the logician it is the sentence susceptible of truth or falsity, that is, the declarative proposition.[4] The logician leaves the other

1. In Aristotle, moreover, *sumbolon* designates the expressive power of voiced sounds with respect to the states of the soul (*ta pathêmata*). A symbol is a conventional sign for the states of the soul, whereas the latter are the images (*homoiômata*) of things. Interpretation has therefore the same extension as symbol; the two words cover the totality of conventional signs, either in their expressive value or in their significative value. The treatise *On Interpretation* does not again speak of symbols (except in 16ª 28), seeing that the theory of expression does not come under this treatise but under the treatise *On the Soul.* The present treatise deals exclusively with signification. Pierre Aubenque, in his *Le Problème de l'être chez Aristote* (Paris, Presses Universitaires de France, 1962), p. 107, remarks that Aristotle sometimes takes the word "symbol" in the sense of signification. The dominant idea remains that of conventional sign; a symbol is the intermediary instituted between thought and being. Thus we are set on the path of Cassirer—through Kant, it is true!

2. "A noun is a voiced sound having a meaning by convention with no reference to time, while no part of it has any meaning when taken separately" (*On Interpretation,* Ch. 2, 16ª 19).

3. "A verb is that which, in addition to its particular meaning, has a reference to time; no part of it has meaning by itself, and it is always a sign of something said of something else" (ibid., Ch. 3, 16ᵇ 5).

4. "An affirmation is a statement asserting something of something; a negation is a statement separating something from something" (ibid., Ch. 6, 17ª 25).

types of discourse to rhetoric and poetics and retains only declarative discourse, the first form of which is the affirmation that "says something of something."

Let us stop with these definitions: they suffice to clarify in what sense the "semantic voice"—the signifying word—is interpretation. It is interpretation in the sense that, for Cassirer, the symbol is universal mediation; we say the real by signifying it; in this sense we interpret it. The break between signification and the thing has already occurred with nouns, and this intervening distance marks the locus of interpretation. Not all discourse is necessarily within the true; it does not adhere to being. In this regard, nouns that designate fictitious things—the "goat-stag" of Ch. 1 of the Aristotelian treatise—clearly show that there can be signification without the positing of existence. But we would not have thought of calling nouns "interpretation" if we did not see their signifying import in the light of that of verbs and that of verbs in the context of discourse, and if, in its turn, the signifying import of discourse were not concentrated in declarative discourse that says something of something. To say something of something is, in the complete and strong sense of the term, to interpret.[5]

How does this "interpretation," proper to the declarative proposition, orient us toward the modern concept of hermeneutics? The connection is not immediately evident. The "to say something of something" interests Aristotle only insofar as it is the locus of the true and the false. Hence the problem of the opposition between affirmation and negation becomes the central theme of the treatise; the semantics of the declarative proposition serves merely as an introduction to the logic of propositions which is essentially a logic of opposition, and the latter in turn leads to the *Analytics,* i.e. the logic of arguments. This logical aim prevents the development of

5. The notion of interpretation comes to the fore in the verb. On the one hand the verb looks to the noun, since it "adds to the meaning of the noun the meaning of present existence." On the other hand "it is always a sign of something said of something else"; Aristotle explains this formula thus: "Moreover, a verb is always a sign of something said of something else, i.e. of something predicated of a subject or contained in a subject" (ibid., Ch. 3, 16^b 10). Thus a verb looks toward the sentence or declarative discourse; in this sense it is as it were an instrument of the attribution which it "interprets," i.e. "signifies."

semantics for its own sake. Further, the way to a hermeneutics of double-meaning significations appears blocked from another side. The notion of signification requires univocity of meaning: the definition of the principle of identity, in its logical and ontological sense, demands it. Univocity of meaning is ultimately grounded in essence, one and self-identical; the entire refutation of the sophistical arguments is based upon this recourse to essence: "Not to have one meaning is to have no meaning." [6] Thus communication between men is possible only if words have *a* meaning, i.e. *one* meaning.

A reflection that extends the properly semantic analysis of the "to say something of something" leads us back to the area of our own problem. If man interprets reality by saying something of something, it is because real meanings are indirect; I attain things only by attributing a meaning to a meaning. Predication, in the logical sense of the term, puts into canonical form a relation of signification that forces us to reexamine the theory of univocity. The study of sophistical reasoning poses not one problem but two: the problem of the univocity of meanings without which dialogue is impossible, and the problem of their "communication"—to use the expression of Plato's *Sophist*—without which attribution is impossible. Without this counterpart univocity condemns one to a logical atomism, according to which a meaning simply is what it is. It is not enough to struggle against sophistic equivocity; a second front must be opened against Eleatic univocity. Nor is this second struggle without an echo in the philosophy of Aristotle. It breaks out even at the heart of the *Metaphysics;* the notion of being cannot be univocally defined: "being is said in several ways"; being means substance, quality, time, place, and so on. The famous distinction of the many meanings of being is not an anomaly in discourse, an exception in the theory of signification. The many meanings of being are the categories—or figures—of predication; hence this multiplicity cuts across the whole of discourse. Nor can it be overcome. Although it does not constitute a pure disorder of words, seeing that the different meanings of the word "being" are all ordered by reference to a first, original meaning, still this unity of reference—

6. *Metaphysics* Γ(IV), 1006^b 7.

pros hen legomenon—does not make *one* signification; the notion of being, it has recently been said, is but "the problematic unity of an irreducible plurality of meanings." [7]

I do not mean to draw from the general semantics of the *Peri Hermêneias* and from the particular semantics of the word "being" more than is allowed; I do not say that Aristotle raised the problem of plurivocal meanings in the way we shall elaborate it here. I merely suggest that his definition of interpretation as "to say something of something" leads to a semantics distinct from logic and that his discussion of the multiple meanings of being opens a breach in the purely logical and ontological theory of univocity. The task of founding a theory of interpretation, conceived as the understanding of plurivocal meanings, has not yet been accomplished. The second tradition will bring us closer to the goal.

The second tradition comes to us from biblical exegesis. Hermeneutics in this sense is the science of the rules of exegesis, the latter being understood as the particular interpretation of a text. There is no question that the problem of hermeneutics has to a great extent been constituted within the boundaries of the interpretation of Holy Scripture. The core of this hermeneutics lies in what has traditionally been called the "four senses of Scripture." It cannot be emphasized too strongly that philosophers should be more attentive to those exegetical discussions in which a general theory of interpretation was operative.[8] There in particular the notions of analogy, allegory, and symbolic meaning were elaborated—notions to which we shall frequently have to return. This second tradition, then, relates hermeneutics to the definition of symbol by analogy, although it does not entirely reduce hermeneutics to this definition.

What limits the definition of exegetical hermeneutics is, first, its reference to an authority, whether monarchical, collegial, or ecclesiastic, the latter being the case of biblical hermeneutics as practiced within the Christian communities. Most of all, however, it is limited by being applied to a literary text: exegesis is a science of writings.

Still, the exegetical tradition affords a good starting point for our

7. Aubenque, p. 204.
8. Henri de Lubac, *Exégèse médiévale* (4 vols. Paris, Aubier, 1959–64).

enterprise, for the notion of text can be taken in an analogous sense. Thanks to the metaphor of "the book of nature" the Middle Ages was able to speak of an *interpretatio naturae*. This metaphor brings to light a possible extension of the notion of exegesis, inasmuch as the notion of "text" is wider than that of "scripture." With the Renaissance the interpretatio naturae was completely freed from its properly scriptural references, with the result that Spinoza could use it to inaugurate a new conception of biblical exegesis. The interpretation of nature, he says in the *Theologico-Political Treatise*, is to inspire a new hermeneutics ruled by the principle of the interpretation of Scripture by itself. This step of Spinoza's, which does not interest us here from the strictly biblical point of view, marks a curious rebound of the interpretatio naturae upon the interpretation of Scripture: the former scriptural model is now called into question, and the new model is henceforward the interpretatio naturae.

This notion of text—thus freed from the notion of scripture or writing—is of considerable interest. Freud often makes use of it, particularly when he compares the work of analysis to translating from one language to another; the dream account is an unintelligible text for which the analyst substitutes a more intelligible text. To understand is to make this substitution. The title *Traumdeutung*, which we have briefly considered, alludes to this analogy between analysis and exegesis.

At this point we may draw an initial comparison between Freud and Nietzsche. Nietzsche borrowed the concept of *Deutung* or *Auslegung* from the discipline of philology and introduced it into philosophy. It is true that Nietzsche remains a philologist when he interprets Greek tragedy or the pre-Socratics, but with him the whole of philosophy becomes interpretation. Interpretation of what? We shall answer that question later, when we enter into the conflict of interpretation. For the present this point can be made: the new career opened up for the concept of interpretation is linked to a new problematic of representation, of *Vorstellung*. It is no longer the Kantian question of how a subjective representation or idea can have objective validity; this question, central to a critical philosophy, gives way to a more radical one. The problem of objective validity still remained in the orbit of the Platonic philosophy of truth and science, of which error and opinion are the contraries. The problem of interpretation refers to a new possibility which is no longer either error in the epistemological sense or lying in the moral sense, but illusion, the status of which we will discuss further on. Let us leave aside for the moment the problem we shall turn to shortly, namely, the use of interpretation as a tactic of suspicion and as a battle against masks; this use calls for a very specific philosophy which subordinates the entire problem of truth and error to the expression of the will to power. The important point here, from the standpoint of method, is the new extension given to the exegetical concept of interpretation.

Freud's position lies at one of the ends of this extension. For him, interpretation is concerned not only with a scripture or writing but with any set of signs that may be taken as a text to decipher, hence a dream or neurotic symptom, as well as a ritual, myth, work of art, or a belief. Thus we return to our notion of symbol as double meaning, with the question still undecided whether double meaning is dissimulation or revelation, necessary lying or access to the sacred. We had in mind an enlarged concept of exegesis when we defined hermeneutics as the science of exegetical rules and exegesis as the interpretation of a particular text or of a set of signs considered as a text.

As may be seen, this intermediate definition, which goes beyond a mere scriptural science without being dissolved in a general theory of meaning, receives its authority from both sources. The exegetical source seems the closer, but the problem of univocity and equivocity to which interpretation in the Aristotelian sense leads us is perhaps still more radical than the problem of analogy in exegesis. We return to this in the next chapter. On the other hand, the problem of illusion, central to the Nietzschian Auslegung, brings us to the threshold of the key difficulty that governs the fate of modern hermeneutics. This difficulty, which we shall now consider, is not a mere duplicate of the one involved in the definition of symbol; it is a difficulty peculiar to the act of interpreting as such.

The difficulty—it initiated my research in the first place—is this: there is no general hermeneutics, no universal canon for exegesis, but only disparate and opposed theories concerning the rules of interpretation. The hermeneutic field, whose outer contours we have traced, is internally at variance with itself.

I have neither the intention nor the means to attempt a complete enumeration of hermeneutic styles. The more enlightening course, it seems to me, is to start with the polarized opposition that creates the greatest tension at the outset of our investigation. According to the one pole, hermeneutics is understood as the manifestation and restoration of a meaning addressed to me in the manner of a message, a proclamation, or as is sometimes said, a kerygma; according to the other pole, it is understood as a demystification, as a reduction of illusion. Psychoanalysis, at least on a first reading, aligns itself with the second understanding of hermeneutics.

From the beginning we must consider this double possibility: this tension, this extreme polarity, is the truest expression of our "modernity." The situation in which language today finds itself comprises this double possibility, this double solicitation and urgency: on the one hand, purify discourse of its excrescences, liquidate the idols, go from drunkenness to sobriety, realize our state of poverty once and for all; on the other hand, use the most "nihilistic," destructive, iconoclastic movement so as to *let speak* what once, what each time, was *said,* when meaning appeared anew, when meaning was at its fullest. Hermeneutics seems to me to be animated by this double motivation: willingness to suspect, willingness to listen; vow of rigor, vow of obedience. In our time we have not finished doing away with *idols* and we have barely begun to listen to *symbols.* It may be that this situation, in its apparent distress, is instructive: it may be that extreme iconoclasm belongs to the restoration of meaning.

The underlying reason for initially posing the problem in the above way is to bring into the open the crisis of language that today makes us oscillate between demystification and restoration of meaning. To my mind, an introduction to the psychoanalysis of culture has had to proceed in this roundabout way. In the next chapter we will try to probe deeper into these prolegomena and relate the crisis of language to an ascesis of reflection whose first movement is to let itself be dispossessed of the origin of meaning.

To finish locating psychoanalysis within the general discussion of language, the terms of the conflict need to be sketched.

INTERPRETATION AS RECOLLECTION OF MEANING

This section is concerned with hermeneutics as the restoration of meaning. The point at issue in the psychoanalysis of culture and the school of suspicion is better understood if we first contrast what is radically opposed to them.

The contrary of suspicion, I will say bluntly, is faith. What faith? No longer, to be sure, the first faith of the simple soul, but rather the second faith of one who has engaged in hermeneutics, faith that has undergone criticism, postcritical faith. Let us look for it in the series of philosophic decisions that secretly animate a phenomenology of religion and lie hidden even within its apparent neutrality. It is a rational faith, for it interprets; but it is a faith because it seeks, through interpretation, a second naïveté. Phenomenology is its instrument of hearing, of recollection, of restoration of meaning. "Believe in order to understand, understand in order to believe" —such is its maxim; and its maxim is the "hermeneutic circle" itself of believing and understanding.

We will take our examples from the phenomenology of religion in the wide sense, embracing here the work of Leenhardt, Van der Leeuw, and Eliade, to which I add my own research in *The Symbolism of Evil.*

It will be our task to disengage and display the rational faith that runs through the purely intentional analysis of religious symbolism and "converts" this listening analysis from within.

The first imprint of this faith in a revelation through the word is to be seen in the care or concern for the *object,* a characteristic of all phenomenological analysis. That concern, as we know, presents itself as a "neutral" wish to describe and not to reduce. One reduces by explaining through causes (psychological, social, etc.), through genesis (individual, historical, etc.), through function (affective, ideological, etc.). One describes by disengaging the (noetic) intention and its (noematic) correlate—the *something* intended, the implicit object in ritual, myth, and belief. Thus, in the case of the symbolism of the pure and the impure alluded to in Chapter 1, the task is to understand what is signified, what quality of the sacred is intended, what shade of threat is implied in the analogy between spot and stain, between physical contamination and the loss of existential integrity. In my own research, concern for the object consisted in surrender to the movement of meaning which, starting from the literal sense—the spot or contamination—points to something grasped in the region of the sacred. To generalize from this, we shall say that the theme of the phenomenology of religion is the *something* intended in ritual actions, in mythical speech, in belief or mystical feeling; its task is to dis-implicate that object from the various intentions of behavior, discourse, and emotion. Let us call this intended object the "sacred," without determining its nature, whether it be the *tremendum numinosum,* according to Rudolf Otto; "the powerful," according to Van der Leeuw; or "fundamental Time," according to Eliade. In this general sense, and with a view to underlining the concern for the intentional object, we may say that every phenomenology of religion is a phenomenology of the sacred. However, is it possible for a phenomenology of the sacred to stay within the limits of a neutral attitude governed by the *epochê,* by the bracketing of absolute reality and of every question concerning the absolute? The epochê requires that I participate in the belief in the reality of the religious object, but in a neutralized mode; that I believe with the believer, but without positing absolutely the object of his belief.

But while the scientist as such can and must practice this method of bracketing, the philosopher as such cannot and must not avoid the question of the absolute validity of his object. For would I be interested in the object, could I stress concern for the object, through the consideration of cause, genesis, or function, if I did not expect, from within understanding, this something to "address" itself to me? Is not the expectation of being spoken to what motivates the concern for the object? Implied in this expectation is a confidence in language: the belief that language, which bears symbols, is not so much spoken by men as spoken to men, that men are born into language, into the light of the logos "who enlightens every man who comes into the world." It is this expectation, this confidence, this belief, that confers on the study of symbols its particular seriousness. To be truthful, I must say it is what animates all my research. But it is also what today is contested by the whole stream of hermeneutics that we shall soon place under the heading of "suspicion." This latter theory of interpretation begins by doubting whether there is such an object and whether this object could be the place of the transformation of intentionality into kerygma, manifestation, proclamation. This hermeneutics is not an explication of the object, but a tearing off of masks, an interpretation that reduces disguises.

Second, according to the phenomenology of religion, there is a "truth" of symbols; this truth, in the neutral attitude of the Husserlian epochê, means merely the fulfillment—*die Erfüllung*—of the signifying intention. For a phenomenology of religion to be possible, it is necessary and sufficient that there be not only one but several ways of fulfilling various intentions of meaning according to various regions of objects. Verification, in the sense of logical positivism, is one type of fulfillment among others and not the canonical mode of fulfillment; it is a type required by the corresponding type of object, namely, the physical object and, in another sense, the historical object—but not by the concept of truth as such, or, in other words, by the requirement of fulfillment in general. It is in virtue of this multiplicity of types of fulfillment that phenomenology, in a reduced, neutralized mode, speaks of religious experience, not by analogy, but according to the specific type of object and the specific mode of fulfillment in that field.

We encountered this problem of fulfillment in the order of symbolic meanings in our investigation of the analogical bond between the primary or literal "signifier" and the secondary "signified"—for example, the bond between spot and stain, between deviation (or wandering) and sin, between weight (or burden) and fault. Here we run up against a primordial, unfailing relationship, which never has the conventional and arbitrary character of "technical" signs that mean only what is posited in them.

In this relationship of meaning to meaning resides what I have called the *fullness* of language. The fullness consists in the fact that the second meaning somehow dwells in the first meaning. In his *Traité d'histoire générale des religions,* Mircea Eliade clearly shows that the force of the cosmic symbolism resides in the nonarbitrary bond between the visible heavens and the order they manifest: thanks to the analogical power that binds meaning to meaning, the heavens *speak* of the wise and the just, the immense and the ordered. Symbols are bound in a double sense: bound *to* and bound *by*. On the one hand, the sacred is *bound to* its primary, literal, sensible meanings; this is what constitutes the opacity of symbols. On the other hand, the literal meaning is *bound by* the symbolic meaning that resides in it; this is what I have called the revealing power of symbols, which gives them their force in spite of their opacity. The revealing power of symbols opposes symbols to technical signs, which merely signify what is posited in them and which, therefore, can be emptied, formalized, and reduced to mere objects of a calculus. Symbols alone *give* what they say.

But in saying this have we not already broken the phenomenological neutrality? I admit it. I admit that what deeply motivates the interest in full language, in bound language, is this inversion of the movement of thought which now addresses itself to me and makes me a subject that is spoken to. And this inversion is produced in analogy. How? How does that which binds meaning to meaning bind me? The movement that draws me toward the second meaning assimilates me to what is said, makes me participate in what is announced to me. The similitude in which the force of symbols resides and from which they draw their revealing power is not an objective likeness, which I may look upon like a relation laid out before me; it is an existential assimilation, according to the movement of analogy, of my being to being.

This allusion to the ancient theme of participation helps us make a third step along the path of explication, which is also the path of intellectual honesty: the fully declared philosophical decision animating the intentional analysis would be a modern version of the ancient theme of reminiscence. After the silence and forgetfulness made widespread by the manipulation of empty signs and the construction of formalized languages, the modern concern for symbols expresses a new desire to be addressed.

This expectancy of a new Word, of a new tidings of the Word, is the implicit intention of every phenomenology of symbols, which first puts the accent on the object, then underscores the fullness of symbol, to finally greet the revealing power of the primal word.

INTERPRETATION AS EXERCISE OF SUSPICION

We shall complete our assigning of a place to Freud by giving him not just one interlocutor but a whole company. Over against interpretation as restoration of meaning we shall oppose interpretation according to what I collectively call the school of suspicion.

A general theory of interpretation would thus have to account not only for the opposition between two interpretations of interpretation, the one as recollection of meaning, the other as reduction of the illusions and lies of consciousness; but also for the division and scattering of each of these two great "schools" of interpretation into "theories" that differ from one another and are even foreign to one another. This is no doubt truer of the school of suspicion than of the school of reminiscence. Three masters, seemingly mutually exclusive, dominate the school of suspicion: Marx, Nietzsche, and Freud. It is easier to show their common opposition to a phenomenology of the sacred, understood as a propaedeutic to the "revelation" of meaning, than their interrelationship within a single method of demystification. It is relatively easy to note that these three figures all contest the primacy of the object in our representation of the sacred, as well as the fulfilling of the intention of the sacred by a type of analogy of being that would engraft us onto being through the power of an assimilating intention. It is also easy to recognize that this contesting is an exercise of suspicion in three different ways; "truth as lying" would be the negative heading under which one might place these three exercises of suspicion. But we are still far from having assimilated the positive meaning of the enterprises of these three thinkers. We are still too attentive to their differences and to the limitations that the prejudices of their times impose upon their successors even more than upon themselves. Thus Marx is relegated to economics and the absurd theory of the reflex consciousness; Nietzsche is drawn toward biologism and a perspectivism incapable of expressing itself without contradiction; Freud is restricted to psychiatry and decked out with a simplistic pansexualism.

If we go back to the intention they had in common, we find in it the decision to look upon the whole of consciousness primarily as "false" consciousness. They thereby take up again, each in a different manner, the problem of the Cartesian doubt, to carry it to the very heart of the Cartesian stronghold. The philosopher trained in the school of Descartes knows that things are doubtful, that they are not such as they appear; but he does not doubt that consciousness is such as it appears to itself; in consciousness, meaning and conciousness of meaning coincide. Since Marx, Nietzsche, and Freud, this too has become doubtful. After the doubt about things, we have started to doubt consciousness.

These three masters of suspicion are not to be misunderstood, however, as three masters of skepticism. They are, assuredly, three great "destroyers." But that of itself should not mislead us; destruction, Heidegger says in *Sein und Zeit,* is a moment of every new foundation, including the destruction of religion, insofar as religion is, in Nietzsche's phrase, a "Platonism for the people." It is beyond destruction that the question is posed as to what thought, reason, and even faith still signify.

All three clear the horizon for a more authentic word, for a new reign of Truth, not only by means of a "destructive" critique, but by the invention of an art of *interpreting*. Descartes triumphed over the doubt as to things by the evidence of consciousness; they triumph over the doubt as to consciousness by an exegesis of meaning. Beginning with them, understanding is hermeneutics: henceforward, to seek meaning is no longer to spell out the consciousness of meaning, but to *decipher its expressions*. What must be faced, therefore, is not only a threefold suspicion, but a threefold guile. If consciousness is not what it thinks it is, a new relation must be instituted between the patent and the latent; this new relation would correspond to the one that consciousness had instituted between appearances and the reality of things. For Marx, Nietzsche, and Freud, the fundamental category of consciousness is the relation hidden-shown or, if you prefer, simulated-manifested. That the Marxists are stubbornly insistent on the "reflex" theory, that Nietzsche contradicts himself in dogmatizing about the "perspectivism" of the will to power, that Freud mythologizes with his "censorship," "watchman," and "disguises"—still, what is essential does not lie in these encumbrances and impasses. What is essential is that all three create with the means at hand, with and against the prejudices of their times, a mediate *science* of meaning, irreducible to the immediate *consciousness* of meaning. What all three attempted, in different ways, was to make their "conscious" methods of deciphering coincide with the "unconscious" *work* of ciphering which they attributed to the will to power, to social being, to the unconscious psychism. *Guile will be met by double guile.*

Thus the distinguishing characteristic of Marx, Freud, and Nietzsche is the general hypothesis concerning both the process of false consciousness and the method of deciphering. The two go together, since the man of suspicion carries out in reverse the work of falsification of the man of guile. Freud entered the problem of false consciousness via the double road of dreams and neurotic symptoms; his working hypothesis has the same limits as his angle of attack, which was, as we shall state fully in the sequel, an economics of instincts. Marx attacks the problem of ideologies from within the limits of economic alienation, now in the sense of political economy. Nietzsche, focusing on the problem of "value"—of evaluation and transvaluation—looks for the key to lying and masks on the side of the "force" and "weakness" of the will to power.

Fundamentally, the *Genealogy of Morals* in Nietzsche's sense, the theory of ideologies in the Marxist sense, and the theory of ideals and illusions in Freud's sense represent three convergent procedures of demystification.

Yet there is perhaps something they have even more in common, an underlying relationship that goes even deeper. All three begin with suspicion concerning the illusions of consciousness, and then proceed to employ the stratagem of deciphering; all three, however, far from being detractors of "consciousness," aim at extending it. What Marx wants is to liberate *praxis* by the understanding of necessity; but this liberation is inseparable from a "conscious insight" which victoriously counterattacks the mystification of false consciousness. What Nietzsche wants is the increase of man's power, the restoration of his force; but the meaning of the will to power must be recaptured by meditating on the ciphers "superman," "eternal return," and "Dionysus," without which the power in question would be but worldly violence. What Freud desires is that the one who is analyzed, by making his own the meaning that was foreign to him, enlarge his field of consciousness, live better, and finally be a little freer and, if possible, a little happier. One of the earliest homages paid to psychoanalysis speaks of "healing through consciousness." The phrase is exact—if one means thereby that analysis wishes to substitute for an immediate and dissimulating consciousness a mediate consciousness taught by the reality principle. Thus the same doubter who depicts the ego as a "poor creature" in subjection to three masters, the id, the superego, and reality or necessity, is also the exegete who rediscovers the logic of the illogical kingdom and who dares, with unparalleled modesty and discretion, to terminate his essay on *The Future of an Illusion* by invoking the god Logos, soft of voice but indefatigable, in no wise omnipotent, but efficacious in the long run.

This last reference to Freud's "reality principle" and to its equivalents in Nietzsche and Marx—eternal return in the former, understood necessity in the latter—brings out the positive benefit of the ascesis required by a reductive and destructive interpretation: confrontation with bare reality, the discipline of Ananke, of necessity.

While finding their positive convergence, our three masters of suspicion also present the most radically contrary stance to the phenomenology of the sacred and to any hermeneutics understood as the recollection of meaning and as the reminiscence of being.

At issue in this controversy is the fate of what I shall call, for the sake of brevity, the mytho-poetic core of imagination. Over against illusion and the fable-making function, demystifying hermeneutics sets up the rude discipline of necessity. It is the lesson of Spinoza: one first finds himself a slave, he understands his slavery, he rediscovers himself free within understood necessity. The *Ethics* is the first model of the ascesis that must be undergone by the libido, the will to power, the imperialism of the dominant class. But, in return, does not this discipline of the real, this ascesis of the necessary lack the grace of imagination, the upsurge of the possible? And does not this grace of imagination have something to do with the Word as Revelation?

This is what is at issue in the debate. Our question now is to determine to what extent such a debate can still be arbitrated within the limits of a philosophy of reflection.

Chapter 3: Hermeneutic Method and Reflective Philosophy

We assigned ourselves the task, in these beginning chapters, of placing Freud within the movement of contemporary thought. Before becoming involved with its technical language and specific problem we wanted to reconstruct the context in which psychoanalysis is set. We first fixed its hermeneutics of culture upon the background of the problematic of language. From the outset we have looked upon psychoanalysis as throwing light upon and contesting human speech; Freud belongs to our time just as much as Wittgenstein and Bultmann. The place of psychoanalysis within the general debate on language might be more precisely described as an episode in the war between the various hermeneutics, though this does not tell us whether psychoanalysis is but one hermeneutic sect among others or whether, in a manner we shall have to discover, it encroaches upon all the others. In this chapter we would like to go further and discern in psychoanalysis, in the hermeneutic war itself, and in the problematic of language as a whole, a crisis of reflection—that is to say, in the strong and philosophic sense of the term, an adventure of the Cogito and of the reflective philosophy that proceeds therefrom.

THE RECOURSE OF SYMBOLS TO REFLECTION

I will begin by retracing the path of my own inquiry. It was as a requirement of lucidity, of veracity, of rigor, that I encountered what I called, at the end of *The Symbolism of Evil,* "the passage to reflection." Is it possible, I asked, to coherently interrelate the interpretation of symbols and philosophic reflection? My only answer to this question was in the form of a contradictory resolve: I vowed, on the one hand, *to listen* to the rich words of symbols and myths that precede my reflection, instruct and nourish it; and on the other hand to continue, by means of the philosophical exegesis of symbols and myths, the tradition of rationality of philosophy, of our western philosophy. Symbols give rise to thought, I said, using a phrase from Kant's *Critique of Judgment*. Symbols give, they are the gift of language; but this gift creates for me the duty to think, to inaugurate philosophic discourse, starting from what is always prior to and the foundation of that discourse. I did not conceal the paradoxical character of this promise; on the contrary, I accentuated it by affirming first that philosophy does not begin anything, since the fullness of language precedes it, and second that it begins from itself, since it is philosophy which inaugurates the question of meaning and of the foundation of meaning.

I was encouraged along these lines by what appeared to me to be a prephilosophical richness of symbols. Symbols, it seemed to me, call not only for interpretation, as we said in the first chapter, but for *philosophic reflection*. If this did not become apparent to us sooner, it is because we have restricted ourselves up to now to the semantic structure of symbols, that is, to the excess of meaning due to their "overdetermination."

That symbols call for reflection, however, is due to a second trait of symbols which we have left in the shadows; the purely semantic aspect is merely their most abstract aspect. Linguistic expressions are embodied not only in rituals and emotions, as was suggested above when we mentioned the symbolism of the pure and the impure, but also in myths, that is, in the great narratives about the beginning and the end of evil. I have studied four cycles of these myths: the myths of the primal chaos, the myths of the wicked god, the myths of the soul exiled in an evil body, and the myths concerning the historical fault of an individual who is both an ancestor and a prototype of humanity. New traits of symbol appear here, and with them new suggestions for a hermeneutics. First, these myths introduce exemplary personages—Prometheus, Anthropos, Adam—who begin to generalize human experience on the level of a universal concept or paradigm in which we can read our condition and destiny. Second, thanks to the structure of the narrative that tells of events that happened "once upon a time," our experience receives a temporal orientation, an *élan* extended between a beginning and an end; our present becomes charged with a memory and a hope. More profoundly still, these myths recount, after the manner of a transhistorical event, the irrational break, the absurd leap, which separates two views, one concerned with the innocence of coming-to-be, the other with the guilt of history. At this level symbols have not only an expressive value, as they do on the merely semantic level, but a heuristic value, since they confer universality, temporality and ontological import upon our self-understanding. Interpretation therefore does not consist simply in extricating the second intention, which is both given and masked in the literal meaning; it tries to thematize this universality, this temporality, this ontological exploration implied in myth. Thus, in their mythical form symbols themselves push toward speculative expression; symbols themselves are the dawn of reflection. The hermeneutic problem therefore is not imposed upon reflection from without, but proposed from within by the very movement of meaning, by the implicit life of symbols taken at their semantic and mythical level.

There is a third way in which the symbolism of evil calls for a science of interpretation, a hermeneutics. Semantically as well as mythically, the symbols of evil are always the obverse side of a greater symbolism, a symbolism of salvation. This is already true on the semantic level: to the impure there corresponds the pure; to the wandering of sin corresponds pardon in its symbol of the return; to the weight of sin, deliverance; and, more generally, to the symbolism of slavery, that of liberation. It is even clearer on the mythical level; the images of the beginning receive their true meaning from the images of the end. The symbolism of chaos constitutes the preface of a poem that celebrates the enthroning of Marduk; to the tragic god corresponds the purification of Apollo, the same Apollo who through his oracle called Socrates to "examine" other men; to the myth of the soul in exile corresponds the symbolism of deliverance through knowledge; to the figure of the first Adam correspond the successive figures of the King, the Messiah, the Just One who suffers, the Son of Man, the Lord, the Logos. The philosopher, qua philosopher, has nothing to say concerning the proclamation, the apostolic kerygma, according to which these figures are brought to fulfillment in the coming of the Christ Jesus; but he can and should reflect upon these symbols insofar as they are representations of the end of evil. What, then, does this one-to-one correspondence between the two symbolisms signify? It signifies, first, that the symbolism of evil receives its true meaning from the symbolism of salvation. The symbolism of evil is only a particular province within religious symbolism; thus the Christian *Credo* does not say "I believe in sin," but "I believe in the remission of sins." More fundamentally, however, the correspondence between a symbolism of evil and a symbolism of salvation signifies that we must cease being totally absorbed in a symbolism of evil that is severed from the rest of the symbolic and mythic universe and reflect upon the totality formed by these symbols of the beginning and the end. Thereby is suggested the architectonic task of reason, which has already been sketched in the interplay of the mythic correspondences; it is this totality, as such, which demands expression at the level of reflection and speculation.

Symbols themselves demand this speculative reflection. An interpretation of symbols that extricated their philosophical meaning would not be something superadded to them. Such an interpretation is required by the semantic structure of symbols, by the latent speculation of myths, and finally by the fact that each symbol belongs to a meaningful totality which furnishes the first schema of the system.

Though we do not yet know what privileged place [1] the symbols and myths of evil have within the empire of symbolism, we will here try to pose the problem in its full generality by asking the question:

1. In giving precedence to the problem of method, we reduce the entire symbolism of evil to the rank of an example. We shall not regret doing so: one of the results of reflection will be precisely that the symbolism of evil is not one example out of many but a privileged example, perhaps even the native land of all symbolism, the birthplace of the hermeneutic conflict taken in its full extent. But this we shall understand only through the movement of reflection—a reflection that at first knows the symbols of evil merely as a given or arbitrarily chosen example.

How can a philosophy of reflection nourish itself at the symbolic source and become hermeneutic?

It must be admitted that the question seems quite perplexing. Traditionally—since Plato, that is—it is put in the following terms: What is the place of myth in philosophy? If myth calls for philosophy, is it true that philosophy calls for myth? Or, in the terms of the present work, does reflection call for symbols and the interpretation of symbols? This question precedes any attempt to move from mythical symbols to speculative symbols, whatever the symbolic area being dealt with. One must first make sure that the philosophic act, in its innermost nature, not only does not exclude, but requires something like an interpretation.

At first sight the question seems hopeless. Philosophy, born in Greece, introduced new demands in contrast to mythical thought; first and foremost it established the idea of a science, in the sense of the Platonic *epistêmê* or the *Wissenschaft* of German idealism. In view of this idea of philosophical science, the recourse to symbols has something scandalous about it.

In the first place, symbols remain caught within the diversity of languages and cultures and espouse their irreducible singularity. Why begin with the Babylonians, the Hebrews, the Greeks—be they tragic or Pythagorean? Because they nourish my memory? In that case I put my singularity at the center of my reflection; but does not philosophical science require that the singularity of cultural creations and individual memories be reabsorbed into the universality of discourse?

Secondly, philosophy as a rigorous science seems to require univocal significations. But symbols, by reason of their analogical texture, are opaque, nontransparent; the double meaning that gives them concrete roots weights them down with materiality. This double meaning is not accidental but constitutive, inasmuch as the analogous sense, the existential sense, is given only in and through the literal sense; in epistemological terms, this opacity can only mean equivocity. Can philosophy systematically cultivate the equivocal?

Thirdly, and this is the most serious point, the bond between symbol and interpretation, in which we have seen the promise of an organic connection between *mythos* and *logos*, furnishes a new motive for suspicion. Any interpretation can be revoked; no myths without exegesis, but no exegesis without contesting. The deciphering of enigmas is not a science, either in the Platonic, Hegelian, or modern sense of the word "science." Our preceding chapter gave a glimpse of the gravity of the problem: there we considered the most extreme opposition imaginable within the field of hermeneutics, the opposition between the phenomenology of religion, conceived as a remythicizing of discourse, and psychoanalysis, conceived as a demystification of discourse. By the same token our problem becomes graver in becoming more precise. The question now is not simply why an interpretation, but why *these* opposed interpretations? The task is not only to justify the recourse to some kind of interpretation, but to justify the dependence of reflection upon preconstituted hermeneutics that are mutually exclusive.

To justify the recourse to symbols in philosophy is ultimately to justify cultural contingency, equivocal language, and the war of hermeneutics within itself.

The solution of the problem hinges on showing that reflection, in principle, requires something like interpretation; starting from that requirement one can then justify, also in principle, the detour through the contingency of cultures, through an incurably equivocal language, and through the conflict of interpretations.

Let us begin at the beginning. Up to the present we have only been considering the recourse of symbols to reflection; what makes that recourse intelligible is reflection's recourse to symbols.

THE RECOURSE OF REFLECTION TO SYMBOLS

When we say philosophy is reflection we mean, assuredly, self-reflection. But what does the Self signify? Do we know it any better than the words symbol and interpretation? No doubt we do, but with a knowledge that is abstract, empty, and vain. Let us start, then, by taking stock of this vain certitude. Perhaps it is symbolism that will save reflection from its vanity, while at the same time reflection will provide the structure for handling any hermeneutic conflict. Therefore, what does Reflection signify? What does the Self of self-reflection signify?

I assume here that the positing of the self is the first truth for the philosopher placed within that broad tradition of modern philosophy that begins with Descartes and is developed in Kant, Fichte, and the reflective stream of European philosophy. For this tradition, which we shall consider as a whole before setting its main representatives in opposition to one another, the positing of the self is a truth which posits itself; it can be neither verified nor deduced; it is at once the positing of a being and of an act; the positing of an existence and of an operation of thought: *I am, I think;* to exist, for me, is to think; I exist inasmuch as I think. Since this truth cannot be verified like a fact, nor deduced like a conclusion, it has to posit itself in reflection; its self-positing is reflection; Fichte called this first truth the *thetic judgment*. Such is our philosophical starting point.

But this first reference of reflection to the positing of the self, as existing and thinking, does not sufficiently characterize reflection. In particular, we do not yet understand why reflection requires a work of deciphering, an exegesis, and a science of exegesis or hermeneutics, and still less why this deciphering must be either a psychoanalysis or a phenomenology of the sacred. This point cannot be understood so long as reflection is seen as a return to the so-called evidence of immediate consciousness. We have to introduce a second trait of reflection, which may be stated thus: reflection is not intuition; or, in positive terms, reflection is the effort to recapture the Ego of the Ego Cogito in the mirror of its objects, its works, its acts. But why must the positing of the Ego be recaptured through its acts? Precisely because it is given neither in a psychological evidence, nor in an intellectual intuition, nor in a mystical vision. A reflective philosophy is the contrary of a philosophy of the immediate. The first truth—*I am, I think*—remains as abstract and empty as it is invincible; it has to be "mediated" by the ideas, actions, works, institutions, and monuments that objectify it. It is in these objects, in the widest sense of the word, that the Ego must lose and find itself. We can say, in a somewhat paradoxical sense, that a philosophy of reflection is not a philosophy of consciousness, if by consciousness we mean immediate self-consciousness. Consciousness, as we shall say later, is a task, but it is a task because it is not a given . . . No doubt I have an apperception of myself and my acts, and this apperception is a type of evidence. Descartes cannot be dislodged from this incontestable proposition: I cannot doubt myself without perceiving that I doubt. But what does this apperception signify? A certitude, certainly, but a certitude devoid of truth. As Malebranche well understood, in opposition to Descartes, this immediate grasp is only a feeling and not an idea. If ideas are light and vision, there is no vision of the Ego, nor light in apperception. I only sense that I exist and that I think; I sense that I am awake; such is apperception. In Kantian language, an apperception of the Ego may accompany all my representations, but this apperception is not knowledge of oneself, it cannot be transformed into an intuition of a substantial soul; the decisive critique Kant directs against any "rational psychology" has definitively dissociated reflection from any so-called knowledge of self.[2]

This second thesis, that reflection is not intuition, enables us to glimpse the place interpretation has in the knowledge of oneself; that place is indirectly indicated by the difference between reflection and intuition.

A new step will bring us closer to the goal. Having opposed reflection and intuition to one another, with Kant and in opposition to Descartes, I would like to distinguish the task of reflection from a mere critique of knowledge; this new step leads us away from Kant in the direction of Fichte and Nabert. The basic limitation of a critical philosophy lies in its exclusive concern for epistemology; reflection is reduced to a single dimension: the only canonical operations of thought are those that ground the "objectivity" of our representations. This priority given to epistemology explains why in Kant, in spite of appearances, the practical philosophy is subordinated to the critical philosophy: the second critique, that of practical reason, in fact borrows all of its structures from the first, that of pure reason. A single question rules the critical philosophy: What is a priori and what is merely empirical in knowledge? This distinction is the key

2. In Husserlian language: the Ego Cogito is apodictic, but not necessarily adequate.

to the theory of objectivity; it is purely and simply transposed into the second critique; the objectivity of the maxims of the will rests on the distinction between the validity of duty, which is a priori, and the content of empirical desires. It is in opposition to this reduction of reflection to a simple critique that I say, with Fichte and his French successor, Jean Nabert, that reflection is not so much a justification of science and duty as a reappropriation of our effort to exist; epistemology is only a part of this broader task: we have to recover the act of existing, the positing of the self, in all the density of its works. Why must this recovery be characterized as appropriation and even as reappropriation? I must recover something which has first been lost; I make "proper to me" what has ceased being mine. I make "mine" what I am separated from by space or time, by distraction or "diversion," or because of some culpable forgetfulness. Appropriation signifies that the initial situation from which reflection proceeds is "forgetfulness." I am lost, "led astray" among objects and separated from the center of my existence, just as I am separated from others and as an enemy is separated from all men. Whatever the secret of this "diaspora," of this separation, it signifies that I do not at first possess what I am. The truth that Fichte called the thetic judgment posits itself in a desert wherein I am absent to myself. That is why reflection is a task, an *Aufgabe*—the task of making my concrete experience equal to the positing of "I am." Such is the ultimate elaboration of our initial proposition that reflection is not intuition; we now say: the positing of self is not given, it is a task, it is not *gegeben*, but *aufgegeben*.

At this point one may wonder whether we have not overly stressed the practical and ethical side of reflection. Is this not a new limitation, like that of the epistemological stream of the Kantian philosophy? Moreover, are we not farther than ever from our problem of interpretation? I do not think so; the ethical stress put on reflection does not mark a limitation, if we take the notion of ethical in its wide sense, as in Spinoza, when he calls the total process of philosophy "ethical."

Philosophy is ethical to the extent that it leads from alienation to freedom and beatitude. In Spinoza this conversion is achieved when the knowledge of self is made equal to the knowledge of the unique substance; but this speculative process has an ethical significance, inasmuch as the alienated individual is transformed by the knowledge of the whole. Philosophy is ethics, but ethics is not simply morality. If we follow Spinoza's use of the word "ethical" we must say that reflection is ethical before becoming a critique of morality. Its goal is to grasp the Ego in its effort to exist, in its desire to be. This is where a reflective philosophy recovers and perhaps also saves the Platonic notion that the source of knowledge is itself *Eros,* desire, love, along with the Spinozistic notion that it is *conatus,* effort. Such effort is a desire, since it is never satisfied; but the desire is an effort since it is the affirmative positing of a singular being and not simply a lack of being. Effort and desire are the two sides of this positing of the self in the first truth: *I am.*

We are now in a position to complete our negative proposition—reflection is not intuition—by a positive proposition: *Reflection is the appropriation of our effort to exist and of our desire to be, through the works which bear witness to that effort and desire.* That is why reflection is more than a mere critique of knowledge and even more than a mere critique of moral judgment; prior to every critique of judgment it reflects upon the act of existing that we deploy in effort and desire.

This third step leads us to the threshold of our problem of interpretation: the positing or emergence of this effort or desire is not only devoid of all intuition but is evidenced only by works whose meaning remains doubtful and revocable. This is where reflection calls for an interpretation and tends to move into hermeneutics. The ultimate root of our problem lies in this primitive connection between the act of existing and the signs we deploy in our works; reflection must become interpretation because I cannot grasp the act of existing except in signs scattered in the world. That is why a reflective philosophy must include the results, methods, and presuppositions of all the sciences that try to decipher and interpret the signs of man.[3]

Such is, in its principle and widest generality, the root of the hermeneutic problem. The problem is posed both by the factual

3. Cf. my article "Acte et signe dans la philosophie de Jean Nabert," *Études philosophiques* (1962–63).

existence of symbolic language which calls for reflection and, conversely, by the indigence of reflection which calls for interpretation. In positing itself, reflection understands its own inability to transcend the vain and empty abstraction of the *I think* and the necessity to recover itself by deciphering its own signs lost in the world of culture. Thus reflection realizes it does not begin as science; in order to operate it must take to itself the opaque, contingent, and equivocal signs scattered in the cultures in which our language is rooted.

REFLECTION AND EQUIVOCAL LANGUAGE

By thus placing the hermeneutic problem within the movement of reflection we are enabled to meet the objections that would seemingly invalidate a philosophy that presents itself as a hermeneutics. In the foregoing we have reduced these objections to three main ones: Can philosophy derive its universality from contingent cultural productions? Can it build its rigor upon equivocal significations? Can it subject its vow of coherence to the fluctuations of an indecisive conflict between rival interpretations?

The aim of these introductory chapters is not so much to resolve the problems as to show their legitimacy when they are rightly posed, to assure ourselves that they are not meaningless but are inscribed in the nature of things and in the nature of language. That philosophical discourse achieves universality only by passing through the contingency of cultures, that its rigor is dependent upon equivocal languages, that its coherence must traverse the war between hermeneutics—all this can and must be seen as the necessary pathway, as the triple *aporia* rightly formed and rightly posed. At the end of this first series of investigations, deliberately called a "Problematic," one point should be assured: the aporias of interpretation are those of reflection itself.

I will say very little here about the first difficulty, since I have discussed it in the introduction to *The Symbolism of Evil.* To start from a pregiven symbolism, I objected, is to give oneself something to think about; but at the same time a radical contingency is brought into discourse, the contingency of the cultures of one's acquaintance. My answer was that the philosopher does not speak from nowhere: every question he can pose rises from the depths of his Greek memory; the field of his investigation is thereby unavoidably oriented; his memory carries with it the opposition of the "near" and the "far." Through this contingency of historical encounters we have to discern reasonable sequences between scattered cultural themes. I should now add that it is only abstract reflection which speaks from nowhere. To become concrete, reflection must lose its immediate pretension to universality, to the extent of fusing together its essential necessity and the contingency of the signs through which it recognizes itself. This fusion can be achieved precisely in the movement of interpretation.

We must now come to grips with the more formidable objection, that the recourse to symbolism hands thought over to equivocal language and fallacious arguments that are condemned by a sound logic. The difficulty in avoiding this objection is increased by the fact that logicians have invented symbolic logic with the express aim of eliminating equivocation from our arguments. For the logician, the word "symbol" means precisely the contrary of what it means for us. The important status of symbolic logic obliges us to say something about this encounter, which at the very least constitutes a strange homonymy; the obligation is all the more pressing in view of the fact that we have constantly alluded to the duality of univocal and equivocal expressions and have implicitly assumed that the latter can have an irreplaceable philosophical function.

The only radical way to justify hermeneutics is to seek in the very nature of reflective thought the principle of a *logic of double meaning*, a logic that is complex but not arbitrary, rigorous in its articulations but irreducible to the linearity of symbolic logic. This logic is no longer a formal logic, but a transcendental logic established on the level of the conditions of possibility; not the conditions of objectivity of nature, but the conditions of the appropriation of our desire to be. Thus the logic of double meanings, which is proper to hermeneutics, is of a transcendental order.

We have now to establish this connection between the logic of double meaning and transcendental reflection.

If the advocate of hermeneutics does not carry the discussion to this level, he will soon be driven into an untenable position. Any effort to maintain the debate on the level of the semantic structure of symbols will be to no purpose. He may of course appeal, as we ourselves have done up to now, to the overdetermination of meaning in symbols and thus defend a theory of two types of symbolism whose respective fields of application must be kept from any overlapping.

But the idea that there can exist two logics on the same level is strictly untenable; a pure and simple juxtaposition can only lead to the elimination of hermeneutics by symbolic logic.

For what advantages can the hermeneutician adduce when faced with formal logic? To the artificiality of logical symbols, which can be written and read but not spoken, he will oppose an essentially oral symbolism, in each instance received and accepted as a heritage. The man who speaks in symbols is first of all a narrator; he transmits an abundance of meaning over which he has little command. This abundance, this density of manifold meaning, is what gives him food for thought and solicits his understanding; interpretation consists less in suppressing ambiguity than in understanding it and in explicating its richness. It may also be said that logical symbolism is empty, whereas symbolism in hermeneutics is full; it renders manifest the double meaning of worldly or psychical reality. This was suggested earlier when we said that symbols are bound: the sensible sign is bound by the symbolic meaning that dwells in it and gives it transparency and lightness; the symbolic meaning is in turn bound to its sensible vehicle, which gives it weight and opacity. One might add that this is also the way symbols bind us, viz. by giving thought a content, a flesh, a density.

These distinctions and oppositions are not false; they are merely unfounded. A confrontation which restricts itself to the symbolic texture of symbols and does not face the question of their foundation in reflection will soon prove embarrassing to the advocate of hermeneutics. For the artificiality and emptiness of logical symbolism are simply the counterpart and condition of the true aim of this logic, viz. to guarantee the nonambiguity of arguments; what the hermeneutician calls double meaning is, in logical terms, ambiguity, i.e. equivocity of words and amphiboly of statements. A peaceful juxtaposition of hermeneutics and symbolic logic is therefore impossible; symbolic logic quickly makes any lazy compromise untenable. Its very "intolerance" forces hermeneutics to radically justify its own language.

We must therefore understand this intolerance in order to arrive *a contrario* at the foundation of hermeneutics.

If the rigor of symbolic logic seems more exclusive than that of traditional formal logic, the reason is that symbolic logic is not a simple prolongation of the earlier logic. It does not represent a higher degree of formalization; it proceeds from a global decision concerning ordinary language as a whole; it marks a split with ordinary language and its incurable ambiguity; it questions the equivocal and hence fallacious character of the words of ordinary language, the amphibolous character of its constructions, the confusion inherent in metaphor and idiomatic expressions, the emotional resonance of highly descriptive language. Symbolic logic despairs of natural language precisely at the point where hermeneutics believes in its implicit "wisdom."

This struggle begins with the exclusion from the properly cognitive sphere of all language that does not give factual information. The rest of discourse is classified under the heading of the emotive and hortatory functions of language; that which does not give factual information expresses emotions, feelings, or attitudes, or urges others to behave in some particular way.

Reduced thus to the informative function, language still has to be divested of the equivocity of words and the amphiboly of grammatical constructions; verbal ambiguity must be unmasked so as to eliminate it from arguments and to employ coherently the same words in the same sense within the same argument. The function of definition is to explain meaning and thereby eliminate ambiguity: the only definitions that succeed in doing this are scientific ones. These are not content with pointing out the meaning words already have in usage, independently of their definition; instead they very strictly characterize an object in light of a scientific theory (for example, the definition of force as the product of mass and acceleration in the context of Newtonian theory).

But symbolic logic goes further. For it, the price of univocity is the creation of a symbolism with no ties to natural language. This notion of symbol excludes the other notion of symbol. The recourse to a completely artificial symbolism introduces in logic a difference not only of degree but of nature; the symbols of the logician intervene precisely at the point where the arguments of classical logic, formulated in ordinary language, run into an invincible and, in a way, residual ambiguity. Thus the logical disjunction sign v eliminates the ambiguity of words that express disjunction in ordinary language (Eng., or; Ger., *oder;* Fr., *ou*); v expresses only the partial meaning common to the inclusive disjunction (the sense of the Latin *vel*) according to which at least one of the terms of the disjunction is true although both may be true, and to the exclusive disjunction (the sense of the Latin *aut*) according to which at least one is true and at least one is false; v resolves the ambiguity by formulating the inclusive disjunction as the part common to the two modes of disjunction. Likewise the symbol $\supset$ resolves the ambiguity inherent in the notion of implication (which may denote formal implication, either logical, definitional, or causal); the symbol $\supset$ formulates the common partial meaning, namely, that any hypothetical statement with a true antecedent and a false consequent must be false; the symbol is thus an abbreviation of a longer symbolism which expresses the negation of the conjunction of the truth value of the antecedent and the falsity of the consequent: $\sim(p \cdot \sim q)$.

Thus the artificial language of logical symbolism enables one to determine the validity of arguments in all cases where a residual ambiguity can be ascribed to the structure of ordinary language. The precise point where symbolic logic cuts across and contests hermeneutics, therefore, is this: verbal equivocity and syntactical amphiboly—in short, the ambiguity of ordinary language—can be overcome only at the level of a language whose symbols have a meaning completely determined by the truth table whose construction they allow. Thus the sense of the symbol v is completely determined by its truth function, inasmuch as it serves to safeguard the validity of the disjunctive syllogism; likewise the sense of the symbol $\supset$ completely exhausts its meaning in the construction of the truth table of the hypothetical syllogism. These constructions guarantee that the symbols are completely unambiguous, while the nonambiguity of the symbols assures the universal validity of arguments.

As long as the logic of multiple meaning is not grounded in its reflective function, it necessarily falls under the blows of formal and symbolic logic. In the eyes of the logician, hermeneutics will always be suspected of fostering a culpable complacency toward equivocal meanings, of surreptitiously giving an informative function to expressions that have merely an emotive or hortatory function. Hermeneutics thus falls under the fallacies of relevance which a sound logic denounces.

The only thing that can come to the aid of equivocal expressions and truly ground a logic of double meaning is the problematic of reflection. The only thing that can justify equivocal expressions is their a priori role in the movement of self-appropriation by self which constitutes reflective activity. This a priori function pertains not to a formal but to a transcendental logic, if by transcendental logic is meant the establishing of the conditions of possibility of a domain of objectivity in general. The task of such a logic is to extricate by a regressive method the notions presupposed in the constitution of a type of experience and a corresponding type of reality. Transcendental logic is not exhausted in the Kantian a priori. The connection we have established between reflection upon the *I think, I am* qua act, and the signs scattered in the various cultures of that act of existing, opens up a new field of experience, objectivity, and reality. This is the field to which the logic of double meaning pertains—a logic we have qualified above as complex but not arbitrary, and rigorous in its articulations. The principle of a limitation to the demands of symbolic logic lies in the structure of reflection itself. If there is no such thing as the transcendental, there is no reply to the intolerance of symbolic logic; but if the transcendental is an authentic dimension of discourse, then new force is found in the reasons that can be opposed to the requirement of logicism that all discourse be measured by its treatise of arguments. These reasons, which seemed to us to be left hanging in air for want of a foundation, are as follows:

1. The requirement of univocity holds only for discourse that presents itself as *argument:* but reflection does not argue, it draws no conclusion, it neither deduces nor induces; it states the conditions of possibility whereby empirical consciousness can be made equal to thetic consciousness. Hence, "equivocal" applies only to those expressions that ought to be univocal in the course of a single "argument" but are not; in the reflective use of multiple-meaning symbols there is no fallacy of ambiguity: to reflect upon these symbols and to interpret them is one and the same act.

2. The understanding developed by reflection upon symbols is not a weak substitute for definition, for reflection is not a type of thinking that defines and thinks according to "classes." This brings us back to the Aristotelian problem of the "many meanings of being." Aristotle was the first to see clearly that philosophical discourse is not subject to the logical alternative of univocal-equivocal, for being is not a "genus"; and yet, being is said; but it "is said in many ways."

3. Let us go back to the very first alternative considered above: a statement that does not give factual information, we said, expresses only the emotions or attitudes of a subject. Reflection, however, falls outside this alternative; that which makes possible the appropriation of the *I think, I am* is neither the empirical statement nor the emotive statement, but something other than either of these.

This case for interpretation rests entirely on the reflective function of interpretative thought. If the double movement of symbols toward reflection and of reflection toward symbols is valid, interpretative thought is well grounded. Hence it may be said, at least negatively, that such thought is not measured by a logic of arguments; the validity of philosophical statements cannot be arbitrated by a theory of language conceived as syntax; the semantics of philosophy is not swallowed up by a symbolic logic.

These propositions concerning philosophic discourse do not enable us, however, to say positively what a philosophical statement is; such an affirmation could be fully justified only by its actually being said. At least we can affirm that the indirect, symbolic language of reflection *can* be valid, not *because* it is equivocal, but *in spite of* its being equivocal.

REFLECTION AND THE HERMENEUTIC CONFLICT

But the reply of hermeneutics to the objections of symbolic logic is liable to be an empty victory. The challenge comes not only from without, it is not only the voice of the "intolerant" logician; it comes from within, from the internal inconsistency of hermeneutics, torn by contradiction. As we already know, not one but several interpretations have to be integrated into reflection. Thus the hermeneutic conflict itself is what nourishes the process of reflection and governs the movement from abstract to concrete reflection. Is this possible without "destroying" reflection?

In our attempt to justify the recourse to hermeneutics that are already constituted—that of the phenomenology of religion and that of psychoanalysis—we suggested that their conflict might well be not only a crisis of language but, deeper still, a crisis of reflection: to destroy the idols, to listen to symbols—are not these, we asked, one and the same enterprise? Indeed, the profound unity of the demystifying and the remythicizing of discourse can be seen only at the end of an ascesis of reflection, in the course of which the debate dramatizing the hermeneutic field shall have become a discipline of thinking.

One trait of this discipline is already clear to us: the two enterprises which we at first opposed to one another—the reduction of illusions and the restoration of the fullness of meaning—are alike in that they both shift the origin of meaning to another center which is no longer the immediate subject of reflection: "consciousness"—the watchful ego, attentive to its own presence, anxious about self and attached to self. Thus hermeneutics, approached from its most opposed poles, represents a challenge and a test for reflection, whose first tendency is to identify itself with immediate consciousness. To let ourselves be torn by the contradiction between these divergent hermeneutics is to give ourselves up to the wonder that puts reflection in motion: it is no doubt necessary for us to be separated from ourselves, to be set off center, in order finally to know what is signified by the *I think, I am.*

We thought we had resolved the antinomy of myth and philosophy by appealing to interpretation itself for the mediation between myth and philosophy or, in a broader sense, between symbols and reflection. But that mediation is not given, it is to be constructed.

It is not given like a ready-made solution. The dispossession of the ego, which psychoanalysis more than any other hermeneutics demands of us, is the first achievement of reflection that reflection does not understand. But the phenomenological interpretation of the sacred, to which psychoanalysis seems to be diametrically opposed, is no less foreign to the style and fundamental intention of the reflective method; does it not oppose a method of transcendence to the method of immanence of reflective philosophy? Does not the sacred, manifested in its symbols, seem to pertain to revelation rather than to reflection? Whether one looks back to the will to power of the Nietzschean man, to the generic being of the Marxist man, to the libido of the Freudian man, or whether one looks ahead to the transcendent home of signification which we designate here by the vague term the "sacred," the home of meaning is not consciousness but something other than consciousness.

Both hermeneutics pose therefore the same crucial question: Can the dispossession of consciousness to the profit of another home of meaning be understood as an act of reflection, as the first gesture of reappropriation? This is the question that remains in suspense; it is more radical than the question of the coexistence of several styles of interpretation, or the whole crisis of language in which the hermeneutic conflict is set.

We suspect that these three "crises"—crisis of language, crisis of interpretation, crisis of reflection—can only be overcome together. In order to become concrete, i.e. equal to its richest contents, reflection must become hermeneutic; but there exists no general hermeneutics. This aporia sets us in movement: would it not be one and the same thing to arbitrate the war of hermeneutics *and* to enlarge reflection to the dimensions of a critique of interpretations? Is it not by one and the same movement that reflection can become concrete reflection *and* that the rivalry between interpretations can be comprehended, in the double sense of the term: justified by reflection and embodied in its work?

For the moment our perplexity is great. What is offered to us is a three-term relation, a figure with three heads: reflection, interpretation understood as restoration of meaning, interpretation understood as reduction of illusion. No doubt we shall have to penetrate quite deeply into the conflict between interpretations before we see appear, as a requirement of the very war of hermeneutics, the means of grounding the three together in reflection. But in its turn reflection will no longer be the positing, as feeble as it is peremptory, as sterile as it is irrefutable, of the *I think, I am:* it will have become concrete reflection; and its concreteness will be due to the harsh hermeneutic discipline.

BOOK II

Analytic: Reading of Freud

Introduction
How to Read Freud

Before entering my "Essay to Understand Freud" I would like to explain how it was written and how it should be read.

What I propose is not an interpretation on a single level but rather a series of readings each of which is both completed and corrected by the following one. Because of the great distance between the first and last readings it may seem that the initial interpretation has been retracted, but such is not the case. Each reading is essential and must be preserved.

Let me explain what I mean by this procedure. I will first say something about the two main divisions of this study, which I have called an "Analytic" and a "Dialectic," and then about the movement of the "Analytic" itself.

1. With a view toward a dialectic between conflicting hermeneutics, I first wrote a separate study dealing solely with the Freudian interpretation. I call this separate interpretation an Analytic because of the mechanical and external nature of its opposition to all the other interpretations. How is the Analytic, taken as a whole, connected with the Dialectic?

The relation between the Analytic and the Dialectic answers to the central difficulty raised in the Problematic. In my introductory presentation of Freud I regarded him, along with Marx and Nietzsche, as one of the representatives of reductive and demystifying hermeneutics. In this view I was guided by a taste for extremes; I saw Freud as having a precise place in the hermeneutic debate, opposed to a nonreductive and restorative hermeneutics, and in league with other thinkers who wage a combat comparable to his. The whole movement of this book consists in a gradual readjusting of that initial position and of the panoramic view of the battlefield governing it. In the end it may seem that in this indecisive combat Freud is nowhere because he is everywhere. That impression is correct: the limits of psychoanalysis will finally have to be conceived not so much as a frontier beyond which exist other points of view, rival or allied, but rather as the imaginary line of a front of investigation which constantly advances, while the other points of view filter through the dividing line. In the beginning, Freud is one combatant among many; in the end, he shall have become the privileged witness of the total combat, for all the opposition will be carried over into him.

We will first come across his allies, now no longer alongside him but within him. The issues raised by Nietzsche and Marx will gradually be seen to rise to the heart of the Freudian question as questions of language, ethics, and culture. The three interpretations of culture that we usually set side by side will encroach upon one another, the question of each becoming the question of the other.

But the greatest change in the course of these successive readings will concern Freud's relationship to what is most opposed to him, namely, a hermeneutics of the sacred. I first wanted to become involved in the liveliest opposition, in order to give myself the widest range of thought. At the start, in an interpretation of psychoanalysis completely governed by Freud's own systematization, all opposition is external; psychoanalysis has its "opposite" outside of itself. This first reading is necessary; it serves as a discipline of reflection; it brings about the dispossession of consciousness and governs the ascesis of that narcissism that wishes to be taken for the true Cogito. Hence this reading and its harsh schooling will not be retracted but rather preserved in the final reading. It is only in a second reading, that of our "Dialectic," that the external and completely mechanical opposition between the contending points of view can be converted into an internal opposition, with each point of view becoming in a way its opposite and bearing within itself the grounds of the contrary point of view.

The basic reason for not going directly to the dialectical view lies in our concern for a discipline of thought. First we must do justice to each point of view separately; we must adopt, so to speak, their instructive exclusiveness. Next we must account for their opposition; we must do away with convenient eclecticisms and posit all the oppositions as external. We will try to maintain this discipline of thought; hence we will enter psychoanalysis from its most demanding side, its systematization, which Freud called his "metapsychology."

2. But our "Analytic" is not a self-enclosed reading on a single level; from the beginning it is oriented toward a more dialectical view, according to the movement from the more abstract to the more concrete that sustains the series of readings. I use the word "abstract" not in the vague and improper sense, according to which an idea is abstract when it is without basis in experience, detached from facts, "purely theoretical," but in the precise and proper sense. The topographic theory and its conjoined economics are not abstract in the sense of being remote from the facts. In the sciences of man, "theory" grounds the facts; the "facts" of psychoanalysis are set up by the theory—in Freudian language, by the "metapsychology"; theory and facts can only be confirmed or invalidated together.

In what sense, then, is the Freudian "topography" abstract? In the sense that it does not account for the intersubjective nature of the dramas forming its main theme. Whether it be the drama of the parental relation or the drama of the therapeutic relation itself, in which the other situations achieve speech, what nourishes analysis is always a debate between consciousnesses. Moreover, in the Freudian topography that debate is projected onto a representation of the psychical apparatus in which only the "vicissitudes of instincts" within an isolated psychism are thematized. Stated bluntly, the Freudian systematization is solipsistic, whereas the situations and relations analysis speaks of and which speak in analysis are intersubjective. Therein lies the abstract character of the first reading we propose in Part I of the "Analytic." That is why the topography, adopted at first as a necessary discipline, will gradually come to be seen as a provisional level of reference which will not be abandoned but surpassed and retained. Gradually, within the "Analytic" itself, the reading of Freud will become enriched and inverted into its contrary, until the moment is reached when it will speak at times in the manner of Hegel.

The main stages of the movement that carries the Analytic toward its Dialectic are as follows. In a first cycle, entitled "Energetics and Hermeneutics," we will set forth the basic concepts of analytical interpretation. This study, properly epistemological in nature, will center on the metapsychological papers of the years 1914–17; in the investigation we will be guided by one question: What is interpretation in psychoanalysis? This inquiry must precede any study of cultural phenomena, for the rights of that interpretation as well as its limits of validity depend exclusively upon the solution of this epistemological problem. This first group of chapters, which will follow fairly closely the historical order of the constitution of the first topography (unconscious, preconscious, conscious) and the gradual introduction of the economic explanation, will place us before an apparent dilemma: by turns we will see psychoanalysis as an explanation of psychical phenomena through conflicts of forces, hence as an energetics; and as an exegesis of apparent meaning through a latent meaning, hence as a hermeneutics. At issue in Part I will be the unity of these two manners of understanding; on the one hand we will see that the only possible way for psychoanalysis to become "interpretation" is by incorporating the economic point of view into a theory of meaning; on the other hand the economic point of view will appear to us to be irreducible to any other by reason of what we will call the unsurpassable character of desire.

The second cycle, entitled "The Interpretation of Culture," will begin the movement by which Freud extends his central ideas to wider areas. Freud's entire theory of culture may be regarded as a merely analogical transposition of the economic explanation of dreams and the neuroses. But the application of psychoanalysis to esthetic symbols, ideals, and illusions will have repercussions calling for a revision of the initial model and the schema of interpretation discussed in Part I. This revision is expressed in the second topography (ego, id, superego), which is added to the first without suppressing it. New relations will be revealed, essentially those concerned with other persons, which only cultural situations and productions can bring to light. In the course of these chapters, then, we will begin to discover the abstract and especially the solipsistic character of the first topography; this will prepare the way for a confrontation with the Hegelian exegesis of desire and of the reduplication of consciousness in self-consciousness, a topic that will occupy us in the "Dialectic." Here too, however, dreams will be a model at once surpassed and unsurpassable, like the emergence of desire in Part I; hence the theory of illusion, at the end of Part II, will appear as a repetition of the starting point at the peak of culture.

A third and last cycle will be concerned with the final reworking of the theory of instincts under the sign of death. This new instinct theory is of far-reaching significance. On the one hand it alone enables us to complete the theory of culture by placing this theory within the field of the struggle between Eros and Thanatos. By the same token it enables us to carry to its completion the Freudian interpretation of the reality principle, which functions throughout as counterpole to the pleasure principle. However, in thus completing the theories of culture and reality the new theory of instincts does not limit itself to questioning the initial dream model: it upsets the topographical starting point itself or, more precisely, the mechanistic form in which the topography was first stated. This mechanism, whose basic hypothesis about the functioning of the physical apparatus we present at the beginning of Part I, was never entirely eliminated from the later presentations of the topography; it resists being integrated into an interpretation of meaning through meaning and renders precarious the connection between energetics and hermeneutics that we present in Part I; it is fundamentally challenged only at the level of this final theory of instincts. But the paradox is that the final development of the theory marks the return of psychoanalysis to a sort of mythological philosophy, the emblems of which are the figures of Eros, Thanatos, and Ananke.

Thus our Analytic progresses, by successive self-surpassing, toward a Dialectic. That is why these chapters should be read as successive strata or episodes in which understanding, by advancing from the abstract to the concrete, changes meaning. On a first and more analytical reading, Freudianism reduces its opposition as something external to itself; on a second and more dialectical reading, it embraces in a certain manner what it seemed to exclude through reduction. I expressly ask the reader, therefore, to suspend his judgment and to engage in moving from a first understanding, which has its own criteria, to a second understanding, in which the opposing thought is heard in the texts of the master of suspicion himself.

PART I: ENERGETICS AND HERMENEUTICS

The Epistemological Problem in Freudianism

Our first cycle of investigation concerns the structure of psychoanalytic discourse. This prepares the way for an inspection of the phenomenon of culture, which will be the subject matter of the second cycle.

For the present inquiry I have used a title that directly indicates the central difficulty in the psychoanalytic epistemology. Freud's writings present themselves as a mixed or even ambiguous discourse, which at times states conflicts of force subject to an energetics, at times relations of meaning subject to a hermeneutics. I hope to show that there are good grounds for this apparent ambiguity, that this mixed discourse is the *raison d'être* of psychoanalysis.

I will limit myself in this introduction to showing the necessity of both dimensions of psychoanalytic discourse. The precise task of the three chapters of Part I will be to overcome the gap between the two orders of discourse and to reach the point where one sees that the energetics implies a hermeneutics and the hermeneutics discloses an energetics. That point is where the positing or emergence of desire manifests itself in and through a process of symbolization.

Within a topographic-economic explanation the status of interpretation, or *Deutung*, presents itself at first as an aporia. If we emphasize the deliberately antiphenomenological bent of the topography, we appear to remove any basis for a reading of psychoanalysis as hermeneutics; the substitution of the economic notions of cathexis—i.e. placement and displacement of energy—for the notions of intentional consciousness and intended object apparently calls for a naturalistic explanation and excludes an understanding of meaning through meaning. In short, it would seem that the topographic-economic point of view can uphold an energetics but not a hermeneutics. And yet there is no doubt that psychoanalysis is a hermeneutics: it is not by accident but by intention that it aims at giving an interpretation of culture in its entirety. But works of art, ideals, and illusions are various modes of representation. And if we move from the periphery to the center, from the theory of culture to the theory of dreams and the neuroses, which forms the hard core of psychoanalysis, we are constantly led back to interpretation, to the act of interpreting, to the work of interpretation. It was in the work of dream interpretation, as we shall fully elaborate, that the Freudian method was forged. All the "contents" with which the analyst works are increasingly representational, from fantasies to works of art to religious beliefs. But the problem of interpretation is exactly coextensive with the problem of meaning or representation. Hence psychoanalysis is interpretation from beginning to end.

This is where the aporia arises: What is the status of representation or ideas in relation to the notions of instinct, aim of instinct, and affect? How can an interpretation of meaning through meaning be integrated with an economics of cathexis, withdrawal of cathexis, anticathexis? At first glance, there seems to be an antinomy between an explanation governed by the principles of the metapsychology and an interpretation that necessarily moves among meanings and not among forces, among representations or ideas and not among instincts. As I see it, the whole problem of the Freudian epistemology may be centralized in a single question: How can the economic explanation be *involved* in an interpretation dealing with meanings; and conversely, how can interpretation be an *aspect* of the economic explanation? It is easier to fall back on a disjunction: either an explanation in terms of energy, or an understanding in terms of phenomenology. It must be recognized, however, that Freudianism exists only on the basis of its refusal of that disjunction.

The difficulty in the Freudian epistemology is not only its problem but also its solution. At the outset, Freud did not clearly see the entanglement of the points of view in the metapsychology. The successive presentations of the topography bear the mark—increasingly less pronounced, it is true—of an initial state in which the topography is cut off from the work of interpretation. What we call the "quantitative hypothesis" weighs heavily upon the economic explanation. The result is that all the later presentations of the topography suffer from a residual dissociation; we will look for the key to the initial divorce between explanation and interpretation in the "Project" of 1895. This will be the object of our first chapter. We will then show how the celebrated Chapter 7 of *The Interpretation of Dreams* takes up the line of thought of the "Project," but also goes beyond it and more clearly paves the way for its integration into the work of interpretation; this will be the concern of our second chapter. Finally, we will look to the "Papers on Metapsychology" of 1914–17 for the most mature expression of the theory and will concentrate at some length on the relationship between instincts and representations or ideas, which is the basis not only for all the difficulties but also for all the attempts at resolution.

It may be that the possibility of moving from force to language, but also the impossibility of completely integrating force within language, lies in the positing or emergence of desire.

Chapter 1: An Energetics Without Hermeneutics

The "Project" of 1895 [1] represents what could be called a nonhermeneutic state of the system. Indeed, the notion of the "psychical apparatus" that dominates this essay appears to have no correlation with a work of deciphering—although, as we shall see, the interpretation of neurotic symptoms is not absent from this notion. The notion is based on a principle borrowed from physics—the constancy principle—and tends to be a quantitative treatment of energy. This recourse to the principle of constancy and the quantitative hypothesis is the aspect of Freudianism that most resists the reading I propose, based on the correlation between energetics and hermeneutics, between connections of forces

1. The essay known as the "Project for a Scientific Psychology" was first published in London in 1950 at the end of a volume of letters from Freud to Wilhelm Fliess (including some drafts and notes), under the general title *Aus der Anfängen der Psychoanalyse* (London, Imago, 1950); Eng. trans. Eric Mosbacher and James Strachey, with an Introduction by Ernst Kris, *The Origins of Psychoanalysis* (New York, Basic Books, 1954), pp. 355–445. The essay has in fact no definite title: Freud sometimes speaks of his "Psychology for Neurologists" (Letter 23 of Apr. 27, 1895, *Origins*, p. 118) or simply of the system $\phi\psi\omega$ (*Origins*, p. 123) for reasons we shall see later (n. 16). Concerning the title and aim of the "Project," see Kris, Introduction to *Origins*, pp. 25–27, as well as his Editorial Note to the "Project," *Origins*, pp. 349–51; also Ernest Jones, *The Life and Work of Sigmund Freud* (3 vols. New York, Basic Books, 1953), *1*, 347. On the term "metapsychology," see Letters 41 and 84. Concerning the first outlines of the "Project," see the letter to Breuer of June 29, 1892 (*GW*, *17*, 5; *Collected Papers*, *5*, 25); this text will be printed in *SE*, Vol. 1 (which has not yet appeared); see also the important "Preliminary Communication" which was written in November 1892, published in Berlin and Vienna at the beginning of 1893, and placed at the head of the *Studies on Hysteria* of 1895 (*GW*, *1*, 77 ff.; *SE*, *2*, 1–17). Among the notes and drafts prior to the "Project," Drafts D and G are especially to be noted.

and relations of meanings. However, the "Project" of 1895 is not meant to be a topography in the sense of the "Papers on Metapsychology"; it is important at the outset not to identify the notion of psychical apparatus with the "topographic point of view"; the first is simply patterned on a physical model, the second is correlative to an interpretation of meaning through meaning. It must be admitted that this quasi-physical conception of the psychical apparatus was never completely eliminated from Freudian theory; however, I think the development of Freudian theory may be looked upon as the gradual reduction of the notion of psychical apparatus —in the sense of "a machine which in a moment would run of itself" [2]—to a topography in which space is no longer a place within the world but a scene of action where roles and masks enter into debate; [3] this space will become a place of ciphering and deciphering.

Of course, because of the constancy principle, the explanation in terms of energy will always remain somewhat external to the interpretation of meaning through meaning; the topography will always retain an ambiguous character: it may be regarded both as the development of the primitive theory of the psychical apparatus and as a sustained movement to free itself from that theory. Accordingly, we will pay close attention to what happens to the quantitative hypothesis through the successive stages that lead from the "Project" to the topography (or topographies). In this connection, it should be mentioned that the four or five ways in which the system is expressed have by no means the same epistemological significance. In particular, Chapter 7 of the *Traumdeutung* holds the most equivocal position, situated as it is between the "Project" and the two topographies. It is truly a development of the "Project," of the principle of constancy, and of the quantitative hypothesis, and yet it is connected with interpretation in a way that suggests the later topography. This situation should not perplex us. As I hope to show later, it is not in the topography that the quantitative hypothesis is radically brought into question, but in the confrontation—

2. Letter 32, *Origins,* p. 129.

3. We read in Draft L (enclosed in Letter 61 of May 2, 1897): "*Multiplicity of Psychical Personalities.* The fact of identification may perhaps allow of this phrase being taken literally" (*Origins,* p. 199).

nontopographical or hypertopographical—of all the forces of desire, of all the forces of the libido, with the death instinct. It is the death instinct that upsets everything: what is "beyond the pleasure principle" cannot help but have repercussions upon the constancy hypothesis with which the pleasure principle was initially coupled (cf. "Analytic," Part III, Ch. 3).

THE CONSTANCY PRINCIPLE AND THE QUANTITATIVE APPARATUS

The opening statement of the "Project" merits citation:

> The intention of this project is to furnish us with a psychology which shall be a natural science: its aim, that is, is to represent psychical processes as quantitatively determined states of specifiable material particles and so to make them plain and void of contradictions. The project involves two principal ideas: 1. That what distinguishes activity from rest is to be regarded as a quantity (*Q*) subject to the general laws of motion. 2. That it is to be assumed that the material particles in question are the neurons.[4]

We are indebted to Bernfeld,[5] Jones,[6] and Kris,[7] for a careful reconstruction of the scientific environment in which such a project could arise. This is also the environment psychoanalysis will have to

4. *Origins*, p. 355. In a letter dated May 25, 1895, Freud says: "I am plagued with two ambitions: to see how the theory of mental functioning takes shape if quantitative considerations, a sort of economics of nerve-force, are introduced into it; and secondly, to extract from psychopathology what may be of benefit to normal psychology" (*Origins*, pp. 119–20). And five months later (Oct. 20, 1895): "The three systems of neurons, the 'free' and 'bound' states of quantity, the primary and secondary processes, the main trend and the compromise trend of the nervous system, the two biological rules of attention and defense, the indications of quality, reality, and thought, the state of the psycho-sexual group, the sexual determination of repression, and finally the factors determining consciousness as a perceptual function—the whole thing held together, and still does. I can naturally hardly contain myself with delight" (*Origins*, p. 129).

5. S. Bernfeld, "Freud's Earliest Theories and the School of Helmholtz," *Psychoanal. Quart.*, *13* (1944), 341.

6. *Life and Work*, *1*, 33–35, 39–43.

7. Introduction, *Origins*, pp. 1–47.

fight against. But in any event Freud will never disavow its fundamental convictions: like all his Vienna and Berlin teachers, Freud sees and will continue to see in science the sole discipline of knowledge, the single rule of all intellectual honesty, a world view that excludes all other views, especially that of the old religion. In Vienna, as in Berlin, *Naturphilosophie* and its scientific counterpart, vitalism, gave way in biology to a physico-physiological theory based on the ideas of force, attraction, and repulsion, all three being governed by the principle of the conservation of energy (discovered by Robert Mayer in 1842 and made prominent by Helmholtz). According to that principle the sum of forces (motor and potential) remains constant in an isolated system. Today we have a better knowledge of the influence of the Helmholtz school in Vienna,[8] as well as of Freud's first scientific works in neurology and embryology; as a result the "Project" of 1895 no longer seems so singular to us. It is of interest not so much because of its presuppositions, which are not peculiar to it, but because of its aim of holding determinedly to the hypothesis of constancy in new areas where it had not been tested: the theory of desire and pleasure, education to reality through "unpleasure," the incorporation within the system of observant and judging thought. In so doing Freud not only extended Helmholtz but also linked up with the tradition of Herbart,[9] who, beginning in 1824, had protested against free will, linked determinism with unconscious motivation, and applied the terminology of physics to a dynamics of ideas. The use of the word "idea" in the sense of perception and representation; the theme that ideas have primacy over affects, which plays an eminent role in the metapsychological papers; and perhaps even the word—if not the notion of—*Verdrängung* (repression) may also be traced to Herbart. Freud's relationship to Herbart on the precise point of

8. Brücke, Freud's first master, is the Viennese link between Helmholtz and Freud; cf. Jones, *1*, 371–79.

9. There are two lines of influence, one from Helmholtz to Freud and one from Herbart and Fechner to Freud; both lines pass through Brücke, and also through Griesinger and Meynert. On Freud's use of the word "idea" in the Herbartian sense, cf. A. C. MacIntyre, *The Unconscious* (London, Routledge, 1958), p. 11. On the Herbartian origin of the word "repression," see the interesting remarks made by Jones, *1*, 280–81.

the principle of constancy is beyond all doubt: the "striving for equilibrium" is the guiding principle of that "mathematical psychology" and its calculus of forces and quantities. Finally, Freud places himself in the company of Herbart and Fechner [10] when he gives up any anatomical basis for his psychical system, thus restoring psychology to the place Herbart wished to give it.

Thus the 1895 "Project" belongs to a whole period of scientific thought. What is most interesting is the manner in which Freud, by extending this thought, transforms it to the breaking point. In this regard the "Project" stands as the greatest effort Freud ever made to force a mass of psychical facts within the framework of a quantitative theory, and as the demonstration by way of the absurd that the content exceeds the frame: not even in Chapter 7 of the *Traumdeutung* will Freud try to make so many things fit together within such a narrow system. Nothing is more dated than the explanatory plan of the "Project," and nothing more inexhaustible than its program of description. As one enters more deeply into the "Project," one has the impression that the quantitative framework and the neuronic support recede into the background, until they are no more than a given and convenient language of reference which supplies the necessary constraint for the expression of great discoveries. The same adventure will be repeated in *Beyond the Pleasure Principle*, in which biology plays the double role of language of reference, and pretext for the discovery of the death instinct.

Let us try to untangle these two developments: the generalization of the constancy principle, and the fact that it is transcended by its own applications.

It should be noted that Freud does not say much about the origin and nature of what he calls "quantity." As for its origin, it comes from external or internal excitations and covers pretty much the idea of perceptual and instinctual stimuli; the notion *Q* serves to unify under a single concept anything that produces energy. As for its nature, Freud simply characterizes it as a summation of excitation homologous to physical energy: it is a current which flows,

10. "The only sensible thing on the subject was said by old Fechner in his sublime simplicity: that the psychical territory on which the dream process is played out is a different one" (Letter 83, *Origins*, pp. 244–45).

which "stores," "fills" or "empties," and "charges" neurons; the all-important notion of "cathexis" was first elaborated within this neuronic framework as a synonym of storing up and filling (*Origins*, pp. 358–62). Thus the "Project" talks about cathected or empty neurons; it will also speak of a rise or fall in level of charge, of discharge and resistance to discharge, of contact barriers, screens, stored quantity, freely mobile or "bound" quantity. Freud adopts this last notion from Breuer; later we will see why. We will meet all of these notions in other contexts, but in an increasingly metaphorical sense. It is to be noted, however, that in the "Project" Freud does not go further along the path of determining *Q*.[11] No measure is stated: the quantities are spoken of as being "of a comparatively low order" (p. 366), as being "large" or "excessively large" (p. 368), but there is no numerical law concerning them. A curious quantity indeed! We shall come back to this point at the end of the chapter.

But if the quantity obeys no numerical law, it is nonetheless governed by a principle, the principle of constancy, which Freud develops from the principle of inertia. The principle of inertia means that the system tends to reduce its own tensions to zero, i.e. to discharge its quantities, to "get rid of" them (pp. 356–57); the principle of constancy means that the system tends to maintain the level of tension as low as possible. The divergence between constancy and inertia is in itself very interesting,[12] for it already points to the intervention of what will later be described as the "secondary process." The impossibility for the system to eliminate all tensions results from the lack of an equivalent of flight regarding dangers from within: the psychical apparatus is forced to store up and cathect a stock of contrivances made up of a permanent group of

11. MacIntyre (pp. 16–22) compares Freud's notion of quantity to Engels' matter in motion and contrasts Freud with Lorenz, for whom the energy model is only a model.

12. Kris (*Origins*, p. 358, n. 1) sees here the sketch of the future distinction between the Nirvana principle and the pleasure principle. One might also ask whether the trend toward zero does not point to the death instinct. In any case, it will be impossible to say that Eros wishes $Q = 0$. Cf. below, "*Analytic*," Part III, Ch. 3.

bound quantities whose object is to reduce the tensions although they cannot completely eliminate them. Freud writes toward the beginning of the "Project":

> The neuronic system is consequently obliged to abandon its original trend towards inertia (that is, towards a reduction of its level of tension to zero). It must learn to tolerate a store of quantity ($Q\dot{\eta}$) sufficient to meet the demands for specific action. In so far as it does so, however, the same trend still persists in the modified form of a tendency to keep the quantity down, at least, so far as possible and avoid any increase in it (that is, to keep its level of tension constant). All the performances of the neuronic system are to be comprised under the heading either of the primary function or of the secondary function imposed by the exigencies of life.[13] (p. 358).

Thus from its first formulation, which distinguishes it from the principle of inertia, the principle of constancy brings into play the secondary process, whose anatomical basis is strictly unknown: indeed, further on Freud will postulate, for reasons of symmetry, a group of neurons which retain a bound stored energy and which he calls the "ego" (pp. 384–86). Freud will always try to regard the principle of constancy as equivalent to the principle of inertia for an apparatus that is forced to act and defend itself against internal dangers for which there is no screen comparable to the sensory apparatus, the latter acting both as barrier and receptor.[14]

The metaphorical character of the constancy principle is heightened when one considers that it extends to a variety of apparatuses

13. The distinction between the primary and the secondary processes will be established at length further on; for the present let us say simply that it is a matter of distinguishing between reaction in a quasi-hallucinatory manner and a correct exploitation of the indications of reality on the part of the ego (*Origins*, pp. 388–89).

14. This will be one of the basic themes of *The Ego and the Id*. Whereas there exists a "perceptual screen," the ego is exposed without any protection to the excitations from its instincts. The notion that perception is a selective system regarding excitations from the external world, whereas desires leave us unprotected, is a profound one. One might compare it to the Nietzschean concept of danger.

at least one of which concerns the contrary of quantity, namely quality.[15] "Consciousness gives us what we call 'qualities'" (p. 369) (we will see the great importance these qualities have for reality-testing); "thus we must summon up enough courage to assume that there is a *third* system of neurons—'perceptual neurons' they might be called,"[16] which are "contrivances for changing external *quantity* into *quality*" (p. 370). Freud tried to attach them to the quantitative system by assigning them a temporal property, periodicity: "the *period* of neuronic motion is transmitted without inhibition in every direction, as though it were a process of induction" (p. 371).[17] This enables Freud to differentiate himself from the school of parallelism and the epiphenomenalists: since it is bound to a specific group of neurons, consciousness is not an ineffectual double of the nervous process in general.

What is yet more serious, however, is the fact that the whole system rests on the simply postulated equivalence between unpleasure and the rise in the level of tension on the one hand, and between pleasure and the lowering of the level on the other:

> Since we have certain knowledge of a trend in psychical life towards *avoiding unpleasure,* we are tempted to identify that trend with the trend towards inertia. In that case *unpleasure*

15. It may be asked whether the difference between the Φ-neurons, which allow a current to "pass through" them and then return to their former state, and the Ψ-neurons, which are "permanently altered" by the current (*Origins,* pp. 359–60), is not the transcription of a fundamentally qualitative distinction, viz. the opposition between receiving and retaining, perceiving and remembering.

16. Freud designates these neurons by the letter *W* (*Wahrnehmung*), which he then jokingly changes to ω so as to call the three kinds of postulated neurons Φ,Ψ,ω. Thus it is that in his letters he speaks of his φψω system (*Origins,* pp. 123–24). The Φ-neurons are essentially "permeable" (i.e. they offer no resistance and retain nothing) and serve the function of perception; the Ψ-neurons are essentially "impermeable" (i.e. they retain quantity) and thus are the vehicles of memory and presumably also of psychical processes in general (*Origins,* p. 360).

17. The introduction of time is of the greatest importance; we will often come back to it. *The unconscious is timeless.* It should be noted that time is intimately connected with quality, which plays a role in reality-testing. Time, consciousness, and reality are thus correlative notions.

> would coincide with a rise in the level of quantity ($Q\dot{\eta}$) or with a quantitative increase of pressure; it would be the perceptual sensation when there is an increase of quantity ($Q\dot{\eta}$) in Ψ. *Pleasure* would be the sensation of discharge. (p. 373)

This is a mere postulate, since unpleasure and pleasure are sensed intensities which Freud localizes along with sensory qualities in a third type of neurons, the ω-neurons, and since he characterizes these intensities as the cathexis of ω by Ψ.[18] In fact, this is a new example of the transformation of quantity into quality, which Freud tries to liken to the previous transformation by again appealing to the phenomenon of periodicity (pp. 373–74) already called upon to account for sensory qualities.[19] Desires or wishes enter this mechanistic theory (pp. 383–84) through the intermediary of the traces left by the experiences of pleasure and unpleasure: it is to be assumed that the cathexis of a pleasant memory in a state of desire is far greater than the cathexis of a mere perception. This assumption allows for a first definition of repression (equated here with primary defense) as the removal of cathexis from a hostile memory image (p. 383).[20]

At this point, however, the system starts to break down: the pleasure-unpleasure combination sets into play much more than the isolated functioning of the psychical apparatus; it sets into play the external world (food, the sexual partner), and with the external

18. ω and Ψ function "to some extent like inter-communicating pipes" (*Origins*, p. 373). MacIntyre (p. 18) is right: the model is taken from hydraulics.

19. Freud will always endeavor to find a law to explain the alternation of sensory qualities with the affective qualities of pleasure-unpleasure: the various sensory qualities lie in a zone of indifference and seem to require an optimum point of reception, linked with the phenomenon of periodicity (*Origins*, pp. 373–74); beyond or short of that point it is the charge (cathexis) or discharge as such that is perceived. Freud rightly saw that this perception obeys the laws of summation and of threshold (ibid., pp. 377–78).

20. On the relation between the notions of defense and repression, see the important work of Peter Madison, *Freud's Concept of Repression and Defense, Its Theoretical and Observational Language* (Minneapolis, University of Minnesota Press, 1961); cf. below, p. 138, n. 58, and p. 355, n. 18.

world other persons appear. It is remarkable that Freud, in designating the overall process that encompasses being aided by others, chose to speak of the *experience of satisfaction:*

> At early stages the human organism is incapable of achieving this specific action. It is brought about by extraneous help, when the attention of an experienced person has been drawn to the child's condition by a discharge taking place along the path of internal change [e.g. by the child's screaming]. This path of discharge thus acquires an extremely important secondary function —viz., of bringing about an *understanding with other people;* and the original helplessness of human beings is thus the *primal source of all moral motives.* (p. 379)

The experience of satisfaction is indeed a sort of "test-experience": it is related to reality-testing and marks the transition from the primary to the secondary process.

Freud tried to maintain this detour through reality within the framework of the principle of constancy by linking the regulation by reality to the sole principle of unpleasure: "Unpleasure remains the sole means of education" (p. 428). But the avoidance of unpleasure in turn implies several processes that are scarcely quantifiable; these come down basically to the work of discriminating between hallucinatory desires and perceptual qualities, a work coupled with the ego organization's function of inhibiting.

When first examined, these themes fit in quite well with the central hypothesis: in the primary process, where the apparatus functions most in accord with the principle of inertia, discharge takes the path of a recathexis of the memory images of the "wished-for" object and of movements to obtain it; it is assumed that this reactivation produces the analogue of a perception, i.e. a hallucination: "I have no doubt that the wishful activation will in the first instance produce something similar to a perception—namely, a hallucination" (p. 381).[21] This mistake produces real unpleasure and an

21. Recognizable here is the condition described by Meynert as amentia (acute hallucinatory psychosis), which Jones (*1,* 353) sees as one of the starting points for the theory of the primary process in Chapter 7 of *The Interpretation of Dreams.*

excessive reaction on the part of the primary defense; together these reactions can be biologically damaging. Chapter 7 of the *Traumdeutung* will again postulate no discrimination between images and perceptions in the primary process, and to account for this will devise a topographical regression within the functioning of the psychical apparatus;[22] the assumption is made that the excessive charge of the desire produces an image similar to the indication of a perceptual quality. We shall have much to say at the proper time about this hypothesis.[23] For the present, how does discrimination come about in the secondary process?

For the first time Freud establishes a connection between discriminating between the real and the imaginary and the function of inhibition, attributing the latter to what has already been called the "ego organization" (pp. 384–86). It is a point that will never change: the constant cathexis of the ego, the function of inhibiting, and reality-testing will always go together.[24] "Where, then, an ego exists, it is bound to inhibit primary psychical processes" (p. 385). To make this new idea accord with the system, Freud postulates an organization of neurons with a constant charge—"a network of cathected neurons, well facilitated in relation to one another" (p. 385). This text also contains the first sketch of a genetic explanation of the ego. As in *The Ego and the Id* later on, this reserve of energy arises by means of cumulative borrowings from endogenous quantity; this bound energy forms a system of tensions at a constant level.

But what is inhibition? Freud puts it as follows: the ego learns *not* to cathect motor images or the ideas of desired objects. This "restriction" or "limitation," which foreshadows the famous *Verneinung,* the movement by way of the *No,* is presented here as a

22. This mechanism is foreshadowed in the "Project," *Origins,* pp. 438–39: "We must necessarily suppose that in states of hallucination the quantity (*Q*) flows back to Φ and at the same time to *W* (ω). Thus a bound neuron does not permit such a flow-back to occur" (p. 438).

23. See below the discussion of Chapter 7 of *The Interpretation of Dreams* and the interpretation of dreams as being quasi-hallucinatory, "Analytic," Part I, Ch. 2, second section.

24. Kris (*Origins,* p. 384, n. 3) sees in this analysis the first anticipation of the theory of the ego in *The Ego and the Id* (1923).

mechanical effect of the threat of unpleasure; it is not clear, however, how the "moral motives" and the "mutual facilitation" alluded to above fit in with this hedonistic principle. Freud admits, moreover, that he is unable to give a mechanical explanation how the threat of unpleasure governs the noncathexis of quantities accumulated in the ego (p. 428); on this occasion he states: "From this point onwards I shall venture to omit any mechanical representation of biological rules of this kind; and I shall be content if I can henceforward keep faithfully to a clearly demonstrable course of development" (p. 428).

It is still more difficult to give a mechanical explanation of the connection between inhibition and discrimination; Freud assumes that discrimination is based on "indications of reality" arising from the system ω: "*It is this report of a discharge coming from W* (ω) *that constitutes an indication of quality or reality to* Ψ" (p. 387). But how does inhibition enable these indications to operate? Freud focuses upon the difficulty in these terms: "*it is the inhibition brought about by the ego that makes possible a criterion for distinguishing between a perception and a memory*" (p. 388). But the explanation he gives is rather a description of the problem to be resolved:

> Wishful cathexis carried to the point of hallucination and a complete generation of unpleasure, involving a complete expenditure of defense, may be described as "psychical primary processes." On the other hand, those processes which are only made possible by a good cathexis of the ego and which represent a moderation of the primary processes may be described as "psychical secondary processes." It will be seen that the *sine qua non* of the latter is a correct exploitation of the indications of reality and that this is only possible when there is inhibition on the part of the ego.—We have thus put forward a hypothesis to the effect that, during the process of wishing, inhibition on the part of the ego leads to a moderation of the cathexis of the object wished-for, which makes it possible for that object to be recognized as not being a real one. (pp. 388–89)

Along with discrimination, certain functions are assigned to the system that are less and less ascribable to measurable energies. In the third part, the "Project" introduces some descriptive themes that will not be developed until much later: "judgment"—a term borrowed from W. Jerusalem [25]—is conceived as the recognition of the identity between a wishful cathexis and a perceptual indication of reality; this real recognition of a wished-for object is the first stage in achieving an estimation of reality, a belief. Freud is confident that he can give a quantitative interpretation of it, but it is clear that "the cathexis of Ψ-neurons" (p. 396) is simply a translation of psychology into a conventional technical language.

The same may be said of "attention," conceived as the interest aroused in Ψ by the indications of reality. The explanation Freud proposes is already an economic one: the interest consists in the fact that the ego has learned to hypercathect perception (p. 419). But does this remain a mechanical and quantitative explanation?

Still more remarkable is the role attributed to the verbal [26] stage of "observant thought." Verbal images—the famous "things heard" which combine with "things experienced" in the childhood seduction scene [27]—contribute not only to the construction of fantasies; their positive function is contemporaneous with attention and understanding (p. 423). Verbal images contribute to the secondary function by becoming indications of thought-reality rather than of perceived reality: "Thus we have found that the characteristic thing about the process of cognitive thought is that the attention is from the start directed to the indications of the discharge of thought—that is, to indications of speech" (p. 424). Freud will remain faithful to this notion of two degrees of reality, the first on the biological and perceptual level, the second on the intellectual and scientific level: "*Thought which is accompanied by the cathexis of indications of thought-reality or of indications of speech is the highest and most secure form of cognitive thought-process*" (p. 431). The sci-

25. Jones, *I*, 371, and *Origins*, p. 120.

26. It would be impossible to overemphasize this theme: Letter 46 connects in the same way the process of becoming conscious and "verbal consciousness" (*Origins*, p. 165). We shall return to this point when dealing with *The Ego and the Id*. The same letter anticipates another basic point: "An increase in the uninhibited processes to the point of their alone being in possession of the path to verbal consciousness produces *psychoses*" (*Origins*, p. 166).

27. Cf. the important Draft M attached to Letter 63 of May 25, 1897 (*Origins*, p. 204).

entist's disinterestedness, his ability to concentrate steadily on an idea, is thus translated into energy terms. To do this, Freud returns to Breuer's notion of bound energy, defining it as a *"condition in the neurons, which, though there is a high cathexis, permits only a small current to flow"* (p. 425). *"Thus the process of thought would be characterized mechanically by this bound condition, which combines a high cathexis with a small flow of current"* (p. 426). But it must be admitted that from now on there is no longer any anatomical basis; moreover, the shortcomings of thought, unlike the confusion between hallucinations and perceptions, do not give rise to biological sanctions of unpleasure: "In theoretical thought no part is played by unpleasure" (p. 443). This is the clearest instance where description is seen to go beyond the mechanical explanation.

TOWARD THE TOPOGRAPHY

If now we step back a bit and place the "Project" on the trajectory of the successive topographies, two sets of remarks present themselves:

1. That which cuts explanation off from any work of deciphering, from any reading of symptoms and signs, is the pretension of making a quantitative psychology of desire, comparable to Fechner's quantitative psychology of sensations, correspond to a mechanical system of neurons. In this regard the "Project" is Freud's final attempt to give an anatomical translation of his discoveries; the "Project" is the final parting of the ways with anatomy in the form of an imaginary anatomy. The topography, to be sure, will always be couched in the language of a quasi anatomy; consciousness, conceived as a sensory organ, a "surface" organ, will remain a quasi cortex; but the attempt to localize the functions and roles attributed to the "agencies" of the later topography will never be made again. We must go even further: this final attempt is also the first step in the emancipation of "psychology": the tenor of the text is psychological, not neurological. At the very time Freud was writing the "Project" the anatomical basis of his system was being undermined.

Divided between the clinic and the laboratory, between Charcot and Brücke, Freud is already closer to the more clinical-minded French than to the more anatomical-minded Germans.[28] At a very early period—1891!—his criticism of theories of localization, which he formulated in his critical study on aphasia, had made him wary of any premature organic explanation of psychical disturbances.[29] But above all, the great discovery of those years, the one that was to estrange him from the scientific milieu of the university and the medical profession—the discovery of the sexual etiology of the neuroses [30]—remains purely clinical and is not paralleled by any properly organic hypothesis; in particular the clinical entity of hysterical paralysis is established in opposition to the anatomists: everything takes place, Freud remarked, as if there were no such thing as anatomy of the brain.[31]

This episode was as decisive as the study of aphasia in detaching Freud from any premature organic explanation. During the same period, his incursion into the cathartic method of Breuer,[32] coupled with his disappointment with electrotherapy,[33] confirmed the properly psychical genesis of symptoms: "hysterical patients," wrote Breuer and Freud in the "Preliminary Communication," "suffer principally from reminiscences"; [34] what disappeared by a

28. Jones, *1*, 185 ff.; *Origins*, pp. 55, 58. What place should be assigned to Freud's three unsuccessful attempts, made in 1878, 1884, and 1885, to handle the experimental method? (Jones, *1*, 54–55). The cocaine episode (1884–87) was perhaps even more decisive (Jones, *1*, 78–97); Freud's self-analysis would later reveal that episode's deep and lasting effect, which he was inclined to interpret in terms of unconscious guilt: cf. the dream of 'Irma's injection' (July 24, 1895), which is related in the *Traumdeutung* (Jones, *1*, 354). On all these points, cf. Didier Anzieu, *L'Auto-analyse* (Paris, P. U. F., 1959), Ch. 1: "L'Auto-analyse de Freud et la découverte de la psychanalyse."

29. Jones, *1*, 212–16; *An Autobiographical Study* (1925), *SE, 20*, 18. In *On Aphasia*, his first book, published in 1891, Freud boldly attacked the localization schemes drawn up by Wernicke and Lichtheim and proposed instead a functional explanation, citing to this effect Hughlings Jackson's doctrine of "disinvolution."

30. Sexuality and speech both share, however, in organic and psychical factors. Jones, *1*, 272.

31. Jones, *1*, 233; *An Autobiographical Study, SE, 20*, 13–14.

32. *An Autobiographical Study, SE, 20*, 19; Jones, *1*, 204.

33. "On the History of the Psychoanalytic Movement" (1914), *GW, 10*, 46; *SE, 14*, 9.

34. "Preliminary Communication," *Studies on Hysteria, GW, 1*, 86; *SE, 2*, 7.

psychical procedure must have come into existence by a psychical means. It is exciting to follow, in the "Letters to Fliess" as well as in the accompanying notes and drafts, the development of the idea that the physical energy of sexuality demands a properly psychical stage; the essential reason for constructing the concept of the libido at its psychological and nonanatomical level was to account for the disturbances that affect this psychical elaboration of sexuality; the libido is the first concept that can be said to be both energic and nonanatomical.[35] The *Three Essays on the Theory of Sexuality* will definitively determine this concept of "the psychical energy of the sexual instincts."

2. Perhaps we can go even further: the "Project" is not merely a mechanical system cut off from interpretation by its anatomical hypothesis; it is already a topography, linked by underground connections to the work of deciphering symptoms. Hermeneutics is already present in this text.

First, the notion of quantity: it is surprising that it is never measured, but from the outset it has a concrete, tangible characteristic that it owes to clinical observation: "This line of approach," Freud says at the beginning of the "Project," "is derived directly from pathological clinical observations, especially from those concerned with 'excessively intense ideas.' (These occur in hysteria and obsessional neurosis, where, as we shall see, the quantitative characteristic emerges more plainly than in the normal)" (p. 356).[36]

35. Concerning the transition from "physical sexual tension" to "psychical libido," see *Origins*, p. 91, Draft E. It is mainly the phenomenon of anxiety that forces Freud to consider that "sexual tension" is "worked over psychically" (p. 93), or more precisely, "transformed into affects." In a note to Draft G of January 7, 1895, Kris cites an important excerpt from the first of Freud's two papers on anxiety neurosis (1895). The role "representations" or "ideas" play, which we shall stress in Ch. 3 of this part of the "Analytic," is expressly set up in that paper: once the excitation has become a psychical stimulus, "the group of sexual ideas present in the mind becomes charged with energy and a psychical state of libidinal tension comes into existence, bringing with it an impulse to relieve this tension" (*Origins*, p. 102, n. 5). Along the same lines Draft G speaks of the "psychical sexual group" (ibid., p. 103). The entire theory of anxiety neurosis is based on the notion that something blocks the psychical elaboration of the excitation. Jones, *1*, 241–50, 258–59.

36. This notion is taken up again in Part II of the "Project" (pp. 405–

In this regard, the phenomenon of anxiety very clearly manifests the tangible presence of quantity; anxiety is quantity laid bare. The mechanical aspect of quantity is ultimately less important than its intensive aspect.

We must go further: all the "mechanisms" described at this period have already been raised to the level of what Freud will soon call work: dream-work, work of mourning, etc. All the dynamic concepts—defense, resistance, repression, transference [37]—are deciphered in the work of the neurosis, in "the psychical elaboration of the libido," as we said above. By the same token the energy concepts are already correlative to the whole activity of interpretation brought into play by the etiology of the neuroses.

Finally, the theory of constancy and its anatomical translation furnish little support to the edifice; when the "Project," barely drafted, succumbs to doubt, only the clinical observations on the neuroses will stand firm.[38] The sexual etiology of the neuroses was actually a much better guide than any mechanism or quantitative system. From the beginning Freud had "the distinct impression" that he had "touched on one of the great secrets of nature" (Letter 18 of 1894).

---

16), which is inserted between the "General Scheme" and the "Account of Normal Ψ-Processes" (the secondary process, etc.): "compulsion, which is operated by means of excessively intense ideas," and which is *found* in hysteria, is at the same time the *demonstration* of quantity. As Freud notes, "The term 'excessively intense' points to *quantitative* characteristics" (p. 407). It is *from* the mechanisms of neurosis (conversion of affects in hysteria, displacement of affects in obsession, transformation of affects in the anxiety neuroses) that Freud, a year before the "Project," "reads off" quantity: " 'Sexual affect,' " he writes, "is, of course, taken in its widest sense, as an excitation with a definite quantity" (Letter 18, *Origins*, p. 85). Draft D clearly shows the correlation between the sexual etiology of the neuroses and the theory of constancy (*Origins*, p. 87).

37. The correlation between clinical and economic concepts is very noticeable in Freud's early remarks about grief, mortification, self-reproach on the one hand and defense, conflict, resistance, repression on the other (*Origins*, pp. 126–31, 136, 146, 164). Particularly to be noted is the definition of grief or mourning as the "longing for something that is lost." The correlation between mourning and melancholy has already been made: "melancholia consists in mourning over loss of libido" (ibid., p. 103).

38. *Origins*, pp. 133, 134. "Perhaps in the end I may have to learn to content myself with the clinical explanation of the neuroses" (p. 137).

However, one should not conclude from this second set of remarks that the constancy principle and the quantitative hypothesis are liquidated along with the pseudoanatomical translation. Affects will continue to be treated as displaceable or bound "quantities" joined to ideas, and the notion of cathexis will remain closely linked with this strange quantity that is never measured. It may even be thought that the discovery and practice of the method of free association, which was substituted for the cathartic method, rather reinforced the idea that the psychism presents some definite agency. The conviction that the psychism is not a chaos but presents a hidden order not only gave rise to the method of interpretation but also reinforced the deterministic explanation; as Jones says toward the beginning of his book, "Freud never abandoned determinism for teleology." [39] The constancy principle was the instrument by which a theory of desire or wishing, with its ideas of purpose, aim, and intention, remained subordinated to a deterministic hypothesis (Jones, *1*, 366). At the end of Chapter 3 we will account for this coincidence between the idea of interpretation as the relation of meaning to meaning and the idea of order and system. Because of this coincidence the principle of constancy, conceived as the self-regulation of a psychical system, will outlast its expression in terms of neurons: for a long time the reality principle will be looked upon as a complication and a detour; it will be seriously challenged only by the death instinct; in the face of death, life will present itself as Eros. Having reached this ultimate phase of the metapsychology, one may then wonder whether the Freudian theory has not restored the Naturphilosophie which the school of Helmholtz endeavored to overthrow, and Goethe's Weltanschauung which the young Freud had admired so much. If so, then Freud will have brought to pass the prophecy he made about himself: to return to philosophy by way of medicine and psychology.[40]

39. Jones, *1*, 45.

40. "I secretly nurse the hope of arriving by the same route [i.e. medicine] at my own original objective, philosophy. For that was my original ambition, before I knew what I was intended to do in the world" (*Origins*, p. 141). On Freud and Goethe, cf. Jones, *1*, 43.

Chapter 2: Energetics and Hermeneutics in *The Interpretation of Dreams*

The difficult Chapter 7 of *The Interpretation of Dreams*[1] (*Traumdeutung*) is unquestionably the heir to the "Project" of 1895; left unpublished by Freud himself, the "Project" found an outlet in *The Interpretation of Dreams.*[2] However, at least two changes have supervened. The first is so great that no one could overlook it: the psychical apparatus of *The Interpretation of Dreams* functions without any anatomical reference; it is a *psychical* apparatus. From this point on, dreams impose a theme that may be called Herbartian: there are dream "thoughts"; a dream is the accomplishment or fulfillment (*Erfüllung*) of a desire or wish (*Wunsch*); that is to say, it is something "psychical" or "ideational." Hence *The Interpretation of Dreams* no longer speaks

1. I shall frequently cite passages from *The Interpretation of Dreams* so as to propose to French readers a more exact translation of the original text. The title itself, which directly concerns the theory of hermeneutics, should be translated literally: *Deutung* does not mean science but interpretation. The French translation to which I refer—with the reservation that I may correct it—is that of I. Meyerson, *La Science des rêves* (Paris, P. U. F., 1950), translated from the 7th German edition; I also indicate in parentheses the pagination of the edition of the *Club français du livre*, 1963. [Translator's note: By the author's directive, nearly all references to the French editions are omitted and all quotations are taken from James Strachey's translation in the *Standard Edition*, Vols. 4 and 5.]

2. The evolution of the theory may be followed in the letters to Fliess written after the "Project"; see particularly Letters 39 and 52, which are still close to the "Project." It is important for our later discussion to note that the theory of the hallucinatory character of dreams—a theory already introduced in the "Project" (*The Origins of Psychoanalysis*, p. 401)—preceded the more general thesis that dreams are a wish-fulfillment: Letters 28, 45, and 62; cf. Anzieu, *L'Auto-analyse*, pp. 82–129.

of cathected neurons but of cathected ideas. This first change entails another one which, though less visible, is perhaps of greater importance for an epistemological reflection on "models": the schema of the psychical apparatus oscillates between a *real* representation, as was the machine of the "Project," and a *figurative* representation, as will be the later schemata of the topography. We shall try to understand this ambiguity and, if possible, justify it to a certain extent.

These two changes disclose a more radical transformation affecting the relationship between the topographic-economic *explanation* on the one hand and *interpretation* on the other. In the "Project" that relation was left unclear: the interpretation of symptoms, which arose from observations of transference in neurotic patients, guided the construction of the system without itself being thematized within the system. As a result the systematic explanation seemed to be independent of the concrete work of the analyst and of the patient's own work on his neurosis. Such is not the case in *The Interpretation of Dreams:* here the systematic explanation is placed at the end of a process of work whose own rules have been elaborated; the express aim of the explanation is to present a schematic transcription of what goes on in the dream-work that is accessible only in and through the work of interpretation. The explanation, therefore, is explicitly subordinated to interpretation; it is not by accident that this book is called *Die Traumdeutung, The Interpretation of Dreams.*

THE DREAM-WORK AND THE WORK OF EXEGESIS

The thesis that dreams have meaning is first of all a polemical thesis which Freud defends on two fronts. On the one hand, it is opposed to the notion that dreams are a chance play of representations, a waste product of mental life, and that the sole problem concerning them is their lack of meaning. From this first point of view, to say that dreams have meaning is to assert that they are an intelligible, and even intellectual, operation of man; to understand them is to experience their intelligibility. On the other hand, the thesis is opposed to any premature organic explanation of dreams; the thesis signifies that one can always substitute for the dream account another account, with a semantics and a syntax, and that these two accounts are comparable to one another as two texts. It sometimes happens that Freud compares, more or less appropriately, this relation of text to text to that of translating from one language to another; we will return to the exactitude of the analogy later. For the present let us take the analogy as unambiguous affirmation that interpretation moves from a less intelligible to a more intelligible meaning. The same may be said of the analogy of the picture puzzle or rebus, which is another example of the relation of obscure text to clear text.[3]

The comparison of meaning to a text enables one to eliminate what remains equivocal in the notion of symptom; a symptom, to be sure, is already an *effect-sign* and presents the mixed structure we wish to delimit in this study; but this mixed structure is more clearly revealed by dreams than by symptoms.[4] Belonging as they

3. "The aim which I have set before myself is to show that dreams are capable of being interpreted [*einer Deutung fähig sind*]. . . . My presumption that dreams can be interpreted at once puts me in opposition to the ruling theory of dreams and in fact to every theory of dreams with the exception of Scherner's; for 'interpreting' a dream implies assigning a 'meaning' [*Sinn*] to it—that is, replacing [*ersetzen*] it by something which fits [*sich . . . einfügt*] into the chain of our mental acts as a link having a validity and importance equal to the rest" (*GW, 2/3,* 100; *SE, 4,* 96). Further on, at the beginning of Chapter 3, Freud compares the situation of the analyst who has surmounted the first difficulties of dream interpretation to that of an explorer who comes upon an open view after passing through a narrow defile: "We find ourselves in the full daylight of a sudden discovery" (*wir stehen in der Klarheit einer plötzlichen Erkenntnis*) (*GW, 2/3,* 127; *SE, 4,* 122; this phrase is omitted in the French translation, p. 94 [77]). Thus dreams are seen to be "psychical phenomena of complete validity [*vollgültiger*]—fulfillments of wishes [*Wunsch*]; they can be inserted [*einzureihen*] into the chain of intelligible [*uns verständlichen*] waking mental acts; they are constructed by a highly complicated activity of the mind [*geistige*]" (ibid.). On the comparison of interpretation to a translation from one language into another, or to the solution of a rebus, see *GW, 2/3,* 283–84; *SE, 4,* 277–78.

4. Chronologically the idea of symptoms, which is common to Breuer and Freud, is certainly first; methodologically, however, the reversal of priority is essential: "Though my own line of approach to the subject of dreams was determined by my previous work on the psychology of the

do to discourse, dreams reveal that symptoms have a meaning; thus dreams enable one to coordinate the normal and the pathological within what might be called a general semiology.

But is it possible to maintain interpretation on this unambiguous level where relations would be those of meaning to meaning? Interpretation cannot be developed without calling into play concepts of an entirely different order, energy concepts. It is impossible to achieve the first task of interpretation—viz. to discover the thoughts, ideas, or wishes that are "fulfilled" in a disguised way—without considering the "mechanisms" that constitute the dream-work and bring about the "transposition" or "distortion" (*Entstellung*) of the dream-thoughts into the manifest content. This study of the dream-work, according to one of the methodological texts of *The Interpretation of Dreams,* constitutes the second task.[5] The

---

neuroses, I had not intended to make use of the latter as a basis of reference in the present work. Nevertheless I am constantly being driven to do so, instead of proceeding, as I should have wished, in the contrary direction and using dreams as a means of approach to the psychology of the neuroses" (*GW, 2/3,* 593; *SE, 5,* 588). The structural identity of neurotic symptoms and dreams as both being "formations of compromise" will be established only at the end of the topography ("Traumbildung und Symptombildung," *GW, 2/3,* 611–13; *SE, 5,* 605–08). But the interpretation of symptoms as *symbols,* in the *Studies on Hysteria,* is the main link; cf. below, p. 97, n. 15.

5. See the important methodological text that terminates Chapter 6: "Two separate functions may be distinguished in mental activity during the construction of a dream: the production [*Herstellung*] of the dream-thoughts, and their transformation into the content of the dream." The dream-thoughts do not have a special nature. On the other hand, the dream-work is peculiar to dreams; this activity "is completely different [from waking thought] qualitatively and for that reason not immediately comparable with it. It does not think, calculate or judge in any way at all; it restricts itself to giving things a new form" (*GW, 2/3,* 510–11; *SE, 5,* 506–07). This theme is taken up again in Chapter 7: *GW, 2/3,* 597; *SE, 5,* 592. The translation of the word *Entstellung,* by which Freud globally designates the dream-work, and which covers displacement, condensation, and other procedures, is difficult: it contains two ideas, that of a violent change of place, and that of a deformation, disfiguring, or disguise which makes something unrecognizable. Both the traditional French translation, *transposition,* and the English translation, "distortion" (*distorsion* is also a good French expression), retain only one of the intentions of the original term. That is why I write: "transposition" or "distortion."

distinction between the two tasks has only a pedagogical value, however: the discovery of the unconscious dream-thoughts shows that they are the same as the thoughts of waking life; all the strangeness of dreams is centered, rather, upon the dream-work. Transposition or distortion, in which the dream-work roughly consists, splits dreams off from the rest of psychical life, whereas the revealing of the dream-thoughts relates dreams to waking life.

Moreover, the first task, which in the course of the book is not clearly distinguished from the second, cannot be accomplished to any great extent without recourse to economic concepts. To find the dream-thoughts is, in fact, to follow out a certain regressive path which, beyond the present impressions and bodily excitations, the memories of waking life or the day's residues, or the actual wish for sleep, discloses the unconscious, that is to say, *the earliest wishes.* It is our childhood that rises to the surface, with its forgotten, checked, repressed impulses, and along with our childhood that of mankind, recapitulated in that of the individual. Dreams provide access to a basic phenomenon that will constantly preoccupy us in this book, the phenomenon of *regression,* of which we shall shortly better understand not only the temporal but the topological and dynamic aspects. In regression, we are led from concepts of meaning to concepts of force by this relation to the abolished, the forbidden, the repressed—this close connection between the archaic and the oneiric; for the realm of dream-fantasy is a realm of desire. If dreams are drawn toward discourse because of their narrative aspect, their relation to wishes or desires throws them back on the side of energy, conatus, appetition, will to power, libido, or whatever one wishes to call it. Thus dreams, inasmuch as they are the expression of wishes, lie at the intersection of meaning and force.

Interpretation (*Deutung*), which has not yet become identified with the work of deciphering correlative to the dream-work, and which has been concerned more with psychical content than with mechanism, nevertheless has begun to receive its proper structure, and this structure is a mixed one. On the one hand, in terms of meaning, interpretation is a movement from the manifest to the latent. To interpret is to displace the origin of meaning to another region. The topography, at least in its static and properly topographical form, will be the pictorial representation of this movement of interpretation from the apparent meaning toward another locality of meaning. But even at this first level it is impossible to look upon *Deutung* as a simple relation between ciphered and deciphered discourse; it is not enough to say that the unconscious is another discourse, an unintelligible discourse. In its transposition or distortion (*Verstellung*) of the manifest content into the latent content, interpretation uncovers another distortion, that of desires into images; Freud investigates this distortion in Chapter 4. To use an expression from the "Papers on Metapsychology," a dream is already a "vicissitude of instinct."

But it is impossible to thematize this Verstellung more precisely without proceeding to the second task of accounting for the mechanisms of the dream-work (*Traumarbeit*), which is the subject of Chapter 6. More clearly than the first, this second task requires combining two universes of discourse, the discourse of meaning and the discourse of force. To say that a dream is the *fulfillment* of a *repressed* wish is to put together two notions which belong to different orders: fulfillment (*Erfüllung*), which belongs to the discourse of meaning (as attested by Husserl's use of the term), and repression (*Verdrängung*), which belongs to the discourse of force. The notion of Verstellung, which combines the two universes of discourse, expresses the fusion of these two concepts, for a disguise is a type of manifestation and, at the same time, a distortion that alters that manifestation: it is the *violence done to the meaning*. Thus the relation of the hidden to the shown in the notion of disguise requires a deformation, or disfiguration, which can only be stated as a compromise of forces. The concept of "censorship," correlative to the concept of distortion, belongs to this same mixed discourse: distortion is the effect, censorship the cause. But what does censorship mean? The word is well chosen: on the one hand, censorship manifests itself at the level of a text on which it imposes blanks, word substitutions, softened expressions, allusions, tricks of arrangement —with suspect or subversive items being displaced and hidden in harmless, out-of-the-way spots; on the other hand, censorship is the expression of a power, more precisely of a political power, which works against the opposition by striking at its right of expression. In the idea of censorship the two systems of language are very closely interwoven: censorship alters a text only when it represses a force, and it represses a forbidden force only by disturbing the expression of that force.

What we have just said of the notions of disguise, distortion, and censorship, which together characterize the "transposition" effected by the dream-work, is still more evident if we consider the diverse mechanisms separately; none of them can be enunciated without recourse to that same mixed language.

On the one hand, the dream-work is the inverse of the analyst's work of deciphering and is homogeneous therefore with the mental operations of interpretation which trace it back. Thus the two main processes studied in Chapter 6 of *The Interpretation of Dreams*, "condensation" (*Verdichtungsarbeit*) and "displacement" (*Verschiebungsarbeit*), are meaningful operations comparable to rhetorical procedures. Freud himself compares condensation to an abbreviated, laconic turn of phrase, to a lacunary expression; it is at the same time a formation of composite expressions each of which belongs to several trains of thought. He compares displacement to a shift away from the central point, or again to an inversion of emphasis or value, whereby the various ideas of the latent content transfer their "psychical intensities" to the manifest content. These two processes attest, on the plane of meaning, to an "overdetermination" which calls for interpretation. Each of the elements of the dream-content is said to be overdetermined when it is "represented in the dream-thoughts many times over." [6] Overdetermination also governs, though in different ways, condensation and displacement. This is clear in the case of condensation, where the problem is to set out or make explicit a multiplicity of meanings through free association. But displacement, which concerns psychical intensities rather than the number of ideas, also requires overdetermination: to create new values, to displace interests, to "disregard" the point of intensity, displacement must follow the path of overdetermination.[7]

But this overdetermination, stated in the language of meaning, is

6. *GW, 2/3,* 289 (*mehrfach in den Traumgedanken vertreten*); *SE, 4,* 283.
7. *GW, 2/3,* 313; *SE, 4,* 307–08.

the counterpart of processes stated in the language of force: condensation means compression; displacement means transference of forces:

> It thus seems plausible to suppose that in the dream-work a psychical force [*eine psychische Macht*] is operating which on the one hand strips the elements which have a high psychical value of their intensity, and on the other hand, *by means of overdetermination,* creates from elements of low psychical value new values [*Wertigkeiten*], which afterwards find their way into the dream-content. If that is so, *a transference and displacement of psychical intensities* occurs in the process of dream-formation, and it is as a result of these that the difference between the text of the dream-content and that of the dream-thoughts comes about. The process which we are here presuming is nothing less than the essential portion of the dream-work; and it deserves to be described as "dream-displacement." Dream-displacement and dream-condensation are the two governing factors to whose activity we may in essence ascribe the form [*Gestaltung*] assumed by dreams.[8]

Thus there is the same relation between overdetermination (or "multiple determination") and displacement as there is between meaning and force.

The same mixed discourse is required by a third process which gives dreams their specific characteristic as "scenes" or "pictures"; whereas condensation and displacement accounted for the alteration of themes or "content," "representation" (*Darstellung*) denotes another aspect of regression that Freud calls formal regression (to distinguish it from temporal regression, of which we have already spoken, and from topographical regression, which we shall speak of later).[9] Such representation lends itself to description in terms of meaning; thus one will note the breakdown of syntax, the replacement of logical relations by pictorial equivalents, the representation of negation through the union of contraries in a single ob-

8. Ibid.
9. On the three forms of regression—formal, topographical, and temporal—see *GW, 2/3,* 554; *SE, 5,* 548 (addition of 1914).

ject, the resemblance of the manifest content to a mime or rebus, and in general the return to concrete pictorial expression. Putting aside for the moment the question of sexual symbolism, which has been too much the center of the discussion and whose exact place we shall see later, let us pose in its full extent the problem that Freud himself describes as "regard for representability."[10] In this connection, what is seen to characterize dreams is the regression beyond memory images to the hallucinatory revival of perception. Thus Freud says that *"in regression the fabric [das Gefüge] of the dream-thoughts is resolved into its raw material."*[11] But this regression to images, just described in terms of meaning as the hallucinatory revival of perception, is at the same time an economic phenomenon that can only be stated in terms of "changes in the cathexes of energy attaching to the different systems."[12]

One will object, before going any further, that the *Traumdeutung* is burdened here with an illusion that Freud was to abandon soon after the publication of his major book. It is not difficult to recognize in the background of this quasi-hallucinatory theory of dreams, just as in the "Project" of 1895, the belief in the reality of the childhood scene of seduction. The perceptual traces corresponding to that scene are eager for revival and exercise an attraction on the repressed thoughts, themselves struggling to find expression: "On this view a dream might be described as *a substitute [Ersatz] for an infantile scene modified by being transferred onto a recent experience.*"[13] According to the pattern of the infantile scene, which Freud regards as a model, the residual core of dreams would consist in a "complete hallucinatory cathexis of the perceptual systems. What we have described, in our analysis of the dream-work, as 'regard for representability' might be brought into connection with the *selective attraction* exercised by the visually recollected scenes touched upon by the dream-thoughts."[14]

These texts clearly show that Freud regarded the predominance

10. *"Die Rücksicht auf Darstellbarkeit," GW, 2/3,* 344 ff.; "Considerations of Representability," *SE, 5,* 339 ff.
11. *GW, 2/3,* 549; *SE, 5,* 543.
12. Ibid.
13. *GW, 2/3,* 552; *SE, 5,* 546.
14. *GW, 2/3,* 553; *SE, 5,* 548.

of pictorial representation in the dream-work as the hallucinatory revival of a primitive scene that had actually been perceived. The objection that may be raised about this assumption, however, is aimed more against the topography of Chapter 7 than against the description of representation in the context of the dream-work. There is no doubt that by interpreting the infantile scene as a real memory Freud is forced to confuse fantasies with the mnemic traces of real perceptions, in which case topographical regression is a regression to perception and the proper dimension of the imaginary is lost. We shall come back to this later. For our present purpose it is important only to notice that formal regression, which characterizes "pictorial representation," that is to say, the return from the logical to the figurative, raises a problem analogous to the problem of condensation and displacement: representation likewise is a distortion—and consequently an obstructing of direct expression, the forced substitution of one mode of expression for another. In all three cases, therefore—condensation, displacement, and representation—the dream is a work. That is why the Deutung corresponding to them is also a work, which, in order to be thematized, requires a mixed language that is neither purely linguistic nor purely energic.

In the notion that interpretation is a work we have the key to a difficulty with which I shall terminate this study of the main concepts of *The Interpretation of Dreams,* before proceeding to the topography of Chapter 7. The difficulty has to do with Freud's use of the notions of symbol and symbolic interpretation.

This use is at first rather disconcerting: on the one hand Freud opposes his own interpretation to a symbolic interpretation, and on the other hand he gives an important place, *precisely within the framework of representation,* to the sexual symbolization of dreams, with which the book itself has too hastily been identified. A clarification of this point is of the greatest importance to us, for in the vocabulary of our "Problematic" the term "symbol" stands for all double-meaning expressions and is the pivotal point of interpretation. If a symbol is the meaning of meaning, then the entire Freudian hermeneutics should be a hermeneutics of symbols inasmuch as they are the language of desire. In fact, however, Freud gives the notion of symbol a much more restricted extension.[15]

15. A systematic study of Freud's notion of symbol remains to be done. M. Guy Blanchet, who has begun such a study, has drawn my attention to the first Freudian conception of symbol, that in *Studies on Hysteria.* In the "Preliminary Communication" of 1892 (the subtitle of the first chapter of the *Studies*) the symbolic connection designates the hidden relation between the determining cause and the hysterical symptom; the symbolic connection is thus distinct from the manifest connection. The same text establishes, for the first time, a parallel between this symbolic connection and the dream process. Limited at first to the sufferings or pains of hysterical patients, this connection is gradually extended to all hysterical symptoms by means of the relation, gradually brought to light, between symbolization and memory; symbols thereby take on the value of recollection of pain, and Freud uses the expression "mnemic symbols" (*Studies on Hysteria, SE, 2,* 90–93, etc.). A symbol is thus a mnemic substitute for a traumatic scene the memory of which has been suppressed. If it is true, as was already said in the "Preliminary Communication," that "hysterics suffer mainly from reminiscences" (*GW, 1,* 86; *SE, 2,* 7), mnemic symbols are the means by which the trauma continues to exist in the form of symptoms. Mnemic symbols, unlike the (chronic) "mnemic residues," are deformed or converted, in the sense that one speaks of hysterical conversion. Symbolization therefore is coextensive with the whole field of distortion connected with repression (the latter being identified at this period with defense). The "Project" of 1895 still bears the imprint of this early conception of symbol as a mnemic substitute for a repressed trauma (*Origins,* pp. 406–07); thus symbolization tends to denote any substitute formation in cases where resistance is exercised against the return of the repressed memory.

This first sense of the word "symbol" is therefore wider than that in *The Interpretation of Dreams,* for it covers everything later called transposition or distortion (*Entstellung*). However, the intermediary role assigned to idiomatic expressions in the formation of hysterical symptoms foreshadows the future restriction of symbolism to cultural stereotypes: "It is as though there were an intention to express the mental state by means of a physical one; and linguistic usage affords a bridge by which this can be effected" (a lecture of January 1893, "On the Psychical Mechanism of Hysterical Phenomena," *SE, 3,* 34). Thus the facial neuralgia of a female patient treated conjointly by Breuer and Freud symbolized an insult, felt as a slap in the face; another patient, who suffered from the feeling that she could not "take a single step forward" in life, symbolized in the pains of her legs—pains which were already present from other sources—her sense of helplessness. In the *Studies on Hysteria* Freud saw therefore that symbolization is not only a distortion of the body through fantasies but a revival of the primitive meaning of words, as he will state in the 1910 paper "The Antithetical Meaning of Primal Words" (*SE, 11*), which we shall study further on.

In his survey of previous dream theories, Freud encounters two popular methods of dream interpretation which he opposes to one another as being "essentially different": symbolic interpretation and the decoding method. "The first of these procedures considers the content of the dream as a whole and seeks to replace it by another content which is intelligible and in certain respects analogous to the original one. This is '*symbolic*' dream-interpreting; and it inevitably breaks down when faced by dreams which are not merely unintelligible but also confused." [16] This was the method Joseph used in interpreting the Pharaoh's dream; it was also used by the novelist Jensen in his *Gradiva*—which Freud was to comment on several years later—when he attributed to the hero of his story a number of artificial but easily interpretable dreams. The second procedure, the *Chiffrier-methode* or decoding method, "treats dreams as a kind of cryptography in which each sign can be translated into another sign having a known meaning, in accordance with a fixed key." [17] This mechanical term-for-term translation has nothing at all to do with the notions of displacement and condensation, but at least it is closer than the symbolic method is to the psychoanalytic method inasmuch as it is an analysis *"en détail* and not *en masse."* [18] Like the decoding method, analysis treats dreams as having a "composite character," as "conglomerates of psychical formations." [19] Thus, what approximates analysis to the *Chiffrierverfahren* and separates it from the symbolic method is the method of free association.

Does this mean that the idea of symbol is excluded from the field of analysis along with the idea of the symbolic method? A second allusion, again a negative one, suggests that there is room for symbols, an idea the succeeding editions of *The Interpretation of Dreams* will pursue with great consistency. This allusion is to be found in the discussion of Scherner, the only person from whom Freud says he retained anything on this subject. The discussion occurs in the context of the somatic theories of dreams. Scherner is

16. *GW, 2/3,* 101; *SE, 4,* 96–97.
17. *GW, 2/3,* 102; *SE, 4,* 97.
18. *GW, 2/3,* 108; *SE, 4,* 104; in French in the text.
19. Ibid.

still held prisoner within that narrow context, but he rightly saw that "the dream-work, when the imagination [*Phantasie*] is set free from the shackles of daytime, seeks to give a *symbolic* representation [*symbolisch darzustellen*] of the nature of the organ from which the stimulus arises and of the nature of the stimulus itself." [20] Thus we are already involved in representation; in spite of his narrow starting point (stimulus and bodily organ), Scherner recognized under the name of symbol the work of representation that tends to derealize the body, to make it, in the proper sense of the term, fantastic. One drawback to this method of interpretation is the same as that found in the method employed in antiquity, with its generalized correspondences; an even greater defect, however, is that this manner of "fantasying" (*phantasieren*) the body reduces dreams to a useless activity. One must relate the body symbolism to the activity of "disposing of the stimulus" and hence to the complex interplay between the underlying forces that are the veritable sources of dreams.

In the series of re-editions [21] the place allotted to symbolism kept expanding, but always within a subordinate setting, first in the context of "typical dreams" (Ch. 5) and then, after 1914, under the heading of "representation" (Ch. 6). What attracted Freud's attention to the peculiar meaning of symbolism was the fact that certain dreams are typical (dreams of being naked, dreams of the death of persons of whom the dreamer is fond, and so on). Very early Freud remarks that these dreams are the hardest to approach by the method of interpretation. Gradually the conclusion is drawn

20. *GW*, *2/3*, 230; *SE*, *4*, 225.

21. Prior to the critical *Standard Edition* by Strachey, it was impossible to distinguish the successive additions from the 1900 text. It is important to know that the essential content of Section E of Chapter 6, the section devoted to "Representation by Symbols in Dreams," was added in 1909, 1911, and 1914, with still more paragraphs or notes added in subsequent editions (1919, 1921, 1922, 1930). In the second and third editions, these additions were included in Section D ("Typical Dreams") of Chapter 5. It was only in the 1914 edition that symbolism was transferred to the context of the theory of representation, a displacement that places symbolism in its true light. In the first paragraph (1925) of this new section, Freud acknowledges his debt to Stekel's work, *Die Sprache des Traumes* (1911); he had already done so in the preface to the third edition. A serious study of the development of Freud's thought should also take note of the influence of Herbert Silberer

that symbolism poses a specific problem, although there is no special symbolic function that deserves to figure among the procedures of the dream-work. All the examples of symbols in dreams have led

> to the same conclusion, namely that there is no necessity to assume that any peculiar symbolizing activity of the mind is operating in the dream-work, but that dreams make use of any symbolizations which are already present in unconscious thinking, because they fit in better with the requirements of dream-construction on account of their representability [*Darstellbarkeit*] and also because as a rule they escape censorship.[22]

That sentence gives the key to the rest: representation poses a problem, and to account for it Freud constructed a whole metapsychology of regression; symbolization does not pose a problem because in symbolism the work has already been done elsewhere; dreams make use of symbolism, they do not elaborate it. One thus understands why the dreamer does not produce associations in connection with his typical dreams: in his dream he has merely utilized,

---

and Havelock Ellis, as well as of Freud's close collaboration during this period with Otto Rank, who published the *Myth of the Birth of the Hero* in 1909; in the fourth, fifth, sixth, and seventh editions Freud included two essays by Rank entitled "Dreams and Creative Writing" and "Dreams and Myths" as appendices to Chapter 6. There would also appear to be an undoubted influence by Karl Abraham, with his work *Traum und Mythus* (1909), and by Ferenczi, who published a number of articles on dreams between the years 1910 and 1917. Finally, such a study should include the whole nexus of relations between Freud and Jung. This conflict is just as important for an understanding of the re-editions of the *Traumdeutung* as for an understanding of *Totem and Taboo* which appeared in 1913, the year of the break with Jung.

22. *GW, 2/3*, 354; *SE, 5*, 349. This is the earliest mention of the relation between representation and symbolization in the whole of the *Traumdeutung*. The passage was present from the first edition of 1900 and may be regarded as the initial nucleus of all later developments concerned with the "Representation by Symbols in Dreams." The transfer of this development, starting with the fourth edition of 1914, to the context of the processes of representation (Section E in Chapter 6) is the logical outcome of what had been seen from the beginning. The sentence we have just quoted was in fact the concluding one of the section on representability in Chapter 6, Section D; it thus served as a lead into the newly constituted Section E of Chapter 6 in 1914.

as in the use of a common expression, symbolic fragments that have fallen to the sphere of the trodden commonplace, phantoms that he has momentarily brought to life. One is reminded of the Husserlian notion of "sedimentation"; Freud grants it: "The question is bound to arise of whether many of these symbols do not occur with a permanently fixed meaning, like the 'grammalogues' in shorthand; and we shall feel tempted to draw up a new 'dream-book' on the decoding principle." [23]

Thus symbols have moved to the other side of the border that at first separated the symbolic method from the decoding method. But there they receive a precise place as a stereotyped code. It is no longer surprising that this general symbolism is not peculiar to dreams, but is also to be found in unconscious ideation among the people, in folklore and myths, legends and linguistic idioms, proverbs and current jokes—and "to a more complete extent than in dreams." [24] In making use of these symbols the dreamer but follows the paths traced out by the unconscious. Here we again come upon Scherner's symbolism and the symbolic extravagances of neurotics: "Wherever neuroses make use of such disguises they are following paths along which all humanity passed in the earliest periods of civilization— paths of whose continued existence today, under the thinnest of veils, evidence is to be found in linguistic usages, superstitions and customs." [25]

This is the reason why analytic interpretation must be supplemented by a genetic interpretation. Symbols have a special overdetermination which is not the product of the dream-work but a pregiven fact of culture: they are often the vestige of a conceptual and linguistic identity now lost. Hence the warning to the reader or overzealous practitioner of psychoanalysis not to reduce the trans-

23. *GW, 2/3,* 356; *SE, 5,* 351. This 1909 text links up with the remarks of the *Studies on Hysteria* concerning the role of idiomatic expressions in the constitution of the symbolic relation. This is doubtless the area, as we suggested above, in n. 15, where we must look for the continuity of the Freudian conception of symbol. A study of Lecture X of the *Introductory Lectures on Psychoanalysis* ("Symbolism in Dreams") (1917), to which we shall return in Chapter 4 of the last part of our work, will confirm this interpretation.

24. Ibid.

25. *GW, 2/3,* 352; *SE, 5,* 347.

lating of dreams to a translating of symbols, but rather to regard symbolism as an auxiliary: the proper path of interpretation is the dreamer's associations and not the pregiven connections in the symbols themselves. Finally, symbolic interpretation and analytic interpretation remain two distinct techniques and the first is subordinate to the second "as an auxiliary method." [26]

Was Freud right in restricting the notion of symbol to these stenographic signs? Should not a distinction be made between levels of actuality in symbols? In addition to the commonplace symbols, worn with use, at the end of their course, and having nothing but a past; and even in addition to the symbols in use, useful and utilized, which have a past and a present and serve in the clockwork of a given society as a token for the nexus of social pacts, are there not also new symbolic creations that serve as vehicles of new meanings? In other words, are symbols merely vestiges? Are they not also the dawn of meaning? Regardless of the outcome of this discussion—which we will return to at the proper moment—it is clear why, in the Freudian vocabulary and also in the framework of the economic explanation, there is no problem of *symbolization,* whereas there is a problem of pictorial *representation.* But even within the narrow limits in which Freud confines symbols the problem is not exhausted, for the psychoanalysis of myths, which we will meet with in the second part of this "Analytic," is elaborated precisely on the symbolic level. It is not accidental that the interpretation of *Oedipus Rex* and *Hamlet,* which we shall later discuss in detail, is elaborated in relation to the analysis of "typical dreams." [27]

THE "PSYCHOLOGY" OF CHAPTER 7

How does the systematization in Chapter 7 relate to the economic and hermeneutic concepts developed in the chapters preceding this difficult final one?

Its relation to the rest of the work is complex: it is partly the elu-

26. *GW, 2/3,* 365; *SE, 5,* 360.

27. It is remarkable that in the later editions the interpretation of the Oedipus myth was left in the section on "typical dreams" in Chapter 5 (Section D) and was not transferred to the section on "representation by symbols" (Section E of Chapter 6) after the major revision of 1914. The analysis of the Oedipus theme remains in the subsection concerning typical

cidation, by means of an "auxiliary representation," of what has already been elaborated and stated in implicit or confused terms; but it is also the imposition of a theory that remains somewhat external to the material it gathers together and coordinates. Hence the theory presents itself as an addition to the half economic, half hermeneutic, more practiced than reflected network of conceptions that we have drawn from the work itself.

The presentation of the topography in Chapter 7 is skillfully divided into three episodes, which are interspersed with descriptive and clinical themes that tend to becloud the reading somewhat. In the first,[28] the psychical apparatus is pictured spatially as functioning in both a progressive and a regressive direction; in the second,[29] the apparatus is viewed as an evolving system endowed with a temporal dimension; in the third,[30] the apparatus is presented as having force and conflict in addition to space and time. This progression parallels the one we tried to establish at the level of interpretation.

Interpretation, we said, aims first of all at locating the actual dream-thoughts, which we look for first in the somatic excitations, then in the residues of the previous day, then in the wish to sleep. The topography serves to determine the region in which the dream-thoughts originate. This is the first function of the topography in its purely static form.

The topographical location of the wish to sleep, as compared with the wishes assigned to dreams as their true origin, will make the problem quite clear. It is well known that Freud assigns dreams a certain function with regard to sleep; the wish-fulfillment that characterizes dreams is a substitute action which protects sleep.[31]

---

dreams containing death wishes, and more particularly, a child's death wish against his father. Regarding the Oedipus myth, Freud was in fact more interested in the "sources of dreams" (the title of Chapter 5), namely their rootedness in childhood desires, than in the role of representation or symbolization in the legendary disguise.

28. *GW*, *2/3*, 541–55; *SE*, *5*, 536–49.

29. *GW*, *2/3*, 570–78; *SE*, *5*, 564–72.

30. *GW*, *2/3*, 604–14; *SE*, *5*, 598–608.

31. "All dreams are in a sense dreams of convenience [*Bequemlichkeitsträume*]: they serve the purpose of prolonging sleep instead of waking up. *Dreams are the* GUARDIANS *of sleep and not its disturbers*" (*GW*, *2/3*, 239; *SE*, *4*, 233).

So important is the wish for sleep that the transformation of external stimuli into images and the entire derealization of the body, of which the symbolic distortion described by Scherner is the counterpart, must be attributed to it. Certain texts would even lead one to think that this wish is the dominant wish, since the censorship admits only those interpretations of the stimuli that are compatible with the wish to sleep.[32] This would seem to take us back to Aristotle, for whom "a dream is thinking that persists (insofar as we are asleep) in the state of sleep." [33] The solution of this difficulty is a topographical one: the wish to sleep is assigned to the preconscious system and the underlying instinctual wishes that instigate dreams belong to the unconscious system.[34] That is why the precise relation between the intermittent wish to sleep and the permanent wishes that seek an outlet in dreams is left in suspense until the celebrated Chapter 7.[35]

The subsidiary thesis in this discussion is that no wish—not even the wish to sleep—is efficacious unless it is joined to the "indestructible" and "so to say, immortal" desires that stem from our unconscious and whose infantile character is attested by the neuroses.[36]

32. *"Thus the wish to sleep (which the conscious ego is concentrated upon, and which, together with the dream-censorship and the 'secondary revision' which I shall mention later, constitute the conscious ego's share in dreaming) must in every case be reckoned as one of the motives for the formation of dreams, and every successful dream is a fulfillment of that wish"* (*GW, 2/3,* 240; *SE, 4,* 234).

33. *GW, 2/3,* 555; *SE, 5,* 550.

34. "I am unable to say what modification in the system *Pcs.* is brought about by the state of sleep; but there can be no doubt that the psychological characteristics of sleep are to be looked for essentially in modifications in the cathexis [*Besetzungsveränderung*] of this particular system—a system that is also in control of access to the power of movement, which is paralyzed during sleep. On the other hand, nothing in the psychology of dreams gives me reason to suppose that sleep produces any modifications other than secondary ones in the state of things prevailing in the *Ucs.*" (*GW, 2/3,* 560; *SE, 5,* 555).

35. "Zur Wunscherfüllung," *GW, 2/3,* 555 ff.; *SE, 5,* 550 ff.

36. An entrepreneur, as Freud reminds us, can do nothing without capital; he needs a capitalist, "and the capitalist who provides the psychical outlay for the dream is invariably and indisputably, whatever may be the thoughts of the previous day, *a wish from the unconscious*" (*GW, 2/3,* 566; *SE, 5,* 561). On the notion of "indestructible" and "immortal," cf. *GW, 2/3,* 559, 583; *SE, 5,* 533, 577.

Thus the first function of the topography is to give a schematic picture of the descending degrees of desire all the way to the *indestructible*. Even at this point, perhaps, we may say that the topography is the metaphorical picture of the indestructible as such: "In the unconscious nothing can be brought to an end, nothing is past or forgotten." [37] This statement foreshadows the formulations of the "Papers on Metapsychology": the unconscious is timeless. The topography is the locality which pictorially represents that "timelessness."

But this pictorial representation is at the same time a snare—the snare of thingness. Hence, from the very first presentation of the topography Freud is careful to soften the spatial aspect of his schema and to emphasize its directional orientation. He makes this adjustment by turning to the well-defined problem of regression. It will be remembered that regression designates both the return of thought to pictorial representation (formal regression) and the return of man to childhood (temporal regression). To these Freud now adds a regression of another kind, topographical regression, viz. the flow of an idea, which is barred from ending in motor activity, back from the motor pole toward the perceptual pole and ending in hallucination. This third type of regression is therefore inseparable from the other two modes of regression whose disclosure was possible only through dream deciphering. The question is whether it adds something to the former regressions or is merely their schematic representation.

In interpreting the famous dream about the dead child whose body is burning and who comes to awaken its father, Freud raises the question of the nature of the "psychical locality" [38] of the *scene of action* of dreams—a psychical rather than anatomical locality. This notion of psychical locality is analogous from the outset: the psychical apparatus functions *like* a compound microscope, or *like* a photographic apparatus; the psychical locality is *like* the place in the apparatus where the image is formed. This point is itself an

37. *GW, 2/3*, 583; *SE, 5*, 577.

38. *GW, 2/3*, 541 (*die psychische Lokalität*); *SE, 5*, 536. It should be noted that the expression comes from Fechner's *Elemente der Psychophysik* (2, 520): "*the scene of action of dreams is different from that of waking ideational life*" (*GW, 2/3*, 541; *SE, 5*, 536).

ideal point to which there corresponds no tangible component of the apparatus. Thus the comparison leads to the paradox of a series of localities that constitute not so much a real extension as a fixed order: "Strictly speaking, there is no need for the hypothesis that the psychical systems are actually arranged in a *spatial* order. It would be sufficient if a fixed order [*eine feste Reihenfolge*] were established by the fact that in a given psychical process the excitation passes through the systems in a particular temporal sequence." [39] Properly speaking, therefore, spatiality is only an "auxiliary representation"; it is meant to represent the mental apparatus as composed of distinct systems which function in determined directions.

At this point it should be remarked that the execution of this program bears the imprint of an illusion we have thus far left undiscussed. Freud is still under the influence of the theory of the child's seduction by an adult; this illusion is what nourishes the interpretation of regression as an attraction exercised by memory traces which arise from and lie close to perception. Thus the two "ends" of the apparatus are defined as motility and perception. The mnemic traces are placed "near" the perceptual end, the critical agency "near" the motor end; the traces are close to perception just as the preconscious is close to motor activity. Finally, the unconscious "lies behind" the preconscious, in the sense that it has no access to consciousness *"except via the preconscious."* The progressive direction of the functioning of waking life lies toward motor activity, whereas the regressive direction designates the movement by which "an idea [*Vorstellung*] is turned back into the sensory image [*Bild*] from which it was originally derived." [40] What renders this topography obsolete is doubtless the fact that the regressive pole is characterized as the perceptual pole. This schema is closely linked with the hallucination theory of wishes that was inherited from the "Project" of 1895 and kept alive by the theory of

39. *GW, 2/3*, 542; *SE, 5*, 537.

40. *GW, 2/3*, 548; *SE, 5*, 543. In this retrogressive movement the tion of the cathexis arising from the unconscious extends backward to the memory traces of perception in such a way as to make possible cathexis of the system *Pcpt.* in the reverse direction, starting from thou [*Gedanken*], to the pitch of complete sensory vividness" (*GW, 2/3*, 5 *SE, 5*, 543).

childhood seduction considered as a real memory. The decisive phenomenon, as Freud sees it, is not that the path toward motor activity is closed off, but that the dream-thoughts, thus thrust back from consciousness, are attracted by childhood memories which have retained a certain closeness to perception by virtue of their sensory vividness: "On this view a dream might be described as *a substitute for an infantile scene modified by being transferred onto a recent experience.* The infantile scene is unable to bring about its own revival and has to be content with returning as a dream." [41] It is understandable that when Freud finally discovered his error, he thought for a moment the whole system was going to collapse.[42]

It would seem that this confusion of a fantasy scene with a perceptual one prevents the topography of *The Interpretation of Dreams* from completely freeing itself from natural spatiality and from drawing all the consequences implied in the idea of a "psychical locality." Thus, the topography wavers back and forth between representing a series of places homologous to physical localities and representing a "scene of action" that is in no way a part of the world but simply the schematic picture of what has been described as "representability" (*Darstellbarkeit*).

I do not think, however, that the objection invalidates the essential elements of this topography; the theory of real seduction explains only the ambiguities of the topography, not the underlying

41. *GW, 2/3,* 552; *SE, 5,* 546.

42. One may follow the phases of this breakdown and also the resistance on the part of the hypothesis in the "Letters to Fliess," *Origins,* pp. 73, 125–28, 132, 163–65, 183–85, 187 (n. 1), 193, 196–98. And yet, even in 1895 Freud was speaking of the "things seen or heard and only half-understood" (ibid., p. 73). Cf. also the allusion to sublimation, ibid., pp. 196–98. It was through his own self-analysis that Freud discovered that the infantile scene of seduction originated in fantasies (Jones, *Life and Work, 1,* 283; Anzieu, *L'Auto-analyse,* p. 61). At the same time his study of folklore and the history of religions—especially those involved with cases of demoniacal possession—confirmed him as to the unreality of the childhood scene ("Letters to Fliess," *Origins,* pp. 187–90). Concerning fantasies, see ibid., p. 204. The question arises whether this is not the same tenacious illusion that will reappear in the Freudian interpretation of religion, where the attempt will be made, with a great array of history and ethnology, to reconstruct a real murder of the father of the horde, and then a real murder of the Egyptian Moses (cf. below, Book II, Part II, Ch. 3).

reason for positing it. We began to discover that reason when we designated the locality of the unconscious as the symbol of "timelessness." The following episodes of the topography will allow us to bring this characteristic into the open.

To account for the temporal aspects of regression Freud introduces time into the system in the form of a history of its functioning. *"Dreaming,"* he reminds us, *"is a piece of infantile mental life that has been superseded."* [43] Freud appeals to this topographic-genetic reconstruction in order to elucidate a puzzling characteristic of wishes, namely their drive toward *fulfillment*. It is assumed that there was a primitive state of the psychical apparatus—one recognizes the primary process of the "Project" here—in which the repetition of experiences of satisfaction created a solid link between the excitation and the mnemic image:

> As a result of the link that has thus been established, next time this need arises a psychical impulse [*psychische Regung*] will at once emerge which will seek to re-cathect the mnemic image of the perception and to re-evoke the perception itself, that is to say, to re-establish the situation of the original satisfaction. An impulse of this kind is what we call a wish [*Wunsch*]; the reappearance of the perception is the fulfillment of the wish [*Wunscherfüllung*]; and the shortest path to the fulfillment of the wish is a path leading direct from the excitation produced by the need to a complete cathexis of the perception. Nothing prevents us from assuming that there was a primitive state of the psychical apparatus in which this path was actually traversed, that is, in which wishing ended in hallucinating. Thus the aim of this first psychical activity was to produce a "perceptual identity"—a repetition of the perception which was linked with the satisfaction of the need.[44]

So much for the shortest path of fulfillment. But the shortest path is not the one reality has taught us; deception and failure have taught us to halt the regression at the mnemic image and to invent the detour of thinking (*Denken*). From the genetic point of view,

43. *GW, 2/3*, 573; *SE, 5*, 567.
44. *GW, 2/3*, 571; *SE, 5*, 565–66.

this secondary system is the substitute (*Ersatz*) for hallucinatory wishing. We now understand in what sense topographical regression in dreams is also a temporal regression: that which animates the regression is the longing for the primitive stage of hallucinatory wishing; this return to the primary system is the key to pictorial representation.[45]

In the third and last episode, under the heading "The Primary and Secondary Processes—Repression," *The Interpretation of Dreams* again revises the theory of the psychical apparatus. Besides space and time, the apparatus now receives force and conflict. This reworking of the apparatus is prescribed by the dream-work and especially by the process of repression to which all the dream mechanisms are related. The purely topographical point of view with which we began was linked to the question of the origin of dream-thoughts *in* the unconscious. It was natural therefore to represent that origin as a locality and the regression toward perception as a regression toward one of the ends of the apparatus. What is important now are the relations at the frontiers of the system; consequently the localities must be replaced by "processes of excitation" and "modes of its discharge": "What we are doing here is once again to replace a topographical way of representing things by a dynamic one."[46] From the dynamic point of view, the primary process is directed toward the free discharge of quantities of excitation, whereas the secondary process aims at inhibiting this discharge and at transforming the cathexis into a quiescent one (*ruhende Besetzung*). This language is familiar to us from the "Project." The problem, then, has to do with the "mechanical conditions" (*mechanische Verhältnisse*) of the discharge of excitation, according to whichever system is in control.

What is the significance of this problem? The point at issue is the

45. "The theory governing all psychoneurotic symptoms culminates in a single proposition, which asserts that *they too are to be regarded as fulfillments of unconscious wishes*" (*GW, 2/3*, 574; *SE, 5*, 569). The reference to Hughlings Jackson's remark is not without interest: "Find out all about dreams and you will have found out all about insanity" (ibid., n. 2); what is inserted here into the purely topographical schema of the psychical apparatus is, in fact, Jackson's schema of functional liberation.

46. *GW, 2/3*, 615; *SE, 5*, 610.

fate of the regulation by the unpleasure principle and, ultimately, the fate of the constancy principle. Freud's whole effort is aimed at establishing the secondary process within the context of the regulation by unpleasure. To that end he reconstructs repression on the model of flight provoked by an external danger and regulated by the anticipation of pain; repression is a sort of "avoidance [*Abwendung*] of the memory which is no more than a repetition of the previous flight from the perception";[47] this affords us, says Freud, "the prototype and first example of *psychical repression.*"[48] The avoidance of the memory image may be interpreted economically as a regulation by the least expenditure of unpleasure; the process that occurs under these conditions of inhibition will be called the secondary process.[49]

There is consequently nothing new here in comparison with the "Project." On the contrary, the attentive reader will note that the "Project" is ahead of *The Interpretation of Dreams* in the description of the secondary process. Perhaps this retreat of *The Interpretation of Dreams* in relation to the "Project" will give us the key to this topography and its consequences.

It is indeed striking that *The Interpretation of Dreams* is sparing in its explanation of the secondary process, as though the functioning of the apparatus in the progressive direction did not interest it. There are, to be sure, some scattered remarks about the role of consciousness that confirm the "Project." Here too consciousness is accessible both to peripheral excitations and to pleasure-unpleasure; it is called *"a sense-organ for the perception of psychical qualities."* Here too the process of becoming conscious depends on verbal images, the core of the preconscious. Because of these images, the pleasure-unpleasure regulation develops complications. The course of cathectic processes is no longer automatically regulated by the unpleasure principle; consciousness is now attracted by other signs besides those of pleasure-unpleasure. This is possible because the system of linguistic symbols constitutes what Freud

47. *GW, 2/3*, 606; *SE, 5*, 600.

48. Ibid.

49. As the *Traumdeutung* says: "Let us bear this firmly in mind, for it is the key to the whole theory of repression: *the second system can only cathect an idea if it is in a position to inhibit any development of unpleasure that may proceed from it*" (*GW, 2/3*, 607; *SE, 5*, 601).

calls a second "sensory surface" (*Sinnesoberflächen*). Consciousness is now turned not only toward perception, but toward the preconscious thought processes as well. One recognizes here the "Project's" two degrees of reality-testing. Oddly enough, however, that is not the aspect *The Interpretation of Dreams* develops; what is encountered on this progressive path is still another process of the dream-work, one we have not yet spoken of and which Freud calls "secondary revision" (*Bearbeitung*). This process consists, within the dream itself, in a first interpretation, a rationalization, which gives dreams an affinity both to waking life and to daydreams.

The brevity of *The Interpretation of Dreams* is still more noticeable in regard to the nature of the secondary process. Thus the problem—of great importance in the "Project"—of the relation between the inhibition exercised by the ego organization and the discernment of perceived qualities is not developed: whence the enigmatic character of the lines dealing with "thought-identity," which Freud distinguishes from "perceptual identity" [50] and takes from the theory of judgment presented above. That is why *The Interpretation of Dreams* appears to come far less close than the "Project" to what seemed to us the breaking point of the system, namely, the liberation from the pleasure principle. To be sure, Freud explicitly says that "thinking must aim at freeing itself more and more from exclusive regulation by the unpleasure principle and at restricting the development of affect in thought-activity to the minimum required for acting as a signal." [51] And in enigmatic terms he describes this task of "consciousness" as a "greater delicacy in functioning," achieved by a "hypercathexis" (*Überbesetzung*).[52] Here one recognizes the problem, raised in the "Project," of the transition from observant thought to the cogitative process, which operates not with indications of perceived reality but with indications of thought-reality.

If *The Interpretation of Dreams* does not enter into the study of

50. *GW, 2/3,* 607; *SE, 5,* 602.
51. *GW, 2/3,* 608; *SE, 5,* 602.
52. A few pages earlier Freud had written: "Under certain conditions a train of thought with a purposive cathexis [*zielbesetzte*] is capable of attracting the attention of consciousness to itself and in that event, through the agency of consciousness, receives a 'hypercathexis' [*Überbesetzung*]" (*GW, 2/3,* 599; *SE, 5,* 594).

the secondary process to the same extent as the "Project," it is because its problem is entirely different. The "Project" aimed at being a complete psychology for the use of neurologists. *The Interpretation of Dreams* aims at accounting for the strange or bewildering (*befremdendes*) phenomenon of dream-work. Why does the apparatus so often function in the regressive rather than in the progressive direction? This problem is faced by *The Interpretation of Dreams*. Here the investigation of "thinking" is of less importance than the "belated appearance" of the secondary process as compared with the primary process, and the compelling force which the latter exercises on the former. The primary process is truly primary: it is present "from the first" (*von Anfang an*); [53] the secondary process makes a belated appearance and is never definitively established.[54]

Thus we see what Chapter 7 is getting at; its true problem is the indestructibility of the primary system. Because the pleasure-unpleasure principle is never completely or definitively replaced, the principle of constancy remains *our* ordinary truth. Consequently, what might have destroyed the system is less important than what confirms it; and what confirms it is man's failure to escape from the pleasure-unpleasure principle; after all, thinking only "aims at" freeing itself from that principle.

That this is indeed the most basic intention of the "psychology" is confirmed by the place given to repression in the final pages.[55] The place is not an indifferent one. Freud's final analysis of repression comes immediately after his pessimistic remarks about the belated

53. *GW, 2/3,* 609; *SE, 5,* 603.

54. "In consequence of the belated appearance [*verspäteten Eintreffens*] of the secondary processes, the core of our being, consisting of unconscious wishful impulses [*Wunschregungen*], remains inaccessible to the understanding and inhibition of the preconscious; the part played by the latter is restricted once and for all to directing along the most expedient paths the wishful impulses that arise from the unconscious. These unconscious wishes exercise a compelling force upon all later mental trends, a force which those trends are obliged to fall in with or which they may perhaps endeavor to divert and direct to higher aims. A further result of the belated appearance [*Verspätung*] of the secondary process is that a wide sphere of mnemic material is inaccessible to preconscious cathexis" (*GW, 2/3,* 609; *SE, 5,* 603–04).

55. *GW, 2/3,* 609–14; *SE, 5,* 604–09.

appearance of the secondary system as compared with the primary system: repression is the ordinary operational mode of a psychism condemned to making a late appearance and being prey to the infantile, the indestructible. The desires arising from the invincible core of our being cannot be stopped on their path toward unpleasure except by a conversion or transformation of affects, an *Affektverwandlung*, which is the essence of repression.[56] Of course, that which produces this transformation is the secondary system, but not through access to what we just called "thinking"; the secondary system is reduced here to operating from within pleasure-unpleasure by the conversion of affects. As a result, the preconscious turns away from its thoughts that have become unpleasant, and thus the principle of pleasure-unpleasure is confirmed. Freud's conclusion serves to confirm the earlier idea of the belated appearance of the secondary system and the indestructible character of the primary system: "the presence [*Vorhandensein*] of a store of infantile memories, which has from the first been held back from the *Pcs.*, becomes a *sine qua non* of repression." [57]

Thus two aspects become intelligible now that we see them together, whereas when taken separately they had puzzled us. On the one hand, *The Interpretation of Dreams* seemed to us less advanced than the "Project" with respect to going beyond the constancy and unpleasure principles; but regression, of which dreams are the witness and model, precisely attests to man's inability to go beyond those principles. On the other hand, the topography of Chapter 7 seemed to us to waver between a realism of things and an auxiliary representation of processes that require a different scene of action than the space of nature. Freud's illusion about the real memory of the infantile scene only partially explains this wavering. In the last analysis, the spatiality of the topography expresses man's inability

56. *"We here recognize the infantile stage of condemnation [Verurteilung], that is, of rejection based on judgment [Verwerfung durch das Urteilen]."* This part of the sentence appears neither in *GW, 2/3*, 609, nor in *SE, 5*, 604, but is present in the first German editions, p. 446; the French translation, p. 492 (328) has preserved this very significant text. Concerning the rejection based on judgment, see the paper called "Repression": "Repression is a preliminary stage of condemnation, something between flight and condemnation."

57. *GW, 2/3*, 610; *SE, 5*, 604.

to go from slavery to freedom and happiness, or in terms less Spinozist and more Freudian (though they are basically equivalent), from the regulation by the pleasure-unpleasure principle to the reality principle. The "apparatus" Chapter 7 focuses upon in its three successive attempts is man insofar as he *has been* and *remains* a Thing.

Chapter 3: Instinct and Idea in the "Papers on Metapsychology"

The Interpretation of Dreams was unsuccessful in harmonizing the theory inherited from the "Project" with the conceptual structure elaborated by the actual work of interpretation. As a result, Chapter 7 seems to remain somewhat external to the organic development of the book. This structural discordance is a sign that the language of meaning implied by the work of interpretation, and the quasi-physical language implied by the language of the topography, are not yet perfectly coordinated.

In the "Papers on Metapsychology," [1] nearly all of which were written in the early war years, this problematic reaches its point of maturity and the two requirements of analytic discourse attain an equilibrium. On the one hand, these papers coherently thematize the topographic-economic point of view in what is called the "first topography": unconscious-preconscious-conscious; on the other hand, they show how the unconscious can be reintegrated into the realm of meaning by a new interrelation—"within" the unconscious itself—between instinct (*Trieb*) and idea (*Vorstellung*): an instinct can be represented (*repräsentiert*) in the unconscious only

1. Five papers written in 1915—"Instincts and Their Vicissitudes," "Repression," "The Unconscious," "A Metapsychological Supplement to the Theory of Dreams," and "Mourning and Melancholia"—are all that remain of a series of twelve papers that Freud had originally planned to publish under the title *Preliminaries to a Metapsychology* (see *SE, 14,* 105–07). The five texts are presented in *GW, 10,* and in *SE, 14.* To them may be added "A Note on the Unconscious in Psychoanalysis," *GW, 8,* 430–39; *SE, 12,* 260–66; *Métapsychologie,* pp. 9–24; and especially the paper "On Narcissism: An Introduction" (1914), *GW, 10,* 138–70; *SE, 14,* 73–102.

by an idea (*Vorstellung*).[2] Our entire discussion will converge on this notion of *Vorstellungsrepräsentanz* or ideational representative; the interpretation of meaning through meaning and the explanation by means of energies localized in systems intersect and coincide in this notion. The first movement, therefore, will be a movement *back to* instincts; the second, a movement *starting from* the ideational representative of instincts. The question is whether the "Papers on Metapsychology" are more successful than *The Interpretation of Dreams* in fusing the two viewpoints of force and meaning.

Thus we are going to follow two paths. The first will lead us back from the supposed self-evidence of consciousness to the origin of meaning in the positing of desire; in this first movement we will attain both the topographic-economic point of view and the concept of instinct (*Trieb*)—of which everything else is a vicissitude (*Schicksal*).

But then we will have to take the reverse path; for instincts are like the Kantian thing—the transcendental = X; they too are never attained except in that which stands for and represents them. In this way we will be led from the problematic of instincts to the problematic of the representatives of instincts.[3]

2. The words *Vorstellung* and *Repräsentanz* pose serious problems for translators. How is one to translate the phrase, *den Trieb repräsentierende Vorstellung?* (*GW*, *10*, 264). The *Collected Papers*, *4*, 98, translates it as "the ideational presentation of an instinct," and *SE*, *14*, 166, as "the idea which represents an instinct." Thus the English translators have abandoned the translation of *Vorstellung* as "representation," in spite of the solid tradition that goes back at least to Kant and Schopenhauer; the words "idea" and "ideational" have serious reasons on their side in the tradition of Locke and Hume. In French, *Vorstellung* can only be translated as *représentation*. The difficulty is then to translate the term *Repräsentanz*, which denotes the psychical expression or representative of an instinct, in either the ideational or the affective order; I propose to follow the suggestion of the translators of the *Collected Papers* and to translate *Repräsentanz* as *présentation*. [Translator's note: With the permission of the author, we shall here follow the *SE* translation; thus *Vorstellung* will be translated as "idea" and *Repräsentanz* as "representative."]

3. In Chapter 2 of the "Dialectic" we will return to this double movement in the framework of a philosophy of reflection. The first movement is one of *dispossession*, whereby reflection completely separates itself from the illusion of consciousness; the second movement is one of *reappropriation*, the re-

Will all incoherence be eliminated? Will the gap between the discourse of energy and the discourse of meaning be closed? This question will remain open at the end of this chapter. But at least we will be able to understand the reasons for this state of affairs.

THE ATTAINMENT OF THE TOPOGRAPHIC-ECONOMIC VIEW AND OF THE CONCEPT OF INSTINCT

At the start of this investigation we take as our guide the paper of 1912 entitled "A Note on the Unconscious in Psychoanalysis" [4] and the first two sections of the celebrated paper of 1915, "The Unconscious."

One of the interesting points in these essays lies in what might be called a Freudian apologetics: the essays attempt to make the concept of the unconscious plausible, the first for a nonspecialized public, the second for a scientific public (both give up trying to convince philosophers infected with the prejudice of consciousness!). More important, however, is the fact that the topography is presented as resulting from a reversal of viewpoint, from an antiphenomenology already put into effect without having been reflected upon in the work of interpreting. We proceed to thematize this reversal under Freud's guidance.

The movement of thought leads from a descriptive concept, where the term "unconscious" is still an adjective, to a systematic concept, where it becomes a substantive; the loss of its descriptive meaning is indicated by the abbreviation *Ubw*, which we translate as *Ucs*. To arrive at the topographic point of view is to move from

---

capture of meaning through interpretation. In order to arrive at the root of desire, reflection must let itself be dispossessed of the conscious meaning of discourse and shifted off center to a different locus of meaning; but as desire is accessible only in the disguises in which it displaces itself, the emergence or positing of desire can be incorporated into reflection only through the interpretation of the signs of desire.

4. First published in English in the *Proceedings* of the Society for Psychical Research, *26* (1912), Part 66; then in German in *Int. Z. Psychoanal.*, *1* (1913).

the adjectival unconscious to the substantival unconscious, from the quality of being unconscious to the unconscious as a system. It is a matter therefore of a reduction, of an *epochê* in reverse, since what is initially best known, the conscious, is suspended and becomes the least known. At the outset the quality of being unconscious is still understood in relation to consciousness: it is simply the attribute of what has disappeared but can reappear; the non-known is on the side of the unconscious; the unconscious is something we assume and reconstruct from signs derived from consciousness, since it is from consciousness that memories disappear and in consciousness that they reappear. Although we do not know how such unconscious representations can persist in the state of unperceived existence, still it is in relation to consciousness that we define this first concept of the unconscious as a state of latency.[5]

The shift from the descriptive to the systematic point of view required by psychoanalysis is made as a result of the dynamic attributes of the unconscious: the facts of posthypnotic suggestion, the terrible power disclosed in hysterical phenomena, the psychopathology of everyday life, etc., compel us to attribute an effective activity to certain "strong unconscious ideas." [6] But the experience of psychoanalysis compels us to go further and to form the notion of "thoughts" (*Gedanken*) excluded from consciousness by forces that bar their reception. The reversal is motivated by this energy schema: first there is the unconscious modality (henceforth Freud speaks of "unconscious psychical acts"); then the process of becoming conscious is a possibility which may or may not eventuate. Consciousness does not occur unconditionally and as a matter of course. The barrier of resistance leads us to represent the process of becoming conscious as a transgression, a crossing of a barrier; to become conscious is to penetrate *into*, to be unconscious is to keep apart *from* consciousness.[7] The topographical presentation is not far off; in effect, the activity of becoming conscious has in turn two modalities; when it occurs without difficulty, one will speak of the

5. *GW*, *8*, 433, *10*, 266; *SE*, *12*, 262, *14*, 167.
6. *GW*, *8*, 434–35; *SE*, *12*, 263.
7. *GW*, *8*, 434; *SE*, *12*, 263.

preconscious; when it is forbidden or "cut off," one will speak of the unconscious. Thus we have three "agencies": *Ucs.*, *Pcs.*, *Cs.* The close connection between the energy point of view and the topographic point of view is already visible: there are topographical places because there are relations of exclusion that are relations of *force* (resistance, defense, rejection). We have thus come back to the level of Chapter 7 of *The Interpretation of Dreams.* Indeed, dreams supply Freud with his ultimate proof of the unconscious: the dream-work, its activity of transposition or distortion, makes us attribute to the unconscious not only a distinct locality, but its own *legality:* "the laws of unconscious activity differ widely from those of the conscious";[8] in turn the discovery of unconscious processes and laws invites us to form the idea of "belonging to a system," which is the true psychoanalytic concept of the unconscious. This point of view is totally unphenomenological. The enigmas of consciousness no longer serve as signs of the unconscious; the unconscious is no longer defined as "latency" as compared with a conscious "presence"; the fact of "belonging to a system" allows the unconscious to be posited for itself.[9]

The text entitled "The Unconscious" ("Das Unbewusste") assumes we have already attained the intermediate dynamic level; the unconscious is the mode of being of that which, having been repressed, has not been suppressed or annihilated. Hence to be excluded from consciousness and to become conscious are two correlative and contrary vicissitudes, which already enter into a perspective that may be called topographical, since a barrier decides the exclusion from or the access to consciousness: it is the barrier that makes the topography. On this level the justification of the unconscious takes on an aspect of scientific necessity: the text of consciousness is a lacunary, truncated text; the assumption of the un-

8. *GW*, *8*, 438; *SE*, *12*, 265–66.

9. "The system revealed by the sign that the single acts forming parts of it are unconscious we designate by the name 'The Unconscious,' for want of a better and less ambiguous term. In German, I propose to denote this system by the letters *Ubw*, an abbreviation of the German word '*Unbewusst.*' And this is the third and most significant sense which the term 'unconscious' has acquired in psychoanalysis" (*GW*, *8*, 439; *SE*, *12*, 266).

conscious is equivalent to a work of interpolation that introduces meaning and connection into the text.[10] Besides being necessary, the hypothesis is also legitimate, for it does not differ basically from the reconstruction we make of the consciousness of other people by inference from their behavior, although in psychoanalysis it is not a second consciousness we infer but a psychism that lacks consciousness. Accompanying this discussion is the idea that consciousness, far from being the first certitude, is a *perception*, and calls for a critique similar to Kant's critique of external perception. By calling consciousness a perception Freud makes it problematic, while at the same time preparing for its subsequent treatment as a "surface" phenomenon. To be conscious and to be unconscious are at most secondary characteristics: what alone count are the relations of psychical acts to instincts and instinctual aims, in accord with their interconnections and the particular psychical system to which they belong.

As a matter of fact, Freud's wish to abstract completely from the characteristics of conscious and unconscious will be realized only in the second topography, which we shall speak of later. In spite of the ambiguity of using the words "conscious" and "unconscious" sometimes in a descriptive and sometimes in a systematic sense, these terms will be retained in the first topography to designate the systems themselves, the systematic sense being indicated by the abbreviations *Ucs.*, *Pcs.*, *Cs.* It is worth noting that Freud presents only one remark to justify a vocabulary that continues to recall the attribute of being conscious, namely, that the latter "forms the point of departure for all our investigations." [11] We will come back to this admission later.

At any rate consciousness has become the least known, since to become conscious is to become an object of perception under certain conditions. The question of consciousness has become the question of becoming conscious, and the latter, in great part, coincides with overcoming resistances.

In order to clarify this shift from a merely dynamic view to a

10. *GW, 10,* 265; *SE, 14,* 166–67.
11. *GW, 10,* 271; *SE, 14,* 172.

topographical view, Freud accepts the risks of an apparently absurd question: If to become conscious is a "transposition" (*Umsetzung*) from the unconscious system into the conscious system, are we to suppose that this transposition is equivalent to a second record (*Niederschrift*) in a new psychical locality (*in einer neuen psychischen Lokalität*),[12] or is it a matter of a change of state involving the same material and occurring in the same locality? An abstruse question, as Freud admits, but it must be raised if we are to take the topographical point of view seriously.[13] The question is serious only if one does not confuse this psychical locality (*Lokalität*) with anatomical localities (*Ortlichkeiten*).[14] And Freud proposes, at least provisionally, to assume the naïve and crude hypothesis of the transition from one location to another and a double registration of the same idea in two different places. Why this absurdity? It should be noted that Freud appeals here to psychoanalytic practice, as if the most naïve and crudely naturalistic explanation were more faithful to what actually takes place in interpretation. If, says Freud, one communicates (*mitteilt*) to a patient the meaning of his trouble by telling him the idea which he has at one time repressed, the patient is neither relieved nor cured, for he remains separated from this idea by his resistances, which only make him reject it again. Thus the idea is recorded both in the conscious region of auditory memories and in the unconscious, where it remains enclosed as long as the resistances are not overcome. The "double registration" is therefore the provisional way of noting the difference in status of the same idea, at the surface of the conscious and in the depths of the repressed. We shall later see how and why this theory of double registration may be transcended.

We have just shown the reason for the shift from a merely descriptive concept of latency to a systematic concept of a topographical system; we must now bring this reversal of viewpoint about. Whereas the Husserlian epochê was a reduction *to* consciousness,

12. *GW, 10,* 273; *SE, 14,* 174. This could also be translated as a second "registration."
13. Ibid.
14. *GW, 10,* 273; *SE, 14,* 175.

the Freudian epochê is seen as a reduction *of* consciousness; thus we speak of it as an epochê in reverse.[15] This reversal is achieved only when we posit instinct (*Trieb*) as the fundamental concept (*Grundbegriff*), with everything else being understood as a vicissitude (*Schicksal*) of instincts. I will attempt to make this substitution understandable by continuing to sift out the antiphenomenological characteristics of Freud's approach. The epochê in reverse implies that we stop taking the "object" as our guide, in the sense of the vis-à-vis of consciousness, and substitute for it the "aims" of the instincts; and that we stop taking the "subject" as our pole of reference, in the sense of the one to whom or for whom "objects" appear. In short, we must abandon the subject-object problematic as being that of consciousness.[16]

Freud abandons the "object" as psychological guide in the paper entitled "Instincts and Their Vicissitudes," which thematizes the earlier findings of the *Three Essays on Sexuality.*

In positing instinct as the basic concept whose function, as in the experimental sciences, is to systematically relate empirical facts, Freud is aware that he has left the field of description for that of systematization.[17] Implied in this systematization are not only conventions (definitions of stimulus, need, and satisfaction) but also hypotheses or postulates (*Voraussetzungen*), the most important of which is the familiar hypothesis of constancy, which states that the

15. This is only a first approximation of the distinction between the epochê of consciousness, which is characteristic of Freudian psychoanalysis, and the Husserlian epochê; we will develop this confrontation at much greater length in the "Dialectic," Ch. 1, where a more precise distinction will be made.

16. I purposely allude to the expressions "object-guide" and "subject-pole," which recall the vocabulary of phenomenology. But the phenomenology that is thus destroyed is only a phenomenology of consciousness; we must lose the object as the vis-à-vis of consciousness and the subject itself as consciousness in order to recapture the object as the transcendental guide and the subject as the reflective and meditating *I*. We will elaborate this theme systematically in the "Dialectic," Ch. 2.

17. Freud took this occasion to write one of his most important texts on methodology: *GW, 10,* 210–11; *SE, 14,* 117–18; the relations that definitions, basic concepts, and conventions have to empirical matter in psychology are established on the pattern of the experimental sciences of nature; cf. below, "Dialectic," Ch. 1.

psychical apparatus "is automatically regulated by feelings belonging to the pleasure-unpleasure series." [18] This hypothesis in turn assumes a correspondence between the qualities of pleasure-unpleasure and "the amounts of stimulus [*Reizgrössen*] affecting mental life." [19] Thus we are back on the familiar ground of the quantitative theory—in fact we have never left it since the "Project."

With the concept of instinct we force the topography into an economics: "Every instinct is a piece of activity." [20] But the economic point of view finds its primary expression in the fact that the concept of aim has primacy over the concept of object: "The *aim* of an instinct is in every instance satisfaction, which can only be obtained by removing the state of stimulation at the source of the instinct." [21] From now on the object is defined in function of the aim, and not conversely:

> The object of an instinct is the thing in regard to which or through which the instinct is able to achieve its aim. It is what is most variable about an instinct and is not originally connected with it, but becomes assigned to it only in consequence of being peculiarly fitted to make satisfaction possible.[22]

As such, it may either be an extraneous object (*Gegenstand*) or a part of one's own body. This dialectic of aim and object was discovered and elucidated by Freud in *Three Essays on Sexuality*.[23]

Starting from the new problematic of aim and object there are "vicissitudes of instincts." Since the study of the sources (*Quelle*) of instincts comes under the jurisdiction of biology, instincts are known to us only in their aims: these alone lie within the scope of psychology. This is another way of saying that the apparatus we are

18. *GW*, *10*, 214; *SE*, *14*, 120.
19. *GW*, *10*, 214; *SE*, *14*, 121.
20. *GW*, *10*, 214 (*jeder Trieb ist ein Stück Aktivität*); *SE*, *14*, 122.
21. Ibid.
22. Ibid.
23. "Let us call the person from whom sexual attraction proceeds the *sexual object* and the act towards which the instinct tends the *sexual aim*" (*GW*, *5*, 34; *SE*, *7*, 135–36). The distinction between deviations "in respect of the object" and deviations "in respect of the aim" is the governing factor in the first essay.

considering is a psychical apparatus and that the regulation by pleasure-unpleasure belongs to an order which, though quantitative, is psychological.

In "Instincts and Their Vicissitudes" Freud presents a systematic but deliberately limited view of these "vicissitudes." Another hypothesis must be made: the distinction between ego, or self-preservative instincts, and sexual instincts. But this hypothesis is not on the same plane as the hypothesis of constancy: the latter is a general hypothesis, whereas the distinction between the two kinds of instincts is only a working hypothesis that will undergo subsequent alteration; it corresponds roughly to the biological distinction between soma and germ-plasm and is seen to be a useful instrument for psychoanalytic practice, since it was in the course of clinical observations that sexual instincts came to be isolated from the others. The primacy of the aim over the object is most clearly seen in the sexual instincts: Freud says they "act vicariously [*vikariierende*] for one another" [24] inasmuch as they can readily change their objects.

Although it is limited to the sexual instincts, the list of the instinctual vicissitudes may be regarded as systematic. Whereas *The Interpretation of Dreams* dealt only with repression, this vicissitude is now inserted among three others: reversal (*Verkehrung*) of an instinct into its opposite, turning round (*Wendung*) upon the subject's own self, and sublimation. (The essay does not treat of sublimation but deals only with reversal and turning round; a separate paper is devoted to repression.)

It is to be noted that it is not in terms of the *intended object* that reversal or turning round can be understood; on the contrary, the intended object will itself be reinterpreted in economic terms. In the reversal from the active to the passive role in the paired opposites voyeurism-exhibitionism, the aim is what changes; in the reversal from an external content to the content of one's self (*inhaltliche Verkehrung*) [25] in the pair sadism-masochism, the object is what

24. *GW, 10*, 219; *SE, 14*, 126.

25. *GW, 10*, 219; *SE, 14*, 127. The text dates from a period when Freud had not yet recognized the idea of primary masochism; cf. "The Economic Problem of Masochism" (1924), *GW, 13*, 371–83; *SE, 19*, 159–70. We shall return to this notion later, Book II, Part III, Ch. 1.

changes, but in relation to an unchanged aim—the causing of pain. But the "reversal" may also be stated in terms of "turning round," for masochism is actually sadism turned round upon the subject's own ego, and exhibitionism includes looking at one's own body. We are not interested here in a detailed study of these diverse vicissitudes, but rather in their underlying structural principle. In this regard the chief thing to notice is that the notion of object is recast in accordance with the economic distribution of libido.

But this economic recasting of the notion of the object entails that of the subject. The exchange of roles between the self and another, both in the pair sadism-masochism and in the pair voyeurism-exhibitionism, forces us to question collectively all the so-called self-evidences concerning the relation between a subject-pole and its objective counterpart. The subject-object distribution is itself an economic distribution. That is why Freud does not hesitate, in the case of the transformation of sadism into masochism, to speak of a return to "the narcissistic object" [26] as the counterpart of the exchange of subjects. To talk of a narcissistic object, in reference to primary narcissism and to any return to narcissism, is simply to apply the definition of the object as the means of attaining instinctual aims. Thus narcissism is set within a vast economics in which not only objects but also the respective positions of subject and object are exchanged for one another. Not only are this and that object interchanged, while subserving the same aims, but also the self and the other, in the reversal from active to passive role, from looking at to being looked at, from inflicting pain on another to inflicting pain on oneself. In relation to these transformations, to these economic exchanges, narcissism serves as a primordial landmark: it represents the primal confusion between thing-love and self-love. To denote this lack of distinction Freud speaks equivalently of the narcissistic object or the cathected ego.

This structure of interchange enabled Freud to adopt an expression from Ferenczi that was destined to great success—and also to great abuses—the term "introjection," as opposed to projection. If one admits a narcissistic phase in which the external world is indifferent and the subject the sole source of pleasure, then the process of

26. *GW, 10,* 224; *SE, 14,* 132.

distinguishing between the external and the internal, between the world and the ego, is a process of economic division between what the ego can incorporate into itself and prize as the possession of the "pleasure-ego" (*Lust-Ich*) [27] and what it rejects as hostile, as the source of unpleasure. This division of internal and external according to the attitude of love (if by love is understood the ego's relation to its sources of pleasure) is further complicated by a different process of division according to the attitude of hate. Love has, indeed, a "second opposite," [28] namely hating: the opposite of the loved object for the pleasure-ego is unpleasure; the opposite of the loved object for the instincts of self-preservation is the hated object. What we ordinarily call the object—the loved or the hated object—is not something immediately given; it is rather the end result of a double series of divisions between the internal and the external; to distinguish this end result from the initial narcissistic stage, we speak of it as the object-stage.[29]

It could be said that what is economically reconstructed at the end of this process is precisely "the object" in the phenomenological sense. At the end of the paper "Instincts and Their Vicissitudes" Freud comes back to ordinary language: we *speak* of the attraction of an object, and *say* that we love that object; we say that it is *we*—the total ego—who love, but not that an instinct hates or loves. Linguistic usage, in which the verbs "to love" and "to hate" are governed by the object, is justified only at the end of a genesis of the object function, at that period of desire when love and hate have constituted, so to speak, their opposed objects and constituted their subject. The history of the object is the history of the object function, and this history is the history of desire itself. What interests us here is not this history—the famous theory of stages [30]—but its methodological import; the object, in Freud, is not something immediately presented to an ego endowed with immediate awareness; it is a variable in an economic function.

The economic interchange between the ego and objects must be

27. *GW, 10,* 228; *SE, 14,* 136.

28. Ibid.

29. *GW, 10,* 229; *SE, 14,* 137.

30. Freud presents an overall view of these phases in the *New Introductory Lectures, SE, 22,* 98–102.

carried to the point where not only is the object a function of the aim of an instinct, but the ego itself is an aim of instinct.[31] This is the meaning of the introduction of narcissism into psychoanalysis. Of course, we never know primary narcissism face to face. Consequently, in his paper "On Narcissism: An Introduction," Freud proceeds by a number of converging signs: narcissism as perversion, in which one's own body is treated as an object of love; narcissism as the libidinal complement to the instincts of self-preservation; the schizophrenic's indifference to reality, as if he had withdrawn his libido from objects, without replacing them by others in fantasy; and the overestimation of the power of thought on the part of primitive peoples and children. Then there is the withdrawal into oneself of the sick person and the hypochondriac; and finally, there is the egoism of sleep. In all these cases we know directly only processes of the withdrawal of cathexis; but in conceiving these withdrawals as the return to primary narcissism (i.e. as secondary narcissism) we *introduce* into the theory a new intelligibility that crowns the attainment of the topographic-economic point of view. The introduction of narcissism deepens our notion of instinct; it forces us to conceive of instincts as more radical than any subject-object relation. Instincts are the reservoir of energy underlying all the distributions of energy between the ego and objects. Object-choice itself becomes a concept correlative to narcissism, as a departure from narcissism; from this point of view there are only departures from —and returns to—narcissism.

At the proper place in our discussion we will see an important application of this theory of narcissism in the theory of identification and sublimation. In this respect, the article on narcissism makes a surprising advance over the writings of the 1920–24 period and foreshadows the reorganization of the topography according to the new sequence of ego, id, and superego. In effect, after consider-

31. "Zur Einführung des Narzissmus," *GW, 10,* 138–70; *SE, 14,* 73–102; *Collected Papers, 4,* 30–59. For a philosophy of reflection, the introduction of narcissism will be the supreme test: it will be necessary to give up the subject of immediate apperception; an abortive Cogito has taken the place of the first truth *I think, I am.* With the extreme point in the reduction of all phenomenology, the extreme point in the crisis of the Cogito is also reached. Cf. below, "Dialectic," Ch. 2.

ing several other applications (the mechanism of paraphrenia, narcissistic object-choice, overvaluation of the sexual object, femininity) Freud introduces the important idea that the formation of ideals is brought about through a displacement of narcissism.[32] We are not yet in a position to develop all the consequences of this important discovery, but at least we learn that the ideal by which the subject measures his actual ego can be brought under the libido theory, precisely through the mediation of narcissism. This connection between *ideals* and *narcissism* is extremely suggestive: thanks to the complicity between what seems to us the height of egoism and the worship of an ideal before which the ego effaces itself, ideals themselves are to be accounted for in terms of the displacement of instincts. This will be the focal point of the second part of our "Analytic."

For the present, however, we are in a position to integrate into our reflection another term that Freud mentions in this context of the relations between idealization and narcissism; this other factor is *sublimation,* which "Instincts and Their Vicissitudes" mentioned as being the fourth vicissitude of an instinct. In the paper on narcissism Freud says:

> Sublimation is a process that concerns object-libido and consists in the instinct's directing itself towards an aim other than, and remote from, that of sexual satisfaction; in this process the accent falls upon deflection from sexuality. Idealization is a process that concerns the *object;* by it that object, without any alteration in its nature, is aggrandized and exalted in the subject's mind. Idealization is possible in the sphere of ego-libido as well

32. "This ideal ego is now the target of the self-love which was enjoyed in childhood by the actual ego. The subject's narcissism makes its appearance displaced onto this new ideal ego, which, like the infantile ego, finds itself possessed of every perfection that is of value. As always where the libido is concerned, man has here again shown himself incapable of giving up a satisfaction he had once enjoyed. He is not willing to forgo the narcissistic perfection of his childhood; and when, as he grows up, he is disturbed by the admonitions of others and by the awakening of his own critical judgment, so that he can no longer retain that perfection, he seeks to recover it in the new form of an ego ideal. What he projects before him as his ideal is the substitute for the lost narcissism of his childhood in which he was his own ideal" (*GW, 10,* 161; *SE, 14,* 94).

> as in that of object-libido. For example, the sexual overvaluation of an object is an idealization of it. Insofar as sublimation describes something that has to do with the instinct and idealization something to do with the object, the two concepts are to be distinguished from each other.[33]

That is one reason for distinguishing between idealization and sublimation. But even more important is the fact that one can submit himself to an ideal without succeeding in sublimating his libidinal instincts; the neurotic is precisely the victim of the heightened demands imposed upon his instincts by the formation of an ego ideal, demands accompanied by a low potential of sublimation. To be successful, of course, idealization requires sublimation; but it does not always obtain it, for it cannot enforce it.[34] We touch here on something very important: there exists a shortcut, a way of violence in the formation of ideals, which we will not understand until we have introduced masochism as another primary phenomenon; by contrast, sublimation would be a kind of gentle conversion. If we understood this, we would see that sublimation is quite a different vicissitude from repression: "sublimation is a way out, a way by which the claims of the ego can be met *without* involving repression."[35]

All this will only become meaningful, however, in the transition from the first to the second topography and through the introduction—already proposed in the paper "On Narcissism"—of "a special psychical agency." This will be the superego. We must say even more: with the question of the superego, there arises the question of the ego, and this question no longer coincides exactly with that of consciousness, which alone was thematized in a topography whose primary concern was to free the positing of the unconscious from dependency on the evidence of consciousness.

Without anticipating too much of the second topography and the new problems it raises, we can take the investigation of the relations between narcissism and object-libido a bit further by mentioning as a final example—perhaps the most striking one of all—the

33. Ibid.
34. *GW, 10,* 161; *SE, 14,* 94–95.
35. *GW, 10,* 162; *SE, 14,* 95.

work of mourning, to which Freud devotes one of his admirable short essays, "Mourning and Melancholia."[36] Mourning is a work: "Mourning is regularly the reaction to the loss of a loved person, or to the loss of some abstraction which has taken the place of one, such as one's country, liberty, an ideal, and so on." [37] The absorbing work of mourning, the exclusive devotion to this work, certain traits of which are well known—the loss of interest in the outside world, the turning away from any activity that is not connected with thoughts of the lost object—raises a tremendous problem, nothing less than the problem of the economics of pain (*Schmerz*) (pain here being quite different from the unpleasure of the pair *Lust-Unlust*). This economics of pain leads us to the heart of the relations between narcissism and object-libido. Reality-testing having shown that the loved object no longer exists, the libido is called upon to withdraw from its attachments to this object; the libido rebels; and it is only bit by bit and with a great expenditure of cathectic energy that the libido carries out piecemeal, and upon each of the memories of the lost object, the orders given by reality. This work is what absorbs the ego and inhibits it; when it is completed the ego once again becomes free and uninhibited. Melancholia, on the other hand, adds to those traits a decisive element: a diminution of one's self-regard (*Selbstgefühl*).[38] To this lowering of self-esteem is joined a heightened self-criticism, which once more brings us to the threshold of the problematic of the superego; that critical and watchful agency (*Instanz*) is, in effect, the basis of moral conscience (*Gewissen*).[39] We are interested here not in the structure of that agency, but in the fact that in the melancholic's self-reproaches the ego has been substituted for the loved object against whom the reproaches had originally been directed (*Ihre Klagen sind Anklagen*). What has happened is this:

36. "Trauer und Melancholia," *GW, 10,* 428–46; *SE, 14,* 243–58.

37. *GW, 10,* 428–29; *SE, 14,* 243.

38. This expression is also found in "On Narcissism," in the context of the discussion of Adler's theories. *GW, 10,* 166–70; *SE, 14,* 98–102.

39. "What we are here becoming acquainted with is the agency commonly called 'conscience'; we shall count it, along with the censorship of consciousness and reality-testing, among the major institutions of the ego, and we shall come upon evidence to show that it can become diseased on its own account" (*GW, 10,* 433; *SE, 14,* 247).

instead of being displaced onto another object, the libido was withdrawn into the ego and employed in establishing an identification of the ego with the abandoned object. Thus the ego receives the blows intended for the object. In this way an object-loss becomes an ego-loss and the ego is mistreated.

We have thus brought to light a new process, which Freud calls narcissistic identification with the object, that is to say, the substitution of identification for object-love.[40] Identification as such will raise serious problems later on; here it serves as a sign that helps us discover a more hidden relation between object-choice and narcissism. For this process to be possible, it is necessary (1) that object-choice can *regress*, given certain conditions, to original narcissism; this seems to imply that the object-choice was made on a narcissistic basis; this regression is what is lacking in mourning. (2) It is also necessary that the love relationships were highly ambivalent, in order that the element of hate, set free by the loss of the loved object, may take refuge in narcissistic identification and thereby turn round upon the subject in the form of self-reproaches; hence there is a second regression, a return to the stage of sadism, which will also be of great significance for the mechanism of conscience, remorse, and self-punishment.

One might expect that mourning, precisely because it is not melancholia, does not present this group of relations to narcissism. But such is not the case. Coming back to mourning, after the discussion of melancholia, Freud remarks,

> Each single one of the memories and situations of expectancy which demonstrate the libido's attachment to the lost object is met by the verdict of reality that the object no longer exists; and

40. In this text Freud suggests a possible connection between object-choice and identification: the two would come together in the oral stage, where to love is to devour (*GW, 10,* 436; *SE, 14,* 249–50). The regression from object-choice to the narcissistic stage would thus include the regression to the oral phase of the libido; this would mean that the oral phase itself still belongs to narcissism. It should be noted at this point that Freud was never overconfident in his explanations of identification; identification is truly the thorn in the side of psychoanalysis. It is no mere accident that Freud admits three times that the economics of mourning eludes him. *GW, 10,* 430, 439, 442; *SE, 14,* 245, 252, 255.

> the ego, confronted as it were with the question whether it shall share this fate, is persuaded by the sum of the narcissistic satisfactions it derives from being alive to sever its attachment to the object that has been abolished.[41]

A cruel but penetrating remark: the work of mourning is undertaken in order to survive the loss of the object; detachment from the object is dictated by self-attachment. But that is not, perhaps, the sole function of narcissism in the work of mourning. An earlier remark has gone unnoticed: the orders given by reality, Freud says, are carried out only bit by bit, with a great expenditure of time and cathectic energy; and he adds: "and in the meantime the existence of the lost object is psychically prolonged."[42] This process of internalizing, of installing the lost object within ourselves, once again links mourning with melancholia, and thus the connection of mourning with narcissism is seen to be less shocking. Narcissism no longer pursues the every-man-for-himself attitude of the survivor, but the survival of the other in the ego; and so we can say with Freud: "by taking flight into the ego love escapes extinction."[43] Further, the obsessional self-reproaches arising after a death has occurred show that mourning too, in some degree, presents aspects of ambivalence between love and hate; whence the regression of this ambivalent libido back into the ego in the form of self-reproaches. At the end of the essay the regression of the libido to narcissism stands as the fundamental precondition of both mourning and melancholia.

Here let us bring to a close the investigation of the relations and exchanges between object-libido and ego-libido. The point we have been trying to make is simply that the ego of psychoanalysis is not what presents itself as subject at the outset of a description of consciousness; the notion of "ego-instinct" (*Ichtrieb*), symmetric with that of "object-instinct" (*Objekttrieb*), makes instinct a structure prior to the phenomenal relation of subject-object. The notion of instinct is seen, then, to be the *quid* aimed at in every endeavor to

41. *GW, 10,* 442; *SE, 14,* 255.
42. *GW, 10,* 430; *SE, 14,* 245.
43. *GW, 10,* 445; *SE, 14,* 257.

work back from the symptom of "being conscious." In effect, instincts have been freed, not only from reference to objects, but from reference to the subject, since the "ego" has itself gone over to the side of objects. In the notion of Ichtrieb, the *Ich* is related to instincts no longer as subject but as object, in the sense, as we have said, of being the variable function of an aim; the ego's position with respect to instincts is now such that the ego can be exchanged with objects by means of substitution or displacement of cathexis. To switch to another terminology, which is called for here because of the quarrel with Adler, the self (*Selbst*) and self-regard (*Selbstgefühl*) (the feeling of inferiority, etc.) by no means escape the economy of the libido; self-regard comes within a generalized erotics (*Erotik*) by means of the great redistributions of erotic cathexes.[44]

In order to understand the topography one must, I think, keep clearly in mind the double *destruction*—of the intended object as supposed guide, and of the subject as supposed pole of reference for all the intentions of consciousness. One might say that the topography is the nonanatomical, psychical locality introduced into psychoanalytic theory as the condition of the possibility of all the vicissitudes of instincts; it is the marketplace of cathexes where ego-instincts and object-instincts are exchanged for one another.

At the end of this epochê in reverse, consciousness is now the least known; it has ceased to be self-evident and has become a problem. This problem, dealt with in the topography, has to do with the process of becoming conscious.

Such is, it seems to me, the meaning of the difficult fifth section of "The Unconscious," entitled "The Special Characteristics of the System *Ucs.*," whose examination we postponed. Freud presents this section as a description, but its meaning is actually opposed to any description; it is rather the transcription in descriptive, quasi-phenomenological terms of the result of the antiphenomenology. That is why I present it here as a result and not as a given: "The distinction we have made between the two psychical systems receives fresh significance when we observe that processes in the one

44. "On Narcissism," *GW, 10,* 167; *SE, 14,* 99.

system, the *Ucs.*, show characteristics which are not met with again in the system immediately above it."[45] We shall likewise use pseudo-descriptive terms when we say: the unconscious is timeless; the unconscious is exempt from contradiction; the unconscious follows the pleasure principle and not the reality principle, etc. But these characteristics are in no way descriptive, for "the attribute of being conscious [*Bewusstheit*], which is the only characteristic of psychical processes that is directly presented to us, is in no way suited to serve as a criterion for the differentiation of systems."[46] And further on: "Consciousness stands in no simple relation either to the different systems or to repression."[47] Whence the conclusion: "The more we seek to win our way to a metapsychological view of mental life, the more we must learn to emancipate ourselves from the importance of the symptom of 'being conscious' [*Bewusstheit*]."[48] In the topography what we transcribe is precisely this emancipation.

REPRESENTATIVES AND IDEAS

We must now go back along the reverse path. From the opening pages of the essay "The Unconscious" the question is asked, How do we arrive at a knowledge of the unconscious? And the answer: "It is of course only as something conscious that we know it, after it has undergone transformation [*Umsetzung*] or translation [*Übersetzung*] into something conscious."[49] And Freud adds: "Psychoanalytic work shows us every day that translation of this kind is possible."[50]

What does such a possibility consist in? Here is where we enter into the most difficult problematic—the one indicated by the title of this chapter: "Instinct and Idea." At a certain point the question of force and the question of meaning coincide; that point is where instincts are indicated, are made manifest, are given in a psychical

45. *GW, 10,* 285; *SE, 14,* 186.
46. *GW, 10,* 291; *SE, 14,* 192.
47. Ibid.
48. *GW, 10,* 291; *SE, 14,* 193.
49. *GW, 10,* 264; *SE, 14,* 166.
50. Ibid.

representative, that is, in something psychical that "stands for" them; all the derivatives in consciousness are merely transformations of this psychical representative, of this primal "standing for." To designate this point, Freud coined the excellent expression *Repräsentanz.* Instincts, which are energy, are "represented" by something psychical. But we must not speak of representation in the sense of *Vorstellung,* i.e. an "idea" *of* something, for an idea is itself a derived form of this "representative" which, before representing things—the world, one's own body, the unreal—stands for instincts as such, *presents* them purely and simply. This function of presentation, or representation, is evoked not only on the first page but in the first sentence of "The Unconscious": "We have learnt from psychoanalysis that the essence of the process of repression lies, not in putting an end to, in annihilating, the idea which represents an instinct [*den Trieb repräsentierende Vorstellung*], but in preventing it from becoming conscious." [51]

What is the nature of this function of presentation or representation that governs not only ideas but, as we shall see, affects as well?

If the problem we enter upon here is not basically a new one,[52] it is new in terms of Freud's position. Freud's originality consists in shifting the point of coincidence of meaning and force back to the unconscious itself. He presupposes this coincidence as making possible all the "transformations" and "translations" of the unconscious into the conscious. In spite of the barrier that separates the systems, they must be assumed to have a common structure whereby the conscious and the unconscious are equally psychical. That common structure is precisely the function of Repräsentanz. This function is what lets us "interpolate" unconscious acts into the text of conscious acts; it assures a close "contact" (*Berührung*) [53] between conscious and unconscious psychical processes and makes it possible that the latter, "with the help of a certain amount of work . . . can be transformed [*umsetzen*] into, or replaced

51. Ibid.

52. In our discussion of this Freudian concept in Chapter 2 of the "Dialectic" we shall see its relationship to similar concepts in Spinoza and Leibniz.

53. *GW, 10,* 267; *SE, 14,* 168.

[*ersetzen*] by, conscious mental processes"; [54] finally, because of it "all the categories which we employ to describe conscious mental acts, such as ideas, purposes, resolutions and so on, can be applied to them. Indeed, we are obliged to say of some of these latent states that the only respect in which they differ from conscious ones is precisely in the absence of consciousness [*Wegfall des Bewusstseins*]." [55]

This function of Repräsentanz is certainly a postulate. Freud gives no proof for it; he assumes it as that which allows him to transcribe the unconscious into the conscious and to group the two together as comparable psychical modalities; that is why he writes this function into the definition of instinct itself. He will one day say, "The theory of the instincts is so to say our mythology." [56] We do not in fact know what instincts are in their own dynamism. We do not talk of instincts in themselves; we talk of instincts in their psychical representatives; and by the same token we speak of them as a psychical and not as a biological reality. True, we were able to call them "a form of activity," thereby designating them as energy, drive, tension, etc. But the psychological qualification of that energy is a part of its definition, for it is an energy that is not represented by, but representative of, organic energies: "If now we apply ourselves to considering mental life from a *biological* point of view, an 'instinct' appears to us as a concept on the frontier between the mental and the somatic, as the psychical representative [*Repräsentant*] of the stimuli originating from within the organism and reaching the mind"; and to emphasize the composite character of this concept, Freud connects with it the notion of work, in which we have recognized a privileged expression of the composite language required by psychoanalysis: an instinct is "a measure of the demand made upon the mind for work [*ein Mass der Arbeitsanforderung*] in consequence of its connection with the body." [57]

54. Ibid.
55. Ibid.
56. *New Introductory Lectures on Psychoanalysis, SE, 22,* 95.
57. *GW, 10,* 214; *SE, 14,* 121–22. In the ensuing terminological discussion Freud again refers to the representative or presentative function in connection with each of the interrelated terms. "By the pressure [*Drang*] of an instinct we understand its motor factor, the amount of force or the measure

Hence, we cannot say simply that instincts are expressed by ideas—this is only one of the derived aspects of the representative function of instincts. More radically it must be said that instincts themselves represent or express the body to the mind (*in die Seele*). This is, perhaps, the most fundamental hypothesis of psychoanalysis, the one that qualifies it as *psycho*analysis. Let us examine this hypothesis in its important consequences.

All the vicissitudes of instincts are vicissitudes of the "psychical representatives" of instincts. This is evident in the instances of "reversal" and "turning round," which alone are treated in detail in the paper "Instincts and Their Vicissitudes." The reversal from looking at to being looked at and from inflicting pain on another to inflicting pain on oneself finds expression in ideas and affects that represent displacements of energy in a psychical field where they can be signified and recognized, and thus become, with the help of a certain amount of work, conscious.

The vicissitude of the "psychical representatives" is far more instructive in the case of repression, which constitutes, it will be remembered, the third vicissitude of an instinct. Repression brings to the psychical representative of an instinct all the complexity that Freud designates by the words "remoteness" (*Entfernung*) and

---

of the demand for work which it represents [*repräsentiert*]" (ibid.). "By the source [*Quelle*] of an instinct is meant the somatic process which occurs in an organ or part of the body and whose stimulus is represented [*repräsentiert*] in mental life by an instinct" (*GW*, *10*, 215; *SE*, *14*, 123). These passages clearly reflect the basic ambiguity in the concept of an instinct: in some texts an instinct is *what* is "represented" (by affects and ideas); in others, it is *itself* the psychical "representative" of organic forces that are not yet clearly known. In his introductory note to "Instincts and Their Vicissitudes" (*SE*, *14*, 111–16), the editor of the *Standard Edition* calls attention to the main passages in Freud concerned with this question: the *Three Essays* (addition of 1915), Section III of the Schreber case (1911), "On Narcissism" (1914), "The Unconscious" and "Repression" (1915), *Beyond the Pleasure Principle* (1920), and the Encyclopaedia Britannica article (1926). I fully agree with the editor that the ambiguity is of little moment; the important point for us is that an instinct is knowable only in its psychical representatives. They are what determine its psychological status. The solution of the ambiguity no doubt lies in the notion of primal repression which establishes the very first "fixation" of the psychical representative to an instinct. We discuss this point further in the following footnote.

"distortion" (*Entstellung*) (the latter term having already served to characterize the group of procedures constituting the dream-work). It is repression, in fact, that cuts instincts off from consciousness; but it does not cut them off from their psychical representatives; it cannot do this, for instincts are themselves representatives of the organic. That is why the Freudian unconscious is a *psychical* unconscious; it is made up of psychical representatives (it being understood that this expression covers not only ideas—what the *Traumdeutung* called dream-thoughts—but also affects, which will subsequently pose a rather difficult problem).

On the other hand, however, repression prevents us from directly grasping the primary psychical expression of instincts: we can only postulate it. The "remoteness" of the known and recognized expressions of an instinct, as compared with its primal expression, is always greater than one might imagine. Freud expresses this by saying that repression proper (*eigentliche*) is a secondary repression as compared with a primal repression (*Urverdrängung*), "which consists in the psychical (ideational) representative of the instinct [*der psychischen* (*Vorstellungs-*) *Repräsentanz des Triebes*] being denied entrance into the conscious." [58] Hence, what we take to be

58. *GW, 10,* 250; *SE, 14,* 148. Any current systematic study of the Freudian concept of repression should pay close attention to the work of Peter Madison, *Freud's Concept of Repression and Defense* (see Part I, Ch. 1, n. 20). In it the author applies the epistemological concerns of the Carnap school and attempts to clarify the Freudian concept by distinguishing and interrelating two levels, an "observational language" and a "theoretical language." The first uses terms that refer to the observable manifestations of the interplay between instincts and anticathexis; the second contains terms that refer to unobservable features of this interaction of forces. The varied manifestations of this hypothesized interaction explain the baffling complexity of Freud's formulations. In the "Preliminary Communication" of 1892 (*Studies on Hysteria,* Ch. 1) "repression" meant unconsciously motivated forgetting of things that the patient wished to forget, as is observable in cases of hysteria; thus repression referred specifically to hysterical amnesia, as Freud himself reaffirmed in the important eleventh chapter of *Inhibitions, Symptoms and Anxiety* (1926). However, the term "defense" was also used synonymously with repression: "defense, that is, repressing ideas from consciousness." A second complication was that there are other defensive mechanisms besides hysterical amnesia, such as conversion, projection, substitution, and isolation (isolation, according to the "rat-man" case, allows the ideational content to enter consciousness but deprived of its affective cathexis). Then the concept of defense was dropped from Freud's

the primal expression of an instinct is in fact the product of a fixation; the relation between expression and instinct never appears to us except as one that has been established, sedimented, "fixed." In order to attain an immediate expression one would have to be able to go back beyond this primal repression. (We are not questioning

terminology and replaced by the concept of repression until 1926; in the 1915 article, repression is formally defined as follows: "the essence of repression lies simply in turning something away, and keeping it at a distance, from the conscious." The concept is taken here in its theoretical dimension: it covers a variety of mechanisms which are operative in three different types of neurosis; but repression is, in turn, only one of the vicissitudes of an instinct; the defensive process would thus seem to cover the whole group of these vicissitudes. Hence it is not exactly correct to say that the concept of repression was substituted for that of defense, even though the latter practically disappeared from Freud's vocabulary until 1926. The revival of the concept of defense in *Inhibitions, Symptoms and Anxiety* to designate all the techniques the ego makes use of in conflicts that may lead to a neurosis is therefore not unexpected: once again Freud mentions—in addition to the keeping away from consciousness, which is seen clearly in hysterical repression—"isolation" and "regression" to an earlier libidinal stage, as in obsessional neurosis; he also mentions a procedure that consists in magically "undoing" what has been done. All these mechanisms are defensive in the sense that they protect the ego against instinctual demands. But it is only in the chapter entitled "Addenda" that the concept of repression is not only subordinated to that of defense but restricted once more to hysterical amnesia; in the main body of the work the other defensive mechanisms are at times treated as forms of repression. Madison suggests that repression and defense were "inextricably linked to consciousness in a way that did not allow separation through a simple agreement on terminology" (p. 27). The first task of an epistemology is to classify the various observable effects resulting from the unobservable inner conflicts and to reserve the concept of defense for those mechanisms that have a basic purpose in common, viz. the preventive protection of the ego against anxiety. Part I of Madison's book is devoted to this classification. Psychoanalysis is mainly concerned with defenses that have failed; the successful ones, Freud said in 1915, escape our examination. Among the successful mechanisms of defense, Freud cites the "destruction of the Oedipus complex" (which is "more than a repression" in that the impulse itself is destroyed in the id), rejection based on judgement, and especially sublimation, which we shall discuss elsewhere in its connection with desexualization. In *Civilization and Its Discontents,* Freud suggests that the instincts themselves may be modified by becoming absorbed, sublimated, or repressed; an example of absorption would be the formation of character traits. As for the unsuccessful defenses, these may be divided into repressive and nonrepressive defenses; the first achieve the effect of ego protection by altering the idea attached to a dangerous impulse; amnesia is but one of the modes of this type of mechanism,

here the clinical reality of primal repression but rather its epistemological implications.) As far as I know, however, Freud never stated the conditions under which one could go back beyond primal repression.

Primal repression means that we are always in the mediate, in

---

along with conversion, displacement, projection, reaction-formation, isolation, undoing, and denial. The criterion of the degree of repression is given by the degree of distortion and remoteness of the derivatives of the unconscious in dreams, symptoms, and the various signs and disguises of the repressed instinct. One may speak of "nonrepressive defense" in the case of regression involving a substitution of one drive for another (for instance, the return to a pregenital sex interest) but with no alteration of the attached idea. Some defense mechanisms, however, do not seem to fall under this alternative of repressive and nonrepressive defenses; these include purely emotional inhibitions, which Freud mentions as examples of vicissitudes separated from affects: here the impulses are prevented from developing into full affective manifestation. Freud still calls this a case of repression (1915), although the affective inhibition is not achieved through distortion of the ideational content. Finally, what is to be said of the concept of resistance? What is its relation to the concept of repression? From certain texts it is clear that resistance is one of the manifestations of repression, the one the therapeutic work encounters as an obstacle to its progress. This manifestation is on the same footing as symptom formation; the patient engages in it as a defense measure against recovery, which the ego regards as a new danger. But resistance also covers a variety of directly observable actions (silence, elusiveness, repetition, etc.). As a hypothesized force resistance belongs to the theoretical concepts; it is the counterpart, in the analytic situation, of anticathexis; and the notion of anticathexis explicitly serves to define primal repression (secondary repression, or repression proper, being a withdrawal of the *Pcs.* cathexis). Thanks to this chain of ideas (resistance-anticathexis-repression) the concept of resistance operates on several levels: on the most general level, it is the name given to repression in the analytic situation; on the theoretical level, the counterforce operative in this situation is identified with what the theory of repression called anticathexis; on the observational level, it includes all the measures the patient uses to evade the rules of therapy; in this connection, the most powerful form of resistance is the one that makes use of the transference to obstruct the work of the analysis.

Thus the theory of repression includes not only a highly complex network of observable effects, but a system of unobservable opposed forces; this system underwent many changes in the Freudian doctrine, for it is inseparable from the theory of sexual organizations and the successive theories of instinct. A highly abstract form of the theory was reached with the distinction between "primal repression" and "after-repression" (or "repression proper"). The former places at the disposition of the latter a store of repressed infantile experiences; thanks to primal repression, all repression

the already expressed, the already said. We are all the more compelled to deal with mere derivatives because of repression proper; "the second stage of repression, *repression proper*, affects mental derivatives of the repressed representative [*psychische Abkömmlinge der verdrängten Repräsentanz*], or such trains of thought [*Gedankenzüge*] as, originating elsewhere, have come into associative connection with it." [59] The unconscious appears, then, as a

---

consists in a transformation of affects, in virtue of which what formerly generated pleasure henceforth generates unpleasure, in the form, for example, of disgust. The most complete analysis of the theory of primal repression occurs in the Schreber case (1911), Section III; the short paper of 1915 is a restatement of that analysis in condensed form. In the earlier text the fixation characteristic of primal repression is the condition of repression proper; this latter is divided into two processes, repulsion exercised by the conscious system and attraction exercised by the unconscious. The theory reached its most abstract form in 1915 with the concept of anticathexis; this notion assumes that the instinctual force and the counterforce operate as constant opposed pressures; the counterforce is defined simply as energy directed against the instincts. This system, mechanistic in appearance, is actually a "motivational" system. This is the whole point of the discussion of the relationship between repression and defense: the entire system is oriented toward the idea of protection against inner dangers (libidinal or moral) even more than against external and physical ones. It is understandable that anxiety, long regarded as an effect of repression (in 1915 it was one of the separate vicissitudes of affect, conversion into anxiety), was able, in 1926, to take on an anticipatory or signal function: whereas traumatic anxiety consists in the wholly passive helplessness of the ego in the face of an overwhelming danger (the traumatic situation), signal anxiety anticipates this traumatic situation; it actively repeats the trauma in a weakened version, with the hope of directing its course. By way of contrast, primal repression seems to be connected with what is now called traumatic anxiety; *Beyond the Pleasure Principle* had already described as "traumatic" any breach in the protective shield against stimuli; before it is able to make use of anticipatory anxiety the ego's only recourse is to act on the innate tendency to restore an earlier state of repose; primal repression, which seems to concern simply the nonsatisfaction of infantile needs, is from now on sharply distinguished from all the mechanisms succeeding the formation of the superego and which Freud now characterizes as anticipatory or signal anxiety; such anxiety functions as a warning that an earlier danger situation is threatening to recur.

So much for the extraordinary network of facts and theories that characterize Freud's concept of repression. In the "Dialectic," Ch. 1, pp. 355–58, we shall speak of Part II of Peter Madison's book and his attempt to apply Carnap's rules to Freudianism.

59. *GW, 10,* 250; *SE, 14,* 148.

ramified network made up of the indefinite branchings of those derivatives or "offshoots"; as such it forms a system and is open to what psychoanalysts call an intrasystemic investigation. But still it is a system of psychical expressions, and the whole of analysis lies in the art of interpreting those derivatives in their relation to ever more primitive expressions of instinct, according to the degree of their remoteness and distortion.[60] Thus the derivatives' relations of remoteness and distortion correspond, on the side of the analyzed psychism, to the aforementioned relations of translation (*Übersetzung*) on the side of analysis itself. Thanks to this correlation, at the level of psychical expressions, between the work of repression and the work of analysis, everything we were able to treat under the heading of "the [energic] vicissitude of instincts" *comes to language* as the vicissitude of their psychical expressions.

It is therefore in this notion of psychical expression, of psychical representative, that the economics and the hermeneutics coincide; the distance between the two psychoanalytic universes of discourse, which appeared insurmountable on the level of *The Interpretation of Dreams,* seems to have vanished in the "Papers on Metapsychology."

We have still not come to the end of the problem. Everything would be fine if we could simply equate psychical expressions (*Repräsentanz*) with representations (*Vorstellungen*), i.e. with ideas of things. Ideas, however, are only one category of psychical expressions; we have pretended to ignore that there is another category, that of affects, and that these have a different vicissitude or

60. "Psychoanalysis is able to show us other things as well which are important for understanding the effects of repression in the psychoneuroses. It shows us, for instance, that the instinctual representative develops with less interference and more profusely if it is withdrawn by repression from conscious influence. It proliferates in the dark, as it were, and takes on extreme forms of expression, which when they are translated and presented to the neurotic are not only bound to seem alien to him, but frighten him by giving him the picture [*durch die Vorspiegelung*] of an extraordinary and dangerous strength of instinct [*Triebstärke*]. This deceptive [*täuschende*] strength of instinct is the result of an uninhibited development in fantasy [*in der Phantasie*] and of the damming-up [*Aufstauung*] consequent on frustrated satisfaction [*infolge versagter Befriedigung*]" (*GW, 10,* 251; *SE, 14,* 149).

destiny which may well be of greater importance for psychoanalysis than the destiny of ideas.

Thus we seem to be set adrift. Will not affects be the refuge of an economic explanation that has been split off from exegetical interpretation? Are not affects purely quantitative? In short, is it not the case that interpretation and the economic explanation coincide in the vicissitude of ideas, that is to say, in the least important vicissitude, only to be separated from each other once again in the vicissitude of affects?

Let us return to the texts.[61] First it should be noted that Freud was very careful to bracket the question of affects and to elaborate his theory of the unconscious contents on the basis of the equivalence between psychical expressions and ideas (Repräsentanz and Vorstellung); in this respect there is a parallel between the initial step of the two texts in question.[62] It is only in a second phase that the content within the brackets is reintroduced: "In our discussion so far we have dealt with the repression of an instinctual representative, and by the latter we have understood an idea or group of ideas which is cathected with a definite quota [*Betrag*] of psychical energy (libido or interest) coming from an instinct [*vom Trieb her*]." [63] This "quota of affect" (*Affektbetrag*) constitutes the "other element of the psychical representative"; [64] and what forces us to study it as a theme in its own right is repression, inasmuch as repression confers on it a different vicissitude. Freud calls this other element "the *quantitative* factor of the instinctual representative," or again "the quota of affect belonging to the representative," or

61. The end of "Repression," *GW, 10,* 254 ff.; *SE, 14,* 152 ff.; and Section III of "The Unconscious," *GW, 10,* 275–79; *SE, 14,* 176–79.

62. "Clinical observation now obliges us to divide up what we have hitherto regarded as a single entity; for it shows us that besides the idea, some other element representing the instinct has to be taken into account, and that this other element undergoes vicissitudes of repression which may be quite different from those undergone by the idea. For this other element of the psychical representative the term *quota of affect* has been generally adopted. It corresponds to the instinct in so far as the latter has become detached from the idea and finds expression, proportionate to its quantity, in processes which are sensed as affects [*als Affekte der Empfindung*]" (*GW, 10,* 255; *SE, 14,* 152).

63. Ibid.

64. Ibid.

again "the instinctual energy linked to [the idea]." Sometimes he even speaks of "the quantitative portion" as opposed to the "ideational portion." [65] Is not this second factor one of pure energy? Are we not thereby reduced to physics? No, for even when separated from the idea, the instinct becomes sensibly observable in affects in which it "finds expression, proportionate to its quantity." The vicissitudes of quantity are vicissitudes of affects. Freud distinguishes three of them: no affect (as in what Charcot called *"la belle indifférence"* of hysterical patients); an affect that is "qualitatively colored"; and finally, "anxiety." Only the last two merit being called a "transformation" (*Umsetzung*) of the psychical energies of instincts into affects.

Thus we again come upon the quantity that has been perplexing us ever since the "Project"! We were correct in saying that such a quantity is not subject to measurement but rather to a process of diagnosis and interpretation, for apart from the vicissitudes of ideas, it can only be grasped in the vicissitudes of affects. We had already remarked, moreover, that the principle of constancy, which concretizes the notion of quantity, is nothing else than the pleasure-unpleasure regulation. The separate vicissitude of affect brings out the meaning of that regulation; it is when repression is struggling with affects that repression discloses its true meaning in relation to the pleasure-unpleasure principle:

> We recall the fact that the motive and purpose of repression was nothing else than the avoidance of unpleasure. It follows that the vicissitude of the quota of affect belonging to the [instinctual] representative is far more important than the vicissitude of the idea, and this fact is decisive for our assessment [of the success or failure] of the process of repression.[66]

That is why Freud undertakes to give a new interpretation of the theory of the neuroses within the double perspective of the vicissitude of the "ideational portion" and the vicissitude of the "quantitative portion." The manner in which he does this is not important for us here except for the conceptualization involved: "substitutive

65. All of these expressions are found in the third part of "Repression."
66. *GW, 10,* 256; *SE, 14,* 153.

formations," "symptoms," the "return of the repressed," and so on.

The paper entitled "Repression" definitely enables us to say that the "quantitative portion" is recognizable only in affects. However, by distinguishing between the vicissitudes of ideas and those of affects, it leaves open the question whether the economic explanation of affects is not irreducible to the interpretation of ideas, or, in other words, whether interpretation is not fixed upon ideas and the economic explanation upon affects. If "the true task of repression" lies in "dealing with the quota of affect," is it not the case that the economics of repression is ultimately irreducible to any interpretation of meaning through meaning?

Section III of "The Unconscious" seems to move in this direction, for it expressly links the economic point of view with the consideration of affects;[67] the topographical point of view, on the contrary, was introduced in Section II on the basis of the identification of psychical expressions with ideas. In a sense that is purely topographic and not yet economic, Freud reminds us, at the beginning of Section III, that "an instinct can never become an object of consciousness—only the idea that represents the instinct can. Even in the unconscious, moreover, an instinct cannot be represented otherwise than by an idea."[68] The triple vicissitude of affects poses a specifically economic problem, that of the "processes of discharge" (*Abfuhrvorgängen*).[69] In this sense we must speak of "access to affects" just as we speak of access to motility; in both cases it is a question of discharge, and in both cases consciousness is the guardian of the discharge. This is quite true; but the separate vicissitudes of affects should not make us forget that affects remain affects of ideas. That is why it was possible and necessary to begin by bracketing affects. We are being duped by language if we think we have established a strict parallel between ideas and affects. Thus, when we speak of an unconscious feeling or emotion—unconscious anxiety, an unconscious feeling of guilt—we forget

67. This section contains a rather systematic enumeration of affects according to their degree of discharge; at one end there are the "instinctual impulses" (*Triebregungen*), and at the other the "sense impressions" or "feelings" (*Empfindungen*).

68. *GW, 10,* 275–76; *SE, 14,* 177.

69. *GW, 10,* 277; *SE, 14,* 179.

that, *stricto sensu,* the feeling is felt, hence conscious: "We can only mean an instinctual impulse [*Triebregung*] the ideational representative of which is unconscious, for nothing else comes into consideration."[70] We always designate an affect by the idea *of which* it is the affect; and when we speak improperly of "unconscious" affects, it is because we misconstrue the original representative connection and regard the affect as the manifestation of an idea that is not proper to it.

It may be objected, however, that this strictness of vocabulary concerns only the descriptive point of view; from the systematic point of view the vicissitude of the quantitative factor remains a distinct vicissitude: the notion of unconscious affect is again required when we consider the specific effects of repression on the discharge of affect and the three vicissitudes of that discharge which we have already mentioned above. But what is an inhibited affect? A repressed idea continues to exist as "an actual structure [*reale Bildung*] in the system *Ucs.*"[71] A repressed affect, on the other hand, is rather obscurely designated as a potential beginning (*Ansatzmöglichkeit*) which is prevented from developing.[72] We know nothing about these "processes of discharge" (*Abfuhrvorgänge*) apart from their psychical expressions or manifestations, which are perceived as "feelings" (*Empfindungen*). At most we can only trace out a certain path, mark off a certain development, starting from those affective potencies of which we know very little, moving thence to instinctual impulses, and finally to explicit affects. This is the path upon which we placed ourselves earlier when we spoke of the conscious system's control over the release of affect in the same terms we use for the control of consciousness over motility.

But even so we should not overlook the fact that a pure affect, an affect that has come directly from the unconscious—such as anxiety with no particular object—is an affect waiting for a substitutive idea to which it can attach itself. An affect that we describe as being severed from its idea is an affect in search of a new ideational support by which it can penetrate into consciousness.

70. *GW, 10,* 276; *SE, 14,* 177.
71. *GW, 10,* 277; *SE, 14,* 178.
72. Ibid.

Therefore we can neither reduce affects and their quantitative factor to ideas, nor treat them as a distinct reality. At any rate, the difference between affects and ideas is the basis for the distinction between the topography and the economics. The theory of affects offers certain possibilities of autonomy to the economic point of view. Section IV of "The Unconscious" goes to the extreme limit of these possibilities by presenting the economics as a third point of view in addition to the dynamic and topographic ones; in this section Freud attempts "to follow out the vicissitudes of amounts of excitation and to arrive at least at some relative estimate of their magnitude." [73] This is the consummation, Freud says, of psychological research: "I propose that when we have succeeded in describing a psychical process in all its dynamic, topographical and economic aspects, we should speak of it as a *metapsychological* presentation. We must say at once that in the present state of our knowledge there are only a few points at which we shall succeed in this." [74]

This "tentative effort" and its "few points" actually amount to a new and systematic treatment of the theory of the neuroses along the lines of the article "Repression." But this time, instead of following the separate vicissitudes of ideas and affects, Freud constructs a sort of typology or combination system by uniting in different ways the two orders of psychical expressions. I will not enter into this sketch of the clinical catalogue of the neuroses either here or elsewhere; I simply wish to point out the shift in language and conceptualization that occurs in this section. The analysis moves in the direction of a pure economics; it is concerned solely with the placement and displacement of cathexis, withdrawal of cathexis, and anticathexis: "Thus there is a withdrawal of the preconscious cathexis, retention of the cathexis, or replacement of the preconscious cathexis by an unconscious one." [75] That Freud envisages here an actual substitution of the economic explanation for the topographical one is clearly implied in the solution he provides to the strictly topographical hypothesis of the double registration; the earlier hypothesis is replaced by the strictly economic hypoth-

73. *GW, 10,* 280; *SE, 14,* 181.
74. Ibid.
75. *GW, 10,* 279; *SE, 14,* 180.

esis of a change in the state of cathexis, and he adds: "The functional hypothesis has here easily defeated the topographical one." [76] To this sequence of withdrawal, retention, and replacement of cathexis Freud adds another economic mechanism, anticathexis, which he says is the sole mechanism of primal repression and the means by which the preconscious system protects itself from the pressure exerted on it by unconscious ideas. A bit further on he will also add the mechanism of hypercathexis.

The theory of the unconscious thus seems to have swung to the side of a pure economics. The dominant factor is no longer the vicissitudes of ideas within a history of meaning; ideas now seem to be but the anchorage point for the genuine processes, which are economic in nature and which Freud schematizes in the ordered play of cathexes.

Must we not go further and say that in the end the Freudian unconscious is characterized more by energy than by meaning? Section V ("Special Characteristics of the System *Ucs.*"), which we have already alluded to as having an antiphenomenological theme but have not really explored, characterizes the unconscious system much more in terms of the discharge of affects than in terms of ideas: "The nucleus of the *Ucs.* consists of instinctual representatives which seek to discharge their cathexis; that is to say, it consists of wishful impulses [*Wunschregungen*]." [77]

That is why the characteristics of the unconscious, which we have already enumerated, all bear the mark of nonmeaning [*du non-signifiant*].[78] If "there are in this system no negation, no doubt, no degrees of certainty," the reason is that impulses coexist without any relations of meaning: "In the *Ucs.* there are only contents, cathected with greater or lesser strength." If the primary process is dominant, it is because the cathexes are more mobile here and the displacements and condensations effected more easily. If the unconscious is timeless (*zeitlos*), it is because it has, properly speaking, no reference to time: we are not yet at the level of a transcendental esthetic; "reference to time," Freud tells us, "is bound

76. Ibid.
77. *GW*, *10*, 285; *SE*, *14*, 186.
78. "The Unconscious," Section V.

up with the work of the system *Cs.*" Lastly, the dominance of the pleasure principle means that the fate of the unconscious processes "depends only on how strong they are and on whether they fulfill the demands of the pleasure-unpleasure regulation."

As for the act of becoming conscious, it too is defined in an economic way, when we consider that it "is no mere act of perception, but is probably also a *hypercathexis,* a further advance in the psychical organization." [79]

All these characteristics of the systems bring us back very close to the "Project," that is, to the two states of cathectic energy, the tonically bound state and the mobile state. The final step in the triumph of the economic over the topographical point of view is taken when the critical frontier is moved back from between the preconscious and the conscious to between the unconscious and the preconscious.[80]

Let us call a halt here and take an overall view of the problem. The path we have taken has consisted in a gradual reversal of priorities. At the start we raised the problem of the psychical representative of instincts; we bracketed affects and started from the primacy of ideas in the topographical structure of the unconscious. Next we removed the parentheses from affects and attempted to subordinate the quota of affect to ideas. We then considered the vicissitude proper to this quantitative factor, and this consideration led us to add the economic to the topographical point of view and to give the interplay of cathexes primacy over meaning.

I think I am being fair to the Freudian systematization in drawing two conclusions from this whole discussion:

First, the irreducible character of affects, from the economic point of view—that is, from the point of view of the interplay of cathexes—exposes a situation whose traits become progressively more precise, if we compare our present conclusion with those of our chapters on the "Project" and *The Interpretation of Dreams:* the language of force can never be overcome by the language of meaning. This does not differ from what we said at the end of the preceding chapters when we posited that the topography and its

79. *GW, 10,* 292; *SE, 14,* 194.
80. *GW, 10,* 291; *SE, 14,* 193.

naturalistic naïveté are suited to the very essence of desire, inasmuch as desires are "indestructible," "immortal," that is to say, always prior to language and culture.[81]

Second, it is impossible to *realize* this pure economics apart from the representable and the sayable; we cannot hypostatize the unnameable of desire, on pain of falling short of a "psycho-logy." That is what prevents us from constructing a theory of *Repräsentanz*. The latter cannot, of course, be reduced to a theory of "representation" in the sense of ideas, since affects "represent" instincts and instincts "represent" the body "to the mind." But the mere verbal assonnance—which so perplexes the translator—betrays a profound kinship between *Repräsentanz* and "representation" in the sense of ideas. In any case, no economics can efface the fact that affects are the charge *of* ideas; the separating of affects from ideas is a further aspect of this intentional connection, which may be stretched out indefinitely but never nullified; that is why affects look for another ideational support to force their way into consciousness.

So little did Freud reduce the interpretation of meaning to the economics of force that the paper on "The Unconscious" ends with a significant circular movement that takes us back to the starting point, that is, to the deciphering of the unconscious in its "derivatives." This return to the point of departure deserves to be examined for the structure of its argumentation. The topography separated the systems from one other, and the economics completed that separation with the theory that each system has its own peculiar laws (the intrasystemic relations). But the economics also requires that we finally come to consider the intersystemic relations; that is why "The Unconscious" ends not with the "special characteristics of the unconscious system" but with a consideration of the "communication between the systems." [82] Only then will there be a

81. We will return to the status of desire in the "Dialectic," Ch. 2; what is represented in affects and does not pass over into ideas is desire qua desire; psychoanalysis is the frontier knowledge of this unnameable factor at the root of speech; it is the factor to which we will look for the ultimate justification of the "economic point of view," within the context of a philosophy of reflection.

82. "The Unconscious," Section VI.

true "recognition" or "assessment" of the unconscious.[83] The communication *between* the systems can only be deciphered, however, in the meaningful architecture of the derivatives: "In brief, it must be said that the *Ucs.* is continued into [*setzt sich in*] what are known as derivatives." [84] Freud especially focuses on those derivatives which present both the highly organized features of the conscious system and the characteristics of the unconscious; we are well acquainted with these hybrid formations as the fantasies of both normal and neurotic people and as substitute formations. The composite nature of fantasies assures us that the unconscious must always be deciphered, or diagnosed, in what we called at the end of our previous analysis the "symptom of being conscious." Furthermore, these derivatives of the unconscious, these "intermediaries between the two systems," not only afford access to the unconscious but open the way to *influencing* it—which is what psychoanalytic treatment is based upon.[85]

What is the meaning of this circular movement of the argumentation? This movement would be unintelligible if the economic point of view were to free itself entirely from the interpretation of meaning through meaning. Psychoanalysis never confronts one with bare forces, but always with forces in search of meaning; this link between force and meaning makes instinct a psychical reality, or, more exactly, the limit concept at the frontier between the organic and the psychical. The link between hermeneutics and economics may be stretched as far as possible—and the theory of affects marks the extreme point of that distention in the Freudian metapsychology; still the link cannot be broken, for otherwise the economics would cease to belong to a *psycho*analysis.

83. "Die Agnoszierung des Unbewussten," Section VII of "The Unconscious." The *Standard Edition* translates this as "Assessment of the Unconscious" (*14*, 196); the translation in *Collected Papers, 4*, 127, is "Recognition of the Unconscious."

84. *GW*, *10*, 289; *SE*, *14*, 190.

85. *GW*, *10*, 293; *SE*, *14*, 194.

PART II: THE INTERPRETATION OF CULTURE

The first part of our "Analytic" was concerned with an epistemology of psychoanalysis, that is to say, an investigation of psychoanalytic "statements" and the position they hold within discourse. The second part will deal with the interpretation of culture. In the "Problematic" we spoke of the importance of Freud's interpretation of culture in relation to a phenomenology of religion and of the sacred in general and placed it, along with the ideas of Marx and Nietzsche, among the forms of the destruction of the sacred and as one of the enterprises of demystification. We shall now proceed to justify that place on the basis of the "Analytic." From this point on, therefore, we shall enter into the great antinomy of hermeneutics, the antinomy of founding and destroying, while reserving the right to reexamine the problem in the "Dialectic."

The analysis we can make of the cultural phenomenon in this second part presents three aspects:

1. In the first place the exegesis of culture is simply an application of psychoanalysis by way of analogy with the interpretation of dreams and the neuroses. By this first trait we characterize both the validity and the limits of a psychoanalytic interpretation of culture. Its validity and limits are not to be found in the object, that is, in what it thematizes, but rather in the point of view, that is, in its operative concepts. The field to which psychoanalysis may be applied has no boundary; in this sense its field is unlimited. But the perspective employed is determined by the topographic-economic point of view which gives psychoanalysis its rights: in this sense psychoanalysis has limits, which, as elsewhere, are a determinant of its validity. Everything psychoanalysis says about art, morality, and

religion is determined in two ways: first by the topographic-economic model which constitutes the Freudian "metapsychology," and second by the example of dreams, which furnish the first term of a series of analogues that can be drawn out indefinitely, from the oneiric to the sublime.

Let us insist upon this double limitation: limitation by the model, limitation by the example. The first limitation means that we must not look to psychoanalysis for what it has forbidden itself to give, namely, a problematic of the primal [*l'originaire*]. Everything that is "primary" in analysis—the primary process, primal repression, primary narcissism, and, later on, primary masochism—is primary in a sense that is completely different from the transcendental: it is not a question of the justification or grounds, but of what takes precedence in the order of distortion or disguise. Thus the primary process expresses the hallucinatory wish-fulfillments that precede all other fantasy formations; primal repression decides which idea will be attached to an instinct first; primary narcissism denotes the reservoir underlying all object-cathexes and the source from which all instincts proceed. But what is first for analysis is never first for reflection; the primary is not a ground. Hence we must not ask psychoanalysis to resolve questions as to root origins, either in the order of reality or in the order of value. It is to be understood that ideals and illusions will be regarded only as the vicissitudes of instincts, as derivatives more or less "distant," more or less "deformed," of the psychical expressions of instinct. Esthetic creativity and pleasure, ideals of moral life, illusions in the religious sphere, will figure simply as elements on the economic balance sheet of instincts, as expenditures in pleasure-unpleasure; one will speak of them and can only speak of them in terms of cathexis, withdrawal of cathexis, hypercathexis, and anticathexis, according to the economic combination system outlined above (p. 147). In this sense the analytic theory of culture is an applied psychoanalysis.

At the same time that it applies the conceptual model elaborated in the metapsychological papers, the exegesis of culture also generalizes the dream exemplar; or rather, we should say it generalizes the pair formed by dreams and the neuroses, according to the key place the *Introductory Lectures on Psychoanalysis* assigns to them at the head of all the applications of psychoanalysis. Dreams propose to applied psychoanalysis precisely the structure defended by *The Interpretation of Dreams* to the point of intransigence under the heading of "wish-fulfillment" (*Wunscherfüllung*). We recall that it was to account for this fulfillment and its triple regression that the topography was worked out, starting from the time of the "Project." Thus psychoanalysis offers to the interpretation of culture the submodel of wish-fulfillment. The psychoanalytic interpretation of culture generalizes this prototype of all cultural phenomena. This is the second sense in which psychoanalysis is limited: it knows cultural phenomena only as analogues of the wish-fulfillment illustrated by dreams. The best way to do justice to Freud's essays on art, morality, and religion is to take them as essays in applied psychoanalysis and as an "analogous" interpretation. We are not, or at least not yet, confronted with a total explanation, but with one that is fragmentary, though extremely penetrating in the narrowness of its attack.

Such is, as I see it, the double internal limitation of this interpretation (which has no external boundaries) of cultural phenomena.

2. But we have not touched upon its essential feature so long as we characterize the psychoanalytic exegesis of culture simply as applied psychoanalysis and as an analogical interpretation. Upon a careful reading, it is evident that the application and transposition have reacted upon and transformed the model itself, the formal model of the economics and the material model of dreams. Consequently, Part II may be taken as a new reading on a deeper level, in the course of which psychoanalysis, by being applied outside the original area of dreams and the neuroses, will unfold its proper meaning and approach its initial philosophical horizon (cf. above, p. 86).

The crucial point is the transition to the second topography of ego, id, and superego. This transition presents special difficulties, for the new triad does not do away with the first, nor can it be said that it is simply an addition, at least not in the same conceptual framework. The consideration of the *roles* or agencies that distinguish the second topography from the first does not stem from a simple correction of the theory of the three *systems* (unconscious, preconscious, and conscious). The second topography is of a different order. That is why we did not introduce it under the heading of the psychoanalytic epistemology, which may be regarded, if not as achieved, at least as sufficiently motivated by the first topography. We preferred to couple it with the interpretation of culture so as to underscore, on the one hand, that the interpretation of culture is much more than a by-product of psychoanalysis, since it is bound up with the conception of the second topography, and on the other hand, that the second topography is not a mere reworking of the first, since it arises from a confrontation of the libido with the nonlibidinal factor that manifests itself as culture. The first topography remained tied to an economics of instinct, with instinct as the one basic concept; the division of the topography into three systems was made in relation to the libido alone. The second topography is an economics of a new type: here the libido is subject to something other than itself, to a demand for renunciation that creates a new economic situation. Hence the topography now sets into play not a series of systems for a solipsistic libido but a series of roles—personal, impersonal, suprapersonal—of a libido situated within a culture. The reason we reserve the second topography for the end of Part II is to stress its intimate connection with the exegesis of culture. It could be said that the theory of culture, as an application of psychoanalysis, proceeds from the first topography, but that, by way of rebound, it gives rise to a new topography which is its culmination; the essay entitled *The Ego and the Id* is the important expression of this expansion of psychoanalysis.

3. However, we have not yet done full justice to the interpretation of culture by linking it to the second topography. To move from a fragmentary, one-sided, and solely analogical view of cultural phenomena to a systematic view of culture, a much more radical recasting of the theory of instinct is required. The problem of culture will be elaborated in a unified manner when we take into account the death instinct and the reinterpretation of the libido as Eros over against death. The final interpretation is not to be sought in *The Ego and the Id,* but in *Beyond the Pleasure Principle*. Between Eros and death, culture will represent the great theater of the "battle of the giants."

At the same time, however, we shall have reached the point where psychoanalysis turns from science to philosophy, perhaps even to mythology. Part II of the "Analytic" will remain on this side of that point, halfway between the still reassuring slopes of applied psychoanalysis and the summits—or chasms—of a new dramaturgy, all the "personages" of which are mythical: Eros, Thanatos, and Ananke. This mythico-philosophical dramaturgy will be the subject of Part III of the "Analytic."

Chapter 1: The Analogy of Dreams

THE PRIVILEGED PLACE OF DREAMS

The privileged place assigned to dreams in the series of cultural analogues is not due to mere chance. Lest one be surprised at the paradigmatic character of the interpretation of dreams, it is important to recall the peculiar affinity between the processes of interpretation and its foremost illustration. What makes dreams a model can be formulated under the following points:

1. Dreams have a meaning: there are dream-thoughts, and these thoughts are not basically different from those of waking life. Everything that places dreams in the same current as the rest of psychical life makes them capable of being transposed into cultural analogues.

2. Dreams are the disguised fulfillment of repressed wishes or desires. This second thesis orients us toward a precise type of interpretation, the hermeneutics of deciphering. Since desires hide themselves in dreams, interpretation must substitute the light of meaning for the darkness of desire. Interpretation is lucidity's answer to ruse. We touch here upon the source of any theory of interpretation understood as the reduction of illusion.

3. Disguise is the effect of a work, the dream-work, the mechanisms of which are far more complicated than might be suggested by a generalization of scriptural exegesis or even by an investigation of the "genealogy of morals" in the manner of Nietzsche. Displacement, condensation, pictorial representation, secondary revision, these well-defined procedures open the way to new structural analogies. If dream interpretation can stand as the paradigm for all

interpretation it is because dreams are in fact the paradigm of all the stratagems of desire.

4. The desires or wishes that dreams stand for are necessarily infantile. Dreams typify the threefold regression of the psychical apparatus: in the formal sense of a return to images, in the chronological sense of a return to infancy, and in the topographical sense of a return to the fusion between desire and pleasure, according to the type of hallucinatory fulfillment called the primary process. Thus dreams give us access to a general phenomenon which will repeatedly claim our attention, the phenomenon of regression; they enable us to grasp the three different forms of this regression. Henceforward we may characterize analogical interpretation not only as a deciphering of hidden meanings, as a struggle against masks, but as the revelation of archaisms of every sort; we shall see the important consequence this has for the ethical sphere.

5. Finally, dreams enable us to elaborate, by means of countless cross-checks, what could be called the language of desire, that is to say, an architectonic of the symbolic function in its typical or universal features. Sexuality, as we know, is what basically sustains this symbolism; it is preeminently susceptible of symbolization; in it *Darstellbarkeit,* representability, reaches its highest point. What dreams encounter as a worn or sedimented language, as symbols in the precise and even narrow sense Freud gives to the term, is the trace in the individual's psychism of the great popular daydreams whose names are folklore and mythology.

The generalization of the oneiric model should not be regarded, however, as a monotonous repetition. At the same time its extension to waking life raises a problem. Each of the traits we have just listed must be disengaged from the nocturnal peculiarity of dreams in order that dreams may become, so to speak, the oneiric in general.

1. If dreams are to provide us with a general theory of meaning, the narcissistic expression of the instinctual life during sleep must be integrated with the manner in which waking life expresses the world.

2. If the Wunscherfüllung of dreams is to have the value of an example, we must, in transposing it to waking life, overcome the attendant character of sleep or the wish to sleep which appears to

be the nontransposable nucleus of dreams. Must sleep also be generalized—metaphorically—as a nocturnal factor immanent to the law of waking life?

3. A more crucial difficulty arises from the fact that the procedures by which the dream-work achieves the distortion of meaning are quite singular and strange, a characteristic Freud stressed in *The Interpretation of Dreams* and contrasted with waking thought.[1] One of the tasks of the theory of culture, therefore, will be to extract from the dream-work a group of structures related to the general function of "fooling the censorship." This relation of structure to function may be seen again in jokes, fairy tales, legends, and myths, and in some way formalized beyond its occurrence in dreams as such. For this, however, the notion of regression must be extended beyond its elementary presentation in *The Interpretation of Dreams*, for the topographical regression toward perception does not appear to be characteristic of fantasy as a whole. In this respect the interpretation of culture will from beginning to end be a struggle with the theme of the "primitive scene" that Freud will always try to connect with real memories, even after he has given up its first expression in the supposed scene of the child's seduction by the adult. It seems highly unlikely that a topographic-economic theory of cultural phenomena can be built on the model of the primary process and the "hallucinatory cathexis of the perceptual systems."

4. The same difficulty, but in different terms, is raised by the theme of the infantile nature of dreams. Here the chronological aspect of regression comes to the fore. How can themes of "progression" be introduced into an interpretation that first and foremost is attentive to the "retrogressive" march of the physical apparatus? As we shall see, in order to maintain the universal validity of the oneiric model Freud refuses as far as possible to oppose progression and regression to each other. His theory of the superego will never give up the idea that at bottom man's fantasies are a restoration of abandoned positions of the libido, a movement of relapse. In this idea is rooted a certain cultural pessimism on the part of Freud, which will be reinforced by the discovery of the death instinct.

5. The theory of culture will enable us to return to the problem

1. Cf. above, p. 90 and n. 5, as well as p. 112.

of symbolization, which in *The Interpretation of Dreams* was said to fall outside the dream-work proper. Freud's reason for turning in that book to the interpretation of myths was precisely to facilitate the interpretation of symbols that resist the method of free association. The decoding method at the level of the individual psychism must give way here to a genetic method at the level of the history of culture.[2] The genetic point of view had been invoked ever since the distinction between the primary and secondary processes; the interpretation of culture will enable us to see how it is connected with the topographic-economic point of view.

For all these reasons the interpretation of culture will be the great detour that will reveal the dream model in its universal significance. Dreams will prove to be something quite other than a mere curiosity of nocturnal life or a means of getting at neurotic conflicts. Dreams are the *royal road to psychoanalysis*.[3] Their function as a model stems from the fact that they reveal all that is nocturnal in man, the nocturnal of his waking life as well as of his sleep. Man is a being capable of realizing his desires and wishes in the mode of disguise, regression, and stereotyped symbolization. In and through man desires advance masked. Psychoanalysis is of value insofar as art, morality, and religion are analogous figures or variants of the oneiric mask. The entire drama of dreams is thus found to be generalized to the dimensions of a universal poetics.

This is not a betrayal of the *Traumdeutung's* method but rather an expansion and deepening of it, for the "disguise" theme, central to the *Traumdeutung*, has itself been deepened and expanded into all the areas where instincts thrust their representatives and derivatives. Among these masks of desire, analogous to our night dreams, we shall encounter the idols that encumber our false cults. "Idols as the daydreams of mankind"—such might be the subtitle of the hermeneutics of culture.

A first confrontation, which does not yet explicitly raise the formidable difficulties attaching to the notion of the superego, will

2. Cf. above, pp. 101–02.

3. *The Interpretation of Dreams, GW, 2/3*, 613; *SE, 5*, 608: "The interpretation of dreams is the royal road to a knowledge of the unconscious activities of the mind."

throw light upon the original style of applied psychoanalysis: the work of art will be the first figure of the daytime nocturnal, the first analogue of the oneiric; it will also place us on the path to the sublime and to illusion, themes to be explored in the following chapters.

THE ANALOGY OF THE WORK OF ART

Freud's application of the topographic-economic point of view to works of art serves more than one design. It was a diversion for the clinician, who was also a great traveller, collector, and avid bibliophile, a great reader of classical literature—from Sophocles to Shakespeare, Goethe, and contemporary poetry—and a student of ethnography and the history of religions. For the apologist of his own doctrine—especially during the period of isolation that preceded the first world war—it was a Defense and an Illustration of Psychoanalysis open to the general, nonscientific public. It was even more a proof and test of truth for the theoretician of the metapsychology. And last, it was a milestone in the direction of the great philosophical design that Freud never lost sight of and which was both masked and manifested by the theory of the psychoneuroses.

Because of the fragmentary character of the essays on psychoanalytic esthetics—a fact we shall admit and even insist upon in our defense of those essays—the exact place of esthetics in that great design is not immediately evident. However, when it is considered that Freud's sympathy for the arts is equaled only by his severity toward religious illusion, and that, on the other hand, esthetic seduction or allurement does not completely measure up to the ideal of veracity and truth which only science serves without compromise, one may expect to discover, beneath analyses that seem highly gratuitous, great tensions which will be brought into the open only at the very end, when esthetic seduction has found its place among Love, Death, and Necessity. For Freud, art is the nonobsessional, non-neurotic form of substitute satisfaction: the charm of esthetic creation does not stem from the return of the repressed. But where, then, is its place between the pleasure principle and the reality principle? This important question will be left in suspense, in the background of the short "papers on applied psychoanalysis."

We must first of all correctly understand the systematic but fragmentary character of Freud's esthetic essays. The systematic point of view is precisely what imposes and reinforces the fragmentary character. The psychoanalytic explanation of works of art cannot be compared to a therapeutic or didactic psychoanalysis, for the simple reason that it does not have the method of free association at its disposal, nor can it situate its interpretations in the field of the dual relation between doctor and patient. In this respect the biographical documents available to art interpretation are of no more significance than the information furnished by a third party during a treatment. The psychoanalytic interpretation of art is fragmentary because it is merely analogical.

This is in fact the way Freud himself conceived his essays; they resemble an archeological reconstruction which, starting from a few architectural details, sketches out the entire monument by affording them a probable context. Later we will examine Freud's general interpretation of cultural productions, but even at this point we can see that these fragmentary essays are held together by the systematic unity of his point of view. Thus is explained the peculiar character of these essays, their amazing minuteness of detail and the rigorousness—rigidity even—of the theory that coordinates these fragmentary studies with the great fresco of dreams and the neuroses. Taken in isolation from one another, each of the studies is neatly delimited. *Jokes and Their Relation to the Unconscious* is a brilliant but prudent generalization of the laws of the dream-work and of fictional satisfaction in the realm of the comic and the humorous. The interpretation of Jensen's *Gradiva* makes no pretension of presenting a general theory of the novel, but aims rather at rejoining the theory of dreams through the fictional dreams that a novelist unversed in psychoanalysis attributes to his hero and through the quasi-analytic cure to which he leads him. In "The Moses of Michelangelo," the statue is treated as a singular piece of art, but no general theory of genius or of artistic creation is proposed. As for the *Leonardo da Vinci*, it does not, in spite of appearances, go beyond the modest title, *Leonardo da Vinci and a Memory of His Childhood;* the only things illuminated are a few peculiarities of Leonardo's artistic destiny, like streaks of light in a painting of a scene in shadows—streaks of light, empty spaces of light, which may be, as we shall see, only voiced darkness.

None of these essays go beyond the simple structural analogy of work to work, of the dream-work to artistic work, and, so to speak, of vicissitude to vicissitude, of the vicissitude of instincts to the destiny of the artist.

To explicate this oblique mode of insight I follow in some detail a few of Freud's analyses. Without limiting myself to a strict historical order, I will begin with the short paper of 1908, "Creative Writers and Daydreaming." [4] Two reasons justify putting it first. In the first place, this short and seemingly insignificant essay is a perfect illustration of the indirect approach to esthetic phenomena through a series of increasingly closer comparisons. The creative writer is like a child at play: "He creates a world of fantasy which he takes very seriously—that is, which he invests with large amounts of emotion [*Affektbeträge*]—while separating it sharply from reality [*Wirklichkeit*]." [5] From play we proceed to fantasy, not through some vague resemblance, but on the assumption of a necessary connection, namely, that man never gives anything up, but only exchanges one thing for another by forming substitutes. In this way the adult, instead of playing, turns to creating fantasies; and fantasies, in their function as substitutes for play, are daydreams, castles in the air. This brings us to the threshold of poetry, the middle link being furnished by the novel, i.e. by art works in narrative form. Freud sees in the fictional history of the novelist's hero the figure of "His Majesty the Ego"; [6] it is presumed that the other forms of literary creation could be linked with this prototype through an uninterrupted series of transitional cases.

Thus the outlines of what might be called the oneiric in general are delineated. In a striking maneuver of abridgment, Freud brings

4. "Der Dichter und das Phantasieren," *GW, 7*, 213–23; "Creative Writers and Daydreaming," *SE, 9*, 143–53.

5. *GW, 7*, 214; *SE, 9*, 144.

6. *GW, 7*, 220; *SE, 9*, 150. Cf. "On Narcissism: An Introduction," *GW, 10*, 157; *SE, 14*, 91.

together the two ends of the chain of the fantastic—dreams and poetry. Both are manifestations of the same fate, the fate of unhappy, unsatisfied man: "The motive force of fantasies [*Phantasien*] are unsatisfied wishes, and every single fantasy is the fulfillment of a wish, a correction of unsatisfying reality." [7]

Does this mean we are simply to repeat *The Interpretation of Dreams?* Two sets of remarks indicate that such is not the case. First, it is no accident that the chain of analogies includes the phenomenon of *play;* we shall learn in the essay *Beyond the Pleasure Principle* that play implies a mastery over absence, and such mastery is of a different nature than the mere hallucinatory fulfillment of desires. Nor, secondly, is the comparison with daydreams devoid of significance; in daydreams fantasies bear a "date-mark" (*Zeitmarke*) which pure unconscious thoughts, being timeless, do not have. Unlike pure unconscious fantasying, imaginative activity has the power of stringing together the present of a current impression, the past of infancy, and the future of a situation to be realized. Later on we shall pursue the connection between these two sets of remarks.

On the other hand, this short study contains in its closing paragraph an important suggestion which takes us back from the fragmentary aspect to the systematic aim. Not being able to penetrate into the innermost dynamism of artistic creation, we might at least be able to say something about the relation between the *pleasure* it gives rise to and the *technique* it employs. If dreams are a work, it is only natural that psychoanalysis approaches the work of art from its "artisanal" side, in order to disclose, with the help of a structural analogy, a far more important functional analogy. Thus the investigation must be oriented toward overcoming resistances. The broadest aim of a work of art is to enable us to enjoy our own fantasies without self-reproach or shame. Two procedures are alleged to serve that intention: the creative writer softens the egoism of daydreams by appropriate alterations and disguises, and he bribes or allures us by a yield of purely formal pleasure attached to the presentation of his fantasies. "We give the name of an *incentive bonus,* or a *fore-pleasure,* to a yield of pleasure such as this, which is

7. *GW, 7,* 216; *SE, 9,* 146.

offered to us so as to make possible the release of still greater pleasure arising from deeper psychical sources." [8]

This sweeping conception of esthetic pleasure as the detonator of profound discharges constitutes the most daring insight of the entire psychoanalytic esthetics. The connection between artistic technique and its hedonistic effect can be used by Freud and his school as a clue in the most penetrating investigations. It meets the conditions of modesty and coherence required of an analytic interpretation. Instead of raising the immense problem of creativity, one explores the limited problem of the relations between the pleasurable effect and the technique employed in producing the work of art. This reasonable question remains within the restricted competence of an economics of desire.

In *Jokes and Their Relation to the Unconscious* (1905), Freud outlines a few precise steps leading to the economic theory of forepleasure. What this brilliant and meticulous essay sets before us is not a theory of art as a whole, but the study of a precise phenomenon, a precise pleasurable effect, pinpointed by the discharge of laughter. Within these narrow limits, however, the analysis goes very deep.

Starting with a study of the verbal techniques of *Witz,* Freud finds therein the essential aspects of the dream-work: condensation, displacement, representation by the opposite, etc., thus verifying the repeatedly postulated reciprocity between work, which is subject to an economics, and rhetoric, which admits of interpretation. But while Witz verifies the linguistic interpretation of the dream-work, dreams in turn furnish the lineaments of an economic theory of the comic and of humor. This is where Freud extends and goes beyond the work of Theodor Lipps (*Komik und Humor,* 1898). But above all, this is where we encounter the enigma of forepleasure. Witz is open to analysis in the proper sense, that is, a separating process that isolates the slight pleasure caused by mere verbal technique from the deeper pleasure set in motion by the technical pleasure and which the play of obscene, aggressive, or cynical words brings to the fore. The connection between technical and instinctual pleasure constitutes the core of Freudian esthetics

8. *GW*, *7*, 223; *SE*, *9*, 153.

and relates that esthetics to the economics of instincts and pleasure. Assuming that pleasure is connected with a reduction of tension, the pleasure arising from technique is minimal and is connected with the economy in psychical expenditure realized by condensation, displacement, etc. For example, pleasure in nonsense frees us from the restrictions that logic imposes on our thinking and makes the yoke of the intellectual disciplines easier to bear. But although this pleasure is slight, as is the economy in expenditure to which it gives expression, it has the noteworthy power of contributing, in the form of a bonus, to erotic, aggressive, and cynical tendencies. Freud here makes use of a theory of Fechner's concerning the "assistance" or convergence of pleasures and integrates it with a scheme of functional release that stems more from Hughlings Jackson than from Fechner.[9]

This link between the technique of a work of art and the production of a pleasurable effect is the thread that serves both as guide and as the element giving rigor to the psychoanalytic esthetics. One could even classify the esthetic essays according to their greater or lesser conformity to the model of the interpretation of *Jokes*. "The Moses of Michelangelo" would be the leading example of the first group, *Leonardo da Vinci* the leading example of the second. (We shall see that what at first perplexes us in the *Leonardo* study is perhaps also what will subsequently be most thought-provoking regarding the true analytic explanation in the field of art as well as in other fields.)

A striking feature of "The Moses of Michelangelo" [10] is that the interpretation of the masterpiece is constructed from details, as in the interpretation of a dream. This properly analytic method enables one to superpose dream-work and creative work, dream interpretation and art interpretation. Instead of seeking to explain in a sweeping generalization the nature of the satisfaction works of art give rise to—a task in which too many psychoanalysts have become lost—the analysis attempts to resolve the general enigma of esthet-

9. *Der Witz und seine Beziehung zum Unbewussten* (1905), *GW, 6,* 53–54; *Jokes and Their Relation to the Unconscious, SE, 8,* 136–38.

10. "Der Moses des Michelangelo" (1914), *GW, 14,* 172–201; *SE, 13,* 211–36.

ics by taking the roundabout path of focusing on one outstanding work and the meanings created by it. The patience and minuteness of this interpretation are well known. Here, just as in a dream analysis, what counts is the precise and to all appearances minor fact, and not the impression of the whole: the position of the index finger of the prophet's right hand, the sole finger to have effective contact with the flow of the beard, whereas the rest of the hand is withdrawn; the tilted position of the tablets about to slip from the pressure of the arm. From the details of this split-second posture, frozen as it were in stone, the interpretation reconstructs the chain of conflicting movements that have found in this arrested movement a sort of unstable compromise. In a gesture of wrath, Moses is thought to have first raised his hand to his beard, at the risk of letting the tablets fall, while at the same time his glance was violently drawn toward the spectacle of the idolatrous people. But a counter movement, canceling the first and incited by the lively consciousness of his religious mission, is supposed to have pulled his hand back. What we have before our eyes is the residue of a movement which has taken place and which the analyst sets out to reconstruct, just as he reconstructs the opposed ideas that give rise to compromise formations in dreams, neuroses, slips of the tongue, and jokes. Digging still deeper beneath this compromise formation, Freud discovers several layers in the thickness of the apparent meaning. Beyond the exemplary expression of a conflict that has been overcome, an artistic expression worthy of guarding the tomb of the Pope, the analyst also discerns a secret reproach against the violence of the dead pontiff and, further still, a warning the artist addresses to himself.

With this last trait, "The Moses of Michelangelo" breaks through the limits of a mere applied psychoanalysis. The essay does not restrict itself to verifying the analytic method; it points to a type of overdetermination that will be seen more clearly in the *Leonardo*, in spite of or because of the misunderstandings the *Leonardo* seems to engender. This overdetermination of the symbol embodied in the statuary indicates that analysis does not close explanation off, but rather opens it to a whole density of meaning. The "Moses" of Michelangelo says more than meets the eye; its overdetermination concerns Moses, the dead Pope, Michelangelo—and perhaps Freud himself in his ambiguous relationship to Moses. An endless commentary opens up, which, far from reducing the enigma, multiplies it. Is this not an admission that the psychoanalysis of art is essentially interminable?

I now come to the *Leonardo*.[11] Why did I begin by calling it an occasion and source of misunderstanding? For the simple reason that this essay, profuse and brilliant, seems to encourage the wrong sort of psychoanalysis of art—biographical psychoanalysis. Did not Freud attempt to capture the mechanism of esthetic creation in general, in its relation to sexual inhibitions or perversions on the one hand and to the sublimation of the libido into curiosity and scientific research on the other? Did he not reconstruct, on the sole basis of his interpretation of the vulture fantasy—which was not, incidentally, a vulture!—the riddle of Mona Lisa's smile? Does he not say that the memory of the lost mother and of her excessive kisses is transformed into the fantasy of the vulture's tail in the infant's mouth, into the homosexual attitude of the artist, and into the unfathomable smile of Mona Lisa? "It was his mother who possessed the mysterious smile—the smile that he had lost and that had fascinated him so much when he found it again in the Florentine lady." [12] The same smile is repeated in the two mother images in the "Saint Anne" grouping: "For if the Gioconda's smile called up in his mind the memory of his mother, it is easy to understand how it drove him at once to create a glorification of motherhood, and to give back to his mother the smile he had found in the noble lady." [13] And further: "The picture contains the synthesis of the history of his childhood: its details are to be explained by reference to the most personal impressions in Leonardo's life." [14]

> The maternal figure that is further away from the boy—the grandmother—corresponds to the earlier and true mother, Caterina, in its appearance and in its spatial relation to the boy. The

11. *Eine Kindheitserinnerung des Leonardo da Vinci* (1910), *GW, 8*, 128–211; *Leonardo da Vinci and a Memory of His Childhood, SE, 11*, 63–137.

12. *GW, 8*, 183; *SE, 11*, 111.

13. *GW, 8*, 183; *SE, 11*, 111–12.

14. *GW, 8*, 184; *SE, 11*, 112.

> artist seems to have used the blissful smile of St. Anne to disavow and to cloak the envy which the unfortunate woman felt when she was forced to give up her son to her better-born rival, as she had once given up his father as well.[15]

What renders this analysis suspect—according to the criteria we have taken from the work on *Jokes*—is that Freud seems to go far beyond the structural analogies that would be authorized by an analysis of the technique of composition and enters into instinctual themes that the painting disavows and conceals. Is this not the very pretension that fosters bad psychoanalysis—the analysis of the dead, the analysis of writers and artists?

Let us take a closer look at the matter. In the first place it should be noted that Freud does not actually speak of Leonardo's creativity, but of his being inhibited by his spirit of research: "The aim of our work has been to explain the inhibitions in Leonardo's sexual life and in his artistic activity." [16] The actual object of the essay's first chapter is Leonardo's creative shortcomings, which occasion some of Freud's most remarkable observations about the relations between knowledge and desire. Within this limited framework, moreover, the transformation of the instinct of curiosity is seen as an irreducible vicissitude of repression. Repression, Freud says, can lead either to the inhibition of curiosity itself, which thus shares the fate of sexuality (this is the type of neurotic inhibition), or to obsessions of a sexual coloring in which thinking is itself sexualized (this is the obsessional type). But

> in virtue of a special disposition, the third type, which is the rarest and most perfect, escapes both inhibition of thought and neurotic compulsive thinking. . . . The libido evades the fate of repression by being sublimated from the very beginning into curiosity and by becoming attached to the powerful instinct for research as a reinforcement. . . . The quality of neurosis is absent; there is no attachment to the original complexes of infantile sexual research, and the instinct can operate freely in the service of intellectual interest. Sexual repression, which has made the in-

15. *GW, 8,* 185 (*verleugnet und überdeckt*); *SE, 11,* 113–14.
16. *GW, 8,* 203–04; *SE, 11,* 131.

> stinct so strong through the addition to it of sublimated libido, is still taken into account by the instinct, in that it avoids any concern with sexual themes.[17]

It is quite clear that with all this we have done nothing but describe and classify, and that by calling the riddle sublimation we only make it the more puzzling. Freud readily admits this in his conclusion. It is all well and good to say that artistic activity derives from sexual desires, and that these deep instinctual layers were released by regression to the childhood memory awakened by his meeting with the Florentine lady: "With the help of the oldest of all his erotic impulses he enjoyed the triumph of once more conquering the inhibition in his art." [18] But this only sketches the outlines of a problem: "Since artistic talent and capacity are intimately connected with sublimation we must admit that the nature of the artistic function is also inaccessible to us along psychoanalytic lines." [19] And a bit further on: "Even if psychoanalysis does not throw light on the fact of Leonardo's artistic power, it at least renders its manifestations and its limitations intelligible to us." [20]

Within this limited scope Freud proceeds, not to an exhaustive inventory, but to a limited excavation *beneath* four or five puzzling traits treated as archeological remains. Here the interpretation of the vulture's tail—treated precisely as a remnant—plays the pivotal role. Such an interpretation, seeing that it cannot be a true psychoanalysis, remains purely analogical. It is arrived at through a number of converging signs taken from disparate sources: first, the psychoanalysis of homosexuals with its own series of themes (erotic relationship to the mother, repression and identification with the mother, narcissistic object-choice, projection of the narcissistic object onto an object of the same sex, etc.); second, the sexual theory held by children concerning the maternal penis; and last, mythological parallels (the phallus of the vulture goddess as seen in archeology). It is in a purely analogical mode that Freud writes: "The child's assumption that his mother has a penis is thus the com-

17. *GW, 8,* 148; *SE, 11,* 80.
18. *GW, 8,* 207; *SE, 11,* 134.
19. *GW, 8,* 209; *SE, 11,* 136.
20. Ibid.

mon source from which are derived the androgynously-formed mother goddesses such as the Egyptian Mut and the vulture's *'coda'* in Leonardo's childhood fantasy." [21]

Now, what insight does this give us into the work of art itself? This is where a misunderstanding of the meaning of Freud's *Leonardo* can be of more help to us than the interpretation of "The Moses of Michelangelo."

On a first reading we think we have unmasked the smile of Mona Lisa and disclosed what lies hidden behind it; we have *shown* the kisses the rejected mother lavished on Leonardo. But let us listen with a more critical ear to this sentence: "It is possible that in these figures Leonardo denied the unhappiness of his erotic life and has triumphed over it in his art, by representing the wishes of the boy, infatuated with his mother, as fulfilled in this blissful union of the male and female natures." [22] This sentence has the same ring as the one we quoted from the "Moses" analysis. What is meant here by "denied" and "triumphed over"? Might the representation that fulfills the boy's wish be something other than a mere repetition of the fantasy, an exhibition of desire, a simple bringing to light of what was hidden? Would interpreting Mona Lisa's smile imply something more than simply to *show*, in the master's paintings, the fantasy disclosed by the analysis of the childhood memory? These questions lead us from an overconfident explanation to a doubt of a second degree. The analsyis has not led us from the less to the better known. The kisses Leonardo's mother showered on the boy's lips are not a reality I could use as a starting point, a solid ground on which I could construct an understanding of the work of art; the mother, the father, the boy's relations to them, the conflicts, the first love wounds—all these no longer exist except in the mode of a signified absence. If the artist's brush recreates the mother's smile in the smile of Mona Lisa, it must be said that the memory of it exists nowhere else but in this smile, itself unreal, of the Gioconda, which is signified only by the presence of the color and pattern of the painting. The Gioconda's smile undoubtedly takes us back to the

21. *GW, 8,* 167; *SE, 11,* 97.
22. *GW, 8,* 189 (*verleugnet und künstlerisch überwunden*); *SE, 11,* 117–18.

"childhood memory of Leonardo da Vinci," but this memory only exists as a symbolizable absence that lies deep beneath Mona Lisa's smile. Lost like a memory, the mother's smile is an empty place within reality; it is the point where all real traces become lost, where the abolished confines one to fantasy. It is not therefore a thing that is better known and that would explain the riddle of the work of art; it is an intended absence which, far from dissipating the initial riddle, increases it.

It is precisely here that the *doctrine*—by which I mean the "metapsychology"—guards us from the excesses of its own applications. We never have access, it will be remembered, to instincts as such, but only to their psychical expressions, their representatives in the form of ideas and affects. Hence the economics is dependent upon the deciphering of a text; the balance sheet of instinctual investments or cathexes is read only through the screen of an exegesis bearing on the interplay between the signifier and the signified. Works of art are a prominent form of what Freud himself called the "psychical derivatives" of instinctual representatives. Properly speaking, they are *created* derivatives. By that I mean that the fantasy, which was only a signified absence (the analysis of the childhood memory points precisely to this absence), finds expression as an existing work in the storehouse of culture. The mother and her kisses exist for the first time among works offered to the contemplation of men. Leonardo's brush does not recreate the memory of the mother, it creates it as a work of art. That is the sense in which Freud could say that "in these figures Leonardo denied the unhappiness of his erotic life and has triumphed over it in his art." The work of art is thus both symptom and cure.

These last remarks enable us to anticipate some of the problems we will be concerned with in our dialectical investigation.

1. To what extent is psychoanalysis justified in submitting works of art and dreams to the unitary viewpoint of an economics of instincts when the former are a durable and, in the strong sense of the term, memorable creation of our days, whereas the latter are a fleeting and sterile product of our nights? If works of art last and live on, is it not because they enrich the patrimony of cultural values with new meanings? And if they have this power, is it not because

they proceed from a specific work, the work of an artisan who embodies meaning in an obdurate matter, communicates this meaning to a public, and thus opens man to a new self-understanding? This difference in value is not overlooked by psychoanalysis; analysis indirectly approaches it through the notion of sublimation. But sublimation is as much a problem as a solution.[23] In any case, it may be said that the object of psychoanalysis is not simply to *accept* the difference between the sterility of dreams and the creativity of art but rather to treat it as a difference that *poses a problem* within a single problematic of desire. Psychoanalysis thereby rejoins Plato's view on the deep-seated unity of poetry and love, Aristotle's view on the continuity of purgation with purification, and Goethe's view on demonism.

2. This common ground between psychoanalysis and a philosophy of creation may be seen in another point. Works of art are not only socially valuable; as was seen in the example of "The Moses of Michelangelo" and in that of *Leonardo,* and as will be strikingly shown in the discussion of Sophocles' *Oedipus Rex,* they are also creations which, as such, are not simply projections of the artist's conflicts, but the sketch of their solution. Dreams look backward, toward infancy, the past; the work of art goes ahead of the artist; it is a prospective symbol of his personal synthesis and of man's future, rather than a regressive symbol of his unresolved conflicts. But it is possible that this opposition between regression and progression is only true as a first approximation. Perhaps it will be necessary to transcend it, in spite of its apparent force. The work of art sets us on the pathway to new discoveries concerning the symbolic function and sublimation itself. Could it be that the true meaning of sublimation is to promote new meanings by mobilizing old energies initially invested in archaic figures? This is the direction, it would seem, in which Freud himself invites us to look when he distinguishes sublimation from inhibition and obsession in *Leonardo,* and when even more strongly he opposes sublimation to repression in the essay "On Narcissism." [24]

23. We reserve the general discussion of sublimation for Chapter 4 of the "Dialectic," where we will also give the reasons for this postponement.
24. Cf. above, pp. 128–29.

But to go beyond this opposition between regression and progression, it is first necessary to have elaborated it and to have carried it to the point where it destroys itself. That will be one of the themes of our "Dialectic."

3. This invitation to deepen psychoanalysis by confronting it with other and seemingly diametrically opposed points of view gives a hint as to the true meaning of the limits of psychoanalysis. Those limits are in no way fixed; they are mobile and they can be transgressed indefinitely. They are not, properly speaking, rigid boundaries, in the manner of a closed door on which would be written "thus far and no farther." A limit, as Kant has taught us, is not an external boundary but a function of a theory's internal validity. Psychoanalysis is limited by what justifies it, namely, its decision to recognize in the phenomena of culture only what falls under an economics of desire and resistances. I must admit that this firmness and rigor makes me prefer Freud to Jung. With Freud I know where I am and where I am going; with Jung everything risks being confused: the psychism, the soul, the archetypes, the sacred. It is precisely this internal limitation of the Freudian problematic that will invite us, in a first phase, to oppose to it another explanatory point of view that would seem more appropriate to the constitution of cultural objects as such, and then, in a second phase, to find in psychoanalysis itself the reason for going beyond it. The discussion of Freud's *Leonardo* gives a hint of that movement. The explanation in terms of the libido has led us not to a terminus but to a threshold; interpretation does not uncover a real *thing,* not even a psychical thing; the desire to which interpretation refers us is itself a reference to the series of its "derivatives" and an indefinite self-symbolization. This abundance of symbolism lends itself to investigation by other methods, phenomenological, Hegelian, and even theological; the justification for these other approaches and their relation to psychoanalysis will have to be discovered in the semantic structure of symbols themselves. The psychoanalyst, it may be noted in passing, should be prepared for this confrontation by his own culture, not, of course, in order to learn to set external boundaries to his own discipline, but in order to enlarge it and find *within* it the reasons for ever extending the boundaries that have

already been reached. Psychoanalysis thus invites us to move from a first and purely reductive reading to a second reading of cultural phenomena. The task of that second reading is not so much to unmask the repressed and the agency of repression in order to *show* what lies behind the masks, as to set free the interplay of references between signs: having set out to find the absent reality signified by desire—the smile of the *lost* mother—we are referred back by this very absence to another absence, to the unreal smile of the Gioconda. The only thing that gives a presence to the artist's fantasies is the work of art; and the reality thus conferred upon them is the reality of the work of art itself within a world of culture.

Chapter 2: From the Oneiric to the Sublime

The sublime refers less to a single problem than to a complex of highly ramified difficulties. Freud speaks not of the sublime but of sublimation, but by this word he indicates the process by which man, with his desires, effects the ideal, the supreme, that is to say, the sublime.

1. First, the word indicates a certain displacement of the center of gravity of interpretation from the repressed to that which represses. Because of this "thematic displacement," interpretation is unavoidably drawn into the area of cultural phenomena. The repressing agency makes its appearance as the psychological expression of a prior social fact, the phenomenon of authority, which includes a number of constituted historical figures: the family, the mores of a group, tradition, explicit or implicit education, political and ecclesiastical power, penal and, in general, social sanctions. In other words, desire is no longer by itself; it has its "other," authority. What is more, it has always had its other in the repressing agent, an agent internal to desire itself. Henceforward it will be even less possible to regard the psychoanalysis of culture as a mere application of the theory of dreams and the neuroses. Of course, psychoanalysis remains bound by its previous hypotheses; all events and situations, including the phenomena of culture, are to be considered only from the viewpoint of the cost of pleasure and unpleasure. Culture comes within the scope of psychoanalysis only as it affects the balance sheet of the individual's libidinal investments or cathexes. The question of ideals is very precisely determined in psychoanalysis by this insertion of the cultural theme into the economic problematic. But the economic problematic is not left unscarred by this confrontation; what is called the second topography,

which finds its most remarkable expression in *The Ego and the Id* (1923), states, at the theoretical level, the profound changes imposed upon interpretation. The second topography expresses the repercussion of the new theme on the earlier problematic. Hence we cannot start from the second topography, but must take it as the point of arrival; it sums up all the revisions of the metapsychology required by the applications of psychoanalysis to culture; these revisions, ruled in the beginning by the first state of the system, have in fact created a new systematic state that is precisely the second topography.

2. But the impact of cultural phenomena on the psychoanalytic "theory" is not a direct one; in order to integrate this new material into interpretation, psychoanalysis has to make extensive use of *genetic* explanation. The reason for this is clear: the repressed, as we have said, has no history ("the unconscious is timeless"); what does is the repressing agency; it is history: the individual's history from infancy to adulthood, and mankind's history from prehistory to history. Hence the thematic displacement requires a methodological displacement; interpretation must now become involved in the construction of a new type of model, genetic models. Their purpose is to coordinate an ontogenesis and a phylogenesis within one fundamental history, which could be called the history of desire and authority. What matters in this history is the way authority affects desire. *Totem and Taboo* is not a book of ethnology, nor is *Group Psychology and the Analysis of the Ego* a book of social psychology, nor is the history of the Oedipus complex a chapter in child psychology. All these writings are a part of psychoanalysis, insofar as the genetic method and the ethnological or psychological documents embodied in that method are but one of the steps in the psychoanalytic interpretation. These genetic models—the formation and dissolution of the Oedipus complex, the killing of the father and the covenant between the brothers, etc.—will have to be understood not only as tools meant to coordinate ontogenesis and phylogenesis, but as instruments of interpretation meant to subordinate every history—that of mores, of beliefs, of institutions—to the history of desire in its great debate with authority. We shall then see that within this debate a more fundamental debate is formed

and mediated, one perceived ever since the beginning of psychoanalysis but fully formulated only at the end: the debate between the pleasure-unpleasure principle and the reality principle. One may presume that the true place of ethnology in Freud's work will not be easy to determine; the ethnology is a necessary step, but one that has no meaning of its own. Nor, consequently, will it be easy to say to what extent psychoanalysis is affected by the frailty—obsoleteness—of its ethnological hypotheses.

3. Thus the thematic and methodological displacements imposed by the consideration of ethical phenomena (in the broad sense where *ethos* means mores or *Sittlichkeit,* i.e. customs or actual morality) are merely steps leading to a new formulation of analytic "theory." We shall have to see how the second topography consolidates these various displacements. Which is more important in this new expression of the topography, the fact that all the processes that were clinically described and genetically explained are reduced to the earlier topographic-economic point of view, or the transformation of the topography under the pressure of new facts? It is easy to foresee that sublimation, so far described merely as one of the vicissitudes of instinct, will be the point where all these discussions crystallize.

THE CLINICAL AND DESCRIPTIVE APPROACHES TO INTERPRETATION

We have roughly characterized the new theme as a thematic shift of attention from the repressed to the agent of repression. Strictly speaking, this point of view was never absent; it even dates from the birth of psychoanalysis, since from its earliest days analysis was understood as a struggle against resistances.[1] Thus, what we will be dealing with under the heading of "the sublime" is something that analytical experience has always had to face. The same theme was prominent in the theory of dreams and the neuroses under the heading of defense or censorship; thus this was the theme at the origin of the process of distortion (*Entstel-*

1. Letter 72 of October 27, 1897, in *The Origins of Psychoanalysis,* p. 226.

lung). Finally, the entire metapsychology, insofar as it was organized about the instinctual vicissitude called repression, was less a theory of the repressed than a theory of the relationship between the repressed and that which represses.

Still, there are legitimate reasons for speaking of a thematic displacement. The agencies of the second topography are not so much places as roles in a personology. Ego, id, and superego are variations on the personal pronoun or grammatical subject; what is involved is the relation of the personal to the anonymous and the suprapersonal in the individual's coming-to-be.[2]

The question of the ego is not, indeed, the question of consciousness, for the question of the act of becoming conscious, a central theme of the first topography, does not exhaust the question of the coming-to-be of the ego. The two questions were never confused by Freud, nor can the two words consciousness and ego be taken as equivalents. Up to now we have seen the question of the ego stated in a series of polarities: ego-instincts and sexual instincts (prior to the essay "On Narcissism"), ego-libido and object-libido (beginning with "On Narcissism"). In the latter theory, which may be called the general libido theory, the ego is thematized and has become interchangeable with objects; it thus admits of being loved or hated. In this sense one may speak of an erotic function of the ego. However, the true problematic of the ego is not yet determined; it lies beyond the alternative of being loved or hated and is expressed basically in the alternative of dominating or being dominated, of being master or slave. This question is not the question of consciousness. Consciousness, increasingly treated according to an embryological model, is the seat of all the relations with exteriority; Freud will say that it is a "surface" phenomenon. Consciousness is being-for-the-outside; this was already apparent in the "Project," where consciousness has to do with the testing of the indications of reality. Of course, the process of becoming conscious is something quite different; but Freud always tried to understand this process as

2. The earliest allusion to the later theory of the superego is to be found in the text of 1897: "*Multiplicity of Psychical Personalities*. The fact of identification may perhaps allow of this phrase being taken literally" (Draft L, joined to Letter 61 of May 2, 1897, *Origins*, p. 199).

a variety of perception—on the model, therefore, of a surface phenomenon; for Freud, internal perception is the analogue of external perception; that is why he speaks, in generalizing, of consciousness-perception (*Cs.-Pcpt.*). All the modalities of consciousness—temporal organization, concatenation of energy, and so on—which in the paper on "The Unconscious" are opposed to the characteristics of the unconscious, stem from its function as a surface. The network of the functions of consciousness constitutes, in Freud's works, the sketch of a true transcendental esthetic, perfectly comparable to Kant's, inasmuch as it groups together all the conditions of "exteriority."

The question of the ego, i.e. of domination, is completely different. This question may be introduced by the theme of danger or threat, the primary phenomenon of nonmastery. The ego finds itself threatened, and in order to defend itself must dominate the situation. From the outset Freud had noted that it is easier to defend oneself against an external danger than against an internal danger; from the former there is often the possibility of flight, and perception itself may be interpreted as a screen or, better, as a barrier against excitations from without. Man is essentially a being threatened from within; hence to external dangers must be added the menace of the instincts (the source of anxiety) and the menace of conscience (the source of guilt). This threefold danger and threefold fear constitute the problematic that gives rise to the second topography. Like Spinoza, Freud approaches the ego through its initial situation of slavery, i.e. of nonmastery. Thus he also rejoins the Marxist concept of alienation and the Nietzschean concept of weakness. The ego is primarily that which is weak in the face of menace. The famous description given in *The Ego and the Id* (Ch. 5) of the "poor creature" menaced by three masters, reality, the libido, and conscience, is well known. The distinction we make between the process of becoming conscious and the coming-to-be of the ego is undoubtedly too schematic; the two processes of vigilance and domination can only be distinguished by abstraction. This is all the more true inasmuch as certain traits attributed to consciousness in the first topography are now assigned to the ego, just as traits attributed to the unconscious are now attributed to the id, although the unconscious and the id do not coincide, since "large portions of the ego and superego are unconscious." [3] However, it is well to hold onto this guide: to be oneself is to maintain one's role, to be master of one's acts, to dominate. The neurotic is essentially one who is not "master in his own house," as we are told in an essay we shall refer to later, "A Difficulty in the Path of Psychoanalysis." [4]

However, this is not what is most remarkable and, at first view, most disconcerting: it is not only the neurotic who is not his own master, but also and above all the man of morality, the ethical man. The value of all the psychoanalytic investigations concerning the moral phenomenon stems from the fact that man's relation to obligation is first described in a situation of weakness, of nondomination. There is obviously a striking affinity here between Freud and Nietzsche.

This condition of weakness, menace, and fear was transcribed by Freud into the relationship of the ego to the superego.

Let us begin with Freud's terminology. In the third chapter of *The Ego and the Id,* Freud speaks of "the ego ideal or superego." Are these terms synonymous? Not exactly. The difference is in fact twofold: whereas the ego ideal designates a descriptive aspect, a manifestation in which the superego is deciphered, the superego is not a descriptive concept but a construct, an entity on a par with the topographic and economic concepts we considered in Part I; hence we shall leave the question of the superego for later and begin with a consideration of the ego ideal. What complicates things, however, is that not only are the concepts of ego ideal and superego on different epistemological levels, but at their respective levels they do not even have the same extension. In the *New Introductory Lectures,* where Freud put the greatest order into his terminology, the ego ideal is regarded merely as the third function of the superego, along with self-observation and "conscience" (*Gewissen*).[5] This fluctuation in terminology is not surprising: in addition to the fact that these concepts all have an exploratory character, the

3. *New Introductory Lectures, GW, 15,* 75; *SE, 22,* 69.

4. See below, "Dialectic," Ch. 2, pp. 426–27.

5. "But let us return to the superego. We have allotted it the functions of self-observation, of conscience [*das Gewissen*] and of [maintaining] the ideal [*das Idealfunktion*]" (*GW, 15,* 72; *SE, 22,* 66).

procedure of psychoanalysis implies that they remain approximate. One reason for this is that they do not designate any primal function. For psychoanalysis, there is no intelligibility peculiar to the ethical phenomenon; to understand the birth of the superego is simply to understand the superego; it is what it has become. Hence we cannot go very far in describing the functions of the superego without appealing to the history of their constitution; what will lead us to a genetic explanation is in fact a certain inconsistency in description. A second reason is that the phenomena to be described necessarily present themselves in a random fashion; what unifies them—the superego—is not a reality subject to description, but rather a theoretical concept. In description, the phenomena are highly disparate and even opposed to one another; the theoretical concept unites them and even identifies them with each other. The third and final reason is that several of the phenomena we are going to consider are themselves the result of interpretation. Resistance, for example, is not a simple phenomenon; it is revealed by the absence of ideas, by amnesia, as well as by flight to another theme, or by the production of painful sensations; thus resistance, like the repressed, is arrived at through inference. The same goes for the "unconscious sense of guilt," which is by no means a phenomenal but rather an inferred reality (I do not dispute here the legitimacy of this expression, which Freud himself questions).[6] Freud places the origin of the theory of the superego in the discovery of the resistance to becoming conscious and in the discovery of the sense of guilt, both of which were encountered in analysis as obstacles to treatment.

Having made these reservations, let us consider the three functions of the superego enumerated in the *New Introductory Lectures:* self-observation, conscience, and the formation of an ideal.

By self-observation Freud designates a certain splitting of the ego, experienced as the feeling of being observed, watched, criticized, condemned: the superego reveals itself as a watchful gaze.

6. Concerning the right of speaking about unconscious feelings, cf. "The Unconscious," Section III. We discussed the problem above, pp. 145–46. The expression "unconscious sense of guilt" occurs very early ("Obsessive Actions and Religious Practices," *GW, 7,* 135; *SE, 9,* 123); it reappears in *The Ego and the Id* at the end of Ch. 2 and is discussed at some length in Ch. 5 in the context of the death instinct.

Conscience, on the other hand, designates the severity and cruelty of the superego; conscience objects to certain actions, like Socrates' demon which says "No," and punishes with reproaches once the action has been taken. Thus the ego is not only watched but ill-treated by its inner and superior other. It scarcely needs emphasizing that these two characteristics of observing and condemning derive not from a Kantian type of reflection upon the condition of the good will, upon the a priori structure of obligation, but from clinical observation. The split between the observing agency and the rest of the ego is revealed, greatly magnified, in the delusions patients have of being observed, and the cruelty of the superego is manifested in the pathology of melancholia.

The ideal-function of the superego is described as follows: the superego "is also the vehicle of the ego ideal by which the ego measures itself, which it emulates, and whose demand for ever greater perfection it strives to fulfill." [7] At first view, it would seem that this analysis is not patterned on pathology. For is it not a question here of moral aspiration, as desire to emulate a model, to measure oneself by it, to alter one's ego according to it? The above text allows this interpretation. However, Freud is more attentive to the forced aspect of the response given by the ego to the demands of the superego than to the spontaneity of that response; he is concerned more with the ego's submission than with its striving. Moreover, when placed next to the first two characteristics, this third function takes on a coloring which may well be said to be pathological, in the clinical and the Kantian sense of the word. Kant spoke of the pathology of desire; Freud speaks of the pathology of duty, in the three modes of observation, condemnation, and idealization.

Will such an analysis be rejected because it views conscience not as a primal given but as something to be deciphered through the screen of the clinical? The advantage of the Freudian "prejudice" is that it begins without taking anything for granted: by treating moral reality as an a posteriori reality, constituted and sedimented, Freud's analysis avoids the laziness that is part of any appeal to the a priori. As for the clinical approach, it enables us, by means of analogy, to denounce the inauthenticity of the ordinary conscience. The approach through pathology reveals the initially alienated and

7. *New Introductory Lectures, GW, 15,* 71; *SE, 22,* 64–65.

alienating situation of morality; a pathology of duty is just as instructive as a pathology of desire: ultimately, the former is merely the prolongation of the latter. The ego oppressed by the superego is in a situation, with respect to this internal foreigner, analogous to that of the ego confronted by the pressure of its own desires; because of the superego we are "foreign" to ourselves: thus Freud speaks of the superego as an "internal foreign territory."[8] This hidden affinity between desire and the sublime—in topographical language, between the id and the superego—is what the genetic interpretation will try to explain and the economics of ideals to systematize.

We must not, of course, demand from psychoanalysis what it cannot give: namely, the origin of the ethical problem, i.e. its ground and principle; but it can give its source and genesis. The difficult problem of identification has its roots here. The question is this: How can I, by starting from another—say, from the father—become myself? Thought that begins by rejecting the primordial givenness of the ethical ego has the advantage of placing the whole focus of attention on the process of the internalization of the external. Thereby is revealed not only an affinity with Nietzsche, but also the possibility of a confrontation with Hegel and his concept of the reduplication of consciousness whereby consciousness becomes self-consciousness. Of course, by rejecting the primordial givenness of the ethical phenomenon, Freud can encounter morality only as a wounding of desire, as interdiction and not as aspiration. But the limitation of his point of view has its counterpart in coherence: if the ethical phenomenon is first given in a wounding of desire, it is open to a general erotic theory, and the ego, exposed to its three masters, remains subject to an interpretation involving an economics.

THE GENETIC WAYS OF INTERPRETATION

"Since [the superego] goes back to the influence of parents, educators, and so on, we learn still more of

8. Ibid., *GW, 15*, 62 (*inneres Ausland*); *SE, 22*, 57.

its significance if we turn to those who are its sources." This statement from the *New Introductory Lectures* [9] aptly expresses the function of genetic explanation in a system that acknowledges neither the primordial givenness nor the ethical dimension of the Cogito; [10] here genesis takes the place of ground.

There is no contesting of the fact that Freudianism, in its basic intention, is not just a variety of evolutionism or moral geneticism. However, a study of the texts bears out the assertion that psychoanalysis, having made a dogmatic beginning, renders its own explanation increasingly problematic in proportion as it puts it to use.

For one thing, the proposed genesis does not constitute an exhaustive explanation. The genetic explanation reveals a source of authority—the parents—that merely transmits a prior force of constraint and aspiration; the text we have just cited continues as follows: "a child's superego is in fact constructed on the model not of its parents but of its parents' superego; the contents which fill it are the same and it becomes the vehicle of tradition and of all the time-resisting judgments of value which have propagated themselves in this manner from generation to generation." [11] There is no question, therefore, of looking to the genetic explanation for a justification of the obligatory or of the acceptable as such; these are given in the world of culture. The explanation simply delimits the earliest phenomenon of authority without truly exhausting it. In this sense, the genesis of morality according to Freudian psychoanalysis is actually a paragenesis. Because of its infinite complexity, the genesis falls back on an economic explanation of the superego as an agency belonging to the same system as the id. The question is whether the economic explanation will completely cover the problem inherited from the individual and collective history of the superego.

Secondly, we must not expect too much from the genetic explanation. Even when reduced to a role of intermediary between clinical description and economic explanation, the genesis proves to be surprisingly complex and ultimately disappointing. Is it a psycho-

9. *GW, 15,* 72–73; *SE, 22,* 67.
10. Cf. below, "Problematic," pp. 44–46.
11. *New Introductory Lectures, GW, 15,* 72–73; *SE, 22,* 67.

logical explanation? Yes, if one considers that the Oedipus complex is the decisive crisis from which arises, by virtue of the well-known mechanism of identification, each individual's structure as a personal ego. But this ontogenesis of the superego—besides leaving untouched the problem of the obligatory as such—makes an appeal on its own historical plane to a sociological explanation: the Oedipus complex involves the family and in general the social phenomenon of authority. Thus Freud is led from ontogenesis to phylogenesis, hoping to find in the institution of the prohibition of incest and in institutions generally the sociological counterpart of the Oedipus complex. But, as an examination of *Totem and Taboo* will make quite evident, psychoanalysis is condemned to have recourse to an ethnology that is fanciful, at times fantastic, and in any event always secondhand; in the end, analysis psychologizes the social phenomenon. Just when it looks to social phenomena for the missing proof of the derived character of the superego, it is reduced to working out a psychological explanation of taboo, thus cutting off the branch on which it placed its credentials. This is a further reason for switching from an infinite genesis to an economic explanation. As may be seen, a number of surprises and deceptions await us on this roundabout path through the genetic explanation. Let us try, then, to retrace this movement from ontogenesis to phylogenesis and back again.

Every reader of Freud's early writings is struck by the decisive manner in which the Oedipus complex was discovered; in one stroke it was revealed both as an individual drama and as the collective fate of mankind, as a psychological fact and as the source of morality, as the origin of neurosis and as the origin of civilization.

Individual, personal, intimate, the Oedipus complex gets its "secret" character from the fact that Freud discovered it in his self-analysis; at the same time, its universality is seen in the details of that singular experience. To begin with, the Oedipus situation immediately takes its place in the etiology of the neuroses, for it replaces an earlier hypothesis of which it is the reverse. We recall the faith Freud had in the theory of the child's seduction by the adult, a theory suggested by the accounts of that scene which his patients related to him during analysis. The Oedipus complex is the theory of seduction in reverse; or rather, the seduction by the father turns out to be the distorted presentation of the Oedipus complex: the father does not seduce the child, but rather the child, in wishing to possess its mother, desires the death of the father. The seduction scene must be understood as a "screen memory" of the Oedipus complex; the latter very naturally takes the place of the earlier fantasy.[12]

Placed within the etiology of the neuroses, it is also located within the structure of culture: "Another presentiment tells me, as if I knew already—though I do not know anything at all—that I am about to discover the source of morality." [13] The amazing thing about this discovery is that it is directly accompanied by the conviction that this singular adventure is also a paradigm of destiny. That is how I interpret the strict parallel between Freud's self-analysis and the interpretation of the Greek myth of Oedipus. Being honest with oneself coincides with grasping a universal drama.[14]

12. The letters to Fliess of 1897 constitute an important document in this connection: whereas previously "blame was laid on perverse acts by the father" (Letter 69), the Oedipus complex now represents "the father's innocence" and a sexual activity must be assigned to the early years of infancy; the primal scene fantasies were intended to cover up this infantile sexuality; see also "On the History of the Psychoanalytic Movement" (1914), *GW, 10,* 55–61; *SE, 14,* 17–18. Concerning Freud's self-analysis and his own Oedipus complex, see Letter 69, 70, 71: the absence of any active role on the part of his father, the pious and thieving nurse of his childhood ("my instructress in sexual matters"), sexual curiosity about his mother, jealousy of his brother, the ambiguous position of his older nephew, etc. On all this see also Jones, *Life and Work, 1,* Ch. 14. In addition, concerning the transfer of the young Sigmund's affection onto his friend Fliess and of his hostility onto his colleague Breuer, cf. Jones, *1,* 305–08; Anzieu, *L'Auto-analyse,* pp. 59–73. The first allusion to the Oedipus complex is to be found in Draft N which accompanies Letter 64 of May 31, 1897. The notion of "screen memories" is treated systematically in an article of 1899, *GW, 1,* 531–54; *SE, 3,* 303–22.

13. Letter 64 of May 31, 1897, *Origins,* p. 206.

14. "Only one idea of general value has occurred to me. I have found love of the mother and jealousy of the father in my own case too, and now believe it to be a general phenomenon of early childhood, even if it does not always occur so early as in children who have been made hysterics. (Similarly with the 'romanticization of origins' in the case of paranoiacs—heroes, founders of religion.) If that is the case, the gripping power of *Oedipus Rex,* in spite of all the rational objections to the inexorable fate that

The relation is reciprocal: self-analysis discloses the "gripping power," the "compulsion" of the Greek legend; the myth in turn is evidence of the fate—I mean the character of nonarbitrary destiny—that attaches to the singular experience. Perhaps in this global insight into the coincidence between singular experience and universal destiny must be sought the underlying motivation, which no ethnological inquiry can exhaust, of all Freud's attempts to relate ontogenesis, the individual *secret,* with phylogenesis, the universal *destiny.*

The scope of this universal drama is seen from the outset; it is shown in the extension of the interpretation of *Oedipus Rex* to the personage of Hamlet: if "the hysteric Hamlet" hesitates to kill his mother's lover, it is because within him lies "the obscure memory that he himself had meditated the same deed against his father because of passion for his mother." [15] A brilliant and decisive comparison, for if Oedipus reveals the aspect of destiny, Hamlet reveals the aspect of guilt attached to the complex. It is no coincidence that Freud cites Hamlet's phrase as early as 1897, and again in *Civilization and Its Discontents:* "So conscience doth make cowards of us all"; on which Freud comments: "His conscience is his unconscious feeling of guilt." [16]

What makes the individual secret a universal—and ethical—destiny, if not the involvement in institutions? The Oedipus complex is incest dreamed; but "incest is anti-social and civilization consists in a progressive renunciation of it." [17] Thus repression, which belongs to the individual's history of desire, coincides with one of the most formidable cultural institutions, the prohibition of

---

the story presupposes, becomes intelligible, and one can understand why later fate dramas were such failures. Our feelings rise against any arbitrary, individual fate such as shown in the *Ahnfrau* [the title of a play by Grillparzer], etc., but the Greek myth seizes on a compulsion which everyone recognizes because he has felt traces of it in himself. Every member of the audience was once a budding Oedipus in fantasy, and this dream-fulfillment played out in reality causes everyone to recoil in horror, with the full measure of repression which separates his infantile from his present state" (Letter 71 of October 15, 1897, *Origins,* pp. 223–24).

15. Letter 71, p. 224.
16. Ibid.
17. Draft N, May 31, 1897, *Origins,* p. 210.

incest. The Oedipus situation sets up the great conflict between civilization and the instincts on which Freud will repeatedly comment from " 'Civilized' Sexual Morality and Modern Nervous Illness" (1908) and *Totem and Taboo* (1912–13), to *Civilization and Its Discontents* (1930) and *Why War?* (1933). Thus repression and culture, intrapsychical institution and social institution, coincide in this paradigmatic case.

From this tangle of insights the psychological genesis proceeds in one direction, the sociological genesis in another. The first line is initiated by *The Interpretation of Dreams* and the *Three Essays on Sexuality*, the second by *Totem and Taboo*.

The Interpretation of Dreams transcribes almost literally the great discoveries of the preceding years, now known to us through the "Letters to Fliess"; but at the same time the cultural import of those discoveries is concealed. The interpretation of the Oedipus complex is placed among the examples of dreams of the death of loved relatives, which come under the heading of typical dreams; the latter appear in the chapter dealing with "The Material and Sources of Dreams"—prior, therefore, to the great chapter on "The Dream-Work." [18] This arrangement is quite misleading, and even more so the treatment of the Oedipus complex as a mere oneiric theme. The Greek legend merely serves to confirm the "universal validity" of the hypothesis "put forward in regard to the psychology of children." [19] Our dreams show that the explanation of the tragedy lies in each of us: "King Oedipus, who slew his father Laïus and married his mother Jocasta, merely shows us the fulfillment of our childhood wishes. . . . Here is one in whom these primeval [*urzeitlich*] wishes of our childhood have been fulfilled, and we shrink back from him with the whole force of the repression by which those wishes have since that time been held down within us." [20] Thus the great conflict between civilization and instincts is projected onto the intrapsychical plane and more precisely onto the screen of dreams: "There is an unmistakable indication in the text of Sophocles' tragedy itself that the legend of Oedipus sprang from

18. Cf. our discussion above, pp. 101–02 and n. 27.
19. *GW*, *2/3*, 267; *SE*, *4*, 261.
20. *GW*, *2/3*, 269; *SE*, *4*, 262–63.

some primeval [*uralt*] dream-material which had as its content the distressing disturbance of a child's relation to his parents owing to the first stirrings of sexuality."[21] Jocasta herself explains to Oedipus his own history as a typical and universal dream:

> "Many a man ere now in dreams hath lain
> With her who bare him. He hath least annoy
> Who with such omens troubleth not his mind."

And Freud concludes: "The story of Oedipus is the reaction of the imagination to these two typical dreams [of possessing one's mother and of the death of one's father]. And just as these dreams, when dreamt by adults, are accompanied by feelings of repulsion, so too the legend must include horror and self-punishment."[22]

Why this apparent reduction of the cultural significance of the Oedipus complex in *The Interpretation of Dreams?* Besides Freud's skill in this book in distilling the truth and presenting it in a semi-concealed fashion, I would also mention his concern to avoid excursions into contingent circumstances of culture, such as his passing explanation of certain traits of the father-son hostility as a residue in our middle-class culture of the *potestas patris familias* of ancient Rome.[23] If one does not wish to limit oneself to a sociocultural explanation, which is precisely what so many neo-Freudians have done, it is necessary to go back to the archaic or primeval constitution of sexuality. That is why Freud here subordinates the institutional aspect of the Oedipus complex to the fantasy aspect and looks for the latter in dreams common to neurotics and to normal subjects.[24] However, within this context peculiar to *The Interpretation of Dreams* definite emphasis is placed upon the aspect of universal destiny that the myth alone reveals—what I will call the hyperpsychological and hypersociological dimension of the myth.

21. *GW, 2/3,* 270; *SE, 4,* 263–64.
22. *GW, 2/3,* 270; *SE, 4,* 264.
23. "All of this is patent to the eyes of everyone. But it does not help us in our endeavour to explain dreams of a parent's death in people whose piety towards their parents has long been unimpeachably established. Previous discussions, moreover, will have prepared us to learn that the death-wish against parents dates back to earliest childhood" (*GW, 2/3,* 263; *SE, 4,* 257).
24. *GW, 2/3,* 263–67; *SE, 4,* 257–61.

The *universal* character of the incestuous impulse is confirmed by the sudden discovery that all men share the destiny of Oedipus; and that common destiny is in turn confirmed by "the profound and universal power" of the legend itself. The myth is of course reduced to a dream fantasy; but this fantasy is universal, for it springs "from some primeval dream-material." Therefore, the complex will forever bear the name of the myth, even when psychoanalysis seems to explain the myth by the oneiric fantasy; the myth alone is what immediately stamps the dream as "typical." [25]

The *Three Essays on the Theory of Sexuality* are an important step toward the strictly psychological interpretation of the Oedipus complex. All the later theses concerning the role of the Oedipus complex in the establishment of the superego presuppose the existence of an infantile sexuality; hence the immense importance of the *Three Essays*. More precisely, the *Three Essays* supply the interpretation of the Oedipus complex with two basic themes: that of the *structure* of infantile sexuality, and that of its *history* or *phases*.

More than this or that particular thesis concerning "the sexual aberrations," "infantile sexuality," or "the transformations of puberty" (the titles of the *Three Essays*), what this short book essen-

25. "If *Oedipus Rex* moves a modern audience no less than it did the contemporary Greek one, the explanation can only be that its effect does not lie in the contrast between destiny and human will, but is to be looked for in the particular nature of the material on which that contrast is exemplified. There must be something which makes a voice within us ready to recognize the compelling force of destiny in the *Oedipus* . . . His destiny moves us only because it might have been ours—because the oracle laid the same curse upon us before our birth as upon him" (*GW, 2/3,* 269; *SE, 4,* 262). A few pages later, speaking of *Hamlet* and *Macbeth,* Freud concludes: "But just as all neurotic symptoms, and, for that matter, dreams, are capable of being 'overinterpreted' [*der Ueberdeutung fähig*] and indeed need to be, if they are fully to be understood, so all genuinely creative writings are the product of more than a single interpretation" (*GW, 2/3,* 272; *SE, 4,* 266). This "overinterpretation" does not seem to me reducible to the ordinary "overdetermination" through condensation or displacement; the latter would seem to lead to a single interpretation—precisely the one that explains the overdetermination. In the fourth chapter of the "Dialectic" I will try to work out a true "overinterpretation." We will discover some new aspects of Freud's text on Sophocles' *Oedipus* that fully justify this notion of overinterpretation; cf. below, "Dialectic," Ch. 4.

tially intended to show is the weight of prehistory in man's sexual history—a prehistory obliterated, as it were, by a careful "amnesia," to which we shall return later. Once the interdict barring us from access to infantile sexuality has been raised, great and terrible truths rise up: the objects and aims with which we are acquainted in an estate of culture are secondary functions of a much broader tendency capable of every sort of "transgression" and "perversion." A disconnected bundle of instincts, including cruelty, is ever on the verge of coming undone, with the resultant formation of neurosis as the negative of perversion. Civilization is built up at the expense of the sexual instincts, through the restriction of their use and in reaction against the threat of their potential perversity (in this period, Freud uses the general term sublimation to cover the diversion of sexual forces from their aims to new aims that are socially useful).[26]

This whole network of ideas is the background for the specific psychology of the Oedipus complex; in fact, there is no discussion of the Oedipus complex which does not sooner or later touch upon the group of themes of the *Three Essays*—the existence of infantile sexuality, its polymorphous structure, its disposition to perversion. Infantile incest, presupposed by the Oedipus complex, is only a particular instance of this general theme.

But the interpretation of the Oedipus complex is also indebted to the *Three Essays* for the first detailed elaboration of the theme of the "stages" or "organizations" of the libido, a genetic theme which is the indispensable complement of the structural theme. It is true that the differentiation of the stages is not yet carried very far in the second essay. In the edition of 1915, the section dealing with the phases of development of sexual organization still recognizes only two "pregenital organizations," the oral organization and the sadistic-anal organization; but the fundamental distinction between the sexual and the genital is established, not only in its structural sig-

26. "Historians of civilization appear to be at one in assuming that powerful components are acquired for every kind of cultural achievement by this diversion of sexual instinctual forces from sexual aims and their direction to new ones—a process which deserves the name of 'sublimation.' To this we would add, accordingly, that the same process plays a part in the development of the individual and we would place its beginning in the period of sexual latency of childhood" (*Three Essays on the Theory of Sexuality*, *GW*, *5*, 79; *SE*, *7*, 178).

nificance, but in its historical elaboration; this distinction is the fundamental condition of all the subsequent analyses. At a later date (1923), and in the following editions of the *Three Essays,* this distinction will enable Freud to modify his account by relating the Oedipus complex to another pregenital organization, the phallic stage, hence to a stage posterior to auto-erotism, a stage where the libido already has a vis-à-vis, but where, in return, sexuality has failed through lack of organization. To this phallic organization will be related the threat of castration, with the result that in 1924, the dissolution of the Oedipus complex can be explained both by the threat of castration and by the lack of organization and maturation of the corresponding stage. All this is present in germ in the theory of stages in *Three Essays.* Even the theme of identification finds support in the theory of stages, inasmuch as the "prototype" of this identification is the incorporation or devouring of the oral or cannibalistic stage.[27]

It is not difficult to see the importance of this brief book, valued very highly by its author, for the explication of the Oedipus complex. It moves in line with one of the most tenacious tendencies of Freud's thought, namely his insistence on "prehistory," [28] a theme shared by Marx and Freud; a prehistory which has its own laws and, so to speak, its own history.

This weight of prehistory promotes a type of pessimism which is very characteristic of Freud and which all the varieties of neo-Freudianism have tried to soften or eliminate. We have already seen it in different forms: the "indestructibility of wishes" in *The Interpretation of Dreams,* the "timelessness" of the unconscious in the "Papers on Metapsychology." What the *Three Essays* add to this basic theme is the idea of an original deviation of sexuality, deviation as to the object, deviation as to the aim: in his conclusion Freud says that "a disposition to perversions is an original and universal disposition of the human sexual instinct and . . . normal sexual behavior is developed out of it as a result of organic changes and psychical inhibitions occurring in the course of maturation." [29] Thus human sexuality is the seat of a debate analogous to the

27. *GW,* 5, 98 (*Vorbild*); *SE,* 7, 198 (prototype).
28. *GW,* 5, 73 (*Vorzeit*); *SE,* 7, 173 (the primeval period).
29. *GW,* 5, 132; *SE,* 7, 231.

one the sophists inaugurated concerning language, the debate between *physis* and *nomos*. Like language, human sexuality is the result of institution as much as of nature; the theme of perversion, which has sometimes been looked upon as a carry-over from middle-class morality, is there to remind us that "by nature" the libido holds in reserve all the "infractions" of ordinary morality. Genital union is always a victory over the libido's original dispersion toward zones, aims, and objects regarded as deviations from the mainstream of genital heterosexuality. Perverts and neuropaths are the human evidence of this original aberration of human sexuality. Fixation and regression to earlier stages are specifically human possibilities inscribed in the structure and history of this "prehistory."

Hence, institutionalization is necessarily painful: man is educated only by "renouncing" archaic practices, by "abandoning" former objects and aims; institutionalization is the counterpart of that "polymorphously perverse" structure. Because the adult remains subject to the infant he once was, because he can lag behind and regress, because he is capable of archaism, conflict is no mere accident which he might be spared by a better social organization or a more suitable education; human beings can experience entry into culture only in the mode of conflict. Suffering accompanies the task of culture like fate, the fate illustrated by the Oedipus tragedy. Possibility of aberration and necessity of repression are correlative;[30] cultural renunciation, similar to the work of mourning men-

30. In the *Three Essays* the expression "mental dams" is frequently encountered (*SE, 7*, 177, 232). This notion does not conflict with the mechanism in question; three "developments" (*GW, 5*, 138–41; *SE, 7*, 237–39) are considered: the first leads to perversion, which results from the failure of the genital zone to dominate the other aims and zones; the second leads to neurosis, when the sexual instinct undergoes repression and continues its existence underground; the third leads to sublimation, when the tendency finds an outlet and use in other fields: "Here we have one of the origins of artistic activity; and, according to the completeness or incompleteness of the sublimation, a characterological analysis of a highly gifted individual, and in particular of one with an artistic disposition, may reveal a mixture, in every proportion, of efficiency [*Leistungsfähigkeit*] perversion and neurosis" (*GW, 5*, 140; *SE, 7*, 238). Repression, sublimation, and reaction-formation (treated here as a subspecies of sublimation—cf. "Dialectic," Ch. 3), are three fairly close mechanisms and come together in what we call a person's character (ibid.).

tioned above, holds the place occupied by fear in the Hegelian dialectic of Master and Slave; identification with the father will enable us shortly to pursue this comparison with the Hegelian notion of recognition. The discovery of the death instinct is already in the *Three Essays;* the many allusions to cruelty will allow us to pursue further the comparison between Hegel and Freud. This is the somber background against which the Oedipus episode unfolds.

Why is this crisis more important than the others, so important that Freud would almost have it be the sole pathway to neurosis and culture alike? [31] Against this apparent aggrandizement of the Oedipus incident, one might legitimately object that all transitions —both in the order of aims and in the order of objects—are crises and renunciations and that the Oedipus drama is but a segment in the general drama which Freud calls "the finding of an object" [32] and which, from nursing to weaning, together with the experience of the absence of loved objects, is simply a long history of the "choosing of objects" and the "giving up of objects," of elections and deceptions; the barrier against incest is, after all, merely one of the ways of checking desire, and one that is quite comparable to the other ways (weaning, absence, withdrawal of affection). However, what gives the prohibition of incest a unique position in this rude schooling of desire, and more particularly in the education in object-choice, is precisely its cultural dimension. The *Three Essays* put this very clearly:

> Respect for this barrier is essentially a cultural demand made by society. Society must defend itself against the danger that the interests which it needs for the establishment of higher social units

31. A footnote added in 1920 is very explicit: "It has justly been said that the Oedipus complex is the nuclear complex [*Kernkomplex*] of the neuroses, and constitutes the essential part of their content. It represents the peak of infantile sexuality, which, through its after-effects, exercises a decisive influence on the sexuality of adults. Every new arrival on this planet is faced by the task of mastering the Oedipus complex; anyone who fails to do so falls a victim to neurosis. With the progress of psychoanalytic studies the importance of the Oedipus complex has become more and more clearly evident; its recognition has become the shibboleth that distinguishes the adherents of psychoanalysis from its opponents" (*GW*, *5*, 127–28; *SE*, *7*, 226).

32. *GW*, *5*, 123 ff.; *SE*, *7*, 222 ff.

> may be swallowed up by the family; and for this reason, in the case of every individual, but in particular of adolescent boys, it seeks by all possible means to loosen their connection with their family—a connection which, in their childhood, is the only important one.[33]

In this text, the horror of incest is seen as an attainment of civilization which every new individual must appropriate to himself if it has not already been fixed by heredity; the explanation of its origin is switched, therefore, from psychology to ethnology.

Does phylogeny take us any further than ontogeny?

That is what an examination of *Totem and Taboo* will enable us to determine. As far as possible we shall put aside the definite problem of the origin of religious belief, that is, belief in the existence of gods, which Freud derives, as we know, from the totemic institution. It will of course be impossible to separate taboo from totem for very long, for it is precisely Freud's thesis that moral prohibitions are derived from primitive taboo prohibitions and that the latter are grounded in the totemic kinship, itself interpreted as a historical and collective Oedipus complex. Nevertheless it is legitimate [34] to make as thorough an investigation of the book as possible without bringing in its weakest point, namely, the historical Oedipus complex of primitive peoples, which is perhaps merely a scientific myth substituted for Sophocles' tragic myth and projected, as a sort of "primitive scene," behind Freud's self-analysis and the psychoanalysis of his patients.

33. *GW, 5,* 127 (*die Inzestschranke*); *SE, 7,* 225. A footnote of 1915 clearly indicates that this is the level on which the correlation is established between the *Three Essays* and *Totem and Taboo*. The former work's notion of a "barrier against incest" coincides with the latter's notion of "taboo."

34. Freud authorizes this relative separation: "It will be found that the two principle themes from which the title of this little book is derived—totems and taboos—have not received the same treatment. The analysis of taboos is put forward as an assured and exhaustive attempt at the solution of the problem. The investigation of totemism does no more than declare that 'here is what psychoanalysis can at the moment contribute towards elucidating the problem of the totem'" (Preface). Toward the beginning of the first essay, Freud adds that "exogamy had originally—in the earliest times and in its true meaning—nothing to do with totemism, but became attached to it (without there being any underlying connection) at some time when marriage restrictions became necessary" (*GW, 9,* 8–9; *SE, 13,* 4).

If, then, we begin by staying clear of the scientific myth of totem, and remain at the level of the book's first two essays ("The Horror of Incest" and "Taboo and Emotional Ambivalence"), what do we find in *Totem and Taboo?* Little more than an applied psychoanalysis, that is to say, one that has been transposed from dreams and the neuroses to taboo. In these two essays, Freud proposes a psychoanalytic interpretation of a rather limited ethnological subject matter. It would be useless to look to them for an ethnological elucidation of the problem of institutionalization; this problem is raised but left unresolved by the psychoanalytic interpretation. It will be the function of the final ethnological myth to make the transition from a mere applied psychoanalysis (in which the model of dreams and neuroses is extended to taboo) to a theory of totem, where ethnology will be regarded as solving the enigma posed by the psychology of the Oedipus complex.

If, in the first two essays of *Totem and Taboo,* the psychoanalysis of taboo scarcely goes beyond an applied psychoanalysis, it is because of the book's two postulates (which are not, however, peculiar to it): on the one hand, primitive peoples give us a well-preserved picture of an early phase of our own development and so constitute an experimental illustration of our prehistory; on the other hand, because of their great emotional ambivalence, they are akin to neurotic patients. By applying psychoanalysis to ethnography, Freud believes he is doing two things at once: he affords the ethnologist an explanation of what the latter describes but does not understand, and he gives the public—and his incredulous colleagues—the experimental proof of the truth of psychoanalysis. The counterpart of this operation is that without the totemic myth the psychoanalytic explanation of taboo goes no further than that of dreams and the neuroses and runs up against the fact of prohibition and, behind prohibition, the fact of institutionalization or authority.

Let us follow the movement of the proof, without dwelling on the details of arguments of no interest to us here. The initial core is the prohibition of incest: the most primitive of primitive peoples—"these poor naked cannibals"—"set before themselves with the most scrupulous care and the most painful severity the aim of avoiding incestuous sexual relations. Indeed, their whole social organization seems to serve that purpose or to have been brought into relation with its attainment."[35] The social instrument of this prohibition is the famous law of exogamy, which was treated extensively by Frazer in his *Totemism and Exogamy,* and according to which there is "*a law against persons of the same totem having sexual relations with one another and consequently against their marrying.*"[36] The basis of the prohibition is therefore the fact of belonging to the same totem; hence, in spite of our effort to bracket the totemic myth and only consider taboo, we must immediately introduce the totemic bond that is the basis of the prohibition; the substitution of a totem kinship for blood relationship is what supports the entire edifice. It may be seen, however, that the important factor at this level of the analysis is not belief in the totem, nor even belief in the mystical nature of the bond of totem kinship, but the social fact of the substitution of "group marriage" for sexual promiscuity. Exogamy is the means of effecting this substitution; in other words, the prohibition is the counterpart of the change of level of sexuality;[37] reduced to this minimum, the interpretation of the prohibition against incest in *Totem and Taboo* rejoins the interpretation of the Oedipus complex in the *Three Essays on Sexuality.*

35. *GW, 9,* 6; *SE, 13,* 2.

36. *GW, 9,* 8; *SE, 13,* 4.

37. Freud, following L. H. Morgan, rightly saw that "classification" is the language of these new relations; speaking of marriage classes in a system of two classes and three subclasses, he notes: "While, however, totemic exogamy gives one the impression of being a sacred ordinance of unknown origin—in short, of being a custom—the complicated institution of the marriage classes, with their subdivisions and the regulations attaching to them, look more like the result of deliberate legislation, which may perhaps have taken up the task of preventing incest afresh because the influence of the totem was waning" (*GW, 9,* 14; *SE, 13,* 9). Thus the classification reinforces and is eventually substituted for the prohibition of sacred origin. Freud is close here to the structuralism of his day, with this difference—which is obviously considerable—that the classification is secondary with respect to the mystical bond of the totem. However, the difference should not be exaggerated: even in this appeal to the totemic bond, what counts is the attainment of culture, which consists in the substitution of a social relationship for spontaneous sexual activity; this biological-social change of level is the positive and primary achievement as compared with the negative and secondary achievement of the prohibition of incest.

That is the extent of the strictly ethnological contribution of the first two essays of *Totem and Taboo*. At this point the book's direction is reversed; what follows is a psychoanalytic explanation of the horror of incest, rather than a sociological explanation of institutionalization whose negative aspect is the prohibition of incest; the enigma of institutionalization is left to the later scientific myth: "All that I have been able to add to our understanding of [the horror of incest] is to emphasize the fact that it is essentially an *infantile* feature and that it reveals a striking agreement with the mental life of neurotic patients." [38] Thus the dominant idea comes from the discovery of the incestuous theme of neurosis; the horror of incest displayed by savages merely supplies proof of the existence, in the open air as it were, of this central complex now lost in the unconscious. The strictly institutional and structuring function of the prohibition is lost sight of. I explain this shift in two ways: first, during the period of the first topography, that is, prior to the discovery of the superego, Freud did not yet possess the theoretical concept of identification but had to rely instead on the rather unwieldy idea of a reaction-formation on the part of a higher psychical organization; [39] we will see the decisive role the essay of 1921, *Group Psychology and the Analysis of the Ego,* plays in this connection. Secondly, Freud is much more concerned with justifying the pathogenic role of the Oedipus complex in the neuroses than in establishing its structuring and institutional role. Ethnology plays the role of experimental verification; that is the most that can be said in defense of the Freudian ethnology: it is merely an accessory scaffolding of the theory of the neuroses. In this respect, *Totem and Taboo* still belongs to the cycle of "analogical" interpretations, by which we have characterized applied psychoanalysis.[40]

38. *GW, 9,* 24; *SE, 13,* 17. When Freud published separately the four essays of *Totem and Taboo* in the review *Imago,* he gave them the title "Some Points of Agreement Between the Mental Lives of Savages and Neurotics."

39. *Three Essays on Sexuality, GW, 5,* 78–79; *SE, 7,* 178. In a footnote in the 1915 edition, Freud distinguishes between sublimation and reaction-formation, whereas the text of 1905 ascribes both of these to the "mental dams"—"disgust, shame and morality" (ibid.).

40. A certain importance must undoubtedly be attached to the dispute with Jung, who published his "Wandlungen und Symbole der Libido" in

The pattern of the analogy is furnished by the structural affinity between taboo and obsessional neurosis: the former functions as a collective neurosis, the latter as an individual taboo. Four characteristics assure the parallel: "(1) the fact that the prohibitions lack any assignable motive; (2) the fact that they are maintained by an internal necessity; (3) the fact that they are easily displaceable and that there is a risk of infection from the prohibited object; and (4) the fact that they give rise to injunctions for the performance of ceremonial acts." [41] But the most important point in this comparison lies in the analysis of emotional ambivalence. Here the interpretation of taboo serves as the pattern; a taboo is both the attractive and the fearful. This emotional composition of desire and fear throws much light upon the psychology of temptation and calls to mind St. Paul, St. Augustine, Kierkegaard, and Nietzsche. Taboo places us at a point where the forbidden is attractive because it is forbidden, where the law excites concupiscence: "the basis of taboo is a prohibited action, for performing which a strong inclination exists in the unconscious." [42]

From this point on, the burden of proof lies on the side of the neuroses. The phenomenon of authority, with which desire is confronted, is presupposed without being made explicit. "Dams" (to use an expression from the *Three Essays*) have already been imposed upon and opposed to desire, which has already become the desire to transgress. Consequently, in the remaining explanation of

---

1912 and his "Versuch einer Darstellung der Psychoanalytischen Theorie" in 1913: "The four essays that follow . . . offer a methodological contrast on the one hand to Wilhelm Wundt's extensive work, which applies the hypotheses and working methods of *non*-analytic psychology to the same purposes, and on the other hand to the writings of the Zurich school of psychoanalysis, which endeavour, on the contrary, to solve the problems of individual psychology with the help of material derived from social psychology" (*GW, 9,* 3; *SE, 13,* xiii). In *An Autobiographical Study* (1925), Freud will be more anxious to acknowledge his debt to Jung: "Later on, in 1912, Jung's forcible indications of the far-reaching analogies between the mental products of neurotics and of primitive peoples led me to turn my attention to that subject" (*GW, 14,* 92; *SE, 20,* 66). But this debt consists precisely in a "psychological" interpretation of ethnology.

41. *GW, 9,* 38–39; *SE, 13,* 28–29.

42. *GW, 9,* 42; *SE, 13,* 32.

taboo[43] Freud continues to pursue his interpretation instead of going back to its conditions and presuppositions. The interpretation spreads out to encompass features that are increasingly further removed from the central core of the ambivalence of the forbidden and the desired, and which are mostly taken from Frazer's *The Golden Bough* (ambivalent attitudes toward enemies, toward chiefs and kings, toward the dead). An intricate psychology or even psychopathology of taboo is worked out, whereas the properly institutional factor of prohibition is never elaborated.[44] The psychopathology often has far-reaching consequences. Thus, in the case of royal ceremonial a comparison with taboo ceremonial and obsessional ceremonial reveals that excessive respect is actually a figurative way of doing what is forbidden, a disguised expression of hostility, and that this hostility is connected with the father complex of childhood. Primitive peoples are the well-preserved evidence of the ambivalence of the psychical life; anxiety ultimately points to the force of desires and the "indestructibility and insusceptibility to correction which are attributes of unconscious processes."[45] Because he is a big child the savage gives us a clear picture on a fantastic scale of what in our present condition we see only in the highly concealed and softened figure of the moral imperative, or in the distorted features of obsessional neurosis. Thus emotional ambivalence is seen to be the "basis" not only of taboo conscience

43. The second essay.

44. In the next chapter we will see how the mechanism of "projection" explains the appearance of transcendence connected with the religious source of the forbidden and the feared; the mechanism of introjection, by which a source of authority is set up within the ego, is thus complicated by the mechanism of projection, by which the omnipotence of thought is projected into real powers—demons, spirits, and gods. Projection is not meant to account for institution as such, but for the illusion of transcendence attaching to the belief in spirits and gods, that is, in the real existence of powers higher than man. Projection is the economic means by which an intrapsychical conflict is, if not resolved, at least lessened; the externality of authority seems indeed to be irreducible; it is presupposed in the very definition of taboo: "Taboo is a primeval [*uraltes*] prohibition forcibly imposed (by some authority) from outside, and directed against the most powerful longings to which human beings are subject" (*GW*, *9*, 45; *SE*, *13*, 34–35).

45. *GW*, *9*, 88; *SE*, *13*, 70.

(and taboo sense of guilt) but also of the moral imperative as formalized by Kant.[46]

Did Freud think he had explained conscience by this emotional ambivalence? Certain texts, which deftly transform the analogy into a real relationship, would lead one to believe so.[47] But such ambivalence is merely the manner in which we experience certain human relations, once given the prohibition that flows from the presence of a tie superior to desire: the father figure in the Oedipus complex, the transition from biological relations to "group kinship" in the totemic system, lead us back to the first phenomenon of authority or institutionalization. But up to this point *Totem and Taboo* has thrown more light on the emotional repercussions of that phenomenon than on its origin "external" to desire. The psychology of temptation, to which the theme of emotional ambivalence belongs, makes us acutely aware of the lack of a more original dialectic of desire and law. What is left unsaid in these two essays is the fact of institutionalization itself.[48]

46. On this occasion, Freud connects *Gewissen* with *Wissen:* "For what is 'conscience' [*Gewissen*]? On the evidence of language it is related to that of which one is 'most certainly conscious' [*am gewissesten weiss*]. Indeed, in some languages the words for 'conscience' and 'consciousness' [*Bewusstsein*] can scarcely be distinguished. Conscience is the internal perception of the rejection of a particular wish operating within us. The stress, however, is upon the fact that this rejection has no need to appeal to anything else for support, that it is quite 'certain [*gewiss*] of itself' " (*GW*, *9*, 85; *SE*, *13*, 67–68).

47. "If I am not mistaken, the explanation of taboo also throws light on the nature and origin of *conscience*. It is possible, without any stretching of the sense of the terms, to speak of a taboo conscience or, after a taboo has been violated, of a taboo sense of guilt. Taboo conscience is probably the earliest form in which the phenomenon of conscience is met with. . . . In fact, one may venture to say that if we cannot trace the origin of the sense of guilt in obsessional neurotics, there can be no hope of our *ever* tracing it. This task can be directly achieved in the case of individual neurotic patients, and we may rely upon reaching a similar solution by inference in the case of primitive peoples" (ibid.). The whole subsequent history of morality seems to reduce itself to a history of ambivalence itself: "The only possible reason why [moral] prohibitions no longer take the form of taboos must be some change in the circumstances governing the ambivalence underlying them" (*GW*, *9*, 88; *SE*, *13*, 71).

48. Freud lifts a corner of the veil when he admits that "taboo is not a neurosis but a social institution [*Bildung*]" (ibid.), and that *"the fact which*

In order to fill in this gap, Freud posits at the origin of mankind a real Oedipus complex, an original parricide, of which all later history bears the scar. The last essay of *Totem and Taboo* works out a theory of totemism whose elements are borrowed from various sources and held together by an Oedipus complex projected into the prehistory of mankind. From Frazer—at least in *Totemism and Exogamy*—and Wundt, Freud derives the conviction that the social function of taboo depends upon the religious function of totemism, that the law of exogamy originates from the totem kinship—although this thesis was subject to much hesitation and changes of opinion on the part of Frazer himself and went against the general tendency of ethnologists to dissociate totemism and exogamy.[49] According to Freud, the savage's belief in actual descent from the totem is the reason why he must not kill the totem (or what stands for it) or marry women of the same group; we recognize here the two major prohibitions of the Oedipus complex. All that remains is to discover the father figure in the totem in order to secure the historical origin of the Oedipus complex.

The decisive link is supplied by psychoanalysis itself. The case of "little Hans" and that of a patient of Ferenczi's convinced Freud that the father is the masked theme of animal phobia in childhood: "The new fact that we have learnt from the analysis of 'little Hans' —a fact with an important bearing on totemism—is that in such

is characteristic of the neurosis is the preponderance of the sexual over the social instinctual elements" (*GW*, *9*, 91; *SE*, *13*, 73). But he immediately goes on to say that "the corresponding cultural formations, on the other hand, are based upon social instincts, originating from the combination of egoistic and erotic elements" (*GW*, *9*, 91; *SE*, *13*, 74). The difference comes up again in another manner: the neurotic, in subjection to the pleasure principle, flees reality, which he finds unsatisfying; but one of the fundamental characteristics of the real world from which the neurotic withdraws and excludes himself is the factor of "human society and of the institutions collectively created by it" (ibid.). How does it happen that this social creation and its resultant institutions are connected with the reality principle rather than with the pleasure principle? This is the question that remains unanswered in *Totem and Taboo*.

49. *GW*, *9*, 132, 146, 176; *SE*, *13*, 108, 120, 146. "Thus psychoanalysis, in contradiction to the more recent views of the totemic system but in agreement with the earlier ones, requires us to assume that totemism and exogamy were intimately connected and had a simultaneous origin."

circumstances children displace some of their feelings from their father onto an animal."[50] Deciphered in infantile neurosis, this displacement of the father theme onto an animal figure will henceforth serve as the guiding thread in the labyrinth of ethnological explanations; Freud is also encouraged in this direction by the parallel already stressed between the savage's emotional ambivalence toward taboo and the ambivalence of the child's relations to his father, the displacement onto the animal figure being the unsuccessful solution of that ambivalence. All that remains is to find a historical equivalent of the fantasy displacement seen in the case of little Hans; what this case presents in small letters must now be found written in the large letters of prehistory.

The discovery of the father complex in animal phobias would seem to be what led Freud to combine two decisive and quite venturesome features with the primary nucleus of the totem theory (the Frazer-Wundt nucleus). From Darwin and Atkinson[51] he takes over a theory of the primal horde, according to which the jealousy of the male is alleged to play the role of excluding the young males from sharing the females whom the leader wishes to monopolize, although it is not clear, at least in Darwin, just how force is transformed into right and jealousy into the law of exogamy.[52] Even more important, however, is the theory he takes from Robertson Smith, the author of *Religion of the Semites* (1889); Smith's theory of the totem meal will enable Freud to patch up the holes in his explanation. It is assumed that sacrifice at the altar plays the same part in all religions, that it is always an act

50. *GW, 9,* 157; *SE, 13,* 129. Ferenczi's contribution is essential, for from him Freud borrows the threat of castration that will later play such a large role, not "in direct relation with [the] Oedipus complex but on the basis of its narcissistic precondition, the fear of castration" (*GW, 9,* 157; *SE, 13,* 130). This theme will be taken up again in the paper on "The Dissolution of the Oedipus Complex" (1924).

51. J. J. Atkinson, *Primal Law* (London 1903).

52. The only allusion pointing toward Freud's explanation is the following: "The younger males, being thus expelled and wandering about, would, when at last successful in finding a partner, prevent too close interbreeding within the limits of the same family" (Darwin, *The Descent of Man* [1871], *2,* 362; quoted in *GW, 9,* 153; *SE, 13,* 125). One might find in this text a slight indication in favor of what we shall later call the covenant of the brothers.

of commensal fellowship between the deity and his worshipers, that the oldest form of sacrifice is the sacrifice of animals, that the slaughter of a victim is permissible for the clan but illegal for the individual, and finally that the sacrificial animal is identical with the ancient totem animal. Thus the totem meal would furnish the ethnological "proof," ever elusive, of the famous totemic kinship. To this schema, already quite simplified, there must be added "a few probable features": [53] the totem animal was cruelly slaughtered, devoured raw, then lamented and bewailed, as a prelude to the festive rejoicing.

The materials have now been gathered together. One has only to combine Frazer, Wundt, Darwin, Atkinson, and Robertson Smith to get the following story:

> One day the brothers who had been driven out came together, killed and devoured their father and so made an end of the patriarchal horde. United, they had the courage to do and succeeded in doing what would have been impossible for them individually. (Some cultural advance, perhaps command over some new weapon, had given them a sense of superior strength.) Cannibal savages as they were, it goes without saying that they devoured their victim as well as killing him. The violent primal father had doubtless been the feared and envied model of each one of the company of brothers: and in the act of devouring him they accomplished their identification with him, and each one of them acquired a portion of his strength. The totem meal, which is perhaps mankind's earliest festival, would thus be a repetition and a commemoration of this memorable and criminal deed, which was the beginning of so many things—of social organization, of moral restrictions and of religion.[54]

It is difficult to resist the impression that the Oedipus complex, deciphered in dreams and the neuroses, is what enabled Freud to select from the available ethnological materials just those factors that allow for the reconstruction of a collective Oedipus complex of mankind in the sense of an actual event that occurred at the begin-

53. *GW*, *9*, 169; *SE*, *13*, 140.
54. *GW*, *9*, 171–72; *SE*, *13*, 141–42.

ning of history. Identification with the totem and ambivalence in its regard are reified, so to speak, in what is now a literal, and not a symbolic, interpretation. If the dreamed animal in animal phobia stands for the father, the ethnological myth allows the father to be substituted for the animal. Thus the symbolic displacement in dreams and the neuroses is paralleled and counterbalanced by a real substitution which is supposed to have taken place in history: "All we have done is to take at its literal value an expression used by these people, which they have therefore been glad to keep in the background. Psychoanalysis, on the contrary, leads us to put special stress upon this same point and to take it as the starting point of our attempt at explaining totemism." [55]

The psychoanalytic interpretation of the Oedipus complex is thus extended into a realistic archeology; it preens itself on being a literal interpretation of totemism. The meaning of the Oedipus complex, deciphered in the semitransparency of dreams and the neuroses, solidifies into a real equivalence: the totem is the father; the father was killed and eaten; the brothers never got over their remorse for the deed; to reconcile themselves with their father and with themselves, they invented morality. We now have a real event in place of a fantasy; upon this first stone it is possible to erect all the other conflict situations which hitherto were only deciphered. Unfortunately, the truth is that the primal parricide is merely an event constructed out of ethnological scraps on the pattern of the fantasy deciphered by analysis. Taken as a scientific document, *Totem and Taboo* is simply a huge vicious circle in which an analyst's fantasy responds to the analysand's.

Consequently, one does psychoanalysis a service, not by defending its scientific myth as science,[56] but by interpreting it as myth. At the end of *Totem and Taboo,* Freud thinks he can derive Greek

55. *GW, 9,* 159–60; *SE, 13,* 131.

56. Freud saw, indeed, the many difficulties involved in this appeal to psychological heredity, that embarrassing version of the inheritance of acquired characteristics (*Totem and Taboo, SE, 13,* 155, 158). With increasing obstinacy, Freud will assume all its inconveniences in *Moses and Monotheism.* For the critique by the ethnologists, cf. B. Malinowski, *Sex and Repression in Savage Society* (New York, Humanities Press, 1927), especially Part III, Ch. 3. A. L. Kroeber, "An Ethnologic Psychoanalysis," *Am. Anthropologist, 22* (1920), 48–57; "Totem and Taboo in Retrospect," *Am.*

tragedy from the historic totem meal.[57] The truth of the matter is just the reverse: the Freudian myth is the positivist transposition, in terms of the ethnography of the beginning of the twentieth century, of the tragic myth itself. By this positivist transposition, Freud believes he is prefacing the fantasies of his patients and of his self-analysis with a true history. But this rational fantasy of Freud the man, later adopted by his school, is comparable to Plato's construction in Book IV of the *Republic,* where the philosopher sets out to read the "small letters" of the human soul, with its three powers, in the "large letters" of the City with its three social classes. The same goes for *Totem and Taboo:* in the father and sons of the Darwinian horde, Freud deciphers the jealousy of the father and the violent birth of society; in the totem meal of Robertson Smith's hypothesis, he deciphers the ambivalence of love and hate, of destruction and participation, which animates the symbolism of the meal through to its most brutal cannibalistic expression; in the mourning that precedes the festival, he deciphers object-loss, the narrow door of every metamorphosis of love; in remorse and deferred obedience, he deciphers the transition to social organization, through the double suffering arising from the crime and from renunciation. In short, by means of this new tragic myth he interprets the whole of history as inheriting the crime: "Society was now based on complicity in the common crime; religion was based on the sense of guilt and the remorse attaching to it; while morality was based partly on the exigencies of this society and partly on the penance demanded by the sense of guilt." [58]

By this new and apparently scientific myth, Freud breaks with

---

J. of Sociology, 45 (1939), 446–50; *Anthropology* (rev. ed. New York, Harcourt Brace, 1948), pp. 616–17. Claude Lévi-Strauss, *Les Structures élémentaires de la parenté* (Paris, P.U.F., 1949).

57. "But why had the Hero of tragedy to suffer? and what was the meaning of his 'tragic guilt'? I will cut the discussion short and give a quick reply. He had to suffer because he was the primal father, the Hero of the great primeval tragedy which was being re-enacted with a tremendous twist; and the tragic guilt was the guilt which he had to take upon himself in order to relieve the Chorus from theirs" (*GW, 9,* 188; *SE, 13,* 156). This interpretation of the tragic hero as the redeemer of the chorus, the chorus itself being identified with the company of brothers, allows Freud to locate Greek tragedy halfway between the totem meal and the Passion of Christ.

58. *GW, 9,* 176; *SE, 13,* 146.

any view of history that would eliminate from history what Hegel called the "work of the negative." The ethical history of mankind is not the rationalization of utility, but the rationalization of an ambivalent crime, of a liberating crime, which at the same time remains the original wound; this is the meaning of the totem meal, the ambiguous celebration of mourning and festival.

By the same token, the problem of institutionalization, or social organization, reappears in full force; in mythical terms, how could the prohibition against "fratricide" arise from a "parricide"? By unmasking the father figure in the alleged totem, Freud intensified the problem he wished to solve, the ego's adoption of external prohibitions. Of course, without the jealousy of the father of the horde, there are no prohibitions; and without the parricide there is no stopping of the jealousy. But the two ciphers, jealousy and parricide, are still ciphers of violence: parricide puts a stop to jealousy; but what puts a stop to parricide as a repeatable crime? This was the problem already faced by Aeschylus in the *Oresteia*. Freud readily acknowledges it: remorse and deferred obedience enable one to speak of a covenant with the father, but at most this explains the prohibition of killing, not the prohibition against incest. The latter requires another covenant, one between the brothers; by it they decide not to repeat the father's jealousy, they renounce the claim to violent possession, even though this had been the motive for the killing: "Thus the brothers had no alternative, if they were to live together, but—not, perhaps, until they had passed through many crises—to institute the law against incest, by which they all alike renounced the women whom they desired and who had been their chief motive for despatching their father." [59] And a bit further on:

> In thus guaranteeing one another's lives, the brothers were declaring that no one of them must be treated by another as their father was treated by them all jointly. They were precluding the possibility of a repetition of their father's fate. To the religiously-based prohibition against killing the totem was now added the socially-based prohibition against fratricide.[60]

59. *GW, 9,* 174; *SE, 13,* 144.
60. GW, 9, 176; *SE, 13,* 146.

With this renunciation of violence, under the goad of discord, there is given the necessary condition for the birth of social organization: the true problem of law is not parricide but fratricide; in the symbol of the brothers' covenant Freud encountered the basic requisite of analytic explanation, which was the problem of Hobbes, Spinoza, Rousseau, and Hegel—namely, the change from war to law; the question is whether this change still falls under an economics of desire. The whole problematic of the superego, which we are now going to consider, centers on this point: the question no longer is the birth of the Oedipus complex, but its dissolution in the building-up of the superego.

THE METAPSYCHOLOGICAL PROBLEM: THE NOTION OF THE SUPEREGO

At the beginning of this chapter we proposed to distinguish between the two Freudian concepts of the ego ideal and the superego by assigning the first to the descriptive, phenomenal, symptomatological plane and the second to the theoretical, systematic, economic plane. The superego is, in effect, a metapsychological construct on a par with those we considered in the context of the first topography. But if the sequence of ego, id, and superego is comparable from the epistemological point of view to the sequence of *Cs.*, *Pcs.*, and *Ucs.*, it may legitimately be asked how it is superimposed upon the latter. To say that the first topography had to do with "psychical localities" and the second with "roles" or personological functions is not very illuminating, for the distinction remains in the metaphorical order.[61] However, the metaphor does orient the research in the right direction, for the difference between roles and localities points to a difference in the manner of treating economic problems. In both cases, of course, the problem remains an economic one; in the second topography as in the first, it is always a question of the changes of cathexis. But

61. For the metaphor of the three territories inhabited by three populations whose distribution partly does and partly does not correspond to the land areas, see *New Introductory Lectures*, *GW*, *15*, 79; *SE*, *22*, 72–73.

whereas the first topography treats these cathectic changes from the viewpoint of exclusion *from* consciousness or access *to* consciousness (whether this access takes place in disguised or substitute, recognized or unrecognized forms), the second topography deals with the cathectic changes from the viewpoint of the ego's force or weakness, hence from the viewpoint of the ego's status of dominance or submission. According to the title of one of the chapters of *The Ego and the Id,* the theme of the second topography is "the dependent relationships of the ego" (Ch. 5). These dependent relationships are first of all the relations of master-slave: the ego's dependence on the id, the ego's dependence on the external world, the ego's dependence on the superego. Through these alienating relations there is formed a personology: the role of the ego, the personal pronoun, is constituted in relation to the anonymous, the sublime, and the real, which are variations on the personal pronoun.

What is the task of this economics?

Its task is to show that what has thus far remained external to desire is actually a "differentiation" of the instinctual substrate; in other words, to make an economic process of the distribution of cathexis correspond to the historic process of the introjection of authority. A new connection is thus set up between hermeneutics and economics: the Oedipus complex was deciphered in myth and history, in dreams and the neuroses: it is now a matter of stating in topographic and economic terms the corresponding energy distribution. The two topographies express two types of differentiation of the instinctual substrate. Parallel to the differentiation of the ego, which Freud attributes to the influence of the external world and assigns to the *Pcpt.-Cs.* system, there must be considered another differentiation, "internal" rather than "superficial," sublime rather than perceptual: this differentiation, this modification of the instincts is what Freud calls the superego. The new economics is accordingly much more than a translation of a mass of clinical, psychological, and ethnographical material into a conventional language. It has the task of solving a problem that has remained unsolvable on both the descriptive and the historical planes; the fact of authority has constantly appeared as the presupposition of the individual or the collective Oedipus complex; it is necessary to introduce the fact of authority, of restrictions, in order to move from individual or collective prehistory to the history of the adult and the civilized person. The entire effort of the new theory of agencies is aimed at bringing authority into the history of desire, at making it appear as a "differentiation" of desire; the institution of the superego will be the answer to this requirement. There is therefore a reciprocal relationship between the genetic and the economic points of view. On the one side, the new theory of agencies reveals the repercussion which the genetic point of view and the discovery of the Oedipus complex have upon the first systematization; on the other, it gives the genesis a conceptual structure which enables it, if not to resolve, at least to pose in systematic terms its central problem: how the sublime arises within desire. If the institution of the superego hinges upon the Oedipus drama, the question is how to interrelate the Oedipus event and the superego's advent and to state this relationship in economic terms.

The solution to this problem—if psychoanalysis may be said to have solved it—is very concisely stated in the celebrated essay of 1923, *The Ego and the Id*. The labored and even problematic character of the solution will be seen more clearly if this text is treated as a synthesis of a series of metapsychological sketches which still date from the period of the first topography. We shall point out three or four of the main steps of the synthesis.

A note added in 1920 to the third of the *Three Essays on Sexuality* indicates in what direction the solution was sought: "Every new arrival on this planet is faced by the task of mastering the Oedipus complex; anyone who fails to do so falls a victim to neurosis." [62] The dissolution of the Oedipus complex is already seen as the key to the institution of the superego. Thus the economic problem of the superego shifts the focus of interest away from the formation of the Oedipus complex toward the dissolution of the Oedipus complex (to anticipate the title of an article of 1924).

A first step is taken in the paper "On Narcissism: An Introduction." [63] It is implied in this essay that the later concept of identi-

62. *GW*, *5*, 127, n. 2; *SE*, *7*, 226, n. 1 (added in 1920).

63. We recall how Freud "introduces" narcissism into psychoanalysis (see above, p. 127 and n. 31). In the "Dialectic" we will show the philosophical significance of narcissism, understood as the abortive Cogito. It is important therefore to grasp just how Freud attempts to derive the sublime, the higher ego, from this abortive Cogito.

fication does not contain the whole economics of the superego, for the essay proposes a schema of differentiation which, it seems to me, was neither absorbed nor abolished by the later theory. According to this schema, the formation of ideals, or idealization, is a differentiation within narcissism. But how? Repression, Freud remarks, arises from the ego, as the pole of the individual's cultural and ethical ideas. However, if one keeps in mind that this ego is at the same time self-love or self-respect (*Selbstachtung*), it is possible to subject the conditioning factor of repression to the libido theory: "We can say that the one man has set up an *ideal* in himself by which he measures his actual ego . . . For the ego the formation of an ideal would be the conditioning factor of repression." [64] But what is idealization? "This ideal ego is now the target of the self-love which was enjoyed in childhood by the actual ego. The subject's narcissism makes its appearance displaced onto this new ideal ego, which, like the infantile ego, finds itself possessed of every perfection that is of value." [65] Incapable of giving up an earlier satisfaction, the "narcissistic perfection of his childhood," "he seeks to recover it in the new form of an ego ideal. What he projects before him as his ideal is the substitute for the lost narcissism of his childhood in which he was his own ideal." [66] Thus idealization is a way of retaining the narcissistic perfection of childhood by displacing it onto a new figure.

What can be constructed on such a narrow basis? Freud himself is not very explicit; he is content with adding two remarks. Idealization is not sublimation; the latter changes the aim of an instinct, and hence the instinct itself in its orientation, whereas idealization only changes the instinct's object, without any alteration in the instinct's basic orientation. Idealization "heightens the demands of the ego," thus raising the level of repression; sublimation is a different vicissitude from repression, a true inner transformation of instinct. This first addition enables Freud to affirm that idealization is just one method of forming the superego, the narcissistic way.[67]

A second remark indicates that this method must be coordinated

64. *GW, 10,* 161; *SE, 14,* 93–94.
65. *GW, 10,* 161; *SE, 14,* 94.
66. Ibid.
67. This discovery is of great importance, for it means that our "better ego" is in a sense in line with the false Cogito, the abortive Cogito.

with another. A bit further on Freud writes: "It would not surprise us if we were to find a special psychical agency which performs the task of seeing that narcissistic satisfaction from the ego ideal is ensured and which, with this end in view, constantly watches the actual ego and measures it by that ideal." [68] Freud had already come upon this observing agency not only in delusions of observation but even within the dream-work, at least in dreams where the dreamer observes himself dreaming, sleeping, and awakening. What Freud is now suggesting is that the self-observation of dreams and delusional insanity, the dream-censorship, the ego ideal, and moral conscience must constitute one and the same agency; but on the whole the manifestations of this one agency indicate a source that is external to narcissism,[69] the parental source. There are good grounds for thinking that if a part of the narcissistic energy is displaced onto an ego that is more ideal than real, it is because that energy is "attracted" by the nucleus derived from the parental complex. To state this in a different way, in order that narcissism may be both displaced and retained in the form of an ideal, it must be mediated by authority. Thus idealization points back to identification.

However, it may be that the narcissistic factor of idealization is what gives a basis to identification and explains how influences from other persons become incorporated into the self; for identification to succeed, it may be necessary that the various influences from other people that form the ego ideal unite into an ideal ego rooted in narcissism. This line of thought would somewhat favor the distinction between ideal ego and ego ideal which has but little support in Freud himself.[70] If Freud did not develop it, it is be-

68. *GW*, *10*, 162; *SE*, *14*, 95.

69. "For what prompted the subject to form an ego ideal, on whose behalf his conscience acts as watchman, arose from the critical influence of his parents (conveyed to him by the medium of the voice), to whom were added, as time went on, those who trained and taught him and the innumerable and indefinable host of all the other people in his environment—his fellow-men—and public opinion. . . . The institution of conscience was at bottom an embodiment, first of parental criticism, and subsequently of that of society—a process which is repeated in what takes place when a tendency towards repression develops out of a prohibition or obstacle that came in the first instance from without" (*GW*, *10*, 163; *SE*, *14*, 96).

70. The expression *Idealich* (ideal ego; Fr., *moi idéal*) rarely occurs. We met it in the paper "On Narcissism" (*GW*, *10*, 161; *SE*, *14*, 94); it reappears

cause he wished to carry his radicalism to its utmost limits: the superego arises from an external source.

The process of identification, to which idealization refers us, also has a long history. In a section dealing with the successive organizations of sexuality, added in 1915 to the second of the *Three Essays*,[71] Freud shows the connection between identification and the so-called oral or cannibalistic pregenital organization; the whole question, however, is whether the identification required by the theory of the superego is a matter of possessing, of having; or whether the desire to be like is not radically different from the desire to have, the most brutal expression of which is the act of devouring. Freud began to recognize the extent of this process in the paper "Mourning and Melancholia." For the first time, identification is conceived as a reaction to the loss of an object, a function appearing in the contrast between melancholia and mourning. In the work of mourning, the libido is obeying the orders of reality to give up all its attachments one by one, to free itself by withdrawal of cathexis; in melancholia the process is entirely different. An identification of the ego with the lost object enables the libido to pursue its cathecting interiorly; by virtue of this identification the ego becomes the ambivalent object of its own love and hate; object-loss is transformed into ego-loss, and the conflict between the ego and the loved person is carried over into the new split between the critical faculty of the ego and the ego as altered by identification.[72]

---

in *The Ego and the Id*, written *Ideal-Ich;* to my knowledge it does not occur elsewhere. The expression *Ichideal* (ego ideal; Fr., *idéal du moi*), on the contrary, is found nearly a hundred times (in this connection, the French translations are misleading for they often translate *Ichideal* by *moi idéal*). In spite of its rarity, the expression *Idealich* should be regarded as intentional: the context indicates that when Freud speaks of the ideal ego it is in contrast with the real or "actual ego." The ideal ego is the displaced narcissistic ego. The expression is strictly synonymous with "the narcissistic ego ideal"; hence it should firmly retain its narcissistic context. This in no way prevents us from stressing the difference, relying here on Freud's remarks about the self-respect originally attaching to narcissism, a factor which Freud calls *Selbstachtung* and which is precisely narcissism's own ideal: in the "narcissism of his childhood" the subject "was his own ideal" (*GW, 10,* 161; *SE, 14,* 94).

71. *GW, 5,* 98; *SE, 7,* 198.

72. "The object-cathexis proved to have little power of resistance and was

This text on identification supplies the bridge between narcissism and the introjection of ideal models that we will need further on. In economic terms, identification—at least in melancholia—is a regression from object-libido to the narcissistic substrate. Following a suggestion by Otto Rank, Freud describes narcissistic identification thus: "Melancholia . . . borrows some of its features from mourning, and the others from the process of regression from narcissistic object-choice to narcissism." [73] It is true that this "narcissistic identification" is a pathological identification; its affinity to devouring, which represents a narcissistic stage of the libido, is evidence that it belongs to the archaic organizations of the libido; nevertheless, through this pathological structure, a general process takes form: the prolongation of the lost object in the ego.

Thus, during the period of the first topography the problem is extremely complex. First, Freud spoke of sublimation as an instinctual vicissitude distinct from all others, especially from repression; secondly, he began to elaborate the concept of idealization on the basis of narcissism; finally, he sketched the concept of identification starting from the oral phase of the libido and he began to link narcissism and identification together on the model of the narcissistic identification in melancholia. But there are a number of things that still remain unclear: the relationship between the three themes of sublimation, idealization, and identification; their common relation to the Oedipus complex; and in particular the connection between identification with the lost object in melancholia and identification with the father in the Oedipus complex—how can the regressive character of narcissistic identification accord with the structuring function of the identification that results in the superego?

The gap between these texts contemporary with the first topography and the great synthesis of *The Ego and the Id* is bridged by

brought to an end. But the free libido was not displaced onto another object; it was withdrawn into the ego. There, however, it was not employed in any unspecified way, but served to establish an *identification* of the ego with the abandoned object. Thus the shadow of the object fell upon the ego, and the latter could henceforth be judged by a special agency, as though it were an object, the forsaken object. In this way an object-loss was transformed into an ego-loss and the conflict between the ego and the loved person into a cleavage between the critical activity of the ego and the ego as altered by identification" (*GW, 10,* 435; *SE, 14,* 249).

73. *GW, 10,* 437; *SE, 14,* 250.

the seventh chapter of *Group Psychology and the Analysis of the Ego* (1921). In this last great text prior to *The Ego and the Id,* Freud inquires into the nature of the "libidinal ties" that "characterize a group [*Mass*]." [74] Just as *Totem and Taboo* examined in psychoanalytic terms the problem raised by Wundt and Frazer of the totemic origin of the prohibition against incest, this important and relatively profuse essay examines Gustave Le Bon's problem of "group psychology" and Theodor Lipps' problem of imitation and emotional contagion. In order to bring his own analysis to bear on the concepts of imitation, emotional contagion, and empathy (*Einfühlung*), then in vogue in social psychology, Freud revises his concept of identification and for the first time gives it a much broader application than it had in the earlier essays. But at the same time the concept of identification becomes a problem rather than a solution, for it now tends to cover the same area as that of imitation or empathy.[75] Chapter 7, entitled "Identification," begins thus: "Identification is known to psychoanalysis as the earliest expression of an emotional tie with another person."

Let us examine this important text. For the first time identification is brought into conjunction with the Oedipus complex. To our great surprise, however, we learn that identification precedes the Oedipus complex as much as it succeeds it. In the early phases of the complex, a little boy shows a special interest in his father; he "would like to grow like him and be like him." Then comes, "at the same time as this identification, or a little later," the movement of the libido toward the mother.

> He then exhibits, therefore, two psychologically distinct ties: a straightforward sexual object-cathexis towards his mother and an identification with his father which takes him as his model [*vorbildliche*]. The two subsist side by side for a time without any

74. *Massenpsychologie und Ich-Analyse, GW, 13,* 110; *SE, 18,* 101.

75. "Another suspicion may tell us that we are far from having exhausted the problem of identification, and that we are faced by the process which psychology calls 'empathy' [*Einfühlung*] and which plays the largest part in our understanding of what is inherently foreign to our ego in other people. But we shall here limit ourselves to the immediate emotional effects of identification, and shall leave on one side its significance for our intellectual life" (*GW, 13,* 118–19; *SE, 18,* 108).

> mutual influence or interference. In consequence of an irresistible advance towards a unification of mental life, they come together at last; and the normal Oedipus complex originates from their confluence.[76]

It seems that the boy's desire for his mother forces the identification to take on the coloring of jealousy; the identification then turns into the wish to replace the father, the wish for his death. At this stage identification is no longer the origin of the Oedipus complex but its result. But if we go back from this identification-result to the identification-condition, the latter turns out to be a great enigma. Freud himself forcefully expresses the enigma as follows:

> It is easy to state in a formula the distinction between an identification with the father and the choice of the father as an object. In the first case one's father is what one would like to *be*, and in the second he is what one would like to *have*. The distinction, that is, depends upon whether the tie attaches to the subject or to the object of the ego. The former kind of tie is therefore already possible before any sexual object-choice has been made. It is much more difficult to give a clear metapsychological representation of the distinction. We can only see that identification endeavours to mould a person's own ego after the fashion of the one that has been taken as a model.[77]

Never will Freud more vigorously express the problematic and undogmatic nature of identification.

How, indeed, is this identification to be related to an economics of desire? There are more questions than answers. In the first place, what about the oral origin of identification? It seems that only the desire to "have," and not the desire to "be like," derives from the oral phase of the libido's organization (the phase "in which the object that we long for and prize is assimilated by eating and is in that way annihilated as such"). Secondly, what about the narcissistic root of identification? Neurotic identification, which is dealt with in the remainder of the chapter, appears to be constructed upon a

76. *GW, 13,* 115; *SE, 18,* 105.
77. *GW, 13,* 116; *SE, 18,* 106.

neurotic leaning toward the father, rather than upon the desire to become like him; the relationship is instanced in the case of Dora, who imitated her father's cough. Freud summarizes his analysis of that case in the following terms: "We can only describe the state of things by saying *that identification has appeared instead of object-choice, and that object-choice has regressed to identification.*" [78] This is a situation, therefore, not of a primordial identification preceding every object-choice, but of a derived identification arising from libidinal object-choice through a regression to narcissism; we are back on the grounds of the narcissistic identification described in "Mourning and Melancholia" and "On Narcissism." And so there are at least two identifications, perhaps even three, Freud notes, if one considers that an identification may occur apart from any emotional attitude toward the person who is being imitated, as in the phenomenon of mental infection; such an identification is frequently seen in cases of hysteria where the imitation occurs independently of any sympathy; this third form rejoins the Einfühlung of the psychologists.

The picture of identification turns out to be more complex than we had counted on. Freud summarizes it thus:

> What we have learned from these three sources may be summarized as follows. First, identification is the original form of emotional tie with an object; secondly, in a regressive way it becomes a substitute for a libidinal object-tie, as it were by means of introjection of the object into the ego; and thirdly, it may arise with any new perception of a common quality shared with some other person who is not an object of the sexual instinct.[79]

There are many indications that the identification that terminates the Oedipus complex manifests the features of this multiple identification.

At the end of the chapter, Freud integrates into his analysis of identification the descriptions that had previously been given in "Mourning and Melancholia" and "On Narcissism." The manner in which melancholia internalizes revenge against the lost object ap-

78. *GW, 13,* 117; *SE, 18,* 106–07.
79. *GW, 13,* 118; *SE, 18,* 107–08.

pears as a new variant of identification; by identifying itself with the object of its hatred, the ego is transformed into a center of hatred against itself, and this is comparable to what we described as the critical agency within the ego that observes, judges, condemns. But Freud does not say, in this text, how the adoption of an external ideal can be likened to the introjection of a lost object based on the model of melancholia on the one hand and to a differentiation of narcissism on the other. By its very composition, the text proceeds more by a series of convergent examples than by a systematic construction. Only the economics of the dissolution of the Oedipus complex will enable us to interrelate the following still disconnected themes: identification with an external ideal, introjection of the lost object into the ego, differentiation of narcissism by the formation of ideals.

The Ego and the Id [80] marks a decisive advance in the integration of these materials because of its resolutely topographic-economic character,[81] which is, moreover, what makes this text so

80. *Das Ich und das Es* (1923), *GW, 13,* 237–89; *SE, 19,* 12–66. Freud expressly takes the term *Es* (Fr., *Ça*) from Georg Groddeck, the author of a book entitled *Das Buch vom Es* (1923), and through him, from Nietzsche. The neuter pronoun is a very good choice to denote the anonymous, passive, unknown, and uncontrollable aspects of the forces previously designated by the term "unconscious." In the *New Introductory Lectures* Freud writes that "it is the dark, inaccessible part of our personality; what little we know of it we have learnt from our study of the dream-work and of the construction of neurotic symptoms, and most of that is of a negative character and can be described only as a contrast to the ego. We approach the id with analogies: we call it a chaos, a cauldron full of seething excitations" (*GW, 15,* 80; *SE, 22,* 73). The rest of the text clearly indicates that the id has taken over all the characteristics formerly attributed to the unconscious: the pleasure principle, timelessness, indestructibility of the primary processes, etc.

81. To what extent are we still dealing with a topography? More stress is put on the figurative and metaphorical character of the second topography than of the first, whose realism we have justified to a certain extent. With the second topography we are obviously dealing much more with a diagram (cf. Fig. 1 of Ch. 2 of *The Ego and the Id*). It should be noted, moreover, that the superego does not figure in this diagram; the diagram tries to combine the two topographies by representing the barrier of repression between the id and the ego in the depths of the sphere of existence, then the preconscious and the acoustic traces halfway to the surface, and finally the system *Pcpt.-Cs.* at the surface. The diagram is thus a compromise between

extremely difficult. One must convince oneself once and for all that it is a question not of phenomenal but of "systematic" entities, in the sense stated in the first chapter of *The Ego and the Id*. This work places the synthesis of the earlier materials on the metapsychological level of the "Project" of 1895, Chapter 7 of *The Interpretation of Dreams*, and the 1915 paper "The Unconscious." Thus the unifying principle of the processes described above is to be sought in the interplay of relations between systems.

The problem that dominates the third chapter of *The Ego and the Id* is this: from the historical point of view the superego is inherited from parental authority, but from the economic point of view it derives its energies from the id. How can this be so? How can the internalization of authority be a differentiation of intrapsychical energies? The intersecting of these two processes, which methodologically belong to two different planes, explains the following: what is sublimation in terms of results and introjection in terms of method may be likened to a regression according to the economic point of view. Therefore the problem of the "replacement of an object-cathexis" by an identification is taken, in its most general sense, as a sort of algebra of placements, displacements, and replacements. So presented, identification has rather the appearance of a postulate in the strong sense of the term, i.e. a demand that must be accepted at the beginning. Consider the following text:

> When it happens that a person has to give up a sexual object, there quite often ensues an alteration of his ego which can only be described as a setting up of the object inside the ego, as it occurs in melancholia; the exact nature of this substitution is as yet unknown to us. It may be that by this introjection, which is a kind of regression to the mechanism of the oral phase, the ego makes it easier for the object to be given up or renders that process possible. It may be that this identification is the sole condition under which the id can give up its objects. At any rate the process, especially in the early phases of development, is a very

two systems of representation, a compromise in which the other dimension of interiority, that of the sublime, has no place. Toward the end of the thirty-first lecture in the *New Introductory Lectures* of 1933, Freud will try to sketch a more complete diagram which will include the superego.

> frequent one, and it makes it possible to suppose that the character of the ego is a precipitate [*Niederschlag*] of abandoned object-cathexes and that it contains the history of those object-choices.[82]

Thus the abandonment of the desired object, which is the beginning of sublimation, coincides with something like a regression. This is a regression, if not in the sense of a temporal regression to an earlier phase of the organization of the libido, at least in the economic sense of a regression of object-libido to the narcissistic libido, considered as a reservoir of energy. If the transformation of an erotic object-choice into an alteration of the ego is indeed a method[83] of dominating the id, the price to be paid is this: "When the ego assumes the features of the object, it is forcing itself, so to speak, upon the id as a love-object and is trying to make good the id's loss by saying: 'Look, you can love me too—I am so like the object.' "[84]

We are prepared for the generalization which henceforth governs the problem:

> The transformation of object-libido into narcissistic libido which thus takes place obviously implies an abandonment of sexual aims, a desexualization—a kind of sublimation, therefore. Indeed, the question arises, and deserves careful consideration, whether this is not the universal road to sublimation, whether all sublimation does not take place through the mediation of the ego, which begins by changing sexual object-libido into narcissistic libido and then, perhaps, goes on to give it another aim.[85]

The only justification for this important hypothesis is that it enables us to understand the following sequence: sublimation (as

82. *GW, 13*, 257; *SE, 19*, 29.

83. I use the word "method" in the sense in which Freud uses it in Chapter 3, when he writes: "From another point of view it may be said that this transformation [*Umsetzung*] of an erotic object-choice into an alteration of the ego is also a method [*ein Weg*] by which the ego can obtain control over the id and deepen its relations with it—at the cost, it is true, of acquiescing to a large extent in the id's experiences" (*GW, 13*, 258; *SE, 19*, 30).

84. Ibid.

85. Ibid.

regards the aim), identification (as regards the method), regression to narcissism (as regards the economics of cathexes).

When we apply this schema to the oedipal situation, identification takes on a concrete historical meaning: that of the child's identification with "the father in his own personal prehistory." [86] To what extent does Freud succeed in integrating the identification with the father into the theoretical schema of identification through the abandonment of object-cathexes?

From the start Freud finds himself faced with the difficulty elaborated in *Group Psychology and the Analysis of the Ego*, namely, that the identification arising from object-cathexis is preceded by "a direct and immediate identification [which] takes place earlier than any object-cathexis." [87] Moreover, this first identification is what explains the ambivalence of love and hate in the child's relationship to the father. The father is both the obstacle to the boy's desire for his mother and the model to be imitated. If identification is not doubled in this way, the economics of the Oedipus complex is unintelligible. Indeed, according to the schema of identification through the abandonment of the object, what should be expected is an identification not with the father but with the mother; the mother is the object the boy abandons and therefore she must have been the one he identified with. Freud admits that the facts do not seem to fit the theory. Consequently, what he calls the "complete Oedipus complex" can be accounted for only by assuming a double identification —that is, by introducing into the conflict a confrontation between an object-choice and an identification prior to any object-choice in such a way that identification with the father presents itself as a double identification, negative by rivalry, positive by imitation. To this must be added the element of bisexuality, a theme going back to the time of Freud's friendship with Fliess,[88] if it is not simply taken from him. Bisexuality requires each of these relations to be doubled again, depending on whether the boy behaves like a boy or like a girl; that makes "four trends" which produce two identifica-

86. *GW, 13,* 259; *SE, 19,* 31.

87. Ibid.

88. Letter 113: "And I am accustoming myself to the idea of regarding every sexual act as a process in which four persons are involved" (*Origins*, p. 289).

tions, a father-identification and a mother-identification, each of them being both negative and positive.

Have we succeeded in making the genesis of the superego coincide with identification through the abandonment of the object? It seems so at first glance, and the following text, which Freud himself places in italics, appears to crown the success of the interpretation: *"The broad general outcome of the sexual phase dominated by the Oedipus complex may, therefore, be taken to be the forming of a precipitate in the ego, consisting of these two identifications in some way united with each other. This modification of the ego retains its special position; it confronts the other contents of the ego as an ego ideal or superego."* [89] This precipitate of abandoned object-cathexes, by which an object-choice becomes a modification of the ego, reminds us somewhat of Kant's notion of self-affection (*Selbstaffektion*). The ego affects itself by its own renunciatory object-choices. This modification of the ego is both a loss for the id—the id lets go, it gets rid of its objects so that the ego may take over—and at the same time an enlarging of the id, for the only way this new formation can be adopted by the id is by making itself loved like the lost object.

> But the derivation of the superego from the first object-cathexes of the id, from the Oedipus complex . . . brings it into relation with the phylogenetic acquisitions of the id and makes it a reincarnation of former ego-structures which have left their precipitates behind in the id. Thus the superego is always close to the id and can act as its representative [*Vertretung*] vis-à-vis the ego. It reaches deep down into the id and for that reason is farther from consciousness than the ego is.[90]

Thus all the scattered elements are brought together: father- or mother-identification, modification of the ego through abandoned objects, enlarging of primary narcissism into a secondary narcissism.

However complicated this schema may be, it is still a long way from satisfying all the requirements of the problem. Besides the fact

89. *GW, 13,* 262; *SE, 19,* 34.
90. *GW, 13,* 278; *SE, 19,* 48–49.

that it leaves intact the distinction between identification with the father or with the mother and object-relation (or again, identification as the desire to be like and identification as the desire to have), secondary identification itself raises a good many problems: how can a precipitate of identification act as "opposition" to the ego? How can the superego be both derived from the id and opposed to it and its first object-choices? We must introduce a further complication, that of reaction-formation. This process goes back to the *Three Essays* and was invoked in the paper "On Narcissism" in order to criticize and propose an alternative to Adler's notion of masculine protest and overcompensation. Its function is to explain the superego's double relationship to the Oedipus complex: the superego arises from the Oedipus complex by borrowing its energy and then turns back against it; the superego is therefore the heir to the Oedipus complex in the double sense that it proceeds from it and represses it. This double sense is implied in the expression of the dissolution (*Untergang*) of the Oedipus complex: the dissolution refers to the exhaustion of a lapsed organization of the libido (the phallic stage), but also to the destruction, the disintegration, the demolition (*Zerstrümmerung*) of an object-cathexis.[91] In order to account for this reaction-formation, Freud was led to underscore the aggressive and punitive character of the parental figure with which the ego identifies itself.

One year after writing *The Ego and the Id,* Freud devoted a separate paper to "The Dissolution of the Oedipus Complex"[92] in which he underscored the repressive function of this "precipitate of identification." No doubt the Oedipus complex is destined to a natural death: it belongs to an organization of the libido that will inevitably experience "disappointments" (the boy will never have a child by his mother and the girl is rejected as a lover by her father); moreover, it is bound to "pass away according to program" (*programgemäss*) when the libidinal organization to which it corresponds gives way to the next phase of development. But what pre-

91. "Along with the demolition of the Oedipus complex, the boy's object-cathexis of his mother must be given up" (*GW, 13,* 260; *SE, 19,* 32).

92. "Der Untergang des Ödipuskomplexes," *GW, 13,* 393–402; *SE, 19,* 173–79; translated in *Collected Papers, 2,* 269, as "The Passing of the Oedipus Complex."

cipitates the *destruction* of the phallic organization is the threat of castration, which is preceded and prepared for by all the other experiences of separation. Although the threat may have been uttered prior to the phallic phase, it does not take effect until the stage when the childhood theory about the loss of the penis in little girls offers it quasi-empirical support.

By thus emphasizing the aggressive and severe character of the parental threat of punishment, Freud improves his interpretation on several counts. For one thing, he strengthens the connection between narcissism and the giving up of the libidinal cathexis of the parental object; indeed, it is in order to save its narcissism that the child's ego "turns away" from the Oedipus complex (*wendet sich vom Ödipuskomplex ab*). Thus this object-cathexis is "given up" and "replaced" by identification. By connecting the abandonment of the object and narcissism, Freud reinforces his theme: "The ego ideal is . . . the expression of the most powerful impulses and most important libidinal vicissitudes of the id." Secondly, one sees more clearly that the superego is opposed to the rest of the ego, for it "takes over" (*entlehnt*) the severity of the father and perpetuates within the ego his prohibition against incest; one might even say that the narcissistic interests and the voice of the superego are in agreement on this point, since the threat of the superego "secures" (*versichert*) the ego against the return of the libidinal object-cathexis. Finally, to a certain extent this "destruction" enables one to interrelate sublimation and repression, which the earlier texts had set in opposition to each other. On the one hand, the destruction is a kind of desexualization; it answers therefore to the definition of sublimation (which is, as we know, a change not only of the object but of the aim); the instincts are "inhibited in their aim" (*zielgehemmt*) and changed into impulses of affection; then begins the latency period. In generalizing these economic relations revealed by the destruction of the Oedipus complex, one may say that desexualization and sublimation happen "with every transformation into an identification." On the other hand, there is no reason for denying the name of repression to the ego's turning away from the Oedipus complex, although later repressions proceed from the superego which it was the function of this repression to set up; however, it must be said that in the normal Oedipus complex this repression, having been successfully carried out, is indistinguishable from a sublimation, since it "destroys" and "abolishes" the complex.[93]

Have we reached our goal? Have we really shown "external" authority to be an "internal" difference?

The last chapters (4 and 5) of *The Ego and the Id* leave no doubt as to the inadequacy of the final results. Identification cannot bear the weight of the economics of the superego all by itself. It is not enough simply to reinforce the *difference* that arises within the id by an opposition or reaction-formation; we must also introduce a factor of *negativity*—a factor taken from another instinctual source, about which we have thus far said nothing and which Freud calls the death instinct. From now on it must be admitted that an economics of the superego requires not only a revision of the first topography and a new kind of differentiation of the libido, but also a revision of the very bases of the instinct theory. We shall accordingly bring the economic genesis of the superego to a halt at this threshold where *The Ego and the Id* must give way to *Beyond the Pleasure Principle;* we shall content ourselves with sketching this conjunction so as to give some idea of the path that remains to be traveled. We shall assume that the death instinct can operate either in "fusion" with Eros or in a state of "defusion";[94] the sadistic component of the libido would be an example of the first mode of operation and the sadism that has become perversion an example of the second mode; this would lead to the conjecture that regres-

93. I have omitted discussion of the feminine Oedipus complex, which Freud frequently dealt with: in *The Ego and the Id,* Ch. 3; at the end of "The Dissolution of the Oedipus Complex"; in "Some Psychical Consequences of the Anatomical Distinction Between the Sexes" (1925); in "Feminine Sexuality" (1931); and in *New Introductory Lectures,* Lecture XXXIII.

94. Strictly speaking, the concepts of fusion (*Mischung*) and defusion (*Entmischung*) apply only to the life and death instincts and their combination, according to *Beyond the Pleasure Principle;* they do have a basis, however, in the conception of the libido (taken from the *Three Essays*) as a loosely connected bundle of tendencies each of which is ready to go off in a separate direction; in this conception there is clearly foreshadowed the separating off of sadism.

sion to a former phase rests upon such a defusion of the instincts. If now we combine the differentiation of the three agencies—ego, superego, id—with the defusion of the two instincts—Eros and death—we catch sight of a new complication in the genesis of the superego. Would not the cruelty of the superego, which we have stressed ever since the descriptive and clinical stage of our investigation, be another representative of the death instinct?

We are not yet in a position to grasp the significance of this complete upheaval of the psychoanalytic edifice; faced with the death instinct, the libido itself reveals new dimensions and changes its name; from now on Freud will speak of Eros. What significance does this have for the pleasure principle, for narcissism? Further, what is the relationship between the death instinct, "by nature mute," [95] and all its representatives, in particular its cultural or anticultural representatives? What relationship is there between sadism and masochism and, within masochism itself, between "moral" masochism, which will be spoken of in "The Economic Problem of Masochism," and the other forms of masochism? We must indeed admit that the theory of the superego remains incomplete as long as we have not understood its "deathly" component.

95. *GW, 13,* 275, 289; *SE, 14,* 46, 59.

Chapter 3: Illusion

It is difficult to pinpoint what is properly psychoanalytic in Freud's interpretation of religion. However, it is essential to put into sharp forcus those elements of his interpretation that merit the consideration of both believers and unbelievers. There is a danger that believers may sidestep his radical questioning of religion, under the pretext that Freud is merely expressing the unbelief of scientism and his own agnosticism; but there is also the danger that unbelievers may confuse psychoanalysis with this unbelief and agnosticism. My working hypothesis, stated in the "Problematic," is that psychoanalysis is necessarily iconoclastic, regardless of the faith or nonfaith of the psychoanalyst, and that this "destruction" of religion can be the counterpart of a faith purified of all idolatry. Psychoanalysis as such cannot go beyond the necessity of iconoclasm. This necessity is open to a double possibility, that of faith and that of nonfaith, but the decision about these two possibilities does not rest with psychoanalysis.

Our procedure will be the same as with the analysis of the sublime. At the first level, corresponding to what we called "the descriptive and clinical approaches to the sublime," we will try to delimit what properly pertains to psychoanalysis and we will concentrate on two themes, observances and illusions. Next we will enter into the "genetic ways of interpretation" and take up the genesis of the gods at the point where we left it in the preceding chapter; we will then attempt to evaluate the significance of a strictly psychoanalytic phylogenesis of religion. Finally, we will enter into the properly economic theme of the "return of the repressed": the entire psychoanalysis of religion is in fact contained in this disclosure of the regressive nature of religion. At the same time the cycle of fantasies will be closed off: from dreams to esthetic seduction, from seduction to ethical idealization, from the sublime to illusion, we shall have returned to our starting point, the quasi-hallucinatory fulfillment of desire. This will involve a change of levels, however, for religion as illusion will no longer be a private fantasy but a public illusion; between dreams and illusion we will have to insert culture itself and understand how illusory wish-fulfillment can operate on two such different levels as the private dreams of our nights and the daydreams of peoples; the task of an economics of culture will be to account for this return to the starting point of the spiral of fantasies.

ILLUSION AND THE STRATEGY OF DESIRE

All of Freud's comments about religion center around two themes, both of them situated in the area of the analogy with neuroses and dreams. The first theme concerns practices or observances; the second concerns belief, that is to say, statements about reality. The second theme, illusion, constitutes the theme proper to religion; but as the first throws more light on the basically analogical character of the psychoanalytic approach to religion, we will begin with it.

This order is backed by the chronology of the texts, for Freud's first work on religion, written in 1907, deals with the resemblance between "Obsessive Actions and Religious Practices." [1] Although this paper does not introduce the theme of illusion, it may be said to contain in germ the entire later theory of religion. The precise level of the comparison, as we must not forget in the later discussion, is that of behavior and gesture, of acting (witness the title itself). Freud finds a resemblance between two types of ceremonials, just as he had previously found a resemblance between the dream-work and the mechanisms of wit. This first approach cannot go beyond a simple analogy; [2] it will be precisely the ambition of the great ethnological and historical constructs in *Totem and Taboo* and *Moses*

1. "Zwangshandlungen und Religionsübungen" (1907), *GW, 7,* 129–39; *SE, 9,* 117–27.

2. H. L. Philp, *Freud and Religious Belief* (London, Rockliff, 1956), has strongly emphasized the analogical character of the psychoanalytic description of religion.

and Monotheism to ground the resemblance in an identity. But it is important to stay at first on the level of the analogy and to realize that it works both ways; we must not forget that Freud was also the one who discovered that the neuroses have meaning and that the ceremonials of obsessed persons have meaning. The comparison is operative, therefore, from meaning to meaning. Hence it is both legitimate and illuminating to point out the many clusters of resemblance: the qualms of conscience brought on by an omission of some ritual action, the need to protect the performance of the ritual against any external interruption, the conscientiousness with regard to detail, the tendency of ceremonials to become increasingly complicated, esoteric, even petty. Moreover, in connection with ceremonials, an early insight is gained into the depths of the "sense of guilt": ceremonials—and included here are acts of penitence and invocations—have a preventive value with regard to an expected and feared punishment; thus religious observances assume the meaning of "defensive or protective measures."

These analogies are all the more instructive in that their many meanings remain in suspense; Freud, of course, had no doubt that the meaning of faith is completely exhausted in them; but that should not stop us. Even the famous formula that will be the leitmotiv of the whole psychoanalysis of religion has more than one meaning. Freud writes, "In view of these similarities and analogies one might venture to regard obsessional neurosis as a pathological counterpart of the formation of a religion, and to describe that neurosis as an individual religiosity and religion as a universal neurosis."[3] This statement opens as many things as it closes. It is an astonishing thing that man is capable both of religion and of neurosis, in such a way that their analogy can actually constitute a reciprocal imitation. As a result of this imitation, man is neurotic insofar as he is *homo religiosus* and religious insofar as he is neurotic. The problematic character of the above formula is brought out by another closely related statement: "An obsessional neurosis presents a travesty, half comic, half tragic, of a private religion."[4] Thus religion can be caricatured as neurotic ceremonial. Is this situation due

3. "Obsessive Actions," *GW*, *7*, 138–39; *SE*, *9*, 126–27.
4. *GW*, *7*, 132; *SE*, *9*, 119.

to the underlying intention of religion, or is it the result of its degradation and regression when it begins to lose the meaning of its own symbolism? And how does the forgetfulness of meaning in religious observances pertain to the essence of religion? Does it pertain to a still more fundamental dialectic, the dialectic of religion and faith? These questions necessarily remain as background, even though Freud does not raise them himself.

Freud was bothered by only one thing: the gap between the *private* character of the "religion of the neurotic" and the *universal* character of the "neurosis of the religious man." The function of phylogenesis will be not only to consolidate the analogy in an identity but to account for this difference on the level of the manifest contents.

The second clinical theme of Freud's psychoanalysis of religion is that of illusion. Here it is even more difficult than with the first theme to distinguish the specific contribution of psychoanalysis from Freud's personal convictions. Yet it must be done, for it is here that the problematic of religion is distinguished from that of the sublime.

For Freud, of course, ethics and religion have a common stem, the father complex originating in the oedipal situation. In this sense the theory of illusion is part of the theory of ideals and constitutes what might be called the fantasy function of the superego—the factor of story-making linked to the factor of prohibition. But the bifurcation of the Oedipus complex into the ethical and the religious branches involves a distinction between two processes, the introjection of ideals and the projection of omnipotence, which latter will presently be at the center of the genetic explanation. It is important therefore to grasp the meaning of this distinction on the descriptive and clinical plane. There are in fact two distinct problematics: ideals and illusion. Ideals represent an internalization of authority in the impersonal manner of the imperative; the existential index of the origin of authority has fallen away and the imperative index alone has been retained, to the exclusion of the indicative. The present problem, concerning religious belief regarded as an illusion, is the positing in reality of figures like the father.

I am not unaware that to a large extent this problematic of illusion is not peculiar to psychoanalysis. It is not difficult to find in Freud's statements the echo of a rationalism and scientism belonging to his time and situation; according to that rationalism, any language that does not give factual information is devoid of meaning. The incompatability of religious dogma and the scientific mind condemns religion beyond appeal: "There is no appeal to a court above that of reason," says *The Future of an Illusion*.[5]

Freud admits that his insistent attack on religion is not based on psychoanalysis.[6] And yet there is a strictly analytic problem about illusion; this problem concerns the deciphering of the hidden relationships between belief and desire; the proper object of the analytic critique of religion is the strategy of desire concealed in religious assertions.

It is here that our second problem is seen to have the same analogous texture as the problem of observances. The essential characteristic of illusions is not their similarity to error, in the epistemological sense of the word, but their relationship with other fantasies and their inclusion within the semantics of desire. This properly analytic dimension of illusion was very precisely delimited by Freud in Chapter 6 of *The Future of an Illusion:* "What is characteristic of illusions is that they are derived from human wishes. . . . Thus we call a belief an illusion when a wish-fulfillment is a prominent factor in its motivation, and in doing so we disregard its relations to reality, just as the illusion itself sets no store by verification."[7] An illusion is constituted by this complicity between wish-fulfillment and unverifiability. Thus the difference between illusion and delu-

5. *Die Zukunft einer Illusion* (1927), *GW, 14,* 325–80; *SE, 21,* 5–56. "Scientific work is the only road which can lead us to a knowledge of reality outside ourselves. . . . Ignorance is ignorance; no right to believe anything can be derived from it" (*GW, 14,* 345–46; *SE, 21,* 31–32).

6. "All I have done . . . is to add some psychological foundation to the criticisms of my great predecessors. . . . Nothing that I have said here against the truth-value of religions needed the support of psychoanalysis; it had been said by others long before analysis came into existence. If the application of the psychoanalytic method makes it possible to find a new argument against the truths of religion, *tant pis* for religion; but defenders of religion will by the same right make use of psychoanalysis in order to give full value to the affective significance of religious doctrines" (*GW, 14,* 358, 360; *SE, 21,* 35, 37).

7. *GW, 14,* 353–54; *SE, 21,* 31.

sion is only one of degree: in an illusion the conflict with reality is hidden, in a delusion it is open; some religious beliefs, Freud remarks, are delusional in this sense.

A second analogical pattern reveals itself as follows: just as religious observances recalled the ceremonials of obsession, so too wishful belief points to a wish-fulfillment on the model of dreams. As *The Future of an Illusion* forcefully states, "Here, too, wishing played its part, as it does in dream-life." [8] Illusions mark the point of return of fantasies toward their primal expression.

The relation of religion to desire and fear is, of course, an old theme: the peculiar role of psychoanalysis is to decipher that relation qua *hidden* relation and to relate the deciphering process to an *economics* of desire. The enterprise is both legitimate and necessary; in conducting it psychoanalysis does not act as a variety of rationalism but fulfills its proper function. The question remains open for every man whether the destruction of idols is without remainder; this question no longer falls within the competency of psychoanalysis. It has been said that Freud does not speak of God, but of god and the gods of men; [9] what is involved is not the truth of the foundation of religious ideas but their function in balancing the renunciations and satisfactions through which man tries to make his harsh life tolerable.

We must now see why the economics of illusion, even more than the economics of the superego, requires the intermediate step of a genetic, and more precisely of a phylogenetic model. We have already stressed the sharp difference between the private religion of the neurotic and the universal neurosis of religion, but there is another difference which individual psychology is likewise unable to account for. Between a dream fantasy—say the dream of animal phobia in the case of little Hans—and the immense figure of the gods there is a huge gap in meaning; here the individual Oedipus complex is not enough. An Oedipus complex of the species is needed. The temporal span of history and the long childhood of mankind are needed to account for the power, solemnity, and sanc-

8. *GW, 14,* 338; *SE, 21,* 17.

9. Ludwig Marcuse, *Sigmund Freud* (Rowohlts Deutsche Encyklopädie, 1956), p. 63.

tity of religious phenomena—that is, in the language of *Moses and Monotheism*,[10] for the "compulsive character that attaches to religious phenomena." [11]

That is why the same theme does not retain, from 1907 to 1939, the same epistemological coefficient; in 1907, it is an analogy whose final meaning remains indefinite; in 1939, Freud claims it is a historically demonstrated identity. All the ethnological and historical investigations separating the two texts have but one aim: to transform into an identity the double analogy of religion with neurosis on the one hand and with oneiric wish-fulfillment on the other.

THE GENETIC STAGE OF EXPLANATION: TOTEMISM AND MONOTHEISM

The genesis of religion differs from the genesis of prohibitions in that it is the genesis of assertions about reality and not simply the genesis of a psychical agency. That is why the concept of projection has the same place in the genesis of religion as the concept of introjection in the genesis of the superego. And it is also the reason why we must go beyond totemism itself in order to grasp the starting point of the process of projection.

In the third essay of *Totem and Taboo* Freud reads the history of religions in a manner reminiscent of Auguste Comte's "law of the three states": "The human race, if we are to follow the authorities, have in the course of ages developed three . . . systems of thought —three great pictures of the universe: animistic (or mythological), religious and scientific." [12] Why these three stages? There is no doubt that from the beginning the choice of this historical sequence is guided by psychoanalytic considerations; indeed, these three states correspond to three exemplar moments in the history of desire: narcissism, object-choice, reality principle.

10. *Der Mann Moses und die monotheistische Religion, GW, 16,* 101–246; *SE, 23,* 7–137. The first two essays of this work appeared prior to World War II in the review *Imago* (1937); the third appeared in London in 1939.

11. *GW, 16,* 208–09; *SE, 23,* 101.

12. *GW, 9,* 96; *SE, 13,* 77.

The intervention of psychoanalysis in the selection of the ethnological materials is quite evident. In order to establish the first level of the correspondence between the history of religion and the history of desire, Freud must postulate a pre-animistic stage of animism, a stage described as "animatism," in which there is as yet no express belief in spirits and therefore no projection into transcendent figures. Freud admits that the ethnological basis is slight, but this first stage enables him to secure the correspondence between the two series from the outset: "This first human *Weltanschauung*," he boldly writes, "is a *psychological* theory." [13] In support of this assertion it is assumed that this first world conception still finds expression today in magic. Freud posits that "magic is the earlier and more important branch of animistic technique," [14] and magic is a technique of desire. This technique, the main description of which is taken from Frazer, is, in its double form of imitative magic and contagious magic, a clear instance of what *The Interpretation of Dreams* and the theory of obsessional neurosis called the "omnipotence of thoughts" or "overvaluation of mental processes": "By way of summary, then, it may be said that the principle governing magic, the technique of the animistic mode of thinking, is the principle of the 'omnipotence of thoughts.' " [15] As we have seen, this technique is the delayed evidence of the primary process which was only postulated in Chapter 7 of *The Interpretation of Dreams*. It is here that desires interfere with reality: the quasi-hallucinatory satisfaction of desire marks the primitive encroachment of desire upon reality; henceforth the true meaning of reality is to be achieved in and through this false efficacy of desire.

This parallel is not free from difficulties. The relationship between narcissism and the omnipotence of thought is not very convincing; there is, indeed, an overestimation of the ego's value in narcissism, but not, strictly speaking, an overvaluation of its effectiveness. Magical acts, for their part, are more a relation to the world than to oneself; nor is it clear what features of magical action

13. Ibid.

14. *GW, 9*, 97; *SE, 13*, 78.

15. *GW, 9*, 106; *SE, 13*, 85. This expression was suggested to Freud by the "rat-man" (cf. "Notes Upon a Case of Obsessional Neurosis" [1909], *GW, 7*, 450–53; *SE, 10*, 233–36).

justify the affirmation that "in primitive men the process of thinking is still to a great extent sexualized. This is the origin of their belief in the omnipotence of thoughts." [16] On the other hand, what to me seems very penetrating in Freud's initial insight is his view that the first religious problematic is a problematic of omnipotence; it was only natural for a psychoanalysis of religion to look for the equivalent of this problematic in the interplay of desires.

Once granted the series of equivalences—pre-animism, omnipotence of thoughts, narcissism—upon which the theory is based, the law of development is clear: essentially it consists in a displacement of that omnipotence that first belongs to desire. The spirits of animism, the gods of religion, bare necessity according to the scientific view of the world—this progression marks off another history, that of the libido, which starts from narcissism, rises to the stage of objectivization characterized by attachment to parents, and ends in genital maturity where the choice of objects is adjusted to the rules and requirements of reality.[17] The parallel allows the corresponding history of religion to be regarded as the history of a dispossession or renunciation of omnipotence. In this sense, the history of religion marks the advance of Ananke, necessity, which opposes human narcissism. But why isn't this abandonment a dispossession to the benefit of nature, to the benefit of reality?

It is here that a new mechanism must be introduced, the mechanism of projection,[18] patterned on paranoia. Freud does not give us a complete theory of projection here, but rather takes it up at the

16. *GW*, *9*, 109; *SE*, *13*, 89.
17. *GW*, *9*, 109; *SE*, *13*, 90.
18. *GW*, *9*, 113–15; *SE*, *13*, 92–94. Freud worked out the theory of projection in the third section of the Schreber case. Cf. "Psychoanalytic Notes on an Autobiographical Account of a Case of Paranoia (Dementia Paranoides)" (1911), *GW*, *8*, 294–316; *SE*, *12*, 59–79. This text is his most important contribution to the study of projection, and more precisely of projection in a religious theme. However, in the picture proposed here of the genesis of paranoia, more light is thrown on the function of projection than on its mechanism, which remains puzzling for Freud himself. Its function is clear: if we assume that the initial core of the Schreber case is a homosexual impulse directed toward his father, and then, by a process of transference, toward his doctor, the principal mechanisms brought into play are "reversal into its opposite," which transforms the loved object into an object of hate and replaces the homosexual impulse with a delusion of sexual persecution (emasculation fantasy), and "projection," which consists

point where it furnishes an economic solution to a conflict of ambivalence comparable to the one we discovered in the behavior of mourning. But whereas melancholia introjects hate that was once

---

in the replacement of Flechsig (his physician) by "the superior figure of God" (*SE, 12,* 48). The economic function of this replacement is clear: the "theodicy" that this figure inspires transforms the emasculation fantasy into a feminine fantasy and makes the subject himself a redeemer through voluptuousness: thus "his ego found compensation in his megalomania, while his feminine wishful fantasy made its way through and became acceptable" (p. 48). The function of projection is, therefore, reconciliation: "the ascent from Flechsig" to God enables him "to become reconciled to his persecution, . . . to accept the wishful fantasy which had had to be repressed" (p. 48). But the mechanism of projection is singularly more obscure than its role: the fact that Flechsig and "Schreber's God" belong to the same class presupposes an identification followed by a division, in which the persecutor is divided into two personalities, God and Flechsig (not to mention the bipartitions of the divine figures themselves). "A process of decomposition of this kind is very characteristic of paranoia. Paranoia decomposes just as hysteria condenses. Or rather, paranoia resolves once more into their elements the products of the condensations and identifications which are effected in the unconscious" (p. 49). Nor does the remainder of the study further elucidate the mechanism. Section III has a different preoccupation: the establishment of the sexual etiology of paranoia. To do this, we must expose the erotic component of social factors (social humiliation, etc.), connect this erotic component to the narcissistic phase of object-choice, and thus discover the "proposition" which the delusions of persecution "contradict"; the original proposition is, "I (a man) love him (a man)"; in persecution, it is transformed into "I do not *love* him—I *hate* him," which is one of the three or four possible ways in which the original proposition may be contradicted. With amazing skill, Freud thus places persecution among the various ways of contradicting the original proposition: delusions of jealousy contradict the subject, delusions of persecution the verb, erotomania the object, sexual overvaluation the proposition as a whole. But just as he is about to tell us the nature of the projection involved in the reversal into its opposite, Freud admits his perplexity. We can, of course, describe projection:

> The most striking characteristic of symptom-formation in paranoia is the the process which deserves the name of *projection*. An internal perception is suppressed, and, instead, its content, after undergoing a certain kind of distortion, enters consciousness in the form of an external perception. In delusions of persecution the distortion consists in a transformation of affect; what should have been felt internally as love is perceived externally as hate. (p. 66)

But projection does not coincide with paranoia; its concept is both narrower and wider; narrower because "projection does not play the same part in all forms of paranoia" (p. 66); wider because "it makes its appearance not

mixed with love and turns it back against the ego, paranoia projects the ego's mental processes outward. Thus spirits are created: they arise from the projection into reality of our own psychical pro-

---

only in paranoia but under other psychological conditions as well" (p. 66)—for instance, when we attribute an external cause to our subjective impressions. The net result is set forth in the following terms:

> Having thus been made aware that more general psychological problems are involved in the question of the nature of projection, let us make up our minds to postpone the investigation of it (and with it that of the mechanism of paranoic symptom-formation in general) until some other occasion; and let us now turn to consider what ideas we can collect on the subject of the mechanism of repression in paranoia. I should like to say at once, in justification of this temporary renunciation, that we shall find that the manner in which the process of repression occurs is far more intimately connected with the developmental history of the libido and with the disposition to which it gives rise than is the manner in which symptoms are formed. (p. 66)

Psychoanalysis is indeed more at ease with the mechanism of repression than with the formation of symptoms by projection. It is in fact on this occasion that Freud presents the clearest analysis of the three phases of repression: fixation, anticathexis, and regression to the original point of the fixation (see above, p. 141, n. 58). Thus the clearest result of the analysis of the Schreber case concerns "the mechanism of repression proper which predominates in paranoia" (p. 68), namely, a preliminary fixation at the narcissistic stage and a regression that is measured by "the length of *the step back from sublimated homosexuality to narcissism*" (p. 72). As for symptom-formation, Freud himself warns us that we have no right to assume that it "follows the same path as repression" (p. 65). We see the reason why: the return of the repressed is one thing, projection another; "*the delusional formation, which we take to be the pathological product, is in reality an attempt at recovery, a process of reconstruction*" (p. 71). This process "undoes the work of repression" by restoring from without, through the detour of externality or transcendence, the lost objects. In conclusion, Freud says: "In paranoia this process is carried out by the method of projection. It was incorrect to say that the perception which was suppressed internally is projected outwards; the truth is rather, as we now see, that what was abolished internally returns from without. The thorough examination of the process of projection which we have postponed to another occasion will clear up our remaining doubts on this subject" (p. 71).

Thus it cannot be said that the Schreber case explains projection; it only marks off the boundaries of projection. It also leaves intact the question whether the genesis of this caricature of God which is "Schreber's god" reveals the complete secret of "the forces that construct religions," as the Postscript to the paper suggests. Man is capable of religion as he is of neurosis, we said; let us add: he is capable of religion as he is of paranoia.

cesses, present as well as latent, conscious as well as unconscious.[19]

It is true that projection does not account for the systematic character of animism, in the sense of the first complete picture of the universe. Therefore we will invoke a subsidiary mechanism,[20] taken here from the dream-work but also seen in paranoia—the mechanism of secondary elaboration, or better, of secondary "revision" (*Bearbeitung*). This rationalization, internal to the dream-work and aimed at giving the dream an appearance of unity, connection, and intelligibility so as to make it acceptable, has its religious counterpart in the work of justification we call superstition. In both cases it is a matter of a screen interposed between knowledge and reality, a provisional construction which we must penetrate in order to reach the underlying conflict. This apparent rationality is itself an instrument of the strategy of desire, an additional factor of distortion.[21]

Upon these basic mechanisms—omnipotence of thoughts and projection of this omnipotence into reality—are built the new mechanisms contemporary with the Oedipus complex.[22] The spe-

---

This proposition—which is considerable indeed—is not so much an answer that closes as a question that opens.

19. The connection is substantiated on the one hand by the role attributed to ambivalence, the importance of which we saw in the interpretation of taboo, and on the other hand by the affinity between "spirits" and the dead; but we also know the seriousness of the ambivalent emotional conflicts the death of loved ones reveals in those who survive them.

20. *GW*, *9*, 116–19; *SE*, *13*, 94–97.

21. In the last pages of the third essay of *Totem and Taboo* Freud softens his pathological interpretation of animism somewhat. "If we take instinctual repression as a measure of the level of civilization that has been reached," superstitious motives are at the same time "disguises" for authentic factors of culture, especially prohibitions; similarly, magical rationalization covers up various esthetic and hygienic purposes.

22. "Into this obscurity one single ray of light is thrown by psychoanalytic observation" (*GW*, *9*, 154; *SE*, *13*, 126). This time it is "little Hans" who supplies the indispensable link; cf. "Analyse der Phobie eines fünfjährigen Knaben" (1909), *GW*, *7*, 243–377; "Analysis of a Phobia in a Five-Year-Old Boy," *SE*, *10*, 5–147. The psychoanalytic materials may seem rather disconnected: paranoia on the one hand, phobia on the other; but there are several symptoms that fill in the gap. The animal phobia of one of Ferenczi's patients is evidence of the part played by the fear of castration, which has to do with the narcissistic elements of the Oedipus complex; and narcissism has been seen to be connected with the omnipotence of thoughts

cific contribution of totemism is the theme of reconciliation. We recall that the ethnological core of this theme, according to the fourth essay of *Totem and Taboo*, is constituted by the totem meal, which is the expression of the communion of god and the faithful. Freud tells us that this meal is the beginning "of social organization, of moral restrictions and of religion." [23] Thus far we have considered only those aspects of this institution that are capable of being internalized in the form of an intrapsychical agency; but what is the properly religious element in the totem meal? Essentially it is the sense of guilt, which derives from the Oedipus complex. From the initial nebula three focal areas have been delineated: the institution of society arises from the covenant between the brothers, and the institution of morality from the deferred obedience that is the result of the covenant; as for religion, it has taken over the guilt. From this point on we can define religion as the series of attempts to resolve the emotional problem posed by the murder and the guilt and to bring about a reconciliation with the offended father.[24]

But that is not all. The totem meal enables us to add an additional feature to the picture. Religion is not only repentance, it is also the disguised remembrance of the triumph over the father, hence a covert filial revolt; this filial revolt is hidden in other features of religion, principally in "the son's efforts to put himself in the place of the father-god." Among all the son religions, Christianity clearly occupies a special place; Christ is the son who "sacrificed his own life and so redeemed the company of brothers from original sin." In this sacrifice the two features of ambivalence come together: on the one hand the guilt from the killing of the father is avowed and expiated; but at the same time the son himself becomes

---

in animism. On the other hand, the ambivalence of the Oedipus complex is akin to the ambivalence of which the paranoiac projection is a solution. In this way the transition between the third and fourth essays of *Totem and Taboo* is made secure.

23. *GW*, *9*, 171; *SE*, *13*, 142.

24. "All later religions are seen to be attempts at solving the same problem. . . . all have the same end in view and are reactions to the same great event [*Begebenheit*] with which civilization began and which, since it occurred, has not allowed mankind a moment's rest" (*GW*, *9*, 175; *SE*, *13*, 145).

the god, replacing the father religion by a son religion. A clear expression of this ambivalence is the revival of the totem meal in the Eucharist: its meaning is both the reconciliation with the father and the substitution of the son for the father, with the faithful consuming the son's flesh and blood.[25]

The striking thing about this history is that it does not constitute an advance, a discovery, a development, but is the sempiternal repetition of its own origins. Strictly speaking, for Freud there is no history of religion: religion's theme is the indestructibility of its own origins;[26] religion is precisely the area where the most dramatic emotional configurations are revealed as unsurpassable. Its theme is preeminently archaic: it speaks of the father and the son, of the killed and lamented father and of the repentant son in revolt; as such it is the area of emotive repetition. That is why in principle the gaps in this history are unessential. *Totem and Taboo* acknowledges two of them: Freud admits that the transition from the totem to god involves "other sources or meanings . . . upon which psychoanalysis can throw no light";[27] this transition will be partly filled out in *Moses and Monotheism*. On the other hand the role of the mother-goddesses, which was already seen in the *Leonardo* in connection with the phallic mother, remains obscure: "I cannot suggest at what point in this process of development a place is to be found for the great mother-goddesses, who may perhaps in general have preceded the father-gods."[28] Freud is much more interested in the repetitive aspect of religion. Omnipotence of thoughts, paranoiac projection, displacement of the father onto an animal, ritual repetition of the killing of the father and of the filial revolt constitute the "indestructible" basis of religion. It is understandable why Freud stated many times over that naïve religion is the true reli-

25. *GW*, *9*, 184–86; *SE*, *13*, 152–55.

26. "The memory of the first great act of sacrifice thus proved indestructable" (*GW*, *9*, 182; *SE*, *13*, 151).

27. *GW*, *9*, 177–78; *SE*, *13*, 147; the humanization of the god figure, which had at first been concealed in animal features, is already a return of the father figure, and one which poses a very complicated problem: Freud views this return as an outcome of the increased longing for the father which arose when the fraternal clan, in order to survive, had to give way to a patriarchal society.

28. *GW*, *9*, 180; *SE*, *13*, 149.

gion; rational and dogmatic theology, far from bringing religion into closer contact with reason and reality, can only be rationalizations adding to the distortion.[29]

It may come as a surprise, therefore, that Freud spent so much time and care composing a new history of origins, not at the level of totemism, but monotheism, and more precisely the ethical monotheism of the Jewish people. But we must not look to *Moses and Monotheism* for some sort of rectification of *Totem and Taboo;* it is rather a completion and reinforcement of the latter's repetitive and regressive theory. What is more, this book stands as an exorcism. It marks the renouncement on the part of Sigmund Freud the Jew of the value that his narcissism could still rightfully claim, the value of belonging to the race that engendered Moses and imparted ethical monotheism to the world. But if Moses is Egyptian and if Yahweh is merely the sublime resurgence of the father of the horde, then there is nothing left but to yield to harsh necessity, over against the claims of narcissism and the pleasure principle. It should perhaps be added that Moses stood as a father image for Freud himself, the same image he had already encountered at the time of "The Moses of Michelangelo"; this Moses had to be glorified as an esthetic fantasy and liquidated as a religious fantasy. One can guess how must it cost Freud to run counter to Jewish pride at the very moment when the storm of Nazi persecution was breaking out, when his books were being burned and his publishing house ruined, and when he himself had to flee Vienna and take refuge in London: all this must have been a terrible "work of mourning" for Freud the man.[30]

What is the theme of *Moses and Monotheism?* Its theme concerns "important considerations regarding the origin of monotheist religions in general." [31] In this book Freud tries to make a plausible reconstruction of a murder that would be for monotheism what the

29. *Das Unbehagen in der Kultur* (1930), *GW, 14,* 431; *Civilization and Its Discontents, SE, 21,* 74.

30. *Moses and Monotheism* begins with this grave declaration: "To deprive a people of the man whom they take pride in as the greatest of their sons is not a thing to be gladly or carelessly undertaken, least of all by someone who is himself one of them" (*GW, 16,* 103; *SE, 23,* 7).

31. *GW, 16,* 113; *SE, 23,* 16.

murder of the primal father had been for totemism, and which would be a continuation, reinforcement, and amplification of the primal murder.

The book contains an impressive number of hazardous hypotheses. The first hypothesis is that of an Egyptian Moses, adherent of the cult of Aten, a god who was ethical, universal, and tolerant. Unfortunately, neither the presumptions derived from the name of Moses nor those suggesting the account of his birth, nor even the Egyptian origin of circumcision, furnish much support to the hypothesis of an Egyptian Moses.

The second hypothesis is that of the monotheism of Aten, which is alleged to have been constructed on the model of an uncontested ruler, the famous Pharaoh Akhenaten, and which Moses imposed upon the Semitic tribes. However, even supposing that neither the Aten religion nor the fascinating personality of Akhenaten has been overestimated, it is doubtful that they have any connection whatsoever with the Hebrew religion.

The third hypothesis assumes that the "hero" Moses—in the sense of Otto Rank, whose influence is considerable here—was killed by the people and that the worship of the god of Moses was merged with the worship of Yahweh, a volcano god, who thus became the disguise behind which the Mosaic god concealed his origin and the people tried to forget the murder of the hero. Unfortunately, the hypothesis of Moses' murder, suggested by Sellin in 1922 in a completely different geographical and historical context, was later abandoned by its author. It presupposes, moreover, that there were two Moses, one of the cult of Aten, the other of the cult of Yahweh, a hypothesis that finds no support in the specialists.

The fourth hypothesis assumes that the Jewish prophets engineered the return of the Mosaic god, reenacting the traumatic event in the name of the ethical god. The return to the Mosaic god would also be the return of the repressed trauma; we thus reach the point where a reawakening on the plane of ideas coincides with a return of the repressed on the emotional plane: if the Jewish people have given Western culture its model of self-accusation, it is because their sense of guilt feeds on the memory of a murder they have all along been trying to forget.

It is with this fourth hypothesis that the mechanism of Freud's thought is perhaps best revealed. Freud is completely uninterested in the development of religious sentiment. He has no interest in the theology of an Amos or an Osee, of an Isaiah or an Ezechiel, nor in the theology of Deuteronomy, nor in the relation between prophetism and the cultural and sacerdotal tradition, between prophetism and Levitism. The idea of the "return of the repressed" enabled him to dispense with a hermeneutics that would take the circuitous path of an exegesis of the texts and rushed him into taking the shortcut of a psychology of the believer, patterned from the outset on the neurotic model. But what is most astonishing is the guiding idea of the enterprise itself. If Freud entered on the path of historical reconstruction in an area in which he was by no means a specialist (*Moses and Monotheism* represents merely a fragment of a huge project in which Freud hoped to apply the psychoanalytic method to the entire Bible!), the reason is that the doctrine, as he saw it, demanded an actual murder; for him, the transition to monotheism required [32] the renewal of the killing itself, so that the father figure might be strengthened and sublimated, the guilt increased, the reconciliation with the father exalted, and later, in Christianity, the substitute figure of the son magnified.

In this history of the return of the repressed, Jewish monotheism takes over where totemism left off. The Jewish people reenacted on the person of Moses, an eminent substitute for the father, the primal forfeiture. The killing of Christ is a further reinforcement of the memory of their origins, while the Passover restores Moses to life. Finally, the religion of St. Paul completes this return of the repressed and relates it to its prehistoric source by giving it the name of original sin: a crime was committed against God and death alone could redeem it. At the same time Freud returns here to his early hypothesis of the revolt of the sons: the Redeemer had to be the main guilty party, the chief of the company of brothers, just like the rebel hero of Greek tragedy. "He was . . . the returned primal father of the primitive horde, transfigured and, as the son, put in the

32. "The killing of Moses by his Jewish people . . . thus becomes an indispensable part of our construction, an important link between the forgotten event of primeval times and its later emergence in the form of monotheist religions" (*GW, 16*, 196; *SE, 23*, 89).

place of the father." [33] This effect of reinforcement to which Freud attributes the transition from totem to god could only be obtained by the reenactment of a real murder.

That is why Freud is unwilling to minimize the historical reality of this chain of traumatic events: "In the group [as in the individual] an impression of the past is retained in unconscious memory traces." [34] For Freud, "the universality of symbolism in language" is far more a proof of the memory traces of the great traumas of mankind [35] than an incentive to explore other dimensions of language, the imaginary, and myth. The distortion of those memories is the only function of the imaginary that is explored. As for the inheritance itself, irreducible to any direct communication, it is indeed embarrassing, but it must be postulated, if we wish to bridge "the gulf between individual and group psychology [and] deal with peoples as we do with an individual neurotic. . . . If it is not so, we shall not advance a step further along the path we entered on, either in analysis or in group psychology. The audacity cannot be avoided." [36] Thus it cannot be said that we are dealing here with an accessory hypothesis; Freud sees it as one of the links that guarantee the cohesion of the system: "A tradition that was based only on communication could not lead to the compulsive character that attaches to religious phenomena"; [37] there can be no return of the repressed unless a traumatic event occurred.

THE ECONOMIC FUNCTION OF RELIGION

The Freudian interpretation of religion will provide us with a final occasion for showing how hermeneutics and economics are interrelated in the Freudian metapsy-

33. *GW, 16,* 196; *SE, 23,* 90.
34. *GW, 16,* 201; *SE, 23,* 94.
35. The "evidential value [of these facts] seems to me strong enough for me to venture on a further step and to posit the assertion that the archaic heritage of human beings comprises not only dispositions but also subject-matter—memory traces of the experience of earlier generations. In this way the compass as well as the importance of the archaic heritage would be significantly extended" (*GW, 16,* 206; *SE, 23,* 99).
36. *GW, 16,* 207; *SE, 23,* 100.
37. *GW, 16,* 208; *SE, 23,* 101.

chology. In Freud's later writings a new theme makes its appearance, the theme of culture, under which Freud groups together various notions—esthetic, ethical, religious—that a phenomenology would split into different regions according to the intentionality of the object. It is in his elaboration of the concept of culture that Freud attempts to account for the economic function of religion. The difference between neurosis as a private religion and religion as a universal neurosis lies essentially in the transition from the private to the public—a transition that has thus far remained unintelligible to us. On the other hand, the successive displacements of the father figure onto the totem, then onto spirits and demons, then onto the gods, and finally onto the God of Abraham, Isaac, and Jacob and the God of Jesus Christ, force us to relocate the production of fantasies within a historical, institutional, linguistic, and literary context which reveals the distance between a mere dream fantasy and a cultural object. If, then, the return of the repressed, taken on the collective scale, has an economic function, it does so through this cultural function; consequently we must elaborate the context in which the displacements of omnipotence, the quasi-paranoiac projection, the reconciliation with the father, and the secret vengeance of the sons occur and become meaningful.

We cannot adequately deal with the problem of culture in this chapter. Following our method of successive readings, we will say just enough about it to account for the religious problematic on the level proper to our investigation at this point, the level of a strategy of desire. Further on we will see the full meaning which a meditation on the death instinct and on the struggle of Eros against death has for culture itself, which is situated at the crossroads of the conflict between the giants Eros and Thanatos. For the present let us remain at this halfway station, which is precisely the level of *The Future of an Illusion*.

What is culture? In the first place let us say negatively that there are no grounds for distinguishing between culture and civilization.[38] This refusal to enter into a distinction that is well on its way

38. *The Future of an Illusion*, *GW*, *14*, 326; *SE*, *21*, 6: "and I scorn to distinguish between culture and civilization"; a similar remark is found toward the end of *Why War?* (1933). The first two chapters of *The Future of an Illusion* are devoted to this "economics" of cultural phenomena in general.

to becoming classical is very illuminating. It is not that there exists on the one hand a utilitarian enterprise of dominating the forces of nature, which would be civilization, and on the other hand a disinterested and idealistic task of realizing values, which would be culture; this distinction may be meaningful from a point of view other than that of psychoanalysis, but it is no longer so once the decision has been made to approach culture from the point of view of the balance-sheet of cathexes and anticathexes of the libido. All the Freudian considerations of culture are dominated by this economic interpretation.

For Freud, the concept of culture represents partly the same thing as the concept of the superego, partly something new and more extensive. As long as its primary task is said to be the proscription of sexual or aggressive desires that are incompatible with a social order, culture is just another name for the superego; in economic language, culture implies instinctual renunciations: we have only to recall the three most universal prohibitions, against incest, cannibalism, and murder. That culture and the superego are here but two names for the same reality is evidenced by the mechanism of introjection.

In passing, Freud adds two complementary features. On the one hand, esthetic satisfaction assures a better internalization of culture, experienced as a sublime desire and not as a mere prohibition; on the other hand, the individual's proud and bellicose identification with his group, all of whose hatreds he adopts, procures for him a narcissistic type of satisfaction which counteracts his hostility to culture and reinforces the corrective action of social models. But these two satisfactions—esthetic and narcissistic—do not remove us from the familiar context of the instincts that lie hidden behind every formation of an ideal.

The point where we go beyond the classical analysis of the superego is in seeing that culture, in addition to its function of prohibiting and correcting, also has the task of protecting the individual against the superior power of nature. Illusions, as we shall presently see, are bound up with this latter task. The task breaks down into three themes: to lessen the burden of instinctual sacrifices imposed upon men; to reconcile individuals to those renunciations that are ineluctable; to offer them satisfactory compensations for those sacrifices. These are what Freud calls "the mental assets of civilization," [39] and it is in these assets that we must search for the true meaning of culture.

That is about the extent to which *The Future of an Illusion* carries the analysis of the phenomenon of culture; *Civilization and Its Discontents* goes much farther, under the guidance of the death instinct; we shall return to the death instinct when we resume the unfinished analysis of the superego.

The properly economic significance of this cultural function comes into view when it is related to another of Freud's familiar themes, that of the *harshness* of life. This theme is developed in several stages. It first of all designates man's natural helplessness in face of the crushing forces of nature, sickness, and death. Next, it concerns man's dangerous situation among his fellow men (*Civilization and Its Discontents* will go rather far in the direction of the famous *homo homini lupus;* man causes pain to his fellow man, exploits him as a worker, and enslaves him as a sexual partner). But life's harshness is also another name for the helplessness of the ego in its primal situation of subjection to its three masters, the id, the superego, reality; the harshness of life is this initial primacy of fear.[40] To this threefold fear—fear of reality, neurotic fear, fear of conscience—*Civilization and Its Discontents* will add a further trait: man is basically a "discontented" being, for he cannot achieve happiness in a narcissistic manner and at the same time fulfill the historic task of culture which his aggressiveness impedes; this is the reason why man, threatened in his self-regard, is so enamored of consolation.[41] At this point culture steps in to meet man's appetite. The new face civilization turns to the individual is no longer one of proscription but of protection, and this benevolent visage is the visage of religion.

Thus, from the economic as well as from the descriptive and genetic points of view, religion is distinct from morality; its point of

39. *GW, 14,* 331 (*der seelische Besitz der Kultur*); *SE, 21,* 10; similarly, further on: "For the principle task of civilization, its actual *raison d'être,* is to defend us against nature" (*GW, 14,* 336; *SE, 21,* 15).

40. *The Ego and the Id,* Ch. 5; *New Introductory Lectures,* No. XXI.

41. On the theme of the "harshness of life," see also *The Future of an Illusion, GW, 14,* 337; *SE, 21,* 16.

contact with man lies beyond man's instinctual renunciations, at the level of the three tasks we assigned to culture; it promises man alleviation of his instinctual burden, reconciliation with his ineluctable fate, and recompense for all his sacrifices. But this movement beyond renunciation is also a return to the hither side of renunciation: for it is to man's desires that the consolation is addressed. Just as all the situations of helplessness and dependency repeat the childhood condition of distress, so too consolation proceeds by repeating the prototype of all the figures of consolation, the father figure. It is because he is forever helpless *like a child* that man remains stricken with longing for the father. Faced with nature, the man-child conjures up gods in the image of the father.

This benevolent figure is precisely what is needed to fulfill the economic task we have just described. By representing the hostile presence of nature in human form, man treats nature as a being that can be appeased and influenced; by substituting psychology for the science of nature, religion fulfills the deepest wish of mankind. In this sense it may be said that desire is what creates religion, even more than fear.[42]

Thus the economic function of culture has enabled us to construct a psychoanalysis of Providence; the god capable of fulfilling this task must be a benevolent figure, beyond all severity; if nature is to be proportionate to man's desires, it must be ruled by such a favorable, wise, and just will.

This direct deduction of what Freud believes to be the highest form of religion has an obvious advantage: it brings to light, by a striking shortcut, the end moment of religion as a return to the historical origins of the idea of God. The deity again becomes a unique person; henceforth man's relationship with him can recapture the intimacy of the child's relationship with his father. Furthermore, it immediately places religion within a cultural context and rescues it from the private circle of the individual's neurosis; religion springs from the same need as the other functions of culture: from the necessity of defending man against the superior powers of nature.

On the other hand, this direct deduction of monotheism, which

42. Ibid., *GW, 14*, 352; *SE, 21*, 30.

appears to do away with the long detour through the earlier figures, from the totem animal to spirits and the gods of polytheism, might give the impression that Freud substituted the motive of human helplessness for the father complex of *Totem and Taboo*. But this motive, considered alone, is "less deeply concealed" [43] than the father complex; it is necessary to point out the connecting links "between the deeper and the manifest motives, between the father-complex and man's helplessness and need for protection." [44] In the language that I have adopted, the hermeneutics of culture in psychoanalysis is always the counterpart of an economics of desire: between the cultural function of consolation as provided by religion and the concealed longing for the father there exists the same relationship as between the manifest and the latent content of dreams. The connection between the two points of view is assured by the very meaning of the adult's helplessness, inasmuch as that helplessness is a continuation and repetition of the helplessness of childhood. Man is "destined to remain a child forever"; [45] therefore he endows the unknown and fearsome powers with the features of his father image.

Such is the specifically psychoanalytic interpretation of religion: religion's "hidden" meaning is the sempiternal repetition of the longing for the father.

We can now set within the framework of this economics the double analogy that has guided us in the clinical description—the dream analogy and the neurosis analogy.[46] This analogy has become an identity; if religion has no truth proper to itself, what is the source of its strength and effectiveness? Religious ideas "are not precipitates of experience or end-results of thinking: they are illusions, fulfillments of the oldest, strongest and most urgent wishes of mankind. The secret of their strength lies in the strength of those wishes." [47] This underlying identity, from the economic point of view, between illusion and dream fantasy has an important corol-

43. On this confrontation with *Totem and Taboo*, cf. *GW, 14*, 344–46; *SE, 21*, 22–24.
44. Ibid.
45. Ibid.
46. *GW, 14*, 367–68; *SE, 21*, 42–45.
47. *GW, 14*, 352; *SE, 21*, 30.

lary, the consequences of which we shall draw when we discuss the meaning of the reality principle in Freud. If religion *is* wish-fulfillment, it is not in essence the support of morality; indeed, history proves that "immorality has found no less support in religion than morality has." [48] If that is so, a fundamental revision of the connections between culture and religion is called for: if religion, as consolation, ultimately has more connection with desires than with their prohibition, it becomes conceivable that culture may outlast religion. In this postreligious culture, cultural prohibitions would have merely a social justification; laws and institutions would have only a human origin.

But, on the other hand, religion is not pure illusion, since it includes "important historical recollections." [49] *Moses and Monotheism* speaks in this sense of "what is true in religion." [50] Freud's insistence on the reality of these recollections provides a historical basis for the analogy between religion and obsessional neurosis. If the analogy of illusion and dreams is based on the infantile character of the father complex, the analogy of religion with neurosis has the same basis, if it is true that "a human child cannot successfully complete its development to the civilized stage without passing through a phase of neurosis sometimes of greater and sometimes of less distinctness." [51]

This theme, clearly delineated in *The Future of an Illusion,* forms the guiding idea of *Moses and Monotheism.* It is particularly operative in the correspondence discovered by Freud between the phenomenon of latency belonging to neurosis and the phenomenon of latency he thinks he has discovered in the history of Judaism, a latency extending from the killing of Moses to the reawakening of the Mosaic religion at the time of the prophets. We thus hit upon the point of intersection of the clinical description, the genetic explanation, and the economic explanation: "Between the problem of traumatic neurosis and that of Jewish monotheism there is . . . one point of agreement: namely, in the characteristic that might be

48. *GW, 14,* 361; *SE, 21,* 38.
49. *GW, 14,* 366; *SE, 21,* 42.
50. *GW, 16,* 230 ff. ("Der Wahrheitsgehalt der Religion"); *SE, 23,* 122 ff.
51. *The Future of an Illusion, GW, 14,* 366–67; *SE, 21,* 42–45.

described as 'latency.' " This analogy, Freud notes, "is very complete, and approaches identity." [52] Once granted the formula for the development of neurosis—early trauma, defense, latency, outbreak of neurosis, partial return of the repressed—the comparison between the history of the human species and that of the individual does the rest:

> Something occurred in the life of the human species similar to what occurs in the life of individuals . . . here too events occurred of a sexually aggressive nature, which left behind them permanent consequences but were for the most part fended off and forgotten, and which after a long latency came into effect and created phenomena similar to symptoms in their structure and purpose.[53]

Such is the well-founded analogy upon which the psychoanalysis of religion ends: it undoubtedly constitutes the most striking example of the interaction, in Freud's works, between the interpretation of dreams and neurosis and the hermeneutics of culture. We will discuss its validity at the end of our "Dialectic."

52. *Moses and Monotheism, GW, 16,* 176–77; *SE,* 23, 72.
53. *GW, 16,* 186; *SE, 23,* 80.

PART III: EROS, THANATOS, ANANKE

Thus far in our reading of Freud we have deliberately skirted the great upheaval brought to light in the celebrated essay of 1920, *Beyond the Pleasure Principle*.[1] This reworking is more extensive than the one that the 1914 paper, with its introduction of the concept of narcissism, had imposed on the notions of subject and object and on the general economy of the human psychism. The introduction of the death instinct into the theory of the instincts is truly a recasting from top to bottom. It is a revision that affects, first, psychoanalytic discourse itself, such as we presented it in its epistemology in Part I; then, by degrees, the interpretation of all the *signs* that constitute the semantics of desire; and finally, the notion of culture itself, the general picture of which we provisionally sketched in Part II.

The new instinct theory questions the initial Freudian hypotheses and especially the conception of a psychical apparatus subject to the constancy principle. We recall that, by postulating the equivalence between the pleasure principle and the constancy principle, Freud thought he was placing psychoanalysis in the scientific tradition of Helmholtz and Fechner. Psychoanalysis could become accredited as a science thanks to the quasi physics of the psychical apparatus and to the quantitative transcription of the economic phenomena underlying the work of interpretation. In Part I we showed that the insight proper to psychoanalysis lies elsewhere, in the reciprocity between interpretation and explanation, between hermeneutics and the economics; but at the same time we had to recognize that the speculation based on the quantitative hypothesis is not in complete harmony with the actual nature of analytical dis-

1. *Jenseits des Lustprinzips, GW, 13,* 3–69; *SE, 18,* 7–64.

course. The new instinct theory involves a type of speculation about life and death that is far different from the quantitative theory; it comes closer to the views of Goethe and romantic thought, and even of Empedocles and the great pre-Socratics. The very title *Beyond the Pleasure Principle* is warning enough that it is to this level—the level of the most general hypotheses concerning the functioning of life—that the conceptual revolution must be carried. In order to account for this switch in tonality, this movement from scientism to romanticism, I have placed Part III under the great emblematic titles of Eros, Thanatos, and Ananke. In face of death, the libido changes meaning and receives the mythical name of Eros. And in face of the pair Eros-Thanatos, the reality principle, the opposite pole of the pleasure principle, unfolds a whole hierarchy of meaning that goes under the equally mythical name of Ananke.

Our first task will be to establish the great polarity present throughout Freud's works, the polarity between the pleasure principle and the reality principle. This will be the object of the first chapter. This antithesis is closely tied in with the initial Freudian hypotheses: constancy hypothesis and quantitative hypothesis, representation of the psychism as a self-regulating apparatus, etc. The tie between the pleasure principle and the constancy hypothesis is so great that one may legitimately ask whether the questioning of the initial hypotheses implies not only a "beyond the pleasure principle" but also a "beyond the reality principle." It is important therefore to accurately locate the meaning of the reality principle and to see how much the initial Freudian hypotheses allow its meaning to vary. Between the perceptual function, which we have often seen associated with consciousness and the ego, and resignation to the ineluctable, there is, no doubt, a rather considerable margin of meaning. The question then will be to what extent the new instinct theory succeeds in displacing the center of gravity of the concept of reality from one pole toward the other.

We will not be able to give a definitive answer to this question until we have made a detailed interpretation of the death instinct. Therefore we will reserve a new and final examination of Freud's notion of reality for Chapter 3, in which we will group together some of the critical questions raised by this new reading of the theory. Let us say immediately that one should not expect too much from this rereading. For reasons bearing closely on the reality principle's critical function toward the world of desire and illusion, the earliest formulation of the reality principle is the one that will offer the most resistance to the doctrinal upheaval caused by the introduction of the death instinct.

The object of Chapter 2 will be to accurately describe the great hypotheses concerning life and death. Part I has taught us that the speculative hypotheses in Freudian theory cannot be justified by themselves. Their meaning is determined in the interplay between interpretation and explanation. The speculative hypotheses are verified by their capacity to interrelate hermeneutic concepts—such as apparent meaning and hidden meaning, symptom and fantasy, instinctual representative, ideas, and affects—with economic concepts, such as cathexis, displacement, substitution, projection, introjection, etc. We have seen that the specificity of analytical discourse ultimately lies in the relation between instinct as the primary energy concept and instinctual representative as the primary hermeneutic concept; such discourse unites the two universes of force and meaning in a semantics of desire. Our first question then is this: What happens to this discourse, this semantics of desire, when a more romantic type of speculation about life and death is joined to a more scientific type of speculation about the constancy hypothesis and its psychological equivalent, the pleasure principle?

Part I of our "Analytic" affords us a good clue: an instinct is always a deciphered reality—deciphered in its instinctual representatives. What are the representatives of the death instinct? With this question a new phase of the work of deciphering is opened and also a new relation between desire and its signs. Starting from this new connection between hermeneutics and economics we will be able to appreciate the scope of the revolution that affects the fundamental hypotheses concerning the functioning of life.

The instinct theory, as we said above, is subjected to a thorough recasting. The revision of the basis of the theory is presented to us in *Beyond the Pleasure Principle*. The revision of the upper reaches of the theory is to be found in the theory of culture, which we presented in part in Part II of the "Analytic" and which finds, if not its completion, at least an extensive development in *Civilization and Its Discontents.*[2]

It is at the level of culture that the death instinct, the "mute" instinct par excellence, makes its way into the "clamor" of history. Thus the basic connection between the economics and the hermeneutics of the death instinct is worked out in the metabiological hypotheses of the 1920 essay and the metacultural theory of the 1929 essay. It is a two-way connection. On the one hand, by ending his theory of culture on the clear note of war, Freud brings out the meaning of the death instinct. On the other hand, by introducing the death instinct into the instinct theory, he can view the meaning of culture as a unified endeavor to which are subordinated the partial phenomena of art, morality, and religion: it is in relation to the "battle of the giants," Eros and Thanatos, that the enterprise of culture assumes its radical and global meaning.

The new reading of the instinct theory requires that the esthetic, ethical, and religious phenomena, which we considered individually in Part II, must now be reread as a group. The previous reading was based on the gradual extension of the model of dreams and the neuroses to all cultural representations. Thus it was an analogical reading, with all the fragmentary and inconclusive character of analogy, for the question remained whether the differences were more significant than the similarities. In placing the task of culture in the field of the struggle between Eros and Thanatos, Freud raises his interpretation to the rank of a single and strong idea. Whereas the first reading, fragmentary and analogical, characterized psychoanalysis as a discipline of thought, the second reading, global and sovereign, characterizes it as a world view. After the analogy step by step, the gaze of the eagle . . .

At the same time, however, the Freudian doctrine clears the way for a more radical questioning which challenges the most assured certitudes. These unresolved questions I would like to group to-

2. *Das Unbehagen in der Kultur, GW, 14,* 421–506; *SE, 21,* 64–145.

gether in Chapter 3 under the three headings: What is negativity? What is pleasure? What is reality? [3]

3. "We would readily express our gratitude to any philosophical or psychological theory which was able to inform us of the meaning [*die Bedeutungen*] of the feelings of pleasure and unpleasure [*Lust und Unlustempfindungen*] which act so imperatively upon us. But on this point we are, alas, offered nothing to the purpose. This is the most obscure and inaccessible region of the mind, and, since we cannot avoid contact with it, the least rigid [*lockerste*] hypothesis, it seems to me, will be the best" (*GW*, *13*, 3–4; *SE*, *18*, 7).

Chapter 1: The Pleasure Principle and the Reality Principle

Beyond the Pleasure Principle—this means, in 1920, the introduction of the death instinct into the theory of the instincts. Yet Freud's doctrine always had a "beyond the pleasure principle," namely, the reality principle. It is impossible therefore to judge the extent of the revolution imposed by the death instinct on the theory of the instincts without first setting up the very first polarity, that of pleasure and reality.

Freud's concept of reality is less simple than it appears. Its development may be outlined as follows:

1. At the start, the two principles of "mental functioning," to use the language of an important short paper of 1911, are coextensive with what was described as the "primary process" and the "secondary process." As we have already analyzed the meaning of these expressions, we will content ourselves with translating that analysis into the terms of the opposition that interests us here. Thus the initial concept of reality is first of all elaborated in the clinical context of the theory of the neuroses and of dreams; the metapsychological papers of 1914–17 enlarge this concept of reality by giving it an economic meaning in accord with the meaning assigned by the first topography to the notions of unconscious, preconscious, and conscious; in general, reality is the correlate of the function of consciousness. By thus moving from a descriptive and clinical meaning to a systematic and economic meaning, we transcribe the initial concept into a new key without actually transforming it.

2. A further enrichment of the reality principle is found in the investigation of the object-relation; we still remain at the level of the first theory of instincts (opposition between sexual instincts and

ego-instincts) and of the first topography (representation of the psychical apparatus as a series of places: unconscious, preconscious, conscious).

3. A more decisive transformation of the notion of reality occurs in connection with the two important revisions of the theory considered in previous chapters: the introduction of narcissism and the switch to the second topography. For different but convergent reasons, these two revisions find expression in a progressive dramatization of the opposition between the pleasure principle and the reality principle. The real is no longer simply the contrary of hallucination; it is harsh necessity, as revealed after the abandonment of narcissism and after the failures, deceptions, and conflicts which culminate in the Oedipus period. At this point reality is called necessity, and at times even Ananke.

The great "remythicizing" of the instinct theory, which we will consider in the following chapter and which is symbolized by Eros and death, will play an important part in this process of dramatization; we will leave the Freudian notion of reality at this threshold, returning to it at the end of our study on death. Thus, we will speak of the reality principle at two different times: before the death instinct and after the death instinct. The transition from a "scientific" picture of the psychical apparatus to a more "romantic" interpretation of the interplay of love and death cannot help but affect the meaning that the notion of reality acquires in Freud's theory. Prior to the death instinct, reality is a regulative concept on the same level as the pleasure principle; that is why it too is called a "principle." After the death instinct, the notion of reality becomes charged with a meaning that raises it to the level of the great quasi-mythical forces that divide up among themselves the empire of the world. This transfiguration will be symbolized by the term Ananke, which calls to mind not only the notion of "destiny" in Greek tragedy, but also that of "nature" in Renaissance philosophy and in Spinoza, as well as of the Nietzschean "eternal return." In short, what at first was merely a principle of "mental regulation" now becomes the cypher of a possible wisdom.

THE REALITY PRINCIPLE AND THE SECONDARY PROCESS

That Freud's remarks about reality began with clinical observations is beyond question. We are reminded of this fact by the opening lines of the short paper of 1911, "Formulations on the Two Principles of Mental Functioning." [1] As Pierre Janet observed, neurotics manifest a loss of "la fonction du réel" ["the function of reality"]; Freud differs somewhat from Janet by maintaining that neurotics turn away from reality because they find it unbearable. Thus at the beginning no special philosophical meaning is attached to the concept of reality. Reality does not pose a problem, it is assumed as known; the normal person and the psychiatrist are its measure; it is the physical and social environment of adaptation.

Still, even on this elementary level it is important to note the lack of homogeneity in the opposition between pleasure and reality. To make the opposition homogeneous, it must be assumed from the start that the pleasure principle interferes with reality as the source of fantasies. Acute hallucinatory psychosis (Meynert's amentia) supplies the initial schema,[2] which Freud extends to all the neuroses: Freud posits that "in fact every neurotic does the same with some fragment of reality." [3] This extension to the neuroses of a schema originally meant for the interpretation of psychosis is based on an early thesis we have already examined—in the neuroses and dreams wish-fulfillment operates in a hallucinatory manner. Start-

1. "Formulierungen über die zwei Prinzipien des psychischen Geschehens," *GW, 8,* 230–38; *SE, 12,* 218–26; *Collected Papers, 4,* 13–21. Cf. Jones, *The Life and Work of Freud, 2,* 312–15.

2. The first formulation of the two principles is found in Letter 105 to Fliess: "My last generalization holds good and seems inclined to spread to an unpredictable extent. It is not only dreams that are fulfillments of wishes, but hysterical attacks as well. This is true of hysterical symptoms, but it probably applies to every product of neurosis—for I recognized it long ago in acute delusional insanity. Reality—wish-fulfillment: it is from this contrasting pair that our mental life springs" (*The Origins of Psychoanalysis,* p. 277). Cf. Jones, *1,* 398.

3. *GW, 8,* 230; *SE, 12,* 218.

ing from this initial nucleus, the task may be reasonably proposed "of investigating the development of the relation of neurotics and of mankind in general to reality, and in this way of bringing the psychological significance of the real external world into the structure of our theories." [4]

The correlation between the pleasure principle and the quasi-hallucinatory function of desire is the basis of the process that Freud, during the period of the "Project" and Chapter 7 of *The Interpretation of Dreams,* called the "primary process"; it also enables him to correlate the reality principle with the secondary process. These two correlations serve as the guiding thread in the remainder of the 1911 paper, although additional themes are indicated which are unintelligible except in relation to the second topography.

The connection between the primary and secondary processes is not a simple one; it reveals two kinds of relations between the pleasure principle and the reality principle. On the one hand, the reality principle is not truly the opposite of the pleasure principle but a detour or roundabout path to satisfaction. The psychical apparatus has in fact never functioned according to the simple schema of the primary process; the pleasure principle, considered in its pure state, is a didactic fiction. Correlatively, the reality principle designates the normal functioning of a psychical apparatus governed by the secondary process. On the other hand, however, the pleasure principle prolongs its reign by assuming many types of disguises. It is the pleasure principle that animates the whole of fantasy existence in all its normal and pathological forms, from dreams to ideals to religious illusions. Taken thus in its disguised forms, it appears quite impossible to go beyond the pleasure principle. From this standpoint the reality principle designates an order of existence difficult to attain.

In our study of the "Project" we mentioned the various reasons why the pleasure principle, taken absolutely, is a fiction that has never been the actual condition of man. For one thing, the internal instincts always break the equilibrium and make the total discharge of tensions impossible; the psychical apparatus is thus forced to de-

4. Ibid.

viate from the simple energy functioning represented by the constancy principle. Secondly, the experience of satisfaction inevitably involves the help of others, object-relations, and consequently the whole circuit of reality. We recall this striking text of the "Project":

> At early stages the human organism is incapable of achieving this specific action. It is brought about by extraneous help, when the attention of an experienced person has been drawn to the child's condition by a discharge . . . This path of discharge thus acquires an extremely important secondary function—viz., of bringing about an understanding with other people; and the original helplessness of human beings is thus the primal source of all moral motives.[5]

Finally, unpleasure, according to another formula of the "Project," is "the sole means of education": [6] unpleasure gives a hedonistic sense to the reality principle itself and sets it within the prolongation of the pleasure principle. As a matter of fact, hallucinatory satisfaction is a biological impasse and would inevitably lead to failure; hence, the setting up of the reality principle is demanded by the pleasure principle itself.

If then the reality principle coincides with the secondary process, every human psychism, so far as it escapes hallucination, obeys that principle.

The third part of the "Project" presents a schematic account of the secondary process understood in the above sense; in this account the reality principle is maintained within the limits of what might be called a calculated or rational hedonism; this schematic picture of the secondary process will never be basically altered. We are acquainted with its main themes: qualitative reality-testing (to which the "Project" assigned a special group of neurons), discrimination between hallucination and perception, attentive exploration of new stimuli; identification of new stimuli with earlier ones by means of judgment (according to a schema close to perceptual judgment in Kant); the movement from observed reality to thought-reality, on the basis of the mnemic traces of heard speech; motor or

5. *Origins*, p. 379.
6. Ibid., p. 428.

muscular domination over reality; control of the delay of discharge with a view toward ideation, etc. Chapter 7 of *The Interpretation of Dreams* adds nothing to this schematic analysis of the secondary process; we have even been able to say that, for reasons of structure stemming from the overall intention of the work, *The Interpretation of Dreams* does not go as far as the "Project."

The main themes of the "Project" are taken up again in the 1911 paper in the first of its eight paragraphs devoted to the reality principle.[7] Once again attention is conceived as anticipated adaptation; memory as the integration of notations of the past; judgment as the comparison and identification between new qualities and memory traces; motor domination as the tonic binding of energy. Finally, the restraint upon motor discharge by means of the process of thinking has the same role as in the "Project"; it may even be said that the text of the "Project" is in every regard the more explicit of the two.

The analysis of the reality principle would be incomplete if we restricted ourselves to this conception of the secondary process, whose contrary remains a theoretical construct. But *The Interpretation of Dreams* already showed, in an inverse manner, why one *cannot go beyond* the pleasure principle. The psychical apparatus, it will be remembered, was pictured as capable of functioning in either a progressive or a regressive direction. This schematic diagram, in many respects a misleading one, at least suggests the notion of a psychism operating in reverse, a psychism that resists the substitution of the reality principle for the pleasure principle. Hence the pleasure principle no longer designates merely an earlier fictive stage, but the reverse movement of the apparatus—what Chapter 7 called the topographical regression or the tendency of the psychical apparatus to restore the primitive form of hallucinatory wish-fulfillment. Thus Freud was able to define a *Wunsch*, which we translate approximately as "desire," as the tendency to restore the hallucinatory form of fulfillment:

> As a result of the link that has thus been established, next time this need arises a psychical impulse will at once emerge which

7. *GW*, *8*, 230–31; *SE*, *12*, 219–21.

> will seek to re-cathect the mnemic image of the perception and to re-evoke the perception itself, that is to say, to re-establish the situation of the original satisfaction. An impulse of this kind is what we call a wish [*Wunsch*]; the reappearance of the perception is the fulfillment of the wish [*Wunscherfüllung*]; and the shortest path to the fulfillment of the wish is a path leading direct from the excitation produced by the need to a complete cathexis of the perception. Nothing prevents us from assuming that there was a primitive state of the psychical apparatus in which this path was actually traversed, that is, in which wishing ended in hallucinating. Thus the aim of this first psychical activity was to produce a "perceptual identity"—a repetition of the perception which was linked with the satisfaction of the need.[8]

This shortest path to fulfillment is no doubt closed to us, but in a figurative and substitute mode it is the path we take in all forms of fantasying; neurotic symptoms, our dreams at night, and our day-dreams are evidence of the supremacy of the pleasure principle and the proof of its power.[9]

From this second point of view, while the pleasure principle represents an actual mode of functioning, the reality principle expresses an aim or task to be achieved. The difficulty of that task is stressed in the remainder of the analysis; the pleasure principle is less costly; the reality principle implies the giving up of the short circuit between desire and hallucination.

This dramatic relation is summed up very briefly in the second paragraph of the 1911 paper:

> A general tendency of our mental apparatus, which can be traced back to the economic principle of saving expenditure [of energy], seems to find expression in the tenacity with which we hold onto the sources of pleasure at our disposal, and in the difficulty with which we renounce them. With the introduction of the reality principle one species of thought-activity was split off [*wurde eine Art Denkbarkeit abgespalten*]; it was kept free from reality-testing and remained subordinated to the pleasure princi-

8. *GW*, *2/3*, 571; *SE*, *5*, 565–66.
9. *GW*, *8*, 234; *SE*, *12*, 222.

> ple alone. This activity is fantasying [*Phantasieren*], which begins already in children's play, and later, continued as *day-dreaming*, abandons dependence on real objects.[10]

Behind these brief remarks must be placed everything that Chapter 7 of *The Interpretation of Dreams* says about the indestructibility of one's earliest desires, about man's inability to move from a rule of fantasy to a rule of reality—in short, everything that makes the human psychism a Thing and justifies the appeal to a topography. The path to reality is indeed the more difficult path. Many allusions, both in the "Project" and in the present paper, imply that reality is actually reached only through thought devoted to scientific work.

Such is, from the "Project" of 1895 to the article of 1911, the conception of the double functioning of the psychical apparatus. Freud will make additions to this conception but basically he will not alter it. The "Papers on Metapsychology" merely present a topographical and economic translation of it, harmonizing it with the first schematic picture of the psychical apparatus that we have called the first topography.

Thus, in the paper "The Unconscious," the opposition between the pleasure principle and the reality principle is incorporated into the great oppositions between the "systems" (*Ucs.*, *Pcs.*, *Cs.*). This translation deserves our attention, since for the first time it makes it possible to relate the reality principle to the system *Cs.* and to define reality as the correlate of consciousness.

This "systemic" translation occurs in the section called "The Special Characteristics of the System *Ucs.*"[11] The pleasure-unpleasure principle is classified with exemption from contradiction (no negation, no doubt, no degrees of certainty), the mobility of cathexes, and timelessness. Inversely, the reality principle is classified with negation and contradiction, the tonic binding of energy, and reference to time.

10. Ibid.

11. "To sum up: *exemption from mutual contradiction, primary process* (mobility of cathexes), *timelessness*, and *replacement of external by psychical reality*—these are the characteristics which we may expect to find in processes belonging to the system *Ucs.*" (*GW*, *10*, 286; *SE*, *14*, 187).

Of all Freud's theoretical writings, the "Metapsychological Supplement to the Theory of Dreams" (1916) [12] contains the most exact formulation of this correlation between the system *Cs.* and the reality principle. Correcting Chapter 7 of *The Interpretation of Dreams,* Freud admits that the topographical regression—that is, the resolution of wishful thoughts into mnemic images derived from earlier experiences of satisfaction, and the revival of those images —does not adequately account for the belief in reality that accompanies hallucination. Hallucination further requires the abolition of the discriminating function of perceptual judgment; hence this discriminating function must be connected with some special psychical institution, with some "contrivance [*Einrichtung*] with the help of which it was possible to distinguish such wishful perceptions from a real fulfillment [*von einer realen Erfüllung*] and to avoid them for the future." [13] Freud calls the function that hallucination abolishes "reality-testing" (*Realitätsprüfung*).[14]

In investigating this function we are led to say that one and the same system regulates the process of becoming conscious and reality-testing. To discriminate between what is internal and what is external pertains to a single function, a function obviously connected with muscular action, for it is by such action that objects are made to appear and disappear. Thus one may speak of a single system *Cs.-Pcpt.,* which has its own cathexis or charge capable of resisting libidinal invasion. Reality-testing is thus intimately linked with the system *Cs.* and its peculiar cathexis. Freud states, "We shall place reality-testing among the major *institutions* [*Institutionen*] *of the ego,* alongside the *censorships* which we have come to recognize between the psychical systems." [15] The censorships that accompany reality-testing are the ones that protect the systems *Pcs.* and *Cs.* against libidinal cathexes; they are the ones that give way in wishful psychosis by a "turning away" (*Abwendung*) or "withdrawal" (*Entziehung*) from reality, or in the state of sleep by a "voluntary

12. "Metapsychologische Ergänzung zur Traumlehre," *GW, 10,* 412–26; *SE, 14,* 222–35; *Collected Papers, 4,* 137–51.
13. *GW, 10,* 422; *SE, 14,* 231.
14. Ibid.
15. *GW, 10,* 424; *SE, 14,* 233.

renunciation." The narcissistic flight into sleep is thus equivalent to a loss of cathexis on the part of the system *Cs.*[16]

Every topographical regression, characteristic of the loss of the function of reality, supposes therefore an alteration of the system *Cs.* itself. But Freud openly admits that the topographic-economic theory of the system *Cs.-Pcpt.* remains to be constructed. Once again the doctrine does not come to decisive conclusions but rather sets the framework for investigation. Our whole previous discussion concerning consciousness as the "surface" of the psychical apparatus (along the lines of Chapter 2 of *The Ego and the Id*) belongs to this investigation of the system *Cs.-Pcpt.*, which we now know is the counterpart to any study of the reality principle. When Freud says that the system *Pcpt.* is the nucleus of the ego,[17] he is in fact stating the reality principle. Thus we can now erect the great function of "externality" over against the demands, ethical as well as instinctual, of the internal world; later on, when we have introduced the superego into the confrontation with reality, we will be able to say with *The Ego and the Id:*

> Whereas the ego is essentially the representative [*Repräsentant*] of the external world, of reality, the superego stands in contrast to it as the representative [*Anwalt*] of the internal world, of the id. Conflicts between the ego and the ideal will, as we are now prepared to find, ultimately reflect the contrast between what is real and what is psychical, between the external world and the internal world.[18]

THE REALITY PRINCIPLE AND "OBJECT-CHOICE"

The pleasure principle is the short and easy path; everything regressive leads back to it. The reality

16. *GW, 10,* 425; *SE, 14,* 234.
17. "Mourning and Melancholia" speaks along the same lines: "We shall count it [conscience], along with the censorship of consciousness and reality-testing, among the major institutions of the ego" (*GW, 10,* 433; *SE, 14,* 247).
18. *GW, 13,* 264; *SE, 19,* 36.

principle is the long and hard path; it entails renunciation and mourning over archaic objects.

This simple schematic picture was developed, without basic alteration, by all the analyses concerning what we have frequently called the history of desire. This schematic "chronology" of desire will reveal further relationships between the pleasure principle and the reality principle.

In his first theory of the libido Freud limited the investigation of the instincts to the domain of the sexual instincts, provisionally opposed to the ego-instincts; thus he delimited the area in which the conflict between the two principles of mental functioning especially occurs. The replacement of the pleasure principle by the reality principle is not accomplished all at once, nor does it take place simultaneously all along the line of the instincts: the domain of the libido is the one in which the change of regime occurs with most difficulty. The libido remains under the dominance of the pleasure principle longer than any other instinct because primitive autoerotism enables it for some time to escape the experience of frustration and, consequently, education by means of unpleasure, and also because the period of latency further delays the confrontation with reality until puberty. Sexuality is thus the seat of archaism, whereas the ego-instincts are directly at grips with the resistances of the real.[19] The pleasure principle continues its dominance mainly in the region of fantasy, where the structure of Wunsch lasts the longest, perhaps even indefinitely. We have often underscored this specificity of the semantics of sexual desire; unlike hunger or even the defense of the ego, sexuality gives rise to imagination and to speech, but in an unrealistic mode; at this point the semantics of desire is a semantics of delusion. That is why the reality principle is seen as the outcome of a battle which takes place no longer merely in the substructures of desire but in the numerous branchings of the realm of fantasy, on the plane of what the "Papers on Metapsychology" call the "offshoots" or "derivatives" of instinct, in all the areas of ideas, affectivity, and the spoken expressions of desire.

In his theory of the "stages" of the libido Freud attempted to

19. "Formulations on the Two Principles of Mental Functioning," *GW*, *8*, 234; *SE*, *12*, 222.

highlight the main steps of this history of desire in which the battle between fantasy and reality takes place. By thus interrelating what he calls in the 1911 paper "the supersession of the pleasure principle by the reality principle" [20] and the theory of stages, he establishes an interesting connection between the reality principle and "object-choice," which forms the central theme of the history of the libido. This connection is more precise and illuminating than the connection we established above between the reality principle and the secondary process.

The point of departure is found in an important remark in the *Three Essays on Sexuality* to the effect that an instinct has a specific "aim" but variable "objects." This original tendency toward deviation on the part of desire is what prolongs the rule of the pleasure principle. Since the relation to the object is not given, it has to be acquired; this problem is designated in the analytic doctrine by the term *Objektwahl*, object-choice, and constitutes the central theme of the theory of the libidinal stages.

Placed within this precise perspective, the reality principle coincides with the institution of the genital stage, and still more precisely, with the subordination of object-love to procreation. On this point Freud never varied; he assumes that there is a correspondence between the reality principle and a specific intrapsychical organization—a form of "organization and subordination to the reproductive function." To this repeated statement of the *Three Essays* [21] there corresponds a similar statement of the 1911 article: "While the ego goes through its transformation from a *pleasure-ego* into a *reality-ego*, the sexual instincts undergo the changes that lead them from their original auto-erotism through various intermediate phases to object-love in the service of procreation." [22] Thus, reality resides in the relation to the other, not only to another body as an external source of pleasure, but to another desire, and finally to the fate of the species. In the area of the sexual libido, the reciprocal relation between complementary partners of the same species and the submission of the individual to the species are decisive for the

20. Ibid. (*die Ablosung des Lustprinzips durch das Realitätsprinzip*).
21. *GW, 5*, 99, 109, 139; *SE, 7*, 199 (1915), 207 (1905), 237 (1905).
22. *GW, 8*, 237; *SE, 12*, 224.

supremacy of the reality principle. The basic contribution of psychoanalysis in this regard is to have shown that this conquest of the most highly complex form of organization is difficult and precarious, not by reason of chance social conditioning, but by reason of a structural necessity. This is what distinguishes Freud from all culturalists who seek to trace the difficulty of living back to the circumstances of the existing social environment. For Freud, the successive phases of sexuality are tenacious and hard to "abandon"; thus the pathway to reality is marked off with lost objects,[23] the first of which is the mother's breast; auto-erotism itself is partly linked with this lost object. Consequently, "the choice of an object" has a nature that is both prospective and nostalgic: "The finding of an object is in fact a refinding of it." [24] For the libido, the future is in the past, in "the happiness that has been lost." [25] Freud often stated that object-choice has, so to speak, no choice; by a kind of inner fate it will pattern itself on the model of the person's own body or on that of the one who was responsible for the child's care: it will be narcissistic or anaclitic.[26]

This dramatic interpretation of the history of desire reaches its climax with the Oedipus complex, which concerns our present investigation by reason of the numerous fantasies it gives rise to. The oedipal crisis is not localized in time; it continues to come to the surface in the form of incestuous fantasies in dreams and the neuroses. Freud's insistence upon the incestuous nucleus of neurosis is well known; it is the point, he says, on which psychoanalysis stands or falls. But the essence of the oedipal drama is itself fantasy; it is a drama enacted and dreamed. Yet it is all the more serious a drama, for it stems from an impossible request on the part of desire. Desire began by wishing for the impossible (a situation which the doctrine expressed in terms that shocked and scandalized: the son wishes to have a child by his mother, and the daughter by her father); because

23. *Three Essays, GW, 5,* 123 ff. (*die Objekfindung*); *SE, 7,* 222 ff.
24. Ibid.
25. Ibid.
26. Ibid. Footnote added in 1915; Freud thus harmonizes his text with the discoveries made in Section II of the paper "On Narcissism," in which are differentiated "two methods"—anaclitic and narcissistic—of "finding an object."

it wished the impossible, desire was necessarily disappointed and wounded. Hence the path to reality is not only lined with lost objects but with forbidden and refused objects as well. Enough has been said about the importance of these abandonments and renunciations in the formation of the superego; we must now speak of their effect on the reality principle.

In the article of 1911, Freud distinguishes the reality-ego from the pleasure-ego (*Lustich*).[27] If desire or wishing (*Wunsch*) is the central drive of the pleasure-ego, the striving for the useful is the central drive of the reality-ego: "Just as the pleasure-ego can do nothing but *wish* [*wünschen*] . . . so the reality-ego need do nothing but strive for what is *useful* and guard itself against damage."[28] Here Freud stands on familiar ground. The early Socratic dialogues revolve around the meaning of the useful. Nor should the Kantian critique conceal the positive significance of this reflection upon the useful; by opposing the useful to the deceitfulness of Wunsch, Freud restores to the useful its role as an indication of reality. This opposition subsumes, at a more complex level of elaboration, the opposition we previously found between the primary and the secondary processes. On the one hand, the useful is the truth of the pleasurable; it is the true pleasurable substituted for the dreamed pleasurable. In this sense, the reality principle is indeed the safeguard of the pleasure principle: "Actually the substitution of the reality principle for the pleasure principle implies no deposing [*Absetzung*] of the pleasure principle, but only a safeguarding [*Sicherung*] of it."[29] On the other hand, the pleasure-ego has so many tricks in its bag, so many ramifications on the plane of the derivatives from the unconscious, that respect for the useful, however modest its claims may be from the standpoint of ethics, already appears as a form of discipline.

The corrective value of the useful becomes evident as soon as one considers that desire or wishing is the infinite source of fantasies and the springboard of illusions. Desire mystifies; the reality principle is desire demystified; the giving up of archaic objects is

27. *GW*, *8*, 235; *SE*, *12*, 223.
28. Ibid.
29. Ibid.

now expressed in the exercise of suspicion, in the movement of disillusion, in the death of idols.

Here the "ethnographical" history of desire cuts across and enriches the "psychological" history of desire. It cuts across it insofar as one can make an exemplary history of belief coincide with a history of the stages of the libido. We recall the terms in which Freud attempted to effect this coincidence in *Totem and Taboo*: [30] to the auto-erotic stage would correspond the omnipotence of thoughts, characteristic of pre-animism and the techniques of magic; to object-choice would correspond the dispossession of the omnipotence of thoughts to the profit of demons, spirits and gods; to the genital stage of the libido would correspond the recognition of the omnipotence of nature. But this ethnographical history of desire, however fanciful it may be, not only cuts across the history of the stages of the organization of the libido, it also adds to it the essential theme of omnipotence. This theme is the "religious" nucleus of the pleasure principle; there is an element of "evil infinitude" in desire; the reality principle—even when stated in the seemingly philistine form of the utility principle—basically expresses the loss of the "evil infinitude," the reconversion to the finite.

That is why *Totem and Taboo* could say that the dispossession of desire's "omnipotence" to the profit of the gods already expresses the first victory of the reality principle. From this point of view, myths present an imaginary expression of this substitution, or, as the 1911 paper says in its fourth paragraph, "a mythical projection of this revolution in the mind." [31] It could be said, in paradoxical terms, that for Freud religion marks the victory of the reality principle over the pleasure principle, but in a mythical mode; thus religion is at once the supreme figure of the abandonment of desire and the supreme figure of the fulfillment of desire.

For Freud the analyst and scientist—I do not return to the difficulty of distinguishing between Freud's personal "prejudice" and the positive achievement of psychoanalysis in this critique of religion—it is science alone that completely satisfies the reality principle and assures the triumph of the useful over the pleasurable, of

30. See above, pp. 236 ff.
31. *GW*, *8*, 236; *SE*, *12*, 223.

the reality-ego over the pleasure-ego. Science alone triumphs over the substitute figures, increasingly complicated and sublimated, in which the pleasure-ego pursues its dream of omnipotence and immortality.

Thus the reality principle is not completely victorious until the adult is capable of giving up not only lost archaic objects of the narcissistic or anaclitic type, not only forbidden objects of the incestuous type, but also mythical objects, through which desire pursues satisfaction in the substitute mode of compensation or consolation. The reality principle might be said to symbolize the access to true utility through the long detour of "mourning" over lost, forbidden, and consoling objects.

I do not argue the point that Freud's "scientism" reduced his vision of reality to observable facts, nor that his critique of idols led him to overlook other dimensions of reality. This narrowness of the Freudian theory is of less importance to me at this stage of reflection than the role he assigns to mourning over the lost object and its derivatives. This loss or renunciation, together with all the pruning it involves of the realm of fantasy, turns the theme of reality toward that of necessity.

Other aspects of the theory, and its entire later development, strengthen this alliance between reality and necessity.

THE REALITY PRINCIPLE AND THE ECONOMIC TASK OF THE EGO

The connection we have established between the ego-agency and the reality principle opens a final field of exploration for us. If reality is that which stands over against the ego, in the topographical sense of the word, then everything that concerns the "economic task of the ego" also concerns the reality principle.

Do we run the risk of dissipating the concept of reality by overextending it? Not if we keep as our guiding thread the differentiation between the "internal" and the "external." To each new complexity of the "internal world" there corresponds a new task for the ego as the representative of the external world.

Freud enriched this world of interiority in two different ways: first, by the revision of the instinct theory, that is, by the introduction of narcissism; second, by the change from the first to the second topography (ego, id, superego). By these two paths he entered more deeply into the unfathomable depths of interiority; at the same time he increasingly dramatized the relation to reality.

Narcissism directly concerns the relation to reality, inasmuch as self-attention is inattention to the other. In the language of the metapsychology, this inaccessibility to the other is expressed by saying that narcissism is the "reservoir" of libido. According to this economy of narcissism, each object-cathexis is a kind of provisional affective investment. Our loves and hatreds are the revocable figures of love derived from the undifferentiated substrate of narcissism: like the waves of the sea, these figures may be effaced without alteration of the substrate. The possibility of sublimation, it will be remembered, stems from the constant return to the "egoistic" libidinal substrate; because of this return we can abandon aims and transform abandoned object-choices into "modifications of the ego"; because of it, consequently, our successive identifications form a precipitate that may be likened to a secondary narcissism by reason of the economic relations between identification, sublimation, desexualization, and narcissism.

Thus is deepened an ever richer and more articulated interiority. The counterpart to this indirect reinforcement of narcissism is, of course, a lack of self-detachment in our consideration of the world. Here we encounter a striking analysis that Freud made in the short paper entitled "A Difficulty in the Path of Psychoanalysis": [32] narcissism opposed acceptance of the discoveries of Copernicus, for they stripped us of the illusion of being at the center of the universe; it opposed Darwin's evolutionist theories, which plunge us into the vast flux of life; finally, it resists psychoanalysis because the latter shakes the primacy and sovereignty of consciousness. A new aspect

32. "Eine Schwierigkeit der Psychoanalyse" (1917), *GW, 12,* 3–12; *SE, 17,* 137–44.

of the conflict between the pleasure principle and the reality principle is brought to light: [33] narcissism interposes itself between ourselves and reality; that is why the truth is always wounding to our narcissism.

These remarks about the power of narcissism to resist truth are greatly corroborated by all that we know about the internal world we call the superego (indeed, the concept of secondary narcissism relates the superego to the primordial inner world or primary narcissism).

Freud did not explicitly treat of the relations between the superego and reality. However, he invites us to explore this path when he states, in *The Ego and the Id,* that "the superego is always close to the id and can act as its representative vis-à-vis the ego. It reaches deep down into the id and for that reason is farther from consciousness than the ego is." [34] The last pages of that essay, devoted to "the dependent relationships of the ego," are a first contribution to this research and foreshadow what a post-Freudian school calls "ego-analysis." Freud's succinct analyses begin by recalling certain functions that have since become classic: order in time, reality-testing, motor inhibition and control; but from now on these functions are considered from the standpoint of the ego's strength and weakness. Thus it is tempting to consider reality as the correlate not only of the ego but of the ego's strength: reality is that which stands over against a strong ego. We thus come back to what seemed to us to constitute the specific problematic of the ego, namely, the problematic of domination and slavery, as in Spinoza's *Ethics.*

The strength of the ego, however, in distinction to the illusory omnipotence spoken of in *Totem and Taboo,* essentially consists in its conciliatory or diplomatic position. In mediating between the id and the superego, between the id and reality, and between the libido and the death instinct, "it only too often yields to the tempta-

33. In the language that we shall use in the "Dialectic" (Ch. 2): the false Cogito is what interposes itself between us and reality; it blocks our relation to the world, it prevents us from letting reality be as it is. If there is, as I believe, a fundamental Cogito, it is first necessary to abandon the position of this screen-cogito, of this resistance-cogito, in order to reach the Cogito that founds in proportion as it lets be.

34. *GW, 13,* 278; *SE, 19,* 48–49.

tion to become sycophantic, opportunist and lying, like a politician who sees the truth but wants to keep his place in popular favor."[35] But this temptation is proper to a mediatory creature, more courtier than arbiter, which must make itself be loved by the id to make the id pliable to the world's order, and which, like a theatrical valet, courts its master's love in order to moderate it. Otherwise the ego would fall under the blows of the superego and once again become prey to the death instincts in their striving to dominate the libido.

A new meaning of the reality principle, intimated rather than expressly formulated, is proposed. I will call it the "prudence" principle, in the full Aristotelian sense; it is opposed to the false idealism of the superego, to its destructive demands, and in general to all the exaggerations of the sublime and to the bad faith of the good conscience.

This prudence principle, which I would like to regard as the culmination of the reality principle, is in sum the ethics of psychoanalysis. In the text we have just commented on, Freud expressly compares the economic task of the ego to that of the analyst: "In point of fact [the ego] behaves like the physician during an analytic treatment: it offers itself, *with the attention it pays to the real world,* as a libidinal object to the id, and aims at attaching the id's libido to itself."[36] The same line of thought is found toward the end of *Civilization and Its Discontents,* where Freud, after having argued that the excessive demands of the superego cannot effectively change the ego, adds: "Consequently we are very often obliged, for therapeutic purposes, to oppose the superego, and we endeavor to lower its demands."[37]

This comparison between the economic task of the ego and the task of psychoanalysis itself is instructive. It may be said that to the patient, the psychoanalyst represents the reality principle in flesh and in act. He does so, however, in proportion as he refrains from judgment and ethical prescription. This abstention from all moral preaching, this analytic detachment, would at first lead one to sup-

35. *The Ego and the Id, GW, 13,* 286–87; *SE, 19,* 56.
36. Ibid. Italics added.
37. *GW, 14,* 503; *SE, 21,* 143.

pose an absence of ethics. But such detachment becomes deeply meaningful when it is placed within the field of the opposition between the pleasure principle and the reality principle. The superego attacks man for being a creature of pleasure, but it demands too much of man and conceals its excesses only by offering the ego the narcissistic satisfaction of being able to think itself better than others; the regard of the analyst, on the contrary, is a regard that has been educated to reality and turned back upon the inner world. Thus the epoche or suspension of value judgments becomes the basic step toward self-knowledge; it is the step that enables the reality principle to gain control of the process of becoming conscious.

Has the whole of ethics been abandoned? The analyst, more than anyone, knows that man is always in an ethical situation; he presupposes this fact at every step; what he says about the Oedipus complex forcefully attests to the moral destiny of man. However, confronted with the fumbling maneuvers of conscience and its strange complicity with the death instinct, the reality principle proposes the substitution of a neutral regard in place of condemnation. There is thus opened up a clearing of truthfulness, in which the lies of the ideals and idols are brought to light and their occult role in the strategy of desire is unmasked. This truthfulness is undoubtedly not the whole of ethics, but at least it is the threshold. No doubt psychoanalysis gives only knowledge, and not veneration.[38] But why should this be asked of it? It does not offer it.

38. Jean Nabert, *Éléments pour une éthique* (Paris, P.U.F., 1943), Ch. 11, "Les sources de la vénération."

Chapter 2: The Death Instincts: Speculation and Interpretation

FREUDIAN SPECULATION ON LIFE AND DEATH

What are the *representatives* of the death instinct? The question arises for two reasons. First, it should be noted that the death instinct was not introduced to account for the factor of destructiveness, as the later papers on culture and especially *Civilization and Its Discontents* might lead us to believe, but to account for a set of facts which center around the compulsion to repeat. It is only afterward that the switch is made from metabiological to metacultural considerations. Thus the connection between the various representatives of the death instinct poses a question. More important, however, is the fact that the link between this instinct and its representatives is not Freud's main concern. *Beyond the Pleasure Principle* is the least hermeneutic and most speculative of Freud's essays; in saying this I refer to the enormous part played in that essay by hypotheses, by heuristic constructs, which are pushed to their extreme consequences.[1] The death instinct is not at first deciphered in its representatives, but instead is posited as a hypothesis or "speculative assumption" about the functioning and regulation of the psychical processes. It is only in a second movement that this instinct is recognized and de-

1. "What follows is speculation, often far-fetched speculation, which the reader will consider or dismiss according to his individual predilection. It is further an attempt to follow out an idea consistently, out of curiosity to see where it will lead" (*GW*, *13*, 23; *SE*, *18*, 24). Further on: "For the moment it is tempting to pursue to its logical conclusion the hypothesis that all instincts tend towards the restoration of an earlier state of things" (*GW*, *13*, 39; *SE*, *18*, 37).

ciphered in a certain number of clinical phenomena, and then, in a third movement, recognized and deciphered as destructiveness, on the individual plane and on the historical and cultural planes. Thus we must always bear in mind that there is an excess of hypothesis compared with its fragmentary and partial verifications.

Let us closely follow the steps in which the concept of death is introduced in *Beyond the Pleasure Principle.*

The speculative side of the notion is evident from the first lines of the essay and even from the title. The concept is not posited in opposition to Eros. On the contrary, Eros will itself be introduced as a revision of the libido theory, a revision imposed by the introduction of the death instinct. As the title suggests, the hypothesis of the death instinct is concerned with the limits of validity (*Jenseits . . . , Beyond . . .*) of the pleasure principle. By the same stroke the essay links up with the earliest set of hypotheses, those of the 1895 "Project." Whereas the notion of libido stems from the deciphering of instincts in their representatives, the pleasure principle belongs to another type of hypotheses which Freud calls the "theory of psychoanalysis."

These hypotheses, we recall, concern the automatic regulation of the psychical processes. They refer to an apparatus that functions on the pattern of an energy system: the apparatus is set in motion by a production of tension and tends to the general lowering of those tensions. This hypothesis is a quantitative one in that the phenomena of pleasure and unpleasure are related to the quantity of excitation present in the mind, unpleasure corresponding to an increase in the quantity of excitation and pleasure to a diminution.[2] There are therefore two hypotheses. The first concerns the correspondence between feelings of pleasure and unpleasure and the increase in the quantity of excitation; the second concerns the effort of

2. Cf. above, "Analytic," Part I, Ch. 1. In the first chapter of *Beyond the Pleasure Principle,* after having recalled these hypotheses, Freud goes on to say that there is no simple relation between the strength of the feelings of pleasure and unpleasure and the corresponding modifications in the quantity of excitation, and that a temporal factor must be considered: "The factor that determines the feeling is probably the amount of increase or diminution in the quantity of excitation *in a given period of time*" (*GW, 13,* 4; *SE, 18,* 8). On this point, cf. "Project," *The Origins of Psychoanalysis,* pp. 371–72.

the psychical apparatus to keep the quantity of excitation present in it as low as possible, or at least to keep it constant. The second hypothesis concerns the work of the psychical apparatus and its direction; it is identical with the hypothesis of constancy; the first hypothesis enables us to transcribe the hypothesis of constancy into the pleasure principle and to say that "the pleasure principle follows from the principle of constancy." [3]

But how is it possible to speak of a "beyond the pleasure principle," if the hypothesis of constancy is the most general hypothesis that can be formed about the psychical apparatus? Just what does the expression "beyond the pleasure principle" refer to? It refers to the "operation [*Wirksamkeit*] of tendencies . . . more primitive than [the pleasure principle] and independent of it." [4] The whole course of the essay is a sustained and skillful movement aimed at uncovering those tendencies. By skirting the reader's resistances and prudently laying siege, Freud lines up facts that could indeed be explained by the pleasure principle but which could also be explained in some other way. Strangely enough, Freud decisively undermines the dominance of the pleasure principle at the very moment he says it might adequately explain the facts. Thus considerations must be brought forward to show that one cannot account for man's psychical life without mentioning the factors that oppose this principle of constancy, that prevent it from being dominant and restrict it to the role of being a *tendency* (Ch. 1).

The surprising thing is that the pleasure principle can only rule over the primary processes, that is, according to Chapter 7 of *The Interpretation of Dreams,* over the short circuit between wishes and their quasi-hallucinatory fulfillment. When faced with difficulties from the external world the pleasure principle is inefficient and even dangerous. Under the influence of the ego's instincts of self-preservation, it is replaced by the reality principle. Thus we have a strange situation: the most general principle of mental functioning is at the same time one of the terms of a polarity, pleasure principle–reality principle. Man is man only if he postpones satisfaction, abandons possibilities of enjoyment, and temporarily tolerates a

3. *GW, 13,* 5; *SE, 18,* 9.
4. *GW, 13,* 15; *SE, 18,* 17.

certain degree of unpleasure on the long indirect road to pleasure.

This is the first breach that Freud hastens to fill in. We still cannot speak, he says, of something beyond the pleasure principle, first, because sexuality is proof that an entire part of the human psychism consistently resists being educated; and secondly, because the admission of unpleasure into any human behavior may be regarded as the roundabout path the pleasure principle takes in order to gain ultimate dominance.

The same remarks are applicable to a second kind of opposition to the pleasure principle. The "Project" had already stated that unpleasure is what educates man. The most notable part of this education consists in the replacement of a libidinal organization by another more highly complex one. The successive organizations of sexuality, which were studied in the *Three Essays* and ever more finely differentiated and articulated in the Freudian school, are the most extensive illustration of this law of development. One of the main things the neuroses have taught us is that earlier phases of development are not simply replaced by succeeding ones, but that conflicts arise between vestiges of the former and demands of the latter. The parts of instinct that are cut off from the possibility of satisfaction seek substitute modes of satisfaction now felt by the ego as unpleasure. This unpleasure is a form of pleasure that cannot be felt as such because it belongs to surpassed organizations of the libido; the neurotic's suffering belongs to this category of unpleasure. Thus psychoanalysis teaches us to discern the pleasure principle in what is felt by the ego as unpleasure.

Thus, each of these two exceptions to the pleasure principle can pass as a modification of the pleasure principle. Strictly speaking, the reality principle may be regarded as the roundabout path adopted by the pleasure principle in order to prevail in the end, and neurotic suffering as the mask that the most archaic pleasure adopts in order to assert itself in spite of everything. But it is clear that the circumstances that confirm the pleasure principle are also the ones that weaken it, for it can be conceived only in opposition to what interferes with it.

Continuing his skillful work of undermining (Ch. 2), Freud sets forth a new series of facts which, he assures us, presuppose the existence and dominance of the pleasure principle and present as yet no evidence of the existence of tendencies more primitive than it and independent of it. Some of these facts are pathological, others normal. Among the former, Freud considers the case of traumatic neurosis and in particular the war neuroses; dreams in such cases have the characteristic of repeatedly bringing the patient back into the situation of his accident, showing that he is fixated to his trauma. We are already in the area of the compulsion to repeat, which is going to become the central reference of the essay. But Freud adroitly steps back and makes a new suggestion drawn from children's play.

We are presented with the case of a little boy, age one and a half. He is a good boy who lets his parents sleep, obeys orders not to touch certain things, and above all never cries when his mother leaves him. He plays at making a wooden reel disappear and reappear, at the same time uttering an expressive "*fort . . . da*" ("gone . . . there"). What does the game mean? It is obviously related to the child's instinctual renunciation that led us to say he is a good boy; it is a repetition of the renunciation, but one in which he is no longer overpowered or passive; the child is staging the disappearance and return of his mother under the symbolic figure of objects within his reach. Thus unpleasure itself is mastered by means of repetition in play, by the staging of the loss of the loved person.

This episode, dear to some French psychoanalysts, is nevertheless inconclusive in Freud's eyes. Once again he minimizes his own findings, with the help of that strategy of lecturer and writer that keeps surprising the reader. Might not the child's efforts, he suggests, be put down to an instinct for domination that is acting independently of whether the memory is pleasurable or not? Or might it not be thought too that the child is revenging himself on his mother by sending her away, as the young Goethe did in throwing the dishes out of the window? Thus domination and revenge do not necessarily incline us to seek something beyond the pleasure principle in this impulse to repeat an unpleasant experience.[5]

5. "This is convincing proof that, even under the dominance of the pleasure principle, there are ways and means enough of making what is in

But why did Freud include this example? Was it not because he saw, mixed in with the motives of domination and revenge, the manifestation of a more essential tendency, driving one to the repetition of unpleasure in the form of symbolism and play? This suggestion has its merits. The *fort-da* example does not simply confirm the example of dreams in traumatic neurosis; traumatic dreams suggest that the "beyond the pleasure principle," the more primitive tendency we are looking for, expresses itself only in the compulsion to repeat; but symbolism and play also repeat unpleasure, not compulsively, but by creating symbolism out of absence. The *fort-da* of the child invites us to reserve for the death instinct a field of expression distinct from the compulsion to repeat or even from destructiveness. Would not this other, nonpathological aspect of the death instinct consist in this mastery over the negative, over absence and loss, implied in one's recourse to symbols and play? It must be admitted that it was not in this direction that Freud developed the theory of the death instinct, but rather in the direction of destructiveness and the compulsion to repeat; perhaps it must be said that in giving this silent instinct a conspicuous and clamorous image, these two representatives have also restricted its scope.

The decisive experience that led Freud (Ch. 3) to the death instinct was a certain difficulty that keeps recurring in analytic treatment in connection with the struggle against the resistances: viz. the tendency of the patient to repeat the repressed material as a contemporary experience instead of remembering it as a past memory. This compulsion is both the ally and the adversary of the physician: his ally since it is inherent in the transference, his adversary since it prevents the patient from recognizing the repetition as a reflection of the forgotten past. Now if the ego's resistance to remembering is attributed to the pleasure principle (unpleasure would be produced by the liberation of the repressed), and if the capacity for tolerating the unpleasure of remembering is attributed to the reality

---

itself unpleasurable into a subject to be recollected and worked over in the mind. . . . [These cases and situations] are of no use for our purposes, since they presuppose the existence and dominance of the pleasure principle; they give no evidence of the operation of tendencies *beyond* the pleasure principle, that is, of tendencies more primitive than it and independent of it" (*GW, 13*, 15; *SE, 18*, 17).

principle, the compulsion to repeat indeed seems to lie outside either one of these principles. What the patient repeats are precisely the situations of distress and failure he underwent as a child, particularly during the oedipal period. This tendency, further evidenced in the strange fate of those persons who seem to call down upon themselves the same misfortunes time and again, appears to justify the hypothesis of a compulsion to repeat that is "more primitive, more elementary, more instinctual than the pleasure principle which it overrides." [6]

Such is the factual basis—rather narrow, it may be said—upon which is built the forthcoming speculation (Ch. 4) concerning the death instinct. With consummate skill Freud prepares the reader for the new aspects of his speculation by relating them to the earliest elements of the metapsychology, those which go back to the period of the "Project" and *Studies on Hysteria.* It will be remembered that Freud had already borrowed from Breuer the hypothesis of two regimes of psychical energy, free energy and bound energy. He now incorporates this conception into his own speculation by relating it to the above-mentioned theory of consciousness as a "surface" function in a quasi-anatomical sense. This comparison, based on reasons of ontogenesis, enables one to contrast the divergent destinies of internal and external perception. The reception of external stimuli is conditioned by the erection of a protective shield: "*protection against* stimuli is an almost more important function for the living organism than *reception of* stimuli." [7] But "toward the inside," i.e. toward the instincts, "there can be no such shield." [8] To this lack of a shield against stimuli, Freud relates Breuer's notion of bound energy. At the same time he opens a breach in his

6. *GW, 13,* 22; *SE, 18,* 23.

7. *GW, 13,* 27; *SE, 18,* 27.

8. *GW, 13,* 28; *SE, 18,* 29. (Cf. "Project," Part I, beginning of Section 10.) The parallel between external and internal protection enables Freud to venture, in passing, a hypothesis concerning projection: when internal excitations produce too great an increase of unpleasure, "there is a tendency to treat them as though they were acting, not from the inside, but from the outside, so that it may be possible to bring the shield against stimuli into operation as a means of defense against them. This is the origin of *projection,* which is destined to play such a large part in the causation of pathological processes" (*GW, 13,* 29; *SE, 18,* 29).

own conception of the self-regulation of the psychical apparatus by the pleasure principle alone. The pleasure principle begins to operate only after a prior task has been assured, that of binding the energy that streams into the psychical apparatus, i.e. of changing it from a freely flowing state into a quiescent one. This is the function, Freud states, that is prior to the pleasure principle. True, we have said nothing as yet about the death instinct; but at least we have limited, on an important point, the dominance of the pleasure principle—namely, the point of defense.

This irreducible and prior function is clearly revealed when it fails. For what is a trauma if not a breach in an otherwise efficacious barrier against stimuli? Prior to pleasure, therefore, there are procedures aimed at mastering the energies that have broken the dikes: reaction to the influx of energy, or, in economic language, anticathexis and hypercathexis.

These speculations on the shield against stimuli and the breaches in that shield are not in vain, for they enable us to explore the relations between defense and anxiety. Freud describes anxiety (*Angst*) as "a particular state of expecting danger or preparing for it, even though it may be an unknown one,"[9] whereas fright (*Schreck*) refers to the state provoked by a danger one encounters unprepared; fright is characterized by the factor of surprise. As for fear (*Furcht*), it arises from an actual encounter with a definite danger. Preparedness for danger, the positive and characteristic function of anxiety, is thus equivalent to a shield against stimuli; when such preparedness is lacking, we have a breach in the shield, or trauma. In light of these considerations about the relations between defense and pleasure, we can now interpret the dreams that occur in traumatic neurosis. Such dreams cannot be classified as fulfillments of wishes and hence subject to the pleasure principle, for they have to do with the task of defense, which precedes the dominance of pleasure: "These dreams are endeavoring to master the stimulus retrospectively, by developing the anxiety whose omission was the cause of the traumatic neurosis."[10] The compulsion to repeat is thus confirmed as an exception to the pleasure prin-

9. *GW, 13,* 10; *SE, 18,* 12.
10. *GW, 13,* 32; *SE, 18,* 32.

ciple, insofar as the task of binding the traumatic impressions is itself prior to the aim of gaining pleasure and avoiding unpleasure.[11]

It will be objected, however, that the priority that the defensive measures, aimed at "binding" free energy, enjoy over the pleasure principle (and over its modification, the reality principle) has no relation to any possible death instinct. This is where the clever tactician suddenly shows his cards: the factor that remains unexplained in the compulsion to repeat is its "instinctual" (*triebhaft*) and even "demonic" (*demonisch*) character. It is necessary to quote the entire paragraph in which Freud achieves the decisive breakthrough, a result disproportionate to all the prudent preparations leading up to it:

> But how is the predicate of being "instinctual" related to the compulsion to repeat? At this point we cannot escape a suspicion that we may have come upon the track of a universal attribute of instincts and perhaps of organic life in general which has not hitherto been clearly recognized or at least not explicitly stressed. *It seems, then, that an instinct is an urge inherent in organic life to restore an earlier state of things* which the living entity has been obliged to abandon under the pressure of external disturbing forces; that is, it is a kind of organic elasticity, or, to put it another way, the expression of the inertia inherent in organic life.[12]

And so, all that preparation was made simply in order to isolate the instinctual character of the compulsion to repeat, which had already been treated as one of the means of defense and was thereby withdrawn from the dominance of the pleasure principle. This instinctual character decisively authorizes us to place inertia on an equal footing with the life instinct.

The rest of the essay consists, on the one hand, in pushing the hypothesis to an extreme, or rather in letting it extend of itself, like a gas that is allowed full scope of extension, and, on the other hand,

11. "If there is a 'beyond the pleasure principle,' it is only consistent to grant that there was also a time [*Vorzeit*] before the purpose of dreams was the fulfillment of wishes" (*GW*, *13*, 33; *SE*, *18*, 33).

12. *GW*, *13*, 38; *SE*, *18*, 36.

in rendering the hypothesis plausible by a method of convergent signs.

Let us go then to the extreme! The extreme is this: Living things are not put to death by external forces which surpass them, as in Spinoza;[13] they die, they go to death by an internal movement: "everything living dies for *internal* reasons . . . *the aim of all life is death.*"[14] Better—or worse?—life itself is not the will to change, to develop, but the will to conserve itself: if death is the aim of life, all of life's organic developments are but detours toward death, and the so-called conservative instincts are but the organism's attempts to defend its own fashion of dying, its particular path to death. Change is imposed by external factors, the earth and the sun, i.e. the inanimate environment of life; progress is disturbance and divergence, to which life adapts in order to pursue its conservative aim at this new level. Dying becomes increasingly difficult, for the paths to death have grown ever more complicated and circuitous. As for the so-called "instinct toward perfection," it must be viewed as a consequence of obligatory adaptation; if all the backward paths are blocked by repression, only forward flight remains, the path of intellectual achievement and ethical sublimation; but none of this requires an "instinct toward perfection" distinct from the conservative tendencies of life.

Would you like proof? Consider the migrations of certain fish and birds returning to the former localities of the species, the embryo's recapitulation of earlier stages of life, the facts of regeneration of organs: does not all this attest to the conservative nature of life, to life's inherent compulsion toward repetition?

The reader will ask what the purpose of all this is. Its purpose is to accustom us to see death as a figure of necessity, to help us submit "to a remorseless law of nature, to the sublime 'Ανάγκη";[15] but above all to enable us to sing the paean of life, of libido, of

13. Spinoza, *Ethics*, Part III, Proposition 4: "Nothing can be destroyed except by an external cause"; and the demonstration of Proposition 6: "Everything, so far as it can (*quantum in se est*), endeavors to persevere in its being."

14. *GW, 13*, 40; *SE, 18*, 38.

15. *GW, 13*, 45; *SE, 18*, 45. We will come back to this mythical term Ananke. Freud, beginning his own critique, observes: "It may be, however, that this belief in the internal necessity of dying is only another of those

Eros! Because life goes toward death, sexuality is the great *exception* [16] in life's march toward death. Thanatos reveals the meaning of Eros as the factor that resists death. The sexual instincts are "the true life instincts. They operate against the purpose of the other instincts, which lead, by reason of their function, to death; and this fact indicates that there is an opposition between them and the other instincts, an opposition whose importance was long ago recognized by the theory of the neuroses." [17]

The result of this tortuous discussion is therefore a straightforward dualism of instincts. Just what is this dualism? And how does it relate to the earlier ways of expressing the dualism of the instincts?

The replacement of the libido by Eros points to a very specific purpose of the new instinct theory. If the living substance goes to death by an inner movement, what fights against death is not something internal to life, but the conjugation of two mortal substances. Freud calls this conjugation Eros; the desire of the other is directly implied in the emergence of Eros; it is always with another that the living substance fights against death, against its own death, whereas when it acts separately it pursues death through the circuitous paths of adaptation to the natural and cultural environment. Freud does not look for the drive for life in some will to live inscribed in each living substance: in the living substance *by itself* he finds only death.[18]

---

illusions which we have created *'um die Schwere des Daseins zu ertragen'* " (ibid.; "to bear the burden of existence" is a citation from Schiller, *Die Braut von Messina,* I, 8).

16. "Is it really the case that, *apart from the sexual instincts,* there are no instincts that do not seek to restore an earlier state of things? that there are none that aim at a state of things which has never yet been attained?" (*GW, 13,* 43; *SE, 18,* 41).

17. *GW, 13,* 43; *SE, 18,* 40.

18. Freud compares his theory with that of August Weismann, who equates the mortal parts of living substance with the soma and the immortal part with the germ-plasm. But he disagrees with Weismann's contention that protozoa are immortal and that death is a late acquisition of organisms. If the death instinct is primal, then not even protozoa may be said to be immortal. Freud aligns himself more with authors who maintained that senescence is a universal characteristic of life due to the impossibility of completely voiding the products of metabolism, and who speculated about the "rejuvenation" of protozoa through "conjugation."

Freud extrapolates this insight to both large and small unities. To large unities: in the 1921 essay *Group Psychology and the Analysis of the Ego,* Freud expressly assigns to Eros, to the libidinal bond, the cohesion of ever wider human groups and more particularly of organized and artificial groups, such as the church and the army. To small unities: the coalescence of unicellular organisms suggests an application of the libido theory to the mutual relationship of cells themselves. Thus a form of sexuality must be attributed to cells, whereby each one would partly neutralize the death instinct of the others: "In this way the libido of our sexual instincts would coincide with the Eros of the poets and philosophers which holds all living things together." [19]

This generalization of sexuality complicates rather than simplifies the situation. Instead of being a clear delimitation of two domains, the dualism of Eros and Thanatos appears as a dramatic *overlapping of roles.* In a sense, everything is death, since self-preservation is the circuitous path on which each living substance pursues its own death. In another sense, everything is life, since narcissism itself is a figure of Eros: we have only to recognize that Eros is the preserver of all things and that the self-preservation of the individual derives from the mutual attachment of the cells of the soma. Thus the new dualism expresses the overlapping of two coextensive domains.

Comparison with the earlier expressions of instinctual dualism confirms this puzzling situation. Freud was always a dualist; what kept changing was the distribution of the opposed terms and the nature of the opposition itself. In the distinction of sexual instincts and ego-instincts he was guided not by an antagonism between instincts, but by the popular division of love and hunger and the polarity between objects and ego. When narcissism was introduced into the theory, the distinction became topographical and economic and indicated a conflict between cathexes.[20] The new dualism does not replace the earlier one but actually reinforces it: indeed, if the narcissistic libido of the ego is a figure of Eros, such libido is on the side of life. Yet we have said that the ego-instincts are opposed to

19. *GW, 13,* 54; *SE, 18,* 50.
20. *GW, 13,* 56; *SE, 18,* 52.

the sexual instincts just as the death instincts are opposed to the life instincts.[21] This comparison is not rejected. We need only consider that the new dualism is located not on the level of purposes, aims, and objects, but on the level of *forces;* hence we must not try to make the duality of ego-instincts and sexual instincts coincide with the duality of life instincts and death instincts. The latter dualism cuts across *each* of the forms of the libido; this will be verified in our study of the representatives of the death instinct. Object-love is both life instinct *and* death instinct; narcissistic love is Eros unaware of itself *and* clandestine cultivation of death. Sexuality is at work wherever death is at work. At this point, however, the dualism of instincts has truly become antagonistic, for it is no longer a question of qualitative differences between hunger and love, as in the first theory of the instincts, nor of differences in cathexis, according to whether the libido turns toward the ego or toward objects, as in the second theory of the instincts; the dualism has become what *Civilization and Its Discontents* will call "a battle of the giants."

THE DEATH INSTINCT AND THE DESTRUCTIVENESS OF THE SUPEREGO

Above we insisted on the excess of meaning that "speculation" gives to the death instinct as compared with the deciphering of that instinct in its representatives, of whatever level or order they may be. We looked upon this discordance

21. "The upshot of our inquiry so far has been the drawing of a sharp distinction between the 'ego-instincts' and the sexual instincts, and the view that the former exercise pressure towards death and the latter towards a prolongation of life" (*GW, 13,* 46; *SE, 18,* 44). And several pages later: "It was not our *intention* at all events to produce such a result. Our argument had as its point of departure a sharp distinction between ego-instincts, which we equated with death instincts, and sexual instincts, which we equated with life instincts. (We were prepared at one stage to include the so-called self-preservative instincts of the ego among the death instincts; but we subsequently corrected ourselves on this point and withdrew it.) Our views have from the very first been *dualistic,* and today they are even more definitely dualistic than before—now that we describe the opposition as being, not between ego-instincts and sexual instincts but between life instincts and death instincts" (*GW, 13,* 57; *SE, 18,* 53).

as an irreducible given of the theory. We must now try to understand it. Why the absence of symmetry between the hermeneutics of life and the hermeneutics of death? Why does conjecture win out over interpretation when we move from the libido theory, taken at its two earlier stages of elaboration, to the theory of the life and death instincts?

An insistent remark of Freud himself may serve to get us started. On various occasions—already in *Beyond the Pleasure Principle,* but especially in *The Ego and the Id* and *Civilization and Its Discontents*—Freud speaks of the death instinct as a "mute" energy, in contradistinction to the "clamor" of life.[22] This disparity between the death instinct and its expressions, between desire and speech—a disparity signified by the epithet "mute"—warns us that the semantics of desire no longer has the same meaning. The desire for death does not speak, as does the desire for life. Death works in silence. Hence the method of deciphering, based on the equivalence of two systems of reference, instincts and meaning, finds itself in difficulty. Yet psychoanalysis has no other recourse than to interpret, that is, to read an interplay of forces in an interplay of symptoms. In his last works, therefore, Freud restricts himself to setting an adventuresome speculation alongside a partial deciphering. Any given representative exhibits only "portions" of the death instinct. But there will be no equivalence between what is deciphered and what has been conjectured.

This point should be kept in mind when one enters into the series of papers that exploited the breakthrough achieved in *Beyond the Pleasure Principle*. One notices a twofold shift of emphasis: first, from the tendency to *repeat* to the tendency to *destroy;* next, from more *biological* to more *cultural* expressions. But this series of manifestations of the death instinct does not exhaust the weight of meaning supplied by speculation; an essential significance may even be lost when this silence is transcribed into clamor. Besides, Freud speaks more readily of the death instincts than of the death instinct (we have ignored this factor in our reconstruction of Freud's speculation), thus reserving the possibility of a great variety of expres-

22. "The death instincts are by their nature mute . . . the clamor of life proceeds for the most part from Eros" (*GW, 13,* 275; *SE, 19,* 46).

sions and of a nonexhaustive enumeration of its manifestations.

The first shift of emphasis is already very noticeable in *Beyond the Pleasure Principle*. The death instinct is introduced by the compulsion to repeat; but it is confirmed and verified by aggressiveness, in its two forms of sadism and masochism. These last two examples do not have the same significance: sadism is simply incorporated into the new theory, masochism is reinterpreted in light of the new theory.

The theory of sadism was formulated very early. Ever since the *Three Essays on Sexuality* the term covers three sets of phenomena. First, it designates a more or less perceptible component in any normal and integrated sexuality; second, it designates a perversion, sadism proper, i.e. a mode of being that has become independent of that sexual component; and last, it also stands for a pregenital organization, the sadistic stage, in which that component plays a dominant role.

The case of masochism is quite different, for up to the present—in the *Three Essays* and in "Instincts and Their Vicissitudes"—masochism was nothing more than sadism "turned round" upon the ego, whereas Freud now regards the forms of masochism as derived phenomena, as a return or regression to a primary masochism. We will soon see the importance this has in the theory of the superego, conscience, and guilt.

All of this is only sketched in a few lines; in 1920, Freud had not yet elaborated the concepts of fusion (*Vermischung*) and defusion (*Entmischung*), by which he will account for the cooperation of the death instinct with sexuality and for its separate functioning.[23] At least these two examples clearly bring out the disparity between the death instinct and its manifestations, where the latter mark the emergence of the instinct at the level of an object-relation. At first view, the case of the death instinct does not seem to differ from that of the life instinct: here too sadism and masochism are able to be interpreted, for they have a particular "aim"—destruction—and definite "objects"—the sexual partner or the ego. But nothing permits one to say that the death instinct is fully manifested in these expressions comparable to the representatives of the life instinct;

23. *The Ego and the Id,* Ch. 4, "The Two Classes of Instincts."

neither the play of the *fort-da* nor even the compulsion to repeat can be reduced to destructiveness. Destructiveness is only one of the death instincts.[24]

This double movement—the replacement of the compulsion to repeat by destructiveness, and the switch from a metabiology to a metaculture—will be completed only in *Civilization and Its Discontents*. Sections IV and V of *The Ego and the Id* supply the indispensable transition between the metabiology of *Beyond the Pleasure Principle* and the metaculture of *Civilization and Its Discontents.*

The stroke of genius in *The Ego and the Id* was to couple the theory of the three agencies—ego, id, superego—with the dualistic theory of the instincts of *Beyond the Pleasure Principle*. This confrontation makes it possible to pass from mere speculation to actual deciphering. Henceforth, instead of considering the death instincts face to face in a dogmatic mythology, we will approach them in the density of the id, ego, and superego.

Strictly speaking, the dualism of the instincts concerns only the id —it is an internal war of the id.[25] But starting from the instinctual interior, the war spreads out until it finally bursts forth in the higher portions of the psychism, in the "sublime." This process of defusion assures the transition from the biological speculation to the cultural interpretation and enables us to set forth all the representatives of the death instinct, to the point where the death instinct becomes inner punishment.

It is necessary to elaborate the concepts of fusion and defusion; they are, assuredly, economic concepts, as are the concepts of cathexis, regression, and even perversion. To give them an energy basis, Freud adopts a hypothesis not unrelated to Hughlings Jackson's concept of "functional liberation": the defusion of an instinct liberates "a displaceable energy, which, neutral in itself, can be added to a qualitatively differentiated erotic or destructive impulse, and augment its total cathexis." [26] Have we come back purely and

24. "The death instinct would thus seem to express itself—though probably only in part—as an instinct of destruction directed against the external world and other organisms" (*GW, 13,* 269; *SE, 19,* 41).

25. It is in these terms that the *New Introductory Lectures* combine the second topography and the dualistic theory of the instincts.

26. *GW, 13,* 272–73; *SE, 19,* 44.

simply to speculation about the quantitative, about free and bound energy? There is no denying the conjectural aspect; Freud himself observes: "In the present discussion, I am only putting forward a hypothesis; I have no proof to offer. It seems a plausible view that this displaceable and neutral energy, which is no doubt active both in the ego and in the id, proceeds from the narcissistic store of libido—that it is desexualized Eros." [27] A sign of this is the looseness or indifference in the "displacements" brought about by the primary process.

Thus the concepts of fusion and defusion have been constructed in order to state in energy language what happens when an instinct places its energy at the service of forces working in different systems. Consequently they are not based upon anything verifiable at the energy level itself where they are assumed to operate: fusion and defusion are simply the correlates, in energy language, of phenomena discovered by the work of interpretation when it focuses on the area of the instinctual representatives.

To see the sequence of the various representatives of the death instinct, it is necessary to examine them from the bottom up, i.e. to proceed from the more biological to the more cultural.

At the lowest level we meet with the erotogenic form of masochism, pleasure in pain (*Schmertzlust*). It is dealt with very briefly in *The Ego and the Id* and at greater length in "The Economic Problem of Masochism." [28] How does it come about that man takes pleasure in pain? It is not enough to say, as in the *Three Essays,* that an excess of pain or unpleasure gives rise to a libidinal sympathetic excitation (*libidinöse Miterregung*) as a concomitant effect (*Nebenwirkung*); granted that this mechanism exists, it provides only a physiological foundation; what is essential takes place elsewhere, on the properly instinctual level. It must be supposed that the destructive instinct is split into two tendencies. One portion, under pressure from the life instinct, which seeks to render it harmless, is diverted outward onto paths of the muscular apparatus; this current of destructiveness places itself in the service of sexuality

27. Ibid.
28. "Das ökonomische Problem des Masochismus," *GW, 13,* 371–83; *SE, 19,* 159–70.

and constitutes sadism proper. The other portion remains inside the organism and "with the help of the accompanying sexual excitation described above, becomes libidinally bound there"; this constitutes erotogenic masochism, pleasure in pain. Erotogenic masochism is therefore the "residuum," remaining within, of a destructiveness which may be viewed either as primal sadism or as primal masochism. There is clearly much that remains puzzling: we do not know how the "taming" (*Bändigung*) of the death instinct by the libido is effected; we can only assume that the libido is at work not only in sadism, that is, in the portion of the death instinct diverted toward external objects, but in the residuum remaining within, hence in masochism itself, which thus appears as the most primitive "coalescence" (*Legierung*) of love and death. Masochism accompanies the libido through all its developmental phases and derives from them its successive "coatings" (*Umkleidungen*): the fear of being eaten up (oral stage), the wish to be beaten (sadistic-anal stage), castration fantasies (phallic stage), fantasies of being copulated with (genital stage). Thus fusion and defusion pinpoint a difficulty rather than provide the solution to a problem.

In *The Ego and the Id* (Ch. 5), it is basically the theory of the superego that profits from this rereading of the agencies from the viewpoint of death. We recall that for psychoanalysis the superego derives from the father complex and is thus a structure closer to the id than the perceptual ego is. But one trait of the superego remained unexplained: its harshness and cruelty. This strange character rejoins other disconcerting phenomena which at first glance seem unrelated to it, such as the resistance to recovery. When one comes to see that this resistance has a "moral" aspect to it, that it is a form of self-punishment through suffering and that it therefore involves an unconscious sense of guilt finding its satisfaction in the illness, a consistent pattern is revealed which includes such different phenomena as obsessional neurosis and melancholia, the resistance to recovery, and the severity of the normal conscience. Let's not go back over the question of whether it is correct to speak of an "unconscious sense of guilt." What is important is the connection discovered between guilt and death. We touch here upon the most extreme consequence of the relationship between the superego and the id. The instinctual character of the superego implies not only that the superego contains libidinal residues from the Oedipus complex, but that it is charged with destructive rage thanks to the defusion of the death instinct. This goes very far, even to the point of diminishing the importance of instruction or reading, of the "things heard"—in short, of word-presentations—in the development of conscience, to the profit of the great obscure forces rising from below. How is it, Freud asks, that the superego manifests itself essentially as a sense of guilt and develops such extraordinary cruelty toward the ego, to the extent of becoming "as cruel as only the id can be"? [29] The case of melancholia leads us to think that the superego has taken possession of all the available sadism, that the destructive component has entrenched itself in the superego and turned against the ego: "What is now holding sway in the superego is, as it were, a pure culture of the death instinct." [30]

In thus emerging at the level of the superego, the death instinct suddenly discloses the dimensions of this pure culture of the death instinct. Caught between a murderous id and a tyrannical and punishing conscience, the ego appears to have no recourse other than self-torment or the torturing of others by diverting its aggressiveness toward them. Hence the paradox: "the more a man checks his aggressiveness towards the exterior the more severe—that is aggressive—he becomes in his ego ideal" [31]—as if aggressiveness either has to be turned outward against others or turned round upon the self. One immediately perceives the religious extension of this ethical cruelty in the projection of a higher being who punishes inexorably.

If we compare the cruelty of the superego with the previous description of "erotogenic masochism," it seems at first glance that any connection with sexuality is lacking; one may assume that there exists a direct link between destructiveness and the superego independently of any erotic factor. In "The Economic Problem of Masochism," Freud attempts to reconstruct the hidden connections

29. *GW, 13,* 284; *SE, 19,* 54. Freud calls the sense of guilt in certain forms of obsessional neurosis "over-noisy" (*überlaut*): it is indeed one of the "clamorous voices" of the instinct which itself is "mute."

30. *GW, 13,* 283; *SE, 19,* 53.

31. *GW, 18,* 283; *SE, 19,* 54.

between erotism and what he calls "moral masochism"—which, it is true, does not cover the whole domain of the superego.

The unconscious sense of guilt, discovered in the tenacious resistance to recovery and more correctly called the need for punishment (*Strafbedürfnis*), throws light on this hidden link between moral masochism and erotism. The link between the fear of conscience and erotism stems from the deep-seated relationship the superego retains with the id by reason of the libidinal ties with the parental source of prohibition; this is the place to repeat it: the superego is the "representative of the id" (*Vertreter des Es*). This libidinal tie may be drawn out indefinitely, in proportion as the father imago is replaced by increasingly distant and impersonal figures, ending with the dark power of Destiny, which only the fewest of men are able to separate from any parental connection.

But at the same time this comparison affords us the occasion to introduce certain nuances that appear to have been overlooked in *The Ego and the Id*, especially a difference between the superego's sadism and the ego's masochism (i.e. "moral masochism"). What was described in *The Ego and the Id* is the *superego's* sadism, which is "an unconscious extension of morality" (*eine solche unbewusste Fortsetzung der Moral*). The *ego's* desire or need for punishment is not exactly the same thing; such a desire is connected with the wish to be beaten by the father, which we have seen to be one of the expressions of "erotogenic masochism." This desire expresses, therefore, a resexualization of morality, in the reverse direction of the normal movement of conscience and morality that arise from the overcoming and hence from the desexualization of the Oedipus complex. With the resexualization of morality the possibility of a monstrous fusion of love and death arises; such a fusion on the "sublime" plane has its counterpart on the "perverse" plane in the phenomena of pleasure in pain.

One can see how dangerous it would be to confuse everything: normal morality, cruelty (the superego's sadism), need for punishment (the ego's masochism). These three tendencies—the cultural suppression of the instincts, the turning back of sadism against the self, and the intensification of the ego's own masochism—do indeed supplement each other and unite to produce the same effects; but, in principle at least, they are distinct tendencies. The sense of guilt results from a combination of these tendencies in various proportions.

If one reexamines the analyses of *The Ego and the Id* in light of the distinctions proposed in "The Economic Problem of Masochism," it must be said that the above description concerns the sadism of the superego rather than the masochism of the ego or "moral masochism." Is this sadism of the superego as clearly opposed to the normal conscience as the masochism characterized above by the resexualization of the Oedipus complex? It is more difficult to decide this. However, it is significant that in Chapter 5 of *The Ego and the Id* Freud limits himself to describing two guilt maladies, obsessional neurosis and melancholia. He shows more interest in their respective differences than in their shared similarity to ordinary morality. In melancholia the superego reveals itself as a pure culture of the death instinct, to the point of suicide. In obsessional neurosis, on the contrary, the ego is protected from self-destruction because of the transformation of its love-objects into objects of hate; the ego struggles against this hate, which is turned outward and which the ego has not adopted, while at the same time the ego undergoes the assaults of the superego which holds the ego responsible; whence the interminable torments of the ego which has to defend itself on two fronts. Are the torments of the obsessed and the melancholic's cultivation of death as clearly opposed to the desexualization of the normal conscience as masochism was? It seems they are not. But the picture is all the more disquieting, for even if the sadism of the superego is independent of any erotic factor, we are presented with a view in which the death instinct is directly included in the sadism of the superego—the result being what might be called a deathly sublimation. Such a view is suggested by the interrelating of defusion, desexualization, and sublimation. Thus the sadism of the superego represents a sublimated form of destructiveness; in proportion as destructiveness becomes desexualized by defusion, it becomes capable of being mobilized to the advantage of the superego; and at this point it becomes a "pure culture of death." The desexualization of sadism is therefore no less dangerous than the resexualization of masochism.[32]

Such is the frightful discovery: the death instinct, too, can be sublimated. To complete this grim picture it might be added that the instinctual basis of this whole process is essentially the fear of castration. In regard to the last text quoted I would like to call notice to a passing remark Freud makes about the relationship between castration and the fear of conscience (a far-reaching remark, if one remembers the role attributed to the dread of castration in "The Dissolution of the Oedipus Complex"). The remark occurs at the end of *The Ego and the Id:* "The superior being, which turned into the ego ideal, once threatened castration, and this dread of castration is probably the nucleus round which the subsequent fear of conscience has gathered; it is this dread that persists as the fear of conscience." [33]

Thus the fear to which we related the genesis of illusions, the properly human fear, the fear of conscience (*Gewissenangst*), remains unintelligible apart from the death instinct.

CULTURE AS SITUATED BETWEEN EROS AND THANATOS

We have not yet considered the broadest impact of the new theory of instincts on the interpretation of culture. The destructiveness of the superego is only one of the components of the individual conscience, on the borderline between the normal and the pathological. The death instinct, however, involves a reinterpretation of culture itself. The confrontation between the definition of culture we gave above, based on the open-

32. "But since the ego's work of sublimation results in a defusion of the instincts and a liberation of the aggressive instincts in the superego, its struggle against the libido exposes it to the danger of maltreatment and death. In suffering under the attacks of the superego or perhaps even succumbing to them, the ego is meeting with a fate like that of the protista [protozoa] which are destroyed by the products of decomposition that they themselves have created. From the economic point of view the morality that functions in the superego seems to be a similar product of decomposition" (*GW, 13*, 287; *SE, 19*, 56–57).

33. *GW, 13*, 288; *SE, 19*, 57.

ing chapters of *The Future of an Illusion*, and the reexamination of that definition as presented in Chapters 3–5 of *Civilization and Its Discontents* points to a deepening and also a unification of the notion of culture as faced by the death instinct.

Of course, in *Civilization and Its Discontents*, Freud is no less anxious than in *The Future of an Illusion* to give a purely economic definition of culture; but the economics of the cultural phenomenon turns out to be profoundly renewed through its relationship to a global strategy, the strategy of Eros versus death.

Let us consider the new economic interpretation of culture in *Civilization and Its Discontents.*

The interpretation is developed in two phases: first, what can be said without having recourse to the death instinct; second, what can be said only after its intervention.

Prior to this turning point, which makes the essay terminate on the tragedy of culture, the essay advances with calculated ease. The economics of culture is seen to coincide with what might be called a general "erotics." The aims pursued by the individual and those which animate culture appear as figures, sometimes convergent, sometimes divergent, of the same Eros: "The process of civilization is a modification which the vital process experiences under the influence of a task that is set it by Eros and instigated by Ananke—by the exigencies of reality; and . . . this task is one of uniting separate individuals into a community bound together by libidinal ties."[34] Thus the same "erotism" forms the internal tie of groups and drives the individual to seek pleasure and flee suffering—the threefold suffering inflicted upon him by the external world, his own body, and other men. Cultural development, like the growth of the individual from infancy to adulthood, is the fruit of Eros and Ananke, of love and work; we must even say, of love more than of work, for the necessity of uniting in work in order to exploit nature is but a small thing compared with the libidinal tie which unites individuals in a single social body. It seems then, that the same Eros inspires the striving for individual happiness and wishes to unite men in ever wider groups. But the paradox soon appears: as the organized struggle against nature, culture gives man the power that

34. *Civilization and Its Discontents, GW, 14,* 499–500; *SE, 21,* 139.

was once conferred on the gods; but this resemblance to the gods leaves man unsatisfied: civilization and its discontents . . .

Why this dissatisfaction? On the basis of this general "erotics" alone one can, no doubt, account for certain tensions between the individual and society, but not for the grave conflict that makes culture tragic. For example, one can easily explain the fact that the family bond resists extension to larger groups; to enter into the wider circle of life necessarily appears to every young person as a breaking of the earliest and closest ties; it is also understandable that something in feminine sexuality resists the transfer of libidinal energy from private sex to social aims. One can adduce many other instances of conflict situations and still not encounter any radical contradictions; it is well known that culture imposes sacrifices in enjoyment upon all sexuality: the prohibition of incest, the proscription of childhood sexuality, the arrogant channeling of sexuality into the narrow paths of legitimacy and monogamy, the insistence upon procreation, etc. But, however painful the sacrifices and however complicated the conflicts, they still do not result in a real antagonism. The most that can be said is, first, that the libido resists with all its force of inertia the task culture lays on it to abandon its old positions, and second, that the libidinal ties that constitute society draw their energy from private sexuality, to the extent of endangering the latter with atrophy. But all of this has so little of the tragic about it that we can dream of a sort of armistice or accord between the individual and the social bond.

And so the question arises again: Why does man fail to be happy? Why is man as a cultural being dissatisfied?

The analysis here reaches its turning point. Confronting man is an absurd commandment: to love one's neighbor as oneself; an impossible demand: to love one's enemies; a dangerous order: to turn the other cheek. These precepts squander love, put a premium on being bad, and lead to ruin anyone imprudent enough to obey them. But the truth behind the irrationality of these imperatives is the irrationality of an instinct that lies outside a simple erotics:

> The element of truth behind all this, which people are so ready to disavow, is that men are not gentle creatures who want to be loved, and who at the most can defend themselves if they are at-

> tacked; they are, on the contrary, creatures among whose instinctual endowments is to be reckoned a powerful share of aggressiveness. As a result, their neighbor is for them . . . someone who tempts them to satisfy their aggressiveness on him, to exploit his capacity for work without compensation, to use him sexually without his consent, to seize his possessions, to humiliate him, to cause him pain, to torture and to kill him. *Homo homini lupus.*[35]

The instinct that thus disturbs man's relations with man and requires society to rise as the implacable dispenser of justice is, of course, the death instinct, here identified with the primordial hostility of man toward man.

With the death instinct there appears what Freud henceforward calls an "anticultural instinct." From now on social ties cannot be regarded as a mere extension of the individual libido, as in *Group Psychology and the Analysis of the Ego*. They are the expression of the conflict between instincts:

> Man's natural aggressive instinct, the hostility of each against all and of all against each, opposes this program of civilization. This aggressive instinct is the derivative and the main representative of the death instinct which we have found alongside of Eros and which shares world-dominion with it. And now, I think, the meaning of the evolution of civilization is no longer obscure to us. It must present the struggle between Eros and Death, between the instinct of life and the instinct of destruction, as it works itself out in the human species. This struggle is what all life essentially consists of, and the evolution of civilization may therefore be simply described as the struggle for life of the human species. And it is this battle of the giants that our nursemaids try to appease with their lullaby about Heaven.[36]

Thus culture itself has been transported onto the great cosmic stage of life and death! In return, the "mute" instinct speaks in its

35. *GW, 14*, 470–71; *SE, 21*, 111.
36. *GW, 14*, 481; *SE, 21*, 122. *Eiapopeia vom Himmel* is a quotation from Heine's poem *Deutschland*, Caput I, Strophe 7.

main derivative and representative. Prior to a theory of culture death is not yet manifested: culture is its sphere of manifestation; that is why a purely biological theory of the death instinct had to remain speculative; it is only in the interpretation of hate and war that speculation about the death instinct becomes a process of deciphering.

There is thus a progressive revelation of the death instinct at three levels, biological, psychological, cultural. Grasped at first in the complexities of Eros, the death instinct remained masked in its sadistic component; sometimes it reinforced object-libido, sometimes it hypercathected narcissistic libido; its antagonism becomes less and less silent as Eros develops, uniting living matter to itself, then the ego to its object, and finally individuals into ever wider groups. At this last level the struggle between Eros and Thanatos becomes declared war; paraphrasing Freud, one might say that war is the clamor of death. The mythical aspect of the speculation is not thereby lessened, however; death now appears not only demonic but demoniacal: Freud now uses the voice of Mephistopheles to speak of death, just as he invoked Plato's *Symposium* to illustrate Eros.

The rebound of the cultural interpretation of the death instinct on the biological speculation has important effects. The final consequence is an interpretation of the sense of guilt quite different from the interpretation in terms of the individual psychology presented in *The Ego and the Id.* Whereas in that essay the sense of guilt leaned toward the pathological, by reason of the resemblance between the cruelty of the superego and the sadistic or masochistic traits of melancholia and obsessional neurosis, Chapters 7 and 8 of *Civilization and Its Discontents* emphasize, to the contrary, the cultural function of the sense of guilt. The sense of guilt is now seen as the instrument which culture uses, no longer against the libido, but against aggressiveness. The switch of fronts is important. Culture now represents the interests of Eros against myself, the center of deathly egoism; and it uses my own self-violence to bring to naught my violence against others.

This new interpretation of guilt entails a complete shift of emphasis. Seen from the point of view of the ego and in the framework of its "dependent relations" (*The Ego and the Id*, Ch. 5), the severity of the superego appeared excessive and dangerous; this remains true and the task of psychoanalysis stays unchanged in this regard: it always consists in attenuating that severity. But seen from the point of view of culture and what might be called the general interests of humanity, that severity is irreplaceable. Thus there is a need to interrelate the two readings of the sense of guilt. Its economics from the point of view of the individual conscience and its economics from the point of view of the task of culture are complementary. So little is the first reading annulled by the second that Freud restates it at the beginning of Chapter 7 of *Civilization and Its Discontents*. According to the second reading, however, the main renunciation culture demands of the individual is the renunciation not of desire as such but of aggressiveness. Consequently, it is no longer sufficient to define the fear of conscience as the tension between the ego and the superego; it must be transported to the larger scene of love and death: "The sense of guilt," we will now say, "is an expression of the conflict due to ambivalence, of the eternal struggle between Eros and the instinct of destruction or death." [37]

The two readings are not merely superimposed, they mesh with one another: the cultural function of guilt necessarily involves the psychological function of the fear of conscience; from the point of view of the psychology of the individual, the sense of guilt—at least in its quasi-pathological form—appears to be merely the effect of an internalized aggressiveness, of a cruelty taken over by the superego and turned back against the ego. But its complete economics is seen only when the need for punishment is placed in a cultural perspective: "Civilization, therefore, obtains mastery over the individual's dangerous desire for aggression by weakening and disarming it and by setting up an agency within him to watch over it, like a garrison in a conquered city." [38]

We are thus at the heart of the "malaise" or "discontent" peculiar to the life of culture. The sense of guilt now internalizes the conflict of ambivalence that is rooted in the dualism of the instincts. Hence, in order to decipher the sense of guilt, one must penetrate to

37. *GW, 14,* 492; *SE, 21,* 132.
38. *GW, 14,* 483; *SE, 21,* 123–24.

this most radical of all conflicts: "It is very conceivable that the sense of guilt produced by civilization is not perceived as such . . . and remains to a large extent unconscious, or appears as a sort of *malaise* [*Unbehagen*], a dissatisfaction [*Unzufriedenheit*], for which people seek other motivations." [39] The extraordinary complexity of the sense of guilt is due to the fact that the conflict between instincts is expressed by a conflict at the level of the agencies; this is why the reading of *The Ego and the Id* is not abolished but incorporated into the second reading.

The same may be said about the interpretation of the Oedipus complex, on the scale of the individual or the species. The ambivalence peculiar to the oedipal situation—feelings of love and hatred toward the parental figure—is itself a part of the larger ambivalence between the life and death instincts. Taken by themselves, the various genetic considerations, which Freud worked out at different periods and which concern the killing of the primal father and the institution of remorse, remain somewhat problematic, if for no other reason than the contingency introduced into history by the sense of guilt which at the same time presents itself as a "fatal inevitability." [40] The contingent character of this developmental process as reconstructed by the genetic explanation is softened as soon as this explanation is subordinated to the great conflicts that dominate the course of culture; the family, which serves as the cultural framework for the Oedipus episode, is itself simply a figure of the great enterprise of Eros of forming ties and uniting; hence the Oedipus episode is not the only possible path leading to the institution of remorse.

Thus the reinterpretation of the sense of guilt at the end of *Civilization and Its Discontents* is seen to be the climax in the series of figures of the death instinct. By mortifying the individual, culture places death at the service of love and reverses the initial relationship between life and death. We recall the pessimistic formulas of *Beyond the Pleasure Principle*: "The aim of all life is death"; the function of the instincts of self-preservation "is to assure that the

39. *GW, 14*, 495; *SE, 21*, 135–36.

40. *GW, 14*, 492 (*die verhängnisvolle Unvermeidlichkeit des Schuldgefühls*); *SE, 21*, 132.

organism shall follow its own path to death . . . Thus these guardians of life, too, were originally the myrmidons of death." But the same text, having reached this critical point, turns back upon itself: the life instincts struggle against death. And now culture comes upon the scene as the great enterprise of making life prevail against death: its supreme weapon is to employ internalized violence against externalized violence; its supreme ruse is to make death work against death.

That the theory of culture thus finds its completion in the reinterpretation of the sense of guilt is expressly desired by Freud. Apologizing for the troublesome and unexpected detours of the discussion of the sense of guilt, he states: "This may have spoilt the structure of my paper; but it corresponds faithfully to my intention to represent the sense of guilt as the most important problem in the development of civilization and to show that the price we pay for our advance in civilization is a loss of happiness through the heightening of the sense of guilt." [41]

Freud illustrates this ruse on the part of culture by citing in support of his interpretation the famous line of Hamlet's monologue, "Thus conscience does make cowards of us all." But such "cowardice" is also the death of death; it is the work of the spy whom culture, in the service of Eros, has "garrisoned" at the heart of the individual, as in a conquered city; for, in the last analysis, the "discontent of civilization" is "the sense of guilt produced by civilization." [42]

41. *GW, 14,* 493–94; *SE, 21,* 134.
42. *GW, 14,* 495; *SE, 21,* 135.

Chapter 3: Interrogations

I would like to pay tribute to Freud by gathering together in this chapter some of the questions he opens up for us but does not completely solve. In spite of the trenchant and even intransigent tone of the master who rarely tolerated disagreement or dissent, the final phase of Freud's doctrine terminates on a number of unresolved questions which we will try to assess in a provisional way:

1. Is it certain that we know the death instinct better as it becomes more manifest and is finally revealed at the level of culture as the instinct of destruction? Don't the biological considerations contain a surplusage of speculation not accounted for in cultural deciphering and which presents matter for further thought? Finally, what is negativity in Freud's doctrine?

2. Must we not also doubt our most confident assertions about pleasure? Throughout, we have regarded pleasure as the "watchman over life"; as such, can it express merely the reduction of tensions? If pleasure is connected with life, and not solely with death, must it not be something more than the psychical sign of the reduction of tensions? Indeed, do we ultimately know what pleasure means?

3. Finally, what about the reality principle, which seems indeed to usher in a wisdom beyond illusion and consolation? How does this lucidity, with its attendant pessimistic austerity, ultimately fit in with the love of life which the drama of love and death seems to call for? Does Freudian doctrine finally find a philosophical unity of tone, or does it remain definitively split between the scientism of its initial hypotheses and the *Naturphilosophie* toward which Eros leads it and which, perhaps, had never ceased being the animating force of this tenacious exploration of the universe of desire?

Such is the meaning of the three questions on which, in my opinion, the final reading of Freud terminates: What is the death instinct and how is it connected with *negativity?* What is pleasure and how is it connected with *satisfaction?* What is reality and how is it connected with *necessity?*

WHAT IS NEGATIVITY?

The death instinct is a problematic concept in many respects.

First of all there is the problem of the relationship between speculation and interpretation. No reader can be insensible to the uncertain, winding, and even "limping" [1] character of this speculation and its set of heuristic hypotheses. Freud himself admits he does not know to what extent he believes in them.[2] At times he talks about an equation with two unknown quantities.[3] Again, he says that the supposition of a tendency to restore an earlier state of things, if comparable to a ray of light in the darkness, is nevertheless "a myth rather than a scientific explanation." [4] No treatise of Freud's is so adventurous as *Beyond the Pleasure Principle.* The reason is clear: all *direct* speculation about the instincts, apart from their representatives, is mythical. Thus the third theory of the instincts is more mythical than the earlier ones, for it claims to reach the very substrate of the instincts. The first concept of libido, sharply distinguished from the ego-instincts, was the unifying concept presupposed by the various vicissitudes or destinies of the instincts; the second concept of libido, covering both object-libido and ego-libido, was wider than the first, for it controlled the various distributions of the libidinal cathexes. The speculation on life and death is an attempt to go beneath these two concepts of libido. The network of "analogies, correlations and connections" [5] involved in

1. In the last lines of *Beyond the Pleasure Principle,* Freud quotes two oriental verses taken from one of the *Maquâmât* of al-Hariri: "What we cannot reach flying we must reach limping. . . . The Book tells us it is no sin to limp."
2. *Beyond the Pleasure Principle, GW, 13,* 64; *SE, 18,* 59.
3. *GW, 13,* 62; *SE, 18,* 57.
4. Ibid.
5. *GW, 13,* 66; *SE, 18,* 60.

the hypothesis is far looser than before; the speculation is disproportionate to the phenomenon meant to verify it; Freud admits that the hypothesis of the death instinct may have led him to overestimate the significance of the facts concerning the compulsion to repeat.[6] We have seen that all the other facts that contribute to this central phenomenon might also be interpreted in another way.

Thus the remainder of our study operated on the plane of analogical interpretation and consisted in a gradual and piecemeal reconquest of what had first been posited on the speculative plane. But we must be aware of the initial excess of speculation over interpretation; from the standpoint of epistemology, this is the most striking feature of the essay. This excess of speculative meaning is essentially due to the fact that the hypotheses at work are directly metabiological in nature: "Biology is truly a land of unlimited possibilities." [7] But the metabiology is itself more mythological than scientific, in spite of the discussions on Weismann and the death of protozoa. The mythical name of Eros is ready proof that we are closer to the poets than to the scientists, closer to the speculative philosophers than to the critical ones. It is no accident that the only philosophical text quoted is taken from the mythical part of Plato's *Symposium* (Aristophanes' discourse about the primeval androgynous men); it is a "poet-philosopher" who teaches that Eros wishes to reunite what a malicious divinity had divided and set asunder. Further, do we not feel that we are listening to one of the pre-Socratics when Eros is called that "which holds all living things together," "the preserver of all things"? [8]

Why did Freud thus venture, hesitancy matching intransigency, into the area of metabiology, speculation, and myth? It is not enough to say that Freud's theorizing was always in excess of interpretation in every field of investigation. What poses a problem is the quasi-mythological nature of this metabiology. Perhaps it must be supposed that Freud was fulfilling one of his earliest wishes—to go from psychology to philosophy—and that in this way he was setting free the romantic demands of his thought which the mechanistic scientism of his first hypotheses had only masked over.

6. *GW, 13,* 66; *SE, 18,* 59.
7. *GW, 13,* 66; *SE, 18,* 60.
8. *GW, 13,* 54, 56; *SE, 18,* 50, 52.

Thus what is most suspect in this essay is also the most revealing: under a scientific surface, or rather under the coating of a scientific mythology, there arises the Naturphilosophie which the young Freud admired in Goethe.

But then, must it not be said that the whole libido theory was already under the control of Naturphilosophie and that Freud's entire doctrine is a protest on the part of the nature-philosophy against the philosophy of consciousness? The patient *reading* of desire in its symptoms, its fantasies, and in general its signs never equaled the *hypothesis* of the libido, of instincts, of desire. Freud is in line with those thinkers [9] for whom man is desire before being speech; man is speech because the first semantics of desire is distortion and he has never completely overcome this initial distortion. If this is so, then Freud's doctrine would be animated from beginning to end by a conflict between the "mythology of desire" and the "science of the psychical apparatus"—a "science" in which he always, but in vain, tried to contain the "mythology," and which, ever since the "Project," was exceeded by its own contents.[10] This muffled conflict will make its appearance again at the end of this chapter, no longer at the level of the initial hypotheses, but at the level of final wisdom.

But the excess of meaning of the death instinct, taken in its most speculative expressions, as compared with the whole series of its biological, psychical, and cultural expressions, reveals another problematic aspect of this strange concept. Is it certain that all the meaning it carries is fully brought out in the cultural interpretation? The speculation's excess of meaning as compared with the interpretation does not seem to indicate a defect in the theory; on the contrary, it suggests that the death instinct, which is finally regarded as anticultural destructiveness, may conceal another possible meaning, as we will suggest further on in the investigation of "Negation."

If one reads the series of representatives of the death instinct in the reverse order, one is struck by the disparity between three themes: the inertia of life, the compulsion to repeat, and destruc-

9. In the "Dialectic" we shall attempt to compare the Freudian libido with the Spinozist *conatus* and the Leibnizian *appetition*, and also with *will* in Schopenhauer and the *will to power* in Nietzsche.

10. Cf. above, "Analytic," Part I, Ch. 1.

tiveness. One begins to suspect that the death instinct is a collective term, an incongruous mixture: biological inertia is not pathological obsession, repetition is not destruction. Our suspicion grows stronger when we consider other manifestations of the negative that are irreducible to destructiveness.

Let us return to the intriguing example of the child's *fort-da* play. This game of making the mother symbolically disappear and reappear consists, no doubt, in the repetition of an affective renunciation; but unlike the dreams that occur in traumatic neurosis, the play repetition is not a forced or obsessive one. To play with absence is already to dominate it and to engage in active behavior toward the lost object as lost. Hence, as we asked when we presented Freud's analysis of children's play, do we not discover another aspect of the death instinct, a nonpathological aspect, which would consist in one's mastery over the negative, over absence and loss? And is not this negativity implied in every appeal to symbols and to play?

This question ties in with the question we asked earlier concerning Leonardo's creations. With Freud, we said that the lost archaic object has been "denied" and "triumphed over" [11] by the work of art which recreates the object or rather creates it for the first time by offering it to all men as an object of contemplation. The work of art is also a *fort-da,* a disappearing of the archaic object as fantasy and its reappearing as a cultural object. Thus, does not the death instinct have as its normal, nonpathological expression, the disappearing-reappearing in which the elevation of fantasy to symbol consists?

This interpretation is not without support in Freud. As a final note to the death instinct we have reserved examination of one of the most remarkable of Freud's short essays, entitled "Die Verneinung." [12] The word *Verneinung* ordinarily designates the contrary of *Bejahung*—affirmation; thus the title of the paper is correctly translated as "Negation," for the term purely and simply designates the sense of "no" as opposed to "yes." By a series of meanders Freud ends up expressly linking negation, the "no," with the death instinct.

11. Cf. above, p. 173, n. 22.
12. *GW, 14,* 11–15; *SE, 19,* 235–39.

But just what type of negation is this? Very definitely it is not located in the unconscious; the unconscious, let us remember, contains neither negation, nor time, nor the function of reality. Therefore negation belongs to the system *Cs.*, along with temporal organization, control of action, motor inhibition involved in every thought process, and the reality principle itself. Thus we meet with an unexpected result: there exists a negativity that does not belong to the instincts but defines consciousness, conjointly with time, motor control, and the reality principle.

The first manifestation of this negativity of consciousness is seen in the process of becoming aware of what is repressed. As Freud notes in the opening lines of his paper, when a patient accompanies an association of ideas or a dream fragment with a protestation such as "It's *not* my mother," the negation does not actually belong to the association that has just come into consciousness; it is rather a condition on which the repressed idea may make its way into consciousness: "Negation is a way of taking cognizance of what is repressed; indeed it is already a lifting [*Aufhebung*] of the repression, though not, of course, an acceptance [*Annahme*] of what is repressed." [13] Freud can even say that "There is no stronger evidence that we have been successful in our effort to uncover the unconscious than when the patient reacts to it with the words 'I didn't think that,' or 'I didn't (ever) think of that.' " The "no" is the certificate of origin—the "Made in Germany"—which attests that the thought belongs to the unconscious. "With the help of the symbol of negation [*Verneinungssymbol*], thinking frees itself from the restrictions of repression and enriches itself with material that is indispensable for its proper functioning." Thus "a negative judgment is the intellectual substitute for repression." [14]

The second function of negation has to do with reality-testing. This new function is actually a continuation of the previous one: we know that the conditions of becoming conscious and those of reality-testing are the same, for they are the conditions that govern the differentiation between the internal and the external. The negative judgment "*A* does not possess the attribute *B*" is truly a judgment of real existence only when it goes beyond the viewpoint of

13. *GW, 14*, 12; *SE, 19*, 235–36.
14. *GW, 14*, 12; *SE, 19*, 236.

the pleasure-ego, for whom to say "yes" means that it wants to introject into itself what is good, i.e. to "devour" it, and to say "no" means that it wants to eject from itself what is bad, i.e. to "spit it out." The judgment of reality is a sign that the "initial pleasure-ego" (*anfängliches Lust-Ich*) has been replaced by the "definitive reality-ego" (*endgültiges Real-Ich*). The question at this point is not whether what has been perceived (*wahrgenommen*) can be taken (*aufgenommen*) into the ego, but whether something that is in the ego as a presentation can be *rediscovered* in reality. Thus is established the differentiation between a presentation, which is only "internal," and the real, which is also "outside." What place does the "no" have in this testing of reality? The function of negation—implicit in every judgment, even positive ones—lies in the interval between "to find" and "to refind" (*wiederfinden*). A presentation is not an immediate presenting of things, but a re-presentation of things that are absent: "A precondition for the setting up of reality-testing is that objects shall have been lost which once brought real satisfaction." It is against this background of absence, of loss, that presentation offers itself to reality-testing: "The first and immediate aim, therefore, of reality-testing is, not to *find* an object in real perception which corresponds to the one presented, but to *refind* such an object, to convince oneself that it is still there." [15] Thus the interval of negation, separating the original presence from the presentation, makes possible the critical testing from which both a *real* world and a *real* ego emerge. If one compares the three analyses—the *fort-da* in *Beyond the Pleasure Principle,* esthetic creation in the *Leonardo,* and perceptual judgment in "Negation"—the traits of the function of negativity start to become clear. The disappearing-reappearing of play, the denying-overcoming of esthetic creation, and the losing-refinding of perceptual judgment all share a common operation.

What connection does this negativity have with the death instinct? Here is what Freud writes at the end of "Negation":

> The study of judgment affords us, perhaps for the first time, an insight into the origin of an intellectual function from the inter-

15. *GW, 14,* 14; *SE, 19,* 238. The same formulation occurs in the *Three Essays:* "The finding of an object is in fact a refinding of it" (*GW, 5,* 123; *SE, 7,* 222).

> play of the primary instinctual impulses. Judging is a continuation, along lines of expediency [*zweckmässige*], of the original process by which the ego took things into itself or expelled them from itself, according to the pleasure principle. The polarity of judgment appears to correspond to the opposition of the two groups of instincts which we have supposed to exist. Affirmation —as a substitute for uniting—belongs to Eros; negation—the successor to expulsion—belongs to the instinct of destruction. The general wish to negate, the negativism which is displayed by some psychotics, is probably to be regarded as a sign of a defusion [*Entmischung*] of instincts that has taken place through a withdrawal of the libidinal components. But the performance of the function of judgment is not made possible until the creation of the symbol of negation has endowed thinking with a first measure of freedom from the consequences of repression and, with it, from the compulsion of the pleasure principle.[16]

Freud does not say that negation is another representative of the death instinct; he only says that negation is genetically derived from it by "substitution," as in general the reality principle is substituted for the pleasure principle (or as a character trait, avarice, for example, is substituted for an archaic libidinal constitution, such as anality). We have no right, then, to draw out of this text more than is warranted and to give it a direct Hegelian translation. We may do this on our own, at our own risk, but not as interpreters of Freud. Freud develops an "economics" of negation and not a "dialectic" of truth and certainty, as in the first chapter of *The Phenomenology of Spirit*. Nonetheless, even within these strict limits this short article makes an important contribution: consciousness implies negation —both in the process of "achieving insight" into its own hidden richness and in the "recognition" of what is real.

It is not surprising that negation is derived from the death instinct by way of substitution. On the contrary, what is surprising is that the death instinct is represented by such an important function which has nothing to do with destructiveness, but rather with the symbolization of play, with esthetic creation, and with reality-testing itself. This discovery is enough to throw into flux the whole

16. *GW, 14,* 15; *SE, 19,* 238–39.

analysis of the representatives of instincts. The death instinct is not closed in upon destructiveness, which is, we said, its clamor; perhaps it opens out onto other aspects of the "work of the negative," which remain "silent" like itself.

PLEASURE AND SATISFACTION

What has become of the pleasure principle at the end of the essay that claims to go beyond it?

To raise this question is to ask: Exactly what is "beyond the pleasure principle"? But there is no definite answer to this question—a surprising situation, when one thinks of the title of the treatise itself. In point of fact, it turns out that the "beyond" cannot be found. Not only is there no final answer, but along the way we have lost even a provisional answer. This is not the least "problematic" aspect of the essay.

Let us recall the initial question and its provisional answer prior to the introduction of the death instinct.

The question did have a definite meaning, insofar as one admitted the equivalence between the constancy principle and the pleasure principle. This being granted—and Freud will not seriously question it in *Beyond the Pleasure Principle*, but only in "The Economic Problem of Masochism"—to search for something beyond the pleasure principle is to question whether there exist "tendencies more primitive than it and independent of it," [17] that is, tendencies irreducible to the effort of the psychical apparatus to reduce its tensions and keep them at the lowest level.

We had found such a tendency, however, even before the introduction of the death instincts. On the one hand, it was manifested by the compulsion to repeat, which operates in spite of the unpleasure which the repetition revives; on the other hand, it was possible to connect it with a task that is prior to the seeking of pleasure, the task of "binding" free energy. Undoubtedly this tendency and this task are not opposed to the pleasure principle; but at least they do not derive from it.

But now the great roles of death and life come upon the scene.

17. Cf. above, p. 283, n. 4.

Instead of reinforcing the first result, the introduction of the death instinct destroys it. The death instinct turns out to be the most striking illustration of the constancy principle, of which the pleasure principle is always regarded as a mere psychological double. It is impossible not to relate the tendency "to restore an earlier state of things," which defines the death instinct, with the tendency of the psychical apparatus to maintain the quantity of excitation present in it at the lowest possible level or at least to keep it constant. Must one go so far as to say that the principle of constancy and the death instinct coincide? But then the death instinct, introduced precisely in order to account for the instinctual character of the compulsion to repeat, is not beyond the pleasure principle, but is somehow identical with it.

This further step must be taken, I believe, at least so long as one assumes the equivalence of the pleasure principle and the constancy principle. If pleasure expresses a reduction of tension, and if the death instinct marks a return of living matter to the inorganic, it must be said that pleasure and death are both on the same side. More than once Freud touches on this paradox:

> The dominating tendency of mental life, and perhaps of nervous life in general, is the effort to reduce, to keep constant or to remove internal tension due to stimuli (the "Nirvana principle," to borrow a term from Barbara Low)—a tendency which finds expression in the pleasure principle; and our recognition of the fact is one of our strongest reasons for believing in the existence of death instincts.[18]

And further on: "The pleasure principle seems actually to serve the death instincts." [19] The same paradox is touched on in *The Ego and the Id,* where the condition that follows complete sexual satisfaction is compared to dying.[20]

But then, it will be asked, what is beyond the pleasure principle? All the terms we have thus far opposed to one another have gone over to the same side, the side of death: constancy, the return to an

18. *Beyond the Pleasure Principle, GW, 13,* 60; *SE, 18,* 55–56.
19. *GW, 13,* 69; *SE, 18,* 63.
20. *GW, 13,* 276; *SE, 19,* 47.

earlier state of things, pleasure . . . And if one considers that the task of "binding" free energy is a preparatory act "which introduces and assures the dominance of the pleasure principle," [21] that task is itself in the service of the pleasure principle and consequently of the death instinct. All the differences are annulled in the general tendency toward annulment.

There remains but one possible answer: if the pleasure principle means nothing more than the principle of constancy, must it not be said that only Eros is beyond the pleasure principle? Eros is the great exception to the principle of constancy. I am well aware that Freud writes that all the instincts are conservative; [22] but he adds that the life instincts are conservative to a higher degree in that they are peculiarly resistant to external influences, and, in another sense, that they preserve life itself for a comparatively long period.[23] Further, the hypothesis of a "sexuality of cells" allows one to interpret self-preservation and even narcissism as an "erotic" sacrifice of each cell for the good of the whole body, hence as a manifestation of Eros. Finally and above all, if Eros is "the preserver of all things," it is because it "unites all things." But this enterprise runs counter to the death instinct: "Union with the living substance of a different individual increases those tensions, introducing what may be described as fresh 'vital differences' which must then be lived off." [24] Thus we have the sketch of an answer: that which escapes the principle of constancy is Eros itself, the disturber of sleep, the "breaker of the peace." However, doesn't this proposition destroy the hypothesis that lies at the origin of psychoanalysis, namely that the psychical apparatus is regulated quasi-automatically by the principle of constancy?

Actually, the questioning of the initial theory's key concepts extends even further: what becomes most problematic is the meaning of pleasure itself. In *Beyond the Pleasure Principle* Freud does not explicitly question the earliest equivalence of the entire metapsychology, that of the pleasure principle and the constancy principle;

21. *Beyond the Pleasure Principle*, *GW*, *13*, 67; *SE*, *18*, 62.
22. *GW*, *13*, 42–43; *SE*, *18*, 40.
23. Ibid.
24. *GW*, *13*, 60; *SE*, *18*, 55.

but the conclusions he draws from it after the introduction of the death instincts simply make the equivalence untenable. What is on the side of death is the Nirvana principle, the only faithful translation of the constancy principle into human affectivity. But is the pleasure principle completely contained in the Nirvana principle? The supposition that pleasure and love may not be on the same side in the battle of the giants waged by life and death is difficult to maintain to the very end. How could pleasure remain foreign to the creation of tensions, that is to say, to Eros? Is not this creation what is felt even in the discharge of tension? Must we not say, then, with Aristotle, that pleasure completes an activity, a function, an operation, as a supervenient end? But then what becomes suspect is the definition of pleasure in purely quantitative terms as a simple function of the increase or diminution of a quantity described as tension due to stimulus. Freud began to draw this conclusion in 1924, in "The Economic Problem of Masochism": the pleasure principle, he concedes, is not the same thing as the Nirvana principle; it is only the latter that is "entirely in the service of the death instincts." [25] It must be recognized that "in the series of feelings of tension we have a direct sense of the increase and decrease of amounts of stimulus [*Zunahme und Abnahme der Reizgrössen direkt in der Reihe der Spannungsgefühle empfinden*], and it cannot be doubted that there are pleasurable tensions and unpleasurable relaxations of tensions." [26] Pleasure, then, would be linked to a qualitative characteristic of the excitation itself, perhaps to its rhythm, its temporal rise and fall.

However, Freud limits the extent of this concession by tying the pleasure principle back in with the Nirvana principle; the pleasure principle is a modification imposed by the life instinct. In this way the pleasure principle incontestably remains the "watchman" over life. Its role as watchman or guardian expresses its ties with the principle of constancy, but it is the watchman over life and not over death.

Is this not an admission that the great dualism of love and death also cuts across pleasure? And does it not imply that the reason we

25. *GW, 13,* 372; *SE, 19,* 160.
26. Ibid.

do not know what is beyond the pleasure principle is that we do not know what pleasure is?

There are numerous reasons in Freud's own writings for having doubts about our knowledge of the nature of pleasure. In the first place it should not be forgotten that the earliest formulation of the pleasure principle is closely connected with a representation of the psychical apparatus which, as we have repeatedly emphasized, is solipsistic in nature. The topographic-economic hypothesis is solipsistic by construction, but this characteristic never attaches to the clinical facts that the hypothesis translates—the relation to the mother's breast, the father, the family constellation, authorities—nor to the analytic experience, dramatized in the transference, in which interpretation takes place. The very notion of impulse or instinct, more basic than all the auxiliary representations of the topography, is distinct from the ordinary notion of instinct inasmuch as an instinct in the Freudian sense involves other persons. Hence, the final meaning of pleasure cannot be the discharge of tensions within an isolated apparatus; such a definition applies only to the solitary pleasure of autoerotic sexuality. Ever since the "Project" Freud used the word "satisfaction" (*Befriedigung*) for that quality of pleasure that requires the help of others.

But then, if we introduce other persons into the circuit of pleasure, other difficulties appear. The structure of *Wunsch* has taught us that a wish or a desire is not a tension that can be discharged; desire, as Freud himself describes it, reveals a constitution that is insatiable. The Oedipus drama implies that the child desires the unobtainable (to possess his mother, or to have a child by his mother); the "evil infinitude" that dwells in him cuts him off from satisfaction.

Moreover, if man could be satisfied, he would be deprived of something more important than pleasure—symbolization, which is the counterpart of dissatisfaction. Desire, qua insatiable demand, gives rise to speech. The semantics of desire, which we are focusing upon here, is bound up with this postponement of satisfaction, with this endless mediating of pleasure.

Strangely enough, Freud has a more finely developed conception of the evils that are "the burden of existence" than he has of pleasure. While he continues to speak of pleasure as a discharge of tension, he very sharply distinguishes between unpleasure—the simple contrary of pleasure—and numerous forms of suffering: the trilogy of fear, fright, and anxiety; the threefold fear due to dangers from the external world, from instincts, and from conscience. Even the fear of death is differentiated into biological fear and fear of conscience, the latter being related to the threat of castration. Freud also stresses the malaise or discontent (*Unbehagen*) inherent in man's cultural existence; man cannot be satisfied as a member of culture, for he pursues the death of others, and culture turns against him the torments he inflicted on others. There is something contradictory and impossible about the task of culture: to coordinate the ego's egoistic urge, which is biologically turned toward death, and its altruistic urge toward union with others in the community. Ultimately, what makes for endless dissatisfaction is the unresolvable struggle between love and death. Eros wishes union, but must disturb the peace of inertia; the death instinct wishes the return to the inorganic, but must destroy the living organism. This paradox continues on into the higher stages of civilized life: a strange struggle indeed, for civilization kills us in order to make us live, by using, for itself and against us, the sense of guilt, while at the same time we must loosen its embrace in order to live and find enjoyment.

Thus the empire of suffering is more extensive than that of mere unpleasure: it extends to everything that makes up the harshness of life.

What is the meaning, in Freud's works, of this disparity between the diversity of suffering and the monotony of enjoyment? Does Freud stand in need of completion on this point? Must we somehow distinguish as many degrees of satisfaction as there are degrees of suffering? Must we restore the dialectic of pleasure, sketched by Plato in the *Philebus*, or even the dialectic of pleasure and happiness in the manner of Aristotle's *Ethics?* Or does the pessimism of pleasure make us admit that man's capacity for suffering is richer than his power of enjoyment? In the face of manifold suffering, does man's only recourse lie in unvaried enjoyment and in bearing the excess of suffering with resignation? I am inclined to think that the whole of Freud's work tends toward the second hypothesis. This hypothesis brings us back to the reality principle.

WHAT IS REALITY?

What is, finally, the reality principle? We left the question in suspension at the end of the first chapter, with the hope of discovering a new dimension in the concept of reality that would correspond to the revision of the pleasure principle imposed by the introduction of the death instinct.[27]

Let us briefly recapitulate the earlier analysis. We started from an elementary opposition concerning the "functioning of the psychical apparatus." Insofar as the pleasure principle had a simple meaning, the reality principle likewise was without mystery. Freud's direct and indirect interpretations of the reality principle are all extensions of the single line sketched by the 1911 article, "The Two Principles of Mental Functioning"—the line of the *useful;* whereas the pleasure principle is biologically dangerous, the useful represents the organism's true and proper interests. All the various levels of meaning of the reality principle that we went on to consider lie within the limits of this notion of utility. Thus, reality is first of all the opposite of fantasy—it is facts, such as the normal man sees them; it is the opposite of dreams, of hallucination. In a more specifically analytical sense, the reality principle indicates adaptation to time and the demands of life in society; thus reality becomes the correlate of consciousness, and then of the ego. Whereas the unconscious—the id—is ignorant of time and contradiction and obeys only the pleasure principle, consciousness—the ego—has a temporal organization and takes account of what is possible and reasonable.

As may be seen, nothing in this analysis bears a tragic accent;

27. Ibid.: "In this way we obtain a small but interesting set of connections. The *Nirvana* principle expresses the trend of the death instinct; the *pleasure* principle represents the demands of the libido; and the modification of the latter principle, the *reality* principle, represents the influence of the external world" (*GW, 13,* 373; *SE, 19,* 160).

nothing foreshadows the world view dominated by the struggle between Eros and death.

Now, what happens to this simple opposition between desire and reality when it is shifted to the area of the new theory of instincts? This question arises because the first term of the pair, pleasure, vacillates in its most basic meaning, and also because reality contains death. However, the death that reality holds in reserve is no longer the death instinct, but my own death, death as destiny; this is what gives reality its inexorable and tragic sense; because of death-destiny reality is called necessity and bears the tragic name Ananke. Let us ask ourselves, then, to what extent the oldest theme of Freudianism—that of the double functioning of the psychical apparatus—was raised to the level of the great dramaturgy of Freud's later writings.

The fact is that Freud's later philosophy did not truly transform, but rather reinforced and hardened the early characteristics of the reality principle. It is only within very narrow and very strict limits that one may say that the "romantic" theme of Eros transformed the reality principle. But this discrepancy between the relative mythicizing of Eros and the cold consideration of reality deserves attention and reflection: this fine discordance reveals perhaps the essence of the philosophical tone of Freudianism.

While emphasizing the dualism of Eros and death, Freud also emphasized the struggle against illusion, the last entrenchment of the pleasure principle; he thus reinforced what might be called his "scientific conception of the world," the motto of which could be, "beyond illusion and consolation."

The last chapters of *The Future of an Illusion* are very significant in this respect. Religion, Freud states, has no future; it has exhausted its resources of constraint and consolation. Thus the reality principle, in which *Totem and Taboo* had already recognized a stage of human history parallel to a stage of the libido, becomes the principle that presides over the postreligious age of culture. In this age to come, the scientific spirit will replace religious motivation and moral prohibitions will be motivated by social interests alone. Coming back to his earlier views about the excessive demands of the superego, Freud suggests that, along with their sanctity, commandments will lose their rigidity and intolerance as well; instead of dreaming of their abolition, it is possible that man will work toward their improvement, finding them in the end reasonable and perhaps even friendly.

All this might make one think of the rationalistic and optimistic prophecies of the last century. But Freud himself objects that prohibitions have never been founded on reason but on powerful emotional forces, such as remorse for the primal killing; besides, was it not Freud who revealed the power of the destructive forces working against the ethical, and even worse, within the ethical? Freud is mindful of all this and will express it even more forcefully a few years later in *Civilization and Its Discontents.* His timid hope is pinned to a single point: if religion is the universal neurosis of mankind, it is partly responsible for the intellectual retardation of mankind; it is as much the expression of the powerful forces that arise from below as it is their educator. The possibility of a nonreligious mankind is supported and measured by the parallelism between the growth of mankind and the growth of the individual: "But surely infantilism is destined to be surmounted. Men cannot remain children forever; they must in the end go out into 'hostile life.' We may call this *'education to reality.'* Need I confess to you that the sole purpose of my book is to point out the necessity for this forward step?" [28] Such is the restrained but hazardous optimism underlying this prophecy of the positive age. Addressing himself to a hypothetical opponent who suggests that religion be retained as a pragmatic illusion, Freud in his reply ventures to give the name of a god—the god Logos—to the central idea of his sober prophecy; but I think this must be looked upon merely as a bit of irony inserted in an *ad hominem* argument:

> The voice of the intellect is a soft one, but it does not rest till it has gained a hearing. Finally after a countless succession of rebuffs, it succeeds. . . . Our god, Λόγος, will fulfill whichever of these wishes nature outside us allows, but he will do it very gradually, only in the unforeseeable future, and for a new generation of men. He promises no compensation for us, who suffer griev-

28. *The Future of an Illusion, GW, 14,* 373; *SE, 21,* 49.

ously from life. . . . Our god Λόγος is perhaps not a very almighty one, and he may only be able to fulfill a small part of what his predecessors have promised. If we have to acknowledge this we shall accept it with resignation.[29]

This kinship between Logos and Ananke—the twin gods of the Dutch writer Multatuli—excludes all lyricism about the totality. Moreover, a proud closing protestation is meant to set the tone for the whole book: "No, our science is no illusion. But an illusion it would be to suppose that what science cannot give us we can get elsewhere."[30]

This text leaves no doubt; reality has the same meaning at the end of Freud's life as it had at the beginning: reality is the world shorn of God. Its final meaning does not contradict but rather extends the concept of utility, long since opposed to the fictions created by desire. This coherence between the final and the initial meanings is borne out by the plea for this world, on which Freud ends one of the last chapters of *The Future of an Illusion*. Borrowing a couplet from Heine, Freud states: "Then, with one of our fellow-unbelievers (*Unglaubensgenossen*), they will be able to say without regret:

Den Himmel überlassen wir
Den Engeln und den Spatzen."[31]

The notion of reality that results from this critique of religion is the least romantic of ideas and seems to have no connection with the term Eros. Even the word Ananke—as set within this context—seems to designate the visage of reality after reality has been stripped of any analogy with the father figure. If religious illusion stems from the father complex, the "dissolution" of the Oedipus complex is attained only with the notion of an order of things stripped of any paternal coefficient, an order that is anonymous and impersonal. Ananke is therefore the symbol of disillusion. This was the sense in which I believe the term made its first appearance in

29. *GW*, *14*, 377–79; *SE*, *21*, 53–54.
30. *GW*, *14*, 380; *SE*, *21*, 56.
31. *GW*, *14*, 374. *SE*, *21*, 50, translates Heine's verse (*Deutschland* [Caput I]) thus: "We leave Heaven to the angels and the sparrows."

the *Leonardo*,[32] even before *Totem and Taboo*. Ananke is the name of nameless reality, for those who have "renounced their father." It is also chance, the absence of relationship between the laws of nature and our desires or illusions.

Is this Freud's final statement on the matter? The very expression "resignation" or "submission" to Ananke points to a total wisdom that is more than the mere reality principle, psychologically considered as the perceptual testing of reality. Is it not the case that it is only when reality is accepted with resignation that it becomes Ananke?

Ananke, it seems to me, is a symbol of a world view, and not merely the symbol of a principle of mental functioning; in it is summed up a wisdom that dares to face the harshness of life. Such wisdom is an art of "bearing the burden of existence," according to Schiller's remark cited in *Beyond the Pleasure Principle*.

One can thus find in Freud the sketch of a Spinozistic meaning of reality, a meaning that is connected, as in the great philosopher, with an ascesis of desire restricted to the body's perspective and with an ascesis of the imaginative knowledge arising from that perspective; is not necessity the second kind of knowledge, knowledge according to reason? And if there is in Freud—we shall go on to discuss this point—the first step of a reconciliation in the form of resignation, is this not an echo of the third kind of knowledge? This sketch, it is true, is so little developed philosophically, that one might just as well speak of a love of fate in a Nietzschean sense. The touchstone of the reality principle, thus interpreted philosophically, would be the victory of the love of the whole over my narcissism, over my fear of dying, over the resurgence in me of childhood consolations.

Let us essay this "second wave," as Plato would have said, taking as our clue the gap the previous analysis kept widening—in spite of the continuity of meaning—between mere perceptual reality-testing and resignation to the inexorable order of nature. Without forcing the texts, I wish simply to gather together certain remarks, certain signs and tentative indications, that broaden this respect for nature in such a way that the reality principle is brought more in harmony with the themes of Eros and death.

32. *GW*, *8*, 197; *SE*, *11*, 125.

Perhaps the most direct approach to the theme of resignation is through the question of death, or rather of dying. Resignation is basically a working upon desire that incorporates into desire the necessity of dying. Reality, insofar as it portends my death, is going to enter into desire itself.

In 1899 Freud recalled the phrase of Shakespeare: "Thou owest Nature a death." [33] He alludes to it again at the beginning of the second essay of "Thoughts for the Times on War and Death," [34] written shortly after the outbreak of World War I.

The natural tendency of desire, he explains, is to put death to one side, to exclude it from the purview of life; desire has the conviction of its own immortality. Such an attitude is an aspect of the absence of contradiction in the unconscious. And so we disguise death in innumerable ways, reducing it from a necessity to a chance event. But in return, "life is impoverished, it loses in interest, when the highest stake in the game of living, life itself, may not be risked." [35] Thus paralyzed, when we exclude death from life, we no longer understand the proud motto of the Hanseatic League: *Navigare necesse est, vivere non necesse* ("It is necessary to sail the seas, it is not necessary to live"). We content ourselves with dying fictionally with our heroes of literature and the theater, while preserving our lives intact.

When Freud wrote these lines he had in mind the lie war deals to this conventional treatment of death; and he dared to write: "Life has, indeed, become interesting again; it has recovered its full content." [36] Of course, Freud knew how odious a remark from the home front, from a noncombatant, could be. What mattered to him was the attainment—through the cruelty of the remark—of truthfulness. When death is acknowledged as the termination of life, finite life recovers its significance.

But the recognition of death is obscured by the fear of death no less than by the disbelief on the part of our unconscious concerning our own death; the fear of death has a different source: it is a by-

33. Letter 104, *Origins*, p. 276. The actual line in Shakespeare runs: "Thou owest God a death" (*I Henry IV*, V. i.126).

34. "Zeitgemässes über Krieg und Tod," *GW, 10*, 324–55; *SE, 14*, 275–300.

35. *GW, 10*, 342; *SE, 14*, 290.

36. *GW, 10*, 343; *SE, 14*, 291.

product of the sense of guilt.[37] At the end of *The Ego and the Id,* Freud will state even more firmly: "I believe that the fear of death is something that occurs between the ego and the superego. . . . These considerations make it possible to regard the fear of death, like the fear of conscience, as a development [*Verarbeitung*] of the fear of castration." [38] The fear of death is therefore no less an obstacle than the invulnerability of the unconscious which proclaims, "Nothing can happen to *me.*" If it be added, finally, that we quite readily put to death enemies and strangers, it appears that the number of inauthentic attitudes in the face of death is considerable; the immorality of the id, the fear of death stemming from guilt, the urge to kill—these are so many screens between the destined meaning of death and ourselves. One thus sees that the acceptance of death is a task: *Si vis vitam, para mortem.* If you want to endure life, be prepared for death.[39]

But then, just what is resignation?

The integration of death into life is symbolically proposed to us by "The Theme of the Three Caskets," [40] that admirable short essay Ernest Jones was so fond of. The third casket, neither of gold nor silver but of lead, contains the portrait of the bride; the suitor who chooses it will also have the beautiful girl as his wife. But if the caskets are women, according to a well-known dream symbol, cannot this comic theme be related to the tragic theme of old King Lear who, to his own ruin, does not choose the third daughter, Cordelia, who was the only one that really loved him? A survey of folklore and literature discloses a series of "the choice of the third woman": the Aphrodite of the Judgment of Paris, Cinderella, the Psyche of Apuleius . . . But who is the third woman? The fairest one, of course, but also the one who "loves and is silent." Now, in dreams, dumbness is a common symbol of death. Hence, are not the three sisters the Moerae, the Fates, the third of whom is called Atropos, the inexorable? If the comparison is correct, "the third woman" signifies that man realizes the full seriousness of the laws

37. *GW, 10,* 350; *SE, 14,* 297.
38. *GW, 13,* 289; *SE, 19,* 58.
39. "Thoughts on War and Death," *GW, 10,* 355; *SE, 14,* 300.
40. "Das Motiv der Kästchenwahl," *GW, 10,* 24–37; *SE, 12,* 291–301.

of nature only when he has to submit to them by accepting his own death.

It will be objected, however, that no one chooses death, nor did Paris choose death, but the most beautiful of women! Substitution, replies Freud: our wishes substitute for death its contrary, beauty, perhaps in accordance with the confusion of contraries in the unconscious; but above all in accordance with the primeval identity of life and death preserved in the myth of the Great Goddess. But if the most beautiful woman is the substitute for death, what does it mean to choose death? Again a substitution, under the dominance of desire: instead of accepting the worst, we substitute the choice of the best. Freud's answer merits quotation:

> Here again there has been a wishful reversal. Choice stands in the place of necessity, of destiny. In this way man overcomes death, which he has recognized intellectually. No greater triumph of wish-fulfillment is conceivable. A choice is made where in reality there is obedience to a compulsion; and what is chosen is not a figure of terror, but the fairest and most desirable of women.[41]

If, then, Shakespeare achieves a profound effect upon us in *King Lear,* it is because he has known how to revert to the primeval myth: if one does not choose the fairest woman, one is necessarily driven to the third, to unhappiness and death. But that is not all: the relation between death and woman is still not clear; once again it is Shakespeare who discloses it: Lear is both the lover and the dying man: Lear is doomed to death, yet he insists on being told how much he is loved. What is, then, the relation between death and woman? The third woman, we said, is death; but if the third woman is death, one must also say, conversely, that death is the third woman, the third form or figure of woman: after the mother, after the beloved mate chosen on the pattern of the mother, finally "the Mother Earth who receives him once more." [42]

Does this mean that man can "choose death and make friends

41. *GW, 10,* 34; *SE, 12,* 299.
42. *GW, 10,* 36; *SE, 12,* 301.

with the necessity of dying" [43] only through regression to the mother figure? Or is it to be understood that the woman figure must become the figure of death for man, so as to cease being fantasy and regression? Freud's final words do not provide a clear answer: "But it is in vain that an old man yearns for the love of a woman as he had it first from his mother: the third of the Fates alone, the silent Goddess of Death, will take him into her arms." [44]

Of course, one might add, along the lines of *The Future of an Illusion*, that the true acceptance of death is distinct from a regressive return in fantasy to the mother's breast only if that acceptance has stood the test of a scientific view of the world. I think this is Freud's actual thought. Even in a Freudian perspective, however, the answer does not completely exhaust the problem; resignation to the ineluctable is not reducible to a mere knowledge of necessity, i.e. to a purely intellectual extension of what we called perceptual reality-testing; resignation is an affective task, a work of correction applied to the very core of the libido, to the heart of narcissism. Consequently, the scientific world view must be incorporated into a history of desire.

The appeal to the poets, to Shakespeare in *King Lear*, invites us to try another path equally familiar to Freud, the path of art. We did not exhaust the resources of Freud's esthetics when we treated the work of art from the standpoint of artistic creation.[45] Because of its analogical character, the investigation of esthetic phenomena remained cautious and fragmentary: the work of art entered the field of psychoanalysis as the analogue of dreams and the neuroses. Nevertheless we did gain two insights into the specificity of works of art: by means of the forepleasure (or pleasure bonus) that the artist's technique offers us, profound sources of tension are liberated; on the other hand, through symbolism, the fantasies of the abolished past are recreated in the light of day.

If we now take up these fragmentary insights from the point of view of the task of culture defined above—to diminish instinctual charges, to reconcile the individual with the ineluctable, to com-

43. Ibid.
44. Ibid.
45. Cf. above, "Analytic," Part II, Ch. 1, pp. 163–77.

pensate for irreparable losses through substitute satisfactions—it is reasonable to ask whether art, now considered from the standpoint of the user or viewer, does not derive its meaning from its intermediate position between illusion represented by religion and reality represented by science. Might it not be that the task of reconciliation and compensation, withdrawn from religion, devolves upon this intermediate function? Is not art an aspect of the education to reality spoken of in the 1911 article, "The Two Principles of Mental Functioning"?

To understand the esthetic function in Freud, one would have to locate the exact place of the *seduction* or *charm* of the work of art on the path leading from the pleasure principle to the reality principle. It is certain that Freud's severity toward religion is equaled only by his sympathy for the arts. Illusion is the way of regression, the "return of the repressed." Art, on the contrary, is the nonobsessional, non-neurotic form of substitute satisfaction; the "charm" of esthetic creations does not stem from the memory of parricide. We recall our earlier analysis of forepleasure or the incentive bonus: the artist's technique creates a formal or esthetic pleasure which brings about a general lowering of the thresholds of inhibition and thereby enables us to enjoy our fantasies without shame. No fictive restoration of the father enters in here to make us regress toward the submissive state of childhood. Instead, we play with the resistances and impulses and in this way achieve a general relaxation of our conflicts. Freud comes very close here to the cathartic tradition of Plato and Aristotle.

What is the relation, then, between esthetic seduction and the reality principle? Freud explicitly treats this point in the 1911 article. In Paragraph 6 [46] he says that art brings about a reconciliation between the two principles in a peculiar way: the artist, like the neurotic, is a man who turns away from reality because he cannot come to terms with the renunciation of instinctual satisfaction that reality demands, and who transposes his erotic and ambitious desires to the plane of fantasy and play. By means of his special gifts, however, he finds a way back to reality from this world of fantasy: he creates a new reality, the work of art, in which he himself be-

46. *GW, 8,* 236; *SE, 12,* 224.

comes the hero, the king, the creator he desired to be, without having to follow the roundabout path of making real alterations in the external world. In this new reality other men feel at home because they "feel the same dissatisfaction as he does with the renunciation demanded by reality, and because that satisfaction, which results from the replacement of the pleasure principle by the reality principle, is itself part of reality."

As may be seen, if art initiates the reconciliation between the pleasure and the reality principles, it does so mainly on the basis of the pleasure principle. In spite of his great sympathy for the arts, Freud has none for what might be described as an esthetic world view. Just as he distinguishes esthetic seduction from religious illusion, so too he lets it be understood that the esthetic—or, to be more exact, the esthetic world view—goes only halfway toward the awesome education to necessity required by the harshness of life and the knowledge of death, an education impeded by our incorrigible narcissism and by our thirst for childhood consolation.

I will give only one or two indications of this. In his interpretation of humor, at the end of his book *Jokes and the Unconscious* (1905), Freud seemed to make much of the ability to create pleasure as a substitute for the release of painful affects. The humor that smiles through tears, and even the dreadful gallows humor (according to which the rogue, who was being led out to execution on a Monday, says: "Well, this week's beginning nicely") seemed to have some credit in his eyes. Interpreted economically, the pleasure of humor arises from an economy in the expenditure of painful feelings. Yet, a brief remark in the 1905 text sets us on guard:

> We can only say that if someone succeeds, for instance, in disregarding a painful affect by reflecting on the greatness of the interests of the world as compared with his own smallness, we do not regard this as an achievement of humor but of philosophical thought, and if we put ourselves into this train of thought, we obtain no yield of pleasure.[47]

In 1927, Freud wrote a separate short paper entitled "Humor,"[48] which is much more severe, and in which he extends humor to

47. *Jokes and the Unconscious, GW, 8,* 266; *SE, 8,* 233.
48. *GW, 14,* 383–89; *SE, 21,* 161–66.

all the sentiments of the sublime. Humor elevates us above misfortune only by saving our narcissism from disaster:

> The grandeur in it clearly lies in the triumph of narcissism, the victorious assertion of the ego's invulnerability. The ego refuses to be distressed by the provocations of reality, to let itself be compelled to suffer. It insists that it cannot be affected by the traumas of the external world; it shows, in fact, that such traumas are no more than occasions for it to gain pleasure. . . . Humor is not resigned; it is rebellious. It signifies not only the triumph of the ego but also of the pleasure principle, which is able here to assert itself against the unkindness of the real circumstances.

And where does humor get this power of withdrawal and rebellion? From the superego, which condescends to allow the ego a small yield of pleasure. Freud concludes: "In bringing about the humorous attitude, the superego is actually repudiating reality and serving an illusion. . . . And finally, if the superego tries, by means of humor, to console the ego and protect it from suffering, this does not contradict its origin in the parental agency."

I am well aware that one cannot judge the whole of art and all of the arts by such a narrow feeling as humor. Still, we had found that humor seems to be a point where the pleasure of esthetic seduction borders on philosophical resignation. It is precisely at this point that Freud opposes a strong negation, as if he said to us: The acceptance of life and death? Yes, but not so cheaply! Everything in Freud implies that true resignation to necessity, active and personal resignation, is the great work of life and that such a work is not of an esthetic nature.

But if art cannot take the place of wisdom, it does lead to it in its own way. The symbolic resolution of conflicts through art, the transfer of desires and hatreds to the plane of play, daydreams, and poetry, borders on resignation; prior to wisdom, while waiting for wisdom, the symbolic mode proper to the work of art enables us to endure the harshness of life, and, suspended between illusion and reality, helps us to love fate.

Let us make a final effort to reach the undiscoverable point in Freud's work where his early and unchanged views concerning the reality principle would be rejoined by his later views concerning the struggle between Eros and Death. Must we leave these two lines of thought unconnected—the one which I will call the path of disillusion, the other that of the love of life? Is it possible that the acceptance of reality has nothing to do with "the battle of the giants"? If the meaning of culture is a struggle of the human species for existence, if love is to be the stronger of the two, what is the meaning of the acceptance of death in relation to the enterprise of Eros? Does not the acceptance of death have to overcome a final counterfeit which would be precisely the death instinct, the wish to die, *against which* Eros is aimed?

I see nothing explicit along these lines in Freud's writings except for some early allusions in the *Leonardo* and a few remarks in *The Ego and the Id* and *Civilization and Its Discontents.* Leonardo's conversion of libido into intellectual curiosity, into the scientific investigation of the external world, teaches us that the force of reflection must express the power of loving, for otherwise it will kill the libido and itself fall into decline; Leonardo himself neither lived nor created according to the standard of the hymn he addresses to "the sublime law of nature (*O mirabile necessità*)." [49] Whereas Faust transformed intellectual curiosity back into an enjoyment of life, Leonardo devoted himself to investigation rather than to loving; and Freud observes: "Leonardo's development approaches Spinoza's mode of thinking" [50]—which would imply that Freud was not satisfied with Spinoza's intellectual love. He continues:

> Lost in admiration and filled with true humility, he all too easily forgets that he himself is a part of those active forces and that in accordance with the scale of his personal strength the way is open for him to try and alter a small portion of the destined course of the world—a world in which the small is still no less wonderful and significant than the great.[51]

Does this mean that the knowledge of necessity, separated from Eros, is also lost in an impasse? Is the sublimation of the libido into

49. *Leonardo, GW, 8,* 141–42; *SE, 11,* 75.
50. Ibid.
51. *GW, 8,* 142; *SE, 11,* 76.

the instinct for research, as in the case of Leonardo, already a betrayal of Eros? Which is the true twin of Ananke—is it Logos, as described at the end of *The Future of an Illusion*, or Eros, as implied in the *Leonardo?* Should we not once again pay heed to the old androgynous myths, evoked in the *Leonardo*,[52] which signify the primal creative force of nature? Do they not say the same thing as the myth of the *Symposium*, cited at length in *Beyond the Pleasure Principle*, the myth of the primeval confusion of the sexes? In short, does not Eros strive to convert the reality principle also, just as it transformed the pleasure principle? Let us listen once more to the *Leonardo*:

> We all still show too little respect for Nature which (in the obscure words of Leonardo which recall Hamlet's lines) "is full of countless causes that never enter experience." (*La natura è piena d'infinite ragioni che non furono mai in isperienza.*) Every one of us human beings corresponds to one of the countless experiments in which these *ragioni* of nature force their way into experience.[53]

This was the final statement of the *Leonardo*.

If these lines have a meaning, do they not say that what is greater than the reality principle, understood as the scientific view of the world, is the respect for nature and for the "countless causes" that "force their way into experience"? But nothing indicates that Freud finally harmonized the theme of the reality principle with the theme of Eros—the first being an essentially critical theme directed against archaic objects and illusions, the second an essentially lyrical theme of the love of life and thus a theme directed against the death instinct. In Freudianism there is undoubtedly no "beyond the reality principle," as there is a "beyond the pleasure principle"; but there is a concurrence of scientism and romanticism. Freud's philosophical temperament consists perhaps in this delicate equilibrium —or subtle conflict?—between lucidity free of illusion and the love of life. It is perhaps in the resignation to death that this equilibrium finds its most fragile expression; but here death figures twice and

52. *GW*, *8*, 162–68; *SE*, *11*, 93–98.
53. *GW*, *8*, 210–11; *SE*, *11*, 137.

with different meanings: lucidity without illusion invites me to accept my death, that is to say, to regard it as one of the necessities of blind nature; but Eros, which wishes to unite all things, calls upon me to struggle against the human instinct of aggression and self-destruction, hence never to love death, but to love life, in spite of my death. It would seem that Freud never unified his early world view, expressed from the beginning in the alternation of the pleasure principle and the reality principle, with the new world view, expressed by the struggle of Eros and Thanatos. That is why he is neither Spinoza nor Nietzsche.

Let us give Freud the last word—which is also his concluding remark in *Civilization and Its Discontents:*

"And now it is to be expected that the other of the two 'Heavenly Powers,' eternal Eros, will make an effort to assert himself in the struggle with his equally immortal adversary." [54]

54. *GW, 14,* 506; *SE, 21,* 145. In 1931, when the menace of Hitler was beginning to be apparent, Freud added a final sentence terminating the work in the second edition: "But who can foresee with what success and with what result?" (Ibid.)

BOOK III

Dialectic: A Philosophical Interpretation of Freud

Our reading of Freud is nearly finished.[1] Our debate with Freud begins. It is reasonable to expect that it will answer the questions left suspended at the end of Book I. But we now see how extensive is the question and how naïve the expectation of a quick and ready answer. We are asking philosophy to do two things at once: to arbitrate the war between two opposed hermeneutics and to integrate into philosophic reflection the entire process of interpretation. Two things, then: to replace an antithesis that left the opposing parties external to one another, with a dialectic in which they are interrelated; simultaneously, and by means of that dialectic, to move from abstract to concrete reflection. But the great philosophy of language and imagination that would give us the integrating principle is not within reach. It is too easily said that symbols carry within themselves, in their overdetermined semantic texture, the possibility of various interpretations, an interpretation that reduces them to their instinctual basis and an interpretation that develops the complete intentionality of their symbolic meaning. This proposition is not a self-evident statement, but is rather the setting of a task. In order to see its truth, one must attain the level of thought on which this synthesis can be understood. That is why I have conceived this dialectic as a patient progression through a series of graduated points of view.

First, a chapter will be devoted to an examination of the *epistemological* status of Freudian psycholanalysis. A philosophic inter-

1. I have purposely reserved for the "Dialectic" the study of several important texts on psychoanalytic technique, and of certain problems, such as sublimation, in the belief that they would stand out more clearly in the new context of the "Dialectic."

pretation must begin with an arbitration at the level of a logic of experience; what is at stake here is the meaning of the statements of psychoanalysis with respect to their validity and limits. If the limits of analytic explanation are given in the structure of its theory and not in some decree proscribing its extension to this or that sphere of human experience, then the search for the philosophical locus of psychoanalysis is subordinate to the understanding of its theoretical structure. The comparison we will make with scientific psychology on the one hand and phenomenology on the other is aimed at determining, by a method of difference, the place of analytic experience in the total field of human experience.

Secondly, moving to a properly philosophical level, we will ask ourselves whether a philosophy of reflection can account for the realist and naturalist concepts that, in Freudian theory, govern this *sui generis* experience. The guiding concept in this *reflective* step will be an *archeology of the subject*. This is not a concept elaborated by psychoanalysis itself; it is rather a concept that reflective thought forms in order to secure a philosophical ground for analytic discourse. At the same time, reflective thought itself undergoes change by incorporating into itself the discourse of its own archeology; instead of abstract reflection, it starts to become concrete reflection.

Thirdly, an archeology remains abstract so long as it is not integrated by way of "complementary opposition" with a *teleology*, with a progressive synthesizing of figures or categories, where the meaning of each is clarified by the meaning of further figures or categories, on the pattern of the Hegelian phenomenology. Thus a third level is formed, which is properly *dialectical;* it is at this level that the possibility of interrelating two opposed hermeneutics comes into view; regression and progression are henceforth understood as two possible directions of interpretation, opposed but complementary. This level of thought is sufficiently important to give its name to the third book—"Dialectic." Still, its importance should not be overestimated. The point of view presented at this level is indeed central, but it is only a transition; the function of a dialectic between regression and progression, between archeology and teleology, is to lead from a reflection that understands its archeology to a symbolic understanding that would grasp the indivisible unity of its archeology and its teleology in the very origin of speech. The dialectic is not everything; it is only a procedure that reflection uses in order to overcome its abstraction and make itself concrete or complete.

Fourthly, I have given the final chapter the subtitle, "The Approaches to Symbol." This subtitle explains the title "Hermeneutics." I do not mean to give the impression that we are at present able to write the general hermeneutics that would reconcile the opposing interpretations; I wish to contribute to that general hermeneutics by trying to resolve some aporias in psychoanalytic interpretation, such as sublimation. The solution I propose to this aporia is only exploratory; but at least it will enable me to attempt a new formulation of the problem that lies at the origin of this book, namely, the conflict—within myself and within contemporary culture—between a hermeneutics that demystifies religion and a hermeneutics that tries to grasp, in the symbols of faith, a possible call or kerygma. It is only at the very end, therefore, that I glimpse the approaches to the solution of a problem that arose at the beginning of my research. It is at the end that one sees not only how large the question was, but also how naïve our demand was for an answer. If the journey to the point of departure is so toilsome, it is because the concrete is the final conquest of thought.

Chapter 1: Epistemology: Between Psychology and Phenomenology

In this first chapter I return to the problems of method discussed in Part I of the "Analytic." There we made an internal examination of Freudian discourse, without trying to locate it within the whole range of discourse about human experience. We are now in a position to confront Freud's discourse with other types of discourse and to justify, with respect to them, its central paradox.

We will take two reference points external to psychoanalysis, scientific psychology on the one hand, phenomenology on the other.

This is not a matter of setting up a balanced comparison and making psychoanalysis oscillate between the two poles. The two phases of the comparison involve a definite progression. If we are to grasp the comparison with phenomenology, we must first understand the difference between psychoanalysis and scientific psychology, the subject of the first two sections. This first confrontation aims above all at doing away with a misunderstanding; it is a question of resisting the temptation to blend psychoanalysis into a general psychology along behaviorist lines; as I see it, such a fusion is a confusion that must be rejected. The second confrontation has a completely different aim and goes much further; it consists in a gradual approximation, by means of the phenomenological method, to what is truly proper to psychoanalysis. Phenomenology likewise fails to produce the equivalent of analytic experience, but this failure, instead of being a misunderstanding, brings to light a difference at the end of an approximation.

THE EPISTEMOLOGICAL CASE AGAINST PSYCHOANALYSIS

The scientific status of psychoanalysis has been subjected to severe criticism, especially in countries of British and American culture. Epistemologists, logicians, semanticists, philosophers of language have closely examined its concepts, propositions, argumentation, and structure as a theory and have generally come to the conclusion that psychoanalysis does not satisfy the most elementary requirements of a scientific theory.

The analysts have answered either by flight, or by the adduction of additional scientific criteria for their discipline, or by attempts at "reformulation" aimed at making it acceptable to men of science. By so doing, they have skirted the "agonizing revision" called for, I believe, by the logicians' critique and which I will express as follows: "No, psychoanalysis is not a science of observation; it is an interpretation, more comparable to history than to psychology."

Let us consider, one by one, the criticisms of the logicians, the reformulations internal to psychoanalysis, and finally the reformulations proposed from without.

The Critique of the Logicians. I purposely begin with the most devastating critique, presented by Ernest Nagel at a symposium held in New York in 1958 on the theme of *Psychoanalysis, Scientific Method and Philosophy.*[1]

If psychoanalysis is a "theory," in the sense of the molecular theory of gases or the gene theory in biology, i.e. a set of propositions that systematizes, explains, and predicts certain observable phenomena, then it must satisfy the same logical criteria as other theories in the natural or social sciences.

In the first place, it must be capable of empirical verification. This assumes that it is possible to deduce determinate consequences

1. Ernest Nagel, "Methodological Issues in Psychoanalytic Theory," in *Psychoanalysis, Scientific Method and Philosophy,* a symposium edited by Sidney Hook (New York, New York University Press, 1959), pp. 38–56. This study was in reply to the methodological paper presented by Heinz Hartmann, "Psychoanalysis as a Scientific Theory," ibid., pp. 3–37.

from its propositions; otherwise the theory has no definite content. In addition, there must be some specific rules of procedure (variously called "correspondence rules," "coordinating definitions," or "operational definitions"), so that at least some theoretical notions may be tied down to definite and unambiguous facts.

However, the energy notions of Freudian theory are so vague and metaphorical that it seems impossible to deduce from them any determinate conclusions; such notions may well be suggestive, but they cannot be empirically verified; further, any coordination with facts of behavior is clouded over with an invincible ambiguity, to such an extent that it is impossible to state on what conditions the theory could be refuted.[2]

Secondly, if the theory is to be regarded as valid, its empirical validation must satisfy the requirements of a logic of proof. Interpretation is said to be its main method (along with confirmation by child development studies and ethnology). However, on what conditions is an interpretation valid? Is it valid because it is coherent, because it is accepted by the patient, because it improves the condition of the patient? But a given interpretation must first be characterized by objectivity; this means that a number of independent inquirers have access to the same data obtained under carefully standardized circumstances. Next, there must be some objective procedures to decide between rival interpretations. Further, the interpretation must lead to verifiable predictions. But, psychoanalysis is not in a position to meet these requirements: its data are enmeshed in the individual relationship of the analyst to the analysand; one cannot dispel the suspicion that interpretations are forced upon the data by the interpreter, for want of a comparative procedure and statistical investigation. Finally, the allegations of psychoanalysts concerning the effectiveness of therapy do not satisfy the minimum rules of verification; since the percentages of improvement cannot be strictly established or even defined by some kind of "before and after" study, the therapeutic effectiveness of psychoanalysis cannot be compared with that of some other method

2. This argument is developed by Michael Scriven, "The Experimental Investigation of Psychoanalysis," ibid., pp. 226–51.

or treatment, or even with the ratio of spontaneous cures. For these reasons, the criterion of therapeutic success is unusable.[3]

The Internal Attempts at Reformulation. As long as one tries to place psychoanalysis among the observational sciences, the preceding attack against psychoanalysis seems to me unanswerable. In order to meet the above requirements, certain psychoanalysts have tried to reformulate the theory in terms acceptable to "academic psychology." Some supporters of that psychology have lent them a hand, not without mixing suspicion with their willingness, and at times with the sincere desire to integrate certain facts and concepts of psychoanalysis into scientific psychology, at the cost of what some have called an "operational reconversion." This attempt comes, moreover, at a moment when the demise of theories is a general phenomenon in the sciences concerned with man.

It is all the more urgent, therefore, to pinpoint just where the original Freudian theory resists these attempts. What resists the reformulation is precisely the hybrid character of psychoanalysis: namely, the fact that it arrives at its energy concepts solely by way of interpretation. Because of this mixed nature, analytic interpretation will always seem an anomaly in the human sciences.

Let us see how far we can go along these lines.[4]

3. Ibid., pp. 228, 234–35.

4. Within the psychoanalytic movement, the origin of this methodological revision goes back to the important work of H. Hartmann, "Ichpsychologie und Anpassungsproblem," *Int. Z. Psychoanal., 24* (1939). Partially translated by D. Rapaport in his *Organization and Pathology of Thought* (New York, Columbia University Press, 1951), the entire work is now available in English: *Ego Psychology and the Problem of Adaptation,* tr. D. Rapaport (New York, International Universities Press, 1958). I have consulted the following works: Hartmann, Kris, Loewenstein, "Comments on the Formation of Psychic Structure," *The Psychoanal. Study of the Child, 2* (1946), 11–38. Kris, "The Nature of Psychoanalytic Propositions and Their Validation," in S. Hook and N. R. Konvetz, eds., *Freedom and Experience* (Ithaca, Cornell University Press, 1947). L. Kubie, "Problems and Techniques of Psychoanalytic Validation and Progress," in E. Pumpian-Mindlin, ed., *Psychoanalysis as Science* (Stanford, Stanford University Press, 1952). Else Frenkel-Brunswik, "Meaning of Psychoanalytic Concepts and Confirmation

First of all, the reformulation must be carried out at the level of the most general presuppositions that make psychology a factual science. Rapaport states three theses that place the facts of psychoanalysis among the "observables" of scientific psychology:[5]

First, the subject matter of psychoanalysis, we shall say, is behavior; in this respect psychoanalysis does not differ basically from the "empirical point of view" of other psychologies except secondarily, because of its stress on "latent" behavior.

Second, psychoanalysis shares the "gestalt point of view" that has conquered the whole of modern psychology; according to this viewpoint all behavior is integrated and indivisible. Hence the "systems" and "agencies" (ego, id, superego) are not "entities," but aspects of behavior; a behavior is said to be "overdetermined" when it can be related to several structures and submitted to multiple levels of analysis.

Third, all behavior is that of the integral personality; in spite of the accusations of atomism and mechanism, psychoanalysis satisfies the "organismic point of view" by reason of all the interconnections it establishes between the systems and agencies of the subject.

If one admits that psychoanalysis can be assimilated, on the level of the "facts" themselves, to these three "points of view" ordinarily assumed by scientific psychology, it is likewise possible to reformulate the "models" used by analytic theory and to assimilate them to

---

of Psychoanalytic Theories," *Scientific Monthly, 79* (1954), 293–300; "Psychoanalysis and the Unity of Science," *Proc. of the Am. Acad. of Arts and Sciences, 80* (1954). Loewenstein, "Some Thoughts on Interpretation in the Theory and Practice of Psychoanalysis," *The Psychoanal. Study of the Child, 12* (1957). David Rapaport and Merton Gill, "The Points of View and Assumptions of Metapsychology," *Int. J. Psychoanal., 40* (1959). And especially Rapaport, "The Structure of Psychoanalytic Theory: A Systematizing Attempt," in S. Koch, ed., *Psychology: A Study of a Science, 3* (New York, McGraw-Hill, 1958), 55–183.

5. Hartmann, in Hook, ed., *Psychoanalysis, Scientific Method and Philosophy*, pp. 3–16. Rapaport, "The Structure of Psychoanalytic Theory," in Koch, ed., *Psychology, 3*, 82–104. Rapaport's work is very significant; since he had to follow Dr. Koch's outline of questions, he had to pose some questions to psychoanalysis that are foreign to that discipline, such as the role of "independent, intervening, and dependent variables" and the "quantification" of its laws.

the points of view familiar to academic psychology.[6] It is interesting to split Freud's metapsychology into a group of "distinct models," with the aim of later reuniting them in a "combined model."

The topographic point of view is thus compared to the reflex-arc model: the psychical apparatus responds by way of distinct parts.

The economic point of view, in turn, is an aspect of the entropy model: from tension to tension-reduction. All motivated behaviors may be placed under this model; its first application is the *Wunscherfüllung* and the pleasure principle and, indirectly, the reality principle itself, so far as the latter remains a mere detour employed by the pleasure principle.

The theory of stages and the role of fixation and regression come under a genetic point of view; moreover, with the help of Haeckel's biogenetic law, it is possible to make phylogeny and ontogeny coincide, as is seen in *Totem and Taboo*. Because of this genetic model, psychoanalysis may be compared to learning theories, although it differs from them in its greater emphasis on the role and weight of early experiences in human experience. But in its own peculiar way, it has developed along the lines of learning theory, as in its investigation of object-choice and in its evolutional history of the systems ego and superego.

Finally, Freud may be said to have used a Jacksonian model: the systems form a hierarchy of integrations, with the higher systems inhibiting or controlling the lower. This model obviously served as the basis for superposing the secondary system on the primary system and for the related notions of censorship, defense, and repression. In this sense, it is the most important model; the topographic, economic, and genetic points of view are associated with this Jacksonian model in all the Freudian concepts involving the notion of conflict.[7]

6. Rapaport, pp. 67–82.

7. Rapaport works out a "combined model" (pp. 71 ff.), starting from the entropic or economic model. The Jacksonian model permits the introduction of a principle of hierarchy between a primary and a secondary form of the economic model. In turn, the pleasure principle, which is characteristic of the primary form, is able to furnish a guiding thread in the three areas of action (impulsive action), perception (quasi hallucination), and affect

These models can be likened to certain points of view universally assumed by present-day psychologists:

1. All behavior, we shall say, is part of a genetic series. Lewin's genotypes and phenotypes come under this same genetic point of view; Freud's contribution was to relate the genetic point of view to the economic point of view.

2. All behavior involves unconscious "crucial determinants." All psychologies deal with unnoticed conditions; but Freud thematizes what is unnoticed, infers it by a method of investigation, discovers the peculiar laws of those factors, thus distinguishing between what can and what cannot become noticeable; at the same time he treats both groups of factors in terms of psychology, not biology.

It was to account for these facts that Freud worked out the topographic point of view (unconscious, preconscious, conscious), and then the structural point of view (id, ego, superego); but this transition, like the technique of handling conflicts, was already implied in the notions of primary and secondary systems. In turn, the structural point of view, with its use of anticathexis, foreshadows the development of recent ego psychology.[8]

(affect discharge, e.g. anxiety). Next, we have the secondary system that superimposes its control and defense structures; anticathexis is thus another name for the integrative control of the Jacksonian model; the heightening by anticathexes of the original thresholds assures the "functional autonomy" —to use Allport's term—of those "structures" which have a slow rate of change and which Freud calls systems or agencies. At the same time the structural point of view reacts on the entropic point of view, since the maintenance of higher structures and their autonomy require not a systematic and general reduction of all tensions, but discharges compatible with the maintenance of tensions appropriate to the maintenance of the control structures.

Thus are preserved the main points of the "Project" of 1895, Chapter 7 of the *Traumdeutung*, "Papers on Metapsychology," and the book *Inhibitions, Symptoms and Anxiety*.

8. "The genetic character of the psychoanalytic theory is ubiquitous in its literature. The concept of 'complementary series' is probably the clearest expression of it: each behavior is part of a historical sequence shaped both by epigenetic laws and experience; each step in this sequence contributed to the shaping of the behavior and has dynamic, economic, structural, and contextual-adaptive relationships to it. Such complementary series do not constitute an 'infinite regress': they lead back to a historical situation in which

3. All behavior is ultimately determined by drives. This dynamic point of view has long prevailed over the preconceptions of the old empirical psychology and its *tabula rasa;* psychology has opted for Kant and against Hume. Freud's contribution consists in his recognition of the preeminent role of sexuality in this drive dynamism, and thus in his rediscovery of the untamed root that exists prior to all cultural development.

4. All behavior makes use of psychological energy and is regulated by it. The main point of interest here is not the energy character of drives, but the energy character of their regulation; everything Freud has said about bound energy, the operation of the psychism with minimal quantities of energy, the diminishing of the tendency toward discharge by the heightening of thresholds, neutralization and desexualization, and deaggressivization and sublimation, finds confirmation and parallels in Lewin, and even more in the notions of power-engineering and information-engineering of cybernetics. What is peculiar to Freud is that he shows how this regulation operates on the borrowed energy of the drive derivatives.

5. All behavior is determined by reality. This adaptive point of view is found not only in psychology, with its basic schema of stimulus-response, but in biology, where reality plays the role of environment, and even epistemology, where reality is called objectivity. Psychoanalysis falls in with this point of view, through its successive conceptions of reality: first, reality was what the neurotic refuses; then, in the object stage of instincts, the correlate of the secondary process; finally, and especially, the field of the ego's preadaptedness.[9]

---

a particular solution of a drive demand was first achieved, or a particular apparatus was first put to a certain kind of use" (Rapaport, p. 87).

9. Rapaport (pp. 97–101) distinguishes five successive conceptions of reality in psychoanalytic theory. Prior to 1900, reality is the target of defense, the defense being directed against the memory of a real event so as to prevent its recurrence. From 1900 to 1923 (with the exception of the article of 1911), the conception of reality is centered on the drive object and is defined by the secondary processes (delays, detour, judgment). The third conception of reality is connected with the first formulation of the ego psychology in the "Two Principles" of 1911; reality is the counterpart of a structure that is no longer merely defensive-conflictful; the ego has a

The "adaptive" point of view has given rise to a corollary that may well constitute a distinct point of view in American psychoanalysis: "All behavior is socially determined"; but in any case classical psychoanalytic theory already contains this theme, which relates it to social psychology (theories of anaclitic object-choice, of the Oedipus complex, of identification, etc.), not to mention the dissidents, the neo-Freudians of the culturalist school.

The above comparisons show how psychoanalysis can be reintegrated into scientific psychology with its dominant themes of adaptation, structurization, and evolution. The contribution of psychoanalysis lies in its stress on the entropic model and thus in its special focus on the instinctual effects related to the primary process, whereas in academic psychology the stress is put on sensory experience and learning. However, these roles are in the process of being interchanged. On the one hand, contemporary psychology of motivation is widening the scope of academic psychology in the direction of psychoanalysis; on the other hand, the reformulation of psychoanalysis in terms of genetic adaptation and progressive structurization places it within the field of general psychology. The development of psychoanalysis in the direction of an *ego psychology,* starting with Hartmann's great work in 1939 (cf. n. 4), has hastened this evolution, for the ego's functions are essentially functions of adaptation.

Thus the lines between psychoanalysis and scientific psychology are constantly being woven more tightly together.

"Operational" Reformulations. Unfortunately, this assimilation of psychoanalysis to observational psychology does not satisfy the psychologist and does not respect the peculiar constitution of psychoanalysis.

What is called for, say those psychologists most conversant with

---

function of its own, namely, that of reconciliation and arbitration. In the fourth conception—Hartmann's—the ego is preadapted, or potentially adapted, to reality by reason of its apparatuses of primary autonomy; but there still remains an essential duality between psychological and external reality. In the fifth conception, developed by Erikson, man is preadapted not only to an average foreseeable environment but to an entire evolving series of environments, which are no longer "objective" but social.

epistemology, is not some vague relationship between psychoanalysis and psychology; if psychoanalysis is to meet the minimal requirements of scientific theory, it must be completely reformulated in what Bridgman [10] calls "operational language."

The only thing that actually meets the conditions of a strict operationalism is behaviorism; in Skinner [11] we find the rigorous conjunction of the operational and behaviorist demands.

In the eyes of this strict operationalism, psychoanalytic theory and all concepts that gravitate around the idea of a mental apparatus can only be regarded as dangerous metaphors of the phlogistic kind; from the epistemological point of view, psychoanalytic theory does not mark a decisive advance over animism and its inventions (demons, spirits, homunculus, personality). "Freud's explanatory scheme," writes Skinner, "followed a traditional pattern of looking for a cause of human behavior inside the organism"; this "traditional fiction of a mental life" [12]—what Ryle called "the ghost in the machine"—led Freud to posit something that is unobservable and cannot be manipulated; for operationalism, however, the sole objects of inquiry are the changes of the organism in relation to environmental variables. Skinner even goes so far as to accuse Freud of exclusive interest in those aspects of behavior that can be regarded as expressions of mental processes, and of having greatly narrowed the field of observation thereby. He concludes that the

10. P. W. Bridgman, "Operational Analysis," *Philosophy of Science, 5* (1938), 114–31; "Some General Principles of Operational Analysis," *Psychological Review, 52* (1945), 246–49.

See also E. Frenkel-Brunswik, "Meaning of Psychoanalytic Concepts and Confirmation of Psychoanalytic Theories," *Scientific Monthly, 79* (1954), 293–300.

11. B. F. Skinner, *Science and Human Behavior* (New York, Macmillan, 1953); "Critique of Psychoanalytic Concepts and Theories," *Scientific Monthly* (1954), reprinted in Herbert Feigl and Michael Scriven, eds., *The Foundations of Science and the Concepts of Psychology and Psychoanalysis*, Minnesota Studies in the Philosophy of Science, *1* (Minneapolis, University of Minnesota Press, 1956), 77–87. This volume is of great importance; in it Herbert Feigl and Rudolf Carnap work out a general theory of the theoretical language of the sciences from the perspective of logical positivism. It also contains articles by Albert Ellis and Antony Flew that will be cited further on, n. 13 ff.

12. Minnesota Studies, *1*, 79–80.

representation of the mental apparatus which Freud imposed upon psychoanalysis has delayed the incorporation of that discipline into the body of science proper. Skinner is right, of course, in asking that all the alleged forces be quantified if they are to be homogeneous with the forces of nature. But he completely misses the point that an operational definition of all the terms of psychonalysis is only an expedient by which one transcribes into terms of behaviorist psychology the results of a completely different work of thought, the work of analytic interpretation. We shall come back to this, for it will be the main point of our discussion.

The reformulation of psychoanalysis can be attempted, therefore, only in a modified or revised form of operationalism.[13] The latter requires that "to be operationally meaningful, a statement must be . . . tied to observables at *some* point." There is therefore only one irreducible requirement: a statement or hypothesis must in some manner be confirmable, that is, it must be related to some kind of observable.[14]

What is thereby aimed at is the exclusion of hypothetical constructs and higher order abstractions, but not of lower order abstractions: the verification of the latter may even be incomplete or indirect. This allows for the introduction of what are called "intervening variables" or "dispositional concepts." Hypothetical constructs, such as essence, phlogiston, ether, id, libido, may be heuristically desirable, but they have done science more harm than good.[15]

If a reformulation of Freudian theory is possible—and to the limited degree that it is so—it must be done in a language entirely derived from two observables or "facts": perception and response. In order to set up this language of reference, it is enough to "an-

13. Albert Ellis, "An Operational Reformulation of Some of the Basic Principles of Psychoanalysis," Minnesota Studies, *1*, 131–54.

14. "Modern empiricism, in fact, seems to have only one invariant requisite: namely, that in some *final* analysis, albeit most indirectly and through a long network of intervening constructs, a statement or hypothesis must in *some* manner (or in principle) be confirmable—that is, significantly tie-able to or correlatable with some kind of observable. It thereby rules out sheer metaphysical speculation but keeps the door widely open for all other hypotheses" (Ellis, p. 135).

15. Ibid., pp. 136, 150–52.

chor" the various constructs necessary or useful for the explanation of human behavior in the empirical concepts of perception and response. Thus the distinction between conscious and unconscious perception is made by saying that the latter occurs when one perceives but does not perceive that he perceives; learning is said to occur when one organizes or reorganizes his perceptions and responds accordingly; the factors of evaluating, emoting, and desiring are regarded as responses to the predicates good or bad, pleasant or unpleasant, beneficial or harmful, which are joined to perceptions.

I will not summarize the operational reformulations [16] that are substituted for Freud's hypotheses, which are taken from the most scholastic of Freud's expository works, *An Outline of Psychoanalysis.* Id, ego, superego, Eros, death instinct, sexual life, anal and oral erotism, phallic phase, repression, libido, sexual libido, Oedipus complex, ego defenses, etc.,[17] are translated thereby into a language entirely derived from the two initial observables.

What is completely overlooked in this reformulation is that none of the above are "observed," even indirectly, as responses to stimuli; prior to the possibility of being "reformulated," they were all "interpreted" in the analytic situation—that is, in a situation of language.

In connection with the enterprise of reformulation, Madison's important work on *Freud's Concept of Repression and Defense* [18] should be mentioned. We previously consulted this book in order to give order to the various senses of the Freudian concept of repression. But we bracketed the author's precise intent, which was to submit this concept to the test of Carnap and Nagel's epistemological requirements. Madison begins by presenting univocal and coherent definitions of all the theoretical terms: the relationship be-

16. Ibid., pp. 140–50.

17. It is interesting to note that among the major Freudian concepts there are two groups that are deliberately not rephrased: (a) the concept of the psyche, of mental life, of mental qualities; (b) the concept of mental energy and energy cathexes; these are outmoded constructs of the nineteenth century and are "redundant" with respect to the "behavioral intervening variables" (ibid., p. 151). As I see them, however, they are two ontic concepts that govern the two universes of discourse, the interpretative and the explanatory, which psychoanalysis combines in its mixed discourse.

18. For a brief summary of this work, see above, p. 138, n. 58.

tween defense and repression, the distinction between successful and unsuccessful defenses, the subdistinction between repressive and nonrepressive defenses, the relationship between primal repression and repression proper (we too followed this path in our analysis of the concept of repression). His main effort consists in establishing a correlation between this theoretical language and an observational language to which the former would be related by means of correspondence rules and coordinating or operational definitions. The conflict between instincts and anticathexis, of which repression and defense are the manifestations, would thus correspond to the unobservable physical concept of "atomic vibrations in solids" or "the speed of random molecular motion in liquids or gases," of which temperature is the manifestation. On the plane of observational language, symptoms, "distorted" and "remote" expression (dreams, fantasies, jokes, etc.), various inhibitions of feeling and behavior, and resistance in therapy would be comparable to the subjective and objective "indicators" of temperature; finally, the specific techniques for quantifying these indicators would have their counterpart in the quantifiable aspects of resistance behavior (periods of silence in free association, changes in the wording of a dream on second telling). Madison holds that the various manifestations of repression lend themselves to translation into observational language just as easily as the manifestations of temperature do, on condition that one correctly subdivides the forms of resistance adopted as 'indicators" of repression (repression resistance, transference resistance, resistance due to secondary gain from illness, resistance of the unconscious, resistance from a sense of guilt).

The point on which Madison's work differs from the other attempts at reformulation is that his is truly located on the plane of the analytic work because of his choice of the indicators of repression: resistance, various defensive processes (amnesia, conversion, isolation, etc.), inhibition of affects and behavior, degrees of distortion or remoteness of the derivatives from the unconscious. For all these indicators, correctly subdivided, Madison proposes appropriate quantitative procedures. He concludes that "repression is measurable in principle, if not presently in fact (due to lack of the necessary techniques)"; [19] the only precaution to be taken is not to leave the therapeutic situation, for an experimental situation can never artificially produce something equivalent to the repression of archaic motivations or of motivations closely linked to them by association. But Madison admits that certain parts of the theory of repression can be neither observed nor measured: he cites infantile repression, castration traumas, and expressions of impulses in dreams; these processes are assumptions and are not observational; an example is Freud's equating little Hans' fear of being bitten by horses with the fear of castration: "In so far as analysts *only* infer the Oedipus complex on such a symbolic basis, it is not statable in observational terms, and, consequently, not measurable even in principle." [20] And further on: "Castration trauma is not observable if it is always inferred on a symbolic or other indirect basis that depends in turn upon further theoretical assumptions involved in Freud's various translation rules." [21] By translation rules the author means symbolism and, in general, all the mechanisms of the dream-work. This limit that Madison recognizes brings us back, in fact, to the problem of interpretation. Interpretation intervenes not only in cases where one can neither observe nor measure; it covers the whole field of investigation, only a part of which can be translated into observational language. For example, the Oedipus complex is so central to Freudian theory that one can hardly regard it as an unobservable and unmeasurable segment of the theory of repression without raising the issue of what Madison finally has to call "Freud's dogmatism about sex." [22] Madison believes the only way he can save an important part of Freud's system is to distinguish *real* sex, subject to observation, from sex merely *statable* in the framework of Freud's translation rules and not subject to an observational language. But is it not evident that this distinction between observed sexuality and interpreted sexuality is the ruination of Freudian theory? Though Madison's enterprise is most interest-

19. Ibid., p. 189.
20. Ibid., p. 190.
21. Ibid., p. 192.
22. Ibid., p. 191.

ing, and though his reading of Freud and his partial translation into observational language are extremely serious, his book underscores the inability of a psychology of positivist inspiration to furnish an equivalent of the relations of signifier to signified that place psychoanalysis among the hermeneutic sciences.

PSYCHOANALYSIS IS NOT AN OBSERVATIONAL SCIENCE

Let us take up in reverse order the stages of this epistemological case against psychoanalysis. First, the critique on the part of the operationalists and their requirement of reformulation offer a good basis with which to begin. Second, having discovered why psychoanalysis cannot satisfy their demand, we shall then be able to understand why the attempts from within the psychoanalytic movement itself to compromise with behaviorism involve a subtle betrayal of the peculiar genius of psychoanalysis. Finally, we shall be led back to the most radical critique, the critique from the logic of the sciences. We shall admit what it insists upon: psychoanalysis is not an observational science. It will remain to turn this admission into a counterattack.

Confrontation with Operationalism. I do not dispute the legitimacy of reformulating psychoanalysis in operational terms; it is inevitable and desirable that psychoanalysis be confronted with psychology and the other sciences of man and that the attempt be made to validate or invalidate its results by those of the other sciences. However, it must be realized that this reformulation is only a reformulation, that is, a second operation with respect to the experience on the basis of which the Freudian concepts have arisen. Reformulation can only deal with results that are dead, detached from the analytic experience, with definitions isolated from one another, cut off from their origin in interpretation, and extracted from academic presentations where they had already fallen to the rank of mere magical phrases.

If one fails to recognize the peculiar origin of these concepts as compared with those of behavioral psychology, there will be no possibility later on of saving psychoanalysis as a distinct branch of an overall psychology of behavior. Inevitably, step by step, one will have to agree with the most radical of the operationalists, regarding psychoanalysis as a retarded form of observational theory and its hypotheses as metaphors of the phlogistic sort. The difference comes at the beginning or never: psychology is an observational science dealing with the facts of behavior; psychoanalysis is an exegetical science dealing with the relationships of meaning between substitute objcts and the primordial (and lost) instinctual objects. The two disciplines diverge from the very beginning, at the level of the initial notion of fact and of inference from facts.

It is noteworthy that those who have come closest to recognizing the peculiar character of psychoanalytic language and its true level of validity are the Anglo-Saxon philosophers concerned with the analysis of language.[23]

One of them, Toulmin, starts from the very anomaly of psychoanalytic language. The statements of the psychoanalyst, he remarks, are not to be classed with those that "explain" human conduct in terms of the "stated reason" (I do this because . . .) (Proposition E_1), or in terms of the "reported reason" (He does this, he says, because . . .) (Proposition E_2), or in terms of the "causal explanation" (Because he was given an injection of cocaine) (Proposition E_3). E_1 cannot be mistaken, nor can it be verified by evidence; E_2 can be mistaken, but verified only by an E_1 proposition; E_3 can be mistaken and verified by factual observations. The analytic explanation is another form of statement, E_4, equally distant from the statements E_1, E_2, and E_3; in other words, psychoanalytic propositions differ as much from causal explanation

23. This discussion about the "logical status" of psychoanalysis began in the journal *Analysis* and centered mainly on the concepts of motive and cause: Stephen Toulmin, "The Logical Status of Psychoanalysis," *Analysis, 9,* No. 2 (1948); reprinted in *Philosophy and Analysis,* Margaret Macdonald, ed. (New York, Philosophical Library, 1954), pp. 132–39. Antony Flew, "Psychoanalytic Explanation," *Analysis, 10,* No. 1 (1949); reprinted in *Phil. and An.*, pp. 139–48. Richard Peters, "Cure, Cause and Motive," *Analysis, 10,* No. 5 (1950); in *Phil. and An.*, pp. 148–54. To these may be added Flew, "Motives and the Unconscious," Minnesota Studies, *1* (1956), 155–73.

as they do from stated or reported motives.[24] At the end of an analytic cure the statement E_4 has become for the patient a plausible stated motive; for a third party, who accepts it as a report, it has become a plausible reported motive; for the analyst, as long as it has not been reintegrated into the patient's psychological field, it is merely a plausible causal history. This way of approaching the epistemological status of psychoanalytic propositions assumes that an explanation through motives is irreducible to an explanation through causes, that a motive and a cause are completely different.

I agree with this analysis: the statements of psychoanalysis are located neither within the causal discourse of the natural sciences nor within the motive discourse of phenomenology. Since it deals with a psychical reality, psychoanalysis speaks not of causes but of motives; but because the topographic field does not coincide with any conscious process of awareness, its explanations resemble causal explanations, without, however, being identically the same, for then psychoanalysis would reify all its notions and mystify interpretation itself. It is possible to speak of stated or reported motivation, provided that this motivation is "displaced" into a field analogous to that of physical reality. That is what the Freudian topography does. But if one does not take this mixed constitution of psychoanalytic statements as the epistemological basis, he is reduced to one of the following three alternatives discussed by the protagonists of the *Philosophy and Analysis* controversy.

One alternative, proposed by Antony Flew, is to point out a contradiction between Freudian practice and Freudian theory: the former appeals to motives (e.g. those of obsessional acts), inten-

24. With much subtlety and precision, Toulmin shows that one can focus in upon this fourth type of proposition, E_4, by means of three mixed types of propositions (E_{14}, E_{24}, E_{34}). E_{14} is closest to the "stated reason" type (e.g. "I found myself wishing that I was alone with her"); E_{24} is closest to the "reported reason" type (e.g. "He behaved for the moment as though he hated the sight of her"); E_{34} is closest to the "causal explanation" type (e.g. "He behaves like that because his father used to beat him violently as a child"). None of these propositions is a psychoanalytic one, but all three focus in on the nucleus: "The kernel of Freud's discovery is the introduction of a technique in which the psychotherapist begins by studying the *motives for*, rather than the *causes of* neurotic behavior" (Toulmin, in *Philosophy and Analysis*, p. 138).

tions (e.g. of unsuccessful acts), meanings (of symptoms, dreams, etc.), whereas Freudian theory treats those same phenomena as "psychical antecedents" to be discovered in some unknown land as Columbus discovered America; this "real cause" of real facts can only lead to a "gratuitous multiplication of dubious entities" which compete with the sole facts open to observation and verification, the facts of physiology.

A second alternative is to try to simplify analytic discourse by assigning it entirely to the realm of motives and not of causes.[25] Freud's contribution, then, would consist in having extended the notions of motive, desire, and intention to two new spheres, the sphere of the nonknown by the subject and the sphere of the non-voluntary; but this extension would not change the basically psychological or mental, i.e. intentional, character of the stream of motivation. If such is the case, the word "unconscious" should remain adjectival, the substantive unconscious being merely a shorthand way of talking about unconscious motives. Through an abuse the logician cannot condone, the adjective became the name for a region of the mind, for a real entity producing real effects. To the contrary, one must preserve the strong sense of the word "intention," where intention is defined as aiming at a goal, with the possibility, at least in principle, of the intention's being raised to the plane of language; because of this intentional factor, Freud's notions are logically irreducible to physicalistic terms. Freud's originality consists in maintaining that the strange phenomena which had previously been left to physiology are explainable in terms of intentional ideas. The relationship between motivation and language means that in principle it is possible to give a verbal account of such phenomena; this is what distinguishes a rational agent—however irrational—from nonrational creatures. The object of analytic therapy is to extend the patient's area of rationality, to replace impulsive conduct by controlled conduct.

25. Flew, "Psychoanalytic Explanation," in *Phil. and An.* In concluding his article, Flew writes: "My two theses have been, *first*, that psychoanalytic explanations or at any rate classical Freudian ones in the first instance are 'motive' and not 'causal' explanations; and, *second*, that these two sorts of explanation are so radically different that they are not rivals at all" (p. 148). In fact, Flew softens this radical difference in his Foreword of 1954 (p. 139).

If this is so, psychoanalysis is more closely related to the historical disciplines that seek to understand the reasons behind human actions than to the psychology of behavior.[26]

Nothing is closer to my position than this article by Antony Flew. My criticism, however, is that he overlooks the specific character of analytic discourse: [27] if there is no possible translation of causal language into motive language and vice versa, how does one account for the mistake of their being combined? It surely seems that the combination, in psychoanlaysis, of a procedure of detection (not to say a detective method), of a technique aimed at producing behavioral changes, and of theoretical propositions, must exclude this type of radical clarification.[28]

The third alternative is an attempt to reduce analytic discourse to empirical propositions. This is the position Peters takes in the *Philosophy and Analysis* discussion. The difference between motive and cause is set aside as inessential and treated as a mere difference of degree or level of generality.[29] If motive is defined as a relation of the type *if . . . then* (in certain kinds of situations a given group of persons will respond in certain typical ways), and if cause is defined as a relation of the type *this . . . because* (the glass broke because it was dropped), the difference between motive and cause is only one of degree; it reduces to the distinction between general laws and initial conditions, between theoretical explanation and his-

26. In his second article, "Motives and the Unconscious," Flew stresses the irreducibly psychological character of such terms as motive, purpose, desire, wish, want, intention; he sets the notion of meaning apart, remarking, "The importance of this notion has not previously been noted either here or in the *analysis* controversy. It would repay special examination: for what is involved seems to range through a spectrum of cases shading from, at one extreme, mere relevance, through the general possibility of motivational interpretation, to the other extreme where the claim is that the performances, dreams, are elements in a full-blown language" (Minnesota Studies, *1*, 159).

27. Flew prefaces his article "Motives and the Unconscious" with a sentence from Kris: "There is, for instance, a lack of trained clarifiers, who might properly coordinate the various propositions with each other or try to eliminate the inequalities of language in psychoanalysis" (ibid., *1*, 155).

28. Peters, "Cure, Cause and Motive," in *Philosophy and Analysis*, pp. 148–50.

29. Ibid., pp. 151–54. Cf. G. Ryle, *The Concept of Mind*, Ch. 4.

torical explanation (Popper), between systematic explanation and historico-geographical explanation (Lewin). Psychoanalysis, by reason of its complex structure, contains both kinds of propositions: general propositions, when for example it assigns a character trait (thrift) to an early libidinal disposition (that of the anal stage); and also historical propositions, when it operates "detectively."

My position in this epistemological controversy is divided. On the one hand, I hold with Toulmin and Flew that the reduction of motives to the type of explanation inaugurated by the Aristotelian formal cause and illustrated in modern epistemology by the notion of functional dependence has nothing to do with motive in the sense of "reason for." [30] The distinction between motive in the sense of "reason for" and cause in the sense of a relation between observable facts in no way concerns the degree of generality of propositions. It is the distinction Brentano, Dilthey, and Husserl had in mind when they sharply distinguished between understanding of the psychical or the historical, and explanation of nature; in this sense motives are on the side of the historical, understood as a region of being distinct from the region of nature and capable of being considered according to the generality or singularity of its temporal sequences. On the other hand, the distinction between motive and cause does not resolve the epistemological problem posed by Freudian discourse: such discourse is governed by a unique type of being, which I call the semantics of desire; it is a mixed discourse that falls outside the motive-cause alternative. From the discussion it is evident that analytic discourse falls partly within the field of motive concepts; that is enough to make the split between psychoanalysis and the observational sciences operative from the beginning. But the sense of this initial difference is missed if one does not carry the difference through to the level of the psychoanalytic "field," that is, to the level of analytic experience in and through which the difference is constituted.

Confrontation with Internal Reformulations. Why is it, now, that the reformulations proposed by cer-

30. Toulmin, Postscript (1954), in *Philosophy and Analysis*, pp. 155–56.

tain analysts in order to meet the requirements of the theory of science do not satisfy us any more than they satisfy the operationalists? The reason, I think, is because they betray the very essence of analytic experience.

The psychologist speaks of environmental variables. How are they operative within analytic theory? For the analyst, these are not facts as known by an outside observer. What is important to the analyst are the dimensions of the environment as "believed" by the subject; what is pertinent to him is not the fact, but the meaning the fact has assumed in the subject's history. Hence it should not be said that "early punishment of sexual behavior is an observable fact that undoubtedly leaves behind a changed organism." [31] The object of the analyst's study is the meaning for the subject of the same events the psychologist regards as an observer and sets up as environmental variables.

For the analyst, therefore, behavior is not a dependent variable observable from without, but is rather the expression of the changes of meaning of the subject's history, as they are revealed in the analytical situation. One may still speak, of course, of "changes in probability of action": in this respect the patient treated by Freud may also be treated in terms of behavioral psychology; but that is not how the behavioral facts are pertinent to analysis. They do not function as observables, but as signifiers [*signifiants*] for the history of desire.[32] This signification is precisely what Skinner casts into

31. Skinner, "Critique of Psychoanalytic Concepts and Theories," in Minnesota Studies, *1*, 81.

32. Hartmann is clearly aware of this difference: "The data gathered in the psychoanalytic situation with the help of the psychoanalytic method are primarily behavioral data; and the aim is clearly the exploration of human behavior. The data are mostly the patient's verbal behavior, but include other kinds of action. They include his silences, his postures, and his movements in general, more specifically his expressive movements. While analysis aims at an explanation of human behavior, those data, however, are interpreted in analysis in terms of mental process, of motivation, of 'meaning'; there is, then, a clear-cut difference between this approach and the one usually called 'behavioristic,' and this difference is even more marked if we consider the beginnings of behaviorism, rather than its more recent formulations" (in Hook, ed., *Psychoanalysis, Scientific Method, and Philosophy*, p. 21). But he does not go on to draw the necessary conclusions, so preoccupied is he with integrating psychoanalysis into general psychology

the outer darkness, into the general catch-all of theories about mental life and of prescientific metaphors.[33] However, this meaning of a history does not concern a less advanced stage along the one and only road of behaviorism: strictly speaking, there are no "facts" in psychoanalysis, for the analyst does not observe, he interprets.

Such is, in my opinion, the analyst's sole reply to the behaviorist. If he accepts the methodology already established upon the axioms of behaviorism, if he begins to formulate his research in terms of "probability of response," he is condemned either to be written off as nonscientific,[34] or to go begging for a partial rehabilitation

---

and with getting confirmation from the other forms of scientific psychology. The question is, however, whether psychoanalysis is a science of "psychological observation." The fact that observations are made "in a clinical setting" (p. 25), that "the psychological object" is studied "in a real-life situation," makes no essential difference; nor even that psychoanalysis thereby discovers "human motivation, human needs and conflicts" (p. 26); more important is the fact that in Freud's "case histories" observation and theoretical elaboration go hand in hand and cannot be separated from each other (p. 27). Hartmann comes very close to giving the essential reason for this when he notes that clinical work is guided by "signs": "A considerable part of psychoanalytic work can be described as the use of signs . . . In this sense one speaks of the psychoanalytic method as a method of interpretation" (p. 28). One may ask, then, whether an investigation of the notions of sign, signal, expressive sign, symbol, and so on, would not break through the epistemological framework taken from the experimental sciences of nature.

33. This signifying function escapes the requirement, formulated by Skinner, of treating behavior as a datum and "probability of response" as the principal quantifiable property of behavior, and of stating learning and other processes in terms of "changes of probability" (Minnesota Studies, *1*, 84). This function is also what prevents one from representing the act of self-observation "within the framework of psychical science" (p. 85).

34. The problem of quantification, which gives Skinner a decisive argument for excluding psychoanalysis from science (ibid., p. 86), considerably embarrasses Rapaport, who, for reasons mentioned above (n. 5), has to devote a section and a chapter to it in his epistemological study (in Koch, ed., *Psychology: A Study of a Science, 3,* 79–82, 124–33). Rapaport rightly sees that the obstacle is not fortuitous, but is due to "the lack of quantitative methods applicable to intrapsychic variables" (p. 80, n. 32); but he attributes this fault to the relatively undeveloped state of psychoanalysis as compared to the other sciences (pp. 81–82). True, he goes on to say that mathematization is not necessarily metric and that "Lewin attempted to introduce topology and Piaget to introduce group theory into psychology as nonmetric mathematizations" (pp. 124 ff.). But he abandons this line of thought to return to the quasi-quantitative character of cathexis; the theory

through what Skinner calls "the simple expedient of an operational definition of terms." The line of defense extends through the outposts and the issue is decided on this basic question: What is pertinent in psychoanalysis? If one answers: Human reality as formulated in operational terms of "observable behavior," the condemnation inevitably follows.[35] If one does not recognize the specificity of the questions of meaning and double meaning, and if one does not relate the question of double meaning to the problem of the method of interpretation, through which this question comes to light, then the "psychical reality" psychoanalysis speaks of will always be one "cause" too many—a redundancy by comparison with what the behaviorist quite competently describes as behavior; ultimately, it will be only a "ritual form of mental alchemy," according to Scriven's harsh phrase.[36] This specificity is what we must now bring into the open, by focusing on the models used in the attempt to liken psychoanalysis to an experimental science.

This attempt misunderstands the essential point: namely, that analytic experience unfolds in the field of speech and that, within

---

of cathexes, he says, includes quasi-quantitative propositions in the form of inequalities (p. 128) concerning mobile, bound, or neutralized energy. As for "dimensional quantification," this will be possible only when we have clarified how processes turn into structures and have understood the process of structure formation in general: "This clarification appears to be the prerequisite for dimensional quantification in psychoanalysis in particular, and perhaps even in psychology at large" (p. 132). But progress in this direction presupposes what is in question, namely, that one can and should submit Freudian propositions to a verification that is experimental in nature.

35. That is why the rejoinders of Michael Scriven are weak ("A Study of Radical Behaviorism," in Minnesota Studies, *1*, 105, 111, 115): it matters little that behaviorism does not conform to its own standards either, that psychoanalysis also has an empirical content, that propositions about "mental states" have a practical utility. In the end, Scriven links the destiny of psychoanalysis to those ordinary language terms that live on in the scientific language of psychology. In a second article ("Psychoanalytic Theory and Evidence," in Hook, ed., *Psychoanalysis, Scientific Method and Philosophy*, pp. 226–51), Scriven is, moreover, much more severe and skeptical about the scientific pretensions of psychoanalysis.

36. Scriven, in Minnesota Studies, *1*, 128. See Hartmann, in *Psychoanalysis, Scientific Method and Philosophy*, pp. 18–19, 24–25; from the standpoint of empiricism, "theory" is justified by its heuristic or synthetic character, or by its ability to interrelate this branch of psychology with medicine, child psychology, anthropology, and the other human sciences.

this field, what comes to light is another language, dissociated from common language, and which presents itself to be deciphered through its meaningful effects—symptoms, dreams, various formations, etc.[37] Not to recognize this specific feature leads one to eliminate as an anomaly the interrelationship of hermeneutics and energetics in analytic theory.

One may indeed discover in psychoanalysis what Rapaport calls the empirical, gestalt, and organismic points of view, but at the cost of a translation that alters the proper meaning of analytic concepts. I will take as a test case the notion of "overdetermination"; translated into the language of behaviorism and causality, this means that every behavior can be described at one and the same time as an id behavior, an ego behavior, etc. That is how a behavior is "multiply determined." [38] The question of double meaning has been

37. J. Lacan, "Fonction et champ de la parole et du langage en psychanalyse," Rapport du Congrès de Rome, 1953, in *La Psychanalyse, 1*, 81–166. My criticism of the behaviorist "reformulations" of psychoanalysis is very close to the one that could be drawn from Lacan's article. We diverge, however, when I go on to criticize a conception that eliminates energy concepts in favor of linguistics. The number of French writings concerned with the epistemology of Freudian theory is still rather small. Cf. D. Lagache, *L'Unité de la psychologie* (Paris, P. U. F., 1949); "Définition et aspects de la psychanalyse," *Rev. fr. de psychan., 14,* 384–423; "Fascination de la conscience par le moi," *La Psychanalyse, 3* (1957), 33–47. Lacan, "Propos sur la causalité psychique," *Évolution psychiatrique,* 1947, fasc. 1; "L'Instance de la lettre dans l'inconscient ou la raison depuis Freud," *La Psychanalyse, 3* (1957), 47–81. M. Gressot, "Psychanalyse et connaissance," *La Psychanalyse, 2* (1956), 9–150. S. Nacht, *De la pratique à la théorie psychanalytique* (Paris, P. U. F., 1950). A. Green, "L'Inconscient freudien et la psychanalyse française contemporaine," *Les Temps modernes, 18* (1962), 365–79. W. Huber, H. Piron, A. Vergote, *La Psychanalyse, science de l'homme* (Brussels, Dessart, 1964), Parts I and IV.

38. "Every behavior has conscious, unconscious, ego, id, superego, reality, etc., components. In other words, all behavior is multiply determined (overdetermination). Since behavior is always multifaceted (and even the apparent absence of certain facets of it requires explanation), the conception of multiple determination (or overdetermination) may be regarded as a purely formal consequence of this method of conceptualization. . . . Overdetermination, to my mind, implies precisely such a lack of *independence* and *sufficiency* of causes and is inseparably connected with the multiple levels of analysis necessitated by this state of affairs" (Rapaport, in Koch, ed., *Psychology, 3,* 83–84). Interpreted in these terms of complex causality, overdetermination loses its specificity; is it enough to write that "Academic

covertly eliminated and translated into that of multiple causal determinations.

Thus the correlation between psychoanalytic "models" and psychological "points of view," which stems from the adoption of the three "fundamental points of view" of scientific psychology, involves a fundamental amputation of the question of meaning.

What is the significance of the topographic point of view, apart from the search for a "place" of meaning that is off-center with respect to the apparent meaning? The problem posed by wish-fulfillment (*Wunscherfüllung*) is illustrative here, for the whole theory of the primary process is built upon its basis. An essential factor in this fulfillment is that fantasies have a relationship of substitution with respect to the lost objects of desire; but they would not be derivatives, nor would those derivatives be remote or distorted, if they did not first of all have a relationship of meaning to something that presents itself as lost. Hence dreams, symptoms, delusions, and illusions pertain to a semantics and a rhetoric, that is to say, to a function of meaning and double meaning that is accounted for neither by the models nor by the points of view enumerated above. To speak of an extension of the economic point of view to cognitive phenomena (Rapaport) [39] is to treat the problem of the relations of meaning in analytic interpretation by way of preterition; it is mainly due to the absence of the object that this problem of meaning arises at every step, whether we are dealing with the absent drive object for which the hallucinatory idea is substituted or with affect discharges in the primary process. As for the secondary process, the Jacksonian model neatly accounts for the facts of structural articulation, automatization, control through anticathexis; but it does not account for the fact that mastery over the absent object and even the discrimination between its presence and its absence manifest themselves in the very birth of language, inasmuch

---

psychologies did not develop such a concept, probably because their methods of investigation tend to exclude rather than to reveal multiple determination"? (p. 84). Hartmann's article (in Hook, ed., *Psychoanalysis*, pp. 22, 43) moves in the same direction.

39. In his sketch of the combined model, Rapaport repeatedly touches on this function of absence. Even on the level of the primary model the absence of the drive object is essential to the production of the hallucinatory idea or affect discharge (Rapaport, pp. 71–73).

as language distinguishes and interrelates presence and absence. Hence, psychoanalysis does not use absence in the same way that scientific psychology, since Hunter and Köhler, uses detour and delay;[40] for psychoanalysis, absence is not a secondary aspect of behavior, but the very place in which psychoanalysis dwells.

The reason for this is that psychoanalysis is itself a work of speech with the patient, which scientific psychology decidedly is not; it is in a field of speech that the patient's "story" is told; hence the proper object of psychoanalysis is the effects of meaning—symptoms, delusions, dreams, illusions—which empirical psychology can only consider as segments of behavior. For the analyst, behavior is a segment of meaning. That is why the lost object and the substitute object are the constant theme of psychoanalysis. Behaviorist psychology can thematize the absence of the object only as an aspect of the "independent variable": something is objectively lacking on the side of the stimuli. For the analyst, this is not a segment in a chain of observed variables, but a fragment of the symbolic world appearing within the closed field of speech that analysis qua "talking cure" is. That is why the absent object, the lost object, the substitute object are misunderstood by any reformulation of the metapsychology that does not take its start from what occurs in the analytic dialogue.

The list of the other models and their correlations with the points of view familiar to academic psychology is the occasion of a similar misunderstanding.

In Freud, the genetic point of view, even in its most scientific or pseudoscientific formulations, never loses the specificity that it receives from the interpretation of fantasies. Of course, it is correct to say that "all behavior is part of a historical series"; it is correct to speak in this way in order to render analytic language homogeneous with the language of the genetic sciences. However, it must not be forgotten that in analysis, the real history is merely a clue to the figurative history through which the patient arrives at self-understanding; for the analyst, the important thing is this figurative history.

As for the "crucial determinants of behavior" which Freud lo-

40. "Here the *psychological* absence of the object plays the same role as its real absence does in the primary model" (ibid., p. 74).

calizes in the unconscious, psychoanalysis never encounters them except as instinctual representatives—ideas or affects—hence as signifiers deciphered in their more or less distorted derivatives.[41] If one eliminates the signifying dimension from these crucial determinants, one will never understand how the pleasure principle can interfere with the reality principle. Their confrontation occurs on the level of fantasy; in deploying its derivatives in the regions of reality, the pleasure principle plays the role of the first kind of knowledge in Spinoza, the role of "false consciousness." Falsification and illusion are possible because from the start the question of pleasure is the question of truth and nontruth.

That is why, indeed, the topographic point of view yielded to the structural point of view, as Rapaport points out. But how are we to account for this shift, unless the structural conflicts—between id, ego, and superego—are set within such meaning-bearers as prohibitions, taboos, the "father complex," which are first of all "things heard," "words"? Ever since *The Interpretation of Dreams*, censorship is nothing else than an erasure of meaning, a rejection into the region of the unconscious of what is forbidden in the official text of consciousness.

The role of signifying also specifies the "dynamic point of view" peculiar to psychoanalysis. It is impossible to overemphasize the distinction, made in *The Interpretation of Dreams*, between need and wish (*Wunsch*); this is the same distinction that the "Papers on Metapsychology" drew between instincts and instinctual representatives. Although instincts are the ultimate origin of behavior, psychoanalysis is not concerned with these ultimates as such, but with the way they enter into the meaningful but distorted history that comes to be told in the analytic situation.

Hence, all the energy exchanges under the heading of the "economic point of view," all the work of cathecting and decathecting, operate at the level of the instinctual representatives and are accessible to analysis only in the distortion of meaning. *The Interpreta-*

41. In speaking of the "unnoticeable" in psychoanalysis, Rapaport states: "While other psychologies treat the unnoticeable in nonpsychological terms (brain fields, neural connections, etc.), psychoanalysis consistently treats it in the psychological terms of motivations, affects, thoughts, etc." (ibid., p. 89).

tion of Dreams is the sure guide here: its field is what it calls the *Traumentstellung*, i.e. the transposition or distortion that manifests itself in the texture of dreams, insofar as they are a type of *Wunscherfüllung*, of wish-fulfillment. The distortion *is* the fictive fulfillment. It is in the area of meaning that the distortion does its "work," in the form of displacement, condensation, pictorial representation. As soon as the economics is separated from its rhetorical manifestations, the metapsychology no longer systematizes what occurs in the analytic dialogue; it engenders a fanciful demonology, if not an absurd hydraulics.

The major difference is found at the level of the adaptive point of view. The reality principle of psychoanalysis is radically distinct from the homologous concepts of stimuli or environment, for the reality in question is the truth of a personal history within a concrete situation. Reality is not, as in psychology, the order of stimuli as known by the experimentalist, but the true meaning the patient is to reach through the obscure maze of fantasies; reality takes on meaning in a conversion of meaning of fantasies. This relation to fantasies, as it presents itself to be understood in the closed field of analytic speech, constitutes the specificity of the analytic concept of reality. Reality always has to be interpreted through the intentionality [*la visée*] of the instinctual object, as that which is both revealed and hidden by this instinctual intending; one has only to recall the epistemological application Freud made of narcissism in 1917, when he exposed narcissism as the principal resistance to truth. That is why reality-testing, the characteristic feature of the secondary process, does not completely coincide with what psychology calls adaptation. The secondary process has to be set within the framework of the analytic situation; in this context, reality-testing is correlative to the *Durcharbeiten*, the "working through," the hard work aimed at true meaning, which has no equivalent except in the struggle for self-recognition that constitutes the tragedy of Oedipus, as Freud himself tells us.[42]

42. "The action of the play consists in nothing other than the process of revealing, with cunning delays and ever-mounting excitement—a process that can be likened to the work of a psychoanalysis—that Oedipus himself is the murderer of Laïus, but further that he is the son of the murdered man and of Jocasta" (*GW*, *2/3*, 268; *SE*, *4*, 261–62).

It will be said that the reality principle finds a more solid basis in present-day ego psychology. But we must always keep reflecting on the implications of Freud's formula: "The ego is a precipitate of abandoned object-cathexes." This reference to the abandoned object, that is, to the work of mourning, brings absence into the very makeup of the ego. Reality, hard reality, is the correlate of this internalized absence. It is impossible to separate the ego's coherence and structural autonomy from the work of mourning without also abandoning the peculiar field of speech in which psychoanalysis operates.

Finally, it seems elementary to recall that the "psychosocial point of view," which has been distinguished from the adaptive point of view, is not a distinct point of view in contrast to the topographic and economic point of view. The reason is, of course, that it is in the dual relationship of speech that all is told. The field of analysis is intersubjective both regarding the analytic situation itself and regarding the past dramas recounted in that situation; this is the reason, moreover, why the drama to be untangled can be transposed into the dual relationship of analysis through the process of transference. The possibility of transference resides in the intersubjective texture of desire and of the desires deciphered within that situation. No doubt this reference to the other person is also present in desire as distinct from need, i.e. in wishes, and even in the psychical as distinct from the biological, i.e. in instinctual representatives. It is because wishes are a demand on another person, a speaking to another, an allocution, that they can enter into a "psychosocial" field where there are refusals, prohibitions, taboos—that is, frustrated demands. The transition to the symbolic occurs at this crossroads, where desires are demands but unrecognized as such. The entire Oedipus drama is lived and enacted within the triangle of demand, refusal, and wounded desire; its language is a lived rather than a formulated language, but at the same time it is a short meaningful [*signifié*] drama in which arise the main signifiers [*signifiants*] of existence. It may be that analysis mythicizes the latter by naming them phallus, father, mother, death; nevertheless these are precisely the structuring myths that psychoanalysis, apart from any problematic of "adaptation," has the task of articulating. What confronts us in this reasoned mythology is the problem of access to true discourse, which is something quite different from the adaptation that some appeal to in their haste to overcome the scandal of psychoanalysis and to render analysis socially acceptable. For who knows where a single true discourse might lead with respect to the established order, that is to say, with respect to the idealized discourse of the established disorder? The question of adaptation is a question which existing society asks on the basis of its reified ideals, on the basis of a false relationship between the idealized profession of its beliefs and the actual reality of its practical dealings. This question psychoanalysis is determined to bracket.

In this regard, the stand taken by orthodox psychoanalysts against culturalism is perfectly sound. To abandon the problematic of instincts in favor of the current factors of social adjustment, they forcefully argue, amounts to a strengthening of censorship and the superego. But all the consequences of this opposition should be spelled out. The psychoanalyst's neutrality between social demands and instinctual demands is well known. But why does the psychoanalyst side neither with society nor with the infantile demands of the patient, unless it is because his problem is not one of adjustment, but of true discourse? And how would the autonomy of the ego avoid taking the same turns as culturalism, if this autonomy is not rooted in a problematic of veridical meaning?

Confrontation with Epistemology.

We can now return to our starting point, the attack of the epistemologists, such as Ernest Nagel, on psychoanalysis.

It is now clear there can be no answer to this attack if one assumes that psychoanalysis is an observational science and if one misapprehends the peculiar nature of the analytic relation. Let us reexamine Nagel's two points in reverse order: the question concerning the evidence of statements from the standpoint of logical proof, and the nature of theoretical propositions with respect to their verifiability.

If we grant that the analytic situation as such is irreducible to a description of observables, the question of the validity of psychoanalytic assertions must be reexamined in a context distinct from a naturalistic science of facts. Analytic experience bears a much greater resemblance to historical understanding than to natural explanation. Take for example the requirement put forward by epistemology of submitting a standardized set of clinical data to the check of a number of independent investigators. This requirement presupposes that a "case" is something other than a history, that it is a sequence of facts capable of being observed by many observers. Of course, no art of interpreting would be possible if there were no similarities between cases and if it were impossible to discern types among these similarities. The question is whether these types are not closer, from the epistemological point of view, to the types of Max Weber, which impart to historical understanding the character of intelligibility without which history would not be a science. Such types are the intellectual instruments of an understanding focused upon singularity. Their function is irreducible to laws in an observational science, although it is comparable to them in its own order. The reason history may be called a science is that the system of types leads to understanding in history just as regularities lead to understanding in the natural sciences. However, the problematic of a historical science does not coincide with that of a natural science. The validity of the interpretations made in psychoanalysis is subject to the same kind of questions as the validity of a historical or exegetical interpretation. The same questions must be put to Freud that are put to Dilthey, Weber, and Bultmann, not those posed to a physicist or a biologist.

It is perfectly legitimate, therefore, to require the analyst to compare his percentage of improvements with the ratios obtained by different methods, or even with the ratio of spontaneous improvement. But it should be realized that one is at the same time requiring that a "historical type" be transposed into a "natural species"; in doing this, one forgets that a type is constituted on the basis of a "case history" and by means of an interpretation that in each instance arises in an original analytic situation. Again, psychoanalysis cannot sidestep, any more than exegesis, the question of the validity of its interpretations; nor even that of a certain sort of prediction (what is the probability, for example, that a patient be accepted for therapy, or that he can then be effectively treated?). Comparisons must surely enter into the analyst's field of consideration; but it is precisely as a problem of historical science, and not of natural science, that analysis encounters and poses the problem.

These remarks about the validation of interpretation enable us to reexamine in new terms the prior question of theory in psychoanalysis. It is completely misleading to raise the question in the context of a factual or observational science. It is surely true that a theory must in general satisfy certain rules of deductibility, which are independent of the mode of verification, as well as certain transformation rules through which the theory may enter some definite field of verification. However, it is one thing to be capable of empirical verification, and another thing to render possible a historical interpretation. The concepts of analysis are to be judged according to their status as conditions of the possibility of analytic experience, insofar as the latter operates in the field of speech. Thus, analytic theory is not to be compared with the theory of genes or gases, but with a theory of historical motivation. What differentiates it from other types of historical motivation is the fact that it limits its investigation to the semantics of desire. In this sense the theory determines, i.e. both opens and delimits, the psychoanalytic point of view on man; by this I mean that the function of psychoanalytic theory is to place the work of interpretation within the region of desire. In this sense, it grounds and at the same time limits all the particular concepts appearing in this field. One may, if he so wishes, speak of "deduction," but in a "transcendental" and not in a "formal" sense; deduction is concerned here with what Kant calls the *quaestio juris;* the concepts of analytic theory are the notions that must be elaborated so that one may order and systematize analytic experience; I will call them *the conditions of possibility of a semantics of desire.* It is in this sense that they can and should be criticized, perfected, or even rejected, but not as theoretical concepts of an observational science.

THE PHENOMENOLOGICAL APPROACH TO THE PSYCHOANALYTIC FIELD

The preceding discussion inclines us to look to Husserlian phenomenology for the epistemological support a logic of the observational sciences was unable to give us. This new critique no longer concerns the results of analytic experience, but rather its conditions of possibility, the constitution of the "psychoanalytic field." What we are seeking to deduce, in the sense just spoken of, are those concepts without which analytic experience would be unthinkable. Thus it is not a matter of reformulating the theory, that is, of translating it into another system of reference, but of approaching the fundamental concepts of analytic experience through another experience that is deliberately philosophical and reflective. We are going to confront Freud's concepts with the resources of Husserl's phenomenology. No reflective philosophy has come as close to the Freudian unconscious as the phenomenology of Husserl and certain of his followers, especially Merleau-Ponty and De Waelhens. It is well to mention at the very start that this attempt is also bound to fail. But this failure does not have the same pattern as the preceding one. It is not a question of a mistake or a misunderstanding, but rather of a true approximation, one that comes very close to the Freudian unconscious but misses it in the end, affording only an approximate understanding of it. In becoming aware of the gap separating the unconscious according to phenomenology from the Freudian unconscious, we will grasp, by a method of approximation and difference, the specificity of the Freudian concepts. If reflection cannot of itself come to the understanding of its archeology, it needs another discourse to speak that archeology.

1. What turns phenomenology directly toward psychoanalysis, prior to any elaboration of a particular theme, is the philosophic act with which phenomenology begins, which Husserl calls the "reduction." Phenomenology begins with a methodological displacement that already affords some understanding of that displacement or off-centering of meaning with respect to consciousness.

The reduction, indeed, has some relation to the dispossession of immediate consciousness as origin and place of meaning; the phenomenological bracketing or suspension is not concerned simply with the "self-evidence" (*Selbstverständlichkeit*) of the appearance of things, which suddenly cease to appear as a brute presence, to be there, to be at hand, with a fixed meaning that one has only to find.

To the extent that consciousness thinks it knows the being-there of the world, it also thinks it knows itself. Furthermore, to the so-called knowledge on the part of immediate consciousness there belongs a pseudo-knowledge on the part of the unconscious, a knowledge that Freud points to at the beginning of the paper "The Unconscious" and which we ordinarily connect with the experience of sleep or the state of unconsciousness, with the disappearance and reappearance of memories, or with the sudden violence of the passions. This immediate consciousness is deposed along with the natural attitude. Thus phenomenology begins by a humiliation or wounding of the knowledge belonging to immediate consciousness. Further, the arduous self-knowledge that phenomenology goes on to articulate clearly shows that the first truth is also the last truth known; though the Cogito is the starting point, there is no end to reaching the starting point; you do not start from it, you proceed to it; the whole of phenomenology is a movement toward the starting point. By thus dissociating the true beginning from the real beginning or natural attitude, phenomenology reveals the self-misunderstanding inherent in immediate consciousness.

This misunderstanding is alluded to in a statement Husserl makes in the *Cartesian Meditations,* § 9: "Adequacy and apodicticity of evidence need not go hand in hand." Of course, a nucleus of primordial experience is presupposed by phenomenology; that is what makes it a reflective discipline. Without the presupposition of such a nucleus—"the ego's living self-presence" (*die lebendige Selbstgegenwart*)—there is no phenomenology; that too is why phenomenology is not psychoanalysis. But beyond this nucleus extends a horizon of the "properly nonexperienced" (*eigentlich nicht erfahren*), a horizon of the "necessarily co-intended" (*notwendig mitgemeint*). This implicit factor is what allows one to apply to the Cogito itself the critique of evidence previously applied to things: [43]

43. "Something similar [*ähnlich also*] is true about the apodictic certitude of the transcendental experience of my transcendental *I am,* inasmuch as the latter also involves the indeterminate generality of an open horizon. Accordingly, the reality of the intrinsically first ground of knowledge is indeed absolutely assured, but such absoluteness does not automatically extend to that which determines its being more particularly and which, during the living evidence of the *I am,* is as yet not itself given but only presumed.

The Cogito, too, is a presumed certitude; it too can be deceived about itself; and no one knows to what extent. The resolute certitude of the *I am* involves the unresolved question of the possible extent of self-deception. Into this fissure, into this noncoincidence between the certitude of the *I am* and the possibility of self-deception, a certain problematic of the unconscious can be introduced. But it is a problematic with which we are acquainted. The first unconsciousness or unawareness [*inconscience*] phenomenology reveals has to do with the implicit, the co-intended: for the model of this implicit—or better, this "co-implicit"—one must look to a phenomenology of perception.

2. A second step toward the Freudian unconscious is represented by the notion of intentionality, a notion both commonplace and unfathomable. Intentionality concerns our meditation on the unconscious inasmuch as consciousness is first of all an intending of the other, and not self-presence or self-possession. Engrossed in the other, it does not at first know itself intending. The unconsciousness that attaches to this bursting forth from self is that of the unreflected; since *Ideen* I, the Cogito appears as "life": [44] the Cogito is operative [*opéré*] prior to being uttered, unreflected prior to being reflected upon. What is more, in the period of the *Krisis,* intentionality in act (*die fungierende Intentionalität*) is broader than thematic intentionality, which knows its object and knows itself in knowing that object; the first can never be equaled by the second; a meaning in act always precedes the reflective movement and can never be overtaken by it. The impossibility of total reflection, hence

This presumption, therefore, which is co-implicit in apodictic evidence, requires a critique that would determine apodictically the range of the possibilities of its fulfillment. How far can the transcendental ego be deceived about itself [*sich über sich selbst täuschen*]? And how far do those components extend that are absolutely indubitable in spite of such possible deception?" Edmund Husserl, *Cartesian Meditations,* tr. Dorion Cairns (The Hague, Nijhoff, 1960), § 9, p. 22 (with changes).

44. "In the natural mode of living-in-the-world [*im natürlichen Dahinleben*], I live continually in this *fundamental form of all 'actual' living,* whether I can or cannot assert [*aussagen*] the cogito, and whether I am or am not 'reflectively' directed toward the ego and the cogitare. If I am so directed, then a new cogito has come to life, which for its part is unreflected upon and so is not an object for me." Husserl, *Ideen* I, § 28 (tr. W. R. Boyce Gibson, *Ideas* [New York, Collier Books, 1962], pp. 93–94 [with changes]).

the impossibility of the Hegelian absolute knowledge, hence the finitude of reflection, as Fink and De Waelhens have deduced it,[45] are written into this primacy of the unreflected over the reflected, of the operative over the uttered, of the actual over the thematic. This unawareness [*inscience*] proper to the unreflected marks a new step toward the Freudian unconscious; it means that the co-implicit or co-intended cannot completely attain to the transparency of consciousness precisely because of the texture of the act of consciousness, i.e. because of the invincible unawareness of self that characterizes intentionality in act.

The corollaries of this second theorem are as follows. First, it is possible to give a direct definition of the psychism—as the mere intending of something, as meaning—without appealing to self-consciousness. But this, as one writer has said, contains the whole of Freud's discovery: "the psychical is defined as meaning, and this meaning is dynamic and historical." [46] Husserl and Freud are seen to be the heirs of Brentano, who had both of them as students.

Second, it is possible to dissociate the actual lived relation from its refraction in representation. In a philosophy of immediate consciousness the subject is first of all a knowing subject, that is to say, ultimately, a look directed to a spectacle; in such a philosophy, the spectacle is at the same time the mirage of self in the mirror of things; the primacy of self-consciousness and the primacy of representation are interconnected; by becoming representation the relation to the world becomes self-knowing. Thus phenomenology should widen the opening made by Husserl himself in the venerable tradition of the knowing subject (although Husserl personally maintained the primacy of objectivizing acts over the grasp of affective, practical, and axiological predicates of things in the world).

45. E. Fink, Appendix XXI to § 46 of the *Krisis* (*Husserliana, 6* [The Hague, Nijhoff, 1954], 473–75). On the difference between the "thematic" and the "operative" [*opératoire*] and on "finite philosophic activity," cf. Fink, "Les concepts opératoires dans la phénoménologie de Husserl," in *Husserl*, Cahiers de Royaumont (Paris, Éditions de Minuit, 1959), pp. 214–41. Also, A. de Waelhens, "Réflexions sur une problématique husserlienne de l'inconscient: Husserl et Hegel," in *Edmund Husserl, 1859–1959* (The Hague, Nijhoff, 1959), pp. 221–38.

46. A. Vergote, "L'Intérêt philosophique de la psychanalyse freudienne," *Archives de philosophie* (Jan.–Feb. 1958), p. 38.

The possibility that man is primarily "concern for things," "appetition," desire and quest for satisfaction, is opened up anew, as soon as the psychical is no longer defined as consciousness, or the actual lived relation as representation.

A further consequence of the primacy of the intentional over the reflective: the dynamics of operative meaning (meaning in act or in operation) is more fundamental than the statics of uttered or represented meaning. Here again Husserl opens the path for his French-speaking successors by introducing, in the fourth Cartesian meditation, the problem of the "passive genesis" of meaning. Husserl approaches this entirely new problem by asking a prior question: How are a diversity of experiences "compossible" in one and the same ego? The "essential laws of compossibility" [47] govern all the problems of *genesis* in the sphere of the ego. Now the form of compossibility, for an ego, is time—not the time of the world, but the temporality by which a series of *cogitationes* forms a sequence, a succession. In phenomenology, then, genesis refers to the operation of linking together the various dimensions of the temporal flux, past, present, and future: "The ego constitutes itself for itself, so to speak, in the unity of a history."

It is here that the idea of "passive genesis" enters in, which in a new way "points toward" the Freudian unconscious. In the active genesis, "the ego operates by productively constituting through specific acts of the ego." This praxis is operative in logical reason, in the sense that logical objects too are "products" (*Erzeugnisse*) of operations such as counting, predicating, inferring, etc.; thus it is possible to regard the in-itself [*l'en-soi*] of these objects as the correlate [*le vis-à-vis*] of a "habitual" operation; the in-itself is an "attainment," abidingly possessed, but which may also be "re-produced" in a new operation. However, Husserl remarks, "every construction on the part of activity necessarily presupposes, at the lowest level, a passivity that receives the object as pregiven." [48] In other words, when we trace back an active production we run into (*stossen wir*) an antecedent constitution through passive genesis. What is the passive genesis? Husserl hardly talks about it except at the level of per-

47. *Meditations*, § 37.
48. § 38.

ception; the passive synthesis is the thing itself as pregiven, as a residue from the perceptual learning experiences of infancy; such experiences make up the ego's "being affected," and the thing itself is found in our perceptual field as a thing with which we are already well acquainted. But the trace of history is not so covered over that reflection cannot explicate the layers of meaning and "thus find intentional references leading back to an [antecedent] 'history.'" These references make it possible to go back to the "first founding," the *Urstiftung*.

A confrontation with the Freudian exegesis of symptoms is possible on this basis. There is always a "goal-form" (*Zielform*) which points back, by means of its genesis, to its own founding: everything known points to an "original becoming acquainted."[49] Thus there is a clear affinity between Husserlian explication and Freudian exegesis by reason of their regressive orientation. Further, by positing "association as the universal principle of passive genesis," Husserl discloses a mode of constitution irreducible to that of logical objects, not only a nonlogical constitution, but a constitution subject to other, albeit essential, laws. Although association is commonly defined in terms of the old psychology, Husserl recognizes that the old concept is "a naturalistic distortion of the corresponding genuine, intentional concepts." He thus provides for its generalization beyond the perceptual sphere. In this sense, association has to do precisely with our existence qua irrational (*irrational*) brute fact (*Faktum*): "Nor should it be overlooked here that [brute] *fact*, with its *irrationality*, is itself a *structural concept within the system of the concrete apriori.*"[50]

Is not such an explication of a meaningful contingency what psychoanalysis proceeds to carry out? Is it not sufficient to extend to desire and its objects this explication of layers of meaning, this investigation of an "original founding"? Is not the history of the libidinal object, through the various stages of the libido, just such an explication by means of successive retroreferences? The linking together of signifiers in what we have called the semantics of desire is the concrete realization of that which Husserl glimpsed under the

49. Ibid.
50. § 39.

old title of association, but of whose intentional significance he was perfectly aware; in short, phenomenology talks about the passive genesis, the meaning that comes about apart from me, but psychoanalysis concretely shows it.[51]

The final corollary to the theorem of intentionality concerns the phenomenological notion of one's own body, or, in the language of the later writings of Merleau-Ponty, the notion of flesh. When asked how it is possible for a meaning to exist without being conscious, the phenomenologist replies: its mode of being is that of the body, which is neither ego nor thing of the world. The phenomenologist is not saying that the Freudian unconscious is the body; he is simply saying that the mode of being of the body, neither representation in me nor thing outside of me, is the ontic model for any conceivable unconscious. This status as model stems not from the vital determination of the body, but from the ambiguity of its mode of being. A meaning that exists is a meaning caught up within a body, a meaningful behavior.

If this is so, it is possible to gradually reexamine, in terms of meaningful behavior, what was said about the genesis of meaning, the psychical character of meaning, and the notion of intentionality itself. Every enacted meaning is a meaning caught up within the body; every praxis involved in meaning is a signifying or intention made flesh, if it is true that the body is "that which makes us be as existing outside of ourselves." [52]

By this thesis, phenomenology moves toward the Freudian unconscious; moreover, once granted this interpretation of the body as incarnate meaning, it is possible to account for the human meaning of sexuality—at least of sexuality in act. Sex in act consists in

51. Vergote, p. 47.

52. De Waelhens, *Existence et signification* (Louvain, Nauwelaerts, 1958), "Réflexions sur les rapports de la phénoménologie et de la psychanalyse," pp. 191–211: "The body is that side of ourself, that dimension originally turned toward the outside, which makes us be as though outside of ourselves" (p. 200). "This radical closeness between things and us is developed and formed within a medium, a mediating element which is neither ego nor thing (or which is both at once): the body. Whether psychoanalysis explicitly formulates the body or not, this same thesis is at the basis of all psychoanalysis and phenomenology must surely come to grips with it" (p. 192).

making us exist as body, with no distance between us and ourself, in an experience of completeness exactly contrary to the incompleteness of perception and spoken communication.[53] It is an experience of completeness in the sense that the body, becoming totally manifest, suppresses all reference to actions in the world. Not only does phenomenology move here in the direction of psychoanalysis, but it offers it a satisfactory schema to account for the relationship between sexuality, as a particular mode, and human existence, regarded as an undivided totality. The relationship is not of part to whole: sexuality is not an isolated function alongside many others; it affects all behavior. Nor is it a relationship of cause to effect, for a meaning cannot be the cause of a meaning; between sexual behavior and total behavior there can only be an identity of style, or, to put it another way, a relationship of homology. Sexuality is a particular manner of living, a total engagement toward reality; this particular mode is precisely the manner in which two partners try to make themselves exist as body, and nothing but body.

3. The reduction is the methodological displacement that defines the phenomenological *attitude;* intentionality is the *theme* of phenomenology. This theme has in turn many implications, of which we have selected only those which have special relevance to psychoanalysis. Two further propositions deserve separate treatment; they are far more than simple corollaries of the phenomenological notion of meaning. The first concerns the dialectical aspects of language; the second concerns intersubjectivity.

At first view the phenomenology of language seems to be merely an extension of the phenomenology of perception; here too, the important thing is to question back from the uttered meaning to meaning in operation. Man is language; in this conviction, phenomenology agrees with Von Humboldt and Cassirer. But the phenomenological problem of language really begins when the act of speaking [*le dire*] is taken on the plane where it establishes a meaning, where it makes a meaning clearly exist, apart from any explicit apophantic, i.e. prior to statements or uttered meanings. The problem raised

53. See De Waelhens' admirable text on sexuality, *Existence et signification*, pp. 204–11.

by perception, of questioning back from representation to the experientially lived relationship, repeats itself on the plane of language. It must be rediscovered with Hegel that language is the being-there of the mind; for phenomenology, as for psychoanalysis, this "reality of language" is nothing other than the meaning achieved by a behavior.

Still, the extension to language of the analysis of perception as meaning in operation is not a mere extrapolation; the comparison also serves to reveal features of perception that can be made explicit only on the plane of spoken signs. These features indirectly throw light upon the Freudian unconscious. I have brought them together under the heading of the dialectic of absence and presence.

This dialectic has at least three aspects. First, man's adoption of language is in general a way of making himself absent to things by intending them with "empty" intentions, and, correlatively, of making things present through the very emptiness of signs.

This dialectic of presence and absence, characteristic of all signs, is specified in two ways, depending on whether one considers speech as the act of the speaking subject, or language as an instrument of communication organized on a level different from consciousness and the intention of each of the speaking subjects. A language has its own way of being dialectical: each sign intends something of reality only by reason of its position in the ensemble of signs; no sign signifies through a one-to-one relation with a corresponding thing; each sign is defined by its difference from all the others. More precisely, it is by combining together the phonemic and the lexical differences, hence by setting into play the double articulation of phonemes and morphemes, that we speak the world.

In turn, the actual use of language in the speech of speaking subjects brings out the ambiguity of all signs. In ordinary language each sign contains an indefinite potential of meaning; a simple glance at the dictionary reveals a sort of gradual slipping into or endless infringement upon the semantic areas of all the other signs. To speak is to set up a text that functions as the context for each word; the potential of words heavily charged with meaning is thus limited and determined by the context, although the rest of the charge of meaning is not thereby done away with; only part of the meaning is thus rendered present, through occultation of the rest of the possible meaning.

By these three types of dialectic of presence and absence the phenomenology of language moves in the direction of psychoanalysis and its unconscious.

First, the interplay of absence and presence characteristic of signs as such is aptly illustrated in the genesis psychoanalysis proposes of the spoken sign; phenomenologists have a special fondness for those pages of *Beyond the Pleasure Principle* in which Freud sketches the genesis of signs starting from the mastery over privation in the game of *fort-da*. By alternately voicing the two words, the child interrelates absence and presence in a meaningful contrast; at the same time, he no longer undergoes absence as a fit of panic massively substituted for a close and saturating presence. Dominated thus by language, privation—and consequently presence as well—is signified and transformed into intentionality; being deprived of the mother becomes an intending of the mother.[54]

The *fort-da* example is not just an isolated case. "Mourning and Melancholia" teaches us that beyond the lost archaic objects, it is possible to establish a relationship to the object that is not simply a repetition of the archaic situation. The manner in which mourning gives up the object as lost recalls the institution of signs, which are universally a giving up of brute presence and an intending of presence in absence.

This recourse to language reinforces the parallel between phenomenology and psychoanalysis. The dialectic of presence and absence, which language sets in motion, is now seen to be operative in all forms of the implicit and the co-intended, in all human experience and at all levels. Thus language makes it possible to generalize the perceptual model of the unconscious. The ambiguity of "things" becomes the model of all ambiguity of subjectivity in general and of all the forms of intentionality.

54. De Waelhens, "Sur L'Inconscient et la pensée philosophique," *Journées de Bonneval sur l'inconscient* (mimeograph, 1960), pp. 16–21; "Réflexions sur une problématique husserlienne de l'inconscient: Husserl et Hegel" (see n. 45), p. 232.

What is more, the dialectic of presence and absence completes the process whereby the initial false knowledge on the part of immediate consciousness is made to waver. From now on the question of consciousness becomes an obscure as that of the unconscious, to paraphrase a celebrated text of Plato on being and nonbeing. Thus phenomenology turns out to be just as radical as psychoanalysis in contesting the illusion of immediate self-knowledge. Every mode of being conscious is for subjectivity a mode of being unconscious, just as every mode of appearing is correlative to a nonappearing or even a disappearing, both signified together, co-signified, in the presumption of the thing itself. Language reveals this co-signifying of the implicit as absence, and it does so more clearly than a phenomenology of mute perception. Thus language brings out the full significance of the perceptual model of the unconscious for phenomenology.

4. The theorem concerning language as a dialectic of presence and absence has to be complemented by a theory of intersubjectivity: *All* our relationships with the world have an intersubjective dimension.

The fact that the perceived thing is perceptible by others brings the reference to others into the very makeup of things qua presumed things; what points to others is precisely the horizon of perceptibility, the invisible other side of the visible. Between the positing of others as perceiving and the assumption of the invisible other side of things there is a reciprocal relation. Every meaning ultimately has intersubjective dimensions; every "objectivity" is intersubjective, insofar as the implicit is what another can make explicit.

This first recourse to intersubjectivity seems unrelated to psychoanalysis; nevertheless, the radical connection phenomenology discerns between intersubjectivity and the unconsciousness peculiar to the implicit is sufficient warning of the danger of defining an unconscious that is not originally implicated in intersubjective relations; this warning concerns psychoanalysis to the extent that the first topography, the one on which its epistemology was structured, remains basically solipsistic. On the other hand, the second topography fundamentally satisfies this requirement of phenomenology, since its agencies and roles are definitely set up in the intersubjective field. Above all, however, the fundamental and absolutely primal role of intersubjectivity takes on its full meaning when it is extended to areas other than representation, according to the suggestions of our second theorem. If the meaning phenomenology speaks of is more "operated" than uttered, more lived than represented, that texture is seen most clearly in the semantics of desire; it seems that desire, as a mode of being in close contact with beings, is human desire only if the intending is not merely a desire of the other but a desire of other desires, that is, a demand. Here all the themes we have touched upon come together: meaning, body, language, intersubjectivity.

The intersubjective structure of desire is the profound truth of the Freudian libido theory; even in the period of the "Project" and Chapter 7 of the *Traumdeutung*, Freud never described instincts outside of an intersubjective context; if desire were not located within an interhuman situation, there would be no such thing as repression, censorship, or wish-fulfillment through fantasies; that the other and others are primarily bearers of prohibitions is simply another way of saying that desire encounters another desire—an opposed desire. The whole dialectic of roles within the second topography expresses the internalization of a relation of opposition, constitutive of human desire; the fundamental meaning of the Oedipus complex is that human desire is a history, that this history involves refusal and hurt, that desire becomes educated to reality through the specific unpleasure inflicted upon it by an opposing desire.

At this point the confrontation, reduced to two terms—Husserl and Freud—should be widened into a triangular relation: Hegel, Husserl, Freud. It has been said [55] that Hegel appears at first to be more suited to a comparison with Freud: the movement to self-consciousness through the reduplication of desire in desire, the education of desire in the struggle for recognition, the inauguration of that struggle in a nonegalitarian situation—all these Hegelian

55. Jean Hyppolite, "Phénoménologie de Hegel et psychanalyse," *La Psychanalyse, 3,* 17 ff., 225 ff. De Waelhens, "Réflexions sur une problématique husserlienne," pp. 225 ff.

themes appear to have more analogies with psychoanalytic themes than does Husserl's labored theory of perceptual intersubjectivity. There is an obvious similarity between the Hegelian struggle of master and slave and the Freudian Oedipus complex.

But if these remarks are true as a first approximation, and if the comparison with Hegel has an undeniable pedagogical advantage, a closer confrontation reveals a more hidden and perhaps more significant affinity. De Waelhens observes that on two basic points Husserl is closer than Hegel, if not to the overt Freudian themes, at least to the ultimate intention of analysis. After Husserl, we cannot lay claim to a completion of the constituting of meaning in an absolute discourse that would put an end to that constituting as an ongoing process; just as meaning remains incomplete for each subject, so too it remains incomplete for all; as De Waelhens remarks, "from the point of view of analysis, absolute knowledge is meaningless." [56] Furthermore, the procedure whereby the Hegelian thinker, that omniscient interpreter, moves ahead of the unfolding of the prototypic history of the mind, is likewise excluded from analytic experience: the analyst, closer in this respect to the maieutic procedure of phenomenological reflection, barely keeps ahead of the progress of the subjectivity he is helping in its enterprise of recognition. The phenomenologist and the analyst both realize that dialogue is endless.

It is not surprising that phenomenology and pyschoanalysis should meet on this level. As we said in the discussion of scientific psychology, it is from the analytic situation itself, as a language relationship, that all discussion must begin. The discourse of the unconscious becomes meaningful only in the interlocutory discourse of analysis; everything we said about the transition from desire to language by means of renunciation finds its manifestation in the psychoanalytic "talking cure"; the constitution of the subject in speech and the constitution of desire in intersubjectivity are one and the same phenomenon; desire enters into a meaningful history of mankind only insofar as that history is "constituted by speech addressed to the other." [57] In return, it is because desire is desire of

56. De Waelhens, ibid., p. 226.

57. In the series of articles by De Waelhens there is a noticeable shift in the discussion from the problem of the unconscious to the problem of

desire, hence demand, hence constituted by language addressed to the other, that analytic dialogue is possible; such dialogue simply transfers into the field of a derealized discourse the drama of desire, insofar as it already was a spoken drama, a demand. It is not surprising therefore that all the problems of the constitution of desire should reappear in the analytic relation. The relation is reciprocal: on the one hand, the intersubjective structure of desire makes it possible to investigate desire in the relationship of transference; conversely, the analytic relationship is able to repeat the history of desire because what comes to speech in the field of the derealized discourse is desire in its original status as demand on the other.

At this point of the approximation, the difference between phenomenology and psychoanalysis seems to be almost nonexistent. Are they not both aiming at the same thing, namely the constitution of the subject, qua creature of desire, within an authentic intersubjective discourse?

When we consider our starting point in the light of our point of arrival, we understand more clearly why the two methods are parallel. Phenomenological reduction and Freudian analysis are homologous in that both aim at the same thing. *The reduction is like an analysis,* for it does not aim at substituting another subject for the subject of the natural attitude; it is not taken up with the attempt to flee "elsewhere." Reflection is the meaning of the unreflected, as avowed or uttered meaning; better, the subject doing the reduction is not some subject other than the natural subject, but the same; from being unrecognized it becomes recognized. In this respect the reduction is the homologue of analysis, when the latter states that "where id was, there ego shall be." But this initial homology between the methods is understood only at the end. Phenomenology attempts to approach the real history of desire *obliquely;* starting from a perceptual model of the unconscious, it gradually generalizes that model to embrace all lived or embodied meanings, mean-

---

language, and then to that of intersubjectivity; his latest study on psychoanalysis, in *La Philosophie et les expériences naturelles* (The Hague, Nijhoff, 1961), is deliberately located in the chapter on "Others" (pp. 135–67). One should take note of the pages concerning the role of the analyst, conceived as the interlocutor who helps to bring about a situation of "disengagement" or isolation with respect to the real, a derealized situation in which repetition and remembering may occur.

ings that are at the same time enacted in the element of language. Psychoanalysis plunges *directly* into the history of desire, thanks to that history's partial expression in the derealized field of transference. But both have the same aim, "the return to true discourse." [58]

PSYCHOANALYSIS IS NOT PHENOMENOLOGY

And yet . . .

And yet phenomenology is not psychoanalysis. However slight the separation, it is not nil, and phenomenology does not bridge the gap. Phenomenology does give an understanding of psychoanalysis, but only through approximation and by way of diminishing differences.

Let us reexamine each of the points of our phenomenological approximation to the Freudian unconscious.

1. Phenomenology is a reflexive discipline; the methodological displacement it sets into operation is the displacement of reflection with respect to immediate consciousness. Psychoanalysis is not a reflexive discipline; the off-centering it brings about is fundamentally different from the "reduction" in that it is very strictly constituted by what Freud calls the "analytic technique," which he breaks down under two headings: the procedure of investigation and the technique of treatment.[59] The Freudian unconscious is rendered accessible through the psychoanalytic technique; but this type of archeological excavation [60] has no parallel in phenomenology. Hence the suspicion analysis professes about the illusions of consciousness is different from the suspension of the natural attitude.[61]

58. De Waelhens, ibid., p. 154.

59. " 'Psychoanalyse' und 'Libido Theorie,' " *GW, 13,* 211; *SE, 18,* 235: "Psychoanalysis is the name (1) of a procedure [*Verfahren*] for the investigation of mental processes which are almost inaccessible in any other way, (2) of a method (based upon that investigation) for the treatment [*Behandlungsmethode*] of neurotic disorders and (3) of a collection of psychological information [*Einsichten*] obtained along those lines, which is gradually being accumulated into a new scientific discipline."

60. Vergote, "L'Intérêt philosophique de la psychanalyse freudienne," *Archives de Philosophie* (Jan.–Feb. 1958), pp. 28–29.

61. Vergote: "Freedom is the correlate of the arbitrariness of con-

If phenomenology is a modification of the Cartesian doubt about existence, psychoanalysis is a modification of the Spinozist critique of free will; analysis begins by denying that the apparent arbitrariness of consciousness is anything more than the nonrecognition of underlying motivations. Whereas phenomenology begins with an act of "suspension," with an epochê at the free disposition of the subject, psychoanalysis begins with a suspension of the control of consciousness, whereby the subject is made a slave equal to his true bondage, to use Spinoza's terms. By starting from the very level of this bondage, that is, by unreservedly delivering oneself over to the domineering flux of underlying motivations, the true situation of consciousness is discovered. The fiction of absence of motivation, on which consciousness based its illusion of self-determination, is recognized as fiction; the fullness of motivation is revealed in place of the emptiness and arbitrariness of consciousness.

Further on we shall speak of how this attack on illusion opens up, as in Spinoza, a new problematic of freedom, a freedom no longer linked to the arbitrary but to understood determination. It was important that the difference in points of view was first of all stated in its full force, on the very basis of the patent similarity.[62]

---

sciousness" (p. 29). And further on: "The inherent law of the problematic of freedom is to go beyond the first and privative notion toward the recognition of a fullness which is at the same time creative. But this latter presupposes that determination and motivation are integrated into freedom" (p. 30).

62. In an important and enlightening text that we will have more to say about later, "L'Inconscient, une étude psychanalytique," *Journées de Bonneval* (mimeograph, 1960), Laplanche and Leclaire sharply distinguish between any phenomenological interpretation of consciousness and the "process of becoming conscious" in psychoanalytic treatment: "In the latter it is rare and even exceptional that the disclosure of the unconscious should occur as a phenomenon that can be located in a single moment or field of consciousness. Generally it is a process of patient work, moving from one particular to another, wherein the revision of perspectives is brought about through discontinuous and isolated moments of consciousness often far removed from one another and none of which are characterized by the sudden reconversion of the ensemble of meanings that the term 'unveiling' might suggest" (p. 10). The process of becoming conscious differs from any sudden remembrance or illumination by reason of its topographic character: it is a matter of a reworking of the systems, aimed at incorporating into "an organized structure of self-apprehension, which includes a

2. It cannot be denied that the perceptual model of the unconscious, in phenomenology, points toward the analytic unconscious, so far as the latter is not a receptacle of contents but a center of intentions, of orientations-toward, of meaning. This signifying character is evidenced by the various derivatives of the primary representatives and by the relations of meaning to meaning which those derivatives have among themselves and with their origin. That remains true; but the important thing, for analysis, is that this meaning is *separated* from becoming conscious by a barrier. This is the essential factor in the idea of repression. The topography represents this essential factor by means of its auxiliary schemata: one moves from phenomenology to psychoanalysis when one understands that the main barrier separates the unconscious and the preconscious, and not the preconscious and the conscious; to replace the formula *Cs./Pcs., Ucs.* by the formula *Cs., Pcs./Ucs.* is to move from the phenomenological point of view to the topographic point of view. The unconscious of phenomenology is the preconscious of psychoanalysis, that is to say, an unconscious that is descriptive and not yet topographic. The meaning of the barrier is that the unconscious is inaccessible unless an appropriate technique is used. From this point on, all the vicissitudes of instincts will be represented by relations of exteriority. Of all the vicissitudes, repression is the one the topography is most anxious to picture; but repression is a real exclusion which a phenomenology of the implicit or co-intended can never reach. These vicissitudes are surely not foreign to the order of the psychical, of motivation, of meaning; that is why the phenomenological approach has not been useless; it is indeed another text that psychoanalysis deciphers, beneath the text of consciousness. Phenomenology shows that it is another *text*, but not that this text is *other*. The realism of the topography expresses this

---

plurality of moments, an entire coherent discourse that is never wholly actualized" (ibid., p. 11). That is why we shall speak later on of becoming conscious as *Durcharbeiten*, as working through. Phenomenology accounts only for "field phenomena" pertaining to a perceptual model (the fringes of the implicit, the horizon of the perceptible, the invisible other side of the visible), that is to say, phenomena at the frontier between the preconscious and the conscious, which Freud, it is true, "barely began to describe" (ibid., p. 12).

otherness of the text, at the limit of an approach that has revealed it as a text.

If we review the series of corollaries to the second point, this understanding by way of approximation becomes more articulated. The psychism, we said to begin with, is defined by meaning and not necessarily by consciousness. To understand this proposition is to approach the Freudian unconscious. But the separation of this meaning we have just spoken of is simply an aspect of what Freud called the "systemic laws." The systems have their own legality, a fact Freud expresses by the list of characteristics of the unconscious we have previously commented on: primary process, absence of negation, timelessness, etc. This legality cannot be reconstructed phenomenologically, but only through the familiarity provided by analytic technique. It is not another consciousness one could grasp through conceptual thought; it is a meaning one must "keep probing into through practice." [63]

Again, phenomenology shows that the lived meaning of a behavior extends beyond its representation in conscious awareness; phenomenology thus prepares us to understand the relations of meaning between the instinctual representatives and their derivatives. But the remoteness and distortion that separate those derivatives from their roots, and the division into two types of derivatives, the ideational and the affective, require an instrument of investigation that phenomenology cannot provide. The notion of ideational representative is approached as meaning, intention, aiming; phenomenology makes that quite clear. But another technique is required in order to understand the remoteness and the division at the basis of the distortion and substitution that make the text of consciousness unrecognizable.

The same may be said of the gap between the passive genesis, in Husserl's sense, and the dynamics of instincts which Freud deciphers by means of the analytic technique. Here it is a question not only of the topographic point of view but of the economic point of view: the notion of cathexis expresses a type of adhesion and cohesion that no phenomenology of intentionality can possibly reconstruct. At this point the energy metaphors replace the inadequate

63. Vergote, "L'Intérêt philosophique de la psychanalyse freudienne."

language of intention and meaning. Conflicts, formations of compromise, facts of distortion—none of these can be stated in a reference system restricted to relations of meaning to meaning, much less, as in Politzer, of literal meaning to intended meaning; the distortion that separates the literal meaning from the intended meaning requires concepts such as dream-work, displacement, condensation, which we have shown to be both heremeneutic and energic in nature; the function of the energy metaphors is to account for the disjunction between meaning and meaning.[64]

To satisfy this requirement, Freud developed the notion of an energy specific to each system and capable of cathecting representations. There is no denying that the difficulties surrounding this notion are numerous and perhaps insurmountable. The roles assigned to this cohesive force are not easy to coordinate; in one role, it is an energy that holds isolated elements together within the whole of a given system; in another, it collaborates in the repression of higher systems through the force of attraction exercised by the previously constituted unconscious system; in a third, it works to promote the process of becoming conscious in opposition to the vigilance of censorship. Nor is it easy to conceive just what relations this cathectic energy proper to each system has with the libido, for the latter, by reason of its organic origin, is neutral with respect to the systems and becomes localized in a given system according to the locus of

64. G. Politzer, *Critique des fondements de la psychologie*, 1. *La Psychologie et la psychanalyse* (Rieder, 1928). Laplanche and Leclaire, "L'Inconscient," *Journées de Bonneval:* "(a) the unconscious is not coextensive with the manifest as its meaning; rather it is to be interpolated in the *gaps* of the manifest text; (b) the unconscious stands in relation to the manifest, not as the intended meaning to the literal text, but on the same level of reality. It is what allows us to conceive a dynamic relationship between the manifest text and that which is absent from and to be interpolated in that text: it is a fragment of discourse that must regain its place within discourse" (pp. 8–9). And further on: "Freud has need of a radical split between two domains located on the same level of reality, for this is the only thing that enables him to account for psychical conflict . . . the lacunary phenomena are still posited here at the origin of the *Ucs.* hypothesis. But the *Ucs.* does not consist in a more comprehensive meaning that would enable one to connect such phenomena to the rest of the text, but is rather a *second structure* in which those lacunary phenomena find their unity, independently of the rest of the text" (p. 14).

the representations to which it attaches itself.[65] The most difficult notion of all is the idea of an "energy that is transformed into meaning."[66]

Nothing, consequently, is firmly settled in this area; indeed, it may be that the entire matter must be redone, possibly with the help of energy schemata quite different from Freud's. For a philosophical critique, the essential point concerns what I call the place of that energy discourse. Its place, it seems to me, lies at the intersection of desire and language; we will attempt to account for this place by the idea of an archeology of the subject. The intersection of the "natural" and the "signifying" is the point where the instinctual drives are "represented" by affects and ideas; consequently the coordination of the economic language and the intentional language is the main question of this epistemology and one that cannot be avoided by reducing either language to the other.

We will focus on this coordination by taking the linguistic aspects of the unconscious as our guide. Nowhere else do phenomenology and psychoanalysis come closer to being one; nowhere else, therefore, will the gap between the two disciplines be more significant.

3. The unconscious is structured like a language, say Lacan and his followers. Isn't this "linguistic" conception of the unconscious indistinguishable from the interpretation of language presented by Merleau-Ponty and De Waelhens? When the latter conceive of language as an instituting [*instauration*] of meaning that takes place prior to any explicit judgment, are they not saying the same thing as those who maintain the linguistic conception of the unconscious? Actually, the latter conception makes sense only in conjunction with the economic concepts of Freudian theory; instead of replacing the Freudian topographic and economic point of view, it paral-

65. Laplanche and Leclaire, pp. 17–18; they appeal to a gestalt interpretation of the cathectic energy of a given system: such energy would be identical to a *prägnanz* of good forms in each system (p. 19).

66. Vergote, pp. 53–54, thus defines the proper object of analytic depth psychology: "the meaning constituted without freedom, by the spontaneity of the instincts. . . . For analysis, the dynamic is an energy that is transformed into meaning. . . . The force of instincts in conflict gives rise to a meaningful history."

lels that point of view in every respect. Thus the linguistic interpretation shows that the unconscious, though separated by repression and the other mechanisms that give it the form of a system, is nevertheless correlative to ordinary language. The linguistic interpretation does not constitute an alternative to the economic explanation; it simply prevents the latter from being reified by showing that the mechanisms that come under the economics are accessible only in their relation to hermeneutics. To say that repression is "metaphor" is not to replace the economic hypothesis but rather to parallel it with a linguistic interpretation and thus relate it to the universe of meaning without reducing it to that universe.

However, before specifying the precise relations between linguistics and the economics, it is perhaps necessary to come to an agreement about the word "linguistic," which up to now we have been hesitant to use when designating the relations of meaning between symptoms, fantasies, dreams, ideals, and unconscious themes. The term "linguistic" may be applied to the field of analysis on the condition that it is taken in a wide sense; it then denotes two distinct but interconnected aspects of the analytic situation. First, the technique of analysis moves entirely within the element of language. Benveniste writes,

> The analyst operates with what the subject tells him, he views the subject in the discourses that the latter makes, he examines him in his locutory and "story-making" behavior, and through these discourses there is slowly shaped for him another discourse that he must make explicit, that of the complex buried within the unconscious. The analyst, therefore, will take the discourse as a stand-in for another "language" which has its own rules, symbols, and syntax and which refers back to underlying structures of the psychism.[67]

Thus, on the one hand there are speech events, a locution, an interlocution, and on the other, through those events, the bringing to light of "another discourse," constituted by the relations of substitu-

67. Émile Benveniste, "Remarques sur la fonction du langage dans la découverte freudienne," *La Psychanalyse, 1*, 6.

tion and symbolization between the motivations belonging to the unconscious. Now, properly speaking, are the laws of that other discourse linguistic laws?

It is indeed difficult to make that other discourse coincide with what, since De Saussure, we call language [*langue*] as opposed to speech [*la parole*], a distinction based on the fact that language has a phonemic articulation, a semantic articulation, and a syntax.

In the first place, it is impossible to make the absence of logic in dreams, their ignorance of "No," accord with a state of real language. Freud once tried to do this, without success, in his essay on "The Antithetical Meaning of Primal Words." [68] It is impossible, however, to make the archaism of the processes of distortion and pictorial representation coincide with a primitive form of language or in general with any chronological reality whatsoever; as Benveniste aptly states, the Freudian archaic "is such only in relation to that which deforms or represses it."

Even in the favorable case of negation (*Verneinung*), which we have previously discussed, the opposition between affirmation and negation is not an extension of the properly libidinal dialectic of admission and rejection, for an expressed negation can only refer to an expressed affirmation. The prior refusal of admission, in which repression consists, is something else: the specific function of repression, in the case of *Verneinung*, consists in admitting a content into consciousness intellectually while at the same time keeping it

68. It would seem that Freud brought the investigation to an impasse in trying to make the *regressive* character of dreams, their disregard of contradiction, coincide with a state of primitive language. In his article "Über den Gegensinn der Urworte" ("The Antithetical Meaning of Primal Words," *GW, 8*, 214–21; *SE, 11*, 155–61), he appeals to the authority of Karl Abel (1884) in order to confirm the regressive and archaic character of dreams by a peculiarity of primitive languages, that of expressing antithetical meanings by the same words. Benveniste pertinently notes that what a language does not distinguish by distinct signs is not thought of as being antithetical: "each language is peculiar and fashions the world in its own way" (p. 10). "It is surely contradictory to impute to a language the knowledge of two notions as being contrary to one another and the expression of those notions as being identical with one another." Benveniste concludes: "Everything seems to take us farther and father away from an experiential correlation between the logic of dreams and the logic of an actual language" (p. 11).

outside of consciousness; but this mechanism sets up a repugnance of identifying oneself with this content, which is not a linguistic phenomenon.

It is not without reason that Freud does not take language [*le langage*] into consideration when he treats of the unconscious but rather restricts its role to the preconscious and the conscious. The signifying factor [*le signifiant*] which he finds in the unconscious and which he calls the "instinctual representative" (ideational or affective) is of the order of images, as is evidenced moreover by the regression of the dream-thoughts to the fantasy stage. Here we must bring together several lines of thought that remain unconnected in Freud. The form by which an instinct reaches the psychism is called a "representative" (*Repräsentant*); this is a signifying factor, but it is not yet linguistic. As for the "presentation" properly so-called (*Vorstellung*), this is not, in its specific texture, of the order of language; it is a "presentation of things," not a "presentation of words." Secondly, in dream regression, the form into which the dream-thought dissolves corresponds to the mechanism which Freud calls regression to "pictorial representation" [*figuration*]. Finally, when he treats of the derivatives substituted for one another and for the instinctual representatives, and when he explains remoteness and distortion, he always relates them to the order of fantasy or images, and not of speech. In these three different circumstances Freud focuses on a signifying power that is operative prior to language. The primary process encounters the facts of language only when words are treated in it as things: this is the case of schizophrenia and also of dreams in their more "schizophrenic" aspects.[69]

69. In the section of *The Interpretation of Dreams* on the work of condensation, in which Freud interprets the dream of Irma's injection, the following assertion is made: "The work of condensation in dreams is seen at its clearest when it handles words and names. It is true in general that words are treated in dreams as though they were concrete things, and for that reason they are apt to be combined in just the same way as presentations of concrete things [*Dingvorstellungen*]" (*GW, 2/3,* 301–02; *SE, 4,* 295–96); there follow a few examples of verbal conceits. In Section VII of "The Unconscious," the discussion of schizophrenia (in a patient of Tausk's) presents the occasion for a more complete treatment of the problem: "In schizophrenia *words* are subjected to the same process as that which makes the dream-images [*Traumbilder*] out of latent dream-

If we take the concept of linguistics in the strict sense of the science of language phenomena embodied in a given and therefore organized language, the symbolism of the unconscious is not *stricto sensu* a linguistic phenomenon. It is a symbolism common to various cultures regardless of their language; it presents phenomena such as displacement and condensation which operate on the level of images, and not that of phonemic or semantic articulation. In Benveniste's terminology, the dream mechanisms will appear now as infra- , now as supralinguistic. For my part, I will say that they manifest the blending [*confusion*] of the infra- and supralinguistic; they belong to the infralinguistic order insofar as they fall short of the level where education brings about the distinctive rule of a language; they belong to the supralinguistic order if one considers that dreams, according to one of Freud's own remarks, find their true

---

thoughts—to what we have called the primary psychical process. They undergo condensation, and by means of displacement transfer their cathexes to one another in their entirety. The process may go so far that a single word, if it is specially suitable on account of its numerous connections, takes over the representation [*Vertretung*] of a whole train of thought" (*GW*, *10*, 297–98; *SE*, *14*, 199). And Freud adds in a footnote: "The dream-work, too, occasionally treats words like things, and so creates very similar 'schizophrenic' utterances or neologisms" (ibid.). This is, then, a very particular process which assures what Freud calls "the predominance of what has to do with words [*Wortbeziehung*] over what has to do with things [*Sachbeziehung*]," in the sense that the similarity between words is substituted here for the resemblance between things, whereas in the transference neuroses the resemblance between things is predominant. Freud proposes the following economic explanation of the process: the object-cathexes have been given up, and only the cathexis of the word-presentations is retained; this implies that what had previously been called the "presentation of the object" can be split up into the "presentation of the *word*" and the "presentation of the *thing*": "the latter consists in the cathexis, if not of the direct memory-images of the thing, at least of remoter memory traces derived from these" (*GW*, *10*, 300; *SE*, *14*, 201). From this Freud draws the important conclusion that an "unconscious presentation" is the "presentation of the thing [*Sachvorstellung*] alone," whereas a conscious presentation comprises both that and the presentation of the word. "The system *Ucs.* contains the thing-cathexes [*Sachbesetzungen*] of the objects, the first and true object-cathexes [*Objektbesetzungen*]: the system *Pcs.* comes about by this thing-presentation being hypercathected through being linked with the word-presentations corresponding to it" (ibid.). This linking of the two orders of presentation is characteristic therefore of the *Pcs.*; it is an approach to the process of becoming conscious insofar as it makes the latter "possible."

kinship in the great unities of discourse such as proverbs, sayings, folklore, myths. From this point of view, it is on the level of rhetoric rather than linguistics that the comparison should be made. Rhetoric, however, with its metaphors, its metonymies, its synecdochies, its euphemisms, its allusions, its antiphrases, its litotes, is concerned not with phenomena of language but with procedures of subjectivity that are manifested in discourse.[70]

To call these mechanisms infra- or supralinguistic is, of course, still to refer them to language. That is precisely what constitutes the soundness of the linguistic interpretation. We are in the presence of phenomena structured like a language; but the problem is to assign an appropriate meaning to the word "like."

It is in the interplay and blending of the infra- and the supralinguistic that we shall find something *like* the instituting of meaning with which phenomenology is familiar.

In order to account for this instituting of meaning, one may start from the fact that the desire or wish (*Wunsch*) disclosed through interpretation is never a pure need, but is rather an appeal and a demand, even if the appeal is presented figuratively through a gesture;[71] this appeal, being a sort of allocution, is like a language. What distinguishes a wish from a need is the fact that a wish is capable of being stated; this capability is exactly coextensive with the celebrated *Rücksicht auf Darstellbarkeit.* Hence it is on the level of the instinctual representatives that we must look for something like a language. The very fact that dreams are expressed in narratives and that their elements cluster around "switch-words" is confirmation that "the capture of instincts in the nets of the signifier" pertains to the order of language in a different way from

70. "Style, rather than language, is where I would see a term of comparison with the properties that Freud has shown to be descriptive of the 'dream language' " (Benveniste, p. 15).

71. In the brief analysis of "Philippe's Dream," proposed by Laplanche and Leclaire ("L'Inconscient, une étude psychanalytique," *Journées de Bonneval,* 1960), the desire to drink is represented by a series of pictorial equivalents of this appeal: the drinking of fountain water from cupped hands, the arrangement of the palms of the hands in the form of a conch. The arrangement of the hands and the phrase "Lili, I'm thirsty" are instinctual representatives; as such "they point, within the text of the interpretation, to the living core of the dream" (p. 28).

what is disclosed through an observation of organized language. What analysis penetrates to is indeed something like a text. The "regard for representability" is itself something like a language, although this is not on the level of "word-presentation" but of "thing-presentation."

But what about language?

We have already noted the parallel between Freud's *Interpretation of Dreams* and *Jokes;* it is based on the fact that the dream mechanisms of condensation and displacement appear to be well-defined figures of classical rhetoric; but we did not go beyond a general analogy. Starting from the role of the switch-words in the unconscious text of dreams, it is possible to develop in detail the interpretation of condensation as metaphor and displacement as metonymy.[72]

Let us follow, with Laplanche and Leclaire, the path of metaphor. In a language without metaphors, there would indeed be relations of signifier to signified [*rapports de signifiant à signifié*], which may be symbolized by $\frac{S}{s}$; but there would be no equivocation in the language, nor any unconscious to decipher. With metaphor, a new signifier S' replaces the signifier (this may be written $\frac{S'}{s}$); but the former S, instead of being suppressed, drops to the rank of the signified (which may be written $\frac{S'}{S}$); the important point is that it continues on as a latent signifier. Thus one does not simply have $\frac{S'}{s}$ in place of $\frac{S}{s}$, but a more complex formula; $\frac{S'}{s}$ would be the reduced

72. In Philippe's dream, the substitution of the village square [*la place*] where the fountain stands, for the seashore [*la plage*], where the sand irritated his feet, is of the order of metaphor; the movement whereby the unicorn [*licorne*] refers to its whole legend and to an entire cycle of signifiers functions as metonymy. Concerning metonymy: "When we speak of the metonymic function of the unicorn, it is not because this signifier refers to an object that would satisfy the thirst in question, but rather because the unicorn, as metonymy, is the representative which points to and covers over the vertiginous gap within being, or, if you will, its 'original castration.' Thus metonymy, by reason of its inexhaustible possibility of displacement, is the proper instrument to designate and mask over the fissure in which desire is born and to which it ceaselessly aspires to return" (ibid., p. 29).

or simplified version of that formula. For its complex form, the authors propose the written formula $\frac{S'}{S} \times \frac{S}{s}$ (Formula 1), of which $\frac{S'}{s}$ is in effect the simplification. But they write it out only to transform it algebraically into $\frac{\frac{S'}{s}}{\frac{S}{S}}$ (Formula 2).

Whatever reservations one may have about these purely algebraic operations (what possible meaning can be assigned to the multiplication $\frac{S'}{S} \times \frac{S}{s}$ which allowed Formula 1 to be transformed into Formula 2?), the final formula deserves to be taken, if not as a true formula, at least as a useful schema for study. It serves the purpose of stimulating reflection about the *bar* that separates the two relations. The authors use the bar to express the double nature of repression: it is a barrier that separates the systems, and a relating that ties together the relations of signifier to signified. Because of its double function, the bar may be said to be not only the symbol of a linguistic phenomenon, a relating of relations consisting solely of signifiers and signified, but also a dynamic phenomenon—the bar expresses repression which impedes transition to a higher system.

The artifice at least enables one to construct a diagram in which repression and metaphor exactly parallel one another. Metaphor is nothing other than repression, and vice versa; but it is just when they are seen to coincide that the irreducibility of the economic to the linguistic point of view reappears in a striking manner.[73] What

73. The cohesive factor binding the systems together can be expressed only in energy language. In the case of "after-repression" (*Nachverdrängung*) or "repression proper," this cohesive force is manifested by the "attraction" exercised by a previously constituted chain, to which must be added the withdrawal of cathexis from the higher system whereby the connection is broken and a hypercathexis whereby a term that has been forced out of the chain is replaced by another one. The case of "primal repression," which has to be reconstructed, is more difficult. Here we are dealing with the origin of the split into systems, prior to any "attraction" exercised by a constituted system; Freud expresses this by saying that anticathexis is the sole mechanism of primal repression. It is possible to make some sort of correlation between language and this original division into two systems, but the correlation is as mythical as the "origin" of the *Ucs.*, as mythical

has been gained, then, by this reading? Everything and nothing. Everything, for there is no economic process to which there cannot be found a corresponding linguistic aspect; thus the energy aspect is completely paralleled by a linguistic aspect that guarantees the correlation of the unconscious to the conscious. Nothing, for the only thing that guarantees the separation of the systems is the economic explanation: withdrawal of cathexis, anticathexis, attraction on the part of the unconscious in secondary repression or repression proper, anticathexis in primal repression. If a fragment of discourse is to set forth an ordered sequence of signifiers, it is necessary, in Freud's words, that "the psychical (ideational) representative of the instinct [be] denied entrance into the conscious";[74] this denial, which precisely constitutes primal repression (*Urverdrängung*), is not a phenomenon of language.

The interpretation of repression as metaphor shows that the unconscious is related to the conscious as a particular kind of discourse to ordinary discourse; but the economic explanation is what accounts for the separation of the two discourses. In the four-stage diagram of secondary repression, repression and metaphor are strictly coextensive; but the barrier functions both as a relation

---

as any "origin" (though not more so). Freud's text on primal repression lends itself to such a step by stating that the action of anticathexis results in a "fixation" of the representative to the instinct, a process which, as we have seen, is understood as the emergence of the instinct into psychical expression, its accession to the order of signifier. Extending this interpretation with the help of the diagram of metaphor, one will conceive "the existence of certain key signifiers [*signifiants-clés*] which function metaphorically and upon which has devolved, because of their particular weight, the property of ordering the whole system of human language. It is clear that we are alluding in particular to what J. Lacan has called the father metaphor" (Laplanche and Leclaire, p. 39). In the example of Philippe's dream, one can see the constitution of a first chain of signifiers in the connection between the need of drinking and thirst, as appeal and demand: the fixation to a representative took place when someone clearly articulated "Philippe's always thirsty" and nicknamed him "thirsty Philippe." "We can now formulate the myth of the origin of the unconscious as follows: *the unconscious results from the capture of instinctual energy in the nets of the signifier*, inasmuch as the signifier there is precisely aimed at covering over the fundamental gap of being which is the unceasing source of the metonymy of desire" (ibid., p. 46).

74. "Repression," *GW, 10,* 250; *SE, 14,* 148.

between signifying or signified factors and as a force of exclusion between dynamic systems.

The strange and, in the proper sense of the term, nonlinguistic characteristics of this discourse are explained, I believe, by the irreducibility of the energy aspect. It is striking indeed that in the diagram of metaphor the original signifier, replaced by the substitute signifier and reduced to a latent signifier, is treated as a double term $\frac{S}{s}$; the same element S has the position of both signifier and signified, a situation for which there is no linguistic parallel. This was an attempt to account for what Freud called "thing-presentation" or "regard for representability." But can one treat as a linguistic element an image that would be in the position of both the signifier and the signified? [75] What linguistic character is left in the imago if the latter functions indifferently as signifier or signified? How can one say of it that it refers to itself and that it remains open to all meaning?

We can retain, then, with the reservations just made, the statement that the unconscious is structured like a language; but the word "like" must receive no less emphasis than the word "language." In short, the statement must not be divorced from Benveniste's remark that the Freudian mechanisms are both infra- and supralinguistic. The mechanisms of the unconscious are not so much particular linguistic phenomena as they are paralinguistic distortions of ordinary language.

For my part I would characterize this distortion as the confusion or blending of the infra- and the supralinguistic. On the one hand,

75. "In a sense, one can say that the signifying chain is pure meaning, but one can just as well say that it is pure signifier, pure nonmeaning, or open to all meanings" (Laplanche and Leclaire, p. 40). Is this not to admit that it is not properly a linguistic phenomenon? The authors frankly recognize the difficulty: "A distinction should be made, however, between the mode of functioning of the primary process in our 'origin fiction' and in the case of the unconscious chain. In the first case there was after all a distinction between the signifier level and the signified level, although the two are constantly infringing upon one another; in the second case, the possibility of 'all meanings' stems from an actual identity of the signifier and the signified. Does this mean there is no possibilty here of infringement? Not at all; but that which infringes or is displaced is instinctual energy, pure and unspecified" (p. 41).

the dream mechanism borders on the supralinguistic when it mobilizes stereotyped symbols parallel to those ethnology finds in the great unities of meaning known as fables, legends, myths; a good part of the "pictorial representation" in dreams is located on this level, which is already beyond that of the phonemic and semantic articulations of language.

On the other hand, displacement and condensation belong to the infralinguistic order, in the sense that what they achieve is less a distinct relating than a confusion of relations. One might say that dreams arise from a short-circuiting of the infra- and the supralinguistic.[76] This jumbling of the infra- and the supralinguistic is perhaps the most notable language achievement of the Freudian unconscious.

In conclusion, the linguistic interpretation has the merit of raising all the phenomena of the primary process and of repression to the rank of language; the very fact that the analytic cure itself is language attests to the mixture of the quasi language of the unconscious and ordinary language. But the distortion—the *Entstellung*—which turns that other discourse into a quasi language is not itself achieved by language. The "infra" or the "supra" with respect to language is what separates psychoanalysis from phenomenology.

76. The fragment of Philippe's dream neatly confirms this confusion. On the one hand the metonymy of desire, sustained by the signifier *licorne* [unicorn], deploys itself not on the plane of the elementary relations of the signifier and the signified but on that of the legend. But at the same time the dream plays upon the homophony of the *G of plage* [seashore] and *j'ai soif* [I'm thirsty]; the wordplay operates through attrition and distortion on the level of the phonemic elements; the homophony $\frac{G}{G}$ is what gives rise to the metonymic displacement through which the need of drinking becomes "thirst for" under the emblem of the unicorn. The *licorne* represents both its own legend (and thus assures what has been called the metonymy of desire) and the word *licorne*, which, on the phonemic plane, divides into li-corne. The unconscious text, which is to be interpolated into the conscious text, must be supplied as a signifying chain between LI and CORNE. The unconscious chain is therefore a complicated patchwork with its various signifiers of ordinary language (*Lili-plage-sable-peau-pied-corne*), whereas condensation condenses the sequence to its two end terms, li-corne. Thus the *licorne* image is both the mythic potential of the fabled animal and the wordplay of li-corne. This is what we call the jumbling of the infra- and the supralinguistic.

This confusion of language is also what raises the urgent and difficult question of an archeology of the subject.

4. The theme of intersubjectivity is undoubtedly where phenomenology and psychoanalysis come closest to being identified with each other, but also where they are seen to be most radically distinct. The narrowest difference is also the most decisive one.

If the analytic relationship may be regarded as a privileged example of intersubjective relations, and if that relationship takes the specific form of transference, it is because the analytic dialogue brings to light, in a special context of disengagement, isolation, and derealization, the demands in which desire ultimately consists.

This analysis has enabled us to relate in principle all the vicissitudes of the analytic situation to the intersubjective constitution of desire; I have nothing to retract from it. Yet it is precisely here that psychoanalysis is most radically distinct from anything phenomenology can understand and produce with its sole resources of reflection. The difference is summed up in a word: psychoanalysis is an arduous technique, learned by diligent exercise and practice. One cannot overestimate the amazing audacity of this discovery. namely of treating the intersubjective relationship as *technique*.

How is the word used here? One of Freud's texts, which we have already cited,[77] binds together inseparably method of investigation, technique of treatment, and elaboration of a body of theories.

77. See above, n. 59: *GW, 13,* 221; *SE, 18,* 235. In other texts Freud takes the psychoanalytic *method* as including both the *method* of investigation and the *technique* of treatment: "The particular psychotherapeutic procedure which Freud practices and describes as 'psychoanalysis' is an outgrowth of what was known as the 'cathartic' method and was discussed by him in collaboration with Josef Breuer in their *Studies on Hysteria* (1895)" ("Die Freud'sche psychoanalytische Methode" [1904], *GW, 5,* 3–10; "Freud's Psychoanalytic Procedure," *SE, 7,* 249–54). The text continues: "The changes which Freud introduced in Breuer's cathartic method of treatment were at first changes in technique" (p. 250): abandonment of hypnosis, conversation between two people equally awake, abandonment of voluntary psychic control, free play of associations, the "rule" of saying everything, even what seems unimportant, irrelevant, nonsensical, embarrassing or distressing. An article of the same period, "On Psychotherapy" (1905), *GW, 5,* 13–26; *SE, 7,* 257–68, speaks of "therapeutic procedure," "technique of treatment," and "method of treatment" in the same context as the preceding article—that of the confrontation with Breuer. In 1914, in "Remembering, Repeating and Working-Through" ("Erinnern, Wiederholen

Technique is here taken in the narrow sense of therapy aimed at healing; the method of investigation is distinguished from it as the art of interpretation. However, a number of other texts dealing with the psychoanalytic technique authorize us to take the word to include both method of investigation, and technique in the narrow sense of therapeutic procedure. This extension is grounded in the nature of the concrete analytic procedure, in which the method of investigation is regarded as the "intellectual" part of a technique. This broad sense of the word "technique" can be broken down into three ideas. From the side of the analyst the analytic procedure, from start to finish, is a "work," to which corresponds, on the part of the analysand, another work, the work of gaining insight whereby he cooperates in his own analysis. This work in turn reveals a third form of work, of which the patient was unaware—the mechanism of his neurosis. These three ideas go together to form the content of the psychoanalytic concept of technique.

Why is analysis a work? Primarily and essentially because analysis is a struggle against the patient's resistances.[78] From this point

und Durcharbeiten," *GW, 10,* 126–36; *SE, 12,* 147–56), the "technique of psychoanalysis" is again opposed to Breuer's catharsis.

On the analytic relation and transference, cf. J. Lacan, "Le Stade du miroir comme formateur de la fonction du Je telle qu'elle nous est révélée dans l'expérience analytique," *Rev. fr. de psychan., 13* (1949), 449–55; "La direction de la cure et les principes de son pouvoir," *La Psychanalyse, 5* (1959), 1–20. D. Lagache, "Le problème du transfert," *Rev. fr. de psychan., 16,* 5–115. B. Grunberger, "Essai sur la situation analytique et le processus de guérison," *Rev. fr. de psychan., 23* (1959), 367–79. E. Amado Lévy-Valensi, *Les Rapports intersubjectifs en psychanalyse* (Paris, P. U. F., 1962). J. P. Valabrega, *La relation thérapeutique* (Paris, Flammarion, 1962). S. Nacht, *La Présence du psychanalyste* (Paris, P. U. F., 1963). C. Stein, "La Situation analytique . . . ," *Rev. fr. de psychan., 28* (1964), 235–49.

78. The struggle against the resistances is at the basis of Freud's rejection of Breuer's cathartic method and his use of hypnosis: "The objection to hypnosis is that it conceals the resistance and for that reason has obstructed the physician's insight into the play of psychical forces" (*SE, 7,* 252). In the 1905 article: "I have another reproach to make against this method, namely, that it conceals from us all insight into the play of mental forces; it does not permit us, for example, to recognize the *resistance* with which the patient clings to his disease and thus even fights against his own recovery; yet it is this phenomenon of resistance which alone makes it possible to understand his behavior in daily life" (*SE, 7,* 261). Speaking in 1910 of "The Future Prospects of Psychoanalytic Therapy" (*GW, 8,* 104–15; *SE, 11,*

of view the art of interpretation is subordinated to the analytic technique as soon as the latter is defined as the struggle against resistances; if there is something to interpret, it is because there is a distortion of the ideas that have become unconscious; but if there is a distortion, it is because a resistance has been opposed to their conscious reproduction.[79] The resistances that lie at the origin of the neurosis are also those obstructing insight and every analytic procedure. Hence the rules of the art of interpretation are themselves part of the art of handling the resistances.

Thus the correlation between hermeneutics and energetics, which we have focused on throughout this chapter, reappears in a decisive manner on the level of praxis, as a correlation between the art of interpretation and the work against the resistances: "to translate" the unconscious into the conscious and "to do away with the constraint" resulting from the resistances are one and the same thing. To interpret and to work coincide. In certain cases, moreover, the art of interpretation must be sacrificed to the strategy of countering the resistances, and hence to technique. Thus Freud advises beginners not to make the art of complete dream-interpretation an end in itself, for to do so would be to fall into the trap of the resistance, which will take advantage of the slowness of the interpretation in order to delay the treatment.[80] This limit case clearly

141–51), Freud characterizes his "innovations in the field of technique" in these terms: "There are now two aims in psychoanalytic technique: to save the physician effort and to give the patient the most unrestricted access to his unconscious. As you know, our technique has undergone a fundamental transformation. At the time of the cathartic treatment what we aimed at was the elucidation of the symptoms; we then turned away from the symptoms and devoted ourselves instead to uncovering the 'complexes,' to use a word which Jung has made indispensable; now, however, our work is aimed directly at finding out and overcoming the 'resistances,' and we can justifiably rely on the complexes coming to light without difficulty as soon as the resistances have been recognized and removed" (*SE, 11,* 144).

79. The earliest text we have cited explicitly ties together analytic technique, resistance, distortion, art of interpretation (*SE, 7,* 251–52).

80. "Die Handhabung der Traumdeutung in der Psychoanalyse" (1911), *GW, 8,* 350–57; "The Handling of Dream-Interpretation in Psychoanalysis," *SE, 12,* 91–96: "I submit, therefore, that dream-interpretation should not be pursued in analytic treatment as an art for its own sake, but that its handling should be subject to those technical rules that govern the conduct of the treatment as a whole" (p. 94). The question as to "the way in which

shows in what sense the rules of interpretation are rules of technique.

The primacy of technique over interpretation brings out the full significance of a Freudian leitmotiv: "It is not easy to play upon the instrument of the mind"; the remark alludes to the words of Hamlet, " 'Sblood, do you think I am easier to be played on than a pipe?"; analytic treatment costs the patient sincerity, time, and money, but it costs the physician study and technical skill.[81] And these two "works" answer to one another; the work of the analyst is like that of the patient: if the analyst wants to play with the terrible forces of sexuality, he must have "overcome in his own mind that mixture of prurience and prudery with which, unfortunately, so many people habitually consider sexual problems"; the requirement that future practitioners undergo training in analysis finds one of its most important justifications here.[82]

---

the analyst should employ the art of dream-interpretation in the psychoanalytic treatment of patients" is a question of "technique" (p. 91). It is in this connection that Freud speaks of the analyst's "work" (p. 92). The expression is appropriate, for this is where the analyst's interest in making an accurate and complete interpretation may collide with the overall strategy unless the analyst has recognized, in the patient's profusion of dreams, a ruse on the part of the resistances; it is for these reasons that the right use of interpretation and the rules governing its use (pp. 92, 94) are part of the analytic "technique." The title of the paper is thus fully justified: "The Handling . . ." (*Handhabung*).

81. One should read the short paper of 1912, "Recommendations to Physicians Practising Psychoanalysis," *GW, 8,* 267–87; *SE, 12,* 111–20, where Freud lays out in detail the rules of this technical skill: the effort of remembering names, dates, associations, and pathological products; the maintenance of evenly suspended attention so that the analyst does not unduly select from the material he hears, etc. All such rules are the counterpart to the fundamental rule laid down for the patient. Corresponding to the "total communication" on the part of the patient is the "total listening" on the part of the analyst. But this total listening relates to the necessary psychoanalytic purification of the doctor himself, and hence, once again, to the reduction of resistances. Other technical rules follow from this affective discipline which cannot be foreseen a priori by a psychology of consciousness: for example, the rule of remaining opaque to one's patients, of foregoing all educative ambition as well as all therapeutic ambition, etc.

82. "On Psychotherapy," *SE, 7,* 267. In 1910, Freud expressly linked the necessity of training analysis to that of recognizing and overcoming the "countertransference" ("The Future Prospects of Psychoanalysis," *SE, 11,* 144–45).

Mastery of the technical rules is what distinguishes authentic psychoanalysis from "wild" psychoanalysis, a compound of scientific ignorance and technical errors. Misunderstanding the mental factors in sexuality and the role of repression in the patient's inability to achieve satisfaction, "wild" analysis commits the major technical error of attributing the patient's illness to his ignorance of the mental forces at work:

> The pathological factor is not his ignorance in itself, but the root of this ignorance in his *inner resistances;* it was they that first called this ignorance into being, and they still maintain it now. The task of the treatment lies in combating these resistances. Informing the patient of what he does not know because he has repressed it is only one of the necessary preliminaries to the treatment. . . . informing the patient of his unconscious regularly results in an intensification of the conflict in him and an exacerbation of his troubles.[83]

This text throws much light on our present discussion: mere improvement in ordinary awareness cannot substitute for analytic technique, for the problem is not to replace ignorance with knowledge, but to overcome the resistances.

At the same time, the text neatly shows the correspondence be-

83. " 'Wild' Psychoanalysis" (1910), *GW, 8,* 118–25; *SE, 11,* 225. The case alluded to in this paper occasions one of Freud's most important discussions of the distinction between mental satisfaction and physical need in human sexuality: "In psychoanalysis the concept of what is sexual comprises far more; it goes lower and also higher than its popular sense. This extension is justified genetically; we reckon as belonging to 'sexual life' all the activities of the tender feelings which have primitive sexual impulses as their source, even when those impulses have become inhibited in regard to their original sexual aim or have exchanged this aim for another which is no longer sexual. For this reason we prefer to speak of *psychosexuality,* thus laying stress on the point that the mental factor in sexual life should not be overlooked or underestimated. We use the word 'sexuality' in the same comprehensive sense as that in which the German language uses the word *lieben* ['to love']. We have long known, too, that mental absence of satisfaction with all its consequences can exist where there is no lack of normal sexual intercourse; and as therapists we always bear in mind that the unsatisfied sexual trends (whose substitutive satisfactions in the form of nervous symptoms we combat) can often find only very inadequate outlet in coitus or other sexual acts" (pp. 222–23).

tween the work of the analyst and the work of the analysand. In the present context, the concept of work does not designate the mechanism of dreams and the neuroses; later I will try to show how this latter work, as applied to the group of processes in which the mental dynamism objectifies itself, is the key concept which reconciles the reality of the energies set in motion and the ideality of deciphered meaning.[84] Here I limit myself to the mental work of the process of achieving insight within the analytic work.[85]

The work of the analyst and that of the analysand are conjoined in the struggle against the resistances.[86] The work on the part of the patient is "to accept, by virtue of a better understanding, something that up to now, in consequence of this automatic regulation by unpleasure, he has rejected (repressed)." For it must not be forgotten, the sole principle of repression is unpleasure. Thus the reeducation involved in overcoming the resistances is a struggle with the pleasure-unpleasure principle. Hypnosis dispensed with this "mental work," but it cannot be avoided. Analysis, Freud repeats, is costly to the patient: it costs time, it costs money; above all it requires total sincerity. The fundamental rule—the famous rule, the single rule, that of saying everything, whatever the cost—is the patient's great contribution to the work of the analysis. Here, to speak is a work. This surrender to whatever comes to mind implies a change in the patient's conscious attitude toward his illness and

84. See below, Ch. 2, second section.

85. Once again Freud remainds us that psychoanalysis is a profession that requires familiarization with a technique acquired through long and slow effort (*SE, 11,* 226); that too is why psychoanalysis must be organized as a recognized profession and the title of analyst guaranteed by an international psychoanalytical association (p. 227). On the relationship between interpretation, the communication of the interpretation, and the dynamics of treatment, see the important paper "On Beginning the Treatment," *GW, 8,* 454–78; *SE, 12,* 123–44, especially pp. 141–44.

86. Under this heading is included not only the patient's regular and punctual attendance at the sessions but also the difficult question as to how long the treatment will take. In this connection we should pause over one of Freud's remarks, in view of the importance we place on all his references to the problem of time: "To shorten analytic treatment is a justifiable wish. . . . Unfortunately, it is opposed by a very important factor, namely, the slowness with which the deep-going changes in the mind are accomplished—in the last resort, no doubt, the 'timelessness' of our unconscious processes" (ibid., p. 130).

hence a different sort of attention and courage than is exercised in directed thinking.

The great work of "becoming conscious" is the process of understanding, of remembering, of recognizing the past and of recognizing oneself in that past. As we have often said in examining Freud's theoretical writings, the process of achieving insight involves an economic problem that completely distinguishes psychoanalysis from phenomenology. What we touched upon from the analyst's point of view is again encountered from the viewpoint of the patient: the communication of an interpretation is of no value unless it can be incorporated into the work of achieving insight. A premature communication will only result in a reinforcement of the resistances. The process of treatment has its own dynamics, according to which the purely intellectual factor of understanding functions as an important but subordinate factor in the liquidation of the resistances; that is why the analyst's interpretation has to be subordinated to the general analytic strategy: the place of "knowledge" within the strategy of resistance must itself be taught by the rules of the art.

"Working-through" (*Durcharbeiten*) [87] is the term Freud proposes for the patient's hard labor with his resistances, a work carried out by means of interpretation and transference and in accord with the fundamental rule of analysis:

> Only when the resistance is at its height can the analyst, working in common with his patient, discover the repressed instinctual impulses which are feeding the resistance . . . This working-through of the resistances may in practice turn out to be an arduous task for the subject of the analysis and a trial of patience for the analyst. Nevertheless it is a part of the work which effects the greatest changes in the patient and which distinguishes analytic treatment from any kind of treatment by suggestion.[88]

The fact that the achieving of intellectual insight is included within the mental work enables us to reexamine a problem we have investigated on the plane of metapsychology—namely, the top-

87. "Remembering, Repeating, and Working-Through," *SE, 12,* 155–56.

88. Similar remarks are to be found in "Lines of Advance in Psycho-analytic Therapy" (1918), *GW, 12,* 183–94; *SE, 17,* 159–68: "The work by which we bring the repressed mental material into the patient's consciousness has been called by us psychoanalysis" (p. 159). Freud then goes

ographic representation of the psychism. The justification for the topographic differentiation into systems is to be found in praxis; the "remoteness" between the systems and their separation by the "barrier" of repression are the exact pictorial transcription of the "work" that provides access to the area of the repressed. "The patients now know of the repressed experience in their conscious thought, but this thought lacks any connection with the place where the repressed recollection is in some way or other contained. No change is possible until the conscious thought-process has penetrated to that place and has overcome the resistances of repression there." [89]

Not only the topographic point of view, but also the economic point of view of the metapsychology is justified by praxis. Therapy derives its energy from the patient's suffering and his wish to be cured; the strength of this energy is countered by various forces, among them the "secondary gain" the patient gets from his illness. The analytic investigation enters into this "economy" by arousing new energies capable of overcoming the resistances, and by showing special paths along which to direct those energies.[90] In this way the economic problem of therapy leads us to the most difficult question of analytic technique, the question of *transference*. For the transference is regarded as supplying the additional energy envisaged in the previous text: a treatment, Freud says, "only deserves the name [of a psychoanalysis] if the intensity of the transference has been utilized for the overcoming of resistances." [91]

The moment has come, therefore, to bring to bear upon this theme the full weight of the difference between phenomenology and psychoanalysis.

Our constant problem—that of the relation between hermeneutics and energetics—arises for the last time: it is now a matter of

---

on to develop the analogy between psychoanalysis and chemical analysis: "We have *analyzed* the patient—that is, separated his mental processes into their elementary constituents and demonstrated these instinctual elements in him singly and in isolation" (p. 160). But Freud rejects the notion of a psychosynthesis and states he finds no meaning in the task that would consist in making "a new and a better combination" (p. 233). We will discuss this point in Chapter 3.

89. "On Beginning the Treatment," *SE, 12,* 142.

90. Ibid., p. 143.

91. Ibid.

understanding how interpretation, its communication, and the gaining of insight are embodied in the dynamics of transference.[92] Freud stresses the fact that the "handling" of the transference is where the technical character of psychoanalysis is evidenced in its highest degree. This too is where the philosopher schooled in phenomenological reflection realizes his exclusion from an experiential understanding of what occurs in the analytic relationship. Ultimately, this is where analytic praxis differs from all its conceivable phenomenological equivalents. With the question of the transference, the strategy concerning the resistances takes on a concrete shape. The transference emerges both as a means of overcoming the early resistances that contributed to the illness and as a new resistance—as Freud says, the most powerful resistance to the treatment.[93] On the one hand, the resistances can be overcome only if the traumatic situation is transposed into the closed field of

92. "Thus the new sources of strength for which the patient is indebted to his analyst are reducible to transference and instruction (through the communication made to him)" (ibid., pp. 143–44). Returning to the same difficulty in 1914, in "Remembering, Repeating, and Working-Through," Freud stresses his opposition to Breuer and adds the following remarks. Breuer's catharsis aimed at the recall of memories, which was to be achieved through the work of interpretation and the communication of its results; but if the essential point is the struggle against the resistances, then the search for former happenings and situations must give precedence to the interpretation of the resistances themselves: "Finally, there was evolved the consistent technique used today, in which the analyst gives up the attempt to bring a particular moment or problem into focus. He contents himself with studying whatever is present for the time being on the surface of the patient's mind, and he employs the art of interpretation mainly for the purpose of recognizing the resistances which appear there, and making them conscious to the patient. From this there results a new sort of division of labor: the doctor uncovers the resistances which are unknown to the patient; when these have been got the better of, the patient often relates the forgotten situations and connections without any difficulty. The aim of these different techniques has, of course, remained the same. Descriptively speaking, it is to fill in gaps in memory; dynamically speaking, it is to overcome resistances due to repression" (*SE, 12,* 147–48).

93. "The Dynamics of Transference" (1912), *GW, 8,* 364–74; *SE, 12,* 99–108. In this text Freud presents as a puzzle the fact that transference is a factor of resistance, "whereas outside analysis it must be regarded as the vehicle of cure and the condition of success" (p. 101). "The solution of the puzzle is that transference to the doctor is suitable for resistance to the treatment only in so far as it is a negative transference or a positive transference of repressed erotic impulses" (p. 105).

the analytic relationship; on the other hand, the transference emerges precisely at the point where it can satisfy the resistance the analytic tactics have tracked down.

In the course of this fight against the resistances in the transference situation there is revealed a further aspect of the dialectic between hermeneutics and energetics. We have seen that the original goal of analytic technique was not only affective discharge or abreaction but also remembering, a process directly aimed at by Breuer's catharsis. But remembering is also an intellectual phenomenon, an insight into the past as past. Little by little it came to be seen that the remembering of unconscious material is of less importance than the recognition of the resistances.[94] But above all, it was seen that remembering is in many cases replaced by an actual repetition of the traumatic situation: instead of remembering the past, the patient repeats it by acting it out, without, of course, knowing that he is repeating it. This strange turn of events is more important than it might at first appear. No phenomenology of intersubjectivity can parallel this automatism of repetition, which is part of a very significant sequence—resistance, transference, repetition; this sequence is the core of the analytic situation.[95] Thus the fight against the resistances, the handling of the transference, and the recourse to repetition form the main constellation of the analytic technique; its tactic consists in using the transference to curb the patient's compulsion to repeat in order to lead him back along the paths of remembering. It is understandable why Freud states that the handling of the transference presents far more serious difficulties than the interpretation of the patient's associations.[96]

94. "Observations on Transference-Love" (1914), *GW, 10,* 306–21; *SE, 12,* 159–71.

95. "We soon perceive that the transference is itself only a piece of repetition, and that the repetition is a transference of the forgotten past not only onto the doctor but also onto all the other aspects of the current situation. . . . The part played by resistance, too, is easily recognized. The greater the resistance, the more extensively will acting out (repetition) replace remembering" ("Remembering, Repeating, and Working-Through," *SE, 12,* 151). The analytic technique consists in letting the repetition occur, and thus it runs counter to the direct technique of remembering that was employed in Breuer's catharsis. On "acting out," cf. "Observations on Transference-Love," *SE, 12,* 65–66.

96. "The main instrument, however, for curbing the patient's compulsion to repeat and for turning it into a motive for remembering lies in the handling

Our main interest here lies less in therapy than in the philosophical implications of this situation. From this point of view the most impressive difficulty, the one offering the greatest challenge to a phenomenological approach to psychoanalysis, is the difficulty concerning the management of transference-love: the height of technique lies in the art of exploiting the transference-love *without satisfying it*. Freud went so far as to write that this is "a fundamental principle which will probably dominate our work in this field"; he enunciates the principle as follows: "Analytic treatment should be carried through, as far as is possible, under privation—in a state of abstinence." [97] This rule, it would seem, has no phenomenological equivalent. What is it getting at? We are here at the heart of the economic problem of the analytic relationship; it is no longer merely upon the patient's resistances that the analyst learns to "play," but upon the other's pleasure and unpleasure in the form of privation or frustration. In order to understand this point one must go back to the original situation and to the frustration generated by the conflict between instinct and resistance; the whole theory of symptoms is based upon that initial frustration; a symptom, from the economic point of view, is nothing else than a substitute form of

---

of the transference. We render the compulsion harmless, and indeed useful, by giving it the right to assert itself in a definite field. We admit it into the transference as a playground in which it is allowed to expand in almost complete freedom and in which it is expected to display to us everything in the way of pathogenic instincts that is hidden in the patient's mind. . . . The transference thus creates an intermediate region between illness and real life through which the transition from the one to the other is made" (*SE, 12,* 154). To these texts should be added the important short paper "Observations on Transference-Love" (cf. above, n. 94); in it Freud deals with the difficulties in the handling of the transference and tell us they are far more serious than the ones encountered in the interpretation of associations (*SE, 12,* 159).

97. "Lines of Advance in Psychoanalytic Therapy," *SE, 17,* 162. The practice of this rule is exemplified in "Observations on Transference-Love": "The patient's need and longing should be allowed to persist in her, in order that they may serve as forces impelling her to do work and to make changes, and . . . we must beware of appeasing those forces by means of surrogates" (*SE, 12,* 165). And further on: "The course the analyst must pursue is . . . one for which there is no model in real life. He must take care not to steer away from the transference-love, or to repulse it or to make it distasteful to the patient; but he must just as resolutely withhold any response to it" (p. 166).

satisfaction; on the other hand, the failure of that tactic of substitution is what sustains the instinctual force impelling the patient toward recovery. When placed within this dynamic context, the frustration, actively sustained by the analytic tactics, is justified. It is important not to diminish the instinctual force; if the patient's suffering becomes mitigated, "we must re-instate it elsewhere in the form of some appreciable privation." [98] Thus the analyst's work, which we described at first as a struggle against the resistances, is now seen as a struggle against substitute satisfactions—precisely in the transference where the patient is particularly looking for such satisfaction. For the phenomenologist, this technique of frustration is the most surprising aspect of the analytic method; he can no doubt understand the rule of veracity, but not the principle of frustration: the latter can only be *practiced.*

If we now connect the point of arrival with the point of departure of these reflections on the technique of the analytic relationship, we have this to say: That which makes the analytic relationship possible as an intersubjective relation is indeed, as we said at the beginning, the fact that the analytic dialogue, within a special context of disengagement, of isolation, of derealization, brings to light the demand in which desire ultimately consists; but only the technique of transference, as a technique of frustration, could reveal the fact that desire is at bottom an unanswered demand . . .

The two attempts to reformulate psychoanalysis, first in terms of scientific psychology, then in terms of phenomenology, have failed, and the unique character of analytic discourse is confirmed by that double failure. On the one hand, the operative concepts of academic psychology do not constitute a better formulation of the analytic concepts; on the other hand, as Merleau-Ponty said in the Preface to Hesnard's *L'Oeuvre de Freud,* phenomenology does not say "in a clear way what psychoanalysis said in a confused way; it is rather by what it only hints at or reveals at its limit—by its latent content or its unconscious—that phenomenology is in harmony with psychoanalysis." [99]

98. "Lines of Advance in Psychoanalytic Therapy," *SE, 17,* 163.

99. Merleau-Ponty, Preface to A. Hesnard, *L'Oeuvre de Freud et son importance pour le monde moderne* (1960). I adopt most of the remarks of this preface as well as its general movement. It is necessary, the author

I have tried to show that psychoanalysis is a unique and irreducible form of praxis; as such, it puts its finger on what phenomenology never perfectly attains, namely, "our relation to our origins and our relation to our models, the id and the superego." [100]

---

says, to go beyond a first formulation of the relations between phenomenology and psychoanalysis, where phenomenology would play the role of an unperturbed mentor correcting misunderstandings and supplying categories and means of expression to a technique that reasons poorly and is poorly thought out. In order to remain itself, in convergence with the Freudian research, phenomenology must first carry through the movement of descent "into its own subsoil" (p. 8). Having started from "that infinite curiosity, that ambition to see everything, which animates the phenomenological reduction" (p. 7), phenomenology must subject its own problematic to the unsettling questions of the body, of time, of intersubjectivity, of the consciousness of things or the world, where being is now "all around [consciousness] instead of laid out before it . . . oneiric being, by definition hidden" (p. 8). This phenomenology, on guard against its own idealism, will then also be able to concern itself with protecting psychoanalysis from its own success, and a contributing factor here could be a phenomenological reformulation. "The idealist deviation in Freudian research is today just as much a threat as its objectivist deviation. One is forced to ask whether it is not essential to psychoanalysis—I mean to its existence as therapy and as verifiable knowledge—to remain, not of course a poor attempt and an occult science, but at least a paradox and a question" (p. 8). I highly value and adopt as my own this remark of one who did so much to break the charm of "the scientistic or objectivistic ideology" (p. 5) of psychoanalysis: "In any case the energic or mechanistic metaphors guard, against any idealistic leanings, the threshold of one of the most valuable intuitions in Freudian theory: the intuition of our *archeology*" (p. 9). To grasp the importance of this preface, see J. B. Pontalis, "Note sur le problème de l'inconscient chez Merleau-Ponty," *Les Temps modernes,* (1961), 287–303.

100. Ibid. Cf. A. Hesnard, *Apport de la phénoménologie à la psychiatrie contemporaine* (Masson, 1959). A. Green, "L'Inconscient freudien et la psychanalyse française contemporaine," *Les Temps modernes, 18* (1962), 365–79; "Du Comportement à la chair: itinéraire dc Merleau-Ponty," *Critique* (1964), 1017–46.

Chapter 2: Reflection: An Archeology of the Subject

The task of this chapter is to bring the results of the preceding epistemological discussion to the level of philosophical reflection. It must be kept in mind that our enterprise is strictly philosophical and in no way binding on the psychoanalyst as such. For the analyst, psychoanalytic theory is sufficiently understood through its relation to the method of investigation and the therapeutic technique. But this "sufficient" understanding—in the sense in which Plato says, in an important methodological text, that the explanations of the geometers stop with "something sufficient," which does not suffice for the philosopher —is not fully transparent to itself. If, as we have asserted in the "Problematic," the ***I think, I am*** is the reflective foundation of every proposition concerning man, the question is how Freud's mixed discourse enters into a philosophy which is deliberately reflective.

In opposing all psychologizing or idealizing reductions of psychoanalysis, and in admitting the irreducibility of the theory's most realistic and naturalistic aspects, we have not made the solution to the problem any easier. The idea guiding me is this: the philosophical place of analytic discourse is defined by the concept of an archeology of the subject. But thus far this concept has remained a mere word. How can we give it a meaning? It is not one of Freud's concepts, nor do we intend to impose it upon the reading of Freud or use some stratagem to discover it in his works. It is a concept that I form in order to understand myself in reading Freud. I stress the peculiar nature of this constituting operation and distinguish it from the preceding methodological discussion, which remained on the sufficient level of as yet unfounded concepts.

The steps of reflection will be the following:

1. First, it must be made clear that it is in reflection and for reflection that psychoanalysis is an archeology; it is an archeology *of the subject.* But of what subject? What must the subject of reflection be if it is likewise to be the subject of psychoanalysis?

2. This twofold adjustment of the question of the subject will enable us finally to assign a philosophical locus to the entire preceding epistemological discussion, and to integrate the methodological paradox of the first chapter into the field of reflection. With this section we conclude our epistemological examination of Freudianism.

3. Turning next to the Freudian theses themselves, we will elaborate the concept of archeology within the limits of a philosophy of reflection. We do not claim that this concept contains a full understanding of Freudianism. The remainder of this book will amply demonstrate that the understanding of Freudianism requires a new advance of thought.

FREUD AND THE QUESTION OF THE SUBJECT

It is one and the same enterprise to understand Freudianism as a discourse about the subject and to discover that the subject is never the subject one thinks it is. The reflective reinterpretation of Freudianism cannot help but alter our notion of reflection: as the understanding of Freudianism is changed, so is the understanding of oneself.

What should point the way for us here is the absence in Freudianism of any radical questioning about the existential and thinking subject. Freud very clearly ignores and rejects any problematic of the primal or fundamental subject. We have repeatedly emphasized this flight from the question of the *I think, I am.* The Cogito does not and cannot figure in a topographic and economic theory of systems or agencies; it cannot possibly be objectified in a psychical locality or a role; it denotes something altogether different from what could be spelled out in a theory of instincts and their vicissitudes. Hence it is the very factor that escapes analytic conceptualization. Are we to look for it in the consciousness? Consciousness presents itself as the representative of the external world, as a surface function, as a mere sign or character in the developed formula *Cs.-Pcpt.* Are we looking for the ego? What we find is the id. Shall we turn from the id to the dominating agency? What we meet is the superego. Shall we try to reach the ego in its function of affirmation, defense, expansion? What we discover is narcissism, the great screen between self and oneself. The circle has come full turn and the *ego* of the *cogito sum* has escaped each time. This flight from the egological foundation is very instructive. It does not at all signify the failure of analytic theory; this very flight from the primal [*l'originaire*] must now be understood as a stage of reflection.

Let us start with the passage in Husserl's *Cartesian Meditations* (§ 9) cited above. "Adequacy and apodicticity of evidence need not go hand in hand." [1] As I see it, this proposition provides the framework in which the Freudian problematic can be thought and reflected upon. It should be read in both directions. On the one hand, it implies that the inadequacy concerning consciousness is accompanied by the apodicticity of the Cogito: there is a point invincible to every doubt, which Husserl calls "one's living self-presence," and to which the phenomenological reduction gives access; without this radical recourse, every problematic concerning human reality is truncated. On the other hand, one cannot attest to the apodicticity of the Cogito without at the same time recognizing the inadequacy concerning consciousness; the possibility that I am deceived, in every ontic statement I pronounce about myself, is co-extensive with the certitude of the *I think:* "The living evidence of the *I am* is no longer given but only presumed." And Husserl could add, "This presumption, co-implicit in apodictic evidence, requires a critique that would determine apodictically the range of its possibilities of fulfillment." [2] At the very heart of the certitude of the *I am* there remains the question: "How far can the transcendental ego be deceived about itself? And how far do those components extend that are absolutely indubitable in spite of such possible deception?" [3]

1. Cf. the rest of the text, p. 377, n. 43.
2. Ibid.
3. Ibid.

Starting from these fundamental propositions, it is possible to work through the entire Freudian metapsychology in a reflective manner that reproduces all the steps of the metapsychology, but in a different philosophical dimension. All that Freud objectifies in a quasi-physical reality, all the models that contemporary epistemological criticism can distinguish in his representation of the mental apparatus, all this must become a stage of reflection.

First and foremost, what must be reproduced is his critique of immediate consciousness. In this regard I consider the Freudian metapsychology an extraordinary *discipline of reflection:* like Hegel's *Phenomenology of Spirit,* but in the reverse direction, it achieves a decentering of the home of significations, a displacement of the birthplace of meaning. By this displacement, immediate consciousness finds itself dispossessed to the advantage of another agency of meaning—the transcendence of speech or the emergence of desire. This dispossession, which the Freudian systematization requires of us in its own way, is to be achieved as a kind of ascesis of reflection, the meaning and necessity of which appear only afterward, as the recompense for an unjustified risk. So long as we have not actually taken this step, we do not really understand what we are saying when we state that the philosophy of reflection is not a psychology of consciousness. If this statement is to be concretely meaningful, we must widen the gap between the positing of reflection, which we have said is apodictic, and the pretension of consciousness, which we have admitted, if only in principle, to be inadequate, capable of mistakes and self-deception. We must really lose hold of consciousness and its pretension of ruling over meaning, in order to save reflection and its indomitable assurance. This is what the path through the metapsychology (short of psychoanalytic practice) can give the philosopher—and I say "give," not "take from."

The necessity of this dispossession is what justifies Freud's naturalism. If the viewpoint of consciousness is—from the outset and for the most part—a false point of view, I must make use of the Freudian systematization, its topography and economics, as a "discipline" aimed at making me completely homeless, at dispossessing me of that illusory Cogito which at the outset occupies the place of the founding act, *I think, I am*. The path through the Freudian topography and economics simply expresses the necessary discipline of an antiphenomenology. At the conclusion of this process, aimed at undoing the would-be evidence of consciousness, I will no longer know the meaning of object, subject, or even thought; the avowed aim of this discipline is to shake the false knowledge which blocks access to the *Ego Cogito Cogitatum*. This dispossession of immediate consciousness is governed by the construction of a model, or set of models, in which consciousness itself figures as one of the places. Thus consciousness is one of the agencies in the triad unconscious-preconscious-conscious. In its turn, this topographical or topological picture of the mental apparatus is inseparable from an economic explanation, according to which the self-regulation of the apparatus is assured by placements and displacements of energy and by mobile or bound cathexes. For those of us who are not psychoanalysts, who do not have to diagnose and heal, the adoption of this topographic and economic discourse can be meaningful, and meaningful within reflection. By definitively dissociating the apodicticity of reflection from the evidence of immediate consciousness, the antiphenomenology of the Freudian topography and energetics can function as a moment of reflection.

I propose that we reexamine this dispossession of immediate consciousness by retracing the movement of the Freudian metapsychology as presented in Freud's language in Chapter 3 of our "Analytic." We saw that this problematic split into two lines or paths. The first path, clearly stated in "The Unconscious," led us from the descriptive point of view, which is still that of immediate consciousness, to the topographic and economic point of view, in which consciousness becomes one of the psychical localities. The second path led us back from the instinctual representatives, which are already psychical factors, to their derivatives in consciousness. This double movement becomes understandable in a discipline of reflection. The dispossession of consciousness implies the attainment of the topographic-economic point of view. In this point of view the place of meaning is displaced from consciousness toward the unconscious. But this place cannot be reified as a region of the world. Consequently, the first task—the displacement—cannot be separated from the second task—the recapture of meaning in interpretation. This alternation of relinquishing [*déprise*] and recapture [*reprise*] is the philosophical basis of the entire metapsychology. If it is true that the language of desire is a discourse combining meaning and force, reflection, in order to get at the root of desire, must let itself be dispossessed of the conscious meaning of discourse and displaced to another place of meaning. This is the moment of dispossession, of relinquishing. But since desire is accessible only in the disguises in which it displaces itself, it is only by interpreting the signs of desire that one can recapture in reflection the emergence of desire and thus enlarge reflection to the point where it regains what it had lost.

Such is the meaning, for reflection, of the two paths of the "Analytic," the path from the descriptive concept of consciousness to the concept of instinct and instinctual vicissitude, and the path from the instinctual representatives to their derivatives in consciousness.

Let us retrace the first path. It starts with a reversal of point of view: the unconscious is no longer defined in relationship to consciousness as a state of absence or latency, but as a locality in which ideas or representations reside; anticipating the present analysis, we called this reversal of viewpoint an antiphenomenology, an epochê in reverse.[4] That remains true, for what we are confronted with is not a reduction *to* consciousness but a reduction *of* consciousness. Consciousness ceases to be what is best known and becomes problematic. Henceforward there is a question of consciousness, of the process of becoming-conscious (*Bewusstwerden*), in place of the so-called self-evidence of being-conscious (*Bewusstsein*). This antiphenomenology must now be seen by us as a phase of reflection, the moment of the divestiture of reflection. The topographical concept of the unconscious is the correlate of this zero degree of reflection.

The second step in the destruction of the pseudo evidence of consciousness was characterized by the abandonment of the concept of object (wished-for object, hated object, loved object, feared object). The object, as it presents itself in its false evidence as correlate of consciousness, must in turn cease to be the guide of analysis: in Freud's terms, it is a mere variable of the aim of an instinct

4. Pp. 117 ff.

(*Three Essays on Sexuality*, "Instincts and Their Vicissitudes"). The notion of instinctual vicissitudes is thus substituted for the laws of representation of the old psychology of consciousness. In the context of this instinctual economy one can attempt to work out a true genesis of the notion of object, in accordance with the economic distributions of the libido. Perhaps this ostensible antiphenomenology is merely the long detour at the end of which the object will again become the transcendental guide, but for a highly mediated reflection, and not for a supposedly immediate consciousness. In this regard the later Husserl indicates the area and direction of research when he structures all investigation of constitution upon a passive genesis. What remains peculiar to Freud is to have linked this genesis of the object with the genesis of love and hate.

The third step of the dispossession is characterized by the introduction of narcissism into psychoanalytic theory. We are now forced to treat the ego itself as the variable object of an instinct and to form the concept of ego-instinct (*Ichtrieb*) in which, as we have said, the ego is no longer the subject of the Cogito but the object of desire. Furthermore, in the economy of the libido, the values of subject and object are constantly being interchanged; there is a pleasure-ego (*Lust-Ich*), correlative to the ego-instinct (*Ichtrieb*), which exchanges itself for object values on the market of libidinal investments or cathexes. This is the supreme test for a philosophy of reflection. What is in question is the very subject of immediate apperception. Narcissism must be introduced, not only into psychoanalytic theory, but into reflection. I then discover that as soon as the apodictic truth *I think, I am* is uttered, it is blocked by a pseudo evidence: an abortive Cogito has already taken the place of the first truth of reflection, *I think, I am*. At the very heart of the Ego Cogito I discover an instinct all of whose derived forms [5] point toward something altogether primitive and primordial, which Freud calls primary narcissism. To raise this discovery to the reflective level is to make the dispossession of the subject of consciousness coequal with the dispossession, already achieved, of the intended object.

Here we have reached a sort of end point of the reduction of

5. Cf. pp. 126–28.

consciousness and, one might say, of phenomenology as well. In speaking of the overestimation of the child by his parents, which Freud regards as a reproduction of their own abandoned narcissism ("His Majesty the Baby" shall fulfill all our dreams), Freud writes: "At the most touchy point in the narcissistic system, the immortality of the ego, which is so hard pressed by reality, security is achieved by taking refuge in the child." [6]

This "touchy point in the narcissistic system" is what I call the false Cogito, coextensive with the primal Cogito. In another famous text, "A Difficulty in the Path of Psychoanalysis" (1917), Freud clearly points out the philosophical issues involved in this challenging of the privileged status of consciousness. In this essay narcissism appears as a veritable metaphysical entity, a veritable evil genius, to which must be attributed our most extreme resistance to truth: "The universal narcissism of men, their self-love, has up to the present suffered three severe blows from the researches of science." First, man regarded the central position of the earth as a sign of his dominating role in the universe, a view that appeared "to fit in very well with his inclination to regard himself as lord of the world." Next, man "acquired a dominating position over his fellow-creatures in the animal kingdom" and presumptuously "began to place a gulf between his nature and theirs." Finally, he was convinced that he was master and lord within his own house, the mind. Psychoanalysis represents the third and "probably the most wounding" of the humiliations dealt to narcissism. After the cosmological blow inflicted by Copernicus, there followed the biological humiliation from the work of Darwin. And now here is psychoanalysis revealing that "the ego is not master in its own house"; having already known he is lord neither of the cosmos nor of the animal kingdom, man discovers he is not even the lord of his own mind. The Freudian thinker turns to the ego and says:

> You feel sure that you are informed of all that goes on in your mind if it is of any importance at all, because in that case, you believe, your consciousness gives you news of it. And if you have had no information of something in your mind you confidently

6. "On Narcissism: An Introduction," *GW, 10,* 158; *SE, 14,* 91.

> assume that it does not exist there. Indeed, you go so far as to regard what is "mental" as identical with what is "conscious"—that is, with what is known to you—in spite of the most obvious evidence that a great deal more must constantly be going on in your mind than can be known to your consciousness. Come, let yourself be taught something on this one point! . . . You behave like an absolute ruler who is content with the information supplied him by his highest officials and never goes among the people to hear their voice. Turn your eyes inward, look into your own depths, learn first to know yourself! Then you will understand why you were bound to fall ill; and perhaps, you will avoid falling ill in future.[7]

"Come, let yourself be taught something on this one point! . . . look into your own depths, learn first to know yourself!" These words of Freud make us realize this humiliation is itself part of a history of self-consciousness. *In te redi*—the phrase is St. Augustine's; it is Husserl's, too, at the end of the *Cartesian Meditations;* but what is peculiar to Freud is that this instruction, this insight, must involve a "humiliation," since it has encountered a hitherto masked enemy, which Freud calls the "resistance of narcissism."

This contrariety of narcissism, as the center of resistance to truth, is what calls forth the methodological decision to move from a description of consciousness to a topography of the psychical apparatus. The philosopher must acknowledge that there is a pro-

7. "A Difficulty in the Path of Psychoanalysis," *GW, 12,* 3–12; *SE, 17,* 137–44. On the Freudian personology, cf. J. Lacan, "Le stade du miroir comme formateur de la fonction du Je . . . ," *Rev. fr. de psychan., 13* (1949), 449–54; "Les Formations de l'inconscient," Séminaire, 1957–58, *Bull. de psych.,* No. 11. D. Lagache, "Fascination de la conscience par le moi," *La Psychanalyse, 3* (1957), 33–45; "La Psychanalyse et la structure de la personnalité," *La Psychanalyse, 6* (1961), 5–54. P. Luquet, "Les Identifications précoces dans la structuration et la restructuration du moi," *Rev. fr. de psychan., 26* (1962), 117–329; P. C. Racamier, "Le moi, le soi, la personne et la psychose," *L'Évol. psychiatr., 2* (1958), 445–66. On the role of the body image, cf. F. Dolto, "Personnologie et image du corps," *La Psychanalyse, 6* (1961), 59–92; S. A. Shentoub, "Remarques sur la conception du moi et ses références au concept de l'image corporelle," *Rev. fr. de psychan., 27* (1963), 271–300; G. Pankow, "Structuration dynamique dans la schizophrénie," *Revue suisse de psychologie, 27* (1956).

found and significant connection between this appeal to a naturalistic model of the ego and the tactic of dislodgment and dispossession directed against the illusion of consciousness, itself rooted in narcissism. The realism of the unconscious, having become a realism of the ego itself, must be viewed as a phase in the struggle against the resistances and as a step toward a self-consciousness less centered on the egoism of the ego, a self-consciousness taught by the reality principle, by Ananke, and open to a truth free of "illusion." Everything we can say, with—and eventually against—Freud, must henceforth bear the mark of this "wounding" of our self-love. In order to express this point of phenomenological impoverishment to which we are invited, I would revert to Plato's remark about being and nonbeing in the *Sophist:* "The question of being," he said, "is as perplexing as that of nonbeing." Similarly, I say, the question of consciousness is as obscure as the question of the unconscious.

That is what can be said in Freud's favor, at the threshold of his theory of agencies. Nor will I hide the fact that this tactic, perfectly adapted to a struggle against illusion, prevents psychoanalysis from ever rejoining the primal affirmation: nothing is more foreign to Freud than the idea of the Cogito positing itself in an apodictic judgment, irreducible to all the illusions of consciousness. That is why Freud's theory of the ego is at once very liberating with respect to the illusions of consciousness and very disappointing in its inability to give the *I* of the *I think* some sort of meaning. But this disappointment, which is properly philosophical, must first of all be attributed to the "wound" and "humiliation" which psychoanalysis inflicts on our self-love.

Hence, in approaching Freud's texts on the ego or consciousness, the philosopher must forget the most basic requirements of his egology and accept the fact that the positing of the *I think, I am* should vacillate. Everything Freud says about consciousness presupposes this forgetfulness and vacillation. Consciousness or the ego never figures in the systematization in the sense of an apodictic positing, but rather as an economic function.

In thus approaching Freudianism through the narrow door of its systematization, we effectively realize the dispossession of consciousness; we "realize" it, moreover, in the proper sense of the word, for what this discipline leads to is a realism of agencies. Considered by itself, however, this realism is unintelligible; the dispossession of consciousness would be *senseless* if it merely succeeded in distorting reflection into the consideration of a thing. Such would be the case if we overlooked the complex connections linking the topographic-economic explanation with the actual work of interpretation, which makes psychoanalysis the deciphering of a hidden meaning in an apparent meaning.

The second path along which the metapsychology has led us has its origin in the difficult concept of "psychical representative of instincts." This concept, more postulated than demonstrated, and which at times might be viewed as an expedient, has an irreplaceable function. It constitutes the main anchorage of the train of reflection. I place it at the point of return where the movement of the "relinquishing" of immediate consciousness is seen as the counterpart of the movement of "recapture," as the start of a "becoming conscious" which seeks to become equal to the authentic Cogito, as the beginning of the reappropriation of meaning.

There is a point, we said, where the question of force and the question of meaning coincide: it is the point where instincts are designated in the psychism by ideas and affects that represent or present the instincts. Leaving aside the problem of affects (we shall return to it in the next section), let us consider only those representatives that Freud calls ideational representatives of an instinct.

An instinct, in its biological being, Freud tells us, is unknowable; the only way it can enter into the psychical field is by means of its ideational representative; thanks to this psychical sign, the body is "represented in the soul." Hence it is possible to use the same language for the unconscious as for the conscious: we can speak of unconscious ideas and conscious ideas; a certain unity of intentional meanings henceforth maintains an affinity of meaning between the systems, in spite of the barrier separating them. This far-reaching thesis is two-pronged. On the one hand, the psychical cannot be defined by the fact of being conscious, by apperception; on this point the affinity with the Leibnizian concepts of appetition and perception, which we shall deal with at greater length further on, is very instructive and renders the Freudian concept of a psychical representative of an instinct highly plausible. On the other hand, the affinity of meaning between the unconscious and the conscious implies that the psychical, as such, cannot be defined apart from the possibility, however distant or difficult it may be, of becoming conscious. The word "unconscious," even when replaced by the abbreviation *Ubw* (*Ucs.*), retains a reference to consciousness; *Bewusstheit,* the attribute of "being conscious," Freud observes, "forms the point of departure for all our investigations"; [8] it is "the only characteristic of psychical processes that is directly presented to us," and consequently it "is in no way suited to serve as a criterion for the differentiation of systems. . . . Hence consciousness stands in no simple relation either to the different systems or to repression." At most, we can and must "emancipate ourselves from the importance of the symptom of 'being conscious.' " [9] This is precisely what we have done in what we have described as the dispossession of consciousness. But the fact of being conscious can be neither suppressed nor destroyed. For it is in relation to the possibility of becoming conscious, in relation to the task of achieving conscious insight, that the concept of a psychical representative of an instinct becomes meaningful. Its meaning is this: however remote the primary instinctual representatives, however distorted their derivatives, they still appertain to the delimitation of meaning; they can in principle be translated into terms of the conscious psychism. In short, psychoanalysis is possible as a return to consciousness because, in a certain way, the unconscious is homogeneous with consciousness; it is its relative other, and not the absolute other.

REALITY OF THE ID, IDEALITY OF MEANING

It is now possible to again take up in reflection, and more precisely in its double movement of relinquishing and recapture, the methodological discussion left in suspense in the first chapter. I will not go back over the status of the

8. "The Unconscious," *GW, 10,* 271; *SE, 14,* 172.
9. Ibid., *GW, 10,* 291; *SE, 14,* 192–93.

hermeneutic concepts and the topographic-economic concepts from the viewpoint of their internal consistency and compossibility within a coherent epistemology. I wish to focus on the mark of "reality" attaching more particularly to the topographic-economic concepts, and on the mark of "ideality" of the concepts of meaning, intention, and motivation.

Freudianism aims at being a realism of the unconscious. In this regard, Freud complains that the prejudice of consciousness prevents "philosophers" from doing justice to the psychoanalytic concepts of the unconscious. He is right; but the question remains of determining what kind of realism we profess and practice when we subordinate the facts of psychoanalysis to the basic concepts of the metapsychology. This is the task of a critique, in the Kantian sense of the word; and this task is now capable of being fulfilled.

That Freud's topography requires a realism of the unconscious is beyond question; we ourselves have endorsed this realism from the viewpoint of reflection, recognizing in it the moment of dispossession, of relinquishing, as contrasted with any premature or illusory achieving of insight. But this disjunction with respect to my consciousness is not a disjunction with respect to all consciousness. The relationship of the metapsychological concepts to the actual work of interpretation implies a new kind of relativity, no longer to the consciousness which "has," so to speak, the unconscious, but to the overall field of consciousness constituted by the work of interpretation. But this new proposition is full of snares; for this work and this field pertain to a scientific consciousness which it is important to distinguish, at least in principle, from any private subjectivity, including that of the analyst; this scientific consciousness must first of all be regarded as a transcendental subjectivity, that is to say, as the locus or home of the rules governing interpretation.

This realism, which we have "disconnected" from ourselves who philosophize, which we have separated off from our immediate consciousness, remains in suspense as long as we have not related the topography to the hermeneutic field within which every realism is constituted. But this relationship must be rightly understood, if we do not wish to annul the gain Freudian realism represents for the progress of reflection. We did not regard this realism as a relapse into naturalism, but as a dispossession of immediate certitude, a withdrawal from and a humiliation of our narcissism. What we now have to say must not be a covert return of that same narcissism, but the achieving of a new quality of consciousness. The dispossession of consciousness has made such an achievement possible, although one discovers afterward that the hermeneutic consciousness is the condition of the possibility of the topographic realism.

There is nothing surprising about this situation, nor is it anything like a vicious circle. It is a situation that in general characterizes the relation between empirical realism, which is presupposed by every scientific enterprise, and the critical idealism governing all epistemological reflection concerning the validity of a science of facts. Hence a critique of the realist concepts of the topography must not revert to the investigation of the consciousness of the analyzed subject, for this would be a step backward in the direction of immediate consciousness, which we have resolutely turned away from. Of course, analysis always starts from the puzzles of meaning *for this* consciousness, from its symptoms *for* it, from the dream narrative it relates to the analyst. That is true, but it is not the crucial factor; what is crucial is the suspension of that immediate meaning, or rather that chaos of meaning, and the displacement of the apparent meaning and its meaninglessness into the field of deciphering constituted by the analytic work itself. It is the topography that makes this suspension and displacement possible. Hence the only possible critique of the realist concepts is an epistemological critique, a critique that "deduces" them—in the sense of the Kantian transcendental deduction—that is to say, justifies them by their power of regulating a new domain of objectivity and intelligibility. It seems to me that a greater familiarity with critical thought would have obviated many scholastic discussions about the realism of the unconscious and of the topography—as though one were forced to choose between a realism of agencies (*Ucs., Pcs., Cs.*) and an idealism of meaning and nonmeaning. In the area of physics, Kant has taught us to combine an empirical realism with a transcendental idealism—I say a transcendental idealism, and not a subjective or psychological one, as would be the case with a too well-intentioned theory which would not be long in annulling the result and gain of the topography. Kant achieved this combination for the sciences of nature; our task is to accomplish it for psychoanalysis, where theory constitutively enters into the facts it elaborates.

First, empirical realism; this means a number of things:

1. The metapsychology is not an optional, adventitious construction; it is not an ideology, a speculation; it has to do with what Kant called the determining judgments of experience; it determines the field of interpretation. Hence we must stop dissociating method and doctrine, stop taking the method without the doctrine. Here, the doctrine is method.

2. At the end of its process of deciphering, analysis reaches a reality just as much as do stratigraphy and archeology. The reality that it encounters, that it finds, surprises us in many ways, and particularly as the requisite of a terminated analysis. A given dream interpretation finally runs up against an ultimate core where it stops. This is the sense in which I understand what Freud says about terminable analysis.[10] At a certain point the analysis terminates *itself*, because it ends with *these* signifiers and not those: the term at which the analysis ends is the factual existence of *this* linguistic sequence and not some other.

3. This is a singular, individual reality, with a particular psychical configuration, but it is a typical reality as well: interpretation is possible because it regularly comes back to the same signifying segments, the same correspondences. These recurrences form a kind of dictionary of preconstituted types; "there is" meaning before "I" speak; "it" (i.e. the id) speaks. Thus analysis is terminable because *certain* singular configurations are discernible; but the singular is discernible, as this and not that, because it carves its singularity out of types that limit the range of possible combinations. To the notion of the terminable must be joined therefore the notion of the finite order of combinations. One is thus oriented toward the idea of a determined structure which analysis both verifies and presupposes.

4. In addition to its grounding in the singularity of meaning and

10. "Analysis Terminable and Interminable," *GW, 16,* 59–99; *SE, 23,* 216–53.

in the finite enumeration of typical structures, Freudian realism is based on the mechanistic nature of the laws governing the unconscious system. The difference between the laws governing that system and the laws of conscious activity is what justifies in Freud's eyes the transition from the descriptive point of view to the systematic point of view. This switch to another legality, in which I encounter myself as mechanism, is not without analogy with the situation described by Hegel in his *Philosophy of Right;* when the understanding grasps the activity of man as that of a being of needs, it grasps it within a system that reifies necessity as mechanism, as external reality; Hegel states, "Political economy is the science which starts from this view." [11] This comparison with political economy is not accidental, for what fills out the topographical framework is an economy of instincts. The analytic method is unfeasible unless one adopts the naturalistic point of view imposed by the economic model and endorses the type of intelligibility it confers; all the power of discovery stems primarily from this model. Consequently, a mere linguistic transcription of analysis seems to me to skirt the basic difficulty proposed by Freud; his naturalism is "well grounded"; and what grounds it is the thing aspect, the quasi nature aspect, of the forces and mechanisms in question. If one does not go that far, sooner or later one comes back to the primacy of immediate consciousness.

But in accepting the realism, one must also ask the question, What sort of reality? Reality of what? This is where one must keep very close to what the topography itself teaches. The reality knowable through the topography is a reality of the psychical representatives of instincts and not of the instincts themselves. An empirical realism is not a realism of the unknowable, but of the knowable; and the knowable, in psychoanalysis, is not the biological being of instincts, but the psychological being of the psychical representatives of instincts. Freud says,

> An instinct can never become an object of consciousness—only the idea that represents the instinct can. Even in the unconscious, moreover, an instinct cannot be represented otherwise than by an idea. If the instinct did not attach itself to an

11. Hegel, *Philosophy of Right,* § 189; tr. T. M. Knox (Oxford, Clarendon, 1942), p. 126.

idea or manifest itself as an affective state, we could know nothing about it.[12]

The realism peculiar to the Freudian topography is first of all, therefore, a realism of the psychical representatives of instincts; starting from there, the same index of reality is gradually extended to everything analysis links with ideas; thus an affective charge (quota of affect) becomes a reality that also has its "place" in the topography, by reason of the connections we have discovered between that charge and the ideational representative: "The nucleus of the *Ucs.* consists of instinctual representatives which seek to discharge their cathexis; that is to say, it consists of wishful impulses"; [13] this connection is what allows one to move from the topographic point of view to the economic point of view, on the same realist level. "Investments" (cathexes) and all the other economic operations can be discerned, recognized, named, only in those ideational representatives and in the quota of affect that constitutes their quantitative aspect. That is why Freud, in his most realist texts, consistently sets forth the vicissitudes of instincts as being the vicissitudes of the instinctual representatives: "Repression is essentially a process affecting ideas on the border between the systems *Ucs.* and *Pcs.* (*Cs.*)." [14] It is because this realism is a realism of the instinctual representatives, and not of the instincts themselves, that it is also a realism of the knowable and not of the unknowable, the ineffable, the unfathomable. One must take both of these texts together: the first, in which Freud says, "The theory of the instincts is so to say our mythology," [15] and the second, in which he states, "Internal objects are less unknowable than the external world." [16] It should be noted that the second text is couched in Kantian language; the context in which it occurs states that Kant corrected our views on external perception and warned us that our perceptions "must not be regarded as identical with what is perceived though unknowable." This is an important remark, for it places the unknowable outside, on the side of things; so too, the text continues,

12. "The Unconscious," *GW, 10,* 276; *SE, 14,* 177.
13. Ibid., *GW, 10,* 285; *SE, 14,* 186.
14. Ibid., *GW, 10,* 279; *SE, 14,* 180.
15. *New Introductory Lectures, GW, 15,* 101; *SE, 22,* 95.
16. "The Unconscious," *GW, 10,* 270; *SE, 14,* 171.

> psychoanalysis warns us not to equate perceptions by means of consciousness with the unconscious mental processes which are their object. Like the physical, the psychical is not necessarily in reality what it appears to us to be. We shall be glad to learn, however, that the correction of internal perception will turn out not to offer such great difficulties as the correction of external perception—that internal objects are less unknowable than the external world.[17]

That having been said, it remains to relate this "reality" to the various operations of interpretation and to show that this reality only exists as a "diagnosed" reality.[18] The reality of the unconscious is not an absolute reality, but is relative to the operations that give it meaning. This relativity presents three degrees, which we shall set out in order from the more objective to the more subjective, or, if you will, from the more epistemological to the more psychological.

1. The unconscious of the first topography is relative to the rules of deciphering which make it possible, for example, to trace the "derivatives" of the unconscious in the preconscious system back to their "origin" in the unconscious system. This relativity must be clearly understood: it does not reduce itself to a simple projection on the part of the interpreter, in a common psychological sense; it means that the reality of the topography constitutes itself within hermeneutics, but in a purely epistemological sense. It is in the movement of tracing the derivative (*Pcs.*) back to its origin (*Ucs.*) that the concept of the unconscious takes on consistency and its mark of reality is tested. This is not to suggest that the unconscious

17. Ibid.

18. I made use of the notions of diagnostic and diagnosed reality in the first interpretation I proposed of the Freudian unconscious (*Le Volontaire et l'involontaire* [Paris, Aubier, 1950], pp. 350–84; tr. Erazim V. Kohák, *Freedom and Nature: The Voluntary and the Involuntary* [Evanston, Northwestern University Press, 1966], pp. 373–409). I return to it here, but with a greater concern for justifying Freud's realism and naturalism. This interpretation may be confronted with that of Politzer, *Critique des fondements de la psychologie*, I. *La Psychologie et la psychoanalyse* (Rieder, 1928), and with that of J.-P. Sartre, *L'Être et le Néant* (Paris, P. U. F., 1943), "La psychanalyse existentielle."

is real for the consciousness of the subject in question. The reference to the consciousness which "has" the unconscious must at first be held in suspension and the relationship disconnected. But this suspension brings to light another relativity, which is not "subjectivist" but epistemological: the topography itself is relative to the hermeneutic constellation formed by the various signs, symptoms, and indications together with the analytic method and the explanatory models.

2. It is in relation to, starting from, and within this first order relativity, which might be called an objective relativity—I mean the relativity to the rules of analysis and not to the person of the analyst—that one may speak of a second order, intersubjective relativity. The facts referred to the unconscious by the analytic interpretation are first of all meaningful for another; this witness-consciousness, which is the analyst's consciousness, is part of the hermeneutic constellation within which the topographic reality is constituted. We are not in a position to spell out the full meaning of these remarks; there is still a long way to go before this coupling or pairing process can be thematized. For the present we can only understand its epistemological significance within the famework of the objective rules governing analysis. In this context the analyst figures simply as the one who practices the rules of the game, and not yet as the second party within a dual relationship through which the consciousness of the one has its truth in the consciousness of the other. The latter meaning will appear only when the analysand himself is revealed as "becoming conscious," as achieving insight, and no longer simply as the object of analysis whose consciousness was bracketed and rejected as the origin of meaning. Let us content ourselves with saying that the unconscious—and in general the reality systematized in the topography—is elaborated as reality by another person in accordance with the rules of interpretation. Later we shall point out that this diagnostic relationship is still very abstract in comparison with the complete and concrete therapeutic relationship which sets in operation, by means of the dialogue and struggle between two consciousnesses, the becoming-conscious of a singular being. What we can say about it at the present stage of our reflection is enough to make precise the objective status of the affirmations about the uncon-

scious. It is in relation to the hermeneutic rules and for another person that a given consciousness "has" an unconscious; but this relation becomes manifest only in the dispossession of the consciousness which has that unconscious.

3. Finally, it is in the dependence of that double relativity that one can account for a third form of dependence which is now merely subjective, although it is still constitutive at its own level: what I am referring to is the constitution of psychoanalytic reality in the transference language. The singularity of the analyst figures here as an indispensable pole of reference; a given analyst is the one who provokes, undergoes, and to a certain extent orients the transference in which the subject matter of the analysis becomes meaningful. We are bordering here on the contingent and the unforeseeable; yet it is not a question of an accidental factor: the transference is not an accidental part of the cure, but its necessary path. Nonetheless in each case the transference unfolds as a unique relationship. It is possible to speak of it only insofar as it is a regulative episode and not an incalculable event. The regulative episode is an object of training; the transference can be taught and learned. The incalculable event is the encounter with the singular personality of the analyst: it is neither taught nor learned. To be sure the regulative episode is inseparable from the incalculable event: but it is the first—separated by abstraction from the second—that figures in the hermeneutic constellation to which the psychical "reality" spoken of in analysis is relative.

I have considered these reflections necessary in order to counteract a certain form of naïve realism. Such a realism would not be an empirical realism, a realism of the instinctual representatives, but a naïve realism which, after the event, would project into the unconscious the final meaning as elaborated by a completed analysis. In such a case psychoanalysis would be a mythology, the worst of all, since it would consist in making the unconscious think. The expressive force of the word "id"—even more than that of the term "unconscious"—guards us from the naïve realism of giving the unconscious a consciousness, of reduplicating consciousness in consciousness. The unconscious is id and nothing but id.

By directly referring the unconscious, essentially and not accidentally, to the hermeneutic constellation, we define both the validity and the limits of any affirmation concerning the reality of the agencies; we exercise a critique of the psychoanalytic concepts—a critique, that is to say, a justification of their meaning-content and a limitation of their pretension to extend beyond the bounds of their constitution. These bounds are the same ones that enclose the hermeneutic constellation, that is, the ensemble made up of (1) the rules of interpretation, (2) the intersubjective situation of analysis, and (3) the language of the transference. Outside of this field of constitution the topography is no longer meaningful.

To sum up, then: reality of the id, ideality of meaning. Reality of the id, inasmuch as the id gives rise to thought on the part of the exegete. Ideality of meaning, inasmuch as meaning is such only at the end of the analysis, a meaning that has been elaborated in the analytic experience and through the language of the transference.

THE CONCEPT OF ARCHEOLOGY

Thus I understand the Freudian metapsychology as an adventure of reflection; the dispossession of consciousness is its path, because the act of becoming conscious is its task.

But it is a wounded Cogito that results from this adventure—a Cogito that posits itself but does not possess itself; a Cogito that sees its original truth only in and through the avowal of the inadequacy, illusion, and lying of actual consciousness.

We must now take a further step and speak no longer merely in negative terms of the inadequacy of consciousness, but in positive terms of the emergence or positing of desire through which I am posited, and find myself already posited. This prior positing of the *sum* at the heart of the Cogito must now be made explicit under the title of an archeology of the subject.

What we must now reexamine in the style of a reflective philosophy is not only the Freudian topography but its economics. We have justified the topographic point of view by the tactic of dispossession through which reflection counters the spell of false consciousness. Advancing in the direction of the central problem of this meditation, we will try to justify the economic point of view as the discourse appropriate to an archeology of the subject.

Starting with our introduction to the reading of Freud, we tentatively proposed, in anticipation of the present discussion, a theme we shall now attempt to tie in closely with a philosophy of reflection. Perhaps, we said, the possibility of moving from force to language, and also the impossibility of completely recapturing that force within language, lies in the very emergence of desire.

The link between that possibility and that impossibility is the present theme of our reflection. Up to now we have regarded the economic point of view as a model, that is, a working hypothesis justified by its epistemological function. But the choice of this economic model remains external to the movement of reflection as long as the relationship of this model to reflection is simply the negative relation described as the dispossession of consciousness. We must now see the underlying compatibility between the economic model and what I henceforth shall call the archeological moment of reflection. Here the economic point of view is no longer simply a model, nor even a point of view: it is a total view of things and of man in the world of things. Such a radical transformation of one's self-understanding cannot be contained in a model or arise from a simple methodological choice. For my part, I regard Freudianism as a revelation of the archaic, a manifestation of the ever prior. Thus Freud's thought has roots, both old and new, in the romantic philosophy of life and the unconscious. A review of Freud's entire theoretical work from the viewpoint of its *temporal* implications would show that its main preoccupation is the theme of the prior, the anterior.

The melodic core of this whole development would be the concept of regression as presented in Chapter 7 of *The Interpretation of Dreams*. As we have analyzed this difficult chapter at length, I will not return to its structure, or to the nature, figurative or realist, of the schema of the psychical apparatus, or to the connection between the topography of 1900 and the theory of the child's seduction by the father; I move directly to what seems to me to be the basic aim of this entire construction. The purpose of the schema, as we pointed out, is to account for the anomaly of an apparatus that functions in reverse, in a regressive and not a progressive direction. Wish-fulfillment (*Wunscherfüllung*), which dreams consist of, is regressive in three ways: it is a return to the raw material of images, a return to childhood, and a topographic return toward the perceptual end of the psychical apparatus instead of a progression toward the motor end. Freud observes that "All these three kinds of regression are, however, one at bottom and occur together as a rule; for what is older in time is more primitive in form and in psychical topography lies nearer to the perceptual end." [19] The topographic regression serves as the pictorial expression of the other two forms of regression, on the one hand the return to images, to scenic representation, to hallucination, and on the other hand the temporal regression. Moreover, these last two forms of regression are closely related: "In regression," Freud says, "the fabric of the dream-thoughts is resolved into its raw material." [20] This decomposition, another name for formal regression, the regression of thoughts to images, is at the service of the return to the past, for the dream-thoughts, subject to censorship, have no way of finding expression except in the hallucinatory mode of pictorial representation: "On this view a dream might be described as a substitute for an infantile scene modified by being transferred onto a recent experience. The infantile scene is unable to bring about its own revival and has to be content with returning as a dream." [21] Finally, it is the temporal direction of regression that is most strongly emphasized: "Dreaming is on the whole an example of regression to the dreamer's earliest condition, a revival of his childhood, of the instinctual impulses which dominated it and of the methods of expression which were then available to him." [22] Expanding this conception, Freud adds that "We can guess how much to the point is Nietzsche's assertion that in dreams 'some primeval relic of humanity is at work which we can now scarcely reach any longer by a direct path'; and we may expect that the analysis of dreams will lead us to a knowledge

19. *The Interpretation of Dreams, GW, 2/3,* 554; *SE, 5,* 548 (an addition of 1914).
20. *GW, 2/3,* 549; *SE, 5,* 543.
21. *GW, 2/3,* 552; *SE, 5,* 546.
22. *GW, 2/3,* 554; *SE, 5,* 548 (these lines were added in 1919).

of man's archaic heritage, of what is psychically innate in him."[23] That this is ultimately the main emphasis of *The Interpretation of Dreams* is confirmed by the last lines of the book: "And the value of dreams for giving us knowledge of the future? There is of course no question of that," Freud answers categorically; for if dreams lead us into the future, by picturing our wishes as fulfilled, this future is "moulded by [the dreamer's] indestructible wish into a perfect likeness of the past."[24] Thus the word "past" is the last word of *The Interpretation of Dreams.* Underlying this entire discussion is the thesis that no desire, not even the wish to sleep—of which dreams are nonetheless the guardian—is efficacious unless it joins itself to the "indestructible" and "virtually immortal" desires of our unconscious.

Reread from this point of view, Freud's entire work—both the metapsychology and the theory of culture—takes on a very definite philosophical tone. I will distinguish between a restricted concept of archaism, directly deduced from dreams and the neuroses and thematized in the "Papers on Metapsychology," and a generalized concept derived analogically from the psychoanalytic theory of culture.

Let us begin within the circle of the restricted archeology.

In Freudianism the sense of depth or profundity lies in the temporal dimension, or more exactly, in the connection between the time function of consciousness and the characteristic of timelessness of the unconscious. We have said that the first function of the topography is to picture schematically the various degrees of desire all the way to the indestructible. Thus the topography subserves the economics as the metaphorical picture of the indestructible as such: "In the unconscious nothing can be brought to an end, nothing is past or forgotten." As we have seen, such formulas are an anticipation of the remarks of the paper "The Unconscious." In that paper, archaism takes on a sense of depth that is far more extensive than any energetics of instincts: "The nucleus of the *Ucs.* consists of instinctual representatives which seek to discharge their cathexis." And Freud continues, "There are in this system no negation, no doubt, no degrees of certainty: all this is only introduced by the

23. Ibid.
24. *GW, 2/3,* 626; *SE, 5,* 621.

work of the censorship between the *Ucs.* and the *Pcs.*" And for us the most important point of all: "The processes of the system *Ucs.* are *timeless;* i.e. they are not ordered temporally, are not altered by the passage of time; they have no reference to time at all. Reference to time is bound up, once again, with the work of the system *Cs.*" These statements are inseparable from the following ones: "The *Ucs.* processes pay just as little regard to *reality*. They are subject to the pleasure principle." All these characteristics are to be taken as a whole: "exemption from mutual contradiction, *primary process* . . . *timelessness,* and *replacement of external by psychical reality.*" [25] It is difficult not to have the impression that the metapsychology is no longer simply the working out of a model, but a penetration and plunging into a depth of existence where Freud rejoins Schopenhauer, Von Hartmann, and Nietzsche.

It is true that in this text Freud does not seem disposed to give the timelessness of the unconscious a meaning other than that of a mere temporal priority: "The content of the *Ucs.,*" he writes at the end of Section VI of the same paper, "may be compared with an aboriginal population in the mind. If inherited mental formations exist in the human being—something analogous to instinct [*Instinkt*] in animals—these constitute the nucleus of the *Ucs.*" [26]

But as Freud reworks his theory of agencies, the metapsychology of time keeps extending beyond the framework of a banal evolutionism. What the paper of 1915 said about the unconscious is now attributed to the id; it is the id that is timeless. Now, the term "id," which was borrowed from Groddeck (*Das Buch von Es*), who in turn was inspired by the example of Nietzsche, has innumerable resonances which cannot possibly be exhausted in a simple energetics. It is a matter not only of an antiphenomenology, but of an inverted phenomenology of the impersonal and the neuter, of a neuter charged with ideas and impulses, of a neuter that, never being an *I think,* is something like an *It speaks,* which expresses itself in laconisms, displacements of emphasis of meaning, and the rhetoric of dreams and jokes. Such is the timeless kingdom, the region of the untimely.

In the *New Introductory Lectures* Freud does not hesitate to say

25. "The Unconscious," *GW, 10,* 285–86; *SE, 14,* 186–87.
26. *GW, 10,* 294; *SE, 14,* 195.

that we have only a borderline view of it: "It is the dark, inaccessible part of our personality; what little we know of it we have learnt from our study of the dream-work and of the construction of neurotic symptoms."[27] "We approach the id with analogies: we call it a chaos, a cauldron full of seething excitations."[28] One would think he is listening to Plato speak of the *Khôra,* which the god shapes into the ordered form of the cosmos. In this context Freud again takes up his earlier statements about the timelessness of the unconscious, but with a quasi-metaphysical accent:

> There is nothing in the id that corresponds to the idea of time; there is no recognition of the passage of time, and—a thing that is most remarkable and awaits consideration in philosophical thought—no alteration in its mental processes is produced by the passage of time. Wishful impulses which have never passed beyond the id, but impressions, too, which have been sunk into the id by repression, are virtually immortal; after the passage of decades they behave as though they had just occurred. They can only be recognized as belonging to the past, can only lose their importance and be deprived of their cathexis of energy, when they have been made conscious by the work of analysis, and it is on this that the therapeutic effect of analytic treatment rests to no small extent. Again and again I have had the impression that we have made too little theoretical use of this fact, established beyond any doubt, of the unalterability by time of the repressed. This seems to offer an approach to the most profound discoveries. Nor, unfortunately, have I myself made any progress here.[29]

These remarks, let us not forget, are those of an old man who reflects back over the whole of his work and underlines its philo-

27. *GW, 15,* 80; *SE, 22,* 73.
28. Ibid.
29. Ibid., *GW, 15,* 81; *SE, 22,* 74. On regression and time in Freud, cf. M. Bonaparte, "L'Inconscient et le temps," *Rev. fr. de psychan., 11* (1939), 61–105; J. Rouart, "La Temporalisation comme maîtrise et comme défense," *Rev. fr. de psychan., 26* (1962), 382–422; F. Pasche, "Régression, perversion, névrose (examen critique de la notion de régression)," *Rev. fr. de psychan., 26* (1962), 161–78.

sophical character; hence the numerous references we make to the *New Introductory Lectures* in these final chapters. The *zeitlos*—timeless—characteristic of the unconscious henceforth belongs to a view of man in which one can rightly speak of the unsurpassable character of desire. Chapter 7 of *The Interpretation of Dreams* was indeed prophetic: the eagle's gaze had at once detected the essential point in the bewildering (*befremdendes*) phenomenon of the dream-work; the bewildering or strange factor is that the secondary process is always posterior to the primary process; the primary process is present from the first, whereas the secondary process makes a belated appearance and is never definitively established. Regression, of which dreams are the witness and model, shows that man is unable to completely and definitively effect this replacement except in the inadequate form of repression; repression is the ordinary rule or working condition of a psychism condemned to making a late appearance and to being ever prey to the infantile, the indestructible. Thereupon the topography receives a second meaning: not only does it picture the degrees of remoteness of the unconscious thoughts, the distribution of ideas and affects all the way to the indestructible; its spatiality likewise represents man's inability to move from the regulation by pleasure-unpleasure to the reality principle, or, in terms that are more Spinozist than Freudian (though they are basically equivalent) man's inability to pass from slavery to beatitude and freedom.

The climax of this archeology, viewed at the instinctual level, lies in the theory of narcissism. Narcissism, it would seem, does not exhaust its philosophical meaning in its role of obstruction and blockage, which made us call it the false Cogito. Narcissism also has a temporal meaning: it is the original form of desire to which one always returns; we recall the texts in which Freud describes it as the "reservoir" of libido; all object-libido is transformed into it; all decathected energy returns to it. Narcissism is thus the condition of all our affective withdrawals and, as we shall repeat further on, of sublimation as well. Thus Freud goes so far as to state that object-choice itself bears the indelible mark of narcissism. All our love-objects, he maintains, are patterned on two archaic objects, the mother who bore us, nursed and cared for us, and our own body;

anaclitic choice or narcissistic choice, our desire has, so to speak, no other choice. Narcissism itself, in its primary form, is always hidden behind its innumerable symptoms (perversion, the schizophrenic's loss of interest, the omnipotence of thought on the part of primitives and children, the withdrawal of the sick person back into his threatened ego, the withdrawal into sleep, the swelling of the ego in hypochondria); one has the impression that if it were possible to pinpoint the nucleus of this *Versagung*, this withdrawal of the ego that shuns and refuses the risk of loving, one would have the key to many fantasy formations in which arises what might be called an egotistic archaism. But primary narcissism is always more deeply embedded than all the secondary narcissisms; the latter are like sedimentations deposited upon an ancient substrate.

It is now possible to move from the circle of the restricted archeology to that of the generalized archeology. As we have shown in Part II of the "Analytic," Freud's entire theory of culture may be regarded as an analogical extension, starting from the initial core formed by the interpretation of dreams and the neuroses. However, as this generalization was the occasion for a doctrinal renovation, manifested particularly in the second topography, the lines of Freud's archeology can be followed in the transformations of the theory.

Insofar as ideals and illusions are the analogues of dreams and neurotic symptoms, it is evident that any psychoanalytic interpretation of culture is an archeology. The genius of Freudianism is to have unmasked the strategy of the pleasure principle, the archaic form of the human, under its rationalizations, its idealizations, its sublimations. Here the function of analysis is to reduce apparent novelty by showing that it is actually a revival of the old: substitute satisfaction, restoration of the lost archaic object, derivatives from early fantasies—these are but various names to designate the restoration of the old in the features of the new. It is obviously in the critique of religion that this archeological character of Freudianism culminates. Under the heading of "the return of the repressed" Freud discerned what might be called an archaism of culture, thus extending the dream archaism into the sublime reaches of the mind. The later works, *The Future of an Illusion, Civilization and Its Discontents,* and *Moses and Monotheism,* strongly emphasize the regressive tendency of the history of mankind. Far from becoming less pronounced, the archeological character of Freudianism has grown progressively stronger.

By no means do I claim that Freudianism reduces itself to this denunciation of cultural archaism; in the next chapter I hope to show that the psychoanalytic interpretation of culture contains not only a highly thematized archeology but also an implicit teleology. But before proposing a more dialectical interpretation of the structure of Freudianism, we can profitably dwell on this one-sided interpretation which emphasizes the critical rather than the dialectical aspects of the doctrine. As a first approximation, it may be said that Freudianism is a reductive interpretation, an interpretation by way of reductive equations, the extreme example of which is the famous formula about religion: religion is the universal obsessional neurosis of mankind. One should not be in a hurry to correct this reductive hermeneutics but should rather stay with it, for it will not be suppressed, but retained, in a more comprehensive hermeneutics (see the last chapter).

The second topography expresses this generalized archeology in its own way by adding to the archaism of the id another archaism, that of the superego. Nor do I claim that the notion of the superego reduces itself to an archeological theme; on the contrary, the theory of identification expresses the progressive and structuring aspect of that agency. But one would not understand the difficulties involved in this theory of identification if one did not keep present in mind the archaic substrate upon which it arises and the archaizing characteristics of the "father complex," to use Freud's terminology again. The father complex has indeed a double valency: on the one hand it forces one to abandon the position of infancy, and thus it functions as law; but at the same time it holds any subsequent formation of ideals within the network of dependence, fear, prevention of punishment, desire of consolation. It is against the background of the archaism of a figure irremediably attached to our infancy that we must overcome, each in his own turn, the archaism of our desire. One would fail to grasp, therefore, the specificity of the Freudian interpretation of morality if one passed too quickly over these archaic features of the superego.

Freud brings this archaism to light when he calls the superego a "precipitate" of lost objects, and when he states that as such, it reaches more deeply into the id than does the perceptual system of the conscious ego. There is a sort of complicity here between two archaisms that gives rise to what Freud calls the internal world, as contrasted with the external world of which the ego is the representative. Let us group together the characteristics of this archaism. We recall that on a purely descriptive plane the conscience of the normal man is approached through a pathological model; the latter, far from disqualifying the description of moral phenomena, enables one to reach them from their inauthentic side. The ego is observed, condemned, mistreated—these are the images or figures that allowed us to say that Freud adds a pathology of duty to what Kant called the pathology of desire. The moral man is first of all an alienated man subject to the law of a foreign master, *just as* he is subject to the law of desire and the law of reality; the apologue of the three masters, at the end of *The Ego and the Id,* is very instructive here. Thus interpretation has not changed its purpose in moving from the oneiric to the sublime: interpretation still consists in unmasking; the superego, because it remains my "other" within myself, must be deciphered. A foreigner, it remains foreign; interpretation has changed its object, but not its purpose or aim. In addition to the exploration of the hidden desires disguised in dreams and their analogues, its function is to unmask the nonprimal or nonprimitive sources of the ego, its foreign and alienating sources. This is the positive gain of a method of exploration that excludes at the start any self-positing of the self, any primal interiority, any irreducible core.

The recourse to a genetic explanation confirms and further emphasizes the archaic features of the ethical world. In Freudianism genesis takes the place of ground; the internal agency of morality derives from an internalized external threat. The same emotional core, that of the Oedipus complex, lies at the origin of neurosis and culture; each man, and the whole of mankind viewed as a single man, bears the scar of a prehistory carefully obliterated by amnesia, a very ancient history of incest and parricide.

The Oedipus episode symbolizes, of course, the achieving of culture, the transition to institutions. But this victory over brute desire bears the archaic marks of fear; it is a giving-up of the object, but under the aegis of fear. The primitive scene to which *Totem and Taboo* assigns the origin of morality is a barbarous history that plunges the sublime into cruelty. From this point on, Freud is fully convinced that our morality preserves the main features that he finds in taboo, namely the ambivalence of desire and fear, fascination and terror. The psychopathology of taboo, which relates taboo to the clinical phenomenon of obsessional neurosis, extends into the Kantian imperative.

I regard this critique of moral alienation as an extraordinary contribution to the critique of "existence under the law," begun by St. Paul, continued by Luther and Kierkegaard, and taken up again in a different manner by Nietzsche. Freud's contribution here consists in his discovery of a fundamental structure of ethical life, namely a first stratum of morality that has the function both of preparing the way for autonomy and of retarding it, of blocking it off at an archaic stage. The inner tyrant plays the role of premorality and antimorality. It is the ethical moment in its dimension of non-creative sedimentation; it is tradition, so far as tradition founds and obstructs moral invention. Each of us is brought into his humanity by this agency of the ideal, but at the same time is drawn back to his own childhood, which is seen as a situation that can never be surpassed. Later I will speak about the problems raised by the fact of social institution as such: the quasi-Hegelian traits which we shall then decipher in the theory of identification must not make us lose sight of the fact that if institutions are always the other of desire, it is because of desire and fear that we are from the outset and for the most part placed in a position of alienating dependence with respect to that law which St. Paul said is "holy and good" in itself.

The metapsychology tries to account for this hidden relationship between the superego and the id. This metapsychology tries to relate the internalization of a foreign authority to the differentiation of desire itself. Its problem is this: How is the sublime brought about within desire? Hence we are not surprised to see Freud compare in various ways the superego and the id. At times he regards the process of idealization as a way of retaining the narcissistic perfection of childhood by displacing it onto an idealized self-image (the ideal ego of the paper "On Narcissism"); thus our better self or ego is, in a certain way, in line with the false Cogito, the abortive Cogito. At times it is in identification itself, the structuring process par excellence, as we shall say further on, that Freud sees a narcissistic component, as in every process of internalization, through which a lost object prolongs its existence within the ego. At times he recalls the ancestry of identification, starting from the oral stage of the libido (in that far-off time when to love was to devour). An important text in *The Ego and the Id*[30] expressly ties together, from the economic point of view, sublimation, identification, and narcissistic regression.

Thus the Oedipus complex represents both a severance in desire —the severance figuratively represented by castration—and the affective continuity between the economics of the law and that of desire. This continuity is what makes it possible to work out an economics of the superego:

> The derivation of the superego from the first object-cathexes of the id, from the Oedipus complex . . . brings it into relation with the phylogenetic acquisitions of the id and makes it a reincarnation of former ego-structures which have left their precipitates behind in the id. Thus the superego is always close to the id and can act as its representative vis-à-vis the ego. It reaches deep down into the id and for that reason is farther from consciousness than the ego is.[31]

All the additions Freud subsequently makes to this economics of the superego, in particular to account for its severity and cruelty, further emphasize its archaizing traits. The superego is a precipitate of identification, hence of abandoned objects, but it is a precipitate that has the remarkable power of turning back against its own instinctual basis. In order to account for this reactive character of the superego Freud will emphasize, in "The Dissolution of the Oedipus Complex," the role of the fear of castration during the period of the "destruction" of the complex; thus the overcoming of the Oedipus

30. Cf. above, pp. 223–25 and n. 85.
31. Cf. above, p. 225 and n. 90.

situation, the main task in the accession to culture, is not at all an escape from the pleasure principle, but is rather its preservation, since it is in order to save its narcissism that the child's ego, under the threat of castration, turns away from the Oedipus complex. Finally, the introduction of the concept of "moral masochism" in "The Economic Problem of Masochism" will make the cruelty of the superego into a representative of the death instinct, interpreted as the impulse of destruction. This "mortifying" component, in the proper sense of the term, is the final element discerned by Freud in the economics of the superego; perhaps it is also the very signature of its archaism.

The death instinct is not simply one out of many archaic figures, but rather the archaic index of all the instincts and of the pleasure principle itself. We should not forget that the death instinct was introduced to begin with in order to account for a peculiar situation in therapy—the resistance to being cured, the impulse to repeat the original traumatic situation instead of raising it to the rank of memory. The function of repetition is thus seen to be more primitive than the function of destruction in the death instinct. Or rather, destruction is one of the ways adopted by a living substance in order to restore an earlier, inorganic state of things. In this regard the statements of the *New Introductory Lectures* are more striking than the ones we took from *Beyond the Pleasure Principle*. The tendency of life to destroy itself appears so primeval that Freud ventures to write that "masochism [self-destructiveness] is older than sadism [destruction of the other]"[32] and that all the instincts aim at restoring an earlier state of things by provoking a process akin to the automatism of repetition: embryology is nothing but a compulsion to repeat. By thus affirming the "conservative nature of the instincts," Freud places death within life, the return to the inorganic within the very furtherance of the organic. Thus the hypotheses of *Beyond the Pleasure Principle* were not simply "heuristic notions," but a profound insight into the nature of things:

> If it is true that—at some immeasurably remote time and in a manner we cannot conceive—life once proceeded out of inor-

32. *New Introductory Lectures*, *GW*, *15*, 112; *SE*, *22*, 105.

> ganic matter, then, according to our presumption, an instinct must have arisen which sought to do away with life once more and to re-establish the inorganic state. If we recognize in this instinct the self-destructiveness of our hypothesis, we may regard the self-destructiveness as an expression of a "death instinct" which cannot fail to be present in every vital process.[33]

It seems to me there exists a mutual harmony and a close affinity between this theme of death-dealing repetition, introduced into the theory at a late date, and all the other forms of archaism. Repetition was already a theme during the period of *The Interpretation of Dreams,* when analysis discovered, beneath the disguises of dreams, "our earliest wishes," "the indestructibility of desire"; repetition is again expressed in all the returns, sublime or not, to narcissism; from *Totem and Taboo* to *Moses and Monotheism* the theme is repetition: man is drawn backward by an agency that constantly draws him away from his childhood desires. The process of temporalization, in which the conscious system ultimately consists, unfolds in a direction opposite to a timelessness which is instinctual in nature, or rather, as *Beyond the Pleasure Principle* would put it, in opposition to an impulse that may be correctly described as detemporalizing. Such is no doubt the most striking transcription we can make of that "battle of the giants" which Freud places under the double emblem of Eros and death. If one interrelates all these modalities of archaism, there is formed the complex figure of a destiny in reverse, a destiny that draws one backward; never before had a doctrine so coherently revealed the disquieting consistency of this complex situation.

ARCHEOLOGY AND REFLECTIVE PHILOSOPHY

We have reached the extreme point of self-estrangement in our own archeology by making use, as Plato would say, of a "bastard reasoning" in order to express the other of oneself within oneself. The philosophical question now arises: Can

33. Ibid., *GW, 15,* 114; *SE, 22,* 107.

we understand this archeology within the framework of a philosophy of reflection? To ask this question is to raise the question of the ultimate meaning of the economic point of view.

This implicit philosophy of our timeless, immortal, indestructible desires justifies not only the realist traits of the topography, but also the naturalistic traits of the economics, and ultimately the differentiation of the economic point of view from the topographic point of view. We recall the difficulties encountered in interpreting the texts concerning the separation of the economic from the topographic point of view. We expressly related this question to that of the peculiar fate or vicissitude of the affective representatives of an instinct; it is when that fate no longer coincides with the fate of the ideational representatives that the economic point of view is truly an addition to the topographic point of view, as is shown in the paper "Repression" and in Section III of "The Unconscious." We followed Freud to the point where the theory of the unconscious seems to swing to the side of a pure economics, with its complex interplay of cathexis (investment), withdrawal of cathexis, anticathexis, and hypercathexis. This movement toward the purely instinctual seemed to us to be a movement toward the presignifying, or even the nonsignifying: "The nucleus of the *Ucs.*," says Freud, "consists of instinctual representatives which seek to discharge their cathexis; that is to say, it consists of wishful impulses [*Wunschregungen*]." And again, "In the *Ucs.* there are only contents, cathected with greater or lesser strength"; the "fate [of the unconscious processes] depends only on how strong they are and on whether they fulfill the demands of the pleasure-unpleasure regulation." [34]

We can now understand, in the context of the archeology of the subject, this problematic of the "affective representatives" as distinct from that of the "ideational representatives"; psychoanalysis is the borderline knowledge of that which, in representation, does not pass into ideas. That which is represented in affects and which does not pass into ideas is desire qua desire. The fact that the economic point of view cannot be reduced to a simple topography shows that the unconscious is not fundamentally language, but only a drive to-

34. "The Unconscious," *GW, 10,* 286; *SE, 14,* 187.

ward language. The "quantitative" is the mute, the nonspoken and the nonspeaking, the unnameable at the root of speech. But in order to speak this muteness, psychoanalysis has only the energy metaphor of charge and discharge, and the capitalist metaphor of placement and investment (cathexis), along with the whole series of their variants. That which, in the unconscious, is capable of speaking, that which is able to be represented, refers back to a substrate that cannot be symbolized: desire as desire. This is the limit the unconscious imposes upon any linguistic transcription that would claim to be without remainder.

Now this regressive movement—well deserving the name of *analysis*—toward the presignifying and the nonsignifying would itself be meaningless unless it were coupled with a problematic of the subject; what this regression designates is precisely the *sum* of the Cogito. Just as the "relinquishing" of consiousness in a topography is intelligible only because of the possibility of a "recapture" in the act of becoming conscious, so too a pure economics of desire is intelligible only as the possibility of recognizing the emergence of desire in the series of its derivatives, in the density and at the borderline of the signifying.

I will try to bring out the intelligibility of this function of desire, at the origin of language and prior to language, by using a comparison taken from the history of philosophy. The priority of instincts to ideas and the irreducibility of affects to ideas are related to a problematic which, without being dominant, is by no means uncommon in the course of our rationalist tradition. The question is shared by all the philosophers who have tried to interrelate the modes of knowledge and the modes of desire and effort. Several great names stand out in this tradition as we look back in reverse chronological order. Thus Nietzsche tries to root values in the will as points of view or perspectives, and to treat them as signs either of resentment or of authentic power. Still more clearly, Freud's problem is Schopenhauer's in *The World as Will and Idea*. But the question has a longer history: it is present in Spinoza, and even more so in Leibniz. Book III of the *Ethics* coordinates the problematic of ideas with that of effort or endeavor. Proposition VI: "Everything, insofar as it is, endeavors to persist in its own being." Proposition

IX: "The mind, both insofar as it has clear and distinct ideas, and also insofar as it has confused ideas, endeavors to persist in its being for an indefinite period, and it is conscious of this endeavor." Proposition XI: "Whatever increases or diminishes, helps or hinders the power of activity in our body, the idea thereof increases or diminishes, helps or hinders the power of thought in our mind." Finally, for Spinoza, the correlation between idea and endeavor is based on the very definition of the mind (*mens*) as the necessary perception of the affections of the body.[35]

But perhaps the one who most clearly prefigures Freud is Leibniz: the Leibnizian equivalent of the function of *Repräsentanz* is the concept of "expression." It is well known that the monad expresses the universe and in this sense perceives it. Expression is not a function solely of monads endowed with reflection, nor even of monads that have consciousness. Every monad perceives, i.e. every being that is one per se and not a mere aggregate. In his correspondence with Arnauld, Leibniz states that the function of expression is common to all forms or souls; expression, therefore, is not defined by a conscious act. More fundamental than consciousness itself is the power of concentrating a diversity within a single act that somehow actively mirrors that diversity. One can even point out the various levels of this power, down to the mineral state.[36] Thus Leibniz's philosophy is better able than Descartes' to incorporate the notion of the unconscious. The *Monadology* states:

> The passing state which involves and represents a multiplicity in the unity or simple substance is nothing but what is called perception; it must be clearly distinguished from apperception or consciousness, as will be seen later on. In this matter the Cartesians have fallen into a serious error, in that they have treated as nonexistent those perceptions which we do not apperceive. (Art. 14)

But there is another aspect of expression: "The action of the internal principle which brings about the change or passage from one perception to another may be called *appetition*. It is true that appe-

35. *Ethics*, Book II, Propositions XII, XVI, XXIII.
36. Cf. *New Essays*, Book II, Ch. 9.

tite may not always entirely attain the whole perception toward which it tends, but it always obtains something of it and arrives at new perceptions" (Art. 15). Thus the notion of soul gets its general definition from the relationship between perception and effort: because of perception, all effort becomes representative of a multiplicity in a unity; because of effort, all perception tends toward further distinctness.

Leibniz thus throws light on a double law of representation: as standing for objects or things, representation is pretension to truth; but it is also the expression of life, expression of effort or appetite. When the second function interferes with the first there arises the problem of illusion; but distortion (*Entstellung*), which served as the title for the various mechanisms of the dream-work (displacement, condensation, pictorial representation), is already included in this overall function of expressivity. Thus the problem posed in the Freudian metapsychology of the relation between representation and instincts goes far beyond the case of psychoanalysis.

But if the basic problem raised by Freud's economic point of view is not completely new, it does retain with respect to Spinoza and Leibniz an undeniable originality. This originality consists entirely in the role played by the barrier between the systems. Spinoza and Leibniz were well aware that effort and ideas, appetition and perception, are bound together on the hither side of consciousness: the mind in Spinoza is the idea of the body prior to being the idea of itself; and in Leibniz perception can operate without apperception. The Freudian paradox of instinctual representatives, especially in the form of affects, consists in the fact that the reflective grasp of this bond is not possible in the direct form of mere conscious awareness; here, the prereflective is inability to reflect. Thus, to find the Freudian equivalent of that increase of power that for Spinoza and Leibniz was the passage from the idea of the body to the idea of the idea or from perception to apperception, one must look to the whole group of procedures listed under the heading of the psychoanalytic technique. This mediating technique does not radically alter the structural problem. The detour through another consciousness, through work or "working-through" (*Durcharbeitung*), which we have commented on above, does not eliminate the structural continuity between the unconscious and consciousness nor between instinctual representatives and ideas. That is why affects, even when split off from ideas, are still called instinctual representatives. Their function of representing the body in the mind gives them a psychical status. Taking up the theory of affects in our present reflective language we shall say this: if desire is the unnameable, it is turned from the very outset toward language; it wishes to be expressed; it is in potency to speech. What makes desire the limit concept at the frontier between the organic and the psychical is the fact that desire is both the nonspoken and the wish-to-speak, the unnameable and the potency to speak.

And did not Leibniz say the same thing, in writing on appetition: ". . . appetite may not always entirely attain the whole perception toward which it tends, but it always obtains something of it and arrives at new perceptions" ? [37]

What is an existent that has an archeology? The answer seemed easy prior to Freud: it is a being who was a child before being a man. But we still do not know what that means. The positing of desire, the unsurpassable character of life—these are expressions that invite us onward, to a greater depth.

The first thing to be reexamined is the status of representation in a concrete anthropology. We proposed placing this status under the laws of a twofold expressivity; representation obeys not only a law of intentionality, which makes it the expression of some object, but also another law, which makes it the manifestation of life, of an effort or desire. It is because of the interference of the latter expressive function that representation can be distorted. Thus representation may be investigated in two ways: on the one hand, by a gnoseology (or criteriology) according to which representation is viewed as an intentional relation ruled by the objects that manifest themselves in that intentionality, and on the other hand by an exegesis of the desires that lie hidden in that intentionality. Consequently a theory of knowledge is abstract, for it is constituted by a sort of

37. *Monadology*, Art. 15. On the meaning of desire, cf. J. Lacan, "Le Désir et ses interprétations," Séminaire 1958–59, *Bull. de psych.* (Jan., 1960); Norman O. Brown, *Life Against Death* (London, Routledge and Paul, 1959); Herbert Marcuse, *Eros and Civilization*.

reduction of the appetition that governs the passing from one perception to another. Inversely, a reductive hermeneutics, bent on exploring only the expressions of desire, proceeds from an opposite reduction, but one that at least has the value of being a protest against the abstract nature of theory of knowledge and its alleged purity. This reduction of the act of knowing as such attests to the nonautonomy of knowledge, its rootedness in existence, the latter being understood as desire and effort. Thereby is discovered not only the unsurpassable nature of life, but the interference of desire with intentionality, upon which desire inflicts an invincible obscurity, an ineluctable partiality. Thereby, finally, is confirmed truth's character of being a task: truth remains an Idea, an infinite Idea, for a being who originates as desire and effort, or, to use Freud's language, as invincibly narcissistic libido.

I rejoin, moreover, the conclusions of my *Philosophy of Will,* in *The Voluntary and the Involuntary*. In that work I said that character, the unconscious, life, are figures of the absolute involuntary; they assure me that my freedom is a "mere human freedom," [38] that is, a motivated, incarnate, contingent freedom. I posit myself as already posited in my desire to be. In such positing, "to will is not to create." [39] I still affirm these conclusions today, but I go beyond them in a decisive point, the one that gave rise to the entire research of this book. A hermeneutic method, coupled with reflection, goes much farther than an eidetic method I was then practicing. The dependence of the Cogito on the positing of desire is not directly grasped in immediate experience, but interpreted by another consciousness in the seemingly senseless signs offered to interlocution. It is not at all a felt or perceived dependence, but rather a deciphered dependence, interpreted through dreams, fantasies, and myths, which constitute somehow the indirect discourse of that mute darkness. The rootedness of reflection in life is itself understood in reflective consciousness only in the form of a hermeneutic truth.

38. *Le Volontaire et l'involontaire*, pp. 453 ff.; Eng. trans., pp. 482 ff.
39. Ibid.

Chapter 3: Dialectic: Archeology and Teleology

Does the philosophical repetition of Freudianism find completion in a philosophy of reflection? To understand Freudianism, is it enough simply to relate it to this philosophy of reflection through the mediating concept of archeology?

The second question is the key to the first. It seems to me that the concept of an archeology of the subject remains very abstract so long as it has not been set in a relationship of dialectical opposition to the complementary concept of teleology. In order to have an *archê* a subject must have a *telos*. If I understood this relationship between archeology and teleology, I would understand a number of things. First of all I would understand that my notion of reflection is itself abstract as long as this new dialectic has not been integrated into it. The subject, we said above, is never the subject one supposes. But if the subject is to attain to its true being, it is not enough for it to discover the inadequacy of its self-awareness, or even to discover the power of desire that posits it in existence. The subject must also discover that the process of "becoming conscious," through which it *appropriates* the meaning of its existence as desire and effort, does not belong to it, but belongs to the *meaning* that is formed in it. The subject must mediate self-consciousness through spirit or mind, that is, through the figures that give a telos to this "becoming conscious." The proposition that there is no archeology of the subject except in contrast to a teleology leads to a further proposition: there is no teleology except through the figures of the mind, that is to say, through a new decentering, a new dispossession, which I call spirit or mind, just as I used the term "unconscious" to designate the locus of that other displacement of the origin of meaning back into my past.

If I understand this connection, at the heart of a philosophy of the subject, between the subject's archeology and its teleology, i.e. between two dispossessions of consciousness, I also understand that the war between the two modes of heremeneutics, which was the main problem of our problematic, is at the point of being resolved. Seen from the outside, psychoanalysis appeared to us to be a reductive, demystifying hermeneutics. As such, it was opposed to a hermeneutics that we described as restorative, as a recollection of the sacred. We did not see, and we still do not see, the link between the two contrary modes of interpretation. We are not in a position to go beyond a mere antithetic, i.e. an opposition whose terms remain external to one another. The true philosophical basis for understanding the complementarity of these irreducible and opposed hermeneutics in relation to the mytho-poetic formations of culture is the dialectic of archeology and teleology. This resolution of the initial hermeneutic problem is therefore the horizon of our whole enterprise. However, we cannot fill out the meaning of such formulas until the present dialectic itself has been understood and seen as central to the semantics of desire.

The reader will not fail to stop us at the threshold of this chapter and object that we are stepping completely outside of a psychoanalytic problematic. Freud expressly stated that the discipline he founded is not a synthesis but an analysis—i.e. a process of breaking down into elements and of tracing back to origins—and that psychoanalysis is not to be completed by a psychosynthesis.[1] I grant the substance of the analyst's objection. But what I am undertaking is altogether different. The present meditation, even more than our investigation of the concept of archeology, is philosophical in nature. I said previously that the only way I can arrive at self-understanding in my reading of Freud is to form the notion of an archeology of the subject. I say now that the only way to understand the notion of archeology is in its dialectical relationship to a teleology. And so I search in Freud's work—in analysis as analysis—for the reference to its dialectical contrary. I hope to show that such a reference actually does exist there and that analysis is inher-

1. "Lines of Advance in Psychoanalytic Therapy" (1918), *GW, 12,* 185; *SE, 17,* 160. Cf. above, p. 412, n. 88.

ently dialectical. Thus, I do not pretend to complete Freud, but to understand him through understanding myself. I venture to think that I advance in this understanding of Freud and myself by revealing the dialectical aspects of both reflection and Freudianism.

What I wish to demonstrate, then, is that if Freudianism is an explicit and thematized archeology, it relates of itself, by the dialectical nature of its concepts, to an implicit and unthematized teleology.

In order to make this relationship between a thematized archeology and an unthematized teleology intelligible, I will make use of a detour. I propose the example—or rather the counterexample—of the Hegelian phenomenology, in which the same problems present themselves in a reverse order. *The Phenomenology of Spirit* is an explicit teleology of the achieving of consciousness and as such contains the model of every teleology of consciousness. But at the same time this teleology arises on the substrate of life and desire; thus we may say that Hegel himself acknowledges the unsurpassable character of life and desire, in spite of the fact that this unsurpassable is always already surpassed in spirit and in truth. In using this detour, I do not at all intend to set Freud within Hegel and Hegel within Freud and to mix everything up. The problematics are too different to shuffle the cards in that way. Moreover, I am too much of the opinion that all the great philosophies contain the same things, but in a different order, to entertain the foolish idea of stringing them together in a facile but absurd eclecticism. My enterprise differs as much as possible from such an eclecticism. Hegel and Freud each stand as a separate continent, and between one totality and another there can only be relations of homology. I will try to express one of these homologous relations by discovering in Freudianism a certain dialectic of archeology and teleology that is clearly evident in Hegel. The same connection is in Freud, but in a reverse order and proportion. Whereas Hegel links an explicit teleology of mind or spirit to an implicit archeology of life and desire, Freud links a thematized archeology of the unconscious to an unthematized teleology of the process of becoming conscious. I do not confuse Hegel with Freud, but I seek to find in Freud an inverted image of Hegel, in order to discern, with the help of this schema, certain dialectical features which, though obviously operative in analytic practice, have not found in the theory a complete systematic elaboration.[2]

A TELEOLOGICAL MODEL OF CONSCIOUSNESS: THE HEGELIAN PHENOMENOLOGY

What Hegel offers for reflection is a phenomenology, not of consciousness, but of spirit or mind. Let us understand by this a description of the figures, categories, or symbols that guide the developmental process along the lines of a progressive synthesis. This indirect method is more fruitful than a direct developmental psychology;[3] the development of consciousness occurs at the point of juncture of two systems of interpretation. The phenomenology of mind engenders a new hermeneutics that shifts the center of meaning no less than psychoanalysis does. The genesis of meaning does not proceed from consciousness; rather, there dwells in consciousness a movement that mediates it and raises its certitude to truth. Here too consciousness is intelligible to itself only if it allows itself to be set off-center. Spirit or *Geist* is this move-

2. This entire chapter is an internal discussion or debate with Herbert Marcuse, *Eros and Civilization*, J. C. Flugel, *Man, Morals and Society;* and Philipp Rieff, *Freud, the Mind of the Moralist*. It will also confront the views of Marthe Robert, *La Révolution psychanalytique* (Payot, 1964).

3. At first glance, it would seem that the process of becoming conscious is a simple problem, which we needlessly complicate by loading psychology down with an unwieldy conceptual apparatus. Certainly consciousness is not a given but a task—in economic terms, a work or "reworking" of all the relevant forces. Is not the transition from infancy to adult life sufficiently accounted for by a psychology of personality, or by what the various neo-Freudian schools have called ego-analysis? I make no secret of my mistrust of these corrections that transform psychoanalysis into an eclectic system. I do not know whether these additions give the analyst more insight; they certainly mask the theoretical problem, which Freud himself was clearly aware of. A dialectic that derives its clarity from opposition is always preferable to a patchwork eclecticism based on an unprincipled empiricism; moreover, these new aspects of psychoanalysis will perhaps be expressed with greater force if they are regarded as the dialectical product of the two opposed approaches. Consequently, I will not first look for the meaning of the psychological process of growth or maturation in a psychology of personality or an ego-analysis, but in a new kind of phenomenology.

ment, this dialectic of figures, which makes consciousness into "self-consciousness," into "reason," and which, with the help of the circular movement of the dialectic, finally reaffirms immediate consciousness, but in the light of the complete process of mediation. The dispossession comes first, the reaffirmation only at the end; what is essential occurs between the two, namely, the whole movement through the constellation of figures: master and slave, the stoic exile of thought, skeptical indifference, the unhappy consciousness, the service of the devoted mind, the observation of nature, the spirit as light, etc. Man becomes adult, becomes conscious, by assuming these new forms or figures which serially constitute "spirit" in the Hegelian sense of the term. For example (an unjustified example if taken in isolation from the total movement), when spirit passes through the dialectic of master and slave, consciousness enters the process of self-recognition in another, it is doubled and becomes a self; thus all the degrees of recognition bring about a movement through regions of meaning irreducible in principle to mere projections of instinct, to "illusions." An exegesis of consciousness would consist in a progression through all the spheres of meaning that a given consciousness must encounter and appropriate in order to reflect itself as a self, a human, adult, conscious self. This process has nothing to do with introspection; nor is it in any way a "narcissism," since the home or center of the self is not the psychological ego, but rather what Hegel calls spirit, i.e. the dialectic of the figures themselves. Consciousness is simply the internalization of this movement, which must be recaptured in the objective structures of institutions, monuments, works of art and culture.

In the next chapter, I will speak of the present-day significance of this Hegelian metapsychology, which I propose to confront with Freud's in order to understand each through the other. I do not think that we can, after more than a century, restore *The Phenomenology of Spirit* as it was written; but it seems to me that we should take as our guide, in any new enterprise of the same style, the two leading themes that characterize a phenomenology of spirit.

The first theme concerns the cast or form of the Hegelian dialectic. This dialectic constitutes a progressive synthetic movement, which contrasts with the analytic character of psychoanalysis and the "regressive" (in the technical sense of the word) character of its economic interpretation. In the Hegelian phenomenology, each form or figure receives its meaning from the subsequent one. Thus, the truth of the recognition of the master-slave relationship is stoicism; but the truth of the stoic position is skepticism, which views the differences between master and slave as unessential and annihilates all such distinctions. The truth of a given moment lies in the subsequent moment; meaning always proceeds retrogressively. Several consequences are connected with this first rule of reading. It is by reason of this retrogressive movement of the true that phenomenology is possible. If phenomenology does not create but only makes meaning explicit as meaning discloses itself, it is because the later meaning is immanent in each of its anterior moments. Hence phenomenology can make this later meaning explicit by examining the prior meaning; the philosopher can pattern himself on what *appears*, he can be a phenomenologist. But if he can state what appears, it is because he sees it in the light of the later forms or figures. This advance of spirit or mind upon itself constitutes the truth, unknown to itself, of the anterior figures; this trait characterizes this phenomenology as a phenomenology of spirit and not of consciousness. For the same reason, the consciousness thus revealed is by no means the consciousness that precedes this dialectical movement. In *The Phenomenology of Spirit* Hegel uses the word consciousness to denote the mere manifestation of the being of the world for a witness who is not reflectively aware of self. Before self-consciousness, consciousness is simply the manifestation of the world.

This first trait, concerning the form of the Hegelian phenomenology, governs the second, which concerns its content (in Hegel the form of the dialectic cannot be separated from its content, for the dialectic is the self-production of the content). The second trait may be stated as follows. In such a phenomenology it is a question of the production of the self (*Selbst*), the self of self-consciousness. When I say that the first trait is the key to the second, I mean that the positing or emergence of the self is inseparable from its production through a progressive synthesis; hence the self does not and cannot figure in a topography; it cannot appear among the vicissitudes of instincts which constitute the theme of the economics.

Let us examine more closely how the self shows itself and appears in *The Phenomenology of Spirit.* It should be noted that the self already prefigures itself and moves toward itself within desire—*Begierde.* On this point, Hegel and Freud agree: culture is born in the movement of desire. The points of identity may be extended quite far: in both Hegel and Freud, the abandonment or death of the object plays an essential role in the education of desire. The Hegelian master who has placed his life at stake and recovers it in the form of mastery realizes the movement Freud will describe as the behavior of mourning and the incorporation of the object within interiority. In this sense there is more than a simple encounter between the Freudian notion of identification and the Hegelian constitution of the self.

But if the one-to-one correspondences may be multiplied, the direction of the genesis is quite different. We have seen that in Freud's view any sublimation that brings out new aims, essentially social aims, must be understood economically as a return from object-libido to narcissistic libido. In Hegel's view, spirit is the truth of life, a truth that is not yet aware of itself in the emergence of desire, but which becomes self-reflective in the life process of becoming conscious. "In this process of becoming conscious," says Jean Hyppolite, self-consciousness is "the origin of a truth which is both for-itself and in-itself, a truth which is constituted in a history through the mediation of different self-consciousnesses, whose interaction and unity constitute spirit." [4] *Unruhigkeit,* the "restlessness" of life, is not at first defined as drive and impulse, but as noncoincidence with one's self; this restlessness already contains within itself the negativity that makes it other and which, in making it to be other, makes it be self. Negation properly belongs to such restlessness. Thus Hegel can say that life is the self, but in an immediate form—the self in itself—which only knows itself in reflection where the self is finally for itself. The light of life, to use the language of St. John, reveals itself in life and through life, but self-consciousness remains nonetheless the birthplace of truth and first of all the truth of life. The Hegelian philosophy of desire derives all its mean-

4. *Genèse et structure de la Phénoménologie de l'Esprit de Hegel* (Paris, Aubier, 1946), *I*, 144.

ing from this recurrent movement of the true, for if one may say that self-consciousness is desire, it is because desire is already illuminated by the dialectic of the reduplication of consciousness into two rival consciousnesses. The earlier dialectic of desire has its truth in the light of the later dialectic of master and slave. Desire is revealed as *human* desire only when it is desire for the desire of another consciousness. The duality of these living self-consciousnesses foreshadows in an external manner the subsequent duplication of self-consciousness within itself; ultimately, "the unhappy consciousness" will be pure self-division. Thus, there is no intelligibility proper to desire as such; the light of life arises only when self-consciousness, in advance upon itself, posits itself as desire. Starting from simple consciousness as the manifestation of the otherness of the world, self-consciousness posits itself as desire and thus takes the pathway of the return into self. In this movement things are no longer mere objects, but a disappearing appearance; and in this disappearance, consciousness with its desires appears to itself. But what is the object of its desire? What it is seeking, with the help of this withdrawal from the sensible world—a withdrawal henceforth related to the unity of self-consciousness with itself—is itself. But it will reach itself only through its relation with another desire, another self-consciousness. In commenting on this difficult passage, Hyppolite refers to a "dialectical teleology" : [5] "The dialectical teleology of the *Phenomenology* gradually unfolds all the horizons of this desire which is the essence of self-consciousness." [6] The desire of self disengages itself from the desire of things by seeking itself in the other. Ultimately, such desire is man's desire to be recognized by man—a desire made explicit only after it has anticipated itself. This anticipation enables Hegel to state that "through such reflection into itself the sensible object has become life"; the reflective mark that distinguishes the object of desire, as something living, from the mere perceived object cannot be generated by mere evolution from the earlier to the later. Consequently, when Hegel discovers in the otherness of desire the intending toward another desire, toward another desiring consciousness that is both object

5. Ibid., p. 155.
6. Ibid.

and self-consciousness, he unequivocally states that we already possess, as philosophers in advance of the movement, the notion of spirit.

The phenomenology of desire, which we have considered at some length because of its affinities with Freudian theory, is the complete contrary of a genesis of the higher from the lower; it consists rather in presenting the meaning and conditions of desire as these appear in the later moments. Desire is desire only if life manifests itself as another desire; and this certainty in turn has its truth in the double process of reflection, the reduplication of self-consciousness. This reduplication is the condition for the emergence of self-consciousness in the midst of life. Reflection can be creative, for each moment includes in its certainty an element of the not-known that all the later moments mediate and make explicit. That is why Hegel links the concept of infinitude to this work of mutual recognition: the concept of self-consciousness, he says, is the concept "of infinitude realizing itself in and through consciousness." The opposition in which each consciousness seeks itself in the other and "does what it does only so far as the other does the same" [7] is an infinite movement, in the sense that each term goes beyond its own limits and becomes the other. We recognize here the notion of Unruhigkeit, the restlessness of life, but raised to the reflective degree through opposition and struggle; it is only in this struggle for recognition that the self reveals itself as never being simply what it is—and therefore as being infinite.

If the Phenomenology of Spirit were only a teleology, as might seem to be the case from the present meditation, and if psychoanalysis were simply an archeology, as the previous study may have suggested, the two approaches would be antithetical to one another. Freudian psychoanalysis and Hegelian phenomenology would together form what we could call an antithetic of reflection. (I take "antithetic" in the sense given the term by Kant in his investigation of the antinomies: viz. a nonmediated opposition, one that either cannot be, or has not yet been, mediated.) This phase of thought,

7. Hegel, *La Phénoménologie de l'esprit*, tr. J. Hyppolite (Paris, Aubier, 1939), *I*, 157; tr. J. Baillie, *The Phenomenology of Mind* (rev. 2d ed. London, 1931), p. 230.

though provisional, is instructive, for the only thing that fully manifests the archeological character of Freudian thought is the contrast with a teleology. The contrast with Hegel reveals in Freud a strange and profound philosophy of fate that is the necessary counterpart of the phenomenology of spirit aimed at the future absolute of total discourse. Archaism of the id and archaism of the superego, archaism of narcissism and archaism of the death instinct form a single archaism as contrasted with the contrary movement of spirit. The antithesis may be summed up in the following terms. Spirit has its meaning in later forms or figures; it is a movement that always destroys its starting point and is secured only at the end. The unconscious, on the other hand, means that intelligibility always proceeds from earlier figures, whether this anteriority is understood in a strictly temporal or in a metaphorical sense. Man is the sole being at the mercy of childhood; he is a creature constantly dragged backward by his childhood. Even if we soften the excessively historical character of this interpretation based on the past, we are still faced with a symbolic anteriority. If we interpret the unconscious as the realm of pregiven key signifiers, this anteriority of the key signifiers as compared with all the temporally interpreted events presents us with a more symbolic notion of anteriority, but it still stands as a counterpole to the inverse realm of spirit. In general terms, spirit is the realm of the terminal; the unconscious, the realm of the primordial. To put the antithesis most concisely, I will say that spirit is history and the unconscious is fate—the early fate of childhood, the early fate of symbolisms, pregiven and repeated without end . . .

THE UNSURPASSABLE CHARACTER OF LIFE AND DESIRE

But we must go beyond this antithetic. The danger is that it will lead to a facile eclecticism in which phenomenology of spirit and psychoanalysis would in some vague manner be complementary to one another. The only way to avoid this caricature of dialectic is to show in each discipline of thought, considered in and for itself, the presence of its other. These two contrary disciplines are not external opposites but are intrinsically interrelated. What I propose to show is that Freud's problematic is in Hegel; we shall then be able to see that Hegel's problematic is in Freud.

To see Freud's problematic in Hegel is to see that the emergence or positing of desire is central to the "spiritual" process of the reduplication of consciousness and that the satisfaction of desire is inherent in the recognition of self-consciousnesses.

Let us return to the difficult transition, in *The Phenomenology of Spirit*, from life and desire to self-consciousness. I do not intend to retract anything from the interpretation I have already given of this transition, but to add to it. Can we not find, no longer outside this dialectic, but in the details of its structure, what I would like to call the unsurpassable character of life and desire? The teleology of self-consciousness does not reveal simply that life is surpassed by self-consciousness; it also reveals that life and desire, as initial positing, primal affirmation, immediate expansion, are forever unsurpassable. At the very heart of self-consciousness, life is that obscure density that self-consciousness, in its advance, reveals behind itself as the source of the very first differentiation of the self.

How does this unsurpassable character of life manifest itself in the sublation effected by self-consciousness? The manifestation occurs in several ways and at several levels of the dialectic of self-consciousness.

First of all it should be said that the dialectic of recognition, which follows that of desire, is not *external* to the earlier dialectic but is rather its unfolding and explicitation. The important concept that joins the two moments together is the notion of satisfaction or *Befriedigung;* it plays the part of the Freudian pleasure principle; Hegel relates it to what he calls the "pure ego." In the Hegelian text, the pure ego is the naïve self-consciousness that thinks it immediately attains itself in the suppression or sublation of the object, in the direct consumption of the object:

> The simple ego is this genus, or the bare universal, for which the differences are of no account; but it is such a genus only by being the negative essence of the moments which have assumed a defi-

> nite and independent form. Thus self-consciousness is certain of itself only through sublating this other, which is presented to self-consciousness as an independent life; self-consciousness is *desire*. Convinced of the nothingness of this other, it affirms this nothingness to be *for itself* the truth of this other, negates the independent object, and thereby acquires the certainty of its own self, as *true* certainty, a certainty which it has become aware of in *objective form*.[8]

The pure ego says: I exist, for I experience satisfaction, and in this satisfaction I see the disappearance and dissolution of that object whose solidity has been assured me by all the physics in the world.

The fruit is dissolved in enjoyment, says the poet. But it is here that desire undergoes the tantalizing experience of the resistance, rebirth, and endless flight of the ripe fruit:

> But in this satisfaction self-consciousness experiences the independence of the object. Desire and the certainty of self obtained in the satisfaction of desire, are conditioned by the object; for the satisfaction comes about through the cancelling of this other. In order that this cancelling may be effected, there must be this other. Self-consciousness is thus unable by its negative relation to the object to abolish it; because of that relation it rather produces it again, as well as the desire.[9]

Expressed in Freudian terms, the pleasure principle runs up against the reality principle. Hegel continues thus: "The essence of desire is, in fact, something other than self-consciousness."[10] In Freudian language, that which thought it was the pure ego is disclosed as foreign to itself, as anonymous and neuter, as id. It is at this point that self-consciousness discovers the other: the independence and the resistance of the object to desire cannot be overcome and satisfaction can be obtained only through the favor of an other which is another person. As the text aptly says, "Self-consciousness attains

8. Ibid., p. 152; Eng. tr., p. 225.
9. Ibid.
10. Ibid.

its satisfaction only in another self-consciousness."[11] Thus the problem of recognition does not follow upon the problem of desire in an external and extrinsic manner, but is rather the unfolding of the egoism of the ego; it is the "mediation" of that which the ego pursued as satisfaction. I would like to cite Hegel's concise text one more time:

> It is in these three moments that the notion of self-consciousness first gets completed: 1. Its first immediate object is the pure undifferentiated ego. 2. But this immediacy is itself absolute mediation; it has its being only by cancelling the independent object, in other words it is desire. The satisfaction of desire is indeed the reflection of self-consciousness into itself, it is the certainty which has become objective truth. 3. But the truth of this certainty is really twofold reflection, the reduplication of self-consciousness.[12]

Consequently the later dialectic will never do anything but mediate this immediacy given in the process of life, which is the substance constantly negated, but also constantly retained and reaffirmed. The emergence of the self will be not outside life but within it.

I find this unsurpassable positing of life and desire at all the other levels of the dialectic of the reduplication of self-consciousness. One must not forget that recognition—the spiritual phenomenon par excellence—is struggle. Struggle for recognition, certainly, and not a struggle for life, but recognition through struggle. This struggle means that the terrible reality of desire is transported into the sphere of spirit in the form of violence. No doubt the passion to achieve recognition goes beyond the animal struggle for self-preservation or domination; the concept of recognition is preeminently a noneconomic concept: the struggle for recognition is not a struggle for life; it is a struggle to tear from the other an avowal, an attestation, a proof that I am an autonomous self-consciousness. But this struggle for recognition is a struggle in life against life—by life. One may say that the notions of domination and servitude,

11. Ibid., p. 153; Eng. tr., p. 226.
12. Ibid.

which belong to the Hegelian language, are, in Freudian language, vicissitudes of instincts: domination, because it has run the risk of death and remains related to life as the enjoyment and destruction of things through the servile work of the loser of the struggle; servitude, because it has preferred immediate life to self-consciousness and has exchanged the fear of death for the security of slave existence, until work, instituting a new mode of confronting things and nature, once again gives the advantage to the slave over the master. Thus it is ever and again life and desire that obtain positivity—or more emphatically, the positional power—without which there would be neither master nor slave. It is always life operations that mark off the dialectic: to risk one's life, to exchange it—to attain satisfaction, to work. It is always the moment of nature, the otherness of life, that, in the proper sense of the word, fosters and nourishes the oppositions of each consciousness to the other than itself.

This is the sense in which desire is both surpassed and unsurpassable. The positing of desire is mediated, not eradicated; it is not a sphere that we could lay aside, annul, annihilate. The illusion of the stoic freedom of thought consists precisely in positing the identity of all reasonable beings in spite of all the differences, in elevating the identity of the emperor Marcus Aurelius and the slave Epictetus above the living and historical struggle. This liberation in mere thought leads back to absolute otherness; the struggling desires no longer have a self and the self no longer has any flesh; this is the sense in which life is unsurpassable. And the very term "self"—*Selbst*—proclaims that self-identity continues to be carried by this self-difference, by this ever-recurring otherness residing in life. It is life that becomes the other, in and through which the self ceaselessly achieves itself.

THE IMPLICIT TELEOLOGY OF FREUDIANISM: THE OPERATIVE CONCEPTS

Let us return to Freud. Psychoanalysis, we said, is an analysis, and there is no possibility of completing it by a synthesis. This cannot be challenged. I believe I can show, however, that this analysis cannot be *understood,* in its strictly "regressive" structure, except by contrast with a teleology of consciousness which does not remain external to analysis but which analysis intrinsically refers to. What, then, are the traits of this implicit teleology which we think we see in Freudian thought? Are we not getting involved in an overinterpretation of Freud? I do not deny that these traits are evident only in a reading of Freud coupled with a reading of Hegel. It is for this reason that I have sharply distinguished the successive moments of my philosophical interpretation: epistemological moment, reflective moment, dialectical moment. But I hope to show that this procedure results in a better reading of Freud and a better understanding of myself in reading Freud.

We may approach this implicit teleology through a convergence of three kinds of indications. The first lies in certain operative concepts of Freudian theory, by which I mean concepts that Freud uses but does not thematize. A second indication appears in certain concepts that are highly thematized, such as the notion of identification, but that remain out of harmony with the dominant conceptualization of psychoanalysis. Finally, an indirect indication of the teleology is present in certain problems which, though clearly belonging to the sphere of competence of psychoanalysis, remain unresolved, such as the problem of sublimation. It has seemed to me that such problems would find, if not a solution, at least a better formulation in a dialectical perspective.

Every theory contains concepts that are employed but not reflected upon in the theory itself. The elimination of such concepts would bring about a state of total reflection or absolute knowledge, which is incompatible with the finitude of knowledge. Hence it is no criticism of psychoanalysis to find in it operative concepts that, in order to be thematized, would require a conceptual framework different from that of its topography and economics.

These operative concepts, which enabled us to distinguish psychoanalysis from scientific psychology and phenomenology, are rooted in the very structure of the "psychoanalytic field," in the sense of a dual relationship of interlocution. Whereas the metapsychology thematizes an isolated psychical apparatus, or, as we have at times put it, whereas the Freudian topography is solipsistic, the analytic situation is directly intersubjective. The analytic situation does not bear merely a vague resemblance to the Hegelian dialectic of reduplicated consciousness; between that dialectic and the process of consciousness that develops in the analytic relation there is a remarkable structural homology. The entire analytic relation can be reinterpreted as a dialectic of consciousness, rising from life to self-consciousness, from the satisfaction of desire to the recognition of the other consciousness. As the decisive episode of the transference teaches us, insight or the process of becoming conscious not only entails another consciousness, the analyst's, but contains a phase of struggle reminiscent of the struggle for recognition. The process is an unequal relation in which the patient, like the slave or bondsman of the Hegelian dialectic, sees the other consciousness by turns as the essential and as the unessential; the patient likewise has his truth at first in the other, before becoming the master through a work comparable to the work of the slave, the work of the analysis. One of the signs that the analysis is ended is precisely the attainment of the equality of the two consciousnesses, when the truth in the analyst has become the truth of the sick consciousness. Then the patient is no longer alienated, no longer another: he has become a self, he has become himself. Furthermore, what occurs in the therapeutic relationship, which is a type of struggle between two consciousnesses, should lead us to something even more important: the transference—in the course of which the patient repeats, in the artificial situation of analysis, important and meaningful episodes of his affective life—assures us that the therapeutic relation acts as a mirror image in reviving a whole series of situations all of which were already intersubjective. A desire or wish, in the Freudian sense, is never a mere vital impulse, for it is from the very beginning set within an intersubjective situation. Hence we can say that all the dramas psychoanalysis discovers are located on the path that leads from "satisfaction" to "recognition." The child's desire involves his mother, then he discovers that his desire for his mother involves his father; therein lies the essence of the Oedipus conflict. The same may be said about the Oedipus conflict that Hegel said about the failure of the immediacy of desire: "but in this satisfaction, self-consciousness experiences the independence of the object." At this point the parallel between hunger and love is at an end: hunger has its object in things, love has its object in another desire. Thus all the phases of the libido are phases of the reduplication of self-consciousness. Moreover, as was intimated by the therapeutic relation itself, in each case such phases are situations in which the division of consciousnesses is not egalitarian. The child's consciousness first has its truth in the father figure, which is the child's first model or ideal; like the slave or bondsman, the child has traded—by a pact no less fictive than the one binding the slave to his master—his security for dependence. But such dependence is the means of achieving independence.[13]

How far is it possible to extend this rereading of Freud in the light of operative concepts homologous with those of Hegel's phenomenology?

A reader familiar with the philosophical mentality of Hegelianism cannot help noticing the constant use of opposition in the structure of Freud's concepts. The three successive theories of instinct are dichotomous ones: sexual (or libido) instincts versus ego-instincts; object-libido versus ego-libido; life instincts versus death instincts. It is true that a dichotomy is not necessarily a dialectic, and that in each instance the dichotomy has a different sense. But this style of opposition is intimately involved in the birth of meaning; the dichotomy is already dialectical.

In the case of the vicissitudes of instincts we have an obvious dialectical structure. Freud combines these vicissitudes into meaningful pairs: voyeurism and exhibitionism, sadism and masochism. These "reversals" and processes of "turning round" entail both a dynamics of desire and a dynamics of meaning, for it is in these vicissitudes that the subject and object are constituted in polar opposi-

13. The discussion concerning the object-relation should be placed in this dialectical field. Cf. M. Bouvet, "Le moi dans la névrose obsessionnelle. Relation d'objet et mécanisme de défense," *Rev. fr. de psychan.*, *17* (1953), 111–96; "La clinique psychanalytique. La relation d'objet," *La Psychanalyse d'aujourd'hui*, *1*, 41–121; "Dépersonnalisation et relation d'objet," *Rev. fr. de psychan.*, *24* (1960), 449–611. G. Grunberger, "Considérations sur l'oralité et la relation d'objet orale," *Rev. fr. de psychan.*, *23* (1959), 177–204; "Étude sur la relation objectale anale," *Rev. fr. de psychan.*, *24* (1960), 137–68.

tion. We may go even further and interpret the topography itself as a dialectic of "systems." What is important here is the communication or relations between the systems; and what are these relations but a further dialectic of instincts? Indeed, Freud explicitly links the constitution of the systems to one of the instinctual vicissitudes, repression. So primal is the conflictual relation that Freud appeals to the notion of primal repression (*Urverdrängung*) as the basis for all later repressions or repression proper. Repression proper presupposes that something has already been repressed; this means that one does not know of any psychical apparatus functioning in a purely nonrepressive manner. In another terminology, the dialectic between the primary system and the secondary system is itself primordial. This primordial aspect of repression is nothing other than the structure of desire insofar as desire is from the very beginning confronted by another desire.

Thus this dialectical structure is to be seen in the topography itself. The topography, as we know, arises from a simple opposition between the conscious and the unconscious; we may say that the topography is the spatial picture of a basically dialectical relationship. The Freudian systematization objectivizes in a solipsistic apparatus relations that owe their origin to intersubjective situations and the process of the reduplication of consciousness. Consequently, even within the topography itself, as an intrapsychical relation, one finds relations that figuratively represent the original intersubjectivity.

I wonder whether we must not also reconsider what seemed to us quite settled in the framework of the metapsychology, namely, the strictly nondialectical characteristics of the unconscious, or rather, to use the expression adopted after 1914, of the id. What I mean here by a nondialectical characterization is the famous description of that locality, called first the unconscious and then the id, as a purely affirmative power, exempt from negation, time sequence, and the discipline of reality, and blindly aiming at pleasure. This absolute desire—absolute in the sense of having no relations—has outside of itself, in another locality, the origin of the negation of time and the relation to reality. That this theory is simply an abstract, though necessary, step in the progress of understanding may be seen from the fact that desire is in an intersubjective situation from the very start. It is desire confronted with the mother and the father, it is desire confronted with desire; as such, it has entered into the process of negativity, the process of self-consciousness, from the outset.

The second topography presents an even more graphic picture of a dialectic. The first topography had to do with intrapsychical localities; the second topography has to do with roles, the roles of a personology in which the impersonal, the personal, and the superpersonal confront one another. The second topography is the dialectic properly so-called in and through which arise the various instinctual dichotomies and the opposed pairs of instinctual vicissitudes mentioned above. The question of the superego lies at the origin of the dialectical situation that made the first topography possible, for this question is at the origin of the intrapsychical conflicts. Desire has its other. Consequently the second topography is more than just a revision of the first topography; it arises from a confrontation of the libido with a nonlibidinal factor that manifests itself as culture. At this point, the economics of instincts is simply the shadow, projected onto the plane of solipsistic cathexes, of the dialectic of roles. That is why the dependent relationships of the ego, to revert to the title of Chapter 5 of *The Ego and the Id,* are more directly dialectical than the topological relationships of the earlier representation of the psychical apparatus. Furthermore, the series of pairs, ego-id, ego-superego, ego-world, which constitute these dependent relations, are all presented, as in the Hegelian dialectic, as master-slave relationships that must be overcome.

THE IMPLICIT TELEOLOGY OF FREUDIANISM: IDENTIFICATION

There is a second way in which the genesis of the superego in Freudian theory relates to an unthematized teleological dialectic. It relates to it not only by reason of the operative concepts used in the construction of the successive topographies, but also by reason of a fundamental and highly elaborated concept which, not finding a suitable conceptual basis in the topographic and economic point of view, remains peripheral to the theory. I refer to the concept of identification, whose gradual formation we have followed in Freud's work. Identification, it seems to me, is a concept that remains unharmonized with the metapsychology.

In Freudian theory the external fact par excellence is authority. Authority is not contained in the proper nature of the libido which seeks satisfaction. It is by means of prohibitions that authority penetrates into the instinctual field and inflicts upon the instincts a specific wound of which the threat of castration is the half-real, half-fictive expression. How then is the encounter between desire and its other to be accounted for on the economic balance sheet as an expenditure of pleasure and unpleasure? The metapsychology states this problem in the following terms. If all instinctual energy derives from the id, how can this instinctual substrate "differentiate" itself, i.e. give a different distribution of its cathexes, according to the various prohibitions? The entrance of authority into the history of desire, this *acquired* differentiation of desire, gives rise to a special type of semantics, that of ideals. I do not mean to return here to the problems of deciphering and interpreting that this new semantics raises; we have already dealt with those problems under the heading of the oneiric and the sublime. Our present interest concerns rather the conceptual structure in which this differentiation may be adequately represented.

My thesis is that this differentiation forms a dialectic homologous to the Hegelian process of the reduplication of consciousness; but this entrance of the other's consciousness into one's self is not completely accounted for in the economics one tries to translate it into. The consciousness that has another consciousness as its paired opposite cannot be treated as an agency in a topography: just as the metapsychology does not theoretically elaborate the analytic relation qua intersubjective drama, neither does it theoretically elaborate the adventure of desire as soon as the desire-pleasure relationship entails the desire-desire relationship. This desire-desire relationship places the libido in the field of a phenomenology of spirit; thus we must speak of this desire of desire in Hegelian terms: "self-consciousness attains its satisfaction only in another self-consciousness."

Freud's puzzlement concerning the concept of identification is the exact expression of this situation. As we have said, identification is more of a problem than a solution. Ultimately, there are two identifications, as we learned from Chapter 7 of *Group Psychology and the Analysis of the Ego*. The one that puzzles us is the identification that precedes the Oedipus complex and is strengthened by the dissolution of the Oedipus complex. According to this primary identification, the father represents what the child would like to be and have; he is a model to be imitated. The Oedipus complex results from the confluence of this identification and the child's attachment to his mother as a sexual object. The attachment to a being as the model of "what one would like to be" is therefore irreducible to the desire to have; *desire to be like* and *desire to have* will come together and intertwine, but they remain two distinct processes. It seems to me the situation might be described rather accurately by saying that psychoanalysis constantly presupposes the intersubjective process of the duplication of consciousness but that the metapsychology, unable to account for that process in its original essence, theoretically elaborates only its side effects on the instinctual plane. In the rest of the same text, it is the regressive aspects of identification that are constantly mentioned and interpreted economically;[14] in examining the case of the Oedipus complex on the part of a little girl in a neurotic context, Freud observes *"that identification has appeared instead of object-choice, and that object-choice has regressed to identification."* Similar terms are used when he speaks of the male homosexual's identification with his mother; because of this identification the young man looks about for sexual objects that can replace his own body, and on which he can bestow such love and care as he experienced from his mother. In this striking case of identification, the regressive character of the replacement of the abandoned or lost object, as well as the regressive character of the introjection of the object into

14. *Group Psychology, GW, 13,* 116–21; *SE, 18,* 106–10. Cf. above, "Analytic," Part II, Ch. 2, pp. 216–21.

the ego, is highly evident. The same remark would apply in the case of melancholia and its characteristic introjection of the object. I would say that what psychoanalysis recognizes under the name of identification is simply the shadow, projected onto the plane of an economics of instincts, of a process of consciousness to consciousness, and that this process has to be understood through another type of interpretation.

Although psychoanalysis grasps only the affective projection of this process, it transforms our understanding of the process by providing us with a completely new frontier view. The energy made available by the dissolution of the object-libido, and hence by the regression of that libido, is what enables us to progress toward affectionate trends of feeling and to invest our emotions in cultural objects. The economics grasps only the reverse side of the phenomenon it calls the introjection or installation of the lost object in the ego. The shadow of the process of consciousness to consciousness, as projected onto the economic plane, is always some kind of regression; the "replacement of an object-cathexis by an identification" is the only method by which an erotic object-choice can become an alteration of the ego, or, as *The Ego and the Id* says, it is a method of obtaining control over the id. Since a detailed exegesis of these texts has already been made,[15] I do not intend to reexamine them here. But I do propose once more to cite the *New Introductory Lectures,* which represent Freud's penultimate reflection on his work; nowhere else does he so clearly express the discrepancy between an economics of desire and a factor that is no longer subject to an instinctual economics. Nowhere else is it so clearly evident that in an economics identification is understood solely as a type of regression, whereas qua founding process it eludes the economics: "If one has lost an object or has been obliged to give it up, one often compensates oneself by identifying oneself with it and by set-

15. Above, pp. 221–26. One should consider here the important work of Erik H. Erikson: *Childhood and Society* (1950), *Young Man Luther* (1958), *Identity and the Life Cycle* (1960), *Insight and Responsibility* (1964). This work may be compared with J. Laplanche, *Hölderlin et la question du père* (Paris, P. U. F., 1961), and with A. Vergote, *La Psychanalyse, science de l'homme* (Dessart, 1964), Part III, "Psychanalyse et anthropologie philosophique."

ting it up once more in one's ego, so that here object-choice regresses, as it were, to identification."[16] That something essential has not been accounted for, at the very moment identification is recognized in its vast dimension, is evidenced by the following admission: "I myself am far from satisfied with these remarks on identification; but it will be enough if you can grant me that the installation of the superego can be described as a successful instance of identification with the parental agency."[17]

This text invites us to place the structure of the Hegelian self-consciousness at the very center of the Freudian desire. The point drawing us onward here is the famous "object-loss," so often treated in the same context as identification and, it seems, always in the perspective of regression, as in "Mourning and Melancholia." But is the loss of the object always and fundamentally a regressive process, a return to narcissism? Does it not indicate, on the contrary, an educative transformation of human desire, a transformation related to the process of reduplication of consciousness not in an accidental but in a fundamental and founding manner? What seems to oppose an interpretation that would place the dialectic of self-consciousness at the very heart of desire is Freud's definition of the libido.[18] This definition seems to be carefully divorced from the whole process of the reduplication of consciousness by reason of the systematic apparatus of the topography. But desire, as we said above, is from the outset in an intersubjective situation; hence the process of identification is not something added on from without but is rather the dialectic of desire itself. Such a remark brings out the profound meaning of the Oedipus complex, in the sense of a "successful" identification, to use an expression mentioned above. Everything is not accounted for in a purely regressive conception of the abandonment of the object. When we say that the superego is the heir of the Oedipus complex, we refer to something much broader than what is meant by an economics of the withdrawal of cathexis: the child's "abandonment" of the Oedipus complex, his "renunciation of the intense object-cathexes which he has deposited

16. *New Introductory Lectures, GW, 15,* 69; *SE, 22,* 63.
17. Ibid.
18. *Three Essays on Sexuality, GW, 5,* 118–20; *SE, 7,* 217–19.

with his parents," are simply ways of designating, in terms of the withdrawal of cathexis, the economic impact of a creative process, viz. the progress of identification and the setting up of a structure. Freud is not far from recognizing that such is the case:

> It is as a compensation for this loss of objects that there is such a strong intensification of the identifications with his parents which have probably long been present in his ego. Identifications of this kind as precipitates of object-cathexes that have been given up will be repeated often enough later in the child's life; but it is entirely in accordance with the emotional importance of this first instance of such a transformation [*Umsetzung*] that a special place in the ego should be found for its outcome.[19]

This text is of great importance for understanding the close connection between loss of the object—the renunciation of libidinal cathexis, which is a vicissitude of the libido—and identification, which pertains to the dialectic of the reduplication of consciousness. As in Hegel, the search for satisfaction undergoes the experience of the negative as soon as that search enters the field of identification, which we have recognized as being homologous with the reduplication of self-consciousness. The fact that desire becomes dialectical is therefore no longer an external vicissitude, as was the case in the texts of the "Metapsychology" which posited an absolute desire, exempt from negation, and assigned the function of negation to the censorship. The censorship escapes the mythology of the watchman or guardian and takes its place in the dialectic of identification. On at least one occasion, in his admirable description of the work of mourning, Freud recognized that the experience of the negative is internal and no longer external to desire itself. I will not go back over these texts, which we have cited and analyzed at length. Do we not find in them the beginning of a genuine dialectic of desire, in which negation is placed at the very center of desire? Are we not invited thereby to reinterpret the death instinct and relate it to the negativity through which desire is educated and humanized? Is there not a profound unity between the death instinct, the mourning of desire, and the transition to symbols?

19. *New Introductory Lectures, GW, 15,* 70; *SE, 22,* 64.

The possibility is thus opened of rereading Freud's writings from the standpoint of the reduplication of consciousness. The rule of this rereading would be the oscillation between a dialectic and an economics, between a dialectic oriented toward the gradual emergence of self-consciousness and an economics that explains the "placements" and "displacements" of desire through which this difficult emergence is effected. I admit that this dialectic of consciousness to consciousness, which operates through identification and has repercussions in the depths of desire in the form of the loss of the object, is not the dominant theme of psychoanalysis. I would say rather that this dialectic has imposed itself upon psychoanalysis in opposition to its metapsychology, its topography, and its economics, i.e. in opposition to the express model that it adopts in order to understand itself and develop its own theory. In an economics the struggle between consciousnesses is not recognized as a dialectic of the self, but only as a vicissitude external to instincts that are moved by the pleasure principle. That is why the economics is at bottom solipsistic. But neither psychoanalysis as therapy nor any of the situations it reflects upon is solipsistic. It is therefore in opposition to the economics that psychoanalysis integrates into itself the Hegelian history of desire wherein satisfaction is attained only through another history, that of recognition. Thus the rereading I have just alluded to is in a certain sense itself in opposition to the Freudian economics.

THE IMPLICIT TELEOLOGY OF FREUDIANISM: THE QUESTION OF SUBLIMATION

If Freud's theory presents a concept of identification, it presents only a question regarding sublimation. The entire preceding problematic is mirrored in this unresolved question. Connected with it are all the other unresolved questions concerning the origin of the ethical sphere, so far as they are not dealt with by the concept of identification.

It will be noticed that our "Analytic" does not present a separate study of sublimation. This is not accidental: in Freud's written work the notion of sublimation is both fundamental and episodic. It is announced as one of the instinctual vicissitudes, distinct not only from the reversal (*Verkehrung*) of instincts into their contrary and from turning round (*Wendung*) upon the subject, but also and especially from repression. Yet Freud has left us no complete and separate work dealing with this original vicissitude. Furthermore, as one of Freud's critics has shown,[20] the rough sketch of a theory found in the *Three Essays* will not be changed appreciably after 1905, except for correlations with desexualization and identification. It is worthwhile, therefore, to examine in detail the text of 1905.

The *Three Essays* treat of sublimation in four separate episodes. The first allusion occurs in the first essay ("Sexual Aberrations") under the heading of "deviations in respect of the sexual aim" and the subheading of "preliminary sexual aims." This location of sublimation is significant. Sublimation is a deviation with respect to the aim of the libido and not a substitution of an object. This deviation is connected with the "preparatory activities" that precede the normal sexual act; more precisely, it is connected with the sensual pleasure resulting from the preparatory acts of touching, seeing, concealing, revealing; such acts can become separate aims that take place of the normal one. This deviation places sublimation in the field of the esthetic, i.e. of cultural phenomena: "[This sexual curiosity] can, however, be diverted ('sublimated') in the direction of art, if its interest can be shifted away from the genitals onto the shape of the body as a whole." [21] By the same token, this lingering over "the intermediate sexual aim of looking" places sublimation in the field of perversion, for perversion too is a lingering and a deviation along the pathway to the normal sexual act. In this first text, the contrast with perversion is attributed to counterforces (shame and disgust) but no distinction is drawn between sublimation and repression.

The second context is that of the second essay, which is devoted to infantile sexuality; thus it is a genetic context. The beginning of

20. Harry B. Levey, "A Critique of the Theory of Sublimation," *Psychiatry* (1939), pp. 239–70.

21. *Three Essays on Sexuality, GW, 5,* 55–56; *SE, 7,* 156–57.

sublimation is connected with the latency period. More clearly than in the preceding text, sublimation is regarded from the viewpoint of the attaining of culture.[22] As for its mechanism, Freud connects it with the role of "mental dams," which he lists as "disgust, shame and morality." These opposing forces run directly counter to the perverse impulses of infantile sexuality, which is related to the erotogenic zones of the body. The opposing forces, or reacting impulses, are evoked to suppress a certain kind of unpleasure that arises because of the individual's subsequent development. Thus in this second text sublimation is linked once again to the erotogenic zones and perversion, as well as to the deviation from the aim because of the activity of counterforces, but still no distinction is drawn between sublimation and repression.

The third allusion is found at the very end of the same essay, in the section on the sources of infantile sexuality. The characteristic deviation of sublimation is compared to the "transfer" or "attraction" that is observed when a sexual function encroaches on another function by reason of their common possession of an erotogenic zone (Freud cites the example of the labial zone: the disturbance of the erotogenic functions of this common zone may result in anorexia):

> The same pathways . . . must serve as paths for the attraction of sexual instinctual forces to aims that are other than sexual, that is to say, for the sublimation of sexuality. But we must end with a confession that very little is as yet known with certainty of these pathways, though they certainly exist and can probably be traversed in both directions.[23]

Thus the factor of inhibition accompanying this deviation from the aim receives less emphasis in this text than in the earlier ones. However, Freud's insistence on linking the problem of sublimation to the fate of the erotogenic zones draws attention to the limited nature of this instinctual vicissitude. One might speak in this sense of a finitude of human desire that develops according to the range of a determinate and relatively limited sensorial constitution (it is true

22. *GW, 5,* 78–79; *SE, 7,* 178–79.
23. *GW, 5,* 123; *SE, 7,* 206.

that the erotogenic zones are not limited in number, but they are limited to the surface of the body).

The fourth and principle treatment of sublimation in the *Three Essays* occurs in the final attempt of synthesis that terminates the book. In this summary, sublimation is viewed as a third alternative result, along with neurosis and perversion.[24] We already know that perversion and neurosis are closely connected, for "neuroses are, so to say, the negative of perversions." [25] We have also learned from the previous texts that sublimation has a close connection with perversions by reason of its economic link with the intermediate aims and erotogenic zones. In the summary, the three "results" (which foreshadow the instinctual "vicissitudes") are clearly distinguished: perversion is interpreted in quasi-Jacksonian terms as being due to the weakness of the integrating function of the genital zone; neurosis, "the negative of perversion," [26] is associated with repression; sublimation is conceived as a discharge and use, in areas other than sexuality, of excessively strong excitations (in this sense, sublimation is still being dealt with in the context of abnormal constitutions). Nevertheless, to these "perilous dispositions" Freud attributes "a not inconsiderable increase in psychical efficiency": esthetic creativity is one of these reactional manifestations. More exactly, artistic dispositions present a mixture, in every proportion, of efficiency, perversion, and neurosis.

What, finally, is the relationship between sublimation and repression? Surprisingly, this last text treats repression as a subspecies of sublimation; connected with this subspecies are a person's character traits, which stem, as we know, from sexual organizations that have been established through fixation, sublimation, and repression. But Freud is quick to add that repression and sublimation are processes "of which the inner causes are quite unknown to us." [27] Freud regards them as "constitutional dispositions." [28] The objection has been made,[29] not unreasonably, that there is no clinical evidence in support of the theory that sublimation derives its energy

24. *GW*, *5*, 140–41; *SE*, *7*, 238–39.
25. *GW*, *5*, 65; *SE*, *7*, 165.
26. *GW*, *5*, 140; *SE*, *7*, 238.
27. *GW*, *5*, 140–41; *SE*, *7*, 239.
28. Ibid.
29. Levey, pp. 247–49.

from infantile erotogenic zones in individuals with abnormally strong sexual constitutions. These texts do not even enable us to form a definite opinion about the causes or mechanism of sublimation. What are the respective roles, or even simply the meaning, of the derivation and the reaction-formation? It is not easy to say; the only factors treated with precision are the reaction-formations of disgust, shame, and morality. Artistic sublimation is mentioned but not developed; instead, a parallel example of reaction-formation is developed—scopophilia. Finally, nothing justifies our saying that the values, esthetic or otherwise, toward which the energy is channeled or displaced, would be created by this mechanism. It would seem that while creativity is derived, its objects are not.

Subsequent texts add more difficulties than solutions. We have already examined the pair sublimation-idealization in the paper "On Narcissism." We recall that idealization concerns the object of an instinct, sublimation its direction and aim; this distinction enables Freud to stress the difference between the two mechanisms, so far as idealization is obtained by force. In this new context, sublimation is contrasted sharply with repression, but a metapsychological revision of the mechanism of sublimation on a par with the revision of the mechanism of repression is not proposed. The more Freud distinguishes sublimation from the other mechanisms, in particular from repression, and even from reaction-formation, the more its own mechanism remains unexplained: sublimation is a displacement of energy, but not a repression of it; it seems to be dependent upon an ability especially pronounced in artists.

The only truly new descriptive characteristics were introduced during the period of *The Ego and the Id*. Sublimation profits from the enormous work that Freud put into the elaboration of a metapsychology of the superego. The abandonment of sexual aims which is required by the process of introjection is described both as an exchange between the object and the ego—object-libido being transformed into narcissistic libido—and as a desexualization. Such desexualization, he adds, is

> a kind of sublimation, therefore. Indeed, the question arises, and deserves careful consideration, whether this is not the universal road to sublimation, whether all sublimation does not take place

> through the mediation of the ego, which begins by changing sexual object-libido into narcissistic libido and then, perhaps, goes on to give it another aim.[30]

The two innovations, then, are as follows. On the one hand, desexualization becomes the central factor in what the earlier texts called deviation or displacement; Freud now assumes the existence of a neutral and displaceable energy which can be added to either the erotic or the destructive instincts. On the other hand, the ego—in the sense of the second topography—is the necessary intermediary in this transformation; thus sublimation is connected with the alteration of the ego that we have called identification; and as identification centers on the model-image of the father, the superego is implied in the process of desexualization and sublimation. We have, therefore, a continuous three-term sequence: desexualization, identification, sublimation. At this point, we have moved away from our initial basis: sublimation is no longer seen as a perverse infantile component that has deviated toward the nonsexual; it is an object-cathexis of the Oedipus period that has been internalized through desexualization and the pressure of forces that brought about the dissolution of the Oedipus complex. But it is difficult to say which notion grounds which: desexualization, sublimation, and identification are rather three enigmas placed end to end. Unfortunately, this does not make for a very clear picture.

Freud's failure to resolve the problem of sublimation gives us matter for reflection. The empty concept of sublimation enables us on the one hand to recapitulate the whole series of difficulties enumerated under the heading of the implicit teleology of Freudianism, and on the other hand to introduce a new train of thought under the very cautious and very propaedeutic heading, "Toward the Problem of Symbol."

It seems to me that the concept of sublimation has two sides. On the one hand it concerns the set of procedures involved in the constitution of the sublime—i.e. the higher or highest—aspects of man; on the other hand it concerns the symbolic instrument of this constitution of the sublime. We shall restrict ourselves here to the problematic of the sublime, apart from its symbolic expression.

30. *The Ego and the Id, GW, 13,* 258; *SE, 19,* 30. Cf. above, p. 223.

By and large, this first side of the problem corresponds to the ethical aspects of sublimation (the second side corresponds in general to its esthetic aspects). Freud himself assigned a privileged status to these ethical aspects by linking sublimation first to reaction-formations (shame, modesty, etc.), then to identification.

Now, all the procedures or mechanisms that are set into operation by the constitution of the higher agency, whether they be called idealization, identification, or sublimation, remain unintelligible in the framework of an economics. The theory of the superego oscillates between a monism of energy, inherited from the first topography, and a dualism of desire and authority. According to the monism of energy, there is only one source of energy—the id, or narcissism in the sense of the reservoir of instincts; according to the dualism of desire and authority, the only figure irreducible to desire is the father figure. From the point of view of energy, everything proceeds from the reservoir of the id; but in order for desire to be torn away from itself, in order for the superego to be differentiated as a reaction-formation, authority must be introduced under the guise of the father. Thus Freud maintains two theses with equal force: the superego is acquired from without and, in this sense, is not primal; on the other hand, the superego is the expression of the most powerful instincts and the most important libidinal vicissitudes of the id. The whole economy of the superego is reflected in the concept of sublimation; this concept forms a kind of compromise between two requirements: to *internalize* an "outside" (authority, father figure, any form of master) and to *differentiate* an "inside" (libido, narcissism, id). The sublimation of the "lower" into the "higher" is the counterpart of the introjection of the "outside." Reaction-formation, the formation of an ideal, and sublimation designate related modalities of this doctrinal compromise. But is such a compromise self-consistent? Does it not conceal an unbridgeable hiatus when taken in separation from a dialectic of archeology and teleology? For my part I doubt that Freud succeeded in reducing the fundamental gap between the externality of authority, to which he is condemned by his refusal of an ethical foundation inherent in the positing of the ego, and the solipsism of desire, which stems from his initial economic hypothesis that every formation of an ideal is ultimately a differentiation of the id. Freudianism lacks a suitable theoretical instrument to render intelligible the absolutely primal dialectic between desire and the other than desire.

The failure of the theory of sublimation thus has the same meaning as the discordance between the concept of identification and the economics: "the desire to be like," we said with Freud himself, is irreducible to "the desire to have." Sublimation conceals an irreducibility of the same order; it too may be said to precede and embrace all the formations derived by way of esthetic transfer of sensual pleasure from erotogenic zones or by way of desexualization of the libido during the dissolution of the Oedipus complex. None of these derived formations accounts for either a primordial identification or the primal power of sublimation. The relationship between sublimation and identification enables us to relate the unresolved enigma of sublimation to the origin of self-consciousness in the dialectic of desire.

The relationship between sublimation and the formation of an ideal, as the latter is developed in the paper "On Narcissism," suggests the same dialectical reinterpretation of all these related mechanisms. I realize that Freud's purpose in bringing sublimation and idealization together is to distinguish them from each other; according to the mechanism of idealization, the ideal remains "the substitute for the lost narcissism of [our] childhood." [31] Nevertheless, this projection of the ideal, a projection stemming from narcissism, presupposes that the ego of this abortive Cogito includes a minimum of ethical meaning, that the ego can have regard for itself, value itself, condemn itself. It is surely not a matter of indifference to learn from psychoanalysis that the formation of ideals stems from the false Cogito, that what we call our ideals are quite often simply projections of that same self-love to which we attributed, in another context, the resistance to truth. Idealization in the Freudian sense is thereby connected with the Nietzschean genealogy of morals. We have already stressed this indisputable contribution of psychoanalysis. But across this narcissistic parentage of ideals there arises a more radical problem. What does it mean that the ego evaluates, is capable of respect or blame, engages in approval and self-

31. "On Narcissism: An Introduction," *GW, 10,* 161; *SE, 14,* 94.

approval, disapproval and self-repudiation? In our presentation of the Freudian theory of idealization, we suggested that this process might give some support to the fleeting and perhaps unintentional distinction between the ideal ego and the ego-ideal; a further basis for the distinction might be the attribution to the ego of a *Selbstachtung*, a "self-regard," [32] initially posited in narcissism itself. If the ego can fear castration, and later on anticipate social blame and punishment and internalize them as moral condemnation, the reason is that it is sensible to threats other than physical danger. For the fear of castration to take on an ethical significance, the threat to one's self-regard must initially be distinct from any other menace; to acquire the meaning of condemnation and punishment, the threat to physical integrity must symbolize the threat to existential integrity.

Thus, whether one links sublimation with identification or with idealization, sublimation takes us back to the central difficulty of the whole Freudian problematic of agencies: ego, id, and superego.

Psychoanalysis is capable of deciphering the ethical characteristics of the ego through affective situations of a regressive nature. This is true not only in practice but in theory; as we have seen, sublimation can be expressed in economic terms only as a regression to narcissism. I grant that this regression, understood as an economic concept, does not coincide with the temporal regression, i.e. with a return to the past, a return to childhood (of mankind or of the individual). But even when it is taken in the most economic and the least temporal sense, when it is conceived as an abandonment of object-cathexis and a return to the narcissistic reservoir, the regression calls for an antithetical concept that seems to have no place in the Freudian economy, the concept of progression. How can narcissism differentiate itself, displace itself? How can a precipitate of identifications deposit itself in the ego and modify the ego, if the process is not a progression by means of a regression? And what is the principle according to which this progression operates? The principle seems quite difficult to elaborate with the resources of the Freudian metapsychology, although it is constantly presupposed in

32. Ibid., *GW, 10,* 160; *SE, 14,* 93.

an unthematized way by analytic practice. These questions do not disqualify psychoanalysis in the least; psychoanalysis greatly benefits reflection by enabling us to raise these questions in the context of the inauthentic modalities of fear and dread, narcissistic self-attachment, and also hate—the hatred of life at the heart of our own existence—and even a hidden complicity with death. Psychoanalysis raises these questions negatively, as it were, by unmasking the archaic, infantile and instinctual, narcissistic and masochistic features of our alleged sublimity.

Ultimately, through the more highly elaborated concepts of identification and idealization, the empty concept of sublimation refers us back to the operative, unthematized concepts of the Freudian economics. I will sum them all up in the unique task of the process of becoming conscious, which defines the finality of analysis. In the *New Introductory Lectures,* Freud writes: "Where id was, there ego shall be." [33] Ultimately, the task of becoming I, of becoming the ego, a task set within the economics of desire, is in principle irreducible to the economics. But this task remains the unspoken factor in Freud's doctrine; the empty concept of sublimation is the final symbol of this unspoken factor. That is why all the difficulties we have encountered under the heading of the implicit teleology of Freudianism are mirrored in this concept. These difficulties may be summed up as follows:

1. If desire is to enter into culture, there must be assumed an initial relationship between desire and a source of valuation external to the field of energy.

2. If the ego's identification with its other is to be possible, a pairing of subjectivities must be postulated.

3. If identification is to be included in a process of idealization of the ego, an original self-regard, a primal *Selbstachtung,* must be assumed.

4. Finally, in a direction contrary to the regressive movement psychoanalysis sets forth in theory, there must be supposed an aptitude for progression, which analytic practice puts in operation, but which the theory does not thematize.

33. *New Introductory Lectures, GW, 15,* 86 (*Wo Es war, soll Ich werden*); *SE, 22,* 80.

I have tried to conceptualize this interplay of progression and regression by means of a radical dialectic, a dialectic of archeology and teleology. Thereby I hope I have advanced, not only in the understanding of Freud, but in the understanding of myself, for a reflective mode of thought that undertakes such a dialectic is already on the path that leads from abstract reflection to concrete reflection. There remains the task of understanding that progression and regression are carried by the same symbols—in short, that symbolism is the area of identity between progression and regression. To understand this would be to enter into concrete reflection.

Chapter 4: Hermeneutics: The Approaches to Symbol

It is only now that we reach the level of the most ambitious interrogations of our "Problematic"; and it is only now that we can glimpse a solution—no longer eclectic, but dialectical—of the hermeneutic conflict. We now know that the key to the solution lies in the dialectic between archeology and teleology. It remains to find the *concrete* "mixed texture" in which we see the archeology and teleology. This concrete mixed texture is *symbol.* I propose to show, at my own risk, that what psychoanalysis describes as overdetermination finds its full meaning in a dialectic of interpretation, whose opposed poles are constituted by archeology and teleology.

It was impossible to understand the overdetermination of symbols without making a long and involved detour; we could not appeal to such overdetermination as our starting point, nor is it certain that we truly can attain to it; that is why I speak of the *approaches to symbol.* As I said in the "Problematic," a general hermeneutics does not yet lie within our scope; this book is no more than a propaedeutic to that extensive work. The task we set ourselves was to integrate into reflection the opposition between conflicting hermeneutics. Now that we have made such a long detour we are simply at the threshold of our enterprise. Let us turn back and consider the path we have taken.

First, it was necessary to pass through the stage of dispossession—the dispossession of consciousness as the place and origin of meaning. Freudian psychoanalysis appeared to us as the discipline best equipped to instigate and carry through this ascesis of reflection: its topography and its economic help displace the locus of meaning toward the unconscious, that is, toward an origin over which we have no control. This first stage terminates in an archeology of reflection.

Next, it was necessary to traverse an antithetic of reflection. Here the archeological interpretation appeared as the counterpart of a progressive genesis of meaning through successive figures, where the meaning of each figure is dependent upon the meaning of the subsequent figures.

Finally, Hegel served as an inverse model and helped us form a dialectic, not *between* Freud and Hegel, but in each one of them. It is only when each interpretation is seen to be contained in the other that the antithetic is no longer simply the clash of opposites but the passage of each into the other. Only then is reflection truly in the archeology and the archeology in the teleology: reflection, teleology, and archeology pass over into one another.

Now that we have thought through in the abstract the reconciliation of these two lines of interpretation, the possibility arises of seeking their point of intersection in the meaningful texture of symbols.

In this sense, symbols are the *concrete* moment of the dialectic, but they are not its *immediate* moment. The concrete is always the fullness or peak of mediation. The return to the simple attitude of listening to symbols is the "reward consequent upon thought." The concreteness of language which we border upon through painstaking approximation is the second naïveté of which we have merely a frontier or threshold knowledge.

The danger for the philosopher (for the philosopher, I say, and not for the poet) is to arrive too quickly, to lose the tension, to become dissipated in the symbolic richness, in the abundance of meaning. I do not retract the descriptions of the problematic; I continue to state that symbols call for interpretation because of their peculiar signifying structure in which meaning inherently refers beyond itself. But the explanation of this structure requires the threefold discipline of dispossession, antithetic, and dialectic. In order to think in accord with symbols one must subject them to a dialectic; only then is it possible to set the dialectic within interpretation itself and come back to living speech. This last stage of reappropriation constitutes the transition to concrete reflection. In returning to the attitude of listening to language, reflection passes into the fullness of speech simply heard and understood.

Let us not be mistaken about the meaning of this last stage: this return to the immediate is not a return to silence, but rather to the spoken word, to the fullness of language. Nor is it a return to the dense enigma of initial, immediate speech, but to speech that has been instructed by the whole process of meaning. Hence this concrete reflection does not imply any concession to irrationality or effusiveness. In its return to the spoken word, reflection continues to be reflection, that is, the understanding of meaning; reflection becomes hermeneutic; this is the only way in which it can become concrete and still remain reflection. The second naïveté is not the first naïveté; it is postcritical and not precritical; it is an informed naïveté.

THE OVERDETERMINATION OF SYMBOLS

The thesis I am proposing is this: what psychoanalysis calls overdetermination cannot be understood apart from a dialectic between two functions which are thought to be opposed to one another but which symbols coordinate in a concrete unity. Thus the ambiguity of symbolism is not a lack of univocity but is rather the possibility of carrying and engendering opposed interpretations, each of which is self-consistent.

The two hermeneutics, one turned toward the revival of archaic meanings belonging to the infancy of mankind, the other toward the emergence of figures that anticipate our spiritual adventure, develop, in opposite directions, the beginnings of meaning contained in language—a language richly endowed with the enigmas that men have invented and received in order to express their fears and hopes. Thus we should say that symbols carry two vectors. On the one hand, symbols repeat our childhood in all the senses, chronological and nonchronological, of that childhood. On the other hand, they explore our adult life: "O my prophetic soul," says Hamlet. But these two functions are not external to one another; they constitute the overdetermination of authentic symbols. By probing our infancy and making it live again in the oneiric mode, symbols represent the projection of our human possibilities onto the area of imagination. These authentic symbols are truly regressive-progressive; remembrance gives rise to anticipation; archaism gives rise to prophecy.

Pursuing this analysis of the intentional structure of symbols more deeply, I would say that the opposition between regression and progression, which we have struggled to establish and to overcome at the same time, throws light on the paradoxical texture described as the unity of concealing and showing. True symbols are at the crossroads of the two functions which we have by turns opposed to and grounded in one another. Such symbols both disguise and reveal. While they conceal the aims of our instincts, they disclose the process of self-consciousness. Disguise, reveal; conceal, show; these two functions are no longer external to one another; they express the two sides of a single symbolic function. Because of their overdetermination symbols realize the concrete identity between the progression of the figures of spirit or mind and the regression to the key signifiers of the unconscious. Advancement of meaning occurs only in the sphere of the projections of desire, of the derivatives of the unconscious, of the revivals of archaism. We nourish our least carnal symbols with desires that have been checked, deviated, transformed. We represent our ideals with images issuing from cleansed desire. Thus symbols represent in a concrete unity what reflection in its antithetic stage is forced to split into opposed interpretations; the opposed hermeneutics disjoin and decompose what concrete reflection recomposes through a return to speech simply heard and understood. If my analysis is correct, sublimation is not a supplementary procedure that could be accounted for by an economics of desire. It is not a mechanism that could be put on the same plane as the other instinctual vicissitudes, alongside reversal, turning round upon the self, and repression. Insofar as revealing and disguising coincide in it, we might say that sublimation is the symbolic function itself. Reflection's initial approach to this function is necessarily divisive. An economics isolates the element of disguise in the symbolic function, insofar as dreams distort the secret intentions of our forbidden desires. The economics must then be counterbalanced by a phenomenology of mind or spirit in order to preserve the other dimension and to show that symbols involve a development of the self that opens up to what the symbols disclose. But one must go beyond this dichotomy which always keeps recurring within symbols; one must see that this second function of symbols runs through and takes into itself the projective function in order to raise it up and, in the proper sense of the term, sublimate it. By means of disguise and projection something further transpires—a function of dis-covery, of dis-closure, which sublimates the oneirism of man.

To what extent does this conception of the dialectical structure of symbols retain a connection with orthodox Freudian doctrine? I do not deny that Freud would reject our interpretation of overdetermination.[1] But the treatment of symbols in *The Interpretation of Dreams* and the *Introductory Lectures* is less unfavorable to our position, because of the ambiguities and unsolved difficulties Freud encounters in that treatment. Let us now relate these difficulties to those of sublimation.

Freud's theory of symbolism is indeed quite disconcerting.[2] On the one hand, symbolism in the mechanism of dreams is very narrowly restricted to the stereotypes that resist the piecemeal method of deciphering dreams through the dreamer's free associations. In this sense there is no strictly symbolic function that might stand as a distinct procedure alongside condensation, displacement, and pictorial representation. Nor does symbolization constitute a peculiar problem from the point of view of dream interpretation, for the symbols used in dreams have been formed elsewhere. Symbols have

1. It is true that the distinction between overdetermination and overinterpretation is to be found in Freud: *GW, 2/3,* 253 (1), 270 (1), 272, 528; *SE, 4,* 248, n. 1, 263, n. 2 (an addition of 1914 concerning the interpretation of the Oedipus myth), 266, and *SE, 5,* 523. But this overinterpretation does not denote interpretations that differ from that of psychoanalysis; cf. above, "Analytic," Part II, Ch. 2, p. 193, n. 25.

2. Besides the works of J. Lacan, which have been already cited, see S. Nacht and P. C. Racamier, "La Théorie psychanalytique du délire," *Rev. fr. de psychan., 22* (1958), 418–574; R. Diatkine and M. Benassy, "Ontogénèse du fantasme," *Rev. fr. de psychan., 28* (1964), 217–34; J. Laplanche and J. B. Pontalis, "Fantasme originaire, fantasme des origines, origine du fantasme," *Les Temps modernes, 19* (1964), 1833–68.

a permanently fixed meaning in dreams, like the grammalogues in shorthand. Consequently their interpretation can be direct and does not require a long and difficult work of deciphering.

Lecture X of the *Introductory Lectures on Psychoanalysis* confirms this first aspect of the problem: the comparisons at the basis of dream-symbols "lie ready to hand and are complete, once and for all." [3] More than fifteen years after *The Interpretation of Dreams,* the question of symbolism is still set within the context of the failure of the method of free association. Symbols are subject to fixed or constant translations—"just as popular 'dream-books' provide [translations] for *everything* that appears in dreams." [4] And Freud expressly states: "A constant relation of this kind between a dream-element and its translation is described by us as a 'symbolic' one, and the dream-element itself as a 'symbol' of the unconscious dream-thought." [5] Thus the symbolic relation becomes a "fourth" relation in addition to condensation, displacement, and pictorial representation.[6] The interpretation of symbols by means of "stable translations" forms a *supplement* to interpretation based on association. As in *The Interpretation of Dreams,* Freud again refers to Scherner as being the first to recognize that symbolism is essentially a fantasying of the body. What is symbolically represented is the human body. The sexual etiology of the neuroses enabled Freud to center this symbolization on sexuality and to link the fantasying of the body with the general finality of dreams, that is, with their function of substitute satisfaction.

If the reader considers only the content this symbolism *thematizes,* he might hastily conclude that Lecture X has nothing interesting to offer. From the standpoint of what is thematized one can only say that, first, the "contents" discovered are monotonous —they are always the same things: the genitals, sexual processes, sexual intercourse; and second, the representations symbolizing them are extremely numerous—the same subject matter can be symbolized by almost anything. This curious fact raises the question

3. *GW, 11,* 168; *SE, 15,* 165.
4. *GW, 11,* 151–52; *SE, 15,* 150.
5. Ibid.
6. Ibid.

of the common element, the *tertium comparationis,* of the supposed comparison.[7] It is precisely the *disproportion* [8] between the number of symbols and the monotony of the contents, especially when "the common element is not understood," [9] that directly poses the problem of the constitution of the symbolic relation. Dreams do not institute this relation; they find it ready made and they make use of it. Hence the elaboration of a dream does not involve any work of symbolization comparable to what was described as the work of condensation, displacement, and pictorial representation. But how then do we "come to know the meaning of these dream-symbols"? The answer is that

> we learn it from very different sources—from fairy tales and myths, from buffoonery and jokes, from folklore (that is, from knowledge about popular manners and customs, sayings and songs) and from poetic and colloquial linguistic usage. In all these directions we come upon the same symbolism, and in some of them we can understand it without further instruction. If we go into these sources in detail, we shall find so many parallels to dream-symbolism that we cannot fail to be convinced of our interpretations.[10]

Thus it is not the dream-work that constructs the symbolic relation, but the work of culture. This means that the symbolic relation is formed within language. But Freud does not draw any consequences from this discovery; the analogy between myths and dreams simply verifies and confirms our dream interpretations. Thus Otto Rank's study of "the birth of the hero" simply furnishes parallels to the symbolic representations of birth that occur in dreams. The confirmation of the sexual symbolism of dreams by the symbolism of myths is equivalent to a reduction of the mythical to the oneiric—even though myths supply the element of speech in which the semantics of symbolism has actually been built up.

The puzzling thing about symbols is not that ships stand for

7. *GW, 11,* 153–54; *SE, 15,* 152.
8. *GW, 11,* 154; *SE, 15,* 153.
9. *GW, 11,* 159; *SE, 15,* 157.
10. *GW, 11,* 160–61; *SE, 15,* 158–59.

women but that women are signified and, in order to be signified on the level of images, verbalized. It is the spoken woman that becomes the dreamed woman; it is the mythicized woman that becomes the oneiric woman. But how is one to examine myths without also examining rituals and cults, emblems and heraldic devices (Freud mentions the French fleur-de-lis and the *triskeles* of Sicily and the Isle of Man)? Freud is well aware that there is more in myths, fairy tales, sayings, and poetry than in dreams. He himself emphasizes this fact at the end of his study of symbolism. But the fact itself is simply the occasion for showing that psychoanalysis is a discipline of "general interest," [11] that it establishes links with other disciplines, and that in these links, as he proudly states, "the share of psychoanalysis is in the first instance that of giver and only to a less extent that of receiver": [12] "it is psychoanalysis which provides the technical methods and the points of view whose application in these other fields should prove fruitful." [13] There is reason to fear that the comparative method is being restricted here to a mere apologetics.

This imperialism was unfortunately reinforced by certain supplementary but disastrous hypotheses concerning language itself. Freud is struck by the fact that the symbolism employed in myths is less exclusively sexual than the symbolism of dreams. He reduces the anomaly in the following way. He supposes a state of language in which all symbols were sexual symbols, a state in which "the original sounds of speech served for communication, and summoned the speaker's sexual partner." [14] Later on, a sexual interest became attached to work; but man accepted this displacement of sexual interest only by treating work as an equivalent of and substitute for sexual activity. The ambiguity of language dates from this period when "words enunciated during work in common thus had two meanings; they denoted sexual acts as well as the working activity equated with them. . . . In this way a number of verbal roots

11. *GW, 11*, 170–71; *SE, 15*, 167–68.
12. Ibid.
13. Ibid.

paper "The Antithetical Meaning of Primal Words," which we discussed above, "Dialectic," Ch. 1, p. 397, n. 68.

would have been formed, all of which were of sexual origin and had subsequently lost their sexual meaning."[15] If this hypothesis, which Freud borrows from the Scandinavian philologist H. Sperber, were correct, the symbolic relation, which dreams preserve better than myths, "would be the residue of an ancient verbal identity."[16] It is clear why Freud adopted this nonanalytic hypothesis; it gives our dreams an advantage over myths; although myths provide the broadest parallels of sexual symbolism, the fact that dream-symbolism is almost exclusively sexual is justified by this "primitive language" of which dreams would be the privileged witness.

But even if we were to credit this hypothesis with some linguistic value, it casts us adrift: all dream-symbolism is found to be related to an activity of language, but the enigma of this activity is simply disguised by the supposition of an original verbal identity where the same words denote the sexual and the nonsexual. The hypothesis of these ancient ambiguous roots is simply an expedient whereby one solves the problem by projecting it into a "basic language" in which similarity would already be identity.[17]

15. Ibid.

16. Ibid.

17. Ernest Jones' essay on symbolism ("The Theory of Symbolism" [1916], in *Papers on Psychoanalysis* [5th ed. London, Baillière, Tindall and Cox, 1948], Ch. 3, pp. 87–144) is no doubt the most remarkable work of the Freudian school that is based on Lecture X of the *Introductory Lectures.* It is of great interest from three points of view: descriptive, genetic, and critical.

Descriptively, the author places symbols, in the psychoanalytic sense, in the general class of indirect representations commonly called symbolic and characterized by the role of double meaning, by the analogy between primary meaning and secondary meaning, by the attributes of concreteness and primitiveness, by the fact that symbols represent hidden or secret ideas, and by the fact that they are made spontaneously. To specify the characteristics of "true symbolism," Jones comments on and modifies the criteria proposed by Rank and Sachs in their *Die Bedeutung der Psychoanalyse für die Geisteswissenschaften* (1913): (1) true symbols always represent repressed unconscious themes; (2) they have a constant meaning, or very limited scope for variation in meaning; (3) they are not dependent on individual factors only; this is not to say that they are archetypes in the Jungian sense, but rather that they are stereotypes that betray the limited and uniform character of the primordial interests of mankind; (4) they are archaic; (5) they have linguistic connections, strikingly revealed by etymology; (6) they have parallels in the fields of myth, folklore, poetry.

In my opinion, these speculations close more paths than they open. By assuming everything at the outset, they imply that thereafter we can never encounter anything but residues. When we presented the theory of symbol as given in *The Interpretation of Dreams,* we asked whether Freud was not mistaken in limiting the notion of symbol to common stenographic signs; are symbols

---

Thus the range of symbolism is candidly restricted to the substitute figures that arise from a compromise between the unconscious and the censorship; moreover, all symbols represent themes relating to the bodily self, immediate blood relatives, or the phenomena of birth, love, and death. This is so because these themes correspond to the earliest repressed functions which were held in such high esteem in primitive civilizations.

Jones then goes on to explain why sexuality, the invariant theme of symbolism, has invested such varied regions of language, and why association operates from the sexual to the nonsexual and never in the reverse direction. It is here that the switch is made from the descriptive point of view to the genetic explanation. As for the origin of the associative connection which is the basis of symbolism, it is not enough to call attention to an incapacity for discrimination (an "apperceptive insufficiency") in primitive minds, which in other respects are so gifted in making distinctions and classifications. Following Freud, Jones adopts the theory of the Swedish philologist Sperber of a primal identity of sexual language and the language of work, the same words having originally served the purpose of calling the sexual mate and of providing rhythmic accompaniment during work; since that time weapons and tools, seed and ploughed land symbolically express sexual things. In my opinion, Jones' paper underscores the expediency of this explanation, which assumes everything by making identity prior to similarity. More seriously still, the explanation glosses over the *prior difficulty concerning the elevation of erotic impulses to language and the fact that such impulses are capable of being indefinitely symbolized.* It is not sufficient simply to invoke "the call of the mate"; one must proceed to reflect on what makes desire speak—namely, the *absence* inherent in instincts and the connection between *lost* objects and symbolization. In answer to the second question concerning the origin of symbolism—why symbolism should take place in one direction only—Jones posits that symbolism has a single function, that of disguising prohibited themes: "Only what is repressed is symbolized; only what is repressed needs to be symbolized. This conclusion is the touchstone of the psychoanalytic theory of symbolism" (p. 116).

This answer, which excludes any doctrinal compromise, leads to the critical part of Jones' paper, the part that directly concerns my own enterprise. The criticism is aimed primarily at Silberer, who, starting in 1909, had developed in a half dozen essays a very detailed theory of the formation of symbols. For Silberer, the production of symbols includes other procedures besides the disguising of sexual themes that have been repressed

merely vestiges, or are they not also the dawn of meaning? We can now take up the question again in the light of our dialectical conception of overdetermination. I suggest that we distinguish various levels of creativity of symbols (before distinguishing, in the following section, various spheres in which symbols actually occur). At the lowest level we come upon sedimented symbolism: here we find

---

by the censorship; thus symbols may be formed of the modes or ways in which the mind is working (slowly, quickly, lightly, heavily, cheerfully, successfully, etc.). Repression would simply be one of these modes of mental functioning. Jones' main objection to this "functional symbolism" is that it has "proceeded, by rejecting the hardly won knowledge of the unconscious, to reinterpret the psychoanalytical findings back again into the surface meanings characteristic of pre-Freudian experience" (p. 117). Thus Jones rejects any attempt to make sexual symbols the *symbols of something else;* in our terminology, the sexual is always *signified,* and never *signifier.* Why this intransigence? The reason, Jones states, is that repression is the sole cause of the distortion operative in the formation of true symbols. The passing of *material* symbolism (mainly representing sexual things) over into *functional* symbolism (representing the modes of mental functioning) is itself a ruse employed by the unconscious and a manifestation of our resistance to the only true interpretation of symbolism. Thus Silberer's interpretation is a defensive or "reactionary" interpretation. Jones grants that any nonsexual idea may indeed be symbolized, but only if it has first had some symbolic connection with a sexual theme; it is precisely the function of metaphor to replace symbolism, which is always grounded in forbidden impulses, by a harmless presentation of the abstract in terms of the concrete; thus the serpent, a sexual symbol, will become the metaphor of wisdom, the wedding ring, a symbol of the female organ, the emblem of fidelity, etc. Every replacement of material symbolism by functional symbolism is an instance of this type of reinterpretation of the repressed in harmless terms.

However great the force of this argumentation may be, it seems to me that Jones' intransigence is not justified; *psychoanalysis has no way of proving that repressed impulses are the only sources of what can be symbolized.* Thus the view that in Eastern religions the phallus became the symbol of a creative power cannot be dismissed for psychoanalytic reasons, but for philosophical reasons which must be debated on other grounds. Jones' disdainful rejection of the view that symbols may have an "anagogic" meaning (Silberer), a "programmatic" meaning (Adler), or a "prospective" meaning (Jung) is characteristic: according to Jones, these authors abandon "the methods and canons of science, particularly the conceptions of causality and determinism" (p. 136). The argument is not psychoanalytical, but philosophical. But that is not the root of the matter; every one-sided theory of symbolism seems to me to break down at a precise point: such theories account for the substitutive or compromise aspect of symbols, but not for

various stereotyped and fragmented remains of symbols, symbols so commonplace and worn with use that they have nothing but a past. This is the level of dream-symbolism, and also of fairy tales and legends; here the work of symbolization is no longer operative. At a second level we come upon the symbols that function in everyday life; these are the symbols that are useful and are actually utilized, that have a past and a present, and that in the clockwork of a given society serve as a token for the nexus of social pacts; structural anthropology operates at this level. At a higher level come the prospective symbols; these are creations of meaning that take up the traditional symbols with their multiple significations and serve as the vehicles of new meanings. This creation of meaning reflects the living substrate of symbolism, a substrate that is not the result of social sedimentation. Later in this chapter we will try to state how this creation of meaning is at the same time a recapture of archaic fantasies and a living interpretation of this fantasy substrate. Dreams provide a key only for the symbolism of the first level; the "typical" dreams Freud appeals to in developing his theory of symbolism do not reveal the canonical form of symbols but merely their vestiges on the plane of sedimented expressions. The true task, therefore, is to grasp symbols in their creative moment, and not when they arrive at the end of their course and are revived in dreams, like stenographic grammalogues with their "permanently

---

their power of denying and overcoming their own origin. Symbolism in the Freudian sense expresses the failure of sublimation and not its advancement, as Jones readily admits: "The affect investing the symbolized ideas has not, in so far as the symbolism is concerned, proved capable of that modification in quality denoted by the term 'sublimation'" (p. 139). Moreover, Jones himself introduces a second pole of the symbolic function when he considers symbolism in terms of the reality principle and not simply in terms of the pleasure principle (pp. 132 ff.) and quite correctly points out that "every step in progress in the line of the reality principle connotes, not only a use of this primordial association [between a new percept and some unconscious complex], but also a partial renunciation of it" (p. 133). However, in the one-sided conception of symbolism, this renunciation can only be a weakening of true symbolism, as in the case where primitive symbols serve to facilitate the formation of objective concepts or scientific generalizations. Such a conception does not account for the immense symbolic domain explored by Western thought since Plato and Origen, but only for the pale metaphors of ordinary language and its rhetoric.

fixed meaning." Further on, the tragedy of *Oedipus Rex* will enable us to recapture the birth of symbol, at the moment when the symbol is itself the interpretation of a prior legendary substrate. But it is impossible to proceed directly to the center of this creative source. We must make use of all the available mediations.

THE HIERARCHICAL ORDER OF SYMBOL

The dialectical interpretation of the concept of overdetermination, understood as the twofold possibility of a teleological exegesis and a regressive exegesis, must now be brought to bear on certain definite problems. What are we to take as our guide? The *Phenomenology of Spirit?* As I have said, I do not think we can restore, after more than a century, The *Phenomenology of Spirit* in the form in which it was written. I propose to put to the test of reflection a principle of hierarchy that I already used in *Fallible Man* to articulate the notion of feeling.[18] The working hypothesis is plausible: feeling, too, is "mixed"; it is that "mixed texture" explored by Plato in Book IV of the *Republic* under the title of *thumos,* i.e. "spiritedness" or "heart." Spiritedness, Plato said, sometimes fights on the side of reason in the form of indignation and courage, and sometimes sides with desire in the form of aggressiveness, irritation, and anger. Spiritedness, I added, is the restless heart that knows not the surcease of pleasure and the repose of happiness, and I suggested that this ambiguous and fragile heart represents the entire middle region of the affective life between the vital affections and the rational or spiritual affections, that is to say, the entire activity that forms the transition between living and thinking, between Bios and Logos. And I had already noted: "It is in this intermediate region that the *self* is constituted as different from natural beings and other selves. . . . Only with *thumos* does desire assume the character of otherness and subjectivity which constitute a self." [19]

18. Ricoeur, *L'Homme faillible* (Paris, Aubier, 1960), Ch. 4, Section 3; tr., Charles Kelbley, *Fallible Man* (Chicago, Regnery, 1965).
19. Ibid., p. 123; Eng. trans., p. 163.

I wish to reexamine this problem of mixed texture in the light of our antithesis between the two hermeneutics. The same feelings that I previously studied under the heading of thumos will now be seen as being subject to two modes of exegesis, one along the lines of the Freudian erotics, the other along the lines of a phenomenology of spirit.

To this effect, I propose to reexamine the trilogy of fundamental feelings that I borrowed from the Kantian anthropology—the trilogy of the passions of having, power, and valuation or worth [*avoir, pouvoir, valoir*]—and to redo the exegesis of the three "quests" that the moralist knows only under the distorted mask of fallen figures—the "passions" of possession, domination, and pretension, or, in another language, of avarice, tyranny, and vanity (*Habsucht, Herrschsucht, Ehrsucht*). What we must discover behind this threefold *Sucht,* with its aberration and violence, is the authentic *Suchen;* "behind this passional pursuit," we must attain to "the 'quest' of humanity, a quest no longer mad and in bondage but constitutive of human praxis and the human self." [20]

I would like to show that this threefold quest pertains to a phenomenology in the style of Hegel and to an erotics in the style of Freud.

It should be emphasized that the three spheres of meaning through which the trajectory of feeling passes as it moves from having, to power, and to worth, constitute regions of human meanings that are in essence nonlibidinal. Not that they are "spheres free of conflict," as certain neo-Freudians say; [21] no region of human existence escapes the libidinal cathexis of love and hate; but the important point is that, whatever be the secondary cathexis of the interhuman relations formed on the occasions of having, power, and worth, these spheres of meaning are not constituted by the libidinal cathexis.

By what, then, are they constituted? It seems to me this is where the Hegelian method is of help. One way of modernizing the Hegelian enterprise would be to constitute through progressive synthesis

20. Ibid., p. 127; Eng. trans., pp. 169–70.
21. Heinz Hartmann, *Ego Psychology and the Problem of Adaptation,* Ch. 1.

the moments of "objectivity" that guide the human feelings as they center on having, power, and worth. Such moments are indeed moments of objectivity: to understand these affective factors, which we name possession, domination, and valuation, is to show that these feelings internalize a series of object-relations that pertain not to a phenomenology of perception, but to an economics, a politics, a theory of culture. The progress of this constitution of objectivity should guide the investigation of the affectivity proper to man.[22] At the same time that they institute a new relationship to things, the properly human quests of having, power, and worth institute new relationships to other persons, through which one can pursue the Hegelian process of the reduplication of consciousness and the advancement of self-consciousness.

Let us examine, from this double point of view, the successive constitution of the three spheres of meaning.

By relations of *having* I understand the relations involved in appropriation and work within a situation of "scarceness." To this day we know of no other condition of human having. In connection with these relations, however, we see new human feelings arise that do not pertain to the biological sphere; these feelings proceed not from life but from the reflection into human affectivity of a new domain of objects, of a specific objectivity that is "economic" objectivity. Man appears here as a being capable of feelings relative to having and of an alienation that in essence is nonlibidinal. This is the alienation Marx described in his theory of the fetishism of money; it is the economic alienation that Marx showed is capable of engendering a "false consciousness," or ideological thinking. Thus man becomes adult and, in the same movement, capable of adult alienation. What is important to note, however, is that the areas in which these feelings, passions, and alienations multiply are new objects, values of exchange, monetary signs, structures, and institutions. We may say, then, that man becomes self-consciousness insofar as he experiences this economic objectivity as a new modality of his subjectivity and thus attains specifically human "feelings"

22. As in *Fallible Man,* I adopt Alfred Stern's idea that feeling internalizes man's relationship to the world; thus new aspects of objectivity are internalized in the feelings of possession, power, and worth.

relative to the availability of things as things that have been worked upon and appropriated, while at the same time he becomes an expropriated appropriator. This new objectivity gives rise to a specific group of impulses, ideas, and affects.

The sphere of *power* should be examined in the same way, that is to say, from the point of view of objectivity and the feelings and alienations this objectivity engenders. The sphere of power is likewise constituted in an objective structure. Thus Hegel used the term "objective spirit" to designate the structures and institutions in which the relation of commanding-obeying, essential to political power, actualizes and engenders itself; as we see at the beginning of the *Principles of the Philosophy of Right*, man engenders himself as spiritual will by entering into the relation of commanding-obeying. Here too the development of self-consciousness is bound up with a development of "objectivity." The "feelings" centering around this "object," which is power, are specifically human feelings, such as intrigue, ambition, submission, responsibility; so too the alienations are specifically human alienations. The ancients already described these alienations in the figure of the tyrant. Plato clearly shows how the maladies of the soul, which are exhibited in the figure of the tyrant, spread out from a center he calls *dunamis*, or power, and even extend into the region of language in the form of "flattery"; thus the tyrant gives rise to the sophist. Hence one can say that man becomes human insofar as he can enter into the political problematic of power, adopt the feelings that center around power, and deliver himself up to the evils accompanying that power. Thus there arises a specifically adult sphere of guilt; power leads to madness, says Alain, following Plato. This second example makes it clear how a psychology of consciousness is simply the projected shadow of this movement of figures that man assumes in engendering economic and then political objectivity.

The same may be said of the third properly human sphere of meaning, the sphere of *valuation* or *worth*. This third moment may be understood as follows: the constitution of the self is not completed in an economics and a politics, but continues on into the region of culture. Here too the psychology of personality grasps only the shadow, that is to say, the aim, present in each man, of being respected, approved, and recognized as a person. My existence for myself is dependent on this constitution of self in the opinion of others; my "self" is shaped by the opinion and acceptance of others. But this constitution of subjects, this mutual constitution through opinion, is guided by new figures which may be said to be "objective" in a new sense. These objects are no longer *things,* as are the objects in the sphere of having; they do not always have corresponding *institutions,* as do the objects in the sphere of power. These new figures of man are to be found in the works and monuments of law, art, and literature. The exploration of man's possibilities extends into this new kind of objectivity, the objectivity of cultural objects properly so-called. Even when Van Gogh sketches a chair, he at the same time portrays man; he projects a figure of man, namely the man who "has" this represented world. Thus, the various modes of cultural expression give these "images" the density of "thingness"; they make these images exist between men and among men, by embodying them in "works." It is through the medium of these works and monuments that a human dignity and self-regard are formed. Finally, this is the level at which man can become alienated from himself, degrade himself, make a fool of himself, destroy himself.

Such is, it seems to me, the exegesis that may be made of consciousness according to a method that is not a psychology of consciousness, but a reflective method that has its starting point in the objective movement of the figures of man. This objective movement is what Hegel calls spirit. Reflection is the means for deriving from this movement the subjectivity that constitutes itself at the same time that the objectivity engenders itself.

It is clear that this indirect, mediate approach to consciousness has nothing to do with an immediate self-presence of consciousness, an immediate self-certainty.

But no sooner have we noted the specificity of economic, political, and cultural objectivity, and the specificity of the related human feelings, than we have to take the reverse path and point out the gradual cathexis or investment of these regions of meaning by what Freud calls the "derivatives from the unconscious." The three spheres we have examined, like the whole life of civilization, are involved in a history of instincts; none of the figures of the phenomenology of spirit escapes the libidinal investment, and consequently the possibilities of regression inherent in the instinctual situation. We shall outline briefly the dialectic of the two hermeneutics at the levels of having and power, and reserve a more extensive analysis for the symbolism of the strictly cultural sphere.

Freud presents a libidinal interpretation of having that is thoroughly compatible with an interpretation that allows the economic sphere, in the sense of political economy, its own specificity. Well known are the attempts made by Freud and his followers to derive the apparently nonlibidinal relations to things and men from the successive phases through which the libido passes: oral phase, anal phase, phallic phase, genital phase. Freud uses the term "transformation" [23] (*Umsetzung*) to designate this displacement of instinctual emotions from certain erotogenic zones onto seemingly quite different objects. Thus Freud borrows the notion from Abraham that after a person's excrement has lost its value for him,

> this instinctual interest . . . passes over onto objects that can be presented as *gifts*. . . . After this, corresponding exactly to analogous changes of meaning that occur in linguistic development, this ancient interest in feces is transformed into the high valuation of *gold* and *money* but also makes a contribution to the affective cathexis of *baby* and *penis*. . . . If one is not aware of these profound connections, it is impossible to find one's way about in the fantasies of human beings, in their associations, influenced as they are by the unconscious, and in their symptomatic language. Feces—money—gift—baby—penis are treated there as though they meant the same thing, and they are represented too by the same symbols.

Freud uses the same terms in speaking of the "formation of character" that begins in the pregenital phases of the libido; he believes that the triad of orderliness, thrift, and obstinacy is connected with anal erotism: "We therefore speak of an 'anal character' in which

23. *New Introductory Lectures, GW, 15,* 106–07; *SE, 22,* 100–01.

we find this remarkable combination and we draw a contrast to some extent between the anal character and unmodified anal erotism." [24]

In this example we can see both the validity and the limits of this type of interpretation. The Freudian interpretation functions as a kind of hyletic of affects (here I take *hylê* or "matter" in the Husserlian sense of the term).[25] It enables us to set forth the genealogy of the main human affects and to establish the table of their derivatives; it verifies Kant's insight that there is only one "faculty of desiring"; in Freudian terms, our love of money is the same love we had as infants for our feces. But at the same time we realize that this kind of exploration into the substructures of our affects does not substitute for a constitution of the economic object. The regressive genesis of our desires does not replace a progressive genesis concerned with meanings, values, symbols. That is why Freud speaks of "transformations of instinct." But a dynamics of affective cathexes cannot account for the innovation or advancement of meaning that is inherent in this transformation.

The same may be said of the political sphere, which constitutes, as we have seen, a specific region of interhuman relationships and an original class of human objects. It is perfectly possible to erect two interpretations upon this single affective complex, an interpretation according to the figures of the phenomenology of spirit and an interpretation of the type that Freud elaborated in 1921 in *Group Psychology and the Analysis of the Ego*. Freud regards the concept of "suggestion," espoused by the social psychology of the beginning of the century, as a screen for the libido: it is Eros, he states, "which holds together everything in the world." [26] And he confidently proceeds to write a chapter on the libidinal structure of the army and the church. We should not be surprised that an enter-

24. *GW, 15,* 107; *SE, 22,* 102.

25. Husserl, *Ideen* I, §§ 85, 97. It is to be noted that in Husserl the words *Formung, Meinung,* and *Deutung* designate the relationship of the intentional act to the matter; the intention "interprets" the matter, just as in Aristotle discourse is the interpretation (*hermêneia*) of the affections (*pathê*) of the soul. The comparison is all the more striking in that for Husserl, the *hylê* includes both affections or feelings and sensations.

26. *Group Psychology and the Analysis of the* Ego, *GW, 13,* 100; *SE, 18,* 92.

prise of this kind never attains to the level of a structural analysis of groups. The key notions here are the concrete tie with the leader and homosexual object-cathexis. The various ideas or causes that might hold a group or society together are regarded as derived from interpersonal ties that ultimately are rooted in the invisible leader. Freud admits that "we are concerned here with love instincts which have been diverted from their original aims, though they do not operate with less energy on that account." [27] This inability on the part of a mere psychoanalysis of the leader to attain to the fundamental constitution of social ties does not prevent the interpretation from being extremely penetrating.

Such an investigation inevitably brings us back to the concept of identification; indeed, Chapter 7 of *Group Psychology* is Freud's most important study of identification. "*A primary group of this kind is a number of individuals who have put one and the same object in the place of their ego ideal and have consequently identified themselves with one another in their ego.*" [28] But Freud himself points out the limits of his enterprise. Ultimately, his investigation is concerned less with the formation and development of social groups than with the regressive characteristics of groups as described by Le Bon at the turn of the century: namely, "the lack of independence and initiative in their members, the similarity in the reactions of all of them, their reduction so to speak, to the level of group individuals"; and at the level of the group as a whole, "the weakness of intellectual activity, the lack of emotional restraint, the incapacity for moderation and delay, the inclination to exceed every limit in the expression of emotion and to work it off completely in the form of action." [29]

Even when he extends his investigation to what he calls "artificial groups"—army or church—the explanation is still in terms of the libidinal ties holding a group or the hypothetical primal horde together:

> The uncanny and coercive characteristics of group formations, which are shown in the phenomena of suggestion that accom-

27. *GW, 13,* 113; *SE, 18,* 103.
28. *GW, 13,* 128; *SE, 18,* 116.
29. *GW, 13,* 129; *SE, 18,* 117.

> pany them, may therefore with justice be traced back to the fact of their origin from the primal horde. The leader of the group is still the dreaded primal father; the group still wishes to be governed by unrestricted force; it has an extreme passion for authority; in Le Bon's phrase, it has a thirst for obedience. The primal father is the group ideal, which governs the ego in the place of the ego ideal.[30]

In conclusion, Freud states: "We are aware that what we have been able to contribute towards the explanation of the libidinal structure of groups leads back to the distinction between the ego and the ego ideal and to the double kind of tie which this makes possible—identification, and putting the [external libidinal] object in the place of the ego ideal." [31] But if we ask psychoanalysis what constitutes the specificity of the political tie, its only answer is to invoke the notion of a "diversion of aim."

In the same text Freud admits that "there is some difficulty in giving a description of such a diversion of aim which will conform to the requirements of metapsychology." [32] And he adds: "If we choose, we may recognize in this diversion of aim a beginning of the *sublimation* of the sexual instincts, or on the other hand we may fix the limits of sublimation at some more distant point." [33] Is this not rather the sign that sublimation is a mixed concept, which designates both a derivation of energy and an innovation of meaning? The derivation of energy shows that there is but one libido and merely various vicissitudes of that one libido, but the innovation of meaning requires another hermeneutics.

A DIALECTICAL REEXAMINATION OF THE PROBLEM OF SUBLIMATION AND THE CULTURAL OBJECT

I now wish to show, in a very precise example, how a dialectical exegesis may be applied to symbols

30. *GW, 13,* 142; *SE, 18,* 127.
31. *GW, 13,* 145; *SE, 18,* 130.
32. *GW, 13,* 155 (*Zielablenkung*); *SE, 18,* 138.
33. *GW, 13,* 155; *SE, 18,* 139.

belonging to the third cycle of man's *Suchen*. I will take this example from the esthetic sphere, where Freud's interpretation is less reductive than it is in the sphere of religious symbolism. It is here that the profound identity of the two hermeneutics, regressive and progressive, may be shown most clearly and forcefully. It is here that the teleology of consciousness will appear in the detailed structure of the archeology itself, and the telos of the human adventure will be foreshadowed in the endless exegesis of the myths and hidden secrets of our childhood and birth.

This privileged example, this prototypic example, will be Sophocles' *Oedipus Rex*. The tragedy is built around a fantasy well known to the interpretation of dreams, the fantasy in which we live through the childhood drama that we call oedipal. In this sense, we may say with Freud that there is nothing more behind the work of art created by Sophocles than a dream. From the start Freud rejects the classical interpretation of the *Oedipus Rex* as a tragedy of destiny, whose effect lies in the contrast between the omnipotence of the gods and the vain efforts of mankind to escape the evil that threatens them. This type of conflict, he thinks, no longer affects a modern audience, whereas spectators are still moved by *Oedipus Rex*. What moves us is not the conflict between destiny and human will, but the particular nature of this destiny, which we recognize without knowing it: "His destiny moves us only because it might have been ours—because the oracle laid the same curse upon us before our birth as upon him." [34] Freud compares the legend and the drama with dreams of incest and parricide.

> King Oedipus, who slew his father Laïus and married his mother Jocasta, merely shows us the fulfillment of our own childhood wishes. . . . Here is one in whom these primeval wishes of our childhood have been fulfilled, and we shrink back from him with the whole force of the repression by which those wishes have since that time been held down within us.[35]

Just as these typical dreams are accompanied by feelings of repulsion whereby we comply with the censorship and make the dream content admissible to consciousness, "so too," says Freud, "the leg-

34. *The Interpretation of Dreams*, *GW*, *2/3*, 269; *SE*, *4*, 262.
35. *GW*, *2/3*, 269; *SE*, *4*, 262–63.

end must include horror and self-punishment."[36] Thus the famous tragic *phobos* would express merely the violence of our own repression against the revival of those childhood wishes. As for the theological interpretation concerning the conflict between Providence and human freedom, Freud casually attributes it to "a misconceived secondary revision of the material."[37]

At this point I would like to counter with a second interpretation, which is in fact contained in the preceding one by reason of the overdetermination of the Oedipus symbol. This interpretation no longer concerns the drama of incest and parricide, a drama that has already taken place when the tragedy begins, but rather the tragedy of truth. It appears that Sophocles' creation does not aim at reviving the Oedipus complex in the minds of the spectators; on the basis of a first drama, the drama of incest and parricide, Sophocles has created a second, the tragedy of self-consciousness, of self-recognition. Thus Oedipus enters into a second guilt, an adult guilt, expressed in the hero's arrogance and anger. At the beginning of the play Oedipus calls down curses upon the unknown person responsible for the plague, but he excludes the possibility that that person might in fact be himself. The entire drama consists in the resistance and ultimate collapse of this presumption. Oedipus must be broken in his pride through suffering; this presumption is no longer the culpable desire of the child, but the pride of the king; the tragedy is not the tragedy of Oedipus the child, but of Oedipus Rex. By reason of this impure passion with respect to the truth, his hubris rejoins that of Prometheus: what leads him to disaster is the passion for nonknowing. His guilt is no longer in the sphere of the libido, but in that of self-consciousness: it is man's anger as the power of nontruth. Thus Oedipus becomes guilty precisely because of his pretension to exonerate himself from a crime that, ethically speaking, he is not in fact guilty of.

It is therefore possible to apply to Sophocles' drama what we have called an antithetic of reflection. One might illustrate this opposition between the two dramas and between the two kinds of guilt by saying that the initial drama, which comes within the province of

36. *GW, 2/3*, 270; *SE, 4*, 264.
37. Ibid.

psychoanalysis, has its antagonist in the sphynx, which represents the enigma of birth—the source, according to Freud, of all the strange events of childhood; whereas the second order drama, which Freud seems to reduce to the status of a secondary revision, and even of a misconception—although it actually constitutes the true tragedy—has its antagonist in Tiresias the seer. In the language of our antithetic, the sphynx represents the side of the unconscious, the seer the side of spirit or mind. As in the Hegelian dialectic, Oedipus is not the center from which the truth proceeds; a first mastery, which is only pretension and pride, must be broken; the figure from which truth proceeds is that of the seer, which Sophocles describes as the "force of truth." [38] This figure is no longer a tragic one; it represents and manifests the vision of the totality. The seer, akin to the fool of Elizabethan tragedy, is the figure of comedy at the heart of tragedy, a figure Oedipus will rejoin only through suffering and pain. The underlying link between the anger of Oedipus and the power of truth is thus the core of the veritable tragedy. This core is not the problem of sex, but the problem of light. The seer is blind with respect to the eyes of the body, but he sees the truth in the light of the mind. That is why Oedipus, who sees the light of day but is blind with regard to himself, will achieve self-consciousness only by becoming the blind seer: night of the senses, night of the understanding, night of the will; nothing more to see, nothing more to love, nothing more to enjoy. "Cease being a master," Creon says harshly; "you won the mastery but could not keep it to the end."

Such is the antithetic reading of *Oedipus Rex;* but we must now combine the two readings in the unity of the symbol and its power to disguise and reveal. I will start with a remark of Freud's which we have omitted and which concerns not the matter of the drama, which we are told is identical with the dream material,[39] but the manner in which the drama unfolds. "The action of the play," he says, "consists in nothing other than the process of revealing, with cunning delays and ever-mounting excitement—a process that can be likened to the work of a psychoanalysis—that Oedipus himself is

38. Sophocles, *Oedipus Rex,* verse 356.
39. *GW, 2/3,* 269; *SE, 4,* 263.

the murderer of Laïus, but further that he is the son of the murdered man and of Jocasta."[40] But we have already seen that psychoanalysis as a therapeutic activity, as a process of reduplicated consciousness, revives the whole history of master and slave. Thus the analytic interpretation, inasmuch as it is itself a struggle for recognition and hence a struggle for truth, a movement of self-consciousness, suggests the other drama, that of anger and non-truth. That is why Freud himself is not content with saying that Oedipus "shows us the fulfillment of our own childhood wishes"; this is the drama's oneiric function. He adds:

> While the poet, as he unravels the past, brings to light the guilt of Oedipus, he is at the same time compelling us to recognize our own inner minds, in which those same impulses, though suppressed, are still to be found. The contrast with which the closing Chorus leaves us confronted—
>
> *. . . Fix on Oedipus your eyes,*
> *Who resolved the dark enigma, noblest champion and most wise.*
> *Like a star his envied fortune mounted beaming far and wide:*
> *Now he sinks in seas of anguish, whelmed beneath a raging tide . . .*
>
> —strikes as a warning at ourselves and our pride, at us who since our childhood have grown so wise and so mighty in our own eyes.[41]

Freud did not clearly distinguish between the mere revival of childhood wishes in dreams and the "warning," addressed to the adult in us, upon which the drama of truth ends. An antithetic method was required to bring this double function of Sophocles' drama to the fore. It is only then that we can see the necessity of going beyond the duality.

In this connection, what is particularly striking about the symbol

40. *GW, 2/3,* 268; *SE, 4,* 261–62.

41. *GW, 2/3,* 269; *SE, 4,* 263. On the Oedipus of fantasy, myth, and tragedy, see C. Stein, "Notes sur la mort d'Oedipe: Préliminaire à une anthropologie psychanalytique," *Rev. fr. de psychan., 23* (1959), 735–56; C. Lévi-Strauss, *Anthropologie structurale* (Paris, Plon, 1958), Ch. 11.

created by Sophocles is the fact that the drama of truth centers precisely around the mystery of birth. The oedipal situation contains all the "spiritual" overtones developed by the process of truth: curiosity, resistance, pride, distress, wisdom. Between the question of the father and the question of truth a secret alliance is formed that resides in the overdetermination of the symbol itself. The father is much more than the father, and the question of the father is much more than an inquiry about my own father. The father, after all, is never *seen* in his fatherhood, but only conjectured. The whole power of questioning is contained in the fantasies of this conjecture. The symbolism of engendering embraces all the questions concerning generation, genesis, origin, development. But if the childhood Oedipus drama is already potentially the tragedy of truth, Sophocles' tragedy of truth is not superimposed upon the drama of origin, for the material of that tragedy, as Freud says, is the same as the dream material. The second order tragedy belongs to the primary tragedy, as is clear from the play's ambiguous and overdetermined ending. The crime of Oedipus culminates in the punishment of mutilation inflicted by the anger of nontruth. What is punishment in the tragedy of sex is the dark night of the senses in the final tragedy of truth. And if we return to an earlier part of the play, we see that the king's anger toward the seer derives its energy from the resistance stemming from the oedipal situation and the dissolution of the childhood complex.

The exegesis of Sophocles' *Oedipus Rex* enables us now to complete the parallel analysis of sublimation and cultural objects, which are in a sense the noematic correlates of sublimation.

We began the dialectical interpretation of sublimation in the spheres of having and power, where we saw the profoundly antithetical nature of sublimation. As we said before, it is on the basis of affects belonging to different libidinal stages that we form the feelings and corresponding meanings that establish us in an economic and a political order. But the example of such an exceptional creation as Sophocles' tragedy reveals more than an antithetic; it reveals, *in the work of art itself,* the profound unity of disguise and disclosure, inherent in the very structure of symbols that have become cultural objects.

It thus becomes possible to locate the oneiric and the poetic on the same symbolic scale. The production of dreams and the creation of works of art represent the two ends of this scale, according to whether the predominant emphasis in the symbolism is disguise or disclosure, distortion or revelation. By this formula I attempt to account both for the functional unity existing between dreams and creativity and for the difference in value that separates a mere product of our dreams from the lasting works that become a part of the cultural heritage of mankind. Between dreams and artistic creativity there is a functional continuity, in the sense that disguise and disclosure are operative in both of them, but in an inverse proportion. That is why Freud is justified in moving from one to the other by a series of imperceptible transitions, as he does in "Creative Writers and Daydreaming." [42] Passing from night dreams to daydreams, from daydreams to play and humor, then to folklore and legends, and finally to works of art, he attests, by this species of increasingly closer analogy, that all creativity is involved in the same economic function and brings about the same substitution of satisfaction as the compromise formations of dreams and the neuroses. But the question remains: Can an economics account for the increasing prevalence, through the functional analogy, of a mythopoetic power that places the oneiric in the area of creations of speech, themselves rooted in the hierophanies of the sacred and in the symbolism of the cosmic elements? Of this other function Freud recognizes only a very partial aspect, which he describes in terms of an "esthetic incentive" and which comes down to the purely formal pleasure produced by the artist's technique in presenting his material. This "incentive" or "allurement" is incorporated into the economy of desire as a type of forepleasure: "We give the name of an *incentive bonus,* or a *forepleasure,* to a yield of pleasure such as this, which is offered to us so as to make possible the release of still greater pleasure arising from deeper psychical sources." [43] Thus

42. Cf. above, "Analytic," Part II, Ch. 1, pp. 165–67. On the relationship between the oneiric and the poetic, see P. Luquet, "Ouvertures sur l'artiste et la psychanalyse; la fonction esthétique du moi," *Rev. fr. de psychan., 27* (1963), 585–618; also the work of La Décade de Cerisy, *Art et psychanalyse,* soon to be published.

43. *GW', 7,* 223; *SE, 9,* 153.

the economic framework of the explanation would reduce the entire Kantian analysis of the "judgment of taste" to a "hedonics." Freud accounts very well for the functional unity of dreams and artistic creation, but the qualitative difference, the difference in "aim" which renders instincts dialectical, escapes him; this is why the question of sublimation remains unsolved.

We thus see in what sense it is true, and in what sense it is not true, that works of art, the lasting and memorable creations of our days, and dreams, the fleeting and sterile products of our nights, are psychical expressions of the same nature. Their unity is assured by the fact that they share the same "hyletic," the same "matter" of desire. But their difference, which Freud himself describes as a "transformation of aim," a "diversion of aim," "sublimation," is bound up with the process of the figures of spirit. We thus relate Freud to Plato, the Plato of the *Ion* and the *Symposium,* who posited the underlying unity of the poetic and the erotic, and who regarded the philosophic mania or madness as belonging to the manifold unity of all forms of enthusiasm and exaltation. Within their intentional structure symbols have both the unity of a hyletic matter and the qualitative diversity of aims and intentions, with the emphasis either upon the disguising of the hylê or upon the revealing of a further, spiritual meaning. If dreams remain a private expression lost in the solitude of sleep, it is because they lack the mediation of the artisan's work that embodies the fantasy in a solid material and communicates it to a public. This mediation of the artisan's work and this communication accrue only to those dreams that at the same time carry values capable of advancing consciousness toward a new understanding of itself. If Michelangelo's *Moses,* Sophocles' *Oedipus Rex,* and Shakespeare's *Hamlet* are creations, they are so in proportion as they are not mere projections of the artist's conflicts, but also the sketch of their solution. Because of their emphasis on disguise, dreams look more to the past, to childhood. But in works of art the emphasis is on disclosure; thus works of art tend to be prospective symbols of one's personal synthesis and of man's future and not merely a regressive symptom of the artist's unresolved conflicts. The same emphasis upon disclosure is the reason our pleasure as viewers of art is not the simple revival, even accompanied by an incentive bonus, of our own conflicts, but the pleasure of sharing in the work of truth that comes about through the hero.

This approach to the intentional unity of symbols has enabled us to overcome the remaining distance between regression and progression. From now on regression and progression do not represent two truly opposed processes; they are rather the abstract terms employed to designate the two end limits of a single scale of symbolization. Are not dreams a compromise fluctuating between these two functions, according as the neurotic aspect inclines dreams toward repetition and archaism, or as they themselves are on the way to a therapeutic action exercised by the self upon itself? Inversely, are there any great symbols created by art or literature that are not rooted in the archaism of the conflicts and dramas of our individual or collective childhood? The most innovative figures that the artist, writer, or thinker can produce call forth ancient energies originally invested in archaic figures; but in activating these figures, comparable to oneiric and neurotic symptoms, the creator reveals man's most open and fundamental possibilities and erects them into new symbols of the suffering of self-consciousness.

But just as there is a scale or gradation in the oneiric, perhaps there is also a scale in the poetic. Surrealism shows quite well how the poetic can return to the oneiric, or even tend to copy neurosis when esthetic creativity gives free rein to the fantasies of obsession, organizes itself around themes of repetition, or even regresses to automatic writing. Thus, not only would works of art and dreams be located at the two ends of a single scale of symbolization, but each of these kinds of production would reconcile, according to an inverse pattern, the oneiric and the poetic.

To overcome what remains abstract in the opposition between regression and progression would require a study of these concrete relations, shifts of emphasis, and inversion of roles between the functions of disguise and disclosure. At least we have shown that the area in which this concrete dialectic must be worked out is that of language and its symbolic function.

Corresponding to this dialectical structure of sublimation is a similar structure of the "cultural objects" that are the correlates of sublimation. These objects pertain to the third sphere of feelings, which we have described as the sphere of worth or valuation. These feelings appeared to us to form a region of meaning irreducible to a political economy and a politics. The process in which man achieves consciousness is not restricted to relationships between the ego and possessions, to relations of appropriation and mutual expropriation, or of exchange, sharing, and giving; nor is it restricted to the relations of dominance and obedience, of hierarchy and sharing of influence. The quest for recognition also extends into a quest for mutual esteem and approval. My existence for myself is thus dependent on the way I am regarded by other people; the self is shaped by the opinion and acceptance of others. This mutual constitution through opinion is still guided by objects, but these objects are no longer "things" in the sense of the goods, commodities, and services of the sphere of having, nor do they have corresponding institutions as in the sphere of power; these objects are the monuments and works of law, art, literature, philosophy. The exploration of man's possibilities extends into this new kind of objectivity, the objectivity of works or cultural objects properly so-called. Painted, sculptured, or written works give these "images of man" the density of thingness, the stability of reality; they make these images exist between men and among men by embodying them in the material of stone, color, musical score, or the written word. It is through the medium of these works or monuments that a certain dignity of man is formed, which is the instrument and trace of a process of reduplicated consciousness, of recognition of the self in another self.

These works or cultural objects, however, cannot be accounted for by a simple antithetic that would see a split between the creative process along which man's human development lies and the affective material upon which the history of spirit works. The only thing that can do justice to both an economics of culture and a phenomenology of spirit is a dialectic based on the overdetermination of symbols. I propose therefore that cultural phenomena should be interpreted as the objective media in which the great enterprise of sublimation with its double value of disguise and disclosure becomes sedimented. Such an interpretation opens up to us the meaning of certain synonymous expressions. Thus the term "education" designates the movement by which man is led out of his childhood;

this movement is, in the proper sense, an "erudition" whereby man is lifted out of his archaic past; but it is also a *Bildung,* in the twofold sense of an edification and an emergence of the *Bilder* or "images of man" which mark off the development of self-consciousness and open man to what they disclose. And this education, this erudition, this Bildung function as a second nature, for they remodel man's first nature. In them is realized the movement so well described by Ravaisson in the limited example of habit; this movement is at the same time the return of freedom to nature through the recapture of desire in the works of culture.[44] Because of the overdetermination of symbols, these works are closely tied in with the world of our experience: it is indeed where id was that the ego comes to be. By mobilizing all our childhood stages, all our archaisms, by embodying itself in the oneiric, the poetic keeps man's cultural existence from being simply a huge artifice, a futile "artifact," a Leviathan without a nature and against nature.

FAITH AND RELIGION: THE AMBIGUITY OF THE SACRED

We have returned to the threshold of our starting point: the interpretation of religious symbolism. It must be confessed, however, that our method of thought does not enable us to solve the question of religious symbolism in a radical way, but serves merely to give us a frontier view of this symbolism.

I do not wish to give the impression that one can get at the radical origin of religious symbolism by a gradual enlargement of reflective thought. I will not employ that astute method of extrapolation. I flatly state that I have no way of proving the existence of an authentic problematic of faith starting from a phenomenology of spirit more or less taken from Hegel's phenomenology; I even grant that such a problematic exceeds the resources of a philosophy of reflection, which the foregoing dialectic has greatly enlarged—but not to the point of making it more than a philosophy of immanence. If there is an authentic problematic of faith, it pertains to a new dimension which I have previously described, in a different philosophical context, as a "Poetics of the Will," because it concerns the

44. Ricoeur, "Nature et liberté," *Études philosophiques* (1962).

radical origin of the *I will,* i.e. the source of effectiveness of the act of willing. In the context of the present work, I describe this new dimension as a call, a kerygma, a word addressed to me. In this sense, I am in accord with the way in which Karl Barth poses the theological problem. The origin of faith lies in the solicitation of man by the object of faith. Hence I will not employ the ruse of extrapolating the question of the radical origin from an archeology of the Cogito, or the question of the final end from a teleology. The archeology only points to what is already there, already posited in the Cogito that posits itself; the teleology only points to an ulterior meaning that holds the earlier meaning of the figures of spirit in suspense; but this ulterior meaning can always be understood as spirit's advance upon itself, as its self-projection into a telos. Compared to *this* archeology of myself and to *this* teleology of myself, genesis and eschatology are Wholly Other. To be sure, I speak of the Wholly Other only insofar as it addresses itself to me; and the kerygma, the glad tidings, is precisely that it addresses itself to me and ceases to be the Wholly Other. Of an absolute Wholly Other I know nothing at all. But by its very manner of approaching, of coming, it shows itself to be Wholly Other than the archê and the telos which I can conceptualize in reflective thought. It shows itself as Wholly Other by annihilating its radical otherness.

But if a problematic of faith has a different origin, the field of its manifestation is the very one we have been exploring. An Anselmian type of procedure, i.e. the movement from faith to understanding, necessarily encounters a dialectic of reflection, which it attempts to use as the instrument of its expression. This is where the question of faith becomes a hermeneutic question, for what annihilates itself in our flesh is the Wholly Other as logos. Thereby it becomes an event of human speech and can be recognized only in the movement of interpretation of this human speech. The "hermeneutic circle" is born: to believe is to listen to the call, but to hear the call we must interpret the message. Thus we must believe in order to understand and understand in order to believe.[45]

By thus making itself "immanent" to human speech, the Wholly

45. Ricoeur, *La Symbolique du mal* (Paris, Aubier, 1960), Conclusion; tr. Emerson Buchanan, *The Symbolism of Evil* (New York, Harper and Row, 1967).

Other becomes discernible in and through the dialectic of teleology and archeology. Although it is completely different from any origin assignable by reflection, the radical origin now becomes discernible in the question of my archeology; although it is completely different from any anticipation of myself I am capable of making, the final end becomes recognizable through the question of my teleology. Creation and eschatology present themselves as the *horizon* of my archeology and the *horizon* of my teleology. Horizon is the metaphor for what approaches without ever becoming a possessed object. The alpha and the omega approach reflection as the horizon of my roots and the horizon of my intendings or aims; it is the radical of the radical, the supreme of the supreme. This is where a phenomenology of the sacred in the sense of Van der Leuuw and Eliade, joined to a kerygmatic exegesis in the sense of Barth and Bultmann (whom I do not regard as differing on this point) can come to the aid of reflection and offer to meditative thought new symbolic expressions situated at the point of rupture and suture between the Wholly Other and our discourse.

This relationship presents itself to reflection as a rupture. The phenomenology of the sacred is not a continuation of a phenomenology of spirit; a teleology along Hegelian lines does not have as its *eschaton,* or final term, the sacred as carried by myth, ritual, and belief. Of itself, this teleology aims not at faith but at absolute knowledge; and absolute knowledge presents no transcendence, but the reabsorption of all transcendence within a completely mediated self-knowledge. Hence one cannot insert this phenomenology of the sacred in place of the eschaton and within the structure of the horizon without challenging the claim of absolute knowledge. But if reflection cannot of itself produce the meaning foreshadowed in this "approach" or "coming" ("the Kingdom of God has come near to you") it can at least understand why it cannot close in upon itself and achieve its proper meaning with its own resources. The reason for this failure is the fact of evil. The area of challenge, which will also be that of the threshold understanding, is the area of discourse where a symbolism of evil is structured upon the successive figures of the world of culture.

Why do we refuse to say that the "end" is absolute knowledge, the fulfillment of all the mediations in a whole, in a totality without remainder? Why do we say this end is only foreshadowed, promised "by prophecy," to use the language of the *Theologico-Political Treatise?* Why do we reassign to the sacred the place usurped by an absolute knowledge? Why do we refuse to transform faith into gnosis? The reason, along with others, why an absolute knowledge is impossible is the problem of evil, the problem we previously regarded merely as our point of departure in raising the problem of symbolism and hermeneutics. At the end of this journey we will discover that the great symbols concerning the nature and origin of evil are not simply one set of symbols out of many, but are privileged symbols. It does not even suffice to say, as we did in the "Problematic," that a symbolism of evil is the counterpart of a symbolism of salvation, which concerns the destiny of man. The symbols of evil teach us something decisive about the passage from a phenomenology of spirit to a phenomenology of the sacred. These symbols resist any reduction to a rational knowledge; the failure of all theodicies, of all systems concerning evil, witnesses to the failure of absolute knowledge in the Hegelian sense. All symbols give rise to thought, but the symbols of evil show in an exemplary way that there is always more in myths and symbols than in all of our philosophy, and that a philosophical interpretation of symbols will never become absolute knowledge. In short, the problem of evil forces us to return from Hegel to Kant—that is to say, from a dissolution of the problem of evil in dialectic to the recognition of the emergence of evil as something inscrutable, and hence as something that cannot be captured in a total and absolute knowledge. Thus the symbols of evil attest to the unsurpassable character of all symbolism; while telling us of the failure of our existence and of our power of existing, they also declare the failure of systems of thought that would swallow up symbols in an absolute knowledge.

But the symbolism of evil is also a symbolism of reconciliation. No doubt this reconciliation is given only in the signs that are its promise. But it is a reconciliation that always invites thought on the part of that understanding of faith I described above as a threshold understanding. Such an understanding does not annul its symbolic origin; it is not an understanding that allegorizes; it is an understanding that thinks according to symbols. Thought, said Nabert, always stands in the "approaches to justification." I shall propose three formulas expressing this link between evil as unjustifiable and the sacred as reconciliation—three formulas in which I discern the lineaments of an eschatology that is both symbolic and reasonable, prophetic and sensible. Although a philosophy of reflection cannot actually encompass this eschatology, it can make an approach to it at the horizon of a teleology of consciousness.

First of all, every reconciliation is looked for "in spite of"—in spite of evil. This "in spite of," this "nevertheless," this "even so," constitutes the first category of hope, the category of confidence. But there is no proof of this "in spite of," but only signs; the area in which this category operates is not a logic but a history, and one that must constantly be deciphered in the sign of a promise, a glad tidings, a kerygma. Next, this "in spite of" is a "thanks to": out of evil the principle of things brings good. The final confidence is also hidden instruction: *etiam peccata,* says St. Augustine, as an inscription, as it were, to the *Satin Slipper*. "The worst is not always sure," replies Claudel; and he adds, in citing the Portuguese proverb, "God writes straight with crooked lines." But there is no absolute knowledge of the "in spite of," nor of the "thanks to." Still less is there an absolute knowledge of the third category of this reasonable history: "Where sin abounds, grace superabounds," says St. Paul; this strange law of superabundance, expressed in the "much more," the πολλῷ μᾶλλον of the apostle, encompasses and enrolls the "in spite of" and the "thanks to." But this "a fortiori" or "much more" is not convertible into knowledge; that which in the old theodicy was only an expedient of false knowledge, modestly becomes the understanding of hope. "In spite of," "thanks to," "much more"—these are the highest rational symbols the eschatology engenders by means of this threshold understanding.

I am not unaware of the fragility of this relationship, *in a philosophy of reflection,* between the figures of spirit and the symbols of the sacred. From the viewpoint of the philosophy of reflection, which is a philosophy of immanence, the symbols of the sacred appear only as cultural factors mixed in with the figures of spirit. But at the same time these symbols designate the impact on culture of a reality that the movement of culture does not contain; they speak of the Wholly Other, of the Wholly Other than all of history; in this way they exercise an attraction and a call upon the entire series of the figures of culture. This is the sense in which I spoke of a prophecy or an eschatology. It is solely through its relation to the immanent teleology of the figures of culture that the sacred concerns this philosophy; the sacred is its eschatology; it is the horizon that reflection does not comprehend, does not encompass, but can only salute as that which quietly presents itself from afar. Thus another dependence of the Cogito or self is revealed, a dependence that is first seen not in the symbol of its birth but in the symbol of an eschaton, an ultimate, toward which the figures of spirit point. The Cogito's dependence on the ultimate, just as its dependence on its birth, its nature, its desire, is revealed only through symbols.

I now wish to show how this hermeneutics, always in a hazardous position in a reflective philosophy because of its horizon-function, can enter into debate with the psychoanalysis of religion with its strong emphasis on demystification. The danger here is of falling back on a purely antithetical conception of hermeneutics where we would lose the benefit of our painstaking dialectic and succumb to an eclecticism we have consistently tried to eradicate. Hence it is important to show that a problematic of faith necessarily implies a hermeneutics of demystification.

I shall start with the function of horizon that we have attributed to the alpha and omega in relation to any purely immanent field of reflection. It seems that such a horizon, by a kind of diabolic conversion, inevitably tends to become transformed into an object. Kant was the first to teach us to regard illusion as a necessary structure of thought about the unconditioned. The transcendental *Schein* is not a mere error, a pure accident in the history of thought; it is a *necessary* illusion. In my opinion this is the radical origin of every "false consciousness," the source of every problematic of illusion, beyond the social lies, the vital lies, the return of the repressed. Marx, Freud, and Nietzsche are already operating at the level of secondary and derived forms of illusion; that is why their problematics are partial and rival. The same may be said of Feuerbach: the movement by which man empties himself into transcendence is secondary as compared to the movement by which he grasps hold of the Wholly Other in order to objectify it and make use of it; the reason man projects himself into the Wholly Other is to grasp hold of it and thus fill the emptiness of his unawareness.

This objectifying process is the origin both of metaphysics and of religion: metaphysics makes God into a supreme being; and religion treats the sacred as a new sphere of objects, institutions, and powers within the world of immanence—of objective spirit—and alongside the objects, institutions, and powers of the economic, political, and cultural spheres. We may say that a fourth sphere of objects has arisen within the human sphere of spirit. Henceforward there are sacred *objects* and not merely *signs* of the sacred; sacred objects in addition to the world of culture.

This diabolic transformation makes religion the reification and alienation of faith; by thus entering the sphere of illusion, religion becomes vulnerable to the blows of a reductive hermeneutics. In our day this reductive hermeneutics is no longer a private affair; it has become a public process, a cultural phenomenon; whether we call it demythologization, when it occurs within a given religion, or demystification, when it proceeds from without, the aim is the same: the death of the metaphysical and religious object. Freudianism is one of the roads to this death.

It seems to me, however, that this cultural movement cannot and must not remain external to the restoration of the signs of the Wholly Other in their authentic function as sentinels of the horizon. Today we can no longer hear and read the signs of the approach of the Wholly Other except through the merciless exercise of reductive hermeneutics; such is our helplessness and perhaps our good fortune and joy. Faith is that region of the symbolic where the horizon-function is constantly being reduced to the object-function; thus arise idols, the religious figures of that same illusion which in metaphysics engenders the concepts of a supreme being, first substance, absolute thought. An idol is the reification of the horizon into a thing, the fall of the sign into a supernatural and supracultural object.

Thus there is a never-ending task of distinguishing between the faith of religion—faith in the Wholly Other which draws near—

and belief in the religious object, which becomes another object of our culture and thus a part of our own sphere. The sacred, as signifying separation or otherness, is the area of this combat. The sacred can be the sign of that which does not belong to us, the sign of the Wholly Other; it can also be a sphere of separate objects within our human world of culture and alongside the sphere of the profane. The sacred can be the meaningful bearer of what we described as the structure of horizon peculiar to the Wholly Other which draws near, or it can be the idolatrous reality to which we assign a separate place in our culture, thus giving rise to religious alienation. The ambiguity is inevitable: for if the Wholly Other draws near, it does so in the signs of the sacred; but symbols soon turn into idols. Thus the cultural object of our human sphere is split in two, half becoming profane, the other half sacred: the wood carver, says the prophet, cuts down a cedar, or a cypress, or an oak:

> Half of it he burns in the fire; over the half he eats flesh, he roasts meat and is satisfied; also he warms himself and says, "Aha, I am warm, I have seen the fire!" And the rest of it he makes into a god, his idol; and falls down to it and worships it; he prays to it and says, "Deliver me, for thou art my god!" They know not, nor do they understand . . . (Isaiah 44:16–18).

Thus the idols must die—so that symbols may live.

THE VALUE AND LIMITS OF A PSYCHOANALYSIS OF RELIGION

The fact that a destructive hermeneutics is justified according to the requirements of faith itself does not imply an acceptance *in toto* of the psychoanalysis of religion within the framework thus outlined. On the contrary, we must once more come to grips with Freud, we must confront his hermeneutics with the hermeneutics of Eliade, Van der Leeuw, Barth, and Bultmann, in order to construct what we can say positively and negatively about the psychoanalysis of religion.

Religion and Instincts. I see three successive focal points of discussion. The first concerns the instinctual substrate of religion. It has been said that "the gods were created through fear." Freud repeats this remark with the fresh resources of analysis and amends it: through fear and desire. Everything he says about the analogy between religion and neurosis is located on this first level of the discussion.[46] Indeed, everything that relates religion to neurosis, also relates it to desire by virtue of the substitute satisfaction attaching to symptoms.

We recall that Freud's point of departure was the parallel between the phenomena of religious practices and the rituals of obsessional neurosis; this parallel on the purely descriptive and clinical plane enabled him to describe religion as the "universal obsessional neurosis of mankind." From the paper of 1907 to *Moses and Monotheism* in 1939, the analogy was constantly extended and reinforced. Thus it is on the model of paranoia that *Totem and Taboo* conceives of the projection, at the narcissistic stage of the libido, of the omnipotence of desire into figures of the divine. Religion is regarded as the refuge of all the individual's repressed wishes—hatred, jealousy, urge to persecute and destroy—which the ecclesiastical institution enables the individual to direct toward the enemies of his religious group. But Freud is no doubt more instructive when he treats religion less as a support of prohibitions than as a function of consolation. This is where the relationship between religion and desire is most evident. Everything centers around the paternal nucleus, the longing for the father. Religion is grounded biologically in the condition of dependency and helplessness peculiar to human childhood. The neurosis that now serves as the point of reference is the one through which the child passes and which is subsequently revived in the adult after a period of latency. So too, religion is the revival of a distressing memory, which the ethnological explanation proceeds to link with a primal killing that would be to primeval mankind what the Oedipus complex is to the childhood of the individual.

If for the moment we leave aside the ethnological explanation,

46. Cf. above, "Analytic," Part II, Ch. 3. Cf. R. Held, "Contribution à l'étude psychanalytique du phénomène religieux," *Rev. fr. de psychan.*, 27 (1962), 211–66.

which allows Freud to move from a descriptive analogy to a structural identity, there remains the analogy with the three basic stages of the childhood condition: neurotic phase, latency period, return of the repressed.

At this first level of the discussion it seems to me important to maintain the purely analogical character of the relationship between religious phenomena and pathological phenomena against any dogmatic reduction to identity, and to reflect upon the conditions of this analogy. Such a procedure does not enable us to escape the Freudian critique but actually exposes us to its strongest point. So fragile are the ethnology of *Totem and Taboo* and the scriptural science of *Moses and Monotheism* that if one is too quick to combine the sociological argument, which claims to furnish the reason for the identity, with the clinical description on which the analogical considerations are based, one only weakens Freud's thesis. It is better to do without the "historical" support of the primal crime and remain on the level of the analogy between the economy of religious phenomena and that of the neuroses, leaving the question of the fantasy of the primal crime for further discussion.

It seems to me that the meaning of this analogy remains and must remain indefinite. All that can be said is that man is capable of neurosis as he is capable of religion, and vice versa. The same causes—life's hardship, the triple suffering dealt the individual by nature, his body, and other men—give rise to similar responses—neurotic ceremonials and religious ceremonials, demand for consolation and appeal to Providence—and obtain comparable effects—compromise formations, secondary gain of illness and discharge of guilt, substitute satisfaction.

But what does the analogy mean? Psychoanalysis as such cannot say. Analysis does indeed throw some light on what we have called the birth of idols; but it has no way of deciding whether that is all that faith is; whether ritual is originally, in its primordial function, obsessional ritual; whether faith is merely consolation on the childhood pattern. Analysis can reveal to the religious man his caricature, but it leaves him the task of meditating on the *possibility* of not resembling his distorted double. For it is truly a matter of distortion, and of self-understanding through distortion: distortion of the infantile, distortion of the neurotic, distortion of the primitive (or of the so-called primitive person, himself interpreted as the analogue of the neurotic and the child).

The value of the analogy, and hence also the limits of the analogy, seem to me to hinge on a crucial point: does the affective dynamism of religious belief have the wherewithal to *overcome* its own archaism? This question can receive only a partial answer in the context of an investigation of the instinctual substrate of religion; it is a question that necessarily relates to the question of the fantasy of the primal killing and more generally of the meaning of the father complex. But even within our present limited framework we can go rather far by critically reexamining what we described in our "Analytic" as the absence of history in religion.

For Freud, religion is the monotonous repetition of its own origins. It is a sempiternal treading on the grounds of its own archaism. The theme of "the return of the repressed" means nothing else: the Christian Eucharist repeats the totem meal, as the death of Christ repeats that of the prophet Moses, which repeats the original killing of the father. Freud's exclusive attention to repetition becomes a refusal to consider a possible epigenesis of religious feeling, that is to say, a transformation or conversion of desire and fear. This refusal does not seem to me to be based upon analysis, but merely expresses Freud's personal unbelief.

In reading Freud's works, one may observe this paring down of religious feeling whenever such feeling is about to go beyond the bounds in which it has been confined. For instance, there is an entire pre-oedipal stratum which is glimpsed, then obliterated. Freud touches on it in the *Leonardo*, when he compares the vulture fantasy to the Egyptian goddess Mut, pictured as a vulture-headed mother deity with a phallus. For a moment Freud glimpses the rich meaning of this representation, but he immediately reduces its scope by explaining Leonardo's childhood fantasy and the representation of the androgynous deities in terms of the infantile sexual theory of the maternal penis. Later we shall discuss the sense in which one and the same representation may be regarded as the common source of both a regressive fantasy and a figure of the sacred. For the present let us keep in mind that there are other affective roots besides the father complex. In contrasting "the primeval days of the human race" with our civilized attitude of depreciating sexuality, Freud himself suggests that primitive men divinized sexuality, and that all other human activities were made to share in its divine nature through transfer of the sexual to the nonsexual. Later on Freud will admit that he does not know what place to assign to the feminine deities in his genesis of religious illusion.

Is this not an indication of a possible religion of life, a religion of love? On at least two occasions Freud touched upon this working hypothesis, only to brush it aside immediately. In the famous myth of the primal murder, Freud encounters an episode that remains unexplained, although it is ultimately the pivot of the drama: this episode is the forming of the covenant among the brothers whereby they agreed not to repeat among themselves the murder of the father. This covenant is highly significant, for it puts an end to a repetition of the act of parricade; by prohibiting fratricide, the covenant engenders a history. But Freud is much more preoccupied with the symbolic repetition of the murder in the totem meal than with the conciliation among the brothers, which makes possible the reconciliation with the father image henceforward engraved in the hearts of men. Why not link the destiny of faith with this fraternal conciliation, rather than with the perpetual repetition of the parricide? But Freud has decided that the son religion is not a true advance beyond the father complex: the fiction that the son is the leader of the revolt, and hence a murderer figure, immediately closes the half-opened door.

A similar difficulty faces the second essay of *Moses and Monotheism*. "If Moses was an Egyptian," he must have taken his ethical god from a religion that was already established. But the cult of Aten, which we are told was built on the model of the benevolent prince Akhenaten, poses the great enigma of a "political" god, by which I mean a god who founds the social covenant and who consequently arises on the substrate of desire and fear and is more closely connected with the conciliation among the brothers than with the murder of the father.

But it is especially the final theory of instincts that might have been the occasion for a fresh investigation of the phenomenon of religion.[47] Such an investigation did not occur. On the contrary, this was the period when Freud hardened his hostility toward religion and was preparing to write *The Future of an Illusion*. Nevertheless, by contrasting Eros with death, Freud recaptured a certain mythical basis preserved by the German romantic tradition; through the latter he was able to go back to Plato and Empedocles and describe Eros as "the power which holds everything together." But he never suspected that this mythology of Eros might concern an epigenesis of religious feeling, nor that Eros might be another name for the Johannine God, and further back, for the Deuteronomic God, and further still, for the God of Osee, when the prophet celebrates in his songs the betrothal in the desert. And why may it not be that "our god Logos, who promises no consolation, whose voice is soft but does not rest till it has gained a hearing," is—in spite of Freud's ironic tone on this occasion—another name for Eros, in the profound unity of the symbols of Life and Light? Freud seems to me to exclude without reason, I mean without any psychoanalytic reason, the possibility that faith is a participation in the source of Eros and thus concerns, not the consolation of the child in us, but the power of loving; he excludes the possibility that faith aims at making this power adult in the face of the hatred within us and outside of us—in the face of death. The only thing that can escape Freud's critique is faith as the kerygma of love: "God so loved the world. . . ." But in return his critique can help me discern what this kerygma of love excludes—a penal Christology and a moral God—and what it implies—a certain coincidence of the tragic God of Job and the lyric God of John.

Religion and Fantasy. The question of the nonregressive, nonarchaizing sources of religion leads to a critical examination of the representational nucleus that Freud thinks he has delimited by the convergent paths of clinical description and ethnology: the fantasy of the killing of the father. For

47. Cf. above, "Analytic," Part III, Ch. 3. Cf. F. Pasche, "Freud et l'orthodoxie judéo-chrétienne," *Rev. fr. de psychan., 25* (1961), 55–88; A. Vergote, "La religion du père face à la raison et à la nécessité," *La Psychanalyse, science de l'homme*, pp. 223–57.

Freud, the return of the repressed is both the return of the affects of fear and love, anxiety and consolation, and the return of the fantasy itself in the substitute figure of god. This substitute figure is the remote derivative of the representations attaching to the instinctual substrate. Consequently, all our remarks about a possible epigenesis of religious feeling become meaningful only through the mediation of an epigenesis at the level of representations.

This epigenesis, however, is simply ruled out in Freudianism because of the status accorded to the fantasy of the murder of the primal father. An essential element of the Freudian interpretation is that this murder actually occurred in the past either once or several times, and that there exists an actual memory of it inscribed in the hereditary patrimony of mankind. The Oedipus complex of the individual is too brief and too indistinct to engender the gods; without an ancestral crime as part of our phylogenetic past, the longing for the father is unintelligible; *the* father is not *my* father. Through the course of the years, Freud kept reinforcing the notion that the memory of the primal killing is a memory of a real event. The most explicit statements in this regard are those in *Moses and Monotheism*, which we have cited at length in the "Analytic." If then, for Freud, religion is archaic and repetitive, it is to a great extent because religion is drawn backward by the remembrance of a murder that belongs to its prehistory and constitutes what *Moses and Monotheism* calls "the truth in religion." The truth resides in memory: whatever is added by the imagination is, as in dreams, distortion; whatever is added by rational thought is, again as in dreams, secondary elaboration, rationalization, and superstition. Thus Freud deliberately turns his back on the demythologizing interpretations which, from Schelling to Bultmann, deprive myths of any etiological function so as to restore to them their mytho-poetic function capable of leading to a reflection or a speculation.

It is strange to note that in order to explain religion Freud held onto a conception he was forced to abandon in the theory of the neuroses. We recall that the true interpretation of the Oedipus complex was achieved in opposition to the erroneous theory of the real seduction of the child by an adult. Unfortunately, the Oedipus episode, which Freud discovered by a sort of reversal of meaning of the seduction scene, was substituted in its place; the Oedipus complex was made the trace or vestige of a real memory (this vestigial function, we recall, is what enabled Freud in Chapter 7 of *The Interpretation of Dreams* to equate formal regression with the quasi-hallucinatory revival of a memory trace). Even more than the individual Oedipus complex, the collective complex of mankind is regarded as the return of a vestigial type of affect and representation.

Freud himself, however, furnishes the means of picturing the matter in another way. There is in Freud a conception of the "primal scene" in which the notion of a nonvestigial function of imagination is sketched. The "scene with the vulture," Freud notes in the *Leonardo,* "would not be a memory of Leonardo's but a fantasy, which he formed at a later date and transposed to his childhood." Freud illustrates this by a comparison with the way in which the writing of history might have originated among the peoples of antiquity, when men entered an "age of reflection" and

> felt a need to learn where they had come from and how they had developed. . . . Historical writing, which had begun to keep a continuous record of the present, now also cast a glance back to the past, gathered traditions and legends, interpreted the traces of antiquity that survived in customs and usages, and in this way created a history of the past.[48]

This "history of a nation's earliest days, which was compiled later and for tendentious reasons" [49]—does it not imply a *creation of meaning,* capable of marking off and carrying what we have called an epigenesis of religious feeling? May not such a primal scene fantasy supply the first layer of meaning to an imagination of origins which is increasingly detached from its function of infantile and quasi-neurotic repetition, and increasingly of service to an investigation of the fundamental meanings of human destiny?

48. *Leonardo da Vinci and a Memory of his Childhood, GW, 8,* 151; *SE, 11,* 83–84. In a footnote added in 1919 (ibid., n. 2), Freud replies to Havelock Ellis, who, in a favorable review (1910) of the *Leonardo,* objected that the memory of Leonardo's may very well have had a basis of reality. Freud continues to emphasize the fantasy character of the vulture scene: even if the scene arose from memories of a real event, the fantasy transfigured this "real event of no importance" (*die reale Nichtigkeit*).

49. *GW, 8,* 152; *SE, 11,* 84.

Freud encountered this nonvestigial product of imagination, this carrier of a new meaning, not when he spoke of religion but when he spoke of art. Let us recall our exegesis of the Gioconda's smile. The memory of the lost mother, we said, is recreated by the work of art; it is not something that lies hidden underneath, like a real stratum that is merely covered over; strictly speaking, it is a creation, and exists only insofar as it is presented in the painting.[50]

Hence one and the same fantasy can carry two opposed vectors: a regressive vector which subjects the fantasy to the past, and a progressive vector which makes it an indicator of meaning. That the regressive and progressive functions can coexist in the same fantasy is intelligible in Freudian terms. Leonardo's vulture fantasy is a first transfiguration of the vestiges of the past; a fortiori, a true work of art like the Gioconda is a creation in which, in Freud's own words, the past is "denied and overcome."[51]

Freud admits, however, that he does not understand this creative function: "Since artistic talent and capacity are intimately connected with sublimation we must admit that the nature of the artistic function is also inaccessible to us along psychoanalytic lines."[52]

Let us apply this remark to the fantasy of the primal crime. Freud writes in the *Leonardo:*

> Psychoanalysis has made us familiar with the intimate connection between the father complex and belief in God; it has shown us that a personal God is, psychologically, nothing other than an exalted father . . . The almighty and just God, and kindly Nature, appear to us as grand sublimations of father and mother, or rather as revivals and restorations of the young child's ideas of them.[53]

Why should not this sublimation of the father involve the same ambiguity, the same double value of oneiric revival and cultural creation? Such must be the case, in a certain sense, even within the framework of Freud's interpretation, if religion is to fulfill its universal and not just its individual function—if it is to acquire cul-

50. Cf. above, "Analytic," Part II, Ch. 1.
51. Cf. above, p. 173.
52. *GW, 8,* 209; *SE, 11,* 136.
53. *GW, 8,* 195; *SE, 11,* 123.

tural importance and assume a function of protection, consolation, reconciliation. But then is it possible that the father figure, as presented by religion and faith, is merely a picture puzzle, hidden in the believer's invocation like Leonardo's vulture in the folds of the Virgin's robe? To my mind one cannot treat the father figure as an isolated figure with its own special exegesis; it is simply one component—the central one, it is true, as we shall say further on—in a mytho-poetic constellation which must first be considered as a whole.

Let us explore the following path. The force of a religious symbol lies in the fact that it recaptures a primal scene fantasy and transforms it into an instrument of discovery and exploration of origins. Through these "detector" representations, man tells the origin of his humanity. Thus the accounts of battle in Hesiod and the Babylonian literature, the accounts of fall in the Orphic literature, the accounts of primal guilt and exile in the Hebraic literature,[54] may indeed be treated, in the manner of Otto Rank, as a sort of collective oneirism, but this oneirism is not a recording of prehistory. Rather, through their vestigial function, such symbols show in operation an imagination of origins, which may be said to be historial, *geschichtlich*, for it tells of an advent, a coming to being, but not historical, *historisch*, for it has no chronological significance. To use Husserlian terminology, I will say that the fantasies explored by Freud make up the hyletic of this mytho-poetic imagination. It is in and through certain primal scene fantasies that man "forms," "interprets," "intends" meanings of another order, meanings capable of becoming the signs of the sacred which the philosophy of reflection can only acknowledge and salute at the horizon of its archeology and its teleology. This new intentionality, through which fantasies are interpreted symbolically, arises from the very nature of the fantasies insofar as they speak of the lost origin, of the lost archaic object, of the lack inherent in desire; what gives rise to the endless movement of the interpretation is not the fullness of memory but its emptiness, its openness. Ethnology, com-

54. *The Symbolism of Evil,* Part II. On religion and fantasy, cf. J. Laplanche and J. B. Pontalis, "Fantasme originaire, fantasme des origines, origine du fantasme," *Les Temps modernes, 19* (1964), 1833–68.

parative mythology, biblical exegesis—all confirm that every myth is a reinterpretation of an earlier account. These interpretations of interpretations are quite capable therefore of operating upon fantasies pertaining to various ages and stages of the libido. But the important factor is not so much this "sensory matter" as the movement of interpretation that is contained in the advancement of meaning and constitutes the intentional transforming of the "matter." This is the reason why a *hermêneutikê technê* can be applied to myths; a myth is already *hermêneia,* interpretation and reinterpretation of its own roots.[55] And if myths assume a theological meaning, as we see in the origin narratives, they do so through this endless process of correction, which has become a concerted and systematic effort.

Thus the father figure cannot be considered apart from the mytho-poetic function in which it is inserted. It is true that this figure is particularly dominant, since it furnishes the prototype of the deity and thus refers, through polytheism and then monotheism, to the unique father figure. This "projective" characteristic is found only in the father figure; that is true. But Freud did not struggle with the difficulties concerning projection as he did with those concerning introjection and identification. The displacement of the father onto the totem animal and the totem god does not perplex him enough. The analogy with animal phobias and with paranoia dispense him from seeking further. Do not the same questions that we asked concerning the mother image in Leonardo's Mona Lisa arise here? Is not the father figure as much "denied and overcome" as it is "repeated"? What have I understood when I have discovered—or divined—the father figure in the representation of the deity? Do I understand both of them better? But I do not know what the father means. The primal scene fantasy refers me back to an unreal father, a father who is missing from our individual and collective history; this is the fantasy in which I imagine God as a father. So great is my ignorance of the father that I can say that the

55. I allude here to the two historical roots of hermeneutics: the "hermeneutic technique" of the interpreters of signs, dreams, and incommunicable speech, and "interpretation" or *hermêneia,* which, according to Aristotle, is the work of meaningful discourse in general. Cf. above, "Problematic," Ch. 2.

father as a cultural theme is created by mythology on the basis of an oneiric fantasy. I did not know what the father was until his image had engendered the whole series of his derivatives. What constitutes the father as an origin myth is the interpretation through which the primal scene fantasy receives a new intention—to the point where I can invoke "our Father, who art in heaven . . ." Stated in the prephilosophical language of myth, the symbolism of the heavens and the symbolism of the father make explicit the origin symbolism that the archaic fantasy virtually contained by reason of the absence, lack, loss, and emptiness of its proper "object."

Why does the father figure have a privilege that the mother figure does not have? Its privileged status is no doubt due to its extremely rich symbolic power, in particular its potential for "transcendence." In symbolism, the father figures less as a begetter equal to the mother than as the name-giver and the lawgiver. Freud's remarks about identification with a model, as distinct from libidinal identification, are applicable here. One does not possess the father of identification, not only because he is a lost archaic object, but because he is distinct from every archaic object. As such, he cannot "come back" or "return" except as a cultural theme; the father of identification is a task for representation because from the start he is not an object of desire but the source of institution. The father is an unreality set apart, who, from the start, is a being of language. Because he is the name-giver, he is the name-problem, as the Hebrews first conceived him. Thus the father figure was bound to have a richer and more articulated destiny than the mother figure. Through sublimation and identification the symbol of the father was able to join with that of the lord and that of the heavens to form the symbolism of an ordered, wise, and just transcendence, as outlined by Mircea Eliade in the first chapter of his *Histoire comparée des religions*.

But then the father figure is not simply a return of the repressed; it is rather the result of a true process of creation. This creation of meaning constitutes the true overdetermination of authentic symbols, and this overdetermination in turn grounds the possibility of two hermeneutics, one of which unmasks the archaism of its fantasy content, while the other discovers the new intention that animates the material content. The reconciliation of the two hermeneutics lies in symbols themselves. Thus one cannot stop with an antithetic that would distinguish between "two sources of morality and religion" for the prophecy of consciousness is not external to its archeology.

One might even say that, thanks to their overdetermined structure, symbols succeed in inverting the temporal signs of the origin fantasy. The primal father signifies the eschaton, the "God who comes"; generation signifies regeneration; birth analogously stands for rebirth; the childhood—that childhood which is behind me—signifies the other childhood, the "second naïveté." The process of becoming conscious is ultimately a process of seeing one's childhood in front of oneself and one's death behind oneself: "before, you were dead . . ."; "unless you become as little children . . ." In this interchange of birth and death, the symbolism of the God who comes has taken over and justified the figure of the primal father.

But if symbols are fantasies that have been denied and overcome, they are never fantasies that have been abolished. That is why one is never certain that a given symbol of the sacred is not simply a "return of the repressed"; or rather, it is always certain that each symbol of the sacred is also and at the same time a revival of an infantile and archaic symbol. The two functions of symbol remain inseparable. The symbolic meanings closest to theological and philosophical speculation are always involved with some trace of an archaic myth. This close alliance of archaism and prophecy constitutes the richness of religious symbolism; it also constitutes its ambiguity. "Symbols give rise to thought," but they are also the birth of idols. That is why the critique of idols remains the condition of the conquest of symbols.

Faith and Speech. It seems to me that the two preceding discussions lead to a third sphere of problems. After seeing the projected shadow or imprint of the advancement of meaning in instincts and fantasies, we must consider speech or the spoken word [*la parole*], for this is the element in which the advancement of meaning occurs. If an epigenesis of instincts and fantasies is possible, it is because speech is the instrument of the hermêneia or "interpretation" that symbols exercise with respect to fantasies, even before symbols are themselves interpreted by the exegetes.

The ascending dialectic of affect and fantasy is thus carried by an ascending dialectic of symbolic language. But this creation of meaning implies that the imaginary of the mytho-poetic function is more closely related to nascent speech than to images in the sense of a mere revival of perception. Unfortunately, the Freudian conception of language is very inadequate; the meaning of words is the revival of acoustic images; thus language itself is a "trace" of perception. This vestigial conception of language can give no support to an epigenesis of meaning. If it is true that the various degrees of fantasy are developed only in the element of language, it is still necessary to distinguish between "things heard" and "things seen." But things heard are first of all things said; and things said, in myths of the origin and the end, are the exact contrary of traces or vestiges. The things said interpret certain primal scene fantasies in order to *speak* of man's situation in the sacred.

The inadequacy of Freud's philosophy of language explains, I believe, what seems to me to be Freud's greatest shortcoming in his theory of religion: he thought he could make a direct psychology of the superego and, on this basis, a direct psychology of belief and the believer, thus circumventing an exegesis of the *texts* in and through which the religious man has "formed" and "educated" his belief, in the sense of the *Bildung* mentioned above. However, it is impossible to construct a psychoanalysis of belief apart from an interpretation and understanding of the cultural productions in which the object of belief announces itself.

What we have said in general about the process of man's "becoming conscious" should be said more specifically about his "becoming religious." For man, to become conscious is to be drawn away from his archaism by the series of figures that institute and constitute him as man. Hence there can be no question of grasping the meaning of the religious man apart from the meaning of the texts that are the documents of his belief. Dilthey very clearly established this point in his famous essay of 1900, "Die Entstehung der Hermeneutik." Understanding or interpretation, he says, does not truly begin until "life-expressions" are fixed in an objectivity that is subject to the technical rules of an art: "We call this technical understanding of durably fixed life-expressions an exegesis or interpretation." [56] If literature is the privileged area of this process of interpretation—though one may also legitimately speak of a hermeneutics of sculpture and of painting— it is because language is the only complete, exhaustive, and objectively intelligible expression of human interiority: "That is why," Dilthey continues, "the art of understanding centers around the exegesis or interpretation of the written testimony of human existence." [57]

There is hardly any need to state that *Moses and Monotheism* does not operate at the level of an exegesis of the Old Testament and in no way satisfies the most elementary requirements of a hermeneutics adapted to a text. Consequently one cannot say that Freud truly made, or even began to make, an "analysis of religious representations," whereas on the esthetic plane the "Moses" of Michelangelo is truly treated as a self-contained work and analyzed in detail, with no concession made to a direct psychology of the artist and his creative activity. The works of religion, the monuments of belief, are treated neither with the same sympathy nor with the same rigor; instead, we are presented with a vague relationship between religious themes and the paternal prototype. Freud has decided once and for all that the truly religious ideas are those that clearly stem from this prototype. A powerful being who rules over nature as an empire, who annuls death and redresses the afflictions of this life—if God is to be God, this is all he can be; naïve religion is religion proper. Philosophic religion and "oceanic" religion,[58] in which the personality of God has been softened, transposed, or abandoned, are derivatives or secondary rationalizations that refer back to the paternal prototype.

I would like to show, in the case of two particular themes central to the Freudian problematic—the themes of guilt and consolation—how a path that Freud has closed may be reopened.

The first theme has to do with religion as the summit of an ethi-

56. Wilhelm Dilthey, "Die Entstehung der Hermeneutik," in *Gesammelte Schriften, 5*, 319; Fr. trans. in *Le Monde de l'esprit, 1* (Aubier), 321.
57. Ibid.
58. *Civilization and Its Discontents*, Ch. 1.

cal view of the world; the second concerns religion as proceeding from a suspension of the ethical. These themes are the two focal points of religious consciousness, as Freud himself acknowledges by viewing religion as a form of interdiction and as a form of consolation.

Now, Freud had no interest whatsoever in what might be called an epigenesis of the sense of guilt, an epigenesis that would be guided by an increasingly refined symbolism. The sense of guilt seems to have no history beyond the Oedipus complex and its dissolution. It remains a preventive procedure with respect to anticipated punishment. In the Freudian literature, the sense of guilt is consistently understood in this archaic sense. But an epigenesis of guilt cannot be directly established by a psychology of the superego; it can only be deciphered by the indirect means of a textual exegesis of the penitential literature. In this literature there is constituted an examplary history of conscience (*Gewissen*). Man arrives at adult, normal, ethical guilt when he understands himself *according to* the figures of this exemplary history. Elsewhere I have tried to investigate the notions of stain, sin, and guilt by means of an exegesis in Dilthey's sense of the term.[59] I found that guilt progresses by crossing two thresholds. The first threshold is that of injustice—in the sense of the Jewish prophets and also of Plato. The fear of being unjust, the remorse for having been unjust, are no longer taboo fears; damage to the interpersonal relationship, wrongs done to the person of another, treated as a means and not as an end, mean more than a feeling of a threat of castration. Thus the consciousness of injustice marks a creation of meaning by comparison with the fear of vengeance, the fear of being punished. The second threshold is that of the sin of the just man, of the evil of justice

59. *The Symbolism of Evil,* Part I. See also my study, "Morale sans péché ou péché sans moralisme," *Esprit,* Feb. 1954 (a review of A. Hesnard, *L'Univers morbide de la faute* and *Morale sans péché*). I also rejoin the remarks of Roy S. Lee, *Freud and Christianity* (London, James Clarke and Co., 1948), p. 93: "Religion is more properly a function of the ego than of the unconscious and the id." On Freud and guilt, see C. Odier, *Les deux sources consciente et inconsciente de la vie morale* (Neuchâtel, La Baconnière, 1943); Hesnard, *L'Univers morbide de la faute* (Paris, P. U. F., 1949) and *Morale sans péché* (Paris, P. U. F., 1954); C. Nodet, "Psychanalyse et sens du péché," *Rev. fr. de Psychan., 21* (1957), 791–805.

proper; here consciousness discovers the radical evil affecting every maxim, even that of the good man.

All we have said above concerning the function of fantasies is relevant here. The myths in which the advance of consciousness is expressed are certainly built upon primal scene fantasies subject to the anxiety of the superego. That is why guilt is a trap, an occasion of backwardness, of fixation in premorality, of stagnation in archaism. But the mythic intentionality resides in the series of interpretations and reinterpretations through which a myth rectifies its own archaic substrate. Thus are constituted the symbols of evil which invite thought and upon which I can form the notion of bad or servile will. Between the sense of guilt in the psychoanalytic sense and radical evil in the Kantian sense there extends a series of figures in which each figure takes up the preceding one to "deny" and "overcome" it, as Freud says of the work of art. It would be the task of reflective thought to show how this progressive consciousness follows the progression of the symbolic spheres we sketched in the first part of this chapter. The same figures that served to mark off the path of feeling—the figures of possession, domination, and valuation—are also the successive regions of our alienation. This is understandable, for if these figures are the symbols of our fallibility, they are also the symbols of our having already fallen. Freedom becomes alienated in alienating its own mediations, economic, political, cultural. The servile will, one might add, mediates itself by passing through all the figures of our helplessness that express and objectify our power of existing.

This indirect method could be the means of elaborating the notion of noninfantile, nonarchaic, non-neurotic sources of our guilt. But just as desire intrudes into these successive spheres and mixes its ramifications with the nonerotic functions of the self, so too the affective archaism of guilt extends into all the regions of alienated possession, of unmeasured power, of vainglorious pretensions of worth. That is why guilt remains ambiguous and suspect. In order to break its false prestige, we must always focus on it the double illumination of a demystifying interpretation that denounces its archaism and a restorative interpretation that places the birth of evil in the mind or spirit itself.

I have taken the example of guilt as the prime example of an ambiguous notion, both archaic in origin and susceptible of an indefinite creation of meaning. This same ambiguity is written into the heart of religion, insofar as the symbols of salvation are on the same level and of the same quality as the symbols of evil. It can be shown that for all the figures of accusation there are corresponding figures of redemption. As a result, the central figure of religion, which psychoanalysis tells us proceeds from the prototype of the father, cannot complete its own genesis until it has traversed all the degrees corresponding to those of guilt. Thus the interpretation of the father fantasy in the symbolism of God extends into all the regions of accusation and redemption.

But if the symbolic representation of God progresses in parallel with the symbols of evil and guilt, it is not completed within this correlation. As Freud well saw, religion is more an art of bearing the hardships of life than an indefinite exorcism of the paternal accusation. This cultural function of consolation is what places religion no longer merely in the sphere of fear, but in that of desire. Plato already said in the *Phaedo* that there remains in each of us an infant to be consoled. The question is whether the function of consolation is merely infantile, or whether there is not also what I should now call an epigenesis or ascending dialectic of consolation.

Once again literature is the medium that marks off the progress of this rectification of consolation. The objection may be made that the critique of the old law of retribution, a critique already made by the wise men of Babylon and even more by the books of the Hebrews, is not a part of religion. But then we must enter into another problematic, which Freudianism seems to be ignorant of, the problematic of the internal conflict between faith and religion: it is the faith of Job and not the religion of his friends that should be confronted with the Freudian iconoclasm. Does not this faith accomplish part of the task Freud assigns to whoever undertakes to "do without his father" (*Leonardo*)? Job receives no explanation of his suffering; he is merely shown something of the grandeur and order of the whole, without any meaning being directly given to the finite point of view of his desire. His faith is closer to the "third kind" of knowledge in Spinoza's sense than to any religion of Providence. A path is thus opened, a path of non-narcissistic reconciliation: I give up my point of view; I love the whole; I make ready to say: "The intellectual love of the mind toward God is a part of that very love of God whereby God loves himself" (*quo Deus seipsum amat*).[60] Through the twofold test of commandment and retribution, faith brings about a single and unique suspension of the ethical. By revealing the sin of the just man, the man of belief goes beyond the ethics of righteousness; by losing the immediate consolation of his narcissism, he goes beyond any ethical view of the world.

Through this twofold test he overcomes the father figure; but in losing it as an idol he perhaps discovers it as a symbol. The father symbol is the surplus of meaning intended by the *seipsum* of the Spinozist theorem. The father symbol is not a symbol of a father whom I can have; in this respect the father is nonfather. Rather, the father symbol is the likeness of the father in accordance with which the giving up of desire is no longer death but love, in the sense once more of the corollary of the Spinozist theorem: "The love of God toward men and the intellectual love of the mind toward God are one and the same thing."

We have reached a point here that seems unsurpassable. It is not a point of repose but of tension, for it is not yet apparent how the "personality" of God who pardons and the "impersonality" of *Deus sive natura* could coincide. I only say that the two ways of suspending the ethical, Kierkegaard's and Spinoza's, may be the same, as we are led to think by the *Deus seipsum amat* of Spinoza and by the dialectic, underlying the whole of Western theology, of "God" and "deity"; but I do not know they are the same.

Starting from this extreme point, a final confrontation with Freud may be proposed. To the very end we must refuse having to choose between two platitudes: that of the apologist, who would completely reject the Freudian iconoclasm, and that of the eclectic, who would juxtapose the iconoclasm of religion and the symbolism of faith. For my part I will apply, as a last and ultimate resort, the dialectic of the *yes* and the *no* to the principle of reality. Ultimately, this is the level on which the "epigenesis of consolation" according

60. *Ethics*, Part V, Proposition 36 and Corollary.

to faith and the "resignation to Ananke" according to Freudianism confront and challenge one another.

I make no secret of the fact that the reading of Freud is what has helped me extend the critique of narcissism—which I have constantly called the false Cogito, or the abortive Cogito—to its most extreme consequences regarding the religious desire for consolation; the reading of Freud is what helped me placc the "giving up of the father" at the heart of the problematic of faith. In return I do not conceal my dissatisfaction with the Freudian interpretation of the reality principle. Freud's scientism prevented him from following to completion a certain path glimpsed in the *Leonardo*, even though this was the harshest book Freud wrote against religion.

As we have said, reality is not simply a set of observable facts and verifiable laws; reality is also, in psychoanalytic terms, the world of things and of men, such as that world would appear to a human desire which has given up the pleasure principle, that is to say, which has subordinated its point of view to the whole. But then, I asked, is reality merely Ananke? Is reality simply necessity offered to my resignation? Is it not also possibility opened to the power of loving? This question I decipher at my own risk—through the questions Freud himself raises concerning the destiny of Leonardo: "Quite apart from doubts about a possible transformation of the instinct to investigate back into an enjoyment of life—a transformation which we must take as fundamental in the tragedy of Faust—the view may be hazarded that Leonardo's development approaches Spinoza's mode of thinking." [61] And further on:

> Lost in admiration and filled with true humility, he all too easily forgets that he himself is a part of those active forces and that in accordance with the scale of his personal strength the way is open for him to try to alter a small portion of the destined course of the world—a world in which the small is still no less wonderful and significant than the great.[62]

And what can be the meaning of the last lines of the *Leonardo?*

61. *Leonardo da Vinci and a Memory of his Childhood*, *GW*, *8*, 142; *SE*, *11*, 75.

62. *GW*, *8*, 143; *SE*, *11*, 76.

> We all still show too little respect for Nature which (in the obscure words of Leonardo which recall Hamlet's lines) "is full of countless reasons that never enter experience." [*La natura è piena d'infinite ragioni che non furono mai in isperienza.*] Every one of us human beings corresponds to one of the countless experiments in which these "*ragioni*" of nature force their way into experience.[63]

I see in these lines a quiet invitation to identity reality with nature and nature with Eros. These "active forces," these "countless reasons that never enter experience," these "countless experiments" in which those reasons "force their way into experience"—these are not observed facts, but rather powers, the diversified power of nature and life. But I cannot apprehend this power except in a mythical symbolism of creation. Is this not the reason why the destroyers of images, ideals, and idols end by mythicizing reality in opposition to illusion—describing illusion as Dionysus, innocence of becoming, eternal return, and reality as Ananke, Logos? Is not this remythicizing a sign that the discipline of reality is nothing without the grace of imagination? that the consideration of necessity is nothing without the evocation of possibility? Through these questions the Freudian hermeneutics can be related to another hermeneutics, a hermeneutics that deals with the mytho-poetic function and regards myths not as fables, i.e. stories that are false, unreal, illusory, but rather as the symbolic exploration of our relationship to beings and to Being. What carries this mytho-poetic function is another power of language, a power that is no longer the demand of desire, demand for protection, demand for providence, but a call in which I leave off all demands and listen.

Thus do I attempt to construct the *yes* and the *no* which I pronounce about the psychoanalysis of religion. The faith of the believer cannot emerge intact from this confrontation, but neither can the Freudian conception of reality. To the cleavage the *yes* to Freud introduces into the heart of the faith of believers, separating idols from symbols, there corresponds the cleavage the *no* to Freud introduces into the heart of the Freudian reality principle, separating mere resignation to Ananke from the love of Creation.

63. *GW*, *8*, 211; *SE*, *11*, 137.

INDEX